We dedicate this book to the people of Shapwick,
past, present and future

Reconstruction of buildings in Old Church field in around 1250, drawn by Victor Ambrus.

Windgather Press
is an imprint of
Oxbow Books, Oxford

ISBN 978-1-905119-45-5

A CIP record for this book is available from the British Library

This book is available direct from

Oxbow Books, Oxford, UK
(Phone: 01865-241249; Fax: 01865-794449)

and

The David Brown Book Company
PO Box 511, Oakville, CT 06779, USA
(Phone: 860-945-9329; Fax: 860-945-9468)

or from our website

www.oxbowbooks.com

Front cover: reconstruction by Victor Ambrus of the church and curia excavated in Old Church field, Shapwick
Back cover: the Old Bakery at Shapwick, reconstructed by Victor Ambrus with selected photographs beneath

Published with the generous assistance of the Marc Fitch Fund

Printed by
Printworks International

Interpreting the English Village

Landscape and Community at Shapwick, Somerset

by

Mick Aston and Christopher Gerrard

WIND*gather*
PRESS

Contents

List of Illustrations

Acknowledgements

The lineage of this Project can be traced to our good friend, the late Professor Harold Fox of the Department of English Local History at Leicester University, who encouraged a generation of research students to work on the records of the Glastonbury Abbey estates. Nick Corcos was one of these: he worked on the enclosure of Shapwick's fields and it was his comments that led to the choice of the parish for this project.

At the outset we would like to take this opportunity to thank the people of Shapwick for having been so accommodating over the years. In particular, Bill Robbins, Bert Hillburn and the Vestey Estate enabled the Project to take place, while the tenant farmers, the villagers, the staff of Shapwick School and other landowners welcomed us into their fields and gardens. Our special thanks must go to Eddie Barrett at Shapwick House and Linda, David and Paul Jenkins at Beerway Farm and to the late Sir David and Lady Margaret Allen.

We also owe an enormous debt to all members of the Shapwick Project. Some are mentioned by name in this book but many more contributed behind the scenes over a decade of fieldwork. Our thanks go firstly to the fieldworkers, who toiled away in all weathers on Thursdays, especially Jon Byron, Nick Corcos, Michael Costen, John and Della Day, Shirley Everden, Sue Fitton, Teresa Hall, Brian Harris, Richard Hayward, John Hedges, Margaret Heslop, the late Dennis Hill-Cottingham, Andrew Jackson (whose PhD research on heavy metals in the soil was an innovative part of the Project), Harry Jelley, Rosie Lishman, Freda Marsden, Richard Pegler, John Richard, Maureen Walter and the late Steve Williams. The Project would have been less than complete without the building survey and we owe much to John Dallimore, the late John Penoyre, Jane Penoyre and their team. We are also very grateful to all the students who worked so hard on the excavations, particularly Kerry Ely, Richard McConnell, Phil Marter and Stuart and Becky Milby. They supervised many of the sites whose results are incorporated here. Vital roles were also played by Geraldine Andrews, Geoff Couling, Fiona Edwards, Mat Jane, Dave Norcott, Claire Rollason (finds), Ross Turle and Alex Turner (geophysics). Colleagues John Creighton, Nick Thorpe and Keith Wilkinson decamped to Somerset summer after summer, rain or shine. A host of others helped with the establishment and running of the Project in many different ways and here we would especially like to single out Dick Broomhead and Charles and Nancy Hollinrake, who provided us freely with their results.

Many different specialists worked on Shapwick finds: Clive Bond (lithics), Richard Brunning (wood), Rowena Gale (charcoal), Louisa Gidney (animal bone), Alejandra Gutiérrez (medieval and later pottery; bone and ivory objects; floor tiles; Roman brick and tile), Deborah Jaques (fish remains), Marek Lewcun (clay pipes), Mary Lewis and Anwen Caffell (human skeletal remains), Jan Light (marine molluscs), Steve Minnitt (coins), Elaine Morris (prehistoric pottery), Mark Robinson (insects), Fiona Roe (stone), Vanessa Straker, Gill Campbell and Wendy Smith (plant macrofossils and waterlogged wood), Jane Timby (Roman pottery), Heather Tinsley (pollen), Linda Viner and Susan Youngs (metalwork), Keith Wilkinson (molluscs) and Hugh Willmott and Jennifer Price (glass). We are grateful to all of them for their hard work. Richard Brunning, Bob Croft, Tom Mayberry, Steve Minnitt and Chris Webster always provided excellent support from Somerset County Council Historic Environment team, as did staff at the Somerset County Record Office and the Somerset Studies Library (now the Somerset Heritage Centre), especially David Bromwich and Ann Nix.

English Heritage made the major financial contribution to fieldwork (for dendrochronology, geophysics, invertebrate analysis, earthworks survey and soils analysis), post-excavation and publication of the Society for Medieval Archaeology monograph, as well as providing help in kind through their Ancient Monuments Laboratory and allowing the former Royal Commission on Historical Monuments (England) to help with earthwork surveys. These contributions were managed on behalf of English Heritage by Andrew Davidson, Rob Iles and Peter Wilson. We would particularly like to thank David Miles, Paul Stamper and Geoff Wainwright for all their help and advice in securing these funds. The Marc Fitch Fund gave a generous grant to enable the use of a lot of colour illustrations. For small grants of £500 or less we gratefully acknowledge the support of the Maltwood Fund for Archaeological Research in Somerset, the Bristol Naturalists' Society, Caja de Ahorros de la Inmaculada de Aragón, the Society for Medieval Archaeology, BT and the research fund at King Alfred's College. Funding for the planning-led excavations came from the Mendip Construction Group, Wessex Water and the Diocese of Bath and Wells. Meanwhile, in exchange for lectures by Mick, many archaeological organisations across the country contributed to a 'slush fund' (ably managed by Nick Corcos) which has helped with incidental expenses. The University of Durham kindly sponsored Chris's research leave in 2003 to write up the results and this was extended by a further three months by the Arts and Humanities Research Council. The University of Bristol supported Mick's involvement in the Project from 1989 until his retirement in 2004.

Finally, for their help with improving this text we would like to thank Teresa Hall, who contributed so much to Chapters 5 and 6 and for work on the Index; Frank and Caroline Thorn, who helped with the Domesday discussion; Martin Ecclestone, who interpreted the historic documentation for both the Shapwick volumes; David Clements, who checked the ecological aspects of the text for us; Richard Kelleher, who researched the coins and coin weight a little further; Eleanor Standley, for her work on the medieval mirror case; and Graham Clarke, who answered our questions about farming. Abby Antrobus, Sue Fitton and Louisa Gidney all read the final text and suggested improvements. Theirs was no small task but, as always, any errors remain our own. Our special thanks go to Alejandra Gutiérrez and Teresa Hall for all they have done to help bring this book to publication.

Illustrations

All the original figures for this volume were drawn by Alejandra Gutiérrez with the exception of finds drawn by Yvonne Beadnell (Figures 3.22A–C, 4.16B, 7.9, 7.20A, 8.9, 9.42), Helena Dennison (9.22), Jacqui Hutton (3.2), Lizzy Indunni (7.10), Rob Reid (9.26) and Jane Timby (4.7A–H). The AP plot in Figure 2.11 is by Caroline Ingle, standing buildings recording by the Somerset Vernacular Buildings Research Group (2.6, 7.2, 7.5A, 7.25C, 7.26, 7.27, 8.1A, 8.5, 8.7, 8.14A, Box 8.2, 9.5, 9.9, 9.10), and graffiti by Nick Barry-Tait (9.19B). Victor Ambrus produced the fine series of twelve coloured reconstructions (3.8, 3.12, 3.18, 4.04, 4.25, 5.12, 6.10, 7.23, 8.21, 9.3, 9.7. 9.32). For their help in searching out specific illustrations we would like to thank David Clements and Rob Witcher and for the scanning of Mick's slides special thanks go to Jeff Veitch, who also tidied Figure 1.4 and took photographs of the finds (Box 3.1, 3.2, 3.10, 4.13A–E, 4.16A, 4.20A–C, 4.23, 6.12, 7.8, 7.9, 7.14, 7.17, 7.29, 8.10, 8.11, 9.13, 9.14, 9.22, 9.42B).

For permission to use their illustrations we are most grateful to: Keith Alexander (2.18B); James Bond (1.4, 7.34A–C, Box 7.2); Dick Broomhead (8.2, 8.4B); Richard Brunning and Chris Webster (4.19, 7.4B, 7.6, 8.4A); David Clements (2.18A, C, D, E, 3.1D, 3.5); John and Bryony Coles (3.7, 3.16, 3.23A, 3.15); John Dallimore, Jane Penoyre and members of Somerset Vernacular Buildings Research Group (2.6, 7.2, 7.5A, 7.25C, 7.26, 7.27, 8.1A, 8.5, 8.7, 8.14A, B.8.2, 9.5, 9.9A–B, 9.10); Durham University Library (8.18); Geoperspectives (3.20); Geophysical Surveys of Bradford (3.24, 4.8, 6.13, 7.18); Teresa Hall (1.7A, B.1.3B, 10.7); English Heritage (3.23B, 4.3, 4.5, 4.11, 8.25A); Charlie and Nancy Hollinrake (6.5, 8.6A–B); Andrew Jackson (4.14); Peter Jacobs (1.6C, 2.20A–B, 2.23C, 2.24A, B.2.2B, C, 6.14, 9.26); Brian Murless (9.40); Dave Norcott (1.7C, F, 2.14, 2.22D, 3.1A–C); Pierre Pétrequin/JADE and Alison Sheridan (B.3.2b); Scottish Universities Environmental Research Centre (2.23A); Stuart Prior (3.13); and Alex Turner (4.18, 7.35). Thanks are also due to those who granted us copyright to use their images: the Bodleian Library, Oxford (B.6.1); FTN Elboru and Cambridge University Press (B.1.1); Somerset County Record Office and Somerset Local Studies Library, now the Somerset Heritage Centre (2.1, 2.2, 3.18A, B.3.2a, B.4.1, 5.1, 7.10A, 8.23A, 8.25B, 9.17B, 9.21, 9.27, 9.34, 9.39, 9.40, 9.43; the Trustees of the British Museum (7.9B); the US Diplomacy Center (9.2, which is extracted from the 'Seals and Symbols in the American Colonies' exhibition poster). Every effort has been made to trace other copyright holders and we apologise in advance for any inadvertent omissions.

Radiocarbon dating

All the dates used here are calibrated at 95 per cent confidence unless otherwise stated. A full discussion can be found in Marshall *et al.* 2007.

Terminology

In this book the term 'medieval' covers *c.*AD 400–1550. We divide this period into 'early medieval' and 'later medieval', separating the two for convenience around the time of the Norman Conquest in 1066. Other authors may use different nomenclatures.

Medieval Settlement Research Group

If you are interested in carrying out a project on settlements in your own local area then you might like to know that there is a long-running Medieval Settlements Research Group with its own annual publication as well as conferences and workshops. Full details can be found on the Group's website.

MA
CMG

Abbreviations

AML	The Ancient Monuments Laboratory, English Heritage	OE	Old English
		OS	Ordnance Survey
BAR	British Archaeological Report	OUP	Oxford University Press
BL	British Library	PCRG	Prehistoric Ceramics Research Group
BNFL	British Nuclear Fuels Ltd		
CBA	Council for British Archaeology	*PSANHS*	*Proceedings of Somerset Archaeology and Natural History Society*
CPR 1354–1358	*Calendar of the Patent Rolls Preserved in the Public Record Office … Edward III … vol. 10 1354–1358* (1898–1916) HMSO, London		
		RCHM	Royal Commission on Historical Monuments
CUP	Cambridge University Press	RCHM(E)	Royal Commission on Historical Monuments (England)
DoE	Department of the Environment	'S'	Sawyer 1968
DRO	Devon Record Office	*SLP*	*Somerset Levels Papers*
GIS	Geographical Information Systems	SMA	Society for Medieval Archaeology
GPS	Global Positioning System	SRO	Somerset Record Office
HBMC	Historic Buildings and Monuments Commission	SVBRG	Somerset Vernacular Buildings Research Group
HMSO	Her Majesty's Stationery Office	TNA	The National Archives
ME	Middle English	VCH	Victoria County History of the Counties of England
MUP	Manchester University Press		

Preface

The Shapwick Project began in October 1988 as a ten-year investigation into the evolution of settlement and landscape. This volume is one of three final publications to arise from that work. The first, published in 2007, was a Society for Medieval Archaeology monograph that presented our findings in detail. That volume, funded by English Heritage, contains sections on methodology, fieldwork, excavations and finds. The third, a pamphlet intended for schools and visitors, is to follow shortly. The present volume places our detailed results into a wider historical and archaeological context and provided an opportunity to develop our ideas much further. To do so an additional two years of research were necessary and, in many cases, we have returned to the documents, maps and archaeological finds to think again about our approaches and conclusions. In the process we have uncovered entirely new sources, particularly for the seventeenth to nineteenth centuries, and those additions make for a more rounded and complete settlement history that helps to bring the Shapwick story up to the present day. Our hope is that this second book will be enjoyed by a broad readership with an interest in the history of the British landscape and that others will be tempted to make use of some of the techniques and ideas described here in projects of their own making. For our own part, even after ten years of research and ten years writing up, we feel that we should be only now just beginning.

CHAPTER ONE

Starting Points

As likely as not you have never been to Shapwick. On the map you will find it marked on the north side of the Polden Hills in the county of Somerset, more or less halfway between the market towns of Glastonbury and Bridgwater (Figure 1.1). Though the village has a church and two grand manor houses, this is not a large place, nor is it obviously picturesque. The low cottages of greyish-white limestone with their red pantile roofs may give the village a traditional 'feel', but this belies significant social and economic change over recent decades (Figure 1.2). In common with many rural communities the length and breadth of Britain, Shapwick no longer has a post office, shops, or a primary school. This is essentially a quiet dormitory and retirement village much like any other.

The inquisitive visitor will find evidence for longstanding links with farming at every turn. Not only are there orchards and agricultural buildings, some of them now converted to housing, but the well-ordered fields that surround the village are dotted with six working farms (Figure 1.3). With the exception of a mixed woodland at Loxley, much of the upland is given over to pasture for cows and the growing of cereals. Walking downhill, where the Polden ridge flattens onto the Somerset Levels, the floodable land or 'moors' was once exploited extensively for peat. Very little is dug there today: the worked-out cuttings lie silent and filled with water. Shapwick Heath, as this northern part of the parish in the Brue valley is known, is now a Nature Reserve of international importance, supporting such rarities as the Large Marsh Grasshopper and Silver Diving Beetles, as well as a diverse ground flora of Sphagnum, sedges, grasses, and wetland herbs between 'wet woodland' of willow, birch and alder.[1] A little more exploring here might lead the adventurous stranger to one of the several abandoned farms subsiding into the soft peat, or to the 'sand islands', named locally as 'burtles'. Like the Nidons that lie closer to the Polden slope, these are important features of the local topography, but they are hardly the 'hills' some older maps extravagantly claim them to be; even the most sensitive of drivers with the least sympathetic of suspensions barely registers their existence.

There is nothing in this picture to suggest that Shapwick is exceptional, at least not in terms of its landscape or its architecture; there is no ruined monastery or castle, for example. Yet, like so many other places in rural England, there are both written records rich in detail and archaeological artefacts buried beneath its gardens and fields that can tell us about the experience of everyday life here and, during the 1990s, this place was chosen as the setting for a wide-ranging historical and archaeological study that aimed to unravel its history and archaeology. This book is the story of that project: a micro-level examination of a well-used English landscape from earliest prehistory to the present day.

Questions and answers

According to recent research, more than half of British people think the countryside is boring and one in ten are hard pressed to recognise a sheep when they see it.[2] Yet, for the other half, there is an enduring infatuation with the countryside, so much so that some claim it lies at the very core of our national identity. We cherish its quirkiness, the bold patterning of fields and hedgerows, the creamy stone and blood-red brick of houses, barns and walls. We marry in its country churches, visit its stately homes and navigate its banked lanes. In this 'forever Ambridge', villages

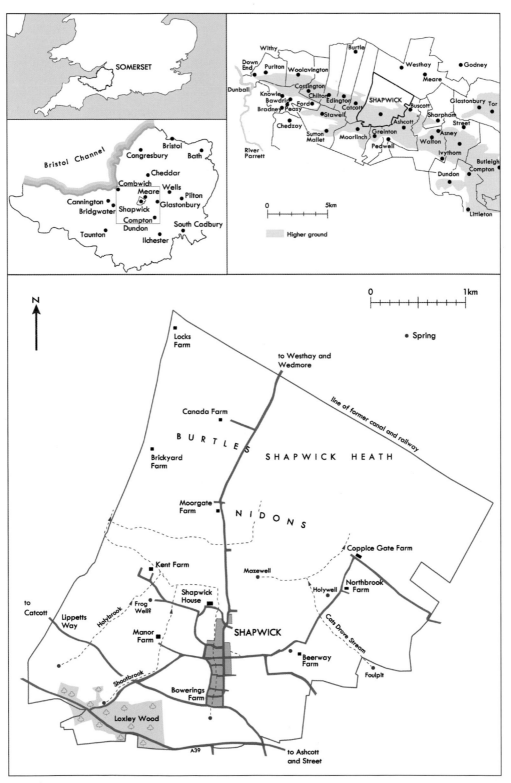

Figure 1.1. Location map for Shapwick showing selected features of the modern landscape.

Figure 1.2. Shapwick village from the south-west with Mendip beyond.

Figure 1.3. Shapwick village from the air, looking north down the Polden slope towards the Brue valley. Manor Farm is visible to the west of the village with Kent Farm beyond.

'nestle', timber-framed buildings are 'handsome' and gardens are never less than 'charming'. The idealised fantasy of our 'green and pleasant land' remains potent, a blur of Brooke, Betjeman, Constable, Elgar and Wordsworth that seems, for some at least, largely untroubled by the harsher realities of multi-cultural expectation, fertiliser-sodden soils, rural recession and the depressing decline in numbers of our native birds and flowers.

It comes as something of a surprise, therefore, to find out just how little we really understand about the development of our rural settlements and their landscapes: the England of village greens and parish churches pictured on jigsaws and the covers of coffee-table books. *When* did villages like these come into being? *Why* exactly did this happen? *What* was there before? *How* did villages develop once they were established, and *what* evidence remains now to show us what life was like in the past? Through the intensive study of historical documents, archaeology, botany and topography, these are the fundamental questions we set out to address in this book.

Beginnings

One of the most intriguing puzzles in the English landscape is quite how the rural settlements we see today came into existence in the first place. Until the mid-1960s even the most enlightened of teachers in schools and universities taught their students that the origins of the village lay in the middle of the fifth century AD. According to near-contemporary annals and later texts such as the writings of the Venerable Bede, it was then that a flood of immigrants sailed from southern Scandinavia, Germany and the Netherlands. On arrival, meeting little resistance from the native British population,[3] they 'established' the English village. This version of events, in which early medieval settlement and its field systems were seen as a 'package' imported by 'German tribes', had first been proposed by distinguished Victorian historians and, in the second quarter of the twentieth century, their claims were further bolstered by new research from place-name scholars who proposed that settlements could be ordered chronologically through an analysis of their names or toponymy.[4] This phasing was backed up by other historical evidence, notably Domesday Book, so often in the past a starting point for economic history, whose contents were thought to provide a moment-in-time snapshot of settlement development around the time of the Norman Conquest in 1066.[5]

All kinds of assumptions necessarily flowed from this simple proposal. For settlement by invaders to be possible at all, the landscape *had*, de facto, to be a blank canvas, and so a depopulated and heavily wooded countryside was envisaged in which major programmes of clearance would be needed to create the open spaces necessary for villages and fields.[6] The imagined existence of primeval forests, undrained marshes and flooded river valleys was only confirmed by the overwhelmingly natural landscapes described in land conveyances known to us as Anglo-Saxon charters. Then, for *so many* settlements to be needed there must have been large numbers of incomers. This last point no-one could doubt because of historical narratives that described the arrival of 'German colonists' and the subsequent displacement of the native 'British' population in a 'bow wave' of conquest. This sort of 'invasion hypothesis' had long been accepted by prehistorians as a way of explaining change in housing traditions, pottery styles and ways of burying the dead, so why should the historic past be any different? And so, block after block, an academic façade came to be constructed that drew its evidence from several different sources, each reinforcing the validity of the others. The most influential of all landscape history books, William Hoskins's *The Making of the English Landscape*, first published in 1955, envisaged a total dislocation of settlement and field system patterns with little or no continuity between Roman and early medieval times.[7] 'The English landscape as we know it today', wrote Hoskins, 'is almost entirely the product of the last fifteen hundred years, beginning with the earliest Anglo-Saxon villages in the middle decades of the fifth century'. Even twenty years later, when respected historical geographer Harry Thorpe came to write up his history of the parish of Wormleighton in Warwickshire, he still envisaged Anglo-Saxon settlers living in compact villages with their characteristic '-ton' and '-ham' place-name endings, and '-worth' and '-field' place-names following on later 'as small groups of venturesome settlers spread north into the dense oak wood making individual hedged clearings'.[8]

Harry Thorpe was in no way unusual among his peers in imagining a country being resettled anew and thus a kind of purity to Anglo-Saxon economy, society and culture which seemed to bear no mark of what had gone before. Settlements, place-names, regulation and legal customs, open-field cultivation – all these were seen to be Germanic introductions.

Thanks to research since the mid-1960s this version of events has now been entirely overturned. First, place-names were found not to be fixed permanently and, contrary to previous assertions, their names could also be quite unconnected with the foundation of settlement.[9] Then, documentary sources, by now being viewed with a more critical eye, showed that William the Conqueror's great census did not in fact provide a comprehensive 'yellow pages' of English villages, as had been assumed, but was in fact largely concerned with those places that owed rent or tax.[10] It did not provide an unambiguous list after all. Archaeologists, too, played an important role in dismantling earlier theories by mapping a far higher density of Roman settlement from aerial photography and fieldwalking than had hitherto been suspected.[11] This not only showed a more sophisticated network of settlements and communications than had previously been accepted by those who saw Roman influence on the fringes of the Empire as weak and easily swept aside, but also raised uncomfortable questions about how such a large 'British' population had *really* been driven out or exterminated with such extraordinary thoroughness and the extent to which settlements *could* have been planted afresh if so many suitable sites were already occupied. There was also the realisation that some Anglo-Saxons had arrived long before, as Roman soldiers. At the same time, environmental scientists re-evaluating the pollen record had concluded that the trees had been substantially cleared from the British landscape by late prehistoric times.[12] This was a telling point because it effectively decoupled any large-scale changes in vegetation from the post-Roman historical events as described by Bede and others. Earlier claims of 'the silent and strenuous conversion of the primeval forests of central and southern England' began to look unduly dramatic.[13] Indeed, viewed in this new light, both charter evidence and early legal documents seemed to depict a landscape brimming with people. By the

seventh century there were food rents of honey, ale, cattle and much else to be honoured and, as historian Peter Sawyer commented, there was 'very little room for unworked resources' in this new vision of the early medieval countryside.[14]

At the same time, archaeological interest in the Anglo-Saxon landscape itself was also strengthening. Until the mid-1950s the focus in research and excavation had been on cemeteries, grave goods and high-status sites rather than what we might think of as 'ordinary' rural settlement. Now, new sites were being identified from pottery scatters and aerial photographs that suggested greater continuity between prehistoric, Roman and Anglo-Saxon landscapes.[15] The most exciting results, however, came from large-scale digging at sites such as Catholme (Staffs), Chalton (Hants), Cowdery's Down (Hants), Mucking (Essex) and West Stow (Suffolk) that discovered the foundations of early medieval structures.[16] Once the postholes were plotted out to reveal timber buildings, it was realised that the layouts of these settlements were not at all similar to the kinds of villages seen on modern Ordnance Survey maps: they seemed to be more loosely structured and less planned, and many of them were short-lived too. There was no sign at all of the classic nucleated village plan that earlier generations of historians had so confidently predicted had been founded in the fifth century AD.[17] Once more, when archaeologists came to excavate beneath villages that had been deserted in the later Middle Ages, Anglo-Saxon deposits were more elusive than they expected. Later medieval villages, it seemed, were not, after all, the successors to Anglo-Saxon villages – so when exactly had the villages we see today come into being and why?

By the time the Shapwick Project was getting underway in the late 1980s the 'invasion' hypothesis was no longer under serious consideration. In its wake were new concepts about how villages might have come into existence. The first was planning: the deliberate creation of larger settlements with ordered layouts to replace an earlier, more dispersed pattern of farmsteads and hamlets.[18] A second mechanism of settlement formation envisaged other villages originating at a cluster of road junctions, small greens, manorial centres and churches, and subsequently growing together as their population

Figure 1.4. A doctored Christmas card sent by landscape archaeologist James Bond to Mick in the mid-1980s. As two peasants ride into their hamlet on a wagon, the son voices his hopes for the future, but the father is disbelieving. Shown to hundreds of undergraduates, extra-mural students at Bristol University, local societies and audiences all over Europe, the card gently pokes fun at the academic agenda for medieval settlement. 'Assarts' is not a known medieval expletive, of course, though it has a good enough ring to it! The term actually refers to an area of woodland which has been cleared for cultivation and enclosed. An example can be seen on Figure 7.39.

increased, leading to what was referred to as a 'composite' or 'polyfocal' village with a very different kind of plan composed of a number of linked nodes.[19] Significant changes in field systems were assumed to accompany these two processes of 'nucleation', earlier forms of cultivation being abandoned in favour of two or more open fields that were worked in common by a number of peasant families.[20] These open-field systems held many advantages: as a means of overcoming shortages in pasture through shared grazing and rotations in land use; as a way to accommodate the new technology of the heavy plough that was cumbersome to manoeuvre around smaller enclosures; and as a measure to ease the inheritance of land (and subsequent exchanges) through the subdivision of holdings into strips. Many of these social and economic explanations were not new,[21] but together they offered a far fuller exploration of the changes that would have had such a profound impact on the lives of those who lived and laboured in the early medieval countryside. This is the back story behind the doctored Christmas card sent to Mick by landscape archaeologist James Bond in the mid-1980s (Figure 1.4).

Where there was less agreement was in the possible timing of this transformation, though some important clues were offered by developing models of the early medieval settlement hierarchy. Figure 1.5a, which derives ultimately from the research of historical geographer Glanville Jones,[22] conveniently summarises in diagrammatic form a hierarchy of settlement on an imagined estate in the seventh century AD. It depicts a settlement landscape with a central 'caput', perhaps a royal centre, vill or *villa regalis*, surrounded by several interdependent hamlets. The 'caput' is envisaged as the most important medieval settlement, perhaps with a hall for royal or elite accommodation, and in many cases a proto-urban centre with its own 'inland'. Any churches or chapels were also dependent initially on the minster there. Further away on the estate the hamlets, with their bond tenants or 'berewicks', supply this centre with specialised products such as lambs, honey, cereals or services and this provisioning role, together with their subsidiary status, is sometimes reflected in their place-names, hence 'Graintun', 'Cattletun', and so on marked on the figure. Crucially, there are no villages in this so-called 'multiple estates' model; instead, these smaller places subsist on their own intensively manured and cropped fields, which are combined with more distant resources such as woodland, pasture and meadow.

As these large estates were broken up and granted away so it is thought that the fragmented parts themselves became self-sufficient (Figure 1.5B), though their earlier interdependence and specialised functions remained 'fingerprinted' to some extent in their place-names ('Lambton' = 'Lambtun', etc.). According to this hypothesis, here drawn diagrammatically for the first time, the process of 'fission' leads to the development of separate field systems for each of the former hamlets ('West Field', 'East Field'), which themselves recombined to emerge as separate villages, in discrete parishes, with their own parish churches and manors. Rising population, the operation of the manorial system and the demands of increased taxation from emerging feudal authorities are all seen to have played their part.[23] These agrarian, demographic and economic changes, it is argued, demanded efficiencies better suited to a cohesive community living in a single settlement, rather than

a population that was dispersed widely in small farmsteads.

Accordingly, at the time when the Shapwick Project was first being discussed in 1987–88, one scheme advocated a middle Anglo-Saxon date (eighth or early ninth century AD) for an initial phase of 'nucleation' – the moment at which villages came into being – with a later phase of replanning in the tenth century.[24] A second scheme preferred a longer and generally later chronology, arguing that nucleation began about AD 850 and was complete by the eleventh century in most areas, but continued as late as the thirteenth century elsewhere.[25] In our project we were keen to test these developing ideas about the timing and reasons behind the origins of the English village and the open-field system, and these are topics to which we shall return in Chapters 5 and 6.

Change and development

Although these questions about how, when and why the English village might have emerged are fundamental, our investigations extend far beyond these themes. In this book we have attempted a series of detailed reconstructions of Shapwick right through to the present day. We therefore begin our story in Chapters 3 and 4 by tracing the development of communities from prehistory and through the Roman period. As our archaeological work will demonstrate, by the early medieval period this was already an ancient landscape, a place where people had lived for thousands of years. We were interested to know to what extent this deeper past had influenced the medieval picture, in the choice of places to live, for example, and in the infrastructure of boundaries and tracks. How had the different topographies and resources of the landscape been exploited by past populations? If we wished to delve deep into our village's genetics it would be vital not only to know how this earlier 'underlay' had influenced the later picture and to view change over a long timescale but also to examine a wide range of settlement types, not just those at the top of the social hierarchy, such as Roman villas.

Over a decade of work we therefore built up a general picture of the development of the landscape before the village even came into existence, mapping prehistoric sites from scatters of flints, aerial

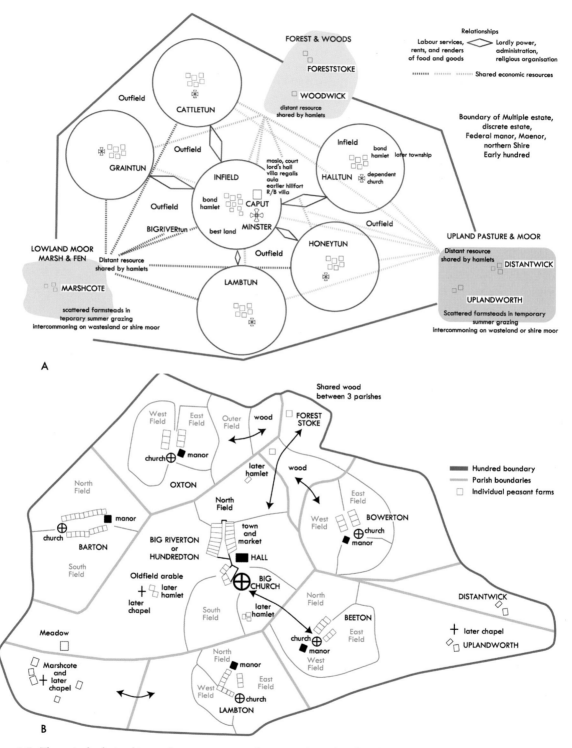

Figure 1.5. Theoretical relationships and arrangements within an early medieval multiple estate. A: an imagined hierarchy of settlement in the seventh century AD *(after Aston 1985, fig. 11). B: the same area around the time of Domesday in the eleventh century.*

photographs, geophysical surveys and excavation and slowly filling out our understanding of early human activity. One key objective here, and for later periods too, was the collection of new information about the environment, not only from faunal remains and pollen sequences but also from any clues lying hidden in the historic ecology of hedgerows and woodland. We hoped these data would tell us when the broad patterns of historic land use were first established and show how local communities adapted to and exploited their environment. But we also knew that to paint a picture of rural history as merely a set of agrarian resources would be to neglect one of the most interesting aspects of our story: the evolution of attitudes towards the 'natural' environment. This we would attempt to understand through a combination of archaeological finds, documents, landscape features and historic maps.

We had many other questions too about the medieval and later village community. As we shall see in Chapter 2, during the Middle Ages Shapwick was part of the very considerable estate of the Benedictine abbey at Glastonbury and an extensive archive of documents is available for that period. Here was an opportunity for us to examine in detail how one part of a monastic estate functioned and to understand the impact of the Abbey on the developing village plan, its churches, farm buildings and agriculture. While others are captivated by the architecture and artistic achievement of the medieval monastery, Chapters 6 and 7 of this book concern the impact of monastic institutions on their agricultural and economic landscapes: the water systems that drove the mills, the fields that grew their barley, the barns that stored the grain and the overgrown quarries that supplied the building stone.

Another key focus of this book is the 'experience' of an English village community over the past 1,000 years and how it has changed. Our interest lies in the full panorama of daily life, from dwellings and gardens to pottery, dress accessories and food on the table. To gain access to this detail we draw upon an interdisciplinary approach that combines a rich body of written material with archaeological evidence and sets our results within a wider social context. We treat the objects that were made and used at Shapwick as expressions of status and identity, structuring the

routines of people's daily lives, even as projections of their owners to some degree. This is especially exciting because it extends our interests right into the living fabric of the settlement, sometimes matching artefacts with houses, families and even individuals. Ultimately, this approach takes us right to people's front doors and introduces us to men and women, past and present, who shaped the local scene. Such a wealth of detail inspired us to preface each of our chapters with a short story that tries to draw upon the particular evidence we have recovered. This commitment on our part to a kind of anthropological history is intended to convey everyday experience more directly and to acquaint the reader with a selection of local 'actors' in the community in an accessible fashion. These narratives, usually called 'interpretive' by archaeologists, ensure that we do not lose sight of the lives of the individual, especially the disadvantaged and the 'marginal', and the social and physical contexts with which they were associated. We found them challenging to write, not least because, to be in any way persuasive, they have to incorporate so many strands of evidence in order to visualise buildings and their environments with any accuracy.[26] They were greatly beneficial, however, when we came to work up the twelve reconstruction drawings undertaken for this volume by Victor Ambrus. Imaginative though it may be, Victor's work draws very precisely on every aspect of the archaeological record as we were able to report it at Shapwick and in itself represents a significant body of work.

We must also acknowledge some constraints. First, no claim is made here that Shapwick is 'typical', some kind of representative 'every-wick', except in so far as many of the processes described in this volume could be documented in other parts of Britain – with corresponding variations. Second, this is a book about villages, but villages are not ubiquitous in Britain; in fact, they are the main form of settlement across only about half of England. Third, Shapwick is very much a 'living village'. The techniques of large-scale open-area excavation, used to such good effect at deserted medieval sites such as Wharram Percy on the Yorkshire Wolds, could not be deployed here and there was no opportunity for us to excavate whole plots or 'tofts'.[27] Nor was this the appropriate place to undertake a detailed investigation of the archaeology of the medieval house, for example – the size of our trenches simply did not allow it and, in any case, a great deal of the medieval archaeology that must once have existed across the village has since been damaged or removed altogether by post-medieval and modern activity.

Given these constraints, our energies were more usefully channelled into other areas. Where we have been able to make a contribution, for instance, is in piecing together archaeological, historical and cartographical evidence. The study of the village plan is a case in point: understanding how and why that plan changed and, in the eighteenth and nineteenth centuries, how the entire 'footprint' of the village was so drastically altered by local landowners, can be achieved only through the analysis of historic maps, the identification of landscape features, including earthworks and ornamental tree planting, and through carefully targeted excavation. As we shall discover in Chapters 8 and 9, our view of Shapwick's medieval past is heavily filtered through eighteenth- and nineteenth-century 'improvements' of this kind, not least the remodelling of spaces and vistas around its manor houses and the reordering of its fields. This is of interest for earlier periods – the modern village plan is not a faithful indication of the medieval layout, for example – but also in its own right, to learn about the historical archaeology of the recent past. From the outset, we were keen to bring the village story right up to the twentieth century, to resurrect the daily lives of these villagers through their artefacts and buildings in much the same way as we have done for prehistory. Post-medieval sites (that is, post-1540) were deliberately selected for excavation to help us achieve that goal. The result is that we have been able to observe the profound changes that have taken place over the past 250 years in domestic architecture and in the suites of objects found inside Shapwick houses.[28] In turn, this introduces us to bigger questions about the changing sociology of the English village, distinctions in food and dining, the emergence of consumerism, capitalism, industrialism and the transition towards modern life.[29] Throughout this book we seek to fit our small-scale observations into the broader backdrop of these major transformations in society.

Finally, this study is an integrated investigation of settlement and land use. In each chapter we address the questions of local industry, communication between settlements along roads and tracks, what crops were grown, how agriculture and field systems were organised and how other resources and rights were allotted. It is important to do this for all periods, first because our investigation constantly makes use of more recent documentary and cartographic sources in order to shed light on the earlier situation in the Middle Ages. This proved particularly important when understanding the settlement pattern in the immediate post-Roman period and emphasises the importance of taking a long chronological view and a more holistic approach whenever studies of this kind are attempted (see Chapter 5). Second, as we shall see, the landscape was not reinvented at each period of the past. There are strong continuities, such as in the alignments of field boundaries and the attraction of specific locations for human occupation.

Why Shapwick?

There are more than 10,000 parishes in England alone, so narrowing down a location for a project of this kind was no simple task. As a rule of thumb, archaeological and historical investigation should always try to build upon previous research, and it must also be practical. So we began close to home. Seven years before our project started Mick had examined the evidence for the origins of nucleated rural settlements in the county of Somerset,[30] close to our Bristol base, and found that only two village plans could be dated with any precision.[31] Although there had been a good deal of archaeological study of the early medieval period in the county over the previous fifty years, much of it directed by Philip Rahtz in the 1960s and 1970s, by 1988 nowhere in the county had there been large-scale excavation on a farm, hamlet or village dated between the fifth and twelfth centuries. Among those sites that had been examined locally were Glastonbury Tor, probably an early eremitic monastery; the cemetery at Cannington; the hillfort of Cadbury at Congresbury, and the adjacent cemetery at Henley Wood (for locations see Chapter 5).[32] Other major work on sites of the same period included the largely unpublished archaeological campaigns at Glastonbury Abbey and the remarkable excavations at Wells cathedral and the hilltop fort of South Cadbury.[33] Many of these sites, however, were high-status secular or ecclesiastical settlements and cemeteries.[34] Virtually no attention had been paid to rural settlements and their contemporary landscapes.[35]

The inspiration for our final choice of Shapwick as the location for our project came from a postgraduate student at the Department of English Local History at the University of Leicester.[36] Nick Corcos had studied the field systems at Shapwick for his Masters dissertation, but it was several almost throw-away remarks about the village plan and the names of the medieval furlongs that were particularly striking.[37] Nick pointed out that Shapwick has a 'regular, grid-iron pattern of roads and lanes ... quite clear on large scale maps even today' and that the village seemed to have been deliberately planned. In addition, Nick had highlighted from a survey of the open fields undertaken in 1515 a group of furlong names at some distance from the modern village that he thought might indicate the locations of 'scattered settlement in the early Anglo-Saxon period'. On that basis, he proposed a drastic recasting of settlement and field systems sometime before the Domesday Book came to be drawn up in the eleventh century.

The more we looked the more Shapwick seemed like a good candidate. If a major focus of the project was to be the origin and development of the medieval village, the first objective was to find a parish, or possibly a series of adjoining parishes, with a single core settlement rather than isolated farmsteads or hamlets: a nucleated rather than a dispersed settlement pattern. Shapwick satisfied that requirement. Furthermore, because archaeological fieldwork was to make a central contribution to our research, it would be vital to have routine access to land, particularly to cultivated fields where fieldwalking would identify new sites, or so we hoped. In the course of his research Nick had also discovered that most of the parish was owned by Lord Vestey of 'Dewhurst the butchers' fame.[38] As a life-long vegetarian, Mick was understandably unenthusiastic about this connection but, as it transpired, dealing with a single land agent, Bill Robbins, who looked after the estate on behalf of Jackson, Stopps, and Staff in Cirencester, proved a tremendous advantage. Any project like this is, of course, totally dependent on the permission (and attitudes) of the landowners and tenant farmers. To have one owner, one land agent and six or so tenant farmers made our negotiations relatively easy.[39] Previous experience also suggested that good sequences of maps and documents would be vital. We therefore pinned our hopes on finding a parish with an existing village, an active farming tradition and a bulging card index at the County Record Office.

Shapwick, it emerged, had all of these plus a few surprises thrown in. True, the parish lies somewhat off the beaten track, but the place is not entirely unknown to archaeologists and historians. Oxford-educated antiquarian John Collinson, for example, incorporated a short history of Shapwick in his *History and Antiquities of the County of Somerset* of 1791, including a valuable plate engraving of one of its manor houses (see Figure 2.5). The archaeological potential of the local peats on the Somerset Levels has also long been appreciated.[40] The Abbot's Way, for example, a prehistoric wooden trackway that runs between Westhay and the Burtle islands, was discovered accidentally in 1834 and a section was excavated by the antiquarian Charles Dymond in 1873.[41] In 1880 local antiquary Arthur Bulleid noted the remains of a wooden trackway in the peats in the north of the parish during his search for prehistoric lake villages.[42] However, it was not until the second half of the twentieth century that the true potential of the peats was more fully realised. Sir Harry Godwin (Box 1.1), a pioneer of the reconstruction of past environments, made it his business to record prehistoric discoveries and their stratigraphy and to take samples for pollen analysis and radiocarbon dating – a race against time as the raised bog peat was sliced away for fuel and gardens. This led to excavation on a larger scale in the 1970s and 1980s by the Somerset Levels Project under the direction of John and Bryony Coles. As digging continued on the Sweet Track, the Shapwick Heath track and other sites in the parish, such as Skinner's Wood and Withy Bed Copse, archaeological teams occasionally made forays upslope onto the drier upland, collecting flints and pottery from the ploughed fields. This fieldwork would provide important clues on which our own project could build.

BOX 1.1

Previous investigations: Harry Godwin, John Coles and the Somerset Levels

Cambridge scholar Harry Godwin (1901–1985) is best known for his studies of fossil plant remains found in waterlogged conditions (Figure B.1.1). He seems to have visited the Somerset Levels for the first time in the 1930s, when excavations by Arthur Bulleid were underway at Meare, and he quickly appreciated the potential of the raised bog for the developing science of peat stratigraphy and pollen analysis.[b1] Godwin realised that the Somerset trackways were prehistoric[b2] and he was able to correlate his findings with the analysis of peat bogs in Denmark, Scandinavia and elsewhere in Britain to produce a comprehensive picture of post-glacial vegetation change over wide areas of northern Europe.[b3] His first paper about Somerset, on the Meare Pool region of the Somerset Levels, was published in 1956, the same year as his major research monograph – *History of the British Flora: A Factual Basis for Phytogeography*. Towards the end of his career, Godwin became interested in radiocarbon as a method of dating deposits and was alive to the implications of the technique for archaeology, publishing several papers on the subject; the Cambridge radiocarbon dating laboratory is, appropriately, named after him. He was also aware just how far climate had changed over the millennia, a very topical consideration today. He was knighted in 1970 for his contributions to Quaternary science.

Figure B.1.1. Harry Godwin, pioneer of palaeo-environmental investigations in the Somerset Levels.

The study of the archaeology of the Somerset Levels has never been a solo effort, however. Godwin was himself a great collaborator, and it was through his local contacts with Stephen Dewar, a retired tea-planter living on the Poldens, that he was able to keep in touch with the latest finds on the Levels.[b4] When John Coles arrived at Cambridge as an assistant lecturer in 1962–63 he then took up the baton. Early excavation concentrated on the Abbots trackway and later, with his future wife Bryony, on the Sweet Track (Figure B.1.2). By 1973 the makings of a multi-disciplinary team had been established and over the next fifteen years the Somerset Levels Project routinely examined the 'heads' as the peat was cut and reported any wood or structures as they were revealed. Hundreds of small excavations were undertaken; in 1974, for example, more than 160 were carried out at Tinney's Ground, and another 100 were undertaken in 1975–76, annual reports appearing regularly in the *Somerset Levels Papers* (1975–89).[b5] This emphasis on immediate and full publication greatly influenced our own approach to the Shapwick Project.

The most exciting discoveries by the Somerset Levels Project were the trackways of the prehistoric period, and of these the most spectacular is the Sweet Track. This plank walkway, much of which crosses Shapwick parish, was excavated in four stretches between 1970 and 1977. Tree-ring dating shows felling dates for the

timber in 3807–3806 BC. The main threat to its survival today is any lowering of the water table that would allow bacteria to attack the wood as it dries out, and it was with this in mind that a water pumping system was installed in 1983. A small museum of objects, replica trackways and displays was opened in 1982 at Roger Rogers's Willows Garden Centre on the road between Westhay and Shapwick, at the heart of the former peat-cutting area. Later on this was to be developed as the Peat Moors Centre, an interpretation centre, now closed, where some of the techniques of environmental archaeology were explained and replicas of finds were put on display. [b6] Today there are more than thirty Sites of Special Scientific Interest on the Levels and further protection is in place to guard its rich biodiversity and archaeology. There is, however, no single conservation designation other than its status as a 'Cultural Landscape' and there have been calls for the whole area to be proposed as a World Heritage Site. The future of the interpretation centre, meanwhile, is again under discussion.

Figure B.1.2. John Coles at work on the Sweet Track. Once the overburden of peat was removed by a mechanical digger, the excavators worked from planks and 'toe-boards' to keep the site from damage. The wood must be kept wet once it is exposed.

As it turned out, what it lacks in architectural jewels Shapwick more than makes up for in folklore and history. This is supposedly the setting for the gruesome tale of St Indracht, an Irish pilgrim, and his companions, whose 'throtes were cut in the night for moneie' by King Ine's men around the year AD 700. Indracht's burial place in Glastonbury was afterwards the scene of miraculous events.[43] Later still, stories connect the village with the tumultuous events of the seventeenth century – with a Civil War escapee,[44] and with the hanging of fugitives after the battle of Sedgemoor in July 1685[45] – and they show how intricately the identities of rural communities were bound up with local allegiances and interests. Shapwick had a colourful cast of characters at this period, among them Sir Henry Rolle (1589/90–1656), a supporter of parliament during the Civil War, best known for his refusal to

act as a judge at the trial of Charles I; and William Bull (1595–1676), who negotiated between hostile forces at Wells in 1642. These two 'county' families, who later supplied three members of parliament for Bridgwater, will figure large in later chapters. They include the eccentric Denys Rolle (1720–1797), who founded colonies in British East Florida in the 1760s and later in the Bahamas; barrister George Warry (1795–1883), railway enthusiast and champion of the Somerset constabulary; and Henry Bull Templer Strangways (1832–1920), who became premier and attorney-general of South Australia 1868–70 before he retired to Shapwick. The town of Strangways, Lake Strangways and the Strangways River in Australia's Northern Territory are named in honour of his role in promoting the exploration of the country's interior. Like those of so many places in Britain, Shapwick's nineteenth-century history is entwined with that of

Empire and its reach is longer than at first might be imagined. For our purposes, however, the important point is that no love was lost between Shapwick's two gentry families. Colonists and travellers of the world they may have been, but they sometimes struggled to adapt to the more familiar environment of home. The two families were forever at each other's throats, so much so that even the local vicar despaired of their interminable fighting. 'Shapwick was eminently respectable', he wrote in his diary, 'so respectable indeed, that it seemed further from the Kingdom of God than most places that I have known'.[46] Lawsuits, however, do have their benefits, not least the generous employment of lawyers and surveyors who drew up documents and maps in support of their client's claims. As we shall see in this book, their disputes can now be turned to our benefit in order to reconstruct everything from the physical appearance of the village and its houses to land use and management practices, as at, for example, Loxley Wood (see Box 8.2).

Only once in history has Shapwick directly drawn the national gaze. In 1845 a local woman, Sarah Freeman, was convicted of poisoning her husband Henry, a glazier and plasterer, and her illegitimate young son James, while they were living at Ashcott. A few months later her elder brother and her mother, who lived in Shapwick, had also fallen victim and Sarah was subsequently implicated in the death of her own daughter and a further five deaths in another family in the parish – a total of ten suspicious 'murders of the most horrible description', as *The Times* put it with grisly relish. Since many of her victims had been buried in Shapwick churchyard, the bodies had to be exhumed and examined there in the presence of the coroner and jury. 'The whole village was in attendance, and although the excitement was intense, yet it was mixed up with a degree of solemnity, awe portrayed visibly upon every countenance, which spoke well for the simple habits of the inhabitants of this retired and quiet village.'[47] White arsenic was quickly detected as the cause of death and, once found guilty of her 'diabolical' crime, Sarah was hanged on top of Wilton gaol outside Taunton. The testimonies of witnesses called to speak at Sarah's trial, like her litigious landlord's maps, proved useful to our project in ways they could never have imagined, this time as an insight into living conditions in the village 150 years ago.

Approaches

Local studies

This book is an intensive dissection of a community and its landscape: Shapwick under the microscope. The unit we have chosen to investigate equates to a parish, the smallest unit of ecclesiastical administration in the medieval and later periods. Although we will be tracing its social and economic links far beyond the parish boundaries and sometimes overseas, this is essentially a small canvas, one which allows a depth of scrutiny and a strong familiarity with the fine grain of the subject matter, rather than a painting done with the broad brush strokes of history. Several projects have followed a similar path and tried to take into account the territory and resources attached to particular settlements.[48] Given that our research covers such a long chronological span and that its source material is both archaeological as well as documentary and cartographical, another appropriate badge for the approach adopted here might be 'local history' – an in-depth portrait of a specific geographical area and its community. It has little in common, however, with histories of institutions or biographies of the great and good. However singular a person's life may have been, our concern here is always a wider cross section of the community and a broader selection of monuments than the church and manor house. We wish to tell the story of the small world of the English village but always through a lens that captures the wider forces of change at work.[49] To do so, our research will have to look outwards to wider communities and culture, touching upon themes drawn from economic and social history and historical geography, though always with an eye for archaeological detail.

Landscape archaeology

A second strand to our study might be broadly characterised as 'landscape archaeology'.[50] This is an exciting branch of research that has developed over the past fifty years through contributions from archaeology, history, geography and historical ecology. Most importantly for our research at Shapwick, landscape archaeology looks beyond the single archaeological monument or any particular excavation to consider the wider geography and a greater chronological depth. Using techniques such as aerial photography and the study of maps, rather than a reliance on excavation for its interpretations, the distinctiveness of the approach lies in the scale of the project and its wide range of intellectual inputs and methodologies.

At around the time when our work on Shapwick was just beginning, several inspirational landscape studies had just been published. Among them was an account of Blenheim Park near Oxford, a fieldwalking survey around the deserted medieval village of Wharram Percy on the Yorkshire Wolds and a project on the Berkshire Downs.[51] The approaches taken by these surveys were all quite different: the first, at Blenheim, had the historic focus and level of detail we wished to emulate; the second used systematic fieldwalking as a platform for the reconstruction of the Roman landscape; while the survey of prehistoric and Roman landscapes on the Berkshire Downs included methodological experiments that we felt could be usefully extended.[52] All of these were influenced, as we were, by earlier surveys in East Hampshire and around Chalton, but none, not even the fictionalised village survey of Ambridge for the BBC radio series *The Archers*, used the range of methods we had in mind.[53] Where one project used fieldwalking as a standard method of prospection, it ignored buildings, historical documentation or geophysics, and vice versa. We insisted upon an integrated project, and one with well-defined outcomes that furthered our understanding of the contemporary experiences of spaces and places.[54]

We also looked with envy at some of the products emerging from Mediterranean surveys. In spite of the obvious impediment of heat, some of these research projects had covered enormous areas and, in doing so, greatly enhanced what was known of their local archaeology – not just sites and monuments but also material culture. And yet they did more than simply describe and document; they had something to offer both in their methodologies and to general theories of landscape.[55] The Bocotia project in Greece, for example, brought home to us the importance of understanding the underlying prehistoric and Roman pattern of settlement and land use, and the need to avoid being sidetracked into the study of just one kind of archaeological site. We wanted to embrace the full variety of settlement forms, from farmsteads to

villages. The Biferno Valley survey in Italy, on the other hand, reinforced to us that landscape archaeology should not be merely a technical application, but must go deeper, to investigate the short-, medium- and long-term processes at work in the landscape, taking our field of enquiry into more recent periods rather than studying any one period in isolation.[56] If a parish-sized study could provide the platform for trying out a whole range of new ideas then it would, in effect, become a kind of outdoor laboratory, pioneering their evaluation and application. In the event, this did indeed prove to be the case: the Shapwick Project opened itself to a great variety of sources of information and, in so doing, was flexible enough to embrace the work of archaeologists, architectural historians, environmental scientists, economic and social historians, chemists, botanists and many more. We believe as firmly now as we did at the outset that some of the most exciting and satisfying advances in any field tend to come from research 'conversations' that cross the traditional disciplinary divides and, at Shapwick, we tried to encourage an environment where that could happen.

Community archaeology

Besides its local scale and landscape approaches, a third distinctive feature of the Shapwick Project was its membership (Box 1.2). Unusually at that time for an academic project, we actively invited community involvement and aimed to provide a place for anyone who wished to participate, whether that be digging holes, walking the fields or helping to wash and identify the finds (Figure 1.6). For those with a particular interest in excavation, Somerset County Council undertook their 'community training dig' at Shapwick, making use of our existing facilities for the processing of their finds. Children too were encouraged (Figure 1.7), watching demonstrations of geophysics as well as attending Open Days while the excavations were underway.[57] The children spent half a day on site on a range of activities and then returned to school to write and draw about their experiences, the best pieces of work being awarded a prize by the project team.

The skills and knowledge of this local community, young and old, were combined with students attending full-time and part-time adult education courses at the

Figure 1.6. Shapwick and the local community. A: test-pitting underway; note the 'surgical' plastic sheets, sieves and a 1m² hole under excavation. B: geophysics (here resistivity) for the visually disabled. C: sieving spoil from excavation and looking for finds. D: local radio. E: the Project's display boards at the village fête. F: Dave Norcott working to update the Project's website.

Figure 1.7. Shapwick, archaeology and local schools. A: Mick visits Shapwick primary schoolchildren at Catcott school. B: Chris Gaffney amazes all with his geophysics plots. C: identifying finds from fieldwalking. D and E: lending a hand on the excavation. F: undertaking educational activities on site.

BOX 1.2

Getting involved

The Shapwick Project was a ten-year investigation with a simple routine. Fieldwork or finds washing and bagging were carried out every Thursday from September to about March with excavation in July and August. To keep everyone informed about our work, to explain our plans for the future and to enlist volunteers the aims and results of the Project were widely advertised. In November or December Mick (sometimes with others) gave an annual lecture in the village hall and answered questions. In May or June, before the excavations got underway, there was also the village fête. This is not usually a fixed date in any archaeologist's diary but it was an essential one for us. We manned a stall with finds and publications, mounted exhibition stands with aerial views and old photographs and took the chance to talk to villagers about existing collections of finds and access to their houses, gardens (for test pitting) and vegetable patches (for finds collection). We came to understand the workings of the village a little better too, and saw how it was changing. The third event in all our diaries was the four- or five-week excavation season. This took place in the summer months and was largely a student affair. People came from all over the country, from many different universities, and stayed for a few days or weeks.

We are sometimes asked *why* all these people wanted to get involved at Shapwick (Figure B.1.3). There was never any financial reward, certainly, but there is something special about any project that can enhance a sense of 'belonging'. As landscape historian William Hoskins once commented, 'we belong to a particular place and the bigger and more incomprehensible the modern world grows the more will people turn to study something of which they can grasp the scale and in which they can find a personal and individual meaning.'[b7] Winning some sense of identity then, is one powerful motive for involvement, though cultural geographer David Lowenthal recognises something further.[b8] 'The surviving past's most essential and persuasive benefit', he says, 'is to render the present familiar'. We routinely use the past to make sense of the present and there is perhaps no more direct way to make this kind of personal connection than to find an artefact for yourself,

---

University of Bristol. Mick felt that a field project could be used as a vehicle to teach adult students the techniques of landscape archaeology. Undergraduate students, too, were welcomed, especially after Chris joined the archaeology department at Winchester in 1993. From that point the Project could count on the support of another institution, King Alfred's College (now the University of Winchester), who were keen to develop their practical provision. Accordingly, the fieldwork component of the Project was stepped up, with annual excavations and increasingly active programmes of survey throughout much of the year. For the next six years we jointly funnelled our interests and what paltry resources we were able to muster into excavation, student projects and research at Shapwick. By the end of the decade Shapwick-related projects could boast several doctoral, MA, BSc and BA dissertations, not to mention hundreds of hours

of finds processing and artefact identification for adult and undergraduate students.[58]

The roots of this decision to mix local volunteers with archaeology students lay with Mick's experiences as a tutor in Extra-Mural Studies at the University of Bristol over many years. After the heyday of local archaeology societies in the 1960s and 1970s, and the lapsing of the Manpower Services Commission (MSC) Community Employment Programme in 1988, it was proving increasingly difficult for students and volunteers to participate in archaeological activities locally, a situation that worsened considerably after changes to planning guidance in 1990. This guidance (known as Planning Policy Guidance 16, or PPG 16) introduced the concept of developer-funded archaeology in England more widely and so 'professionalised' excavation activities, bringing with it more rigorous health and safety considerations and handle it, identify it and learn to place it within a wider historical and social context.

Equally potent motivations for doing community archaeology, though by no means ones exclusive to it, are physical exercise, a basic need for the company of others, for team-working and friendship, and collaboration in an endeavour in which men and women are treated equally. There *is* an important social aspect to all archaeology that feeds basic human needs for companionship and that sense of satisfaction which comes from working on something less run-of-the-mill, something for which you have a passion. Though few were probably inspired by the quality of Mick's coffee, brewed up on site in his trusty van, an important aspect of field archaeology is sharing: working in a group, eating the same food, drinking the same beer, sheltering from the weather, digging a test pit together, building trust, encouraging accountability, participating in the process of enquiry and creation. For many people, just spending time with others as a group is an unusual experience these days.[b9]

Figure B.1.3. Above: the fieldwalking team in good weather. There were usually about fifteen people on any one Thursday. Below: a mud-splattered Mick.

concerns about client confidentiality. Although there were benefits, the guidance had the less desirable effect initially of pushing away the unpaid part-timer.[59] At the same time, many archaeology departments in universities were diversifying from their traditional British focus, so that more staff were to be found working on projects abroad or concentrating on their publications. With archaeologists in local authorities increasingly swamped with planning applications, by the mid-1990s it was only museums and local societies who had any spare capacity to help the interested amateur. For them funding was a key issue. It was therefore a conscious decision on our part to buck this trend and sign up local people wherever possible.

From our own perspectives, we both hankered after a stimulating field project, one that engaged teaching and research and through which we could indulge our love of fieldwork. Mick in particular, faced with

the arid Higher Education philosophies of the early 1980s, cuts in financial support for adult teaching and the increasing bureaucracy required to put on even the simplest or shortest course, felt the need to get out into the field again and do some archaeology for sanity's sake. In the days before mobile phones he was, to all intents and purposes, 'off the grid' when he was out in the field. Being in the open air, even in bad weather, and with a group of like-minded people who became good friends, was a refreshing escape, 'a kind of therapy', as he claimed to one journalist.[60] It was certainly hard physical work, lugging equipment about over ploughed fields and walking many kilometres while fieldwalking, but even this was stimulating and helped alleviate stress. At the end of the day the café at the Peat Moors Centre, with its famous coffee and cakes, provided a safe haven when the afternoon light failed in the winter months.

CHAPTER TWO

Ways of Seeing

Methods for the Analysis of a Landscape

This chapter explores the sources of information available for a study of the historic environment of the parish and describes the many techniques we employed. The details are specific to Shapwick, but the principles hold for any parish in the country and further afield.[1] What follows, therefore, is the kind of basic checklist that any archaeologist and local historian should recognise whenever they contemplate a landscape project.

Preparing the ground

Historical documents

The sheer number of sources available for the history of an English parish can be overwhelming, documents can be hard to decipher and their purpose may be less clear still. Faced with bundles of vellum and spidery handwriting, early enthusiasm can soon turn to a nagging headache. Better progress can often be made by consulting one of the useful general guides to county and national archives,[2] or by enrolling with a local study group – though if detailed interpretation is required then historians must form part of any project team.

The name 'Shapwick' is not recorded until William I's assessment of holdings and valued possessions for tax in 1086, otherwise known as the Domesday Book, but there is considerable evidence, first compiled by Nick Corcos and later by Michael Costen and Lesley Abrams,[3] to suggest that by the mid-seventh century AD the parish area was included within a large royal estate called *Pouholt*. This estate, whose identity and purpose is discussed in Chapter 5, was probably already of some antiquity, and seems to equate broadly to the area of the Polden Hills.[4] During the eighth century it was granted in parcels to the Abbey at Glastonbury by successive kings of Wessex and these land charters provide an unusually detailed picture of changing ownership at an early date.

By the time of the Domesday Book Shapwick was therefore a fairly self-contained estate, nearly all of it in the hands of Glastonbury Abbey. Although a mention in Domesday in no way 'proves' the existence of a village, the entry for four ploughs 'in lordship' does suggest that the Abbey maintained a substantial demesne farm there for its own benefit; the tenants owned a further twelve. These figures confirm that the agricultural year at Shapwick at the turn of the millennium revolved around arable cultivation. Sadly, Domesday tells us nothing about the organisation or layout of these lands but, as we shall see in Chapter 6, it is likely that there was already an open-field unit providing supplies to the monastery. Judging by the number of tenants listed, forty in all, with a further six slaves,[5] there may have been a population of up to 200 people.

From early in the eighth century until the terrible death of Glastonbury's last abbot on the gallows on the Tor in 1539, the fate of Shapwick remained entwined with the Abbey. This fact determines the range, quality and survival of medieval documents. Apart from the Abbey's published charters[6] and an unusual number of early manorial surveys (see below), nearly all the Shapwick documents are court rolls and manorial accounts of the fourteenth century. From the mid-thirteenth century onwards the proceedings of courts tended to be written down by clerks in abbreviated Latin, in this case on parchment; they are called 'rolls' because they were not stitched side-by-side, like a paperback, but end-on-end in one long roll. These documents provide evidence for customary and monetary obligations and transfers of land, although women, the young and the poorest sub-tenants tend to be less well represented. In principle, however, Shapwick villeins, tied to the land, sought justice through the court because the land on which they laboured belonged to the Abbey and it was at the manor court that the Abbey exercised its jurisdiction. The invaluable information that the rolls contain was collated and interpreted by historian Martin Ecclestone.[7]

Of greatest interest to the Abbey was the income expected of the manor, evidence for which includes rents and court receipts, as well as accounts for purchases, wages, repairs and payments (or debts). This kind of information is found in Shapwick's manorial accounts, together with the labour services owed by tenants on the lord's demesne land, such as ploughing, haymaking and harvesting.[8] These records make it clear that, in the heyday of demesne farming between 1250 and 1350, the Abbey exploited its lands at Shapwick chiefly to produce wheat, most of the grain finding its way to the granary at Glastonbury.

Through the course of the Middle Ages more and more demesne land was leased out, so that labour services became theoretical obligations and were replaced by cash payments (plus a few eggs at Easter). The Abbey's administration reflects this shift by compiling surveys that were focused on either its income from rents (listed in the 'rental') or descriptions of the ownership or tenancy of every piece of land (known as a 'terrier'). For Shapwick there are important surveys for c.1260, 1325 and 1515 which provide significant landscape detail, especially when combined with other sources. Most of these medieval documents are kept today at Longleat House in Wiltshire, where there is an archive office. Typically they are written on vellum (calf skin) in Latin in small cursive writing with many medieval letter forms, minims and clerical abbreviations.[9] As we shall see in Chapter 7, it is the survey of 1325 that provided

the basis for our topographical reconstruction of the medieval manorial precinct around Shapwick House (see Figure 7.30), while the 1515 survey was used to reconstruct the medieval parish and its fields (see Box 5.2).

Following the Dissolution of Glastonbury Abbey on 15 November 1539, all the Abbey's property, including Shapwick, was seized by the Crown. A fierce struggle then ensued among courtiers, royal servants, local gentry, lawyers and former monastic officials who were intent on securing a share of these valuable estates. This story was unpicked by historian Joe Bettey.[10] Land at Shapwick passed through numerous hands as manors were purchased, leased and sub-let, often for short periods. These records can be found in the National Archives (TNA) at Kew, as can the documents of the Courts of the Exchequer, Chancery, Requests and Star Chamber, which contain numerous legal disputes, notably those involving several dubious members of the Walton family, who were major lessees and landowners in Shapwick during the later sixteenth century. The quantity of legal disputes and grants of manorial tenancies for this period is large and made more than usually difficult to untangle at Shapwick by the later medieval division of the manor between two holdings, or estates: the 'main' holding that had been vested in the abbot and the 'rectorial' holding that had been attached to the office of the almoner of the Abbey before the Dissolution. Tenants in the village often held lands in both holdings, and it is not always clear to which holding the documents refer.[11]

In approaching the large body of archive material available for the later periods we have tried to deal thoroughly with the evidence most relevant to our concerns, such as the proceedings of the Somerset Justices of the Peace at their Quarter Sessions[12] and, of course, family archives, principally those of the Rolle and Strangways families. These invaluable sources, to be found largely in the record offices for Devon and Somerset,[13] give details of land use, farms and cottages, and the changing landscape of the parish through episodes of drainage and enclosure. Economic activities as diverse as milling, woodland management, peat extraction, quarrying and duck decoys are all covered here. Particularly interesting for our purposes are the depositions made by elderly

Shapwick residents in 1754 during a legal dispute over rights of common in Loxley Wood (Box 8.2).[14] In addition, these parish records provide details of church affairs, from the maintenance of the fabric and parochial government to provision for the poor and education. Unfortunately, the earliest surviving churchwardens' account books for Shapwick are relatively late; they cover the years 1712–53 and list items as diverse as payments of bounty for killing vermin and small sums given in charity to poor travellers.[15] Further personal tragedy is revealed by the accounts of the Overseers of the Poor, the earliest of which survive for 1745–65 (see Chapter 8).[16] Finally, information on the nineteenth-century population was compiled from the national census and other sources by Shapwick villager Dennis Hill-Cottingham.[17]

Maps

Shapwick is unusually rich in its historic maps. Not only are Ordnance Survey maps and the tithe map of 1839 available at Somerset County Record Office, there are also numerous earlier records of drainage on the wetland,[18] together with sixteen surviving eighteenth-century maps and their field books.[19] Details of properties, streams, roads and tenants are sometimes included, while others are surveys of parts of common fields before and after enclosure; one unusual plan shows all the houses in the village liable to repair the churchyard wall (see Figure 7.36). Most of these maps were intended to define ownership and to formalise financial responsibilities, though some are clearly preparatory versions and roughly drawn on both sides of the vellum.

Two maps of the village, drawn up only about a decade apart (Figures 2.1 and 2.2) illustrate some of the problems of interpretation. Not only do the scales differ but their surveyors also had slightly different purposes in mind. To relate what we see here with a spatially accurate modern map, the answer is to standardise the scales. To begin with, the 25-inch (1:2,500) 1970 map of the parish was reduced to produce versions at a quarter of their original size but still retaining all the detail. Mick then drew up his own version of the parish on a drawing board and produced a totally up-to-date modern map by adding more recent buildings and altered boundaries, simply

by walking around the village and fields and checking what he saw against the 1970 original. By doing this the landscape detail also became more familiar.

Rectified earlier maps were then created by transcribing the information from historic maps at the same standardised scale as the modern map, sometimes using photocopies obtained from the County Record Office at modest cost, sometimes working with the originals. The end result is a folder of maps showing the parish at different dates, all reproduced at the same scale without the inconvenience of many square metres of tracing paper. For example, the original 1839 tithe map of the parish of Shapwick,[20] an extract of which is shown in Figure 2.3, is quite large (1.2m × 1.5m), but all its detail for the village can be traced satisfactorily onto an 1885 6-inch base map (Figure 2.4). This provides a reasonable point of departure for understanding the plan of the village in about 1750. The same principle can also be applied to the wider parish, the details for which have to be compiled from several different maps from field books.[21] Taken together, this sequence of standardised maps provides a rich source of detail that, among other uses, enabled us to locate post-medieval monuments on the ground[22] and to analyse changing field and boundary patterns.

Modern computer systems undoubtedly have something to add to this manual process. Maps of convenient size can be scanned and rescaled without the distortions introduced by the photocopier; geographical software can collate and analyse several layers of maps and fieldwork data in ways that were not possible when the Shapwick Project began. Computer software is not cheap, however, and there are some fundamental reservations to a wholly digitised approach. The best analogy is to compare drawing or painting with photography. When drawing or painting, the detail must be closely observed, whereas with a camera the recording can be done instantaneously, without much thought. While the process of drawing out maps is certainly laborious, far more of the landscape detail is observed and committed to memory.

Field, place- and furlong names

In our view, field names are a severely under-researched resource for most parts of Britain. The

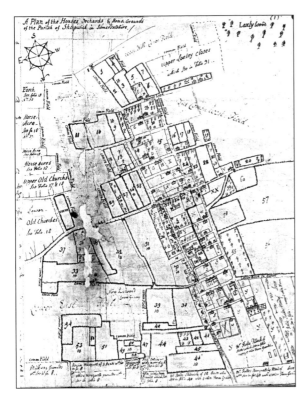

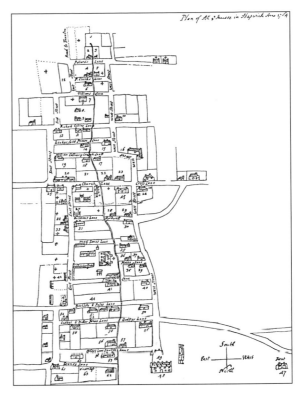

Figure 2.1. 'A Plan of the Houses, Orchards & Home Grounds of the Parish of Shapwick in Somersetshire' (SRO DD/SG 36 c/206 1754). North is towards the bottom of the map. The church is in the centre of the map and the 'Comon West Field' lies to the west of the village.

Figure 2.2. 'Plan of All ye Houses in Shapwick Anno 1764' (SRO DD/SG 41 c/206 1764). North is towards the bottom of the map, where number 48 is Shapwick House with the Great Barn immediately to the south-west.

most complete sequences for the later medieval period at Shapwick were extracted from manorial surveys, with later evidence being taken particularly from maps.[23] A modern list was also drawn up, and the result is a database of all recorded field names, compiled by historian Michael Costen, that shows their evolution over a 700-year period. These names span various categories.

One group of field names at Shapwick might be described as topographical. *Langlond*, in 1515, for example, is an early reference to shape, 'the long furlong' in that case, while *Meswelle* (later *Mazewell*), in 1301–2, points towards OE *(ge)mære*, 'a boundary' + OE *wiell*, 'a spring'. These names are evocative of their physical location and sometimes go further to indicate shape, land use and relative location.

Brodemedeshende, from the 1307 court rolls, is one example of this: OE *brād* is 'wide' + *mæd*, 'meadow' + *hende*, 'near, close at hand'. Clues to past tenants and owners are embedded in Kent Farm, whose name seems to refer to the mill tenant of 1325, John de Kent. A more recent example, *Constable Leaze* in 1771 (and later), probably refers to the grazing ground allocated to the village constable as payment for his services.

Other names are more subjective. *Swetefurlong* recorded in 1304–05 clearly brought greater pleasure than the *Shytbrok* in 1311–12 or, arguably, the *Horepytt* in 1515. Agriculture, too, figures prominently. *Bereweye* (the modern *Beerway*) of 1302–3 is OE *bere*, 'barley' + OE *weg*, 'a road along which the barley was carried', *Broderixon* of 1515 (later *broad rushen* in

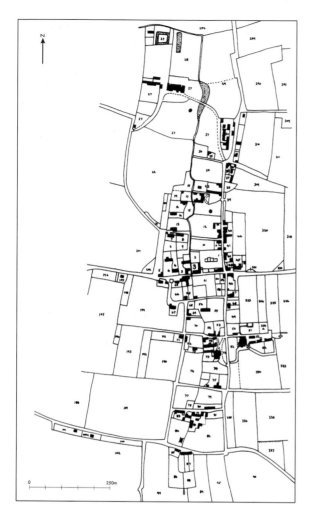

CF   Church Farm
DH   Down House
HF   Home Farm
HlF   Hill Farm
KF   King's Farm
KL   Kent Lane
LF   Lawn Farm
LH   Lawn House
M   Shapwick flour mill
NF   New Farm
Q   Quarry
S   Primary School
SH   Shapwick House
SM   Smithy
SMC   St Mary's Church
SP   Spring
V   Vicarage

p   pump
w   well

Figure 2.3. Shapwick village as depicted on the 1839 tithe map. Here north is to the top of the map and the houses are shown 'in plan' rather than three dimensions. The church is plot number 1.

Figure 2.4. Shapwick village in 1885 (after Ordnance Survey 25-inch map) with additional letter codes for major buildings.

1839) is OE *brædu*, 'a broad strip of land' + OE *riscen*, 'growing with rushes', while *Benham* of 1260, is OE *bean*, 'bean, pea, legume' + *hamm*, 'enclosure'. It is no surprise to find references to farm animals in *Melkweye* (1302–3) and *Oxleaze* (1771), but wild fauna is also unusually well represented. The crane, or possibly the grey heron, a large bird that would presumably once have nested in the wetlands of Shapwick Heath, gave its name to *Cranefurlang* in 1313[24] but there is also *Goselond* in 1302–3 and *Froggewell* and *Hawkeshull*

in 1515.[25] Even industrial activities can be pinpointed in *Higher and Lower Lime Kiln* in 1839, and less obviously in *Collegh* (later *colley*) in 1325, which is OE *col*, 'charcoal' + *leah*, 'a clearing' or 'a wood'. This last site is adjacent to Loxley Wood.

Finally, some field and furlong names refer to lost structures and, in some cases, furnish clues as to their function. Thus the *Sheephouse* of 1643 was probably where sheep were corralled for the winter or where their fodder was stored; *Oldschupene* of 1311–14

Figure 2.5. Reproduction of an engraving from John Collinson's 'History of Somerset' (1791), after an original drawing by Thomas Bonnor undertaken sometime between January 1785 and late summer 1790. The view shows the south side of Shapwick House with its Jacobean fenestration and adjacent medieval barn. Mendip lies in the distance with a rather foreshortened perspective. The dedication reads: Shapwick, The Seat of George Templer Esq to whom this Plate is inscribed by his Obliged Servant J COLLINSON.

is OE *eald*, 'old, former' + *scypen*, 'a cowshed'; and *Stenehulk* of 1515 is OE *stan*, 'stone' and *hulc*, 'a barn'. *Windmill field*, recorded in 1790, speaks for itself, while *Furches* in 1515 is derived from the Latin *furcas*, for gallows. They stood just over the parish boundary in Ashcott. More intangible beliefs find witness in the *Nuthergoldhurd* of 1313, presumably the site of a coin hoard, probably Roman, and the *Halghebrok* of 1325 (*hollybrooks* in 1839), which is derived from OE *halig*, 'holy, sacred' + *broc*, 'stream'.[26]

Illustrations

By far the most useful antiquarian illustration of Shapwick is that by topographical draughtsman Thomas Bonnor (*c.*1743–1807×12), published in John Collinson's county history of 1791 (Figure 2.5). Bonnor was an engraver-publisher for works by, among others, Samuel Richardson and Henry Fielding, but in 1781 he was imprisoned for debt, escaping poverty only by drawing churches, monuments and large mansions such as Shapwick House.[27] In addition, there are four watercolours of three different locations around the parish by John Claude Nattes (*c.*1765–1822), a noted draughtsman and drawing master and one of the founders, in 1804, of the Watercolour Society. Nattes, too, had something of a chequered career. He was eventually disgraced for exhibiting the drawings of others under his own name,[28] but as a young man he was commissioned by George Templer to paint views of Shapwick estate and its houses, more or less at the same time that Bonnor was sketching his view across the park (for example, Figure 8.23). It is conceivable that their work represents a single commissioned set. On the other hand, there may once have been more pictures that are now lost.[29]

Antiquarian sources

Somerset is not particularly well served by early topographical accounts. Of an early county history by geologist John Strachey only a rough draft survives, and this is very much a work in progress, with crossings-out and glued-in bits of paper. One of these additions, possibly dated after 1741/2, mentions the moat around Shapwick House (see Chapter 8).[30] Strachey died in 1743 leaving his work incomplete and unpublished. Collinson's 1791 county history is more useful because it includes a cursory topographical description of the parish, a translation of the Domesday entry and a brief sketch of the ownership of the manor after the Dissolution. Sadly, Collinson did not live long enough to enjoy the fruits of his three-volume labours. He died in 1793 at Long Ashton near Bristol, where he was vicar, aged just 36.[31]

Later antiquarian accounts contain only occasional items of interest. Richard Warner's *History of Glastonbury Abbey* of 1826, written while he was living at Newton St Loe near Bath,[32] featured the first published translation of Abbot Richard Beere's terrier of 1515, a description of medieval lands belonging to the Benedictine abbey which included Shapwick.[33] William Phelps, meanwhile, certainly visited the parish ten years later while he was gathering material for his new county history. Phelps was vicar of nearby Meare between 1824 and 1851 and quite possibly introduced to Shapwick though his fellow clergyman Elias Taylor, the owner of Shapwick House from 1809 until his death in 1827. Certainly Phelps visited the parish's 'pump room' (see Chapter 8), though the site was evidently not deemed worthy of a detour by the Somerset Archaeology and Natural History Society by the time its members visited Shapwick in 1880. The Society were addressed on that day by George Warry, a former director of the Somerset and Dorset railway then in his 85th year; the 'slow and doubtful', as the railway was known locally, ran within earshot of his home at Shapwick House (see Chapter 9). Thereafter, over the course of the twentieth century,

the Victoria County History volumes of 1906 and 1915 noted the discovery of Roman coins 'in the marsh' and the 'homestead moat' at Shapwick House, but the parish as a whole was never the subject of any more focused research, though the Ordnance Survey Archaeology Division visited in the 1960s and 1970s, recording flints and pottery and inspecting the moat at Shapwick House. In addition, there is a useful church guide and a survey of farm buildings from the early 1980s.[34]

Out and about

Geology and soils

The interpretation of any archaeological landscape requires an understanding of what lies beneath. The underlying bedrock here is of Upper Triassic Rhaetian and Lower Jurassic Lias age, with a superficial covering of Quaternary peats in the north.[35] Although temporary exposures of solid rock were recorded whenever possible, and aerial photographs examined (Figure 2.6A),[36] there are few natural exposures of rock *in situ* across the parish to add significant further detail to the geological map. Vertebrae of both ichthyosaurs and plesiosaurs were regularly bagged by fieldwalkers[37] and probably represent complete skeletons in the bedrock from which fossil bones have become detached by the plough. Bands of ammonites also outcrop across the parish. *Psiloceras planorbis*, for example, is found at Beerway Farm and west of Manor Farm. Other common fossil finds include bivalve molluscs such as the oysters *Gryphaea* (Devil's Toenails), *Liostrea* and the larger smooth-shelled *Plagiostoma giganteum* and mussels of the genus *Modiolus*, all of which occur in the lower Jurassic beds in the middle of the parish. The most abundant fossil, however, is the brachiopod *Calcirhynchia calcaria*, which is extremely common in one band that can be traced over hundreds of metres along the crest of the Nidons. When the fieldwalkers reached *Blacklands*, a Roman settlement east of Coppice Gate Farm (see Chapter 4), Peter Hardy, our team geologist, was immediately able to confirm that there must once have been stone buildings on the site, because the blocks of stone in the soil contained fossils not naturally found there. Clues such as these proved to be essential pointers to past activity, not least for the

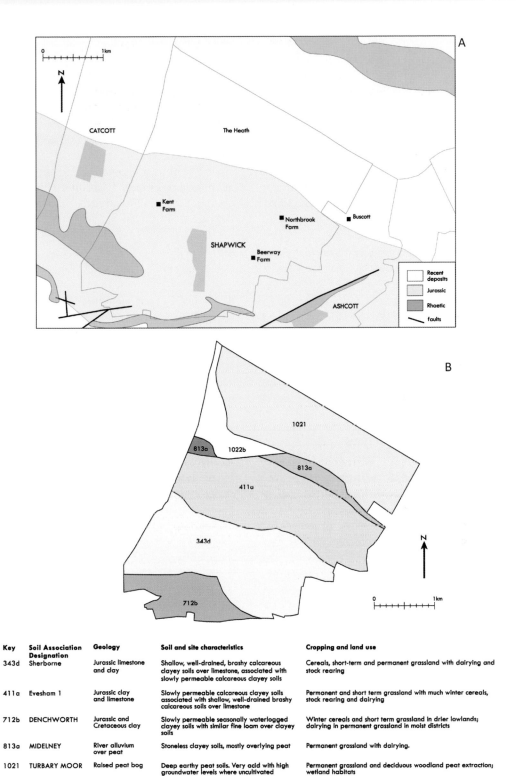

Key	Soil Association Designation	Geology	Soil and site characteristics	Cropping and land use
343d	Sherborne	Jurassic limestone and clay	Shallow, well-drained, brashy calcareous clayey soils over limestone, associated with slowly permeable calcareous clayey soils	Cereals, short-term and permanent grassland with dairying and stock rearing
411a	Evesham 1	Jurassic clay and limestone	Slowly permeable calcareous clayey soils associated with shallow, well-drained brashy calcareous soils over limestone	Permanent and short term grassland with much winter cereals, stock rearing and dairying
712b	DENCHWORTH	Jurassic and Cretaceous clay	Slowly permeable seasonally waterlogged clayey soils with similar fine loam over clayey soils	Winter cereals and short term grassland in drier lowlands; dairying in permanent grassland in moist districts
813a	MIDELNEY	River alluvium over peat	Stoneless clayey soils, mostly overlying peat	Permanent grassland with dairying.
1021	TURBARY MOOR	Raised peat bog	Deep earthy peat soils. Very acid with high groundwater levels where uncultivated	Permanent grassland and deciduous woodland peat extraction; wetland habitats
1022b	ALTCAR 1	Fen pea	Deep earthy peat soils	Wetland and woodland habitats and rough grazing; cereals, sugar beet and field vegetables with groundwater control

Figure 2.6. A: geology (Glastonbury Geology Sheet 296). B: soils and their characteristics with land use (Avery 1955; Soil Survey of England and Wales 1983).

fieldwalkers, who quickly learnt the importance of collecting any unusual pebbles and stones. After a good wash to dissolve the heavy clay, they were often recognisable as prehistoric stone tools, whetstones and gun flints.

It is the 'layer cake' effect of the local limestone bedding, with its interleaving of dark grey shales and clay bands, that explains the curious ponding of water across the upland. Vertical displacements from faulting and the juxtaposition of limestone against clay create an underground reservoir which is then released onto the surface. Other springs can be found wherever limestones cap the clay beds, as at the foot of the southern slope of the Nidons and along the southern slopes of the main Polden ridge. In the past these water sources were of fundamental significance for human activity and, even though they may be forgotten today, they are still marked out in the landscape by changes in vegetation that can be seen from the air.[38] These flexures in the geological bedding are also responsible for the distracting 'tiger stripe' effect sometimes observed on aerial photographs. This is particularly noticeable in spring, when the early leaf growth of young crops responds to the differing water content of the limestone and clay bands beneath. The same banding can also be observed sometimes on resistivity plots and is easily mistaken for archaeological features.

Since the Roman period quarrying activity in the parish has targeted the upper beds of the Triassic white limestones of Rhaetic Age, and probably the so-called 'Sun Bed'. This hard, pale grey, splintery limestone can be seen in the foundations of several farm buildings. At around 0.3m thick, it is the toughest, thickest stone available locally for construction, though the thin, hard limestone employed for local walling is also distinctive. This Blue Lias is cut from beds that accumulated in very uniform thicknesses, and requires only dressing to length from any cut edge. Exploiting this, Shapwick became one of a number of workshops in the locality producing funerary monuments. Though the quarries competed against much larger operations, such as the Purbeck marblers,[39] Shapwick stone is documented as being used for the tomb of the Glastonbury abbot Nicholas Frome (d.1455), while an engraved medieval grave-cover of local Blue Lias was uncovered by the Project team during excavations at the site of St Andrew's church in *Old Church* field (see Figure 7.21C). Quite possibly the stone was quarried to the west of the village in a furlong identified as *stonequarrie* in 1515 (see Figure 7.1 for location). This industry continued later on a small scale[40] and was commented upon by the rural economist William Marshall in the eighteenth century:[41]

> Marble quarries on either side of the road. Many men at work; and teams waiting. Mostly raised in large slabs, six or eight inches thick, and several feet in dimensions ie horizontally, and near the surface of level ground men employed in polishing them. The colour a blue grey.

Even in the middle of the nineteenth century local topographical guides record under the Shapwick entry that 'the substratum contains blue lias, which is quarried as occasion requires'.[42] Sedimentary rock of just this type is still worked by hand in Somerset and, in the past, it could be dug out anywhere along a line from north of Beerway Farm towards Kent Farm. Fortuitously, the parish's major archaeological sites seem to have escaped any adverse impact.

Marshall saw the Poldens as 'thin limestone land',[43] and at the time of the 1839 tithe map the parish was a mosaic of meadow, pasture and arable with some woodland and a few orchards. As Figure 2.6b illustrates, these different land uses reflect the pattern of soils across the parish with uncanny accuracy. In the south of the parish the heavier Denchworth soils are covered by the woodland at Loxley, while the lighter calcareous Sherborne soils on the higher Polden slopes, about 688ha (1,700 acres) in all, were mostly where the medieval open fields once lay. These are what the eighteenth-century agricultural reformer John Billingsley recognised as 'corn-lands'[44] and, to get the best from them, they were extensively drained in the early nineteenth century. The Midelney soils to the north are grassland and, beyond this, the northern third of the parish is covered by 405ha (1,000 acres) of earthy peat soils. Up to the eighteenth century this wetland provided common grazing, fuel and wildfowl, among other benefits. But in the days long before its ecological and archaeological value came to be recognised, agricultural 'improvers' such as Billingsley saw some financial reward to be had, proposing that the clay of the Poldens be dug out and 'laid on this land by means of a portable railway'.[45] His drastic plan would have done little for the archaeological potential of this project, but fortunately an alternative was adopted. In 1784 the Levels were finally enclosed and drained by open surface drains called 'gripes' and marl-drains that were gorged deeply through the peat and then backfilled with broken marl.[46] The peat itself was put to many uses, from fire lighting to horticulture, and, as Figure 2.7 shows, Shapwick Heath is today a mosaic of rough grazing land, tree cover and open pools of worked-out peat.

Fieldchecking and earthwork survey

During the life of the Shapwick Project Mick visited every field in the parish, sometimes on more than one occasion. These reconnaissance visits were prompted by routine fieldwalking, by the sort of map analysis described above, by aerial photographs and sometimes as a result of information from villagers. Archaeological earthworks were noted on the individual sheets compiled for each field and on a duplicate set of 1:2,500 maps reduced to a scale of 1:5,000.[47] For more enigmatic sites, or where there were substantial remains, a more prolonged visit was arranged.

Most of the detailed topographical survey carried out for the Project was undertaken by landscape archaeologist James Bond.[48] The areas to be examined were first divided into 10m squares using tapes, ranging poles and canes. Measurements were then taken from the earthworks along the main axes of the grid, with offsets being taken as appropriate to locate selected details (Figure 2.8A). This is low-cost and low-technology surveying, but entirely adequate. The sites were visited only when conditions were optimum, when the grass was short and the sunlight low and oblique, so as to show up the slightest feature. Using these methods, James was able to produce some extraordinarily detailed plots, such as that of the parkland south of Shapwick House (e.g. Figure B.7.2). Professional archaeological surveyors Dave McOmish and Graham Brown recorded a post-medieval ornamental pond and its associated garden earthworks outside the village, at Henhills Copse (see Figure 8.25A), as well as the site of the former medieval church in *Old Church* field (Figure 2.8B) – a site that proved so complex that the exercise was

Figure 2.7. Former peat workings on Shapwick Heath. Looking south-east towards Glastonbury. The former Glastonbury canal divides Westhay Heath (to the left) from Shapwick Heath (to the right). Alongside the canal is the track of the Somerset and Dorset railway. The kink in the canal is the north-west corner of Shapwick parish.

attempted by both teams and by Mick (Figure 2.8C). All the sites were surveyed at a scale of 1:200 and then reduced in size for publication.

Fieldwalking

Fieldwalking creates a record of archaeological material exposed on the surface of ploughed fields. It is cheap (at least in equipment costs), relatively rapid, enjoyable (mostly), non-destructive and produces plenty of data that are usually conveyed in the form of distribution plots of diagnostic artefacts.[49] Fieldwalking began at Shapwick in June 1989 and

Figure 2.8. Surveying. A: students surveying the earthworks south of Shapwick House using plane tables. B: Dave McOmish of the (then) Royal Commission on Historical Monuments (England) (now English Heritage) surveying the site of the former church near Beerway Farm. C: Mick with Harry Jelley, sketch-plotting the same earthworks while geophysics was underway by GSB.

continued for the next decade under Mick's direction (Box 2.1). Line-walking was the standard technique used,[50] targeting fields only once they had been ploughed, harrowed and rolled, though they were also sometimes already seeded and ideally weathered in the rain. Once the fields were selected, changes to field boundaries were noted on reduced 1:2,500 OS maps and an appropriate OS number allotted.

BOX 2.1

A day in the life of a Shapwick fieldworker

We generally met at 9.00 am at the former Post Office and stores, the preferred day being Thursday so that if a fieldworker missed a week they would still know which day to turn up. The first task was to pick up the equipment from one of the derelict cottages lent to us by the Vestey estate. These cold, bleak buildings were vermin-infested, with no other comforts beyond a roof over our heads, but they were invaluable for the washing and drying of the finds from fieldwalking (Figure B.2.1A), as well as the storage of ranging poles, canes, measuring tapes, plastic bags and waterproof labels. Meanwhile, Mick went off to look at the state of the fields and visited the tenant farmers to update them on progress and to gain access. This often took some time, as the 'public relations' side of the project was considered to be very important; it was essential not only to explain what we were doing but also to find out about the farming regime, future cropping arrangements and so on.

The fieldwalking grid was established using tapes strung out along the sides of the fields. Between these two sides, lines of canes were laid out at 25m intervals and an alphanumeric code provided a reference for each stint within the lines (A1, B1, etc.). The team became very efficient at this and once the direction of the lines had been decided upon groups of two or three fieldworkers went into action (Figure B.2.1B). Back at the van the lines would be plotted on the map and bags and labels made out. These were then distributed at coffee time, when the teams returned. After coffee the fieldwalkers proceeded to walk the field, moving as a group from one end to the other, thus keeping to a minimum any potential problems with people fieldwalking the wrong stint. A warm camaraderie and mutual support quickly

Figure B.2.1. Shapwick fieldwalking. A: washing the finds from fieldwalking outside one of the Vestey owned cottages, here at High Lane. B: line-walking across a ploughed and harrowed field. Note canes marking 25m stints; finds are placed into plastic bags with identifying tags.

developed between the Continuing Education students, local volunteers, Shapwick residents, schoolchildren and university undergraduates who formed our fieldwalkers. In the final years, on a good day, three to five fields would be walked each Thursday, and a very soggy and muddy group of people would then wend their way home.

This fieldwalking programme was made a lot easier by 1:5,000 maps marked up at the very earliest stages of the project which showed tenants and the areas of their farms, and by the copies of 1:2,500 maps loaned to us by Bob Croft, the county archaeologist, at the start of the project. In addition, Mick's four-wheel-drive Volkswagen Transporter served as a mobile office and coffee bar. 'The van' could transport up to seven fieldworkers across the fields, along with all the survey equipment, and return with all the bags of finds crammed into banana boxes pillaged from supermarkets in Weston-super-Mare. Each person brought their own food, drink and waterproofs, and it became a Shapwick maxim never to become separated from your lunch.

It may be asked why we worked in this simple, low technology way, but it must be remembered that this was not a permanently available paid team of fieldworkers but a group of volunteers who gave of their time freely for one day of the week. To make steady progress everything had to be laid out, the work completed and the equipment packed away within the daylight hours of any one day. Farming requirements dictated that poles and canes could not be left in the fields from one week to the next. Aligning the laid-out stints on the fields rather than the national grid maximised the amount of time available.[51]

Before walking began, a field sheet (Figure 2.9A) was filled out with the field number and other information needed to enable later sorting to take place accurately.[52] Any unusual features, such as mounds or burnt soil, were also marked on the map. Then, once lines and stints had been laid out, bags and labels were distributed (Figure 2.9B). New fieldwalkers were instructed and shown different categories of finds as they appeared during the day. An attempt was made to spread the fieldwalkers (and therefore biases in collection results) so that no individual fieldwalker walked adjacent stints. Walking could then start. Generally, everyone timed themselves on ten minutes per stint, about five stints being walked by each person in an hour. Fieldwalkers walked along the lines between the canes, first in each direction and then slightly off the line on either side if time allowed. During the ten minutes the line would be walked four to six times (100–150m walking) and all the finds picked up and bagged. We estimate that strips about 2.0–2.5m wide, and therefore about 10 per cent of the total area of every field was thoroughly examined.

Once the finds were washed and dried they were bagged up, labelled and boxed, ready to be driven over to Chris in Winchester.[53] As soon as possible, Mick would draw up a plan of the walked area at 1:2,500, marking the position of numbered lines and stints. The sorters at Winchester could then check that all the numbers, lines and stints for each field were

Figure 2.9. Fieldwalking. A: field sheet. B: Teresa Hall writing labels for bags of fieldwalking finds. C: finds sorting underway by Winchester students.

accounted for and correctly labelled. Until 1993 all the finds sorting was undertaken by Chris Gerrard and Alejandra Gutiérrez, but later the process was carried out under supervision by undergraduate students at Winchester. During these practical sessions, what began the day as a single bag of mixed finds became three to ten smaller bags containing glass, tile, pottery, flint and so on, which would be rapidly quantified (Figure 2.9C). The task should not be underestimated. Four groups of fifteen students worked for two hours each per week for thirty weeks of the year over a five-year period. As might be imagined, every student came to be confident in the recognition of a wide variety of artefacts of different periods. A database of finds per field was then created by Alex Turner from the paper record and, using digitised versions of Mick's field maps, distribution maps could later be plotted.[54] In particular, we analysed densities per field (rather than raw numbers), examined the 'character' of the assemblage in each field (for example, the different pottery fabrics present) and highlighted any unusual clustering of artefacts.[55]

By comparison with other archaeological projects, the area walked by Shapwick fieldwalkers was not large – some 430ha (1,060 acres) in all. As Figure 2.10A shows, this represents more than half of the dry land on the Polden slope within the parish, to which should be added a further 19ha on the peat.[56] Altogether, 6,877 stints were examined, the equivalent of a total distance walked by a single individual of perhaps 800km: say, the distance from Shapwick to the Spanish border in south-west France. The important thing, however, is the quality of the data. We did not walk selectively over sample areas or 'sites', as many other surveys do, nor did we restrict ourselves to material from a particular period or artefact class. We collected everything, some 96,452 items in all (Figure 2.10B), at an averaged recovery rate of 0.28 finds per square metre of plough soil. Put another way, Shapwick fieldwalkers were bending to pick up finds every three or four paces on average, and in many parts of the parish considerably more frequently.[57] Somewhat against academic fashion, the Shapwick Project opted for full coverage of the study area, feeling that a larger (though far from perfect) universe of archaeological data was superior to a sampled subset of smaller size. Only the

systematic examination (itself, of course, a sample) of a contiguous block of terrain, one that fully defined sites and their surroundings of all periods, would provide the rigorous control we wanted and allow us to be confident about site functions, dates and land use. Once more, there was a strongly felt need to 'understand' the landscape we were investigating. This meant experiencing it in the raw, thinking about sites *in their settings*, rather than in the abstract on paper. Where it can be achieved, full coverage survey provides the optimal conditions for perceiving and understanding in this more anthropological sense.

Aerial photographs

The principal collections of aerial photographs for Shapwick are held by Somerset County Council, the National Monuments Record and Cambridge University.[58] These include RAF pictures and verticals for the county taken in 1971, 1981 and 1992, together with digital coverage for 2001. Twelve flights were also made specifically for this Project and more than 300 photographs were taken by Mick, mostly from a solid (high) wing microlite aeroplane with the advantage of unrestricted all-round vision and a low stalling speed. A flexible wing microlite, used once, proved unsatisfactory because there was no windscreen and the helmet impeded the use of the camera. Use of the best platform, a helicopter, was only possible once as part of another project and in any case would have been prohibitively expensive (Figure 2.11A).[59]

The highlights from aerial survey are two photographs of probable prehistoric enclosures, both of them from archives (see Figures 3.20 and 3.23). Shapwick's Roman sites, however, proved surprisingly elusive, far more being visible at the multi-period site at *Old Church* (Field 4016). Two of the slides taken there by Mick show the lost church building quite clearly (Figure 2.11B), together with enclosures of different dates. A transcription based on these parchmarks suggests a three-part structure of nave and chancel with a central tower and possible aisles to north and south (Figure 2.11C). There is also the hint of a square stone feature nearby that might be a cross base in the medieval churchyard, another rectangular building to the west of the church and, in the south-west corner of the church enclosure, a

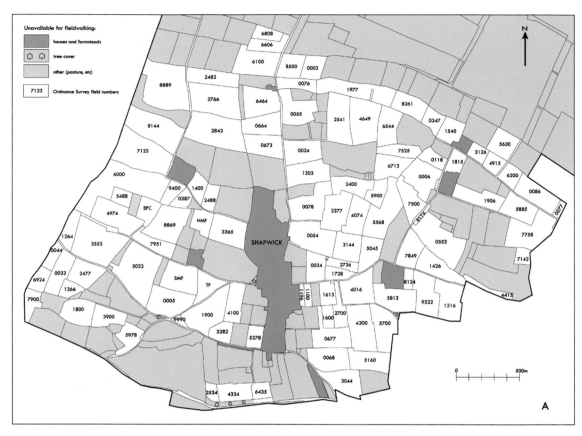

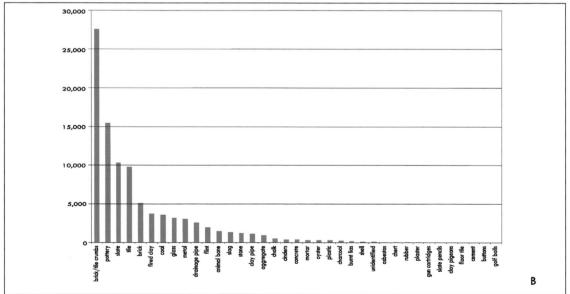

Figure 2.10. Fieldwalking. A: walked fields with their reference numbers; B: the total numbers of artefacts recovered from line-walking over 429.8ha at Shapwick.

Figure 2.11. Aerial survey. A: men in their flying machines! B: Old Church (4016) from the air, looking east. C: a plot of the parchmarks by Caroline Ingle.

roughly circular parched area now preserved as a low mound. On higher ground, other photographs show a series of mounds in the south-east of the parish close to the ridgeway, several of which have since been identified as medieval and later windmills, while others, and indeed the windmill mounds themselves, may have their origins as prehistoric barrows. For later periods, several runs of air photographs show the earthworks in the parkland south of Shapwick House, usually picked out clearly in intense low-level sunlight (see Figure 9.24). Evidence for field drains (see Figure 7.39) and stone quarrying (see Figure 9.36A) is also extensive.

Geophysical survey

Geophysical survey was always intended to be at the heart of the Shapwick Project.[60] Some 41ha in fifty-five fields was investigated in detail across the parish, together with a further 40ha in thirteen fields that was scanned more cursorily. In all, just over 10 per cent of the dry land area of the parish was examined, most intensively to the east of the village (Figure 2.12a).[61] The most useful initial prospection tool was 'magnetic scanning' – the observation of fluctuations in the magnetic signal caused by archaeological or geological anomalies as the operator traverses across the field. No data are recorded in this process but any significant variations are staked with canes so that they can be returned to for more detailed survey. This technique, used by Geophysical Surveys of Bradford (GSB) teams at Shapwick, is one we would have liked to have used much more. It is very rapid, though to be successful it relies on the right soil conditions and, as may be imagined, requires considerable expertise to gauge the magnetic background and pick out anomalous anthropogenic readings. For more detailed magnetic survey, the target areas were divided into 20m × 20m grids and readings were logged at intervals that became steadily more intensive as computer power increased over the course of the Project (Figure 2.12B). The data were then manipulated using computer software and interpreted. A number of resistance surveys were also carried out, mainly by University of Winchester students under Alex Turner's supervision. As its name implies, this type of survey measures the electrical resistance of the earth using electrodes that are inserted into the ground, usually at 1m intervals. Like magnetic survey, the data are also collected in 20m blocks, though the process is far slower (Figure 2.12C).

The results of geophysical surveys appear throughout this book, but it is worthwhile reflecting on the contribution of the technique overall. In effect, two strategies operated. The first, a more traditional approach, took 'sites' selected on the basis of their presumed archaeology, usually from field names, fieldwalking results, topographical survey and so on, and then targeted them for detailed geophysical survey. In that sense the Shapwick Project helped pioneer the integration of geophysical techniques with traditional archaeological fieldwork. On the other hand, magnetic scanning, a prospection tool in its own right, had the advantage of identifying 'hot spots' for detailed survey. This was an important methodological advance because the geophysics could be integrated into the assessment of the landscape rather than simply adding further detail to known sites. From the geophysicist's point of view, it felt more proactive.[62]

Fortunately, Mick's original suggestion that entire landscapes might be investigated by geophysical means as part of a research-driven agenda is now becoming achievable. At Heslerton in North Yorkshire and during the South Cadbury Environs Project in Somerset, geophysics has led as a prospection tool rather than following along behind.[63] That said, the pinpointing of post-Roman sites, one of the prime aims of the Shapwick Project, was never one that geophysics alone could easily address. All geophysics techniques rely on a measurable contrast between the underground target and its surroundings; if the contrast is poor or severely reduced because of agricultural damage then the chances of locating archaeology are diminished. Since this is likely to be true of many low-status post-Roman settlements, geophysics can struggle to make any real contribution. This was realised early on in the life of the Project and methodological interest was duly channelled towards other techniques, among them the potential of 'trace element' signatures in the plough soil.

Soil analyses

The Shapwick Project was one of the first to assess the potential of heavy-metal soil analysis as a tool for archaeological prospection,[64] and it is perhaps worth explaining how this came about. Once Mick realised that the chances of finding early medieval settlement using geophysics and fieldwalking were thin, he began to think about other ways and means. Over coffee one day, Mick relayed his concerns to team botanist David Hill, who described some research by Dr Mike Martin at the Biological Sciences department at Bristol University on pollutants and heavy metals in the soil. David wondered whether there might be an archaeological application. The heavy metal credentials appealed to Mick – some subliminal connection with Led Zeppelin and Deep Purple perhaps! In subsequent meetings back at the university Mick and Mike then discussed

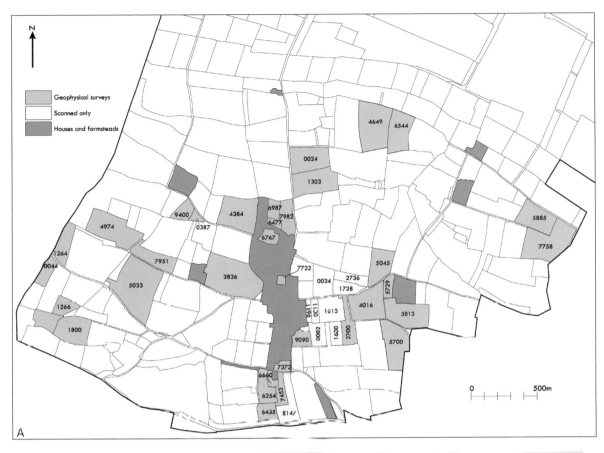

Figure 2.12. Geophysical survey. A: coverage across the parish. B: magnetometry by Chris Gaffney of Geophysical Surveys of Bradford (GSB) in 1991. C: resistivity survey by Alex Turner of the University of Winchester in 1997.

the feasibility of identifying human activity in the soil from traces of various heavy metals. It seemed possible, theoretically at least, but it was a largely untried field of research so some pilot studies would be necessary. The initial plan was to analyse woodlice, which concentrate heavy metals in their bodies, but as we were working in a mostly arable environment we had to settle for soil sampling, a rather laborious process. As a first step we chose a field that we knew a lot about as archaeologists, so that the soil results could be compared against other evidence.[65] Sure enough, the plots of zinc, lead and so on seemed to reflect the known archaeology, giving us confidence to try the method elsewhere.

Fancifully (and only briefly) christened the Aston Martin method, this work was undertaken by Andrew Jackson as one part of his doctoral research.[66] Field workers took many thousands of soil samples from the plough soil within measured grids (shown in Figure 2.13A, marked out with canes and ranging poles), then Andrew sieved the soil to remove roots and stones and allowed the samples to dry slowly. After readings of pH and magnetic susceptibility were taken, the samples were thoroughly dried in an oven and a proportion of the residues boiled in concentrated nitric acid. Once filtered and diluted, the samples could be analysed for a range of heavy metals, including zinc, copper, lead and manganese, using an atomic absorption spectrophotometer at the University of Bristol (Figure 2.13B).[67]

The basic principles of this method are readily appreciated. Evidence of past human activity survives in the soil as organic waste, mainly in the form of faeces and urine and, in analytical terms, phosphorus, persistent forms of organic carbon and heavy metals. Relatively large amounts of phosphorus are excreted daily[68] and, if a cocktail of these residues then becomes inter-mixed with the soil at an archaeological site over the course of many years, those soils will become enriched. The spectrophotometer, an instrument widely used in fields such as physics and chemistry, is able to determine what substances, and exactly how much, are present in each sample. Overall, the heavy metals that show the greatest enhancement from human activity are phosphorus, cadmium, zinc, copper, lead and manganese (Figure 2.13C).[69]

After mapping relative geochemical concentrations from the topsoil and down through the soil profiles

across various sample areas, Andrew concluded that the effects of human activities can persist in the plough soil and he then developed a method to identify suites of heavy metals. The difficulty he found was in distinguishing between recent and ancient activities: on several occasions trenches dug to examine positive results were found to be devoid of any visible trace of archaeology. Like geophysics and fieldwalking, soil analyses cannot reliably be used as a stand-alone prospection tool, but need to be employed in combination with other techniques. After Andrew's pioneering work, further testing on a wider range of geologies and archaeology is badly needed, and in particular more detailed research is required into what might cause the observed concentrations.[70] The benefits for the archaeologist should be clear; for those periods of the past or for those parts of the world where little trace of settlement survives, among them the early medieval period over much of England, soil analysis could offer a valuable prospection tool.[71]

Metal detecting

If this project were to be set up today we would make certain that metal-detector surveys were carried out as part of the fieldwalking strategy, so that any metal objects not picked up by fieldwalkers could be collected alongside other objects. There is absolutely no reason why metal detecting should not be an essential and beneficial tool on any landscape survey, and the decision at the outset not to include it more widely was taken for two reasons. First, when we began in 1989, the County Archaeologist, Bob Croft, felt unable to recommend anyone reliable who could help. The undisciplined way in which some detectorists work, their inability to record accurately where they find things, their inclination to regard objects as personal rather than common property and their overbearing attention to the monetary value of finds all make archaeologists suspicious of their motives. Second, we felt that any positive message to detectorists at that time could have led to the unwanted and irresponsible collection of finds which might have then slipped through the Project's recording systems.[72] To our certain knowledge some Shapwick farmers did allow detectorists onto their land in the mid-1990s and, given the paucity of non-ferrous objects retrieved by fieldwalkers, it seems certain that many finds escaped unrecorded into

Figure 2.13. Archaeological soil analysis. A: samples of topsoil were taken with a trowel. B: Andrew Jackson (left) and Mike Martin (right) in the lab in Biological Sciences at the University of Bristol with the spectrometer. C: the results of 7ha of sampling on a 15m grid across Old Church superimposed onto an aerial photograph (looking south-east with Beerway Farm to the left). Here phosphorus is concentrated over archaeological features visible on aerial photographs (Figure 2.11C) and geophysical survey (Figure 4.11), most notably the medieval graveyard to the south of the church site, which is indicated in blue.

Figure 2.14. Controlled metal detecting at Shapwick. Finds identified by Winchester student Nigel Campbell are surveyed in by Becky Hammond (now Milby). The field has been deturfed but digging has yet to begin.

Figure 2.15. Sue Fitton collecting finds from a vegetable plot at Hollybrook House.

private collections. The loss of this material has serious implications for any assessment of the function and date of scatters of archaeological material. Our conviction is that diagnostic material, even if it is unstratified in the plough soil, should never be removed unless the necessary permissions have been sought and the material is properly identified, recorded, conserved and held in a public archive such as a museum. Given that these conditions were rarely satisfied at that time, we had no wish to promote extensive unregulated metal detecting.

We did, however, welcome detectorists as part of our excavation teams. At first, metal detecting was used only as a 'predictive' tool in areas yet to be excavated, later being employed more systematically once the turf was removed (Figure 2.14). At the Nidons villa site, controlled metal detecting was undertaken in 1998 as part of the operation to recover and record the coin hoard (see Chapter 4). Spoil heaps at all excavations were also routinely scanned and there is no doubt that the use of a metal detector not only hugely boosted the recovery rate of artefacts but also provided distribution data that would have been completely lost otherwise.[73]

Garden survey

Anyone who gardens regularly finds objects in the tilled earth among their vegetables and roses, yet the collection of pottery and other artefacts from garden beds is not often considered by professional archaeologists; not only is the material unstratified, it may have been introduced inadvertently with topsoil dressings brought from elsewhere.[74] We decided, however, that it was time to take a fresh look at the method,[75] and began to retrieve artefacts from flower beds or other areas of exposed soil (Figure 2.15), marking their position on simple sketch maps. A total of thirty-seven beds/areas were examined in this way and some 1,232 sherds of pottery collected, the largest group being from New Farm, where 336 sherds were recovered, though several other gardens produced more than 100 sherds. As expected, the collection was dominated by nineteenth-century pottery, mainly plain pearlwares. Presumably this is broken crockery that found its way into garden beds mixed in with composted kitchen and farmyard waste. Many gardens, however, also produced fragments of later medieval pottery.

Shapwick garden beds are, it seems, merely exposed patches of topsoil, reworked with some additions and garnished with plant life. The pattern of finds needs to be interpreted with a degree of caution, but a comprehensive and systematic study of garden beds in any village could yield useful results. We found that the value of the technique for the Shapwick Project went far beyond its academic benefit. Picking through the dahlias and courgettes forced the archaeologist to confront the interested villager – in our view an encounter beneficial to both sides, but one in which the archaeologist usually has most to learn.

Buildings

A significant contribution to the Shapwick Project was made by Jane and John Penoyre, John Dallimore and other members of the Somerset Vernacular Buildings Research Group.[76] They undertook detailed surveys of the historic buildings in the parish, including all the outlying farms and farm buildings,[77] and made some quite unexpected discoveries in the process (Figure 2.16). Shapwick House, for example, was found to be a later medieval structure fundamentally altered in the seventeenth century and then refaced in the nineteenth century, while Forsters, in Bridewell Lane, proved to be the oldest of the houses in the village; its low proportions, thatched roof and rubble walls are little changed since at least the fifteenth century (see Chapter 7).

The discovery of early buildings such as these is in itself important for, unlike across much of southern and eastern England, few later medieval houses belonging to socially middling groups still survive in this region. Buildings are a microcosm of the village's developing social order and some of the Project's most rewarding moments happened when we were able to link lists of occupiers first to their surviving wills and inventories and then to the emerging archaeological and architectural record. A case in point is yeoman Thomas Prewe, who made his will in 1630 and probably occupied the house we know today as the old Post Office and Stores. In spite of many changes in the intervening 400 years, Thomas's home would still be familiar to him today, and we were able to reconstruct the original locations of many of his most prized belongings (see Figure 8.12).

Buildings survey is not just about the 'earliest' or the 'best' – few of the houses described in this book

Figure 2.16. The standing building team of the Somerset Vernacular Buildings Research Group recording the medieval house at Forsters in 1999. John Dallimore and Jane Penoyre measuring, John Penoyre sits recording.

are grand architectural statements – but it can be a potent tool with which to explore the changing appearance of a village. In this process buildings of all periods and types become important, from the agricultural labourer's modest accommodation to the most imposing of Victorian villas. Not only can these dwellings reveal something about the developing plan of the village, they reflect the region's character in their choice of building materials and house plans. Historic farm buildings, for example, have evolved to suit the needs of the agricultural community and equal merit is given here to ancillary structures such as barns, stables, dairies and dovecotes in understanding how farmsteads were organised and how their functions changed, particularly after the late eighteenth century

Figure 2.17. Species of shrub and climber recorded in the Shapwick hedgerows. A: guelder rose with heavy clusters of berries. B: spindle, a hard yellow wood ideal for knitting needles. The pink and orange berries are purgative. C: wayfaring tree; its white flowers are followed by red berries which turn black. D: dogwood; the first-year stems are red.

(see Chapter 9). In a sense, surviving buildings are the topmost layer of archaeology, the parts that are still in use, and it is important to investigate this stratum before looking earlier.[78]

Plants and hedgerows

With an eye for its developing historic landscape, we also reflected on the modern ecology of the parish and, in particular, the botanical composition of Shapwick's hedgerows. The idea of using elements of the flora of hedges to determine their putative age dates back over thirty-five years, to Max Hooper's suggestion that the number of woody species in a length of hedgerow thirty yards long (27.3m) rises with age by approximately one species for every century of its existence.[79] To investigate this hypothesis and any variations in the occurrence of plant communities across the parish, David Hill and Maggie Williams examined over 70km of hedgerow in the parish and compiled species lists for 10m lengths for every hedge (Figure 2.17). Over 7,015 lengths were surveyed in all, identifying not just woody species (trees and shrubs) but also the herbaceous species and climbers as well as the 'physical' characteristics of the hedges, such as ditches and banks. The Project, with its abundance of documentation about the history of enclosure, provided an ideal opportunity to compare botanical composition with the known history of the hedgerows, as well as to investigate any correspondence with geology, soils, drainage, aspect and management history (see Chapters 6 and 9). As

we shall see, there is no simple way to read the age of a hedge or determine its origin.

Invertebrates and hedgerows

A second ecological study, this time undertaken by David Clements and Keith Alexander, compared the invertebrate faunas from a sample of thirty hedgerows with differing dates of origin. Research elsewhere has long suggested that some plant and animal species are restricted in varying degrees to ancient woodlands or to habitats with a long continuity of large trees ('old growth'), and that they are correspondingly scarce where habitats have been interrupted by clearance or replanted with non-native species and where the habitats have arisen secondarily in recent times.[80] These 'indicator species' range from those that appear to be wholly confined to ancient woodland or old-growth habitats, perhaps indicating a link that might extend back as far as the original 'primary woodlands' that grew in Britain after the last ice age, through to species that show increasing degrees of tolerance to disturbance or modification by mankind. This range of 'indicator species' includes vascular plants, lichens, fungi and various insects (particularly beetles and true flies), as well as land molluscs and other invertebrates, such as pseudoscorpions and millipedes. Studies using invertebrate 'indicator species' have been carried out previously in a very wide range of woodland, parkland and other habitats containing trees but, until this Project began, there had been little effort made to apply such an approach to hedgerows.

For the Shapwick study a range of hedgerows of differing ages, as determined by the archaeological and documentary evidence, were selected at locations scattered across the parish, and these were each sampled for invertebrates in their central 50–60m section, well away from intersections with other hedgerows (Figure 2.18). The foliage and canopy of each hedge was netted and 'beaten' for approximately thirty minutes by two workers, with the dislodged invertebrates being collected either in 0.5m diameter sweep-nets or in 1m² beating trays. In addition, the leaf litter beneath the hedgerow was sampled using two petrol-driven vacuum suction-samplers converted from Sabre BLU25 leaf-blowers, with six suction-samples of approximately two minutes each being taken from different areas of the hedgerow base. Quite what Shapwick farmers made of their hedgerows being hoovered we never found out! Standing and fallen deadwood was subject to *ad hoc* investigation by means of beating, bark-picking, splitting and the collection of fungal fruiting bodies, the latter for subsequent rearing-out of adult invertebrates. The sampling was carried out in May and June, the peak time of year for emerging 'saproxylic' beetle and fly species – in other words, those species that are associated as larvae with the morbidity, death and decay of trees and shrubs, and that tend to be the most valuable as 'indicator species'. The invertebrates collected were initially sorted by hand in the field, and samples of target taxa were collected either in tubes or with the aid of a suction device for subsequent desk-based identification. Critical species were dissected where necessary to confirm their identity.

Woodland surveys

Separate surveys were also carried out on the flora in Shapwick's woodlands. The most interesting proved to be Loxley Wood, which contains some ancient woodland indicators at its core, where the greatest diversity of flora can also be found. To create a more detailed picture of the development of the wood, botanical mapping was combined with maps, documentary sources, aerial photographs and earthwork evidence by John Knight.[81] The woodland name is itself a significant clue to age. *Locheslega*, the name given to Loxley Wood around the time of Domesday as a hundred name in the Geld Inquest, may be interpreted as 'Locc's clearing in woodland'

and probably refers to open ground on the ridge to the west. The suffix 'leah' indicates woodland that was already recognised as ancient by the Anglo-Saxons. During the later medieval period the wood belonged to the main Shapwick holding, though documents intimate that the land was open to all for common grazing through the autumn and winter.[82] This public access was gradually extinguished in the eighteenth century so that the wood could be managed privately for its timber (Box 8.2).

Most of Shapwick's smaller woodlands, Fifteen Acre Copse and Beggars Bush Copse among them, contain few large trees and have ground floras typical of secondary woodland. They were probably created at the time of enclosure to provide shelter for game and foxes for hunting. Beggars Bush Copse, for example, contains the earthworks of ridge and furrow, so the wood was clearly created *after* enclosure over former common field. Henhills Copse is of far greater interest. The woodland there today is mainly ash with a scatter of oak and field maple and a mixed understorey which is abundant in hazel; the ground flora is dominated by ramsons (wild garlic) and dog's mercury. On the face of it, there is little to suggest other than this being non-ancient secondary woodland that regenerated naturally once the post-medieval 'pleasure gardens', indicated by the earthworks there, were abandoned (see Chapter 8). However, the number of ancient woodland indicators – eleven vascular plants in all – hints at a more complex history. David Clements and Keith Alexander suggest that Henhills Copse may in fact stand close to the site of an ancient woodland, perhaps Caterwood, and so retain remnants of its original vegetation. Alternatively, the ancient woodland species may have colonised the copse more recently from neighbouring hedgerows, something that could also be hinted at by the higher than average totals of saproxylic invertebrates to be found there (see above).

Some holes to be dug

Test pits

The villagers of Shapwick were understandably reluctant to allow archaeologists to wreck their lawns and flower beds; it was far easier to persuade people to let us dig a more modest test pit. Once they saw what was going on, however, neighbours soon volunteered

Figure 2.18. Collecting samples for the survey of invertebrate fauna across thirty hedgerows. A: Keith Alexander examining deadwood. B: David Clements beating and catching invertebrates in a sweep-net. C: Keith using a petrol-driven vacuum sampler converted from a leaf-blower to suck along the base of the hedgerow. D: sorting. E: Anaglyptus, a long-horn beetle; here an adult is attracted to blossom.

their gardens and pressed others to participate, so that by the end of the Project a total of eighty-one test pits had been dug across the village (Figure 2.19). This work was supervised initially by Mick, Michael Costen and Paula Gardiner and latterly by Teresa Hall and Sue Fitton.

We found that four people could dig a 1m × 1m hole from the present-day ground surface down to the natural clay or bedrock, sieve half the contents, clean the sides, photograph and draw the sections, backfill and returf all in a six-hour working day. It was hard work, though the camaraderie seemed to make up for it; the most time-consuming part of the process was the sieving of half the spoil through a 10mm mesh, with breaks periodically to record layers and features. Any archaeological material then entered the Shapwick processing system alongside artefacts from excavation and fieldwalking.

The digging of test pits has long been part of the archaeologist's toolkit, first in America and later on Mediterranean surveys.[83] In Britain they have typically been used to map buried deposits and sample ancient land surfaces, as happened nearby at Brean Down in Somerset,[84] rather than to identify 'sites', though one exception to this was the work of Richard Hodges and a team from the University of Sheffield, who excavated nearly 1,000 0.5m × 1m test pits at 10m intervals across pasture at Roystone Grange in Derbyshire.[85] More recently a team exploring Mesolithic sites on Islay in the southern Hebrides used the same method to obtain a 'grab sample' of artefacts.[86] Our own introduction to the technique came when Chris was working for the Cotswold Archaeological Trust in 1990–91.[87] Working in the environment of commercial archaeology, the Trust, under the guidance of Tim Darvill, was busy developing sampling techniques to evaluate buried archaeology prior to building development, mainly in urban settings where the stratigraphy tended to be deep. The Shapwick Project seemed an ideal opportunity to test the value of this technique in a living village where larger-scale work was similarly impractical.

Rather like pixels on a computer screen, the more test pits dug the finer-grained the picture of the underlying archaeology, and a steady pattern of results soon began to emerge.[88] Generally, garden soil overlay less regularly tilled and paler subsoil into

which pits and ditches had been cut. Occasionally waterlogging prevented progress and on one occasion an electrical cable was uncovered, but otherwise most test pits at Shapwick were consistently 0.40–0.65m deep before they hit bedrock or the natural Lias clays. We had expected the older houses to have deeper stratigraphies around them, but this was not the case; in fact, some modern houses are surrounded by deep soil profiles because they are built in former gardens and paddocks, while older houses often seem to have their foundations on surfaces which have been stripped of all topsoil. Few finds were of intrinsic interest; the typical assemblage was seventeenth–nineteenth century in date, with large quantities of structural debris such as tile and slate, as well as pottery, clay pipes and bottle glass. Nevertheless, the overall results were extremely important for the aims of the Project as a whole because they provided important information concerning the origins and evolution of the village (see Chapter 6).

As a result of the test-pit programme at Shapwick the method has now been adopted on other medieval landscape projects. At Whittlewood it was a core technique for the examination of medieval settlements[89] and Carenza Lewis has now used the method successfully with groups of schoolchildren in villages in eastern England.[90] This followed its application in a series of community archaeology projects that were part of several *Time Team* programmes.[91] Nevertheless, in spite of their current popularity, test pits are not entirely unproblematic as an archaeological technique, the main disadvantage being their restricted size. This not only limits the effective interpretation of archaeological features, where they are recognised at all, but also restricts the recovery of dateable objects, something that can make the accurate dating of stratigraphy especially hazardous. The main strength of the technique, on the other hand, is the relative speed with which a small hole can be dug down to the bedrock and then backfilled again after recording. In a community project this is vital because the task can be completed, with satisfaction and a tangible result (records, photos and finds) within the day. For the 'apprentice' fieldworker, in particular, test pits are the ideal learning opportunity; a range of finds are handled and observation skills honed.

Figure 2.19. Test pitting 1m × 1m squares in gardens and paddocks across the village. A: removing and sieving the topsoil. B: in among the beans. C: in open spaces. D: test-pitting in progress at Church Close. E: recording the test pit. F: quantities of medieval pottery plotted out at Hill Farm. Note the grid and frequency of test pits.

Shovel pits

Shovel-pitting, or shovel-testing as it is sometimes called, is the controlled examination of a standard volume of sieved topsoil from multiple locations across a measured grid. The method, first introduced to the project by Nick Thorpe, was pioneered in the north-east woodlands of the United States[92] as a rapid means of identifying sites with dense concentrations of archaeological material and quantifying artefact distributions over sizeable areas. A handful of landscape projects in Europe – in Denmark, for example[93] – as well as more locally, as at the Roman site at Sigwells,[94] have since adopted the technique. Because the holes are shallow, archaeological features are not disturbed; the objective is to minimise the number of shovel pits dug and to maximise the probability of detecting archaeological sites.

Depending on their aims, projects select different sampling regimes. At Shapwick one team laid out a grid of 50m squares aligned on the national grid using a compass and tapes.[95] A second team then proceeded to dig five shovel pits in each square: one at the centre and the others 15m in from the corners (Figure 2.20), like the five-dot pattern on dice. Two bucketfuls (about 30l) of soil were extracted from each shovel pit and sieved for finds through a standard 10mm mesh before the site was returfed. Sieving ensured that little was missed. A complete square was therefore one in which all five tests were carried out and 150l of soil were processed in all.[96] After a pilot project to calibrate the size of the soil sample, we were able to cover up to ten 50m squares per day in this way; work then continued across the parish for several weeks each year.

There are, of course, many circumstances in which the character of the artefact assemblage in the topsoil does not reflect what lies beneath. Original ground surfaces may be buried by dumping, for example, or along the sides of watercourses they might be smothered by alluvium. In such cases shovel-pitting is unlikely to be helpful. The exercise is most accurate when finds are present in quantities and they have not been disturbed too far or buried too deeply. The technique is also rapid and low-cost, while close control is exercised over the recovery of every sample; there are none of the walker or environmental biases that can complicate the interpretation of fieldwalking

results. In particular, shovel-pitting provided an innovative way to assess the archaeological potential of pasture fields that otherwise would have remained inaccessible to our field teams because they had not been ploughed. This included the sand islands at Shapwick Burtle and Brickyard Farm and the Levels edge near Moorgate Farm: both areas that produced important results.

Boreholes

A major ambition of the project was to examine a well-dated environmental sequence that would provide information about the palaeoecology and post-glacial geological sequence for the area.[97] This work was intended to complement that of Godwin and the Somerset Levels Project (Box 1.1). With this in mind, in 1998 Keith Wilkinson undertook a manual auger survey of thirty-four boreholes up to 8m in depth along a transect parallel to the Shapwick–Westhay road. Once a suitable site had been identified with good potential for pollen analysis and radiocarbon dating, a team returned with a pneumatic auger to drill out 'Borehole A'. As we shall see in Chapter 3, the results made an important contribution to our understanding of the local vegetation and environment, particularly for the Mesolithic period.

Evaluations and excavations

Between 1992 and 1999 some sixty-six trenches of varying size were dug across the parish. Most of our excavations were research-driven, the choice of sites being dictated largely by academic questions (see Chapter 1), though others did come about as a result of routine planning applications, among them sites investigated by the University of Bristol Archaeological Services and by Dick Broomhead, as well as two substantial projects directed by Nancy and Charlie Hollinrake (Figure 2.21A). These latter investigations made an important contribution to answering the research objectives of the Shapwick Project, though they differed from our research-driven exercises in being funded by a 'developer' and excavated according to a specification agreed first with the local planning authority.[98] On-site, there was greater use of machinery to remove the overlying soil, sieving was not undertaken and fewer personnel were generally present, though all the

Figure 2.20. Shovel pit testing. A: sieving. B: digging and sieving, with a further team beyond. C: teams digging. D: sieving and bagging up the finds.

staff were professionals.[99] Each evaluation almost instantaneously generated its own separate typescript report and archive to fulfil the immediate needs of curator and client, and this sometimes led on to watching briefs and excavation.[100] These mitigation strategies were carefully targeted, problem-orientated programmes of work. In the case of the water pipeline through Shapwick Park in 1994, archaeological work was strictly restricted to the corridor of disturbed ground,[101] while only the footprint of a proposed new building was excavated at Shapwick Sports Hall in the area where damage to underlying deposits was most likely to occur.[102]

Only one piece of fieldwork sat outside the framework described above. The discovery in 1998 of a hoard of 9,238 Roman coins via metal detecting led to the excavation of six trenches as well as to fieldwalking, geophysics and a metal-detecting survey by Somerset County Council, directed by Richard Brunning.[103] The purpose of this exercise was to assess the potential for further finds and to identify any related archaeological features. As we shall see in Chapter 4, these proved to include the foundations of a Roman villa together with outlying prehistoric settlement, field systems and enclosures.

With few exceptions, the Shapwick sites were buried only shallowly. Archaeology generally lies only 0.15–0.25m below the turf line, with the stratigraphy

Figure 2.21. Excavations underway. A: excavation by Charles and Nancy Hollinrake along the line of the Polden pipeline; work undertaken on behalf of Wessex Water. B: trowelling. C: sieving at Bridewell Lane using metal trays hooked onto an A-frame. Two people operated each sieve, tipping in bucketfuls brought by excavators, pushing and pulling the tray to empty it of soil and then decanting the residue once the finds had been extracted and bagged.

beneath only 0.3m deep. This usually presents few problems, but, where more than one period is present and deposits are severely truncated by ploughing, interpretations and dating become more complex. In order to maximise the potential of every hole dug, less-disturbed lower layers were trowelled (Figure 2.21B) and the distribution of diagnostic finds was recorded. All excavated spoil was also dry sieved (Figure 2.21C)

Figure 2.22. Environmental archaeology. A: Keith Wilkinson and Vanessa Straker from English Heritage taking monolith samples for palynological study from the moat at Shapwick House. B: the flotation tank in action. Soil samples are poured into an adapted oil tank which is filled with water and fitted with a 1mm mesh. Charred remains, encouraged to float by pumping a jet of water from beneath, are caught by fine sieves (here inside the bucket). This is the 'flot'. C: the flot drying. Note the abundant carbonised seeds and charcoal which are later sifted under a microscope and identified. D: cleaning out the tank.

and an extensive programme of wet sieving carried out (Figure 2.22). Where possible, 60l of soil, measured as four bucketfuls, were taken as a sample of a context and processed through a flotation machine, built by Kerry Ely according to a design by Vanessa Straker. Given their enormous weight and bulk the samples were best processed at Shapwick, both 'float' and heavy residue being retained for future analysis. Their main purpose was as environmental samples for plant macrofossils but the residues often contained minute slivers of pottery as well as other finds that would otherwise have gone unnoticed.

Dating

For certain periods of the past archaeologists know enough about flint tools, pottery and metalwork to ascribe a rough date to the human activities they represent. To some extent the accuracy of that date will be dependent upon how many other sites have been dug in the area and what is known of local material culture. Thus, the manufacture of some post-medieval pottery from Shapwick can be pinpointed to within twenty-five years, whereas some diagnostic prehistoric flint tools, such as scrapers, have a much longer date range stretching over thousands of years. In those cases where there is no material culture available or dating is insufficiently precise then several alternatives are available, among them radiocarbon dating, which provided an absolute chronology for our pollen sequences and for a selection of organics present in prehistoric and early medieval layers.[104] Radiocarbon was, however, only one of several methods tried at Shapwick (Figure 2.23A).[105] For those buildings with suitable timbers tree-ring dating, or dendrochronology was employed (Figure 2.23B),[106] and an unsuccessful attempt was made to use archaeomagnetism, a technique that measures the thermoremanent magnetism of iron grains, in this case to try and date the fired clay base of a limekiln (Figure 2.23C).[107]

And after the digging is done …

Finds processing and analysis

At least as much effort goes into the processing of artefacts and samples from archaeological fieldwork as it does into their initial collection. Many of the Shapwick finds were processed while excavation was underway, students and volunteers alternating between the two tasks (Figure 2.24). In the latter half of the Project, when most finds were recovered, the responsibility for coordinating this operation fell

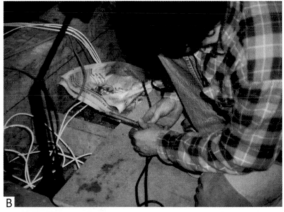

Figure 2.23. Dating techniques. A: radiocarbon dating is commonly used by archaeologists to date wood, charcoal, bone and sediments. Many of the Shapwick samples were processed by the Scottish Universities Environmental Research Centre (SUERC) using a method known as Accelerator Mass Spectrometry (AMS). The samples are cleaned and then combusted to produce CO_2 gas before being chemically reduced to graphite (elemental carbon). The graphitisation process is seen here. A particle accelerator is then used to count the carbon isotopes present and calculate the time elapsed since the sample was 'alive'. B: Dan Miles takes samples for dendrochronology from the roof timbers at Shapwick House. C: Paul Linford takes samples for archaeomagnetic dating from one of the kilns in Old Church.

BOX 2.2

A day in the life of the Shapwick excavator

The majority of those who worked during the summer on Shapwick excavations were undergraduate students from Winchester. They were accommodated on the campsite at Rose Farm in Westhay and, for the final few years, at Garslade Farm at Godney. The Holy Grail for any successful archaeological project is that prized combination of campsite, rented accommodation and decent food (and a glass of beer). The academic aims of a project may be laudable (even important), and the merits of each trench were debated at great length (Figure B.2.2A), but unless the infrastructure is right and appropriately priced, loftier ambitions can quickly disintegrate. In our case diggers arranged their own breakfast and we had sandwiches, made by a rota of volunteers, delivered to the various excavations at lunchtime. One priority was for everyone to eat together in the evening, diggers and supervisors alike, and this forced the group (who sometimes didn't know one another before they arrived) to mix socially and guaranteed one hearty hot meal a day (two courses £4.20 in 1996). We fondly imagined that this bonding would inspire common academic aims, but perhaps that was wishful thinking. At least a decent calorific intake prevented diggers from crumbling physically, and it was a chance to catch up on events and to allot tasks for the following day.

The day began on site at about 9.00 a.m. and finished at 5.30 p.m., with an hour for lunch and two half-hour tea breaks. Tasks such as excavation, finds processing, geophysics, shovel-pitting and sometimes fieldwalking were all undertaken simultaneously, each student taking a turn at every task (Figure B.2.2B). Excavation, the core activity, could be accelerated or slowed by adding numbers or deploying them elsewhere. Usually numbers on site were maximised at the beginning and at the end of the summer's work, which generally lasted for five or six weeks overall, with each crew of students working for two weeks apiece. Not all stayed the course. One volunteer arrived, saw what was required, became dizzy, spent five days in a tent and then went home! For the main supervisors, Kerry Ely, Phil Marter, Richard McConnell and Alex Turner (Figure B.2.2C), the excavations meant a lengthy spell away from family, though the team did take off one day in every fifteen and a short break of two or three days in the middle of the season to recuperate.

Generally three sites were open at any one time, each with a site director and supervisors and volunteers. For four years one of these sites was set up by Somerset County Council as their community archaeology dig, though local volunteers and students from other universities regularly joined in elsewhere. These teams, generally of between six and thirty, removed the topsoil, excavated and recorded the site, and backfilled it too, taking turns at tasks such as drawing and heavy or lighter site work. Occasionally, when time was short, a JCB was used to replace the spoil, though the returfing mostly had to be done by hand. Once completed, the records for each site comprised plan and section drawings (on permatrace film at various stages of excavation), context sheets (describing numbered layers and features) and photographs (colour slide and black and white, sometimes video). Back at the Vestey cottage, finds were washed, dried, marked and bagged by context and the soil samples were run through the flotation machine. Unusual finds in need of more delicate attention or conservation were kept to one side and taken away by Steve Minnitt of Somerset County Museums, who usually visited every two to three weeks. Otherwise, runs were made back to Winchester to store the finds there.

It can well be imagined that 'managing' the off-site activities of between fifty and a hundred 18 to 22-year-olds for a five-week period has its moments. There were the distractions of the Glastonbury Festival to contend with, when archaeological skills were honed by burrowing beneath security fencing. Such desperation can only be fully appreciated after several weeks in local pubs listening to line dancing and, on one occasion, an accordion version of *Smoke on the Water*! There was at least one fight with local youths (over a pool game), smouldering tensions at a barn dance and, most memorably, the arrival of the local constabulary on site one morning to inquire over the whereabouts of several hundredweight of cheese that had been 'liberated' by enterprising dairy-lovers from a refrigerated lorry parked up nearby overnight. The robbers had cut an enormous hole in the side of the vehicle with a blow-torch. Of this we were innocent. Also among the high drama were several dashes to Musgrove hospital in Taunton with beleaguered excavators suffering from rashes, wrecked backs, slipped discs, twisted and pulverised fingers, mattock wounds to the legs and food allergies, though Shapwick diggers remained on the whole blessedly free from illness and breakage. Our most serious injury in ten years was an accident in the skittles alley!

Behind the scenes, the longest hours for the director and the core team are often before the excavation gets underway: booking accommodation (apologising for last year's mess!), arguing food prices and menus, visiting the sites and laying them out, administering the finances, health and safety, websites and equipment (wheelbarrows, shovels, cameras, survey instruments, drawing boards) and purchasing the many consumables (bags, pens, string, dish cloths, mugs, tea spoons, chopping boards, ink). The excavation headquarters had to be erected (a cavernous and ancient army tent) and the latrines dug before the main excavating crew arrived, so there was usually an advance 'reconnaissance' team that set off from Winchester a few days before the others. At the end of six weeks this process was reversed: equipment was dismantled and cleaned and finds and records verified. Often a core team of three or four people stayed behind to make sure everything was packed away (though inexplicably we did forget the site loo one year and Mick found it, in bits, in a hedge several weeks later!). Each site supervisor at Shapwick was then asked to write up their own excavation for completion by the autumn.

A

B

C

Figure B.2.2. Shapwick excavations. A: considering soil chemistry plots and planning the location of trenches. From left to right: Mick Aston, Christopher Gerrard, Teresa Hall, Shirley Everden, Mike Martin and Andrew Jackson. B: measuring and drawing a section. C: deep thoughts at the Old Bakery excavations; from the left, site supervisors Alex Turner, Kerry Ely and Richard McConnell.

Figure 2.24. Finds processing. A: finds washing. B: Clare Rollason hanging finds out to dry. In a damp summer this was the best way to dry finds quickly. C: finds marking. Once they have been dried in old egg boxes, the finds can be marked up with the year, parish code, trench and context numbers.

to Clare Rollason. Once washed, bagged and boxed, finds from excavation were roughly quantified over the following autumn by Winchester students as part of their coursework.

The first stage in the post-fieldwork phase of any archaeological project is the assessment of the size and academic potential of the archaeological materials collected. Chris undertook this review between July and October 2000 after he moved to the Department of Archaeology at Durham University, and then managed the project through its final stages, monitored by Dr Peter Wilson from English Heritage who were the sponsor for this part of the project. The archive of Shapwick materials included voluminous photographic, paper and digital archives as well as boxes containing the bulk finds such as pottery and bone and smaller collections of charcoal, marine molluscs, waterlogged wood, plant macrofossils, insect remains, fish remains, samples for radiocarbon dating and soil samples for pollen. For our finds specialists the chronological range of the material collected and the diversity of sites explored opened up the possibility of comparison *between* sites in the parish as well as with other rural and urban assemblages both locally and nationally.

Reporting

We reported on our results in different ways. For three years (1996–1999) BT provided us with a small grant to experiment with archaeology on the Internet. In the days before 'blogs' and webcams, one of the Winchester students, Dave Norcott, produced a daily bulletin board with photographs to show progress at each of our excavations, a kind of diary of events as they unfolded on site, to which we added not-so-serious competitions and invited contributions to our 'chat room' (see Figure 1.6F). We were rather taken aback when contact was made by people from all over the world, from as far afield as Australia and South America, and the novelty of medieval archaeology in cyberspace attracted enquiry from other archaeologists interested in doing something similar, including the French archaeological magazine *Archéologia* who featured an article on us.[108] When, in 1998, we found ourselves in *New Scientist* as 'website of the week', with 8,000 'hits', we briefly congratulated ourselves on leading the digital age and imagined bringing

Shapwick (and British archaeology) to every one of the-then 23 million users of the Internet![109]

The academic 'profile' of the project was served, as might be expected, by a flow of articles over a fifteen-year period in local, national and international journals.[110] There were also contributions to more popular publications, including *Current Archaeology* among others.[111] Most of our effort, however, was put into writing, editing and distributing 'The Shapwick Reports' which were modelled on those produced by the Somerset Levels Project (Box 1.1). To begin with these were no more than an elaborate newsletter, containing reports on what had been done and what we would like to do next. About 200 copies were distributed to landowners, tenants, fieldworkers and so on as a means of communication. Later on they became more ambitious. At 150–250 pages in length with a contents list stretching to twenty or more articles, they were time-consuming to produce, rather like typesetting and printing a home-made archaeological journal every year, but they were to become a vital chronicle of the project. Many of our most important ideas and methods were first worked through in their pages. Funded by the Department for Continuing Education at the University of Bristol, eight Reports were produced in all.[112]

The Shapwick Reports served several purposes, some more clandestine than others. Obviously they were excellent publicity and we sold copies at lectures to interested members of the general public as well as to university and local libraries. We also sometimes gave them away, begrudgingly to the influential, sometimes to the plain mean, but mostly to those in the village who had contributed to the Project in some way during the course of the year. This included a 'thank you' copy for every fieldworker and a copy for every tenant and landowner who had allowed us onto their land. In a project of this sort some people show active and positive interest immediately; they usually attended the annual lectures and sometimes helped out with the fieldwork. But not everyone has the time for that, nor, because of the social dynamics of the village, do they feel comfortable in doing so. These other people have to be reached, and the Shapwick Project Reports provided an excellent opportunity to do just that; to knock at the door, go in for a cup of tea and explain what the Project was all about.

CHAPTER THREE

Once Upon a Time

From the Hunter-Gatherers of the Mesolithic
to the Agricultural Communities of the Iron Age

By the time he returned to the clearing under the ancient oak it was already dark. They had seen the glow of camp fires in the distance and heard the chatter of low voices as they walked briskly down the track by the watercourse. The sound of the water always led him home, just as it had for his ancestors. All day long they had been cutting the hazel rods higher up the slope, gathering them in bundles and stripping away the side shoots. Tomorrow they would bend and weave them together into lengths, windbreaks against the colder wind that always blew from the north across the marsh. The threading of the poles always seemed to scrape his knuckles, even though his hands were so calloused and hardened. It was not a task he enjoyed – there were others who worked faster and more neatly.

Already that day he had broken the tip of his axe and spent time with the antler hammer scarring the stone edge sharp again. It was too fine a piece to throw away; the colour was unusual and it had come from mines far away, people said. Under his bedding of hides he kept a spare nodule with its skin still intact, a gift from his father. He had stopped it jangling inside the leather pouch by wrapping it in cotton grass. Before dusk he would begin to work on it, his own discarded flakes adding to the accumulation of shattered stones and flint dust. By its weight and shape and by turning it in his hands he knew how the stone would splinter, thick or fine, what to keep and what to throw away. First he would strike off the rind, then work at the core with the antler hammer, and finally etch the cutting edge of a long blade.

And all the while they sat around the fire telling stories. He knew the tales almost by heart; of strangers who lived out on the islands, travels to meet the cousins and of the exotic stone they might bring. There were celebrations and feasting to be planned, down by the water, with thanks to be offered for their game. The women would sway and hum to the songs, glowing from the fat they had rubbed into their skins, while the men held back out of sight until their part came, pounding the earth with their feet. One day soon he would go that way with the others to hunt for wildfowl, listening for the bird calls, watching always for the churned ground where animals had dug. He would take some hazelnuts, he thought, they were light to carry and good to eat. Some of his kin had already gone down to the water's edge, cutting their way through the reeds there. Perhaps when he saw them again they would have some feathers for him to make his arrowheads fly true and straight. He shivered. Tonight, he promised himself, the fire could not be allowed to go out. It would not be long now, one more moon perhaps, before the older men said they should move the stock back towards the pointed hill. If the tethered calf would only stop crying for its mother, he was sure he would sleep the sleep of the dead.

This story takes place in about 2200 BC, in the early Bronze Age, and is based on the evidence gathered for this chapter. We emphasise our individual's knowledge of the natural landscape and the many practical tasks in which he is engaged, such as the weaving of hurdles, the flaking of flint and the cutting of reeds. Some of the activities mentioned here, including the management of woodland and the use of cotton grass as a wrapping for valued flints, are known from the archaeological record. The practical and supernatural role of the peat bog is highlighted here, as it should be for all periods of prehistory when doubtless it held a mysterious allure: a nether world of land and water. The 'pointed hill' is, of course, Glastonbury Tor.

Hunting and gathering on the Poldens

The earlier Mesolithic landscape (c.10,000–6500 BC)
No authentic glimpse of Shapwick's earliest prehistoric world is possible without first establishing something of its landscape and, until very recently, little was known about the Mesolithic environment of this area. The results from 'Borehole A' have changed that by providing the first radiocarbon-dated pollen diagram, which now enables changes in vegetation to be tracked over several millennia (Figure 3.1A–C). To understand these changes we must imagine ourselves high above the Polden Hills in the early Mesolithic at the turn of the seventh millennium BC. Looking down, at first the view is unfamiliar. What we know today as the Levels is a shallow inland embayment of tidal mudflats and gravels, fissured by the braided channels of minor streams that join together to form wider watercourses wending their way out to sea (Figure 3.1D–E). Evidence for this is the freshwater molluscs in the laminated muds and tufas at the very bottom of the Holocene borehole sequence.[1] The estuary below us is dotted with wooded islands, the largest being Wedmore, with Burtle, Westhay and a scatter of smaller islands closer to the Polden ridge. A trio of these so-called 'sand islands' lie within the present parish, at Brickyard Farm, Canada Farm and the Shapwick Burtle; these are the product of freshwater and marine conditions during the Middle Palaeolithic, over 100,000 years ago.[2] In the past they were far more substantial than they are today. Mapping a cross section of the valley bottom beneath the later accumulations of clays and peats reveals that the top of the Shapwick Burtle was almost 8m above the surrounding marsh at this date. Sealed well below the depth of commercially exploited peats, future archaeological investigation may be rewarded by the discovery of waterlogged Mesolithic occupation dipping below the marine silts.[3]

Seen from our prehistoric vantage point, the Poldens are a long finger of dry land projecting out into the sea. Unlike today, the whole of this ridge

is covered by pine, hazel and elm, and any signs of human presence are at first lost among the trees, but here and there smoke rises from fires out on the islands and on the Polden slopes. The microscopic charcoal fragments identified in the borehole sediments are almost certainly from domestic fires, unless the reed beds were being deliberately burnt off, as has been suggested at Goldcliff East on the other side of the Severn estuary at the same date.[4] The majority of the pollen and the charcoal cannot have come from more than 500m away from the borehole, which must place human activity either on the Shapwick Burtle itself or on the higher ground of the Nidons.

The people who laid these fires were skilled and proficient hunter-gatherers. They relied on neither domesticated animals nor crops. Instead, they hunted and trapped wild animals, foraged for wild plant foods, collected fuel and fished. Among the surviving populations today who still gather their resources from the animal and plant communities around them are the Inuit of the Arctic, the Mbuti of Africa and the Australian Aborigines. There is enormous diversity in the organisation and practices of these groups, though anthropologists recognise common strands between them: a lack of possessions that might inhibit movement; the sharing of food that guards against shortfalls and provides opportunities for attention-getting displays of costume, music and dance; egalitarian group structures and a division of labour so that men are more often the hunters, women the more reliable provider of gathered foods. The Shapwick populations would probably have shared these attributes too and they certainly would have been mobile, moving on routinely to new ground once the resources around about became depleted.

For some time researchers have known that there are Mesolithic flints on Shapwick's three sand islands, though no structural evidence has ever been found there or indeed anywhere else in the parish.[5] Modern land use, mostly pasture, precludes fieldwalking, but shovel-pitting confirms two distinct clusters of earlier

Figure 3.1. Auger survey and reconstructed environments. A: auguring along a transect parallel to the Shapwick–Westhay road to examine the sediment stratigraphy. B: examining one of the cores. C: a pneumatic auger being used to recover samples for pollen analysis. D: mudflats at Caldicott in South Wales. Pollen analysis at Shapwick undertaken by Heather Tinsley suggests a shallow inland embayment of tidal mudflats with gravels fissured by braided channels and wider watercourses wending their way out to sea. The modern environment at Caldicott is analogous. E: aerial photograph of mudflats at Stogursey (Somerset); note the medieval fishtraps in the foreground.

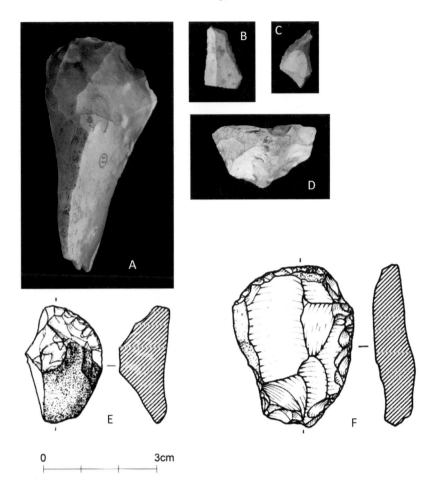

Figure 3.2. Mesolithic flints. Earlier Mesolithic – A: two platformed blade core. B: possible microlith. F: round scraper. Later Mesolithic – C: microburin. D: adze fragment. E: end and side scraper.

Mesolithic flint at opposite ends of the Shapwick Burtle, perhaps marking look-out points.[6] It may be that the vegetation here on the islands was more readily cleared than it was on the Polden slopes; food resources a little way out in the estuary would certainly have been closer at hand, with a rich birdlife and opportunities for fishing both from the water's edge and from waterborne craft, not to mention the natural resources needed to fashion spears, feathered arrows and traps. Knowing now that the Burtle stood out so prominently above the surrounding land surface, which was itself often under water, one wonders how this topography might have affected activities there.[7] It would have been an impressive vantage point, and an unusual one. Little evidence for Mesolithic activity has so far been found on the rock islands of Westhay and Meare, to the north, so perhaps the isolated location of this little island with its views in all directions across the watery landscape, played some part in its selection.[8]

While the wetland may have supplied contributions to diet as well as estuarine transport, other strategies were also available for exploiting local animals and plants. Seasonal campsites were certainly not restricted to the sand islands, in fact about 20 per cent of all the lithics collected by Shapwick fieldwalkers on the upland have been assigned to the earlier Mesolithic (Figure 3.2A, B and F). In the past, individual finds

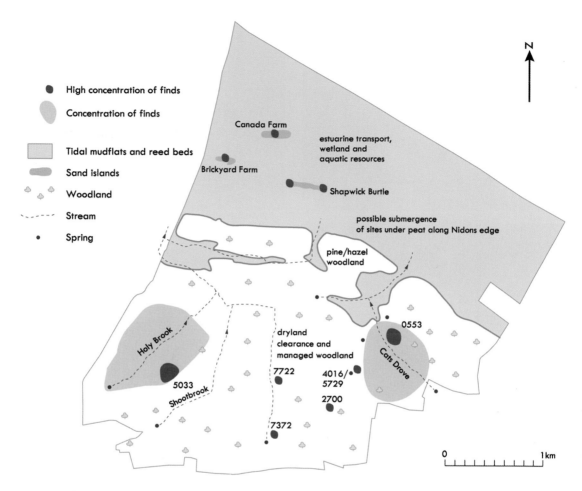

High concentration of finds

Concentration of finds

Tidal mudflats and reed beds

Sand islands

Woodland

Stream

Spring

N

Canada Farm

estuarine transport,
wetland and
aquatic resources

Brickyard Farm

Shapwick Burtle

possible submergence
of sites under peat along Nidons edge

pine/hazel
woodland

0553

Holy Brook

dryland
clearance and
managed woodland

Cats Drove

7722

4016/
5729

5033

2700

Shootbrook

7372

0   1 km

Figure 3.3. Early Mesolithic landscape, 10,000 to 6500 BC. Note the heavy concentrations of lithics close to the Holy Brook and Cats Drove streams and the importance of the wetland. The parish boundary has no significance at this date.

have sometimes been reported on the Poldens, but the scale of fieldwalking at Shapwick and the precision with which the finds have been recorded now reveals broad blade microliths and other flints considered typical of this period across the entire upland, from the lowest slope at the Levels edge to the highest contours of our study area. These scatters are notably denser on the lighter calcareous soils close to freshwater springs and streams.

Mesolithic sites are often found in topographical situations like this, close to rivers and lakes, and certain locations at Shapwick are worth highlighting, not least because they retain their interest for human groups in later periods. One notable concentration

of earlier Mesolithic stone tools and the debris from their manufacture lies mid-slope, close to the course of the Holy Brook (Figure 3.3). Findspots here exist in two bands to the east and west of the stream and there are noticeable clusters of flints, the most striking being in the centre of Field 5033, clearly a spot that was visited repeatedly during cycles of human movement through this area. Similarly, the Cats Drove stream (Field 0553) was another important focus for activity and there are also clusters of lithics on the higher ground near the spring at *Old Church* (Fields 4016/5729; 2700) and close to water within the footprint of the modern village, at Field 7722 and 7372 (Bridewell Lane and Hill Farm). Here our test pits produced a core fragment and seven flakes[9] of earlier Mesolithic date, a single core rejuvenation flake being later Mesolithic. These assemblages could not be considered large. Major concentrations elsewhere in southern England have produced over 100,000 worked Mesolithic flints whereas the total assemblage from the area within the modern village amounts to fewer than thirty pieces. Once more, the Shapwick flints must have been displaced during the cultivation of back gardens and orchards and the digging of foundations for houses.

To learn more about the significance of these scatters more intensive archaeological investigations are needed, perhaps initially through test-pitting, to evaluate the densest clusters and to assess whether anything survives that has not been scoured away by the plough. Glosses and abrasion on the surface of the flints, together with a more detailed analysis of the composition of each lithic scatter, might also reveal whether skins were being prepared there or if antler and timber were being worked, or even whether human activity was seasonal or year-round. At Mount Sandel, overlooking the River Bann not far from the Antrim coast in Ireland,[10] a site with the benefit of good preservation, excavation showed that substantial shelters had been constructed that covered about 30m² of floor space around a central hearth. These were far more than simple windbreaks, and saplings were probably flexed over to create a suitable dome to which animal skins could be lashed. The whole 'tent' may have been weighed down with heavy turves to prevent the saplings from springing upright again. There is no reason why such an arrangement could not have been made warm and comfortable inside while around about meat and fish may have been dried or smoked on racks out in the open air. All this is possible, too, at Shapwick and, though the camp at Holy Brook had limited views upslope, it certainly commanded panoramic vistas out across the Brue valley. The choice of site here, by the watercourse, would have been advantageous not only for plant gathering but also for hunting. The stream defined a natural route that was probably followed by both people and the seasonal movements of deer, wild pigs, horses, wild cattle and other large game. The linear shape of Mesolithic scatters of lithics might even suggest pathways, and the Holy Brook and Cats Drove stream were probably well known to those who

followed tracks from the higher Polden slopes down to the prominent sand islands and travelled further afield to Mendip and the coast. The overall impression is that flint knapping and activities which made use of lithics were taking place repeatedly at defined locations, in all probability at places with mythical and ancestral meanings that would have been known and named.[11] As an observation, there are few obvious physical features along Holy Brook today other than the spring site itself, so perhaps trees, flowering plants or even the water itself fulfilled a symbolic as well as practical role.[12] Gaps or blanks in the distribution of lithics, which are equally interesting, presumably indicate parts of the landscape that were used in a rather different way, though they too may have been rich in cultural understandings now lost to us. It is noticeable, for example, how the line of the Shoot Brook (located on Figure 3.3) was not much visited even though, on the face of it, this is a location that confers exactly the same advantages as the Holy Brook immediately to the west.

Figure 3.4 is a speculative attempt to reconstruct activities in the Shapwick area during the Mesolithic. The Holy Brook area is envisaged as a *home base* for a large semi-sedentary group, a focal point for exploration where human activities were concentrated until resources became depleted. Most of the group assembled here, a band of several families whose occupation shifted about along either side of the brook. Much of the camp's discarded rubbish and some 'dirty' tasks such as butchery would perhaps have lain on the periphery of occupation so that, if it can be assumed that the centre of the camp was kept clean, it is the *gaps between* the scatters and not the scatters themselves that may define the 'residential' area with its hearths and shelters. In fact, it is possible to read the lithic scatters at Holy Brook as at least half a dozen crescent-shaped accumulations, though we should bear in mind that much of this material will have been spread about through the action of the plough.

This camp at Holy Brook may have been occupied for several months of the year rather than just a few days, though one of the perils of interpreting flint scatters is that repeated short-lived activities at the same spot are easily mistaken for something more substantial, particularly since the time span is so long. Overall, we imagine population densities to have been

Figure 3.4. The early Mesolithic activities and resources hypothetically reconstructed for the Shapwick area. Note how the home base shifts along the Polden slope as resources become depleted.

low, and this is one of the characteristics of the hunter-gatherer way of life. One estimate of population numbers for deciduous woodland is as low as 0.16 people per square kilometre, which would multiply up to just twelve people on the entire Poldens ridge west of Street.[13] Clearly, however, this number would depend upon the availability of essential 'nutritionally critical' foodstuffs and it may be too low for our area given the rich variety of resources that lay all around: nuts, berries and tubers from the woodland; browsing ungulates such as deer and wild cattle; and smaller game, waterfowl and fish.

We have also noted a clear association between spring sites and human occupation. There are good practical reasons for this: the availability of clean fresh

water must have been valued, given that people could be made ill by drinking from contaminated sources. The mineral content of the water, too, would have been appreciated through smell and taste, and it may have been considered to have had healing properties. Perhaps our hypothetical Mesolithic band was exclusively associated with the brook or the spring, even sharing its name. From the Holy Brook smaller groups would have foraged further afield to reach specific resources. The killing and butchery of animal prey would lead to more ephemeral archaeological traces that might lie well outside our parish-sized study area, for example. More frequently used sites would have been linked to the home base by paths, and some of the items found by fieldwalkers could be casual losses from just this sort of expedition. From a camp at Shapwick a mobile group walking out only a modest distance of 10km could almost reach the westerly tip of the Poldens ridge and might range as far to the east and south as Glastonbury and High Ham respectively. The many different local terrains encountered along the way provided opportunities for stalking and ambush, as well as for the gathering of the plant foods that made such an important contribution to the diet.

We have also suggested that those hunter-gatherers who visited this earlier Mesolithic landscape probably did so during seasonal forays between upland, lowland and coastline, but in which season of the year they visited Shapwick is not known. The flint assemblage we recovered is broadly comparable with that from the Greylake quarry further south,[14] a site that also overlooks a shallow river valley (the forerunner to the River Cary). At Greylake, microliths are outnumbered by scrapers, possibly indicating the preparation of animal skins. Given that deer hides are at their best in autumn this may be the best clue as to which months were favoured, but other functions for flint scrapers are also possible. A particular feature of the Shapwick flint assemblage is the high proportion of broken pieces, from which heavy use, such as cutting, woodworking, the processing of plants and the preparation of carcasses, might be deduced. Even a winter stay might be feasible, though the Polden slope here is north-facing and the Mendip caves would have provided better shelter. With the spring came plentiful opportunities to catch migrating fish and wildfowl and, of course, other game were attracted to drink at the freshwater streams and browse the wild plants. Contact between groups brought opportunities for exchange and both flint and chert were probably acquired from a variety of regional sources. Our flint specialist, Clive Bond, thinks that some of this material came from the chalklands of Wessex but that most of it was picked out from smaller gravel deposits, perhaps near Frome and Warminster, as well as further south from the Blackdown Hills near Wellington.

The later Mesolithic landscape (c.6500–4000 BC)
During the later Mesolithic there were repeated and sometimes dramatic episodes of environmental change in the Brue valley. After 5720–5530 BC the clay silts were replaced by peats, now only 0.5–0.7m deep but so compacted that the auger had difficulty penetrating through the tangled mat of wood fragments. The peat accumulated rapidly, continuing to do so for at least the next 300 years and for perhaps as much as 900 years, though the low pollen concentrations suggest a time span near the lower end of this range. Some of the algal spores and pondweed found at this date are characteristic of open water, around which there was a fern-rich flora – bur-reeds and sedges, with a range of flowering herbs such as meadow sweet, water parsnips and yellow loosestrife on wetter ground. Willow grew at the edges of the mire together with some alder. On the higher, drier ground the pollen diagram indicates mixed deciduous woodland that was dominated by oak, elm and hazel, though birch, pine, ash and lime were also present in the late Mesolithic woodlands. Of greatest interest, perhaps, is the low frequency of pollen grains from plants characteristic of open, disturbed ground and which might be indicative of clearance and therefore human activity.

Between 5630 and 5420 BC there was a marked change in the woodland near the borehole, as alder spread rapidly around the edges of the peat basin and possibly onto the peat itself. This carr-type wet woodland was interspersed with large tussocks of sedge and patches of open water (Figure 3.5). It was shadier here than before and this may be what reduced the number of ferns, though other wetland herbs did flower. Willow, shrubs such as guelder rose and climbers such as honeysuckle and ivy continued to thrive and the dry woodland remained much as it had previously.

Between 5210 and 4800 BC estuarine clay silts were again washed over the fen in a major marine transgression when salt water inundated the peats, flooding the alder woods on the wetland. More than 2m of blue-grey estuarine clays were deposited and, although local circumstances would have depended upon the direction of flooding and the micro-topography, there is little to indicate a gradual response to the changing water quality by local vegetation, so this may have been a rapid and dramatic event. What had been well-wooded wet fen was now transformed into tidal salt marshes with wooded islands and ridges standing above (Figure 3.6). This pre-Neolithic marine transgression is widely known from a number of other sites in south-west Britain,[15]

Figure 3.5. Wet woodland ('carr') at Crymlyn Bog, South Wales, developing as a succession on wet ground at the edge of open water through colonisation of marshy acidic fern-rich grassland with flowering herbs by willow scrub.

where it has been associated with the post-glacial rise in sea level that was eventually to separate mainland Britain from continental Europe.[16]

The marine incursion came to an end around 4460 BC when, once again, herbaceous peat 3–4m deep began to accumulate over the salt marsh. This date compares closely with other fifth millennium dates for the interface between the clay and upper peats in this part of the Levels. Our borehole data show that the environment was probably a reed swamp that became established once the sea had retreated (Figure 3.7). Pollen from the borehole includes the common reed, which is moderately tolerant of saline water, and what may be a range of common salt-loving plants such as sea beet and glassworts. Evidently salt marsh conditions were not far distant. Gradually, however, freshwater plants such as marsh marigolds came to colonise this transitional environment. On the adjacent dry land, unaffected by the marine transgression, there was little change in the

Figure 3.6. Tidal salt marsh, Essex.

Figure 3.7. Reed swamp.

composition of the upland woodland. The clearance of the elm and oak forests, associated with the first Neolithic farmers, had yet to begin, explaining why herb pollen is scarce and percentages of arboreal pollen so high.

During the later Mesolithic, as the valley landscape at Shapwick was transformed from salt marsh to fen, to salt marsh again and back to a reed swamp, there is little to demonstrate a sustained human presence. Virtually no charcoal was identified in the lower peat and, as we have seen, the pollen evidence for a human presence is equivocal at best. The lithics record is also weak, there being a marked decrease in worked flints diagnostic of the 'narrow blade' industries in the Brue valley as a whole.[17] Overall, only about 2 per cent of all the lithics recovered by Shapwick fieldwalkers are of later Mesolithic date (see Figure 3.2C, D and E).[18] Conventional wisdom dictates that some form of crisis, quite possibly in the ready availability of resources, brought foraging lifestyles to an end, yet all that was truly disrupted in the Shapwick area were marine resources, albeit on several occasions. This seems curious, especially given how dramatic these ecological changes would have appeared to people at the time; surely humans cannot have perceived these changes as startling given the length of time they took to take hold. Yet,

rather than have to adapt to their new circumstances, some sort of 'tipping point' seems to have been triggered and most Mesolithic people simply walked away.[19] One can only conclude that the importance of estuarine resources and/or waterborne communication must have been fundamental in the choice of Shapwick as a preferred location for hunter-gatherers and that, with seasonal rounds of hunting and collecting now disrupted by changing habitats, this part of the Polden slope at least became marginal to their interests.

Communities in transition

The early Neolithic landscape (c.4000–3500 BC)

The wooden trackways of the Somerset Levels are among the best-known monuments of prehistoric Europe. Theirs is a tradition that began at least 6000 years ago in the early Neolithic and continued right through to the middle of the Iron Age at 300 BC (Shapwick Heath track) and on into the medieval period. In the form of woven panels for fencing gardens and stock, it is still maintained today. Many of the trackways lie outside Shapwick and they are fully described elsewhere,[20] but the earliest known alignment does fall within our study area. This trackway was constructed in two phases: the earliest is

Figure 3.8. Reconstruction of the Sweet Track by Victor Ambrus. Note the submerged pots and the beaver. With remarkable precision, sapwood from the Sweet Track is calculated by dendrochronology to have been felled during the winter of 3807/3806 BC.

known as the Post Track, wood for which was felled in 3838 BC,[21] and this was followed by the Sweet Track a little more than thirty years later, in 3807–3806 BC. These, and all the later tracks, carried the walker dry-footed through the reed swamp across the watery pools and soft ground of fen peat (see Box 1.2)

The different techniques on display in the construction of the trackways show a sophisticated understanding of the properties of wood. The Post Track consisted of ash and lime planks that were laid on the boggy ground, the route marked by vertical posts every few metres. The Sweet Track, on the other hand, was a walkway raised 0.2m or so above the water. Victor Ambrus's reconstruction shows this very clearly (Figure 3.8). Guiding rails were first held firm by sharpened 'tent' pegs of alder, ash, elm, hazel and holly, and these acted as a foundation that was topped with a bedding of peat and a planked oak walkway that was held rigid by the tops of the pegs, themselves 'nailed' into the underlying peat by long vertical pegs at the end of each plank. In all the Sweet

Track extends over some 1.8km, but it is estimated to have taken only five days to build and was in use for as little as ten to fifteen years.[22] A short-lived exercise this may have been, but this one structure has told us most of what is known about woodworking in early Neolithic Britain and its construction implies both coordinated manpower and the necessary resources to plan such an undertaking.

The builders of the Sweet Track were, in part at least, farmers, and the grass and cereal pollen present after about 4100 BC confirms their pasture and arable cultivation. While they continued to hunt and to exploit abundant wild foodstuffs such as hazelnuts and fungi, they now also planted crops and harvested them and tended their pigs and cattle. The 'sheep' suggested by the place-name Shapwick have grazed the Polden slopes for 6000 years and the pollen and insect records show that this was now an altogether more managed landscape. Some woods were cleared to create space for rough pasture and for cultivated fields, while others were managed to provide a

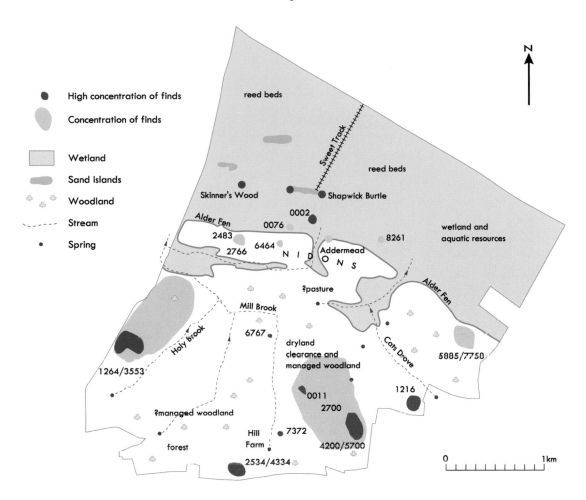

Figure 3.9. Early Neolithic landscape, c.4000 to 2900 BC. This plot may be contrasted with that for the earlier Mesolithic (Figure 3.3) and Bronze Age (Figure 3.14).

continuous supply of wooden poles of hazel and ash, some of which were used as rails and pegs. This was done by cutting tree growth back at the base, encouraging shoots to sprout, and then cropping the poles a few years later, assuming cattle, sheep and deer could be kept from nibbling at the new growth. In amongst this coppice there must also have been timber trees, the mature and ancient examples of oak, lime and ash used for building. Nearly 4km of planks were needed for the Sweet Track alone.

At Shapwick we know nothing of the settlements of these trackway builders. What does remain behind for the archaeologist to find are their flint tools and debitage, the waste flint flakes from their knapping,

and mapping these out on the ground reveals a series of weak clusters right along the edge of the Nidons (Figure 3.9). Fields 0076/0002 represent the best evidence so far for occupation at the southern terminal of the Sweet Track, while 'Addermead', a site originally identified by the Somerset Levels Project,[23] can now be seen to lie on the northern and eastern edge of a larger spread of flint stretching over more than 1.5km and consisting of three or four foci of more intense activity.

A discovery of major importance by the Shapwick Project is that most of the Neolithic activity lies not on the Nidons but on the mid-slope of the Poldens between the 40m and 55m contours. One of these scatters lies in the block of land between the Holy Brook and the western parish boundary with Catcott, the highest density of lithics being concentrated within an area of 600m × 500m in Fields 1264/3553 (*Abchester*). Among this scatter there are three undated quern fragments, a polisher of Mendip Old Red Sandstone and a small fragment of blade from a stone axe. The axe is made of greenstone, probably a gabbro from Cornwall.[24] A second location, centred on Fields 4200/5700 (to the south of *Old Church*), shows rather similar patterning, with a core area and a series of peripheral foci running south as high as the 60m contour, as well as north-west and as far downslope as the 30m contour. More concentrated scatters of early Neolithic flints can be seen in Fields 2534/4334 and Field 1216. All lie on lighter calcareous soils suitable for small-scale farming (see Chapter 2) and reasonably close to water, though never immediately adjacent to it; 2534/4334 is the most distant, at *c*.450m. Whereas the Mesolithic scatters lie along linear corridors either side of watercourses, these later scatters of narrow flake cores, scrapers and other tools (Figure 3.10A–C) are more tightly concentrated and at their centre form less diffuse, sub-circular shapes.

Once again, blanks in the distribution of flints on Figure 3.9 are interesting for what they might tell us about the wider landscape context. There is little to suggest activity below the 15m contour and above the level of the peat, so that in the west of the parish the fields between the Mill Brook and the Nidon 'ridge' are largely devoid of any findspots. Whether this is a reliable picture or whether it simply defines those parts of the parish in which the Neolithic land surface has been masked by later flooding could only be resolved by more intensive geomorphological studies. We can be more certain that the 'blanks' are meaningful over the whole of the land block north of the Cats Drove stream between 15–30m and over most of the south-west corner of the parish, immediately to the north of what is today Loxley Wood. With the exception of Fields 2534/4334, both these areas contain very few finds indeed and they may well define blocks of denser woodland.

Although flint collecting has a long tradition in Somerset, there are few assemblages as well recorded as Shapwick with such potential for spatial and compositional analysis. To find such apparently well-preserved resolution for Neolithic activities

is a rarity for fieldwalkers and the density of the upland scatters surely implies an intensive use of the landscape, some places evidently being visited time and time again. Unusually, this extensive use of the Neolithic landscape seems to have no late Mesolithic precedent. That, at least, is what the lithics on the surface of the ploughed fields seem to indicate, but clearly a follow-up project is needed to examine what these data might represent. A further dissection of the plough soil in some areas, complemented by large-scale stripping of other lithic-rich areas, would reveal whether negative features survive or not, while areas apparently devoid of lithics might also be tested. This strategy has sometimes met with spectacular results, most notably at Barnhouse in Orkney.[25] Its success is far from guaranteed at Shapwick, but some promise at least is indicated by our excavation at 2700/N: this trench produced a relatively large assemblage of earlier Neolithic flint despite lying on the fringes of one of the less dense lithic scatters immediately east of the village. In spite of the intensive regimes of modern agriculture, buried prehistoric land surfaces may still survive in 'islands' of better preservation beneath thicker accumulations of soils on later medieval headlands, baulks and boundaries (for example, Figure 7.38).

These conclusions seem to be borne out by the results of test pits and excavations in the village itself. Hill Farm produced the largest assemblage of early Neolithic flint and there are higher densities of material, too, from Shapwick Park. Moderately large assemblages came from 6767/A and the various pipeline trenches, with two small excavations immediately to the south of Shapwick House mansion producing earlier Neolithic finds.[26] Presumably the location here – on dry land yet close to a freshwater stream and adjacent to the Levels – was an attractive interface between wet and dry landscapes, being suitable for pasture and small-scale arable as well as other animal and plant resources. That Neolithic communities lived in and managed this landscape has never been in doubt; the surprise lies in the overall number and density of 'settlements' identified by the Shapwick Project, a pattern that is likely to be replicated all along the Polden flank. It is simply not justifiable to see the upland as being marginal to the wetland, and our results lead us to raise previous estimates of four or five communities occupying the

Figure 3.10. Lithics from fieldwalking and shovel pits. Earlier Neolithic – A: end and side scraper. B: awl. C: transverse burin. Later Neolithic – D, G and H: petit tranchet derivative arrowheads. E: horseshoe scraper. F: semi-circular scraper. Earlier Bronze Age – I and J: barbed-and-tanged arrowheads.

Figure 3.11. Neolithic activities and resources as reconstructed hypothetically for the Shapwick area. Note the importance of the sand burtle for the Sweet Track and the high degree of mobility along the upland slope. A larger study area is needed to understand the activities represented here more fully.

Brue valley between 3600 and 2900 BC to a figure that is closer to thirty or forty.[27]

Such a bold recalculation returns us once again to the question of what exactly might be represented by these scatters, admittedly in themselves a much-damaged record of human activity. Certainly, we should not imagine Neolithic settlements to be anything like post-medieval farmsteads – there may instead have been a high degree of residential mobility (Figure 3.11). Prehistorians have argued for some time that people followed or drove herds from place to place, though some people may have stayed behind to look after cultivated fields,[28] and thus the places that we can identify in the archaeological record in

Shapwick might represent stopping-off points within a round of seasonal movement. Fencing, clearance and cultivation are all probable activities and, like the trackways, settlements of this date were short-lived. On a day-to-day basis, therefore, the lives of Neolithic communities were in many respects comparable with those of hunter-gatherers; as the reconstruction in Figure 3.12 shows, the search for wild resources did not simply end at the dawn of the fourth millennium BC.[29]

Not all the sites identified at Shapwick would have served the same function. The spread of lithics west of Holy Brook is suggestive of the constant replacement of structures and shifting activities over a block of

Figure 3.12. Reconstruction by Victor Ambrus of earlier Neolithic activities on the Polden slopes. Here a small family fishes, cooks and knaps flint.

land measuring at least 500m × 750m. This site confers many advantages. It lies close to fresh water with easy access to lowland and upland resources; arable, pasture, woodland and wetland were all within striking distance. It seems to be a pre-eminent locality with good views out across the lower valley and, at times of flood, it was particularly well connected with other settlements out on the dry islands and along the Polden flank. In the absence of excavation we can only speculate on the detailed cycle of abandonment and occupation, but the broad similarity in lithics distributions and patterns of activity in the early and later Mesolithic, and on into the early Neolithic, should not unduly surprise us. Some places in the landscape already had a long ancestry even at this early stage in the Shapwick story. Camp sites may have been abandoned and re-established comparatively often, perhaps creating occasional surpluses of second-hand material such as the reused planks that were incorporated into the Sweet Track.[30]

Other sites register only as small, discrete

concentrations between 100m and 200m across. *Addermead* is one, Fields 2534/4334 another (Figure 3.9). These could both be places at which the duration of occupation was short-lived. If *Addermead* was indeed associated with the Sweet Track, as has been suggested, then that structure is estimated to have functioned for only a decade or so. On the other hand, these discrete scatters may represent sites with more specialised functions. Were the sites in Field 2483 or Fields 5885/7758 specialised bases for fishing and fowling on lower ground, for example, whereas the upland site in Fields 2534/4334 was devoted to hunting? It is doubtful whether the character of these sites could be clarified merely by additional study of the lithics already recovered from fieldwalking. More intensive collection is necessary and could be supplemented by test-pitting or, if appropriate, excavation. Nevertheless, several characteristics of the early Neolithic settlement record in Shapwick do echo patterns seen elsewhere in southern Britain: repeated, shifting settlement

BOX 3.1

Leaf-shaped arrowheads and Neolithic worlds

Leaf-shaped arrowheads are characteristic of the early Neolithic period. They were finished by minutely flaking both surfaces and the edges of the tool (called invasive retouch). The finest of flakes was removed by applying pressure with a pointed implement such as an antler tine (known as pressure flaking) (Figure B.3.1), the result being a delicate patterning of the surface that seems to go beyond any basic functional requirement. The arrows would have been used in archery, probably for both hunting and fighting. Arrowheads just like the one shown here have been found embedded in human bone and would certainly have formed part of an efficient killing weapon.[b1] Judging by the burials in which they are found, they were an item of personal gear for some males and, if the flights of their arrows were also coloured, perhaps they marked out group identity too.

In all, seven Neolithic arrowheads of this type have been recovered at Shapwick. Five of them, one retaining a patch of resin glue and another a fragment of the hazel arrow shaft with its fibre binding, were excavated from beside the Sweet Track between the 'island' of Westhay and the Shapwick Burtle. Among other prehistoric artefacts were fragments of between ten and fifteen pottery vessels, including a smashed bowl of fine burnished pottery that contained hazelnuts and another equipped with a wooden stirrer (Figure B.3.2A). Organic residues still present on these potsherds demonstrate that the vessels had been used to process carcass meat, plants and dairy products such as butter or milk.[b2] A wooden dish, in the form of a small trough, was also found together with spades, digging sticks, a possible mattock, roughly made bows and a wooden tomahawk and smoothed and bent pins made of yew-wood, perhaps for holding clothing in place (or for nose piercings?). There was also an unused chipped flint axehead from a source in Sussex and another of jadeite that came from the southern Alps near Liguria (Figure B.3.2B).[b3] Of the other two arrowheads recovered by the Shapwick Project, one came from the Nidons immediately to the west of a recently excavated dump of split oak timbers that may mark the south end of the Sweet Track,[b4] while the other is from the Shapwick Burtle itself. The latter is such a close match to another from the Sweet Track that it may even be possible to see the same hand at work more than 5,800 years ago.

There has always been debate about how these artefacts came to rest next to the Sweet Track. It is easy to imagine even the most careful walker losing their footing on a wet oak plank or two individuals pushing past each other and pots being knocked from the hand. At the time of their discovery such a rational explanation fitted the mood of many British prehistorians. Today, the

Figure B.3.1. Leaf-shaped arrowhead, Neolithic.

0　　　　　　　　　　2cm

for some sites and distinctive, perhaps specialist and short-lived occupation elsewhere. As yet, however, no ritual monuments are known in the parish or nearby and there are no human remains of this date, either on dry land or from the bog.

The middle and late Neolithic landscape (c.3500–2600 BC)

During the middle and late Neolithic, pollen results indicate that the woodland cover was regenerating, while the evidence from fieldwalking suggests less formal deposition of selected objects is well recognised in prehistoric times. Archaeologist Clive Bond[b5] points out the exceptional quality of some of the artefacts along the length of the Sweet Track, noting the presence of arrowheads of rarer and aesthetically pleasing types. In his opinion, these artefacts were not accidentally lost, and the presence of wooden and pottery vessels is consistent with votive offerings that had either been placed down into the water or deliberately smashed on either side of the trackway at set points along its length. We might add that, as well as exotics, there are also ordinary objects, ones that may have held some personal significance and many of them associated with the routines of daily life; the spade, digging stick and possible mattock are among those with agricultural associations.

It seems very likely that the leaf-shaped arrowheads from Shapwick were one of the many ways in which prehistoric groups differentiated themselves, particularly individual males. Because of their intimate association with person, community and place, the arrowheads probably had symbolic roles as well as real practical uses. It is easy to imagine their use being restricted to special occasions or to display alongside exotic dress fittings as part of a performance. Perhaps the arrowheads represented gender and personal authority, rather like ceremonial shields and swords in our own day; they were certainly portable enough to be gifts. By carrying these arrows along the trackway and giving them up to nature, bonds and obligations may have been renewed, statements of territory re-emphasised or, since the artefacts are deposited down into the water, perhaps the continued or renewed regeneration of land and hunting grounds was being wished for. It is certainly an arresting image to visualise a walk down the Sweet Track at a time when the water level was low and imagine the carefully chosen artefacts laid out to left and right; an act more reminiscent to our eyes of an artwork installation or theatre, perhaps, though one that in Neolithic times must have been performed out of sight of any onlookers.[b6]

Figure B.3.2. A: pottery bowl (c.200mm diameter) and wooden stirrer: two of the artefacts abandoned along the length of the Sweet Track. B: Neolithic Jadeite axe recovered from the side of the Sweet Track at the Railway Site excavation in 1973 by the Somerset Levels Project. The rock source has been pinpointed as Liguria on the France–Italy border, the axe itself being worked or reworked in Brittany before it was deposited in 3807–3806 BC (Alison Sheridan and Richard Brunning pers. comm.). One of three such axes from Somerset, it is probably a prestigious or ceremonial object rather than being of practical use.

intense human activity, at least on this section of the Poldens; the settlement west of Holy Brook, among others, was abandoned, for instance. Lithics collection across the parish showed a marked drop in numbers and the lithic scatters recognised by Shapwick fieldwalkers are discrete and smaller, sometimes consisting of just single diagnostic artefacts such as *petit tranchet* arrowhead forms (see Figure 3.10D, G and 11) and scrapers (F).

On the lower ground the wetland continued to

Figure 3.13. In June 1961 one half of a wooden flat-bow was discovered in the peats. A: the original Meare Heath bow alongside a working replica made by Stuart Prior in 1977. Note the clear traces of cross-banding with strips of strengthening material, probably sinew. The original bow was broken across the central hand-grip. B: the bow, which is made of yew and had a length of 1.905m, is capable of killing a deer at 50m in just over a second.

evolve. The reed swamp had become buried beneath the dead vegetation of alder and birch, and willow trees were growing in the fen wood. Our borehole data indicate that ferns grew there as an understorey. Slowly, raised bog began to establish itself, the hummocks of the peat being capped by drier heath flora of cranberry and ling beside wetter pools fringed with bog moss and bog bean. The many opportunities for taking wildlife and gathering wild plants in this environment makes the lack of any notable human

presence on the upland all the more surprising. Elsewhere in the Brue valley and along the Polden slopes human activity certainly did continue. Sherds of a highly decorated round-bottomed pot found in 1936 on Meare Heath belong to the middle or later Neolithic (3400–2500 BC) and, like the Neolithic axe discovered on Shapwick Heath, this pot probably carried a special significance. The axe was certainly far from its place of origin, the Graig Lwyd axe factory in north Wales.

Only a little way to the east there are trackways on Walton Heath, dated to 3300–2800 BC, as well as accompanying settlement on the adjacent dry land.[31] Since some of the tracks here, and elsewhere, were made of short pegged lengths of interwoven hurdles laid over wetter hollows (one can be seen preserved in Somerset County Museum in Taunton), we may safely deduce that management of the local hazel coppice must also have continued. Artefacts such as the well-known mallet head and the longbow (Figure 3.13), both of yew wood, illustrate human activity nearby. Perhaps the intensity of land use specifically within the area of the modern parish in the early Neolithic led to a degradation of soils and, as a result, settlement merely shifted to more fertile ground further along the slope. Some initial clearances, by now infertile ground, may have been lost to the encroaching woodland, while others were being opened up; settlement on the sand island at Burtle, for example, seems to have been extensive. A more accurate picture of the later Neolithic landscape on the Poldens might one day be established by a project to examine prehistoric settlement patterns on a wider regional scale but, for the present, the difficulty of correlating radiocarbon and dendrochronological dates from wooden artefacts and trackways with diagnostic suites of artefacts cannot be entirely resolved. While the Shapwick lithics data seem to confirm the pollen evidence for a negligible human presence, this cannot easily be squared with the rather busier picture of activity that is apparent down on the Levels.[32] The Abbot's Way, for example, which runs between Westhay and Burtle islands and was laid over the raised bog in about 2500 BC, is 2.5km long and its construction required 30,000 alder planks or split logs. Why was so much effort made here when the Polden slopes

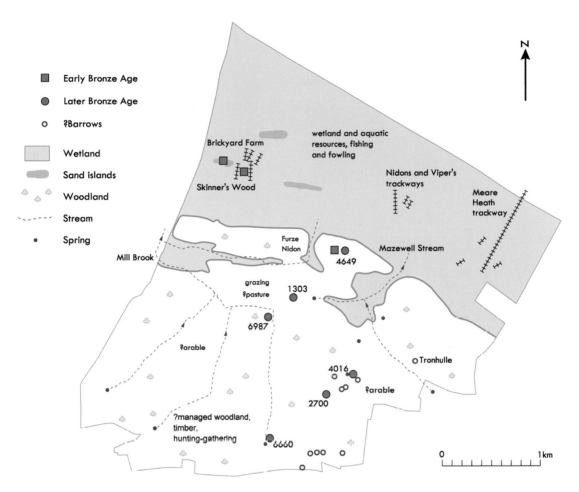

Figure 3.14. Bronze Age landscape c.2000 to 700 BC. Much of the information on the upland comes from excavation by the Shapwick Project and complements earlier work in the wetland by the Somerset Levels Project.

were barely visited? One possibility may be that farmers isolated themselves out on the islands in the bog and used the uplands for summer pasture, or perhaps the islands were themselves sacred.

Tradition and innovation

The early Bronze Age landscape (c.2600–1400 BC)

Although there are some signs of human activity on the Levels early in the Bronze Age, among them the construction of the Eclipse Track that probably linked Meare island to the Polden slopes just to the east of Shapwick parish, they are few and far between.

This seems to equate well with the continuing near-absence of settlement on dry land. Only a single sherd of possible grog-tempered early–middle Bronze Age pottery was recovered from excavation, from Field 4649 (the Nidons villa) (Figure 3.14). Unlike many other survey projects elsewhere in Wessex, comparatively little Bronze Age flint was collected by Shapwick fieldwalkers, much of it being widely scattered and amounting to little more than the occasional arrowhead lost during hunting forays.

For the period between about 2000 BC and 1700 BC this rather deserted picture is supported by pollen evidence, which suggests an episode of forest

Figure 3.15. A: a handful of flint flakes, already put to good use cutting reeds and hides, was found wrapped in moss and cotton-grass sunk in the marsh at Skinner's Wood. Here they are seen photographed in situ. B: a wooden fork for hay or harvesting reeds shaped out of hazelwood.

regeneration on the valley slopes and the continuing development of the raised bog below. Wet and soft, with an uneven surface and pools of standing water, the low ground could have been crossed on foot only during drier summer conditions and even then with care. This does not explain, however, how people used the dry Polden slopes. One suggestion is that people were present only on a seasonal basis and migrated to and fro across the Wessex region, perhaps driving transhumant flocks. If this were so, habitation sites could perhaps have been short-term with impermanent agricultural activities, which may help to explain their archaeological invisibility. Occasionally evocative finds put us in more direct touch with these visitors. A handful of flint flakes, already put to good use cutting reeds and animal

hides, were found sunk in the marsh at Skinner's Wood wrapped in moss and cotton-grass (Figure 3.15A). They have been dated to 2200 BC on the basis of the peat layer from which they were recovered. A little higher in the peats, at 1600 BC, was a wooden hayfork or reed-harvesting fork shaped out of hazel (Figure 3.15B).[33] What were the circumstances in which they were lost? Several types of tools that are diagnostic of this period were also recovered by fieldwalkers and during excavation, among them flint horseshoe scrapers (see Figure 3.10E) and the distinctive barbed and tanged arrowheads, of which five examples were found during fieldwork by the Shapwick Project (see Figure 3.10I and J). Only a handful of other examples are known from the Poldens. Unlike the rougher scrapers, these pieces might have been produced by specialist knappers, the finest examples perhaps being reserved for display rather than the daily hunt, a reminder of the extent to which local tensions among competing groups may have led to raiding and ritualised confrontation.[34]

Funerary monuments were also part of this landscape. There is a possible group of six barrows in the south-east corner of the parish and another on the western edge of the parish. A boundary description of 1325 refers to 'Tronhulle', a name that may mean 'round hill', so this could be another tumulus in the east of the parish. None of these monuments, the first permanent man-made markers in the landscape, have been excavated – as far as is known, anyway – but they are likely to have once concealed burials: male and female, cremation and inhumation, as well as combinations of grave goods and gifts. Figure 3.14 intimates that ritual and settlement landscapes were spatially discrete from one another, but this does not stand up to closer analysis. The closest of the larger group of barrows in the south-east corner of the parish lies only about 300m from the settlement at the spring (6660), and geophysical evidence from Field 4016 (*Old Church*) indicates an arc of three, maybe four, ring ditches, one of which may contain internal features. We must also be alive to the possibility that the former church may itself sit on a large artificial prehistoric mound (which may be Neolithic rather than Bronze Age). Notably, as a group, these barrows do not lie on the highest or most visible locations, possibly because the upper slopes were at that time occupied by woods, or perhaps because they served some other purpose, such as to define the margins of grazing lands. They would have been very visible from the islands out to the north and for groups moving along the mid-slope contour they made an enduring visual statement about connections between people and land.[35] There are no causewayed enclosures, long barrows or henges anywhere in the vicinity, the nearest other ritual monuments being some distance away on Mendip.[36]

The later Bronze Age landscape (c.1400–700 BC)

That numbers of people *were* present later in the Bronze Age is undeniable, since trackways were constructed on the raised bog peats that now began to develop in the northern third of the parish. These were the 'durable skin', as Sir Harry Godwin[37] put it, which allowed the 'mosaic of pools and hummocks' to be bridged. From time to time conditions underfoot must have been even wetter than this, with widespread flooding frustrating movement and transport. Part of the problem was the deteriorating climate, but over-exploitation of the more open upland was probably at least partly to blame because it increased the run-off of surface water from the Polden slopes. Within our small study area there were trackways in three parts of the bog between 1300 and 400 BC; the Meare Heath trackways, the Viper's-Nidons-Platform complex and the Skinner's Wood trackway. In detail their construction differs somewhat and they may originally have differed in purpose too. The Meare Heath trackway (Figure 3.16) is particularly interesting because of the range of techniques used to retrieve information about its date and the environment around it.[38] One of the most informative pollen diagrams for the Somerset Levels came from this work and the dating of the timbers has been refined using radiocarbon dating and dendrochronology to 1445–1270 BC.[39] Once again, these trackways are associated with the deposition of numerous artefacts. Many of them are ordinary, like handles and clubs, while others are exceptional, such as the biconical amber beads from Westhay Moor and the so-called Coppice Gate bronze spearhead from Shapwick Heath – one of a number of metal axes, daggers, palstaves and spearheads recovered from the Brue valley.[40] It is hard to see how objects

Figure 3.16. The Meare Heath trackway. In some cases oak planks, cross-beams and stakes can be matched together from single trees (after Coles and Coles 1980, 46).

like these could have been retrieved easily and they may represent a continuing tradition of deliberate deposition of artefacts in watery places, evidence for which is well documented at this date. At Flag Fen near Peterborough, for example, metalwork was laid in the water from a wooden walkway over an extended period between the late Bronze Age and the Roman Conquest.[41] The walkway there is suggested to be a visual and symbolic representation of the great 'crossing' of life. In the case of Shapwick, however, the finds do not seem to be clustered in a way that might suggest trackways or causeways; they are more dispersed across the bog. Their patterning would repay investigation, especially alongside a detailed environmental history.

Until the Shapwick Project began its work, signs of contemporary activity on the upland had proved elusive. No later Bronze Age pottery has survived on the surface of the plough soil to be collected by fieldwalkers, so our knowledge of sites is restricted to those places where excavation has happened for other reasons. In all, five later Bronze Age sites have now been identified. The best dated of these lies within a few metres of the spring at *Old Church* (4016), where three radiocarbon dates on charcoal are tightly grouped at 1010–820 cal BC, 1130–900 cal BC and 1050–860 cal BC. From the same general area there are also nineteen sherds of prehistoric pottery whose fabrics could be dated broadly between the later Bronze Age and the middle Iron Age, though the identifiable forms were considered by Elaine Morris to be no later than the early Iron Age (see Figure

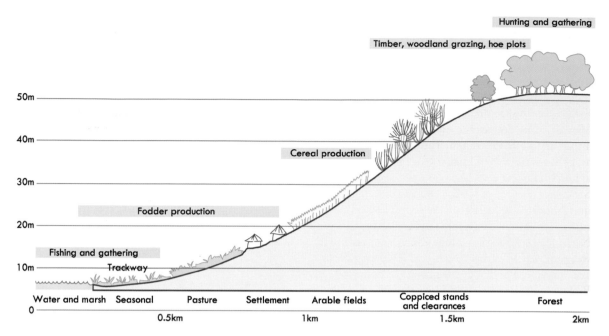

50m

40m

30m

Cereal production

20m

Fodder production

Fishing and gathering

10m

Trackway

0

| Water and marsh | Seasonal | Pasture | Settlement | Arable fields | Coppiced stands and clearances | Forest |

0.5km   1km   1.5km   2km

Hunting and gathering

Timber, woodland grazing, hoe plots

Figure 3.17. The Concave Landscape Model (redrawn from Coles 1982, fig. 5.13). The basic premise remains sound but the model should be modified in the case of Shapwick by adding the Nidons at the base of the slope with wetland behind. Our work considerably amplified details of activities on the slope.

3.22A and B). Little can be said at present about the extent or nature of activities here except to note the chaff from hulled wheat and the presence of emmer or spelt grains, two of the staple cereals of prehistory. Bronze Age features probably do survive in more deeply stratified areas closer to the spring site, though they may have been damaged by later drainage schemes.

Residual sherds of later Bronze Age–early Iron Age pottery were also recovered during excavations of later features at *Sladwick* (Field 1303) and the Nidons Roman villa (Field 4649), and from two sites in the present village, one near the village spring (Field 6660) and another north of Shapwick House (Field 6987). Whether these sites are contemporary is not clear but, from parallels elsewhere, some are likely to be unenclosed clusters of roundhouses and pits which might be expected to contain evidence for a mixed agricultural economy and crafts. We can deduce little more at this stage, except to affirm that settlements were probably very much more common

than our present distribution map allows for. Certainly, the density of Bronze Age settlement has been underestimated previously, but this new picture is more consistent both with the pollen evidence for intensive clearance and for our claims for the laying-out of the wide tracts of the landscape in field systems well before the beginning of the Roman period.

The results of the Somerset Levels Project provide a very complete reconstruction of Bronze Age exploitation of the Polden slopes. In his 'Concave Landscape Model' (Figure 3.17), John Coles[42] describes fixed settlements with their own woodlands and fields located in 'compartments' defined by natural boundaries and set well above the trackway terminals. These settlements enjoyed vistas out over the pasture beneath, the bog and open water of the Brue valley and beyond to the landmarks of Glastonbury Tor, Brent Knoll and Brean Down. The pollen evidence after 1700 BC and the trackways and artefact distributions all point to increasing open ground with light cereal production and managed woodland: the 'considerable expansion of the curves of agricultural indicators' noted by Dewar and Godwin.[43] The upland provided timber for trackway planking, hunting and gathering resources, while the settled intermediate slopes allowed limited arable cultivation and garden plots and the lower slopes were seasonal pasture with fishing and fowling on the bog and along stretches of open water. Viewed from the islands or even as far as Mendip, 11km away to the north, the scale of settlement and the bands of land use would have been clearly appreciable with the naked eye. On the basis of the Shapwick Project evidence, we find little cause to quibble with the basics of the Coles model, except to note the omission of the Nidons. Between the Nidons and the Polden slope there was presumably wet ground and marsh, perhaps with rough pasture and scrubby woodland. The zone occupied by late Bronze Age settlement could also be extended from the mid-slope at 25–35m (4016, 6987) up higher at 60m (6660) as well as down into pasture areas at less than 15m OD (1303 and 4649). This suggests rather more specialisation in dairying and arable than the original model allowed for. Notably, ritual monuments are absent and we know that the barrow burial tradition had by now ended.

It would be satisfying to report that these five newly identified occupation sites, if that is indeed what they are, could be paired up with trackways, but prehistory is rarely so neat. Instead, the late Bronze Age sites are clustered in the centre of the parish and only one partnership between trackway and settlement readily suggests itself: that between the Nidons Roman villa site (Field 4649) and the Nidons and Viper's trackways that appear to join at the foot of the ridge immediately to the north-west. With a previously claimed trackway, known as Tully's Track, now discounted as tree roots, we are left with two contemporary timber trackways, Nidons and Viper's, which converge on the higher ground here. At their apex and apparently at a location that would have optimised views through the sedge, there were at least four wooden platforms, the Viper's Platforms, one of which has been investigated archaeologically. Described as a sub-circular 'mattress' of securely pinned brushwood bundles encircled by vertical sharpened stakes, this is thought to be the remains of a screen, some sort of look-out post for

the adjacent trackways.[44] Similar examples have been found elsewhere in the Brue valley and they may be 'hunting blinds', designed to conceal the hunter from the prey, rather like modern shooting butts. Quite where the trackways themselves join or strike the higher ground may not now ever be known because the peats have long since been cut away. However, this new information from the Shapwick Project certainly suggests contemporary late Bronze Age activity on the higher ground to the south-west about 200–300m away, with the approach from the north capable of being 'monitored' by screened watchers. That Nidons and Viper's trackways were well-used routes is not in doubt, and their multiple *ad hoc* repairs are ample evidence of traffic.[45]

Agriculture and settlement

The Iron Age landscape (c. 700 BC–AD 43)

Finds from the Iron Age wetland echo earlier themes. The Levels environment was diverse and changing. Godwin's excavations on the Shapwick Heath (Foster's) Track showed it to be late Bronze Age or early Iron Age but by the middle of the Iron Age the oak log canoe discovered in 1906 near Shapwick Station would have been fully deployed. Using peat-bog stratigraphy as a proxy climate record, Dewar and Godwin (1963) argued for a flooding horizon during which the 'monoxylous boat', as they referred to it (meaning that it was cut from a single trunk of oak), might have been floated in c.335 BC (Figure 3.18). Climatic deterioration may have led to a total hiatus in trackbuilding in the period 700–400 BC, when transport by boat would have been preferable, if not essential. But while this decline to a cooler climate re-emphasises the importance of water for communication and trade along the Brue valley during wetter episodes throughout prehistory, the unpublished assemblage retrieved from an extinct stream channel at Skinner's Wood by the Somerset Levels Project also indicates that there was continuing activity around the 'islands' at about this date or slightly later.[46] Quite what went on here is unclear – the extraction of bog peat for fuel is one possibility, or perhaps the peat itself was used as a larder; all sorts of perishables might have been stored there, even butter and cheese. Occasional finds of late

Figure 3.18. After its discovery in 1906, the Iron Age log canoe from Shapwick was conserved in a water trough at the nearby Griffin's Head Inn (see Chapter 10). It is now on display at Taunton Museum. Below, Victor Ambrus' reconstruction shows the log boat passing the Glastonbury Lake Village. A replica of the log boat was built and paddled successfully on the River Brue in 1996. It easily carried three adults and still had more than 0.20m of freeboard.

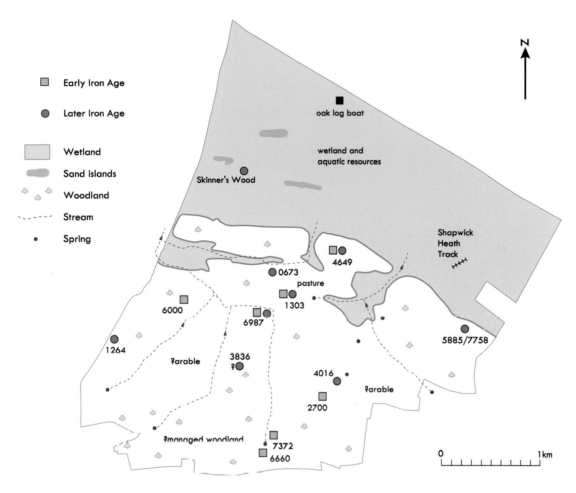

Figure 3.19. Iron Age landscape, c.700 BC to later first century AD.

prehistoric objects by peat cutters in more remote areas of the wetland[47] suggest a more significant link than merely food storage or casual loss, however: given the importance of bogs and rivers in the Celtic world, such artefacts may be offerings to spirits or perhaps pleas for fertility.[48] We can only speculate on what may have been missed or ignored by medieval and later peat cutters, bog bodies included.[49]

To understand the upland environment in the first millennium BC we must again look to the Levels. The impression from pollen diagrams is of a more open landscape in the Iron Age, with increasing pasture and arable. The earlier part of this period is the least visible of all in the archaeological record at Shapwick, partly because the use of flint was negligible by this

time, partly because pottery fabrics from this period are fragile and do not survive weathering in the plough soil, but also because unenclosed settlement patterns tend to be more elusive for the geophysicist and from the air (Figure 3.19). Nevertheless, Shapwick excavations routinely produced fragments of pottery of early–middle Iron Age date, including those at the Fields 6660 (village spring), 7372 (Hill Farm), 4016 (*Old Church*), 4649 (Nidons villa), 1303 (*Sladwick*) and 6987 (Shapwick House). A pit and ditch at 2700/N (*Buddle/Bassecastel*), excavated by Nick Thorpe, were securely dated to the middle or late Iron Age (Box 3.2; Figure 3.22C) and the small enclosure in Field 6000, south-west of Kent Farm, known only from aerial photographs, may well be of the same

BOX 3.2

Field geometries

Anyone who has looked at a map of Shapwick notices the regular arrangement and prevailing orientation of its field boundaries and roads. In other parts of southern England, notably in the Thames valley and the Fens of East Anglia, as well as along the Channel coast, similar alignments have proved to be ancient, in some cases Roman or earlier. The 'reave-like' or 'linear' systems found on Dartmoor, for example, are thought to be Bronze Age in date and seem to be distinguished by long continuous boundaries that run for several kilometres, with an infilling of regular, rectilinear fields in between.[b7] There is nothing as obvious as these so called 'co-axial' field systems at Shapwick, though many boundaries do seem to be consistently aligned along one axis, with others at right angles to them.

Figure B.3.3 shows that boundary alignments at 105° (and at right angles to that) cover most of the west of the parish and spread westwards into Catcott. Another large block to the east of the village suggests that this system might once have extended further. To the east and south-east of the village, meanwhile, there is a large area with alignments at 85° and at right angles to that, while between these two major blocks there is a third at about 95°. Besides these, the field boundaries along the Nidons and around Loxley Wood seem to have had a very different landscape history. The Nidons remained as pasture or wood well into the later medieval period, while Loxley has been the woodland of the parish for a long time, although it was not always the same size or shape as it is today. Its curvilinear outline is best explained as a result of 'assarting', the encroachment of arable that has taken bites out of the fringes of the woodland (see Figure 7.39).

Across the country so-called 'coaxial' fields, like the ones at Shapwick, are thought to have been laid out between the middle of the second millennium BC and the early first millennium AD. Middle Bronze Age dates are suggested by excavation at a number of sites[b8] and it is clear that a managed and controlled landscape was being put in place at this time. Elsewhere, one clue to age is the spatial relationship of the fields to monuments of known date, such as Roman roads, but no such associations are available to guide us at Shapwick. What we can say, on the basis of topography and route names, is that the east–west tracks are plausibly some of the earliest features in the Poldens landscape. The modern A39 is probably a Romanised earlier route, while the *harepath*, now the Lippetts Way that runs from Catcott to Ashcott, and the *verysway*, parts of which are preserved in Kent Lane, are probably ancient.

Dating one of the cross-country east–west routes through archaeological excavation would be the ideal, but they are still used by local traffic and, in any case, the precise dating of roads is fraught with difficulty. The field boundaries themselves have greater potential and, with this in mind, excavations were undertaken *across* them by the Project team, something that has rarely been done before. One of these excavations, within the block of 85° alignments in Field 2700 just west of *Old Church*, identified a series of parallel east–west ditches, the earliest of which may date to the later Bronze Age (Figure B.3.4). This boundary has certainly marked the edge of the field since the eighteenth century, as our sequence of maps demonstrates, and before that it was probably a medieval furlong boundary, possibly a hedge but more probably a headland between blocks of strips out in the common fields. It is thus possible to see the excavated ditches as part of a continuously defined boundary over at least a 3,000-year period. On that basis, the east–west route that is today the back road to Ashcott, together with the three tracks emerging from the west side of the modern village to Kent Farm, to Manor Farm and along Lippetts Way (formerly *verysway*), all of which form part of the same group with 85° alignments, might be Bronze Age in origin. Equally, the boundaries aligned 105° correspond better with the later Iron Age and Roman evidence for settlement in the west of the parish.

Unfortunately, the dimensions of the original fields are obscured by later changes. A simple interpretation, however, might favour an intensification of agriculture in the later Bronze Age with coaxial field systems being set aside in blocks of cultivation and pasture together with droveways to facilitate the movement of livestock. These fields were defined by boundaries laid out in a consistent manner along two axes set at right angles to each other, exhibiting a conformity that some believe goes beyond practical requirement and could be symbolic, perhaps even linked to a particular cosmology. During the later Iron Age and Roman periods, as the number and size of settlements increased, these field systems were added to and probably replaced in some areas by fields on a slightly different alignment. Parts of the modern landscape still broadly reflect this later prehistoric and Roman framework and we must conclude that a proportion of pre-existing boundaries (though not all) have continued to find a purpose for the local Shapwick farmer from later prehistory to the present day. As we shall see, this observation has important implications for the fate of the countryside during the post-Roman period because it suggests that these ancient boundaries were never lost or forgotten (see Chapter 5).

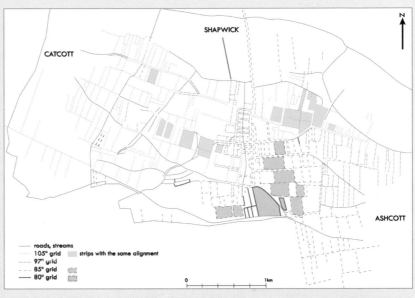

Figure B.3.3. Field boundary alignments taken from a composite of mid-eighteenth-century maps.

Figure B.3.4. Excavation underway in Field 2700, facing west. The earliest of the ditches in this trench was later Bronze Age. Roman and later boundaries on the same alignment lie parallel to the modern hedge line.

Figure 3.20. Aerial photograph of middle or late Iron Age small enclosure in Field 6000 with Kent Farm alongside. North towards the top.

chronolgy. Had the enclosure been of any other date we might have expected something diagnostic to be recovered by fieldwalkers (Figure 3.20).

For the later Iron Age in the immediately pre-Roman period the picture is somewhat clearer, with diagnostic pottery being recovered from several of the sites we excavated. To the north of Shapwick House (Field 6987) geophysical survey looking for medieval gardens found instead circular and oval features more characteristic of later prehistoric sites. The geophysics results are superimposed onto an aerial photograph on Figure 3.21. Excavations by John Creighton in two trenches, labelled here as A and B, then revealed a pit alignment and several ditches containing typical hand-made calcite-tempered sherds of Durotrigian-type sandy ware as well as large quantities of other 'native' wares, more than 100 sherds in all, making up nearly half the total recovered from the site (Figure 3.22E and F). One ditch at least seems to date to the early first century AD. A broken saddle quern from Field 0673, a little way to the north, is similar to one

found at South Cadbury and could indicate a wider spread of occupation. Like many of the other pre-Roman sites, it would appear that this one continued to be inhabited after the Conquest (see Chapter 4), so that pre-Roman late Iron Age sherds occur alongside others of later date.

The most significant quantities of late Iron Age material came from *Old Church* (4016), where more than 2,000 sherds of native and pre-Roman pottery were recovered from the plough soil above trench Z; these included Glastonbury-style wares, Durotrigian wares (which span the late Iron Age and early Roman periods), hand-made calcite-tempered wares and grog-tempered pottery. Other finds of probable Iron Age date included one of the three pebble polishers collected by fieldwalkers; these are shaped from Hangman Grit, a fine-grained sandstone. In its own right this assemblage strongly suggests occupation from at least the first century BC or even slightly earlier, but when this evidence is combined with that from the early–middle Iron Age and further back

Figure 3.21. Aerial photograph of two excavations under way to the north of Shapwick House (Field 6987). The trench closest to the house (A) produced evidence of later prehistory and Roman archaeology as suggested by the geophysics, here superimposed in grey.

into the Bronze Age and earlier it is already clear that *Old Church* was a favoured choice of site over many thousands of years. Unfortunately, it is hard to add much detail. Most of the Iron Age phases had been ploughed away, though a curving ditch at one edge of the trench may be a gully around an Iron Age roundhouse. The ten perinates (stillborn or newborn babies) also recovered from this trench are considered in the next chapter, though their radiocarbon dates (AD 70–225 and AD 20–210) could plausibly place some of them into the late Iron Age. These disarticulated bones are likely to derive from a

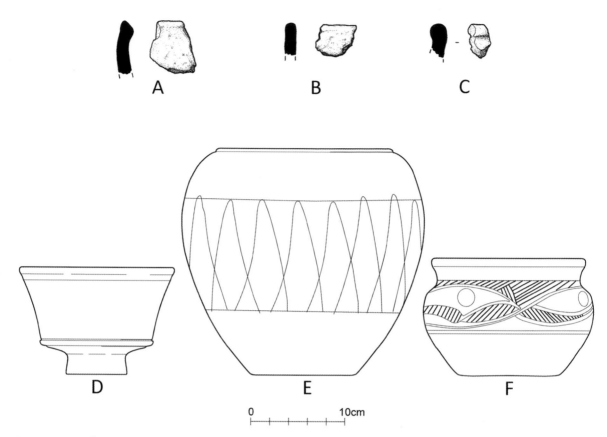

Figure 3.22. Prehistoric pottery. A: rim, ovoid neckless jar with angled edge, late Bronze Age–early Iron Age, from Old Church (4016). B: rim, ovoid neckless jar with rounded rim, late Bronze Age–early Iron Age, earlier first millennium, from Buddle/Bassecastel (Field 2700). C: rim, squat jar, middle–late Iron Age, third to first centuries BC, from Buddle/Bassecastel (Field 2700). D: bowl or large cup. Durotrigian ware with black burnished exterior, from mid–first century BC, from north of Shapwick House. E: jar, beaded rim, Durotrigian ware, from north of Shapwick House. F: bowl, Glastonbury-type with incised curvilinear decoration, from north of Shapwick House.

cluster of infant burials that were disturbed and then incorporated into the fills of ditches that were finally backfilled in the late third or early fourth century AD. That there was late Iron Age domestic occupation here seems certain, but infant burials like these are also a known feature of Iron Age shrines such as those at Uley (Glos) and Maiden Castle (Dorset). In addition, infant and neonatal interments are sometimes found in other late Iron Age contexts such as pits and rubbish dumps – Glastonbury Lake Village is one such site not far away – so the role of *Old Church* in the late Iron Age must remain uncertain for now.

More significant evidence comes from Field 4649 on the Nidons, the site of a later Roman villa

(see Chapter 4). The full extent of this site was first indicated by aerial photographs and later defined more clearly by geophysics (Figure 3.23). It appears to consist of several curvilinear enclosures with a straight east–west boundary at the north end of the field and a length of double ditch along the south side. These southern ditches, which are easily distinguished from the sub-rectangular Roman features of later date, are estimated to be up to 5m wide in places and run along the highest part of the Nidons ridge. The herringbone pattern of post-medieval field drains, marked in yellow on Figure 4.5, indicates this high point very clearly.

Other features to note include a clear break in the

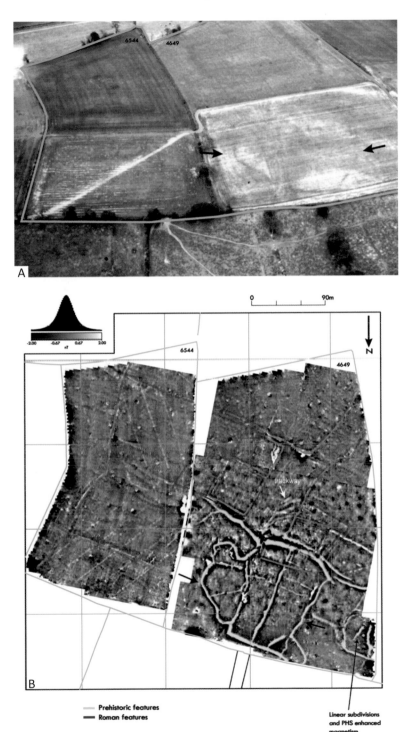

Figure 3.23. The large late prehistoric enclosure on the Nidons west of Northbrook Farm (Field 4649). A: infra-red aerial photograph, looking south with the boundary ditch on the geophysics survey indicated. B: magnetometry survey with broad linear anomalies defining a series of enclosures which continue into the field to the west (north has been reversed to match the aerial photograph).

circuit of ditches at one corner of the main enclosure and a set of linear anomalies that coalesce as they funnel towards this entry point. These may well be trackways. Within the interior, geophysical survey also identified pits, linear subdivisions and several areas of enhanced magnetism, including the fill of the exterior ditches. Industrial processes of some sort are suggested. An excavation trench immediately west of the entry identified a pit containing large quantities of burnt cereal. This was dated by radiocarbon to 50 BC–AD 90, placing it in the late Iron Age or possibly the early Roman period. Julie Jones was able to identify thousands of grains of hulled wheat from here, together with spelt wheat spikelet forks, smaller quantities of barley, oats and vetches, and crop weeds such as meadow grass. Besides cereals there were also a few celtic beans; the most likely interpretation being that part of a crop of spelt was accidentally burnt while it was being lightly roasted in the hollow. All the excavated areas nearby, whether inside or outside the enclosures, yielded at least some evidence of late pre-Roman Iron Age activity, and a Durotrigian bronze coin was also picked up here during metal detecting. Clearly this was a settlement with multiple phases (see above) and the prehistoric ditches must have been filled by the time 'Roman occupation' began, perhaps in the second century AD.

All the above sites may be categorised as 'enclosed settlements' rather than the hillforts that have been the traditional focus of Iron Age settlement studies.[50] Of the latter, the closest to Shapwick is the univallate hillfort at Compton Dundon and, while it does not occupy such a prominent hilltop location, _Borgh/Chestell_ (Field 3836) may be another example of a pre-Roman enclosed settlement with multiple ditches (Figure 3.24). There are several parallels for pre- and post-Roman enclosures in mid-slope locations with annexes of this kind, including Clovelly Dykes in Devon, which also has a sub-rectangular inner enclosure and four outer enclosures, two of them concentric.[51] This site, and others like it, such as Groundwell Farm in the Upper Thames valley,[52] are thought to have been dedicated to pastoral activities, the inner enclosure being inhabited while the outer enclosures were arranged to facilitate the herding of animals on and off the adjacent grassland. The enclosure would be sufficiently sizeable for a

handful of houses – circular structures constructed of timber uprights with thatched roofs such as those reconstructed at the experimental Iron Age farm at Butser in Hampshire (Figure 3.25). That said, our (very limited) excavations produced just nine sherds of pre-Roman late Iron Age pottery from an assemblage of more than 2,200 fragments so, for the moment, any Iron Age attribution for this site must remain extremely doubtful. Late pre-Roman Iron Age pottery was also recovered from later archaeological contexts at _Sladwick_ (Field 1303), _Abchester_ (Field 1264) and _Blacklands_ (5885/7758), but quantities were insufficient to demonstrate convincingly that these sites were occupied in the second or first century BC.

There is still much to learn about the detail of settlements, the treatment of the dead, material culture, crafts, fields, boundaries and farming life. Indeed, the site-specific data for these sites are, for the most part, inconsequential at this stage; our excavations never deliberately focused on prehistoric sites and the data retrieved are therefore, inevitably, limited. However, the identification of so many hitherto unknown late pre-Roman Iron Age sites at Shapwick does at least serve to underline our inadequate understanding of the density and variety of pre-Roman settlement in the area. Whereas three sites of this period are now confirmed within the parish, only another four possible sites are known in the 30km along the Poldens between Butleigh and Puriton (Figure 3.26).[53] Indeed, with the exception of hillforts, comparatively little is known about late prehistoric settlement in Somerset other than the remarkable 'lake villages' of nearby Glastonbury and Meare with their wealth of finds and well-preserved prehistoric carpentry.

The 'lake villages', exceptional though they are in some respects, are useful in filling out some of the missing pieces of the jigsaw for our dry land Shapwick sites. Where archaeological stratigraphy has survived the plough, further excavation might find superimposed clay floors 5–8m across and hearths of baked clay or stone inside thatched roundhouses with walls of wattle and daub. The daub recovered at Shapwick (for example, from 6987) would lead us to expect this. Wood and thatch must have been the key building materials at this period but it seems

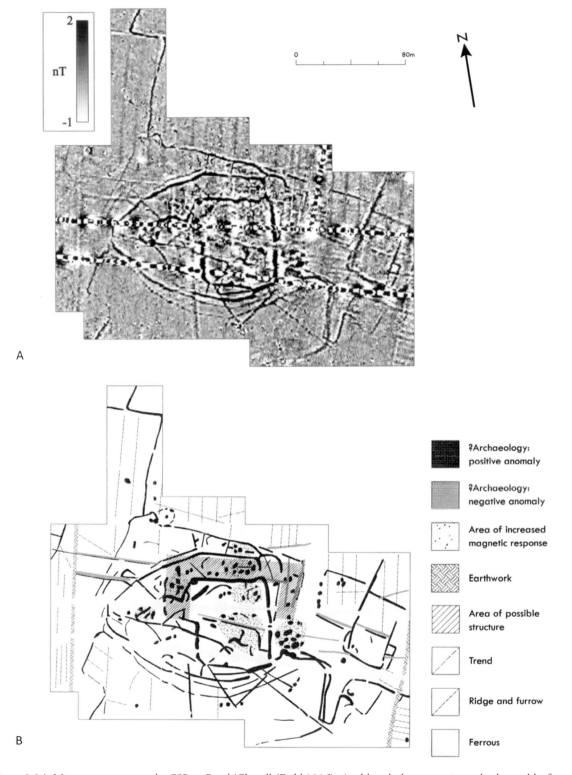

A

B

?Archaeology:
positive anomaly

?Archaeology:
negative anomaly

Area of increased
magnetic response

Earthwork

Area of possible
structure

Trend

Ridge and furrow

Ferrous

Figure 3.24. Magnetometry survey by GSB at Borgh/Chestell (Field 3836). A: although the pattern is partly obscured by ferrous disturbance, the core of this plot shows a rectangular enclosure with subdivisions and clusters of pits surrounded by concentric 'bullet-shaped' enclosures. Medieval ridge and furrow causes the broad (grey) linear north–south trends. B: the magnetic response is poor at defining stone structures but a possible outline of a Roman villa is suggested (see Chapter 4).

Figure 3.25. Butser Iron Age experimental farm in Hampshire. This full-scale reconstruction of a round house is based on archaeological data; here the roof thatch is being replaced. Note the woven panel fencing behind. All that remained at Shapwick was postholes and a drip gully beneath the eaves.

unlikely that there was any need to raise the houses up on brushwood and timber foundations, as was the case in the wet ground conditions at Glastonbury.[54] The principal activity in the Shapwick late Iron Age was agriculture, and cereal cropping is confirmed by both pollen evidence and the contents of late Iron Age plant macrofossil samples from excavations in Field 4649 (see above). Other agricultural features suggested by better-preserved sites include tracks and pathways, ancillary sheds, windbreaks, fences and pens for animals. Doubtless every community made good use of natural resources such as coppiced hazel for their fencing, just as their predecessors had done before them. The small faunal assemblage from excavations in Field 6987 produced cattle-sized bones from animals about the size of modern Dexters, and sheep or goat akin to the modern Soay type that were probably kept for their wool and milk. There were also the bones of small horses, some of which,

together with the cattle, would have been working animals. That dogs ran loose on the site is known from gnawed bones and they too were found at Meare, where a far larger faunal sample produced an almost identical species list, though with the addition of pigs and a range of small animals including birds.[55] The apparent absence of pig from the Shapwick assemblages may have more to do with the small size of the Iron Age faunal sample, though if the Shapwick sites were located with the exploitation of the wetland in mind there is little to suggest any specialisation. It seems that these were agricultural communities with mixed farming economies, presumably surrounded by enclosed rectilinear fields that became in part the framework for later fields. Superficially, at least, we might expect the landscape to look a little like the present one, with hedges and ditches defining square fields running across the slope.

Meare, just a few kilometres to the north of

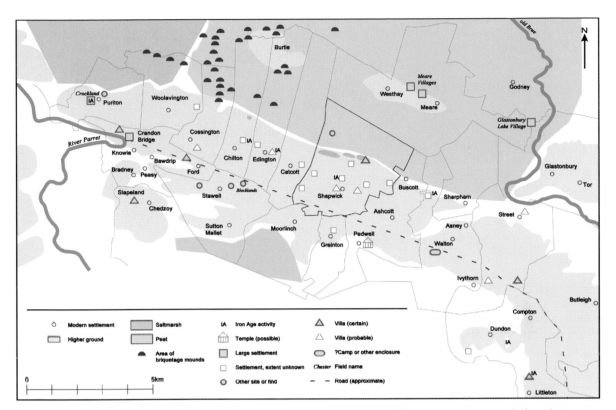

Figure 3.26. Known Iron Age and Roman settlement along the Poldens. Adapted from various sources, including the Somerset County Council Historic Environment Record and Rippon 1997.

Shapwick and visible from the Polden slope, is likely to have been a temporary settlement occupied only when conditions on the raised bog were dry enough; the Glastonbury site, on the other hand, appears to have been a more substantial undertaking that was occupied continuously, houses being built on an artificial island surrounded by a palisade. Settlement at Meare may have begun in about 300 BC and that at Glastonbury about fifty years later. Both sites came to an end around 50 BC,[56] though there is some debate about precise dates.[57] As we have seen, the earliest dateable Iron Age archaeological features from the Shapwick sites begin only in the first century BC. However, there are residual sherds of late Bronze Age–middle Iron Age pottery from at least seven sites in the parish which may well represent earlier phases, so there could have been contact with Meare

and Glastonbury; the Nidons site in Field 4649, in particular, lies close to the wetland edge. Given this evidence for an intensification of settlement and land use in the late Iron Age, one wonders whether it was pressure on dry land resources that lay behind the decision to occupy remote and challenging locations out in the bog.

By the beginning of the Roman period, which we will discuss in the next chapter, Shapwick was already an 'old' landscape. Iron Age boundaries were merely the latest of a series of overlays in a man-made countryside that had already been occupied for 10,000 years. Glimpses of this countryside, as we have seen, are revealed through flint scatters, aerial photographs and pollen diagrams, and this close link between humans and environment is a particular theme of this landscape to which we shall return.

CHAPTER FOUR

In the Shadow of an Empire

Life and Landscape during Roman Times, AD 43–*c.*AD 350

Cunobelinos pushed on faster now, ticking off the milestones as he rode. That plate of oysters had given him indigestion, or worse, and it had taken him most of the day to reach home from Lindinis. He had stopped only once to fodder the horse beneath the oaks by the temple. Entering, he left a few coins as an offering for the return of the three ewes stolen from his pens the night before, but once the rain cleared he was eager to be on his way again. The horse knew his own way down the lane, past the old grassy barrow where the sheep had gathered in the lee out of the driving rain.

As he rode Cunobelinos reflected on his day, the long hours he had spent recording his new purchases of woodland on writing tablets, struggling with the Latin words, keen to grasp the unfamiliar language of business. Tomorrow seemed an altogether better prospect; he would drive the sheep down to the moor's edge and mend the wattle fence where the thieves had trampled it down. He often spent time down there with his fowling nets at this time of year, before the winter struck hard, and flocks of teal would be out feeding on the seeds that floated in the water pools. It was, he thought, a magical sight, the flashes of green, gold and chestnut on their bodies and wings catching the sun at the end of the day. Soon enough they would fly away, though he did not know where.

For now, his woollen cloak was soaked through but at least the house would be warm when he finally arrived. There was nowhere to bathe in the warmth as there was in town but the fires would be well stoked, and in places the floor could burn your feet if you forgot your sandals. One relative or another was always taunting him to do more with the house, but the time was never right, the gods had indicated as much, and why was it always so important? Wasn't the food enough, the Gallic wines, the Spanish olive oil and those plates he had paid so much for? He preferred a drink of beer himself. Only last week the neighbours had been round for honey omelettes and hot lamb stew, a dish he particularly liked, with the meat simmered in a broth of crushed coriander seed, lovage, pepper and fish sauce in a cauldron over the raised charcoal hearth. Everyone seemed to enjoy that well enough, eating noisily with their fingers and supping the sauce from his bone spoons until it was all gone. So much tastier than those gritty oysters he had eaten at lunchtime. They hadn't been properly cleaned, and the owner of the tavern knew as much, but every time he went there the prices had shot up again. Still, his wife would be pleased with the pewter flagon he'd bought cheaply in the market. Most of those jugs looked identical, probably made from local lead in the same stone mould, but he had found an unusually large one that would suit their needs well. It would look fine in the dining room next to the old red Samian wares and those conical green beakers. How all the neighbours had commented on those when he first brought them home. Now everyone seemed to have them.

The small Roman town of *Lindinis* or *Lendiniae*, modern Ilchester, is thought to have been a late civitas capital, the tribal area of the Durotriges being divided between here and Dorchester in the third century AD. The Roman town stands at the junction of major roads to Exeter, Dorchester and Bath, the latter branching off along the Poldens. For British farmers such as Cunobelinos, a visit to *Lindinis* would have been an opportunity to buy from craftspeople and to sell to shopkeepers. Lead-working, specifically mentioned in our story, is one of the industries known from excavations in the town. *Lindinis* may have been his local administrative centre too, with an earthwork perimeter by the early third century and important public buildings, though we do not know whether the town had a forum and basilica. In his negotiations Cunobelinos would perhaps have spoken British Celtic, possibly Latin, maybe both.

In this text, our central character shows his awareness of the inheritance of the prehistoric and natural landscape, while the Roman temple mentioned in the story is that presumed to exist at nearby Pedwell. The names of the deities venerated there are unknown, but among those most commonly depicted in southern Britain were Mercury, Mars, Venus and Hercules. We emphasise in particular the social competition that may have surrounded the acquisition of foods and products such as pottery. Needless to say, we did not find direct evidence for his favourite dish at Shapwick, but the recipe, or something like it, was eaten. Mineralised black peppercorns have been recovered from excavations elsewhere and lovage grows well in the British climate. The 'fish sauce', sometimes called garum, may well have come from Spain but the beer was local and probably made from wheat rather than barley. By no means everyone used oil in their cooking and drank wine, as the low-level occurrence of amphora sherds on some British archaeological sites demonstrates. Most of the continental pottery imports found on our excavations peter out in the third century, so we envisage this story taking place around AD 250.

After the Conquest (AD 43–75)

When the army of Emperor Claudius landed in southern Britain in the summer of AD 43 much of the island was formally annexed into the Roman Empire, and it was to remain as the province of *Britannia* for more than 350 years. For a little while Shapwick lay beyond the western edge of the conquered area, an uncertain frontier zone marked by the Fosse Way and a line of military installations, but this was no more than a temporary pause before another Roman advance into Wales during the decade after AD 47.[1] Images of 'troops', 'conquest' and 'military operations', however, should not be confused with the realities of day-to-day life in the aftermath of conquest. For nearly 100 years southern Britain had lain on the fringes of an Empire with which it had enjoyed many cultural and trading links. There is little to indicate military activity along the Polden Hills and nothing to suggest the kind of large-scale movement of families we might associate with war zones today.[2]

Among the first changes to the daily lives of local people would have been the laying out and construction of new roads under the supervision of

military engineers, for which purpose local labour was doubtless conscripted. The main arterial route though the region was the Fosse Way from Exeter to Lincoln, built by AD 49, which ran locally from *Lindinis* (Ilchester) through the Roman settlement at Shepton Mallet and on northwards to *Aquae Sulis* (Bath) (Figure 4.1). From the Fosse, three parallel Roman roads struck west to the Bristol Channel: one in the north to *Abonae* (Sea Mills), a second past the lead and silver mines on Mendip towards Brean Down[3] and a third, more southerly, along the Polden Hills. Excavation and a watching brief show this last road to have been no more than roughly laid metalling 0.2m thick and 2–3m wide, partly on the same alignment as the modern A39 road.[4] The straightness of its course and the road's embanked construction are best appreciated today just west of Loxley Wood, on the southern fringe of Shapwick parish. Its destination was Crandon Bridge in the parish of Bawdrip, where excavations have recovered evidence for a large site extending over at least 7ha with 'warehouses' designed for the storage and redistribution of all kinds of goods. Tellingly, most of the pottery was from large storage vessels or amphoras, so this was perhaps a small

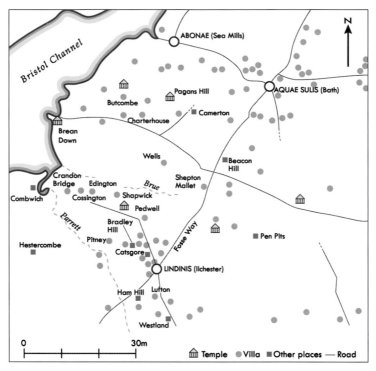

Figure 4.1. Location map for Roman Shapwick, showing places mentioned in the text (adapted from Rahtz 1983, fig. 16).

Roman town with a riverside quay.[5] Judged from a Shapwick perspective, therefore, the Poldens road linked to the west with trading routes down rivers and along the coast and to the east with a major local market at *Lindinis*. Today it is just over 21km by road from Shapwick to Ilchester – approximately three hours on horseback and less than a day's travel along more direct Roman roads. Outgoing products might have included grain and salt, perhaps, with tiles, pottery and construction timber being carted in the opposite direction.

Compiling what is known from recent archaeological fieldwork, field names and lists of casual finds in the surrounding area creates at least the beginnings of a regional Roman atlas of settlement and other monuments. Among the best known of these is the villa complex with its mosaics to the south in High Ham parish,[6] but there are possibly sites of similarly high status at Cossington, Edington and a number of locations around Street. In addition, more modest rural settlements could be found all along the north

flank of the Poldens, perhaps as many as sixteen in all. To these must be added an unknown number of as yet unidentified sites, perhaps as many as thirty-six if our results from Shapwick can be considered representative of densities locally. How many of these places would have been in existence at any one time is less certain – very few have benefited from modern excavation – but it is clear that the whole upland area was extensively farmed and populated and, over time, that it came to be well served with new roads, towns and markets that generated new demands on the countryside and brought new goods and fashions into local households. This new taste for consumption is chiefly visible to the archaeologist as broken pots, metalwork such as brooches that indicate new styles of dress, novel forms of architecture and more abundant coinage. And while these new fashions were not imposed, entirely new or unilaterally adopted they do represent a deep-rooted 'Romanisation' of many aspects of life in Britain between the late pre-Roman Iron Age and the fourth century.[7]

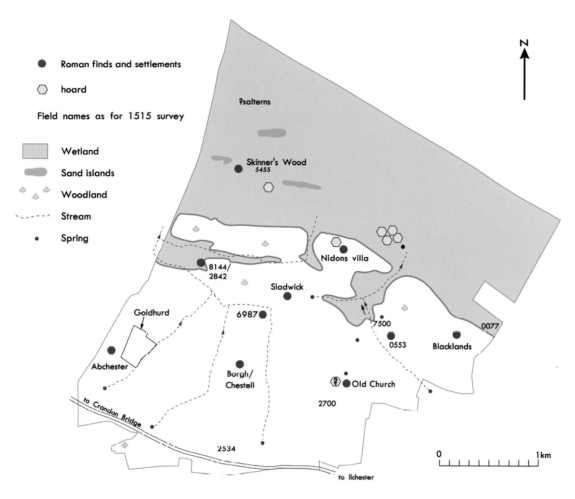

Figure 4.2. Roman Shapwick. When this map is compared against the Iron Age picture in Figure 3.19 the continuity is striking.

The extent to which this Roman settlement pattern duplicates the late prehistoric distribution of sites is striking (Figure 4.2). Locations preferred for human activities appear to remain unchanged for hundreds if not thousands of years. A case in point is the fields in the eastern half of the parish in the vicinity of *Old Church*, where fieldwalkers collected not only flints of earlier Mesolithic and earlier Neolithic date but also debris from every archaeological period between the early Bronze Age and the fourteenth century. Admittedly, when these spreads of material are plotted out on maps there is a degree of lateral shift, but at least some of this can be attributed to changing patterns of rubbish disposal and the spreading of

middens this way and that. New structures tended to migrate short distances around a previously existing core,[8] hemmed in perhaps by cultivated fields but also drawn by ancestral ties and the convenience of handy building materials, a combination that seems to have pulled people back repeatedly to the same places in the landscape. Continuity seems to be a marked feature of the settlement archaeology, an observation that should underline the importance of local cultural patterns and regional diversity.[9]

That said, the distribution of settlement continued to evolve. Several new sites with no underlying late prehistoric presence appeared for the first time in the first and second centuries AD. Both *Abchester* and

Borgh/Chestell are examples of this, and no pre-Roman occupation is known at either of the unnamed sites in Fields 8144/2842 or 0553, though these were not selected for excavation and our understanding of them is much poorer. The broad picture, therefore, is that the late prehistoric pattern of settlement at Shapwick was added to; that it was complemented, but not displaced, with the most significant intensification taking place during the second century AD. That change was driven, at least in part, by the emergence of new markets at military forts and urban centres on both sides of the Severn estuary,[10] among them Caerwent in south Wales and *Lindinis*. It is probably the growing economic and administrative status of these places that explains why so many villas cluster in the countryside nearby.[11]

What we have learnt so far about early Roman Shapwick is that the arrival of Emperor Claudius did not bring with it an upheaval in the everyday life of local farming communities. Quite the opposite: annual cycles of seeding, harvesting and nurturing animals continued just as they had in AD 42; few people lost their homes or moved. Although there is archaeological evidence of local skirmishes in the form of suggestive skeletal material at South Cadbury,[12] probably in response to the Boudiccan revolt of AD 60, the broader picture is one of political takeover, a conquest of minds rather than a fight for land. Clan and tribal groupings had been fluid in their allegiances in the years between Caesar's expedition of 55–54 BC and the Claudian conquest, so disruption was nothing new and Romanisation did not destroy all traces of what had gone before. If anything, over the next 100 years the population of Shapwick increased as new farms and settlements were established in what was already a crowded landscape.

The developing pattern of Romano-British settlement (AD 75–350)

Our understanding of Roman rural settlement in the region has traditionally been focused on the structural history of villas and military sites. The objectives of the Shapwick Project were more inclusive, embracing a fuller range of sites and attempting a more integrated understanding of the landscape.[13] In all, ten Roman sites are now known from the parish, many more than

had been expected at the outset of the Project. Most of them survive in very poor condition, only one having very slight but visible earthworks (*Borgh/Chestell*). Because the soils are generally shallow over the natural bedrock, many sites have been removed altogether by ploughing, leaving only rock-cut features. At others only the thinnest skin of archaeological layers remains. On the one hand, this provides a real problem for the excavator. On the other, it generates a huge quantity of finds that have made their way into the plough soil and, as a result, into the bags of fieldwalkers. Almost all the Shapwick Roman sites were first discovered during field survey and not one, contrary to the usual situation in southern Britain, is readily identifiable from aerial photographs.

Four different forms of settlement can be picked -out from our fieldwork: high-status sites or villas – that is to say, rural buildings with stone foundations, tiled roofs and some evidence for underfloor heating, painted wall plaster or other luxuries;[14] a possible shrine; a large agricultural settlement or village; and farmsteads. The evidence for each of these is considered below.

High-status sites or 'villas'
The Nidons villa (Field 4649)

A concentration of Roman material on the crest of the Nidon ridge was first noted by fieldwalkers in 1995 but, as we discovered in Chapter 3, a much longer prehistory of occupation is now apparent on this site.[15] The magnetometry survey in Figure 4.3A shows the wide meandering ditches of the southern end of the Iron Age enclosure (numbered [1] on Figure 4.3B) with the rectilinear layout of the Roman phase of the site superimposed over the top.

The detail shown in Figure 4.3B illustrates a major phase of development in the site's history in the second century AD, when a southern range at [2, 6] and a western range at [3] were erected around a rectangular courtyard. The southern half of this western range seems to have been built out across one of the earlier enclosure ditches [4] as the complex expanded towards the south. There may also have been a northern range and an eastern one at [5] but this is unclear. Particularly intriguing is what appears to be a room with an apsidal end in the eastern range, possibly a *triclinium* or dining room, or even part of

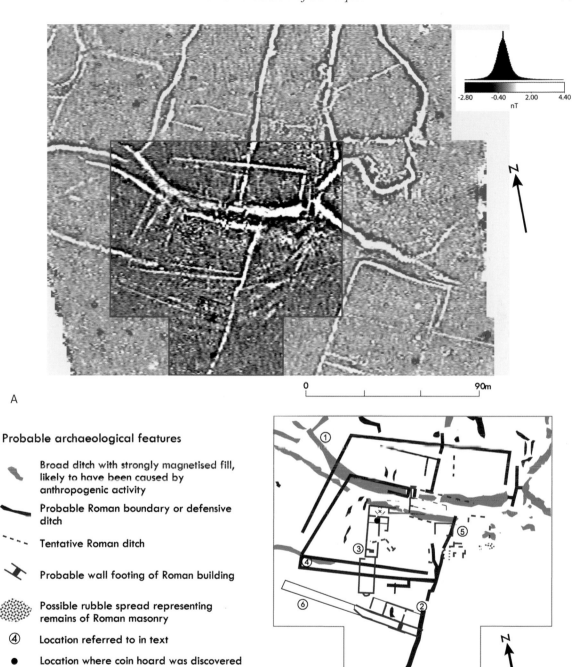

A

B

Probable archaeological features

Broad ditch with strongly magnetised fill, likely to have been caused by anthropogenic activity

Probable Roman boundary or defensive ditch

Tentative Roman ditch

Probable wall footing of Roman building

Possible rubble spread representing remains of Roman masonry

④ Location referred to in text

● Location where coin hoard was discovered

Figure 4.3. Geophysical survey over the Nidons Roman villa. A: magnetometer plot with Roman activity highlighted. B: an interpretation of the results combining magnetometer and resistivity surveys. Figure 3.23 sets these results into a wider spatial context and identifies probable prehistoric features.

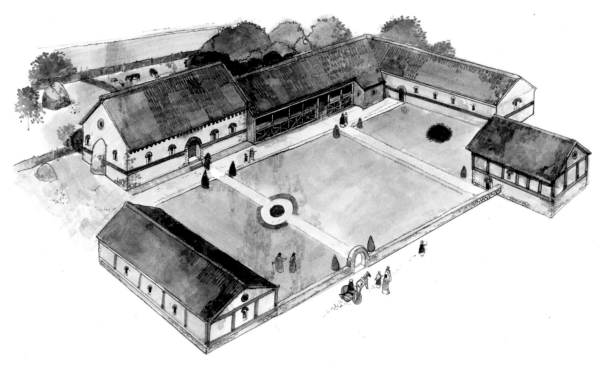

Figure 4.4. Reconstruction of the courtyard Roman villa on the Nidons, by Victor Ambrus. For similar complexes locally see Figure 4.6.

a bath-suite given the increased magnetic disturbance that was registered here, something which is usually indicative of heat.[16] Our interpretation of this sequence is that, over several generations, what may well have been a native family invested their wealth in a more 'Romanised' dwelling.[17] This expansion was incremental, something that may reflect an increase in the size of the family group or a change in the composition of the household, or quite possibly both. Presumably sites such as the Nidons villa would have also accommodated servants or slaves.

Our reconstruction of the final phase of the site shows a modest villa with two or three ranges set around a central courtyard, the whole complex covering about 60m^2 (Figure 4.4). A large hoard of silver coins (discussed in greater detail below) was concealed in about AD 224 under the floor of what was probably a small strongroom in the north-western corner of the complex. Excavation strongly suggests that the villa was still occupied at the time. As for other parts of the villa complex visible on the wider

geophysics plot (Figure 4.5), magnetic susceptibility indicates that heating and burning took place close to [1], which was perhaps the site of a corn-drying oven. Also visible are trackways such as that which linked [2] and [3], field boundaries such as [4], pits such as [5] and [6] and enclosures of different shapes and sizes, such as those at [7], [8] and [9]. These may be paddocks, kitchen gardens,[18] orchards or even vineyards, while the inner court might have been an ornamental garden rather than a farmyard; our reconstruction shows grassy lawns and paths. Historically, most villa excavations have tended to concentrate on the buildings rather than garden design, but there is no reason to think that at least some of the buildings identified could not be pavilions. While no material suitable for palaeobotanical study could be obtained from the excavations, the scale of investment in these enclosures and the clear demarcation of property boundaries is a significant statement of ownership in itself. In terms of the whole layout, the positioning of the villa buildings

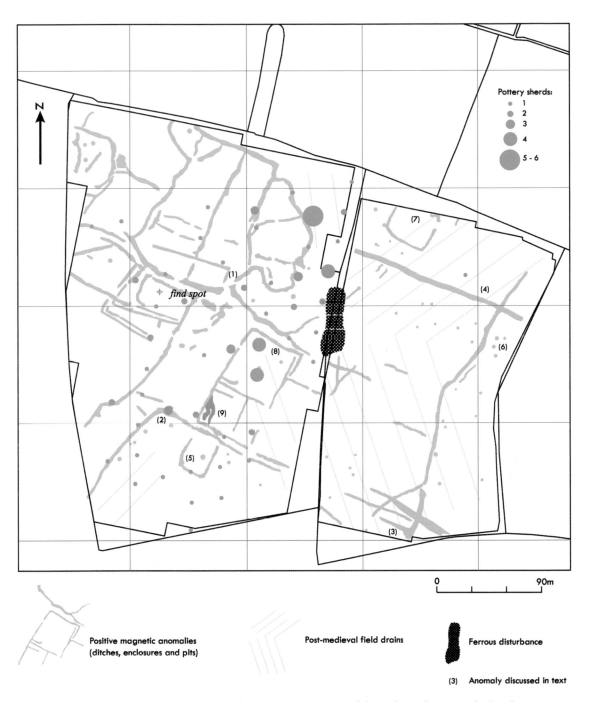

Figure 4.5. Geophysical anomalies identified from the magnetometry survey of the Nidons villa site overlaid with Roman pottery distributions from fieldwalking (in green). This plot also shows field systems, trackways and enclosures as well as prehistoric features and post-medieval drains (in yellow).

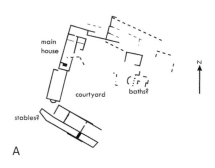

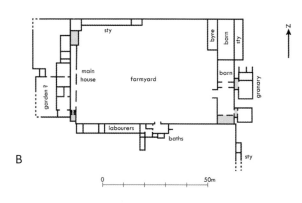

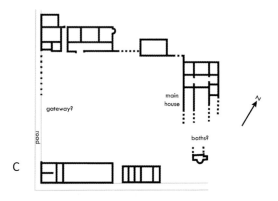

Figure 4.6. Examples of 'courtyard' villas in Somerset. A: Shapwick Nidons. B: Pitney (with tentative functions from Branigan 1976). C: Yeovil Westland. A complex of domestic and agricultural buildings offering accommodation for farmer, family and perhaps servants.

'off-centre' from the eastern approach to the complex and the location of the domestic 'wing' furthest away from the entrance suggests a desire for privacy.

All these buildings were apparently demolished in the early third century, though coins recovered from the plough soil suggest that occupation continued nearby until at least the end of the fourth century, the latest evidence being a copper coin of the House of Theodosius (AD 388–402). Excavated occupation features from this later period were limited to a recut of the ditch of the enclosure immediately south-east of the villa. All in all, the archaeological record gives a strong sense of a pre-Conquest farm progressing, in a series of phases, towards villa-style buildings during the later second century AD, with more modest living conditions both before and after that date. Dramatic shifts in what we might call the 'consumer conduct' of the villa's successive owners were apparently afoot, with innovations in architectural style suggesting upward social mobility initially and a lack of investment later. A change of ownership is one interpretation of this, but it is always possible that the family's wealth was by now more fully displayed at another site elsewhere.[19]

Figure 4.6 compares the plan of the Nidons villa against those from Pitney and Westland at Yeovil, which are of the same 'courtyard' type.[20] Like these other local examples, the Nidons villa was never planned as a single complex of domestic accommodation running around three or four sides of a central area, as was the well-known 'residential villa' at Chedworth near Cirencester (Glos), for example. Rather, this was a series of buildings constructed in successive phases, perhaps with fifteen to twenty rooms in all, grouped around a courtyard. It had more of the appearance of a farm than a country residence, even if it did enjoy striking views to the east towards Glastonbury Tor.[21] The finds from the site are curiously contradictory: the amassing of the hoard appears to be convincing evidence of wealth, as is a diet that included duck, teal, corncrake and possibly rooks or crows, as well as a single bone from a member of the fulmar/petrel/shearwater family. These birds must surely indicate fowling near pools on the nearby wetland, where they were probably snared, trapped or netted; even the last listed might have been considered edible, though shearwaters spend much of their life on the wing and nest only on islands, so an occurrence here is unexpected. On the other hand, neither the architectural fittings nor the finds from the site are especially sophisticated. Objects such as the stone rubber, for example, are routine household items (Figure 4.7L). Finewares normally associated with villas were sparse (Figure 4.7A–H) and, though Lias and ceramic roof tiles were plentiful (Figure 4.7I–K), no hypocaust tiles were recovered – the sort of evidence we might expect for underfloor heating. Likewise, there were no *tesserae* from mosaics, fragments of painted wall plaster or fine pottery. With the notable exception of the coins the metalwork assemblage is also poor, with little to indicate a Roman presence at all except for nineteen hobnails, no more than the number needed for a single pair of shoes. Perhaps these were simply less Romanised landowners, perhaps the residents were themselves tenants for much of the time, or perhaps this was never a permanent residence but something akin to a weekend retreat for fishing and hunting.[22]

One of the Shapwick finds that most cries out for explanation is the spectacular third-century coin hoard from this site (Box 4.1). Just how valuable was it? When all the gold and silver deposits in the late Roman and Byzantine periods between AD 193 and AD 711, within and beyond the frontiers of the Roman Empire, are considered together, the Nidons hoard ranks 57th in its estimated gold equivalent value. In Britain only the hoards from Hoxne (Suffolk), Eye (Suffolk), Cleeve Prior (Worcs), Mildenhall (Suffolk) and *Cunetio*, near Marlborough (Wilts), rank higher, and the first four of these include gold coinage as well as objects such as plate. *Cunetio* (AD 260–74), at over 50,000 items, is the only deposit of base silver coins that is larger. The Shapwick hoard is, therefore, very sizeable by any measure. While there are gold coin hoards of greater value from the period AD 222–237, this is the largest and most valuable of all the silver hoards so far found across the Empire; only a find of about 6500 coins from Rome comes close to matching it.[23] This gives us a starting point for an assessment of the status of the owners of the coins; relatively speaking, these must have been wealthy people. Steve Minnitt[24] estimates the value of the hoard to be equivalent to about a quarter of a million pounds in today's money.

The archaeological detail of the hoard provides further clues. The coins were deposited with considerable forethought, first being arranged in neat single rows then wrapped in some now-perished material such as textile or leather before being placed into a larger sack[25] and dumped into their hiding place beneath the floor. The obvious care taken in this process shows that this is no accidental loss; the hoard must have been buried deliberately. To begin with, we should not completely dismiss the possibility that this was an offering, a generous sacrifice to secure better harvests – and there is certainly a long history of similarly precious deposits in the immediate vicinity throughout prehistory (see Chapter 3). Yet there is little about the archaeology or topography of this particular site to suggest that it was a place of religious significance other than its situation close to the wetland edge. It seems far more likely that this was a burial for safekeeping by some person or persons and the fact that the coins were wrapped and readied for extraction rather than dumped together into a single container would add some credence to the view that the coins were intended to be retrieved. But what could the danger have been? There are no strong clusters of hoards in Britain at this period, let alone in central Somerset, something that we might expect had there been a threat of raiders from Ireland or some more serious military situation locally. Nor do the AD 220s mark any sort of monetary or economic crisis, unlike the second half of the third century, though the value of silver coinage was in decline as the purity and weight of coins slowly decreased.[26] With more coins being produced inflation resulted and, fearing for the value of their savings, one very human response would have been to hide things away for a better day.[27] This does not explain, however, why these particular owners were so acutely aware of the impending economic situation.

A more likely cause, we think, is something that specifically relates to this Nidons site and to the particular circumstances of its owners. It appears significant that the dates of the deposition of the hoard and the demolition of the villa lie so close together. These two events are likely to be connected in some way. But how? One possibility is that whatever circumstances led to the demolition of the villa's buildings they were foreseen by the

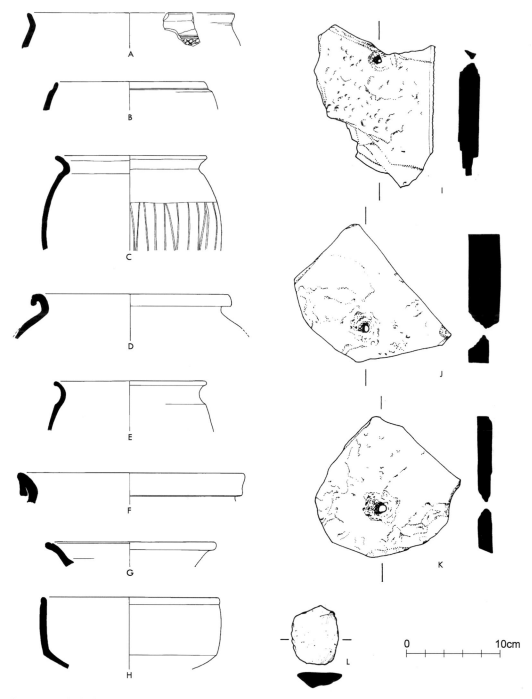

Figure 4.7. Roman finds from the Nidons villa, Shapwick: 775 pottery sherds from six trenches, including A: wide-mouthed bowl with lattice decoration, Glastonbury Group 3, c.250–50 BC. B: jar or bowl, Durotrigan type sandy ware, mid–first century BC. C: jar, black burnished ware from Poole/Wareham area, probably third century. D: jar, grey ware with hooked rim, third century or later. E: jar with everted rim, grey ware, third century or later. F: large storage jar, grey ware, second–fourth century AD. G: shallow dish, black burnished ware from Poole/Wareham area, probably third century. H: deep bowl with beaded rim and chamfered base, south-west black burnished ware, probably mid–second century. I–K: Blue Lias roof tiles. L: a possible Blue Lias rubber, smoothed through grinding.

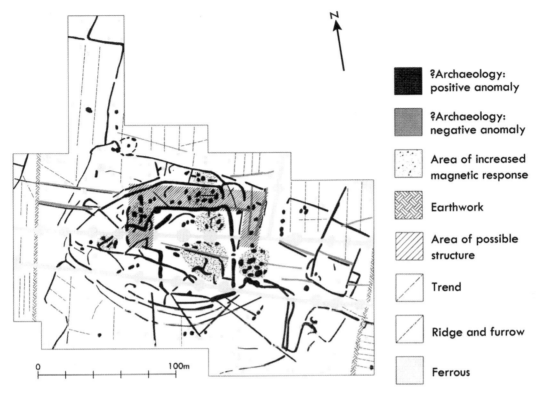

Figure 4.8. Interpretation of gradiometer data from Borgh/Chestell. Enclosures, ditch systems and dense clusters of pits. There is a square enclosure 60m × 60m at the core and a stone building is suggested measuring 100 m east–west with shorter wings at either end – a possible villa whose identification awaits further investigation. A copy of the original plot can be seen in Figure 3.24.

owner and the hoard was buried in anticipation of that occurrence. Another possibility is based on the observation that many of the coins in the hoard come from the reign of Septimius Severus (AD 193–211), an emperor who led a military campaign against the north of Britain for which large numbers of denarii were struck to pay his troops. If the owner of the Nidons villa had been a member of Severus' legions years before, or someone who had benefited financially from the army's presence, such as a doctor or a grain merchant, they might have moved away again and perhaps perished far from home without informing anyone else of the whereabouts of the hoard. This might have led to a financial crisis and, ultimately, to the loss of the villa. We shall perhaps never know the full story, though a review of hoarding practice right across the wetland region and beyond, one that took a longer perspective,

might reveal much about the wider context of this remarkable find.

Borgh/Chestell (Field 3836)

Immediately west of the modern village lies a second possible high-status Roman site. The later medieval names for the fields in this area are *Borgh* and *Chestell*. The former has associations with OE *burh*, 'a fortified place', or perhaps with *beorg*, 'a hill', while *Chestell* is derived from OE *ceastel*, a 'heap (of stones)', and had become *Chessell* by 1638. Both names intimate that crumbling stone buildings were to be found here in the Anglo-Saxon period. Immediately to the west in 1515 lay *Stonyland*, another possibly significant name.

The results of geophysical survey (Figure 4.8), remarkable for their clarity, show a bewildering pattern of enclosures, ditches and densely clustered pits with an enclosure 60m × 70m at its centre. This

BOX 4.1

The Shapwick 'treasure'

On 14 September 1998 Kevin Elliot and his cousin Martin unearthed 9238 Roman coins in a field of barley stubble on the Nidons. Though Martin was an experienced metal detectorist, Kevin, whose family had purchased the land only in January of that year, had been using the detector for just a few minutes when the first coins began to turn up. Half an hour later they were so numerous that the cousins were removing them in milking buckets. At almost 30kg, the coins weighed as much as a sack of cement. Even so, the Shapwick 'treasure', as it came to be called, was green with corrosion and mostly unidentifiable. Only careful cleaning at the British Museum in the months that followed was to reveal the full story.

The coins are mostly silver denarii struck in Rome and span a 250-year period from 32–31 BC to AD 224, from Mark Antony to Severus Alexander, 'a virtual who's who of Roman corruption, lunacy and depravity', as one newspaper reported. More than half are issues of the reign of Septimius Severus (AD 193–211), a period during which large numbers of denarii were struck and the silver content of coins was vastly reduced (Figure B.4.1). Steve Minnitt speculates that some of the coins in the Shapwick hoard may have originated as part of the war chest needed by Severus to pay his troops during their campaigns in northern Britain.[b1]

As might be expected in a coin hoard of this size, there are some unusual inclusions. These include six coins of Didius Julianus, emperor for just sixty-six days before he was murdered in AD 193, and two of his wife Manlia Scantilla. Mints as far afield as Syria and Egypt are represented; there are even four rogue Greek drachmae from Lycia, today in south-west Turkey, and Cappadocian Caesarea, now known as Mazaca/Kayseri in Turkey. The images on the coins celebrate the achievements of the emperors, from the elephants of Roman entertainments to Venus, goddess of love and beauty. There are also twenty-five forgeries of silver and plated copper alloy, three of them probably from the same pair of dies. These particular coins may have been made locally; clay moulds for casting denarii have been found in the parishes near Shapwick, so counterfeiting almost certainly took place.

What lessons are there to be gleaned from this extraordinary discovery? The finders must be congratulated for reporting their discovery so promptly, as should the landowners, for allowing the excavation and geophysics survey that then established the archaeological context for the hoard. Of course, such a process is one not without its costs, which must in the end be borne by others, but all too often in the past hoards like this one have been broken up and dispersed among collectors. Once they come to the attention of the archaeological world we are then left with no real understanding of where they came from, the details of their finding or

core is composed of irregular compartments dotted with darkened magnetic responses, perhaps pits or hearths, while around the perimeter there are loops of parallel ditches that are clearly subdivided and which themselves contain archaeological anomalies. The overall impression is of a bullet-shaped enclosure, entered from the east, with multiple enclosures for corralling and protecting livestock. In the margins of the survey area further fields and later phases of occupation are hinted at by the rectilinear block of lines overlapping the north-east of the enclosure.

Ridge and furrow is also visible as broad parallel lines running north–south up and down the slope, but medieval cultivation seems to have done remarkably little damage.

When excavation began, the uncovering of the debris from a collapsed Roman stone building on the eastern side of the central enclosure caught everyone by surprise. The initial processing of the geophysical results had led us to assume that we would be dealing with late prehistoric ditch features, but the first finds to turn up immediately under the turf of our small even what kind of site they were originally associated with. That was not the case here; we even know the room the hoard was deposited in. The authorities too, including the coroner, Somerset County Council, English Heritage and the British Museum, all acted in exemplary fashion under the terms of the then-new Treasure Act 1996 and the cousins were eventually paid the full market value for their find: £265,000.

For the Shapwick Project the hoard find was not quite such a positive experience. We had known of the existence of the Nidons Roman site for three years, ever since it was partly fieldwalked in 1995. Considerable quantities of Roman pottery were recovered there at that time, together with a single Mark Anthony legionary denarius which, as it turns out, must have been one of the coins dislodged from the hoard. These finds were duly reported in October 1997 in the seventh report of the Shapwick Project, but shortly afterwards members of the project were denied all access to complete their work. Indeed, with the exception of the Somerset County Council-led investigations following the discovery of the hoard, no further work was permitted there at all during the lifetime of the Project. Happily, the coins themselves can now be seen on display at the Somerset County Museum in Taunton and there is an accompanying booklet written by Stephen Minnitt, *The Shapwick Treasure*, as well as an academic volume about the hoard by the Royal Numismatic Society.[b2]

Figure B.4.1. A: issues of the reign of Septimus Severus (AD 193–211) make up more than half the Shapwick hoard; here Severus is shown with his son, Geta, on horseback on the reverse (B). C: Greek drachma of Julia Domna with Aphrodite on the reverse (D). E: coin of Septimus Severus depicting elephants entertaining the people of Rome. F: coin of Julia Domna depicting Venus, goddess of love and beauty on the reverse. G: denarius of Severus Alexander; on the reverse (H) Providentia holds a wand and sceptre with a globe by her feet. This is one of the latest coins in the hoard, suggesting that burial took place in or shortly after AD 224.

trench were Roman hobnails, roofing nails, fragments possibly from a nearby hearth or oven, eight or nine ceramic *tesserae*, cubes of cut tile and plain wall plaster. Among the fragments of pottery were continental imports such as Samian and Moselle black slip table wares and amphoras from Spain.[28]

As the excavators continued to trowel and clean, walling, a doorway and rooms all came to light. Our trench had clearly fallen within the outline of a large Roman structure and this sent us scurrying back to the geophysics plots to reprocess the results. What

emerged was the footprint of a U-shaped building, either a villa of winged corridor plan or a courtyard house. Directly associated with this structure is pottery of late third- or fourth-century date, including sherds from a variety of local workshops as well as Gallic amphoras and Central Gaulish Samian (Figure 4.9). A Roman coin found here is also of later third-century date (AD 270–290), and among the miscellaneous finds were Roman hobnails, oyster shell, a small amount of animal bone, an iron spike, twenty-four iron nails and what may be a pottery

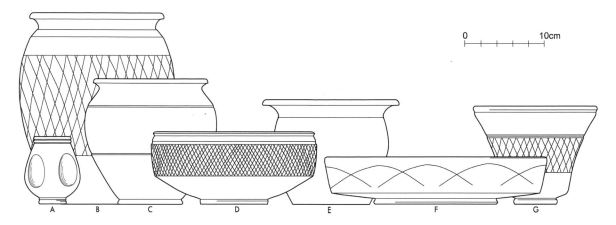

Figure 4.9. Roman pottery from Borgh/Chestell reconstructed by Alejandra Gutiérrez, including A: indented colour-coated beaker, locally produced. B: black burnished ware jar with everted rim and burnished lattice from Poole Harbour area. C: local grey ware jar with everted rim. D: carinated bowl with incised latticework, probably local. E: jar with everted rim, black burnished ware, second–fourth century AD. F: dish with burnished intersecting arcs, black burnished ware, second–fourth century AD. G: flared tankard with tooled lattice decoration, grey ware, probably local. Occupation here dates from the later second or early third century into the fourth century.

burnisher or mosaic polisher. If further work became a possibility here in the future there would doubtless be far more to say, but for now there is at least enough to demonstrate a sizeable Roman stone structure, very probably a large 'villa' site, whose origins may lie in the mid–late second century.

A second small trench in the same field, this time on the eastern edge of the geophysical anomalies, provided plenty of supporting evidence for later second- to mid-fourth-century activity in *Borgh/Chestell*. There was a flat-bottomed beam-slot of a possible timber building here that was provisionally dated to the third century AD, clearly seen in the far left-hand corner of the trench in Figure 4.10. The trench also struck the T-junction of two ditches which, judging by the ceramics they contained, were backfilled sometime after AD 270. Several of the pottery forms intimated a fourth-century source and this is corroborated by an adult burial (see Figure B.4.2) that was cut into the upper layers of the ditch infills. The burial has since been radiocarbon dated to AD 220–390. We may infer that the ditches seen on this part of the geophysics plot had ceased to be cleaned by the early fourth century; the latest coin found on the site dates to the mid-fourth century.[29]

In spite of the quality of the geophysics survey at *Borgh/Chestell*, the two small evaluation trenches that we dug were insufficient to clarify the nature of the site to our satisfaction. The finds assemblage as a whole suggests a well-appointed site with views out across the Brue valley from its plastered and tessellated rooms. Its occupants were familiar with Gaulish wine, uniquely so among Shapwick sites, while the distinctive globular two-handled amphoras had travelled from near Seville in southern Spain with their contents of olive oil or preserved olives. Imports such as these may have been unloaded at the quayside at Crandon Bridge. On the face of it, this is a Roman villa of some standing dating between the later second or even early third century and the mid-fourth century AD, with a heavier emphasis towards material of later Roman date. No earlier material, such as native wares, was identified.

A possible shrine or villa by the spring at Old Church (Field 4016)

The complex of buildings immediately south-east of the spring in Fields 4016 and 5813 is perhaps the most significant and long-lived of the four higher-status Roman sites at Shapwick, as well as being the most frustrating in an archaeological sense. The partial plan recovered from magnetometry survey (Figure 4.11A) shows a remarkable number of potential anomalies, reflecting the site's long occupancy and use from prehistory to the later medieval period. Plainly, the problem in this instance is to work out which anomalies might belong to what phases, and Figure 4.11B is an attempt to disentangle the geophysics results with the benefit of the results of our fieldwork. Overall, the broad and dense scatter of material collected during fieldwalking firmly indicates a sizeable group of buildings covering an area about 185m east–west by 140m north–south, while the finds assemblage suggests a date range between the late Iron Age and the mid-fourth century AD.

Excavation of several trenches across the field quickly demonstrated that the archaeological layers are frustratingly shallow and badly truncated by ploughing (Figure 4.12A). What had survived was just the last 'skim' of late prehistoric and early Roman features, which were inadequate to provide a coherent layout. Postholes sometimes hinted at wooden buildings but even stone buildings had remained only where they had been protected by medieval structures and Lias debris (Figure 4.12B). Elsewhere there were patches of cobbling, most notably on the slopes dipping down into the spring, as well as bedrock-cut ditches that had served for drainage.

Fortunately, the finds assemblage from this site has an interesting story to tell in its own right. The highest densities of pottery of first-century BC/AD date were found disturbed in later contexts in the trench to the south of the spring site in Trench Z (Figure 4.12C). Glastonbury-style wares, hand-made calcite-tempered wares and grog-tempered pottery were recovered: more than 300 sherds of native Iron Age and pre-Roman wares in all (Figure 4.13J). Six brooches were also found here, three dating to *c.*AD 43–70: two were of Aucissa type, with highly ridged bows and decorated central ribs, and a third was of strip bow type (Figure 4.13A–E). Together with a fragment of nail cleaner of mid-first- to second-century date, two lead pot-mends, a Roman shoe cleat and a single hobnail, these finds came from truncated ditches and occupation layers immediately below the surface.

Later pottery from the site includes Dorset black burnished wares and regional imports such as colour-

Figure 4.10. Borgh/Chestell under excavation with the edge of Shapwick village beyond a little way to the east. A beam slot and drip gully in the left background; ditch with a Lias fill exposed in section to the left of the ranging pole. The burial shown in Figure B.4.2 was excavated here.

coated wares and mortaria, particularly those from the New Forest and Oxfordshire industries, marking activity into the early–mid fourth century (Figure 4.13F–H, K). Other mortaria include sherds of Mancetter-Hartshill ware from the Warwickshire–Leicestershire border, Shepton Mallet red-slipped ware and south-west white-slipped ware. The total absence of later fourth-century shelly wares suggests abandonment by the mid fourth century or earlier. Many of these finds are such as might be expected on any other rural settlement locally. There was, for example, a fragment of a possible palette of Roman

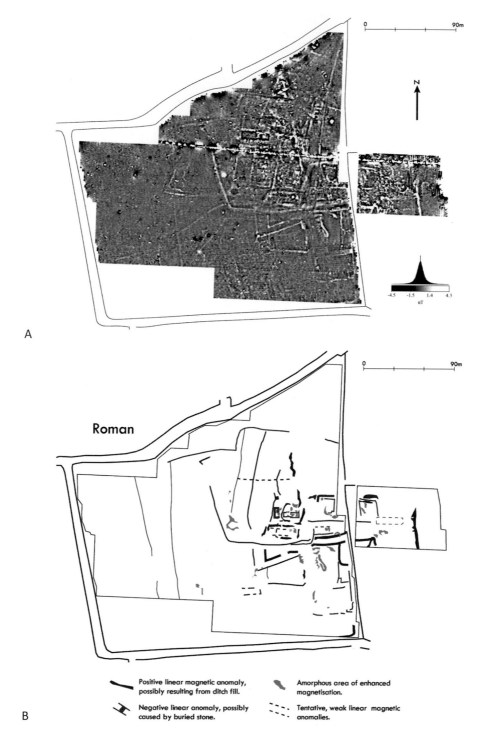

Figure 4.11. A: greyscale plot of the magnetometer data from Old Church by the English Heritage Ancient Monuments Laboratory. A water pipe runs across the field but a large number of archaeological features can be identified, most obviously the imprint of the medieval church of St Andrew and many other enclosures and structures. Beerway Farm lies under the north sign. B: the Roman features only. Note that the complex crosses the modern field boundary into the field to the east.

Figure 4.12. A: aerial photograph of the excavations under way in Old Church (4016), looking west. B: Harry Jelley cleaning a Roman wall (4016/F). C: multiple ditches of late Iron Age and Roman date (4016/Z).

type from *Old Church* made of Coal Measures Sandstone, together with a wide range of other stone objects such as a shale spindlewhorl of later Roman date and so-called 'gaming counters' that may actually be weights or pot lids. Large quantities of fired clay suggest at least one hearth or corn drier nearby. At

least one other building had a stone roof of pegged Lias, the tiles being cut into a diamond pattern with a single nail hole for securing to the roof. These would have been laid across the roof in an overlapping pattern but they were not easily mixed with ceramic tiles, fragments of which were also plentiful. At the

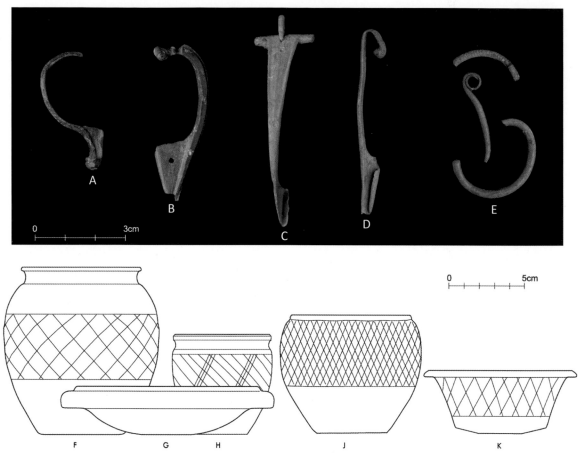

Figure 4.13. Roman brooches and pottery from Old Church reconstructed by Alejandra Gutiérrez, including A and B: Aucissa type brooches, first century AD. *C: T-shaped brooch, mid-first to second century* AD. *D: strip bow brooch, first century* AD. *E: penannular brooch, mid-first to third century. F: jar, black burnished ware from Poole Harbour/Wareham area. Repaired with a lead rivet. Second–fourth centuries* AD. *G: red-slipped mortarium, Shepton Mallet. From early second century* AD. *H: jar with diagonal burnished line decoration, grey ware, probably local. Second–fourth centuries* AD. *J: jar, with burnished lattice decoration, Durotrigan ware from Dorset region. Introduced mid-first century* AD. *K: dish with grooved rim, south-west black burnished ware from Poole Harbour area.*

same time, an impression of modest affluence is corroborated by finds of Roman bottle glass and coal in a third- or fourth-century context, the latter a unique find among Roman sites at Shapwick and possibly intended for a brazier.[30] Also significant among the finds was a single fragment of cast window glass, seven box flue tile fragments and a white chalk *tessera* of the kind used elsewhere for colouring Roman mosaics. This squared-off cube of chalk, whose nearest source would be either to the south-east in Dorset or to the east in Wiltshire, would have been bedded onto a firm base of coarse mortar, several fragments of which were also collected. Their presence here implies that there were tessellated pavements, hypocausts and heated rooms, some at least with translucent window glass to keep out the damp and allow in the sunlight. More than 300 fragments of vesicular tufa, a material which might have been put to use as lightweight roofing or aggregate in a domestic bath-house, were also recovered from excavation and fieldwalking.

A good standard of accommodation seems certain, but the absence of a clear plan inevitably leaves the site open to competing interpretations. Nick Corcos argues that the proximity of the Nidons villa, visible only 1.5km away, 'diminishes the likelihood' that this is also a villa site.[31] His words are chosen carefully, for in an area in which villa architecture is relatively common (on a national scale) such a close spacing of sites is not unknown, especially if the short chronology of the Nidons site is kept in mind. Corcos suggests that 'some kind of religious/ritual complex associated with the adjacent spring is looking an increasingly plausible explanation'. Although no votive objects were recovered, he sees this as the site of a modest rural Roman shrine or estate temple, one that was perhaps being recycled for the Christian church that later stood very close by.

Since there is no structural evidence for a Roman temple or for the living quarters, guest accommodation or shops that we might associate with such a site, we must turn to the finds assemblage for answers. A useful comparison can be made with the temple site at nearby Brean Down, located on a headland projecting out into the Bristol Channel, which also contained very few votive objects when it was excavated in the late 1950s. This was explained by the excavator as being due to the continued post-Roman use of the building, and precisely the same logic could be offered for *Old Church*. Elsewhere in the county, temples sites such as Henley Wood and Lamyatt Beacon[32] exhibit unusual frequencies of certain types of artefact and that is also true here. The first peak is for Roman brooches. One trench alone, 4016/Z, produced six (of a total of fourteen from the parish), a selection of which are illustrated in Figure 4.13. Three date to the period *c*.AD 43–70, two being the 'soldier's brooch', the Aucissa type commonly associated with the Roman army.[33] The second unusual peak is for coins. There are fifteen Roman coins from *Old Church*, most of which date to the mid-fourth century.[34] Four of these were found close together in one trench, the others immediately to the west. The tight focus of dates and location suggests a very disturbed hoard that must have been deposited towards the end of the occupation of the site.

Another obvious place to look for unusual signatures in the archaeological record is among the faunal remains. In this case there is some suggestion of a higher-status diet, one dominated by sheep/goat, cattle, pig and piglets and supplemented on occasion by poultry, venison, hare and teal. Perch and eel were among the fish bones recovered and the presence of oyster, cockle and mussel all show further awareness of natural resources, though marine molluscs were not found in large quantities either here or elsewhere on Shapwick's Roman sites. A dairy-based cattle herd was probably tended nearby, to judge from the ages of the stock indicated by the animal bones, but there were also horses, dogs and domestic fowl outside among the farmyard animals and mole, shrew, mouse and vole underfoot.

Several aspects of this faunal assemblage are worthy of comment. The venison (in this case, red deer) would have been eaten only on special occasions and the wild birds, assuming that they were not chance mortalities, suggest wildfowling rather than opportunistic consumption. The recovery of rook bones is especially curious, given that birds such as this tend to be found in ritual or religious contexts in the Roman period; it may, however, have been kept as a pet if it was not caught for food. Also notable is the high proportion of first molars of sheep in the early stages of wear, something that suggests the seasonal consumption of prime grass-fed fat lamb. This was not commonly done in the past, so were the lambs killed for table provisions, as sacrificial offerings or for their fine lambskins? Either way, there are aspects of the faunal assemblage at this site that are not perfectly in tune with the archaeological signatures of other domestic sites of the same date.[35]

It is unfortunate that we cannot reconstruct the plan of the Roman complex at *Old Church* with any confidence. However, the idea that the site might have combined the functions of agricultural estate centre, domestic accommodation, industry and craft centre and local shrine should not surprise us. There need not have been a formal temple here, as Corcos implies, but we should take his suggestion seriously, and there may have been a chamber with a dedication close to the 'sacred spring' for the spirits who protected the household: a house shrine.[36] Given the local produce on offer at the feast table there were obvious pleasures to be had both socially and gastronomically from hosting deities and there may have been economic and political benefits, too, in a fusion of Celtic and Roman cultures. It is even possible that there were cult centres (Roman or otherwise) at other spring sites. Not a great deal of archaeological work has been done at any of them, although there was some excavation at the village spring and the areas around the springs at *Mazewell* and *Frogwell* were fieldwalked without revealing any notable finds concentrations of any particular date.

Sladwick (Field 1303) – family farmhouse or villa?

The field name *Sladwyke*, as it was recorded in 1303–4, is interpreted by Michael Costen as derived from the OE *slaed*, a 'valley' or 'marshy ground', with the second element being OE *wic*, a farm or settlement. The correlation of *wic* names and Roman settlement has long been known,[37] but on looking over the gate into the field there was absolutely nothing to excite even the most credulous archaeologist. Fieldwalking, too, offered little of interest, and a likely target for excavation was only finally provided by a combination of geophysics, a rectangular spread of buried masonry and soil geochemistry that registered higher than expected concentrations of nickel, cobalt, manganese and lead (Figure 4.14). Mick remembers well the considerable excitement of receiving the geophysics results[38] and the heavy metals data on the same day and realising that the two could be matched up. For the first time it looked as if geophysical and geochemical data could be combined in order to highlight a previously unsuspected site (see Chapter 2 for method).

Trenches were opened at *Sladwick* in 1996 and again in 1998 (Figure 4.15). Collapsed stonework revealed beneath the turf and topsoil was carefully cleaned, drawn and removed to expose the foundations of a rectangular building of fourth-century date. This debris had shielded the building from the plough and so prevented any archaeological finds from being dispersed through the plough soil and thus being collected by fieldwalkers – hence our unpromising results.[39] Figure 4.15B shows the accumulation of fallen rubble over the top of a hearth. The late Roman building, aligned north–south, was 5.5–5.8m wide internally with a length of about 7.5m; the northern end lay outside the trench (Figure 4.15C). The walls were 0.70m thick, with a foundation of pitched limestone cobbles

onto which Lias slabs had been laid in horizontal courses. Subsequent robbing of the site had removed much of the walls and no obvious entrance or window apertures had survived, though Lias tiles provided some indication of roofing materials and, unusually for Shapwick Roman sites, there were large quantities of slate which came from either the Brendon Hills or possibly from North Cornwall.[40] There was also a patchy Lias slab floor laid onto compacted yellow clay that produced pottery sherds dating after *c.*AD 325, among them an Oxfordshire colour-coated bowl, New Forest parchment ware and a range of regional products of varying sizes and functions (Figure 4.16C–F). Where slabs were missing attempts had been made to level the floor either by laying additional slabs or by patching up the holes with mortar-rich soil. No internal divisions within the building were identified but in the south-east quadrant there was a sub-circular hearth base about a metre across that had been cut down into the natural clay (see Figure 4.15B and C). The hearth was made up of reddened and burnt sandstone blocks, and possibly once had an oxidised clay lining, now very degraded.

Externally, a substantial L-shaped wall projected from the building's south-east corner, turning a right angle to run roughly east–west, perhaps as far as 18m according to the geophysics (see Figure 4.15D). Immediately to the north a surface of compacted Lias formed a level hardstanding and there is some suggestion from the geophysics of further buildings here and perhaps an enclosing east–west wall to parallel that excavated on the south side. Including this intra-mural yard, the whole precinct measures around 24m east–west by 20m north–south and lay within a grid of field ditches that ran away from the site in all directions, as our excavations further north in Field 0024 were later to demonstrate. Overall, the coin chronology from the site was third and fourth century.[41] The absence of later Roman shelly ware suggests abandonment by the mid-fourth century, at which time the charcoals recovered from the site show that the derelict building was engulfed by invasive vegetation, such as ivy, elder, blackthorn and hawthorn/*Sorbus*, with saplings of oak and field maple sprouting through the rubble.

Sladwick has the feel of a cottage-type 'villa' similar to that excavated at Barton Court Farm in Berkshire,[42]

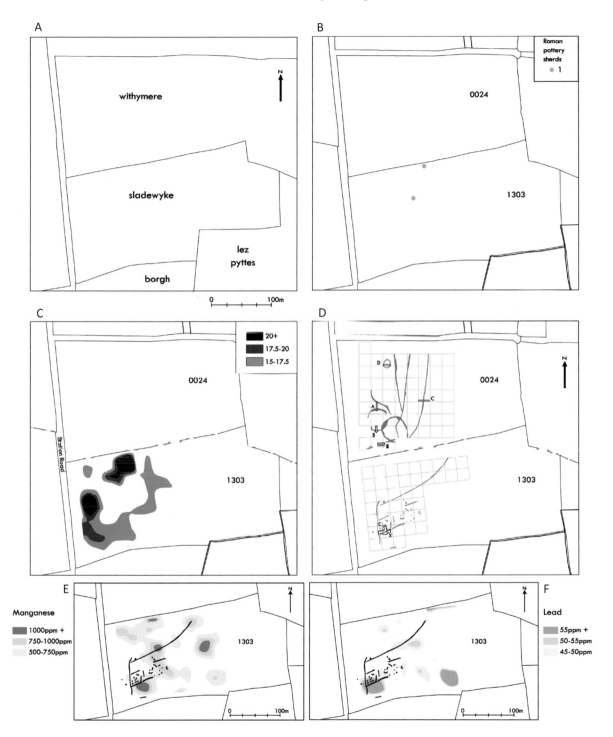

Figure 4.14. Sladwick (Field 1303). A: furlong names in 1515; our reconstructed medieval map identified the location of Sladwick (for method see Box 5.2). B: Roman pottery from fieldwalking. C: magnetic susceptibility. D: geophysics and trench layout. E: manganese concentrations in soils. F: enhancement of lead in soils around site of excavated Roman building.

Figure 4.15. Roman phases under excavation at Sladwick. A: Mick with his broken leg reclines in a wheelbarrow! Behind, Chris Webster (white hat approaching trench edge) and Richard Brunning (blue hat on trench edge) direct the 1996 season of excavations here. B: the hearth and east wall of the building together with the rubble tumble (right). The longevity of species recovered from the hearth fills precluded a tight radiocarbon date. C: Kerry Ely re-opened this site in 1998. The rubble is more fully cleared, exposing the south and east walls of the Roman building, looking south. D: the foundation of the courtyard wall, looking north-east. There is a yard surface of compacted Lias immediately to the north under the ranging pole.

a modest rectangular farmhouse with just one or two rooms. A dozen similar structures are known from the small town at Camerton,[43] and also at Butcombe in north Somerset, where one late third-century building was also found to be single-roomed with a partially paved floor (see Figure 4.1 for locations). Closer to Shapwick, at Bradley Hill near Somerton, both of the two dwellings of the mid-fourth-century farmstead there had stone foundations and flagged floors and there may have been an enclosed yard on

one side of the buildings as there was at *Sladwick*.[44] The added complication here, however, is that the pottery assemblages might be regarded as typical of a late Roman villa, so that, while this was a short-lived establishment with modest architectural pretensions, its occupants owned a decent complement of fine tablewares and mortaria. Among the traded wares present were Samian, Moselle black slipped beakers and products of the New Forest and Oxfordshire industries, including mortaria. Of particular note is

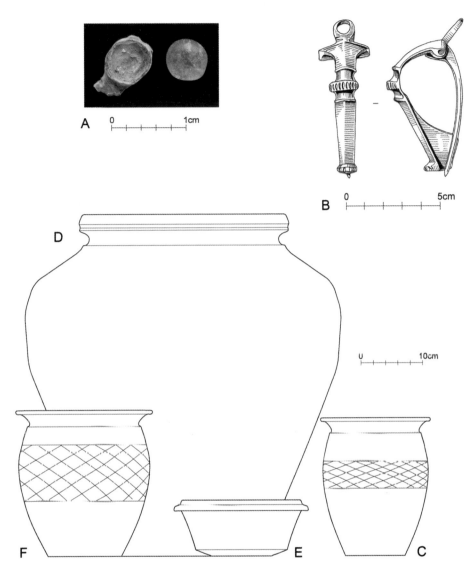

Figure 4.16. Roman objects and pottery from Sladwick reconstructed by Alejandra Gutiérrez including A: fragment of finger ring with green glass inset; B: trumpet brooch, south-west derivative, late first to mid-second century AD; *three Dorset black burnished ware forms: a jar (C), a flanged bowl (E), an everted rim jar (F); and a large storage vessel (D).*

the presence of a number of large vessels and this is a marked feature of the Roman pottery assemblage generally at Shapwick which is presumably linked to the processing and storage of agricultural products.

Thus *Sladwick* does not fit tidily into any prescriptive classification of Roman settlement. A dozen fragments of an igneous rock that was probably dressed for querns confirm the agricultural role of

the site and architecturally it seems more akin to a farmstead at the base of the social pyramid rather than one towards the top. On the other hand, its inhabitants did enjoy a wide range of Roman pottery and this was the only Roman site at Shapwick to produce a finger ring: a hexagonal bezel with a pale green glass inset (Figure 4.16A). While the house was modest, its occupiers apparently sought fashion in other senses.[45] Clearly, there was no standard process of acculturation to 'Roman ways'.

Although as a group there are considerable differences between the four high-status sites or 'villas' at Shapwick, there is perhaps sufficient evidence to group them together on the basis of their plans and finds. Only these sites yielded Roman mortars and plasters and presumably had interior 'finishes' of quality for their walls and floors. Although none of the 'villas' here was palatial, like that at Fishbourne in West Sussex, their owners were also able to select from a range of local building materials, including Lias slabs and lightweight tufas for roofing and walling, soft calcareous sandstone from Wedmore or Moorlinch and honey-coloured stone from the quarries at Ham, 21km to the south. These last two stone types are easily shaped and may well have been carved for doorways and windows, at least some of which were filled with glass. At other villa sites in the region, such as Lufton near Yeovil, Ham stone was used for floor surfaces, door sills and as the lining for hypocaust channels between heated rooms.[46] All this suggests readily available resources, possibly with the intention to impress, but not exceptional luxury. In the complex hierarchy of Roman society these were modest villas, the strongest hints of finer decoration and fittings being the *tesserae* collected from *Old Church* and *Borgh/Chestell* and the box tiles from *Old Church*.[47] These two properties at least incorporated 'luxury' elements that were designed to impress; perhaps they were even two-storied structures, though our excavations did not establish this.

What can be said about their occupants? One theory is that these small villa sites are the houses of disrupted Gallic landowners who set up new homes in western Britain in Romanised taste in the late third century.[48] Agricultural settlements, too, might have been caught up in this injection of foreign investment into the rural economy and, as Roger Leech notes,[49] this could also help explain the rebuilding and reordering of large agricultural settlements such as Catsgore and *Blacklands* in Shapwick (see below). An alternative suggestion, and one that we would subscribe to, is that our villas are the homes of local families who were investing in Roman fashions in diverse ways. The best evidence for this lies in their long histories. The general locations of the Nidons villa,

Old Church and *Sladwick* were all first occupied in the Bronze Age and then throughout the Iron Age. These were places of long tradition for an indigenous society. The impression is of families who were adapting their native customs, rather than outsiders coming into the area with new forms of material culture. While material culture did change, there were in fact long periods of stability in farming and continuity in the families who worked the land.[50] We might assert blandly that native elites sought to demonstrate their social standing through the deliberate adoption of fashionable Roman amenities and products, but the architecture and objects we found at Shapwick better reflect something more complex: in effect, the varying attitudes of consumers who chose their villas as a focus for investment.[51] There is little to suggest a standardised cultural package and there was no single identity to which everyone aspired.

Quite how this cluster of villas could have existed in such a tiny area is an intriguing question. Many, if not all, of these sites must have based their wealth on supplying either the major local market at *Lindinis* or the port at Crandon Bridge, and some of the finds speak of direct links with these places. Large agricultural estates supplying cereals and meat would certainly have benefited from higher demand (from the army and local administrators based here, for example) as well as from the improved roads and trading infrastructure. There would have been a ready market for wool, too, not to mention other products, such as salt from the Somerset Levels and quarried stone. But perhaps not all of the sites we have identified had the same purpose. Some villas may never have been the primary residence of their owners and were perhaps visited only occasionally for pleasure and hunting. The image of a Russian *dacha* springs to mind. Others may have been retirement homes for high-ranking Roman officials with an eye for an attractive landscape. This was certainly the case for country estates later on in the Middle Ages and after, so why not in the Roman period? The obvious place to look for evidence is in the animal bone assemblages, but only further excavation and the analysis of larger samples of objects and animal bone will enable us to probe the differences between sites with any confidence. For now there is only the suggestion of distinctive

Figure 4.17. Blacklands (Fields 5885 and 7758). A: hypothetical reconstruction of the open-field furlongs in 1515, showing the location of Blakelond. Stenehulke, immediately to the east, is OE stan, 'stone' and hulc, 'a barn'. Perhaps it was constructed from stone robbed from the Roman site? B: plot of Roman pottery from fieldwalking with geophysics plot inset (see Figure 4.18 for detail).

patterns of use in the concentration of pig, game and poultry from *Old Church* and high numbers of bird bones at the Nidons villa.

Blacklands (Fields 5885/7758) – a large agricultural settlement

At the north-east edge of the parish on a shallow north-facing slope to the east of Northbrook Farm lies a very different kind of Roman site, called *Blacklands* or *Blakelond*, as the furlong was known in 1515 (Figure 4.17). The name means 'black or dark coloured ploughland' and is often taken to indicate the presence of underlying archaeology: the Roman town at Westland near Yeovil is a local example of this.[52] Roman pottery was first collected at *Blacklands* some twenty years ago by members of the Somerset Levels Project[53] and our fieldwalkers soon collected many sherds of Dorset Black Burnished Ware of second- to fourth-century date, together with a single illegible fourth-century coin. Subsequently, magnetometry revealed a complex of linear anomalies

suggestive of enclosures and at least two ditched tracks running from east to west (Figure 4.18).

Though the evidence is limited, *Blacklands* looks like a small Roman village which can be read as having a planned layout. The geophysical plots and excavation suggest a metalled trackway and accompanying ditch of several phases (Figure 4.19) with a series of rectilinear enclosures appended on its northern side, perhaps laid out in the second century. These enclosures contain buildings towards their northern end, probably domestic housing. Many of the daub fragments recovered had the tell-tale flattened surfaces and wattle impressions created by pressing wet clay into the woven panels of coppiced poles, presumably the structural sections of standing buildings. Among the finds were a plain Colchester Derivative brooch with a pointed foot and hinged pin (Figure 4.20A), bone gaming counter (Figure 4.20B), two Lias discs (Figure 4.20C), two blue-green fragments of late first- to second-century AD glass from prismatic bottles, a second-century brooch

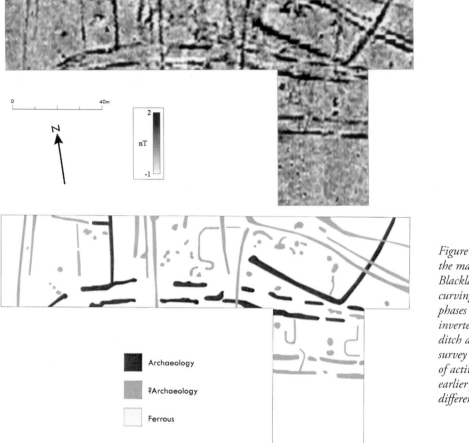

Archaeology

?Archaeology

Ferrous

Figure 4.18. Greyscale plot of the magnetometer data from Blacklands. Pits, ditches, a curving trackway and several phases of activity. The large inverted 'L' of the enclosure ditch at the eastern end of the survey is clearly a later phase of activity because it cross-cuts earlier features and strikes at a different angle.

Figure 4.19. Blacklands under excavation. A: looking south across stone spread of road metalling, second century. B: Roman ditch, probably second century, containing pottery and undiagnostic metalworking residues, looking south.

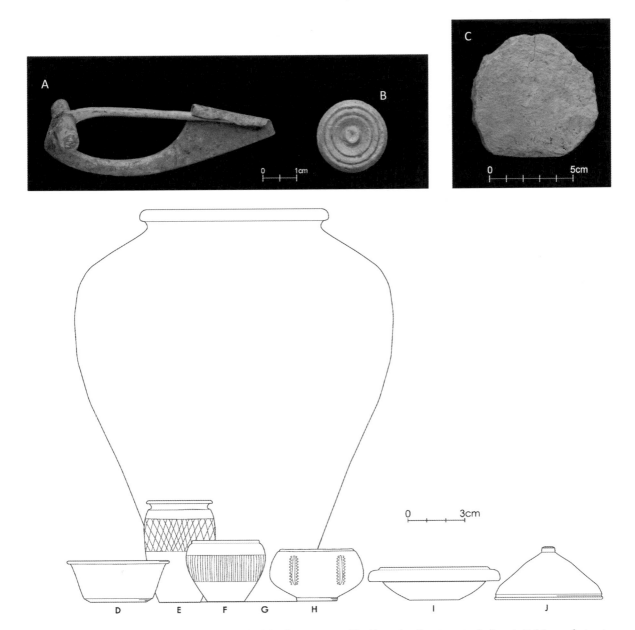

Figure 4.20. Roman artefacts and pottery from Blacklands reconstructed by Alejandra Gutiérrez, including A: Colchester derivative brooch. B: bone 'game counter' with central pivot point, concentric grooves and bevelled edge, from a second-century context. C: Lias disc, possibly cut out from a roofing tile. Among more than 1,000 sherds from fieldwalking and excavation were D: flat rim bowl with black, burnished finish. E: everted rim jar decorated with an acute lattice, Dorset black burnished ware. F: hand-made jar with beaded rim and vertical burnished lines, Dorset black burnished ware. G: large storage jar with expanded rim and incised triangles on the inner rim. H: hand-made jar with beaded rim and applied vertical ribs bordered by incised zig-zag lines. I: mortarium in soft orange fabric, probably Shepton Mallet. J: conical lid with black burnished external finish, south-west black burnished ware.

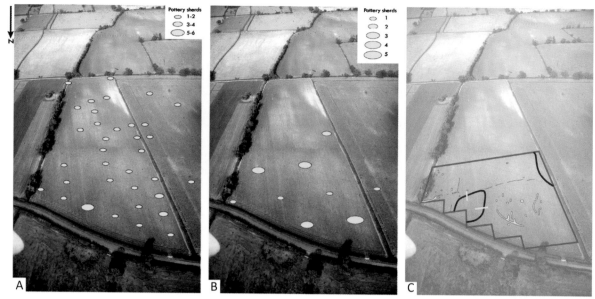

Figure 4.21. Abchester, geophysics and fieldwalking results. A: fieldwalking results showing the distribution of Roman pottery, here superimposed onto an aerial photograph. Material is concentrated close to the road but has also been dragged downhill by the plough. There is no doubt that the site is bisected by the lane, the medieval 'harepathe', and this could well be an earlier route. B: shovel-pitting focused the target area more narrowly. C: magnetometry plot for Abchester showing clear archaeology (in red) including a trapezoid enclosure 40m × 25m with areas of increased magnetic response (in blue) and trenches (in yellow).

and a nail cleaner. All these are typical of household material and reflect the acquisition of some Roman fashions, though the lack of early pottery imports in an assemblage of almost 1,000 sherds emphasises the earlier indigenous character of the site (Figure 4.20D–J).[54] Finally, there is a small collection of cinders and slags – metalworking residues that are suggestive of essential blacksmithing tasks such as the making of nails, knives and farming tools.[55]

The scale and layout of *Blacklands* are highly reminiscent of nearby Catsgore, 4km north of Ilchester, which was excavated by Roger Leech in the early 1970s.[56] That site consisted of several farms within embanked enclosures whose standard dimensions are reminiscent of a planned medieval village, just as they are at *Blacklands*.[57] Like Catsgore, *Blacklands* was not a new location for settlement; pre-Roman late Iron Age pottery was recovered from three of the four trenches excavated. There were also signs at Catsgore of widespread rebuilding in the late third century, coupled with a shift in its economy. The same

might also be argued for *Blacklands*, where analysis of the geophysics plot suggests that the east end of the site was overlain by a large new enclosure in the later Roman period. This implies a major replanning of at least this part of the site and, bearing in mind that the farms may have been linked by tenure to nearby villas, this was perhaps a decision taken by a particular landowner. His or her home may not have been far away, possibly at *Borgh/Chestell*, while those who lived at *Blacklands* might have laboured on the villa estate as tenant farmers. Although these families had fewer means to fulfil any aspirations to mosaics and heated rooms, they too were 'Romanised' in some respects.

A farmstead at Abchester

The field name *Abchester* is no longer familiar to Shapwick villagers, but in the eighteenth century it was still applied to several fields at the extreme western edge of the parish. Since the OE element *ceaster* is so commonly associated with Romano-

Figure 4.22. Excavations at Abchester. Roman enclosure ditch, looking west. Two phases are visible here, the first a narrow cut behind the ranging pole, the second much broader. The site has been excavated down to bedrock here. Note the shallowness of the deposits.

British archaeology (see above for *Borgh/Chestell*) this area was an early target for the Project team. The fieldwalking results revealed a scatter of Roman pottery across Field 1264 and adjacent fields (Figure 4.21) and this was immediately confirmed by shovel-pitting, isolating a site that was then submitted to both geophysical and geochemical survey followed by the briefest of excavations over a three-day period. This was sufficient to investigate a section of enclosure ditch and establish the nature and condition of the site, but little more.

As Figure 4.22 shows, the enclosure ditch had been recut several times but plough damage had removed all traces of occupation except for a single posthole which contained small fragments of bone and burnt wheat grains in its fill. The earliest occupation of *Abchester* is suggested by the recovery of Drurotrigan pottery of the later first century AD. This is confirmed by three pieces of brooch of Aucissa type identical to those from *Old Church* (Figure 4.23A), together with a stone polisher that is considered to be Iron Age.[58] An

Oxfordshire colour-coated bowl, dating between c.AD 325 and the end of the fourth century, and two coins, one minted in AD 318, the other an illegible late third- to fourth-century coin from fieldwalking, confirm that the ditches of the enclosure were backfilled at some point around the mid-fourth century.[59] More than half the pottery came from the plough soil and any archaeological layers other than the postholes and ditches that cut through the bedrock have long since been swept away downslope. Little trace survives, therefore, of what was probably a modest domestic farmstead and, although there were a small number of Lias roofing tiles, the lack of ceramic brick or tile suggests that the major buildings here were either thatched or covered with wooden shingles.

Other sites

The distribution of Roman pottery collected by fieldwalkers shows most of the major sites we have discussed quite clearly (Figure 4.24). Strong concentrations of material were recovered from

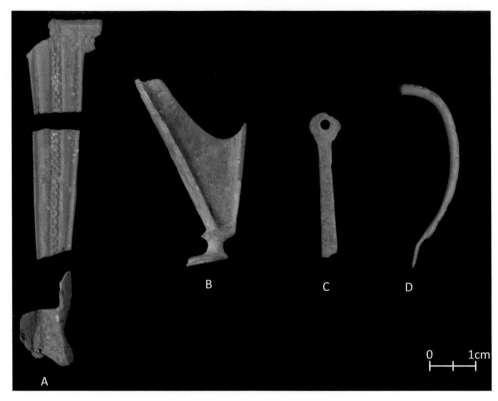

Figure 4.23. Roman objects from Abchester and north of Shapwick House, including A: Aucissa-type brooch. B: bow brooch. C: nail cleaner or ear scoop. D: penannular bracelet, late fourth century.

Abchester (Field 1264 and others), the Nidons villa (4649), *Old Church* (4016 and others) and *Blacklands* (5885 and others). *Borgh/Chestell* (3836) was under pasture and so could not be fieldwalked, while special circumstances inhibited the discovery of *Sladwick* using this technique. As the distribution plot shows, several other fields across the parish did produce low densities of Roman pottery and, occasionally, more significant finds such as the *tessera* from Field 2534 on the Polden slope above the village. Three other areas also produced higher densities of fieldwalked material: one in the west of the parish in Fields 8144/2842, where a second polisher of possible Iron Age date was recovered, another in the east, south of Brickhills Copse (Field 0553), and a third at Skinner's Wood, at the northern edge of the distribution map, where second- to fourth-century sherds were collected by the Somerset Levels Project. The first two scatters

also included Roman brick and tile, an ubiquitous find on all Shapwick Roman sites with the exception of *Abchester*. These might be modest or temporary sites, though, as we have seen in the case of *Sladwick*, in some circumstances the densities of material on the surface are not always an accurate guide to the underlying archaeology.

Residual Roman pottery was also recovered from several locations across the village, mostly from the excavations north and south of Bridewell Lane. The densities of material are very low indeed and could easily derive from manuring during the Roman period; nearby *Borgh/Chestell* is one likely source. However, immediately beyond the northern limits of the later medieval village, the Iron Age site north of Shapwick House (Field 6987) continued to be occupied until at least the second century AD. There is a fragment of brooch and a nail cleaner or ear scoop

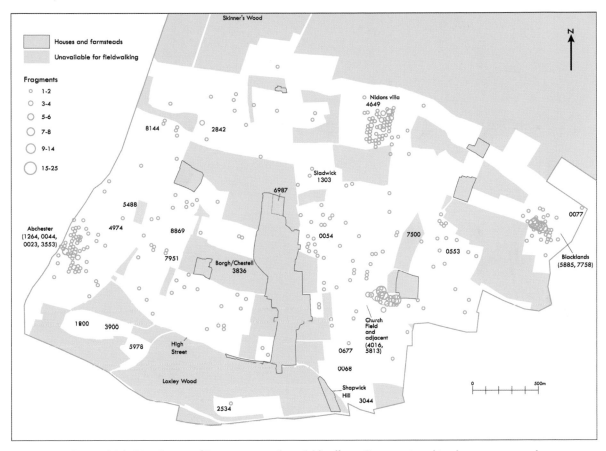

Figure 4.24. Distribution of Roman pottery from fieldwalking. Sites mentioned in the text are named.

of that date from the site (see Figure 4.23B and C). Occasional later sherds, a fourth-century penannular bracelet (see Figure 4.23D) and a possible Roman hairpin were all residual in later contexts, suggesting that the chronology of the site may in fact be rather longer.

In all, ten sites of Roman date were identified in the parish, at an overall density of 1.28 sites per square kilometre, a figure that is rather higher than the average rural site density of 0.8 ± 0.5 sites per square kilometre recorded from surveys elsewhere in Roman Britain.[60] Taking multipliers of twenty and fifty people per site we obtain very rough estimates of 200–500 people in the study area, with a mid-point in that range of 315 inhabitants. However, as the reader will already have appreciated, the 'biography' of each site is subtly different and not all co-existed

throughout the period in question. The degree to which settlements changed in scale and influence over time is often ignored but it may not be stretching the evidence too far to imagine the Nidons villa (early–mid second century to third century) as the centre of a small estate succeeded by a new, grander location at *Borgh/Chestell* (later second or third century to fourth century). Also possibly associated tenurially with these more spacious and sophisticated architectural statements of Romanisation were the site north of Shapwick House (Iron Age to early second century) and a successor at nearby *Sladwick* (third–fourth centuries AD), not forgetting the small farmstead at *Abchester* and the 'planned' agricultural settlement at *Blacklands*, where the majority of the rural population on this part of the Poldens might well have lived between the first and the fourth centuries

AD.[61] Even a comparatively small land area such as Shapwick contained a spectrum of the rich and the poorer, each engaging with Roman material culture in different ways, while *Old Church*, with its long sequence of occupation (Iron Age to fourth century), may have fulfilled a slightly different function. Sadly, there is as yet no solid basis for reconstructing a Roman estate at Shapwick, let alone for making any claims for the continuity of its perimeter or internal boundaries into later periods, as has been claimed for the nearby Vale of Wrington. There is simply no way to establish whether villas and other settlements were part of the same estate, whether they were autonomous or whether historic land divisions, such as Shapwick's modern parish boundary, might fossilise earlier land divisions.[62]

Burials and beliefs

Over much of Britain the predominant burial rite in the first and second centuries AD was cremation, a rare find in this region and probably a continuation of earlier practice. Cremation was replaced later by inhumation. From Shapwick no large inhumation cemeteries are known, though we would expect them to lie outside the main settlements. The only adult Roman burial excavated lay immediately east of *Borgh/Chestell*. This male skeleton, which has been radiocarbon dated to the third–fourth century (see above), lay extended in an unlined grave cut orientated north-east to south-west, with no sign of a coffin or stone-slab lining. There were also no grave goods and the body had been laid into the fill of an enclosure ditch. Note should also be taken of the human tooth from Field 0077 in the north-east corner of the parish (see Figure 4.24). This came from a child with a dental age of 2–4 years. It is undated and might, of course, be a casual loss or one that was manured into the topsoil, but the findspot is not incompatible with the likely location of a Roman cemetery and the location is not far from *Blacklands*. A fragment of tibia mid-shaft was also recovered from Field 7500, immediately west of the known Roman site in Field 0553. This is more likely to be significant archaeologically, but the bone is undated. At the 'villa' sites temple-mausolea are also possible, though none have so far been identified at Shapwick.

One feature of the Roman archaeological record routinely encountered by archaeologists at Shapwick was the skeletons of newborn babies. Unlike the adults, who were buried outside settlements, infants were buried within them, in some cases beneath the floors of houses. At *Old Church* the remains of ten perinates, children who died during or around the time of their birth, were recovered from eight different contexts. Two radiocarbon dates[63] on the human remains have end dates embracing the second century AD – so an early Roman date is possible, though it is not possible to establish their original context. They may be disturbed late Iron Age burials, which were commonly placed in partly filled ditches (see Chapter 3) or, and certainly in one case, they may be Roman-period infants disposed of in a ditch or under a floor. The number of infants and their concentration in this one area of the site might even suggest a discrete children's cemetery such as that at Barton Court near Abingdon (Berks) or Bradley Hill near Somerton, where burials had been inserted into the floor of a byre.[64] However, the numbers of burials at *Old Church* are well within the range expected of a large establishment with several females present among the household.

At the Nidons villa second- or third-century infant bones, seemingly all from the same individual, came from the fill of a ditch. Another infant was found under the floor of one of the interior rooms. This burial had been placed under a Lias slab that was held in place on three sides by vertically set stones. Associated with it was the partial skeleton of a sheep, mostly bones from the left side with knife cuts on the astragalus. Neither of these deposits cut the floor and they appear to have been placed within the room during its construction. Similarly, two burials were found under the clay make-up layer of the floor of the fourth-century building at *Sladwick*: one the ulna of a perinate together with the lower leg of a sheep,[65] another a human infant bone with a young sheep's skull and five hind feet deriving from one younger animal and probably two older animals. Whatever the ceremony was, it necessitated the discrete disposal of these human remains in isolation and in a context that was set apart from normal domestic refuse. The reconstruction by Victor Ambrus (Figure 4.25) illustrates the moment of burial, though the faunal

Figure 4.25. Reconstruction by Victor Ambrus of a child burial at Sladwick. This was one of several Roman sites at which evidence was found for infant bones inside dwellings, in this case accompanied by sheep bones, which were probably the remains of a meal.

remains might equally well represent, rather than a sheep skeleton or a skin with the head and feet left attached (as shown here), what was left of a dish of sheep's head and trotters, a popular plate of food well into the nineteenth century.

This association between buildings and infant burials at the Nidons villa and *Sladwick* is one commonly found across the south-west of Britain (Box 4.2),[66] but these were not places formally dedicated to Romano-Celtic religion. No temples housing deities like those excavated at Brean Down and Lamyatt Beacon[67] are known on the Poldens, though the hill-top location at Pedwell in the adjacent parish of Ashcott has produced coins, pottery and painted plaster (see Story, above). This may possibly be a fourth-century shrine, though no structural evidence has so far been recovered.[68] Its location, midway between Ilchester and Crandon Bridge alongside the Roman road, may be significant. Sites like this, at some distance from a major town, must have served as semi-official meeting places for local communities as well as for the exchange of ideas and news. In addition, every one of the larger houses in

Roman Shapwick and the village at *Blacklands* may have had a small household shrine of some sort and we have already suggested that the Roman complex at *Old Church* hints at something more than domestic occupation. Given the topography of the site, ritual activity may have been based around offerings at the spring, perhaps focusing on its life-giving or healing properties.

Industry and agriculture

During the Roman period agricultural production continued to form the basis of the economy, just as it had done in later prehistory. There may have been other industrial activities too, such as small-scale quarrying of Lias limestone, but there is nothing at Shapwick to suggest the processing of lead ores from Mendip. As at other sites around the Levels, small-scale ironworking took place at *Blacklands*, at the Nidons villa perhaps and also at *Abchester* (although outside the excavated area). There is, however, no evidence whatsoever for salt-making, perhaps a surprise given the proximity of Roman

BOX 4.2

Death and burial in Roman Shapwick

It is easy to make the mistake that the Romano-British people of third-century Shapwick were 'exactly like us', when many customs of the time were very different from our own. One practice referred to by Roman writers such as Juvenal and Pliny and now confirmed by the osteological evidence from Roman sites is the burial of very young infants in and around houses.[b3] In the past this was thought to be highly unusual and explained away as infanticide or the disposal of the unwanted offspring of slaves, though archaeologists have noted for many years that children are under-represented in Roman cemeteries, especially when the enormously high mortality rates of pre-industrial populations are taken into consideration.

The most likely explanation, put forward by Peter Ucko, is that these infants lacked the social identity or status that would have entitled them to burial in cemeteries alongside adults.[b4] Until a child teethed or had begun to walk and talk, they had not yet entered 'personhood'. Adults were not necessarily indifferent to these deaths, but childbirth was far more hazardous and the concept of childhood was not the same as our own. Whereas in western European society today a (disputed) distinction may be drawn between foetuses and newborn babies, in Roman Britain the identity of the individual came to be recognised only at a later stage of life.

It is also difficult to explain how infant remains came to be incorporated into the construction of buildings, as does seem to be the case at several of Shapwick's Roman sites. This was certainly not casual 'rubbish' disposal and a more reasoned interpretation, proposed by osteo-archaeologist Becky Gowland,[b5] is that the house represented the social world of the child in some way. In other words, burial was conducted within the spaces immediately associated with the infant and the child's presence 'reabsorbed' into daily life in that way.

Another feature of the infant burials at Shapwick and elsewhere is their association with faunal remains. These are likely to be the remains of a meal which formed part of the ceremony of burial rather than merely left-over bones placed casually under the floor of the building. The deposition of pairs of animal heads and feet has been noted at other sites, such as Barnsley Park (Glos) and Brislington near Bristol, so in some cases the formalised consumption of food seems to have been integral to the burial ritual. This is, however, not the only explanation. In the late Roman infant cemetery at Barton Court Farm (Berks) three burials of newborn babies were accompanied by the skulls of two dogs and a sheep.[b6] These animals have obvious associations

---

briquetage mounds in the Brue valley immediately to the north-west of Shapwick but easily explained as the easternmost limit of the salt marsh lies to the west of Burtle (and thus to the west of Shapwick parish). Possibly the raised bogs of Shapwick Heath were cut for fuel but no attempt seems to have been made to reclaim the peats, unlike in the Brue valley further north.[69]

Out in the fields the most important contributors to the stock-raising economy were sheep and cattle, and the faunal remains from Shapwick firmly suggest that this was a 'producer community' with evidence for lamb/mutton, beef, milk/cheese production and wool. Both *Borgh/Chestell* and *Sladwick* could have

obtained their meat from dairy-based cattle stock and there is some support for this in the case of *Borgh/Chestell*, where geophysical survey seems to show appended corrals around the main buildings; *Sladwick*, meanwhile, is located in an area of traditional pasture. Fieldwalkers at *Abchester* collected a Roman goad, once used for urging on plough or draught oxen.[70] The material culture of agriculture includes the spindlewhorls from *Old Church*, which show that the spinning of wool took place.[71] Since dogs are evident on every site, either as remains or evidenced by tell-tale gnawing marks on other bones, these may have been guard dogs.[72] A single cat bone found at *Sladwick* may be a wild cat hunted for its with qualities such as loyalty; likewise, they could have been associated with deities – the spirits who presided over the household, the *Lar familiaris*.[b7] Another hypothesis, offered by Eleanor Scott,[b8] sees the deposition of animals and infants as being linked to fertility, rebirth, the economic productivity of the land and therefore the inauguration and long life of agricultural buildings or farms.

A final recurrent characteristic of Roman burial practice at Shapwick is the disposal of the dead, both adult and non-adult, in boundary features. The third- to fourth-century adult burial at *Borgh/Chestell* is one example of this (Figure B.4.2), while the ditch burial at the Nidons villa is another. Inhumations inserted into plots have been found elsewhere, south of the defences at *Lindinis* (Ilchester), for example,[b9] in a fourth-century context where burials were close to and sometimes placed in boundary ditches. At Yeovilton (Somerset) and at Shepton Mallet (Somerset) there

Figure B.4.2: Borgh/Chestell adult burial.

were also small groups of burials within ditched enclosures that sometimes contained buildings.[b10] Recent writers have noted how 'backland' burial of this kind blurs the distinction between cemeteries and settlement.[b11] Of course, it also emphasises the special relationship between certain individuals and particular places, perhaps because they are the burials of the family who inhabited the property and the act of burial reinforced their rights. It could also be argued that burial 'off-site' in a ditch signifies a certain depreciative attitude on the part of the mourners; ditches are places for waste and carrion at Shapwick in the Roman period. However, the careful positioning of bodies seems to go against that idea and suggests a more symbolic purpose. Perhaps the ambiguous status of boundaries (neither here nor there; at an interface; liminal) makes them ideal for burial, a similarly uncertain spiritual state. The practice was not new; there is a considerable literature on human remains in Iron Age boundary contexts.[b12]

fur or killed as vermin, though a domestic cat would certainly have been welcome to keep down the small mammal population.

Such an economy indicates extensive pasture and the sort of short, dry grassland well suited to riding or driving horses. The bones of pony-sized animals perhaps rather like the modern Exmoor pony, around thirteen to fifteen hands high, were found at all the excavated sites and they may have been preferred for field work, for rounding up cattle and for haulage, as well as being a familiar sight up on the Roman road and pasturing on the moors in summertime. Speculatively, one of the long narrow structures at the Nidons villa ([6] on Figure 4.3) could be a stable

block, while an oval chain link from *Borgh/Chestell* might have been lost from a Roman cart fitting or harness. The local blacksmiths at *Blacklands* were presumably kept busy. Pigs, poultry and wild resources, on the other hand, were apparently not widely exploited. Given the proximity of wetter and wooded pasture, the reasons for this may have been cultural,[73] but it is hard to see exactly what, if any, economic benefits were derived from the Roman wetland, other than it being a convenient fuel supply and an occasional source of game and fish for those at the Nidons villa or *Old Church*. Perhaps access rights were reserved in some way.

There was little evidence for the use of wild

plants, with only a single hazelnut shell fragment and no fruit stones or bramble pips preserved, but it seems very likely that the Shapwick villas would have had vegetable and fruit gardens or orchards in their courtyards and out in the enclosures that were picked up on geophysics plots (for example, enclosures [8] and [9] on Figure 4.5). A modified red deer antler with an oval hole for hafting found during excavations at Shapwick Sports Hall probably functioned as a Y-shaped rake or hoe for preparing the ground (see Figure 7.10). More typically, crops such as hulled wheats, emmer and, in particular, hulled barley and spelt wheat were identified from our botanical samples. The latter is a tall-strawed hardy cereal with good baking and milling qualities. Possible evidence for a corn-drying oven, a malt house or even a smoking chamber came from excavations at *Old Church*, where many hundreds of fragments of fired clay weighing 526g were found in a single trench.[74] Grain must have been stored too, partly to provide for the following year's crop and partly for milling into flour, and the large southern building in the west range of the Nidons villa (Figure 4.3) may perhaps be a barn with an entrance at its southern gable end. Among the products stored here may have been straw, either for animal bedding or for thatching; archaeobotanists Vanessa Straker, Gill Campbell and Wendy Davies were able to deduce this from the weeds present on the site.[75]

Also at the Nidons villa a small pit was found to contain thousands of grains of charred wheat cereal and cereal chaff, mainly of hulled wheat and spelt, the latter being particularly favoured during the Roman period. These remains are probably the result of a 'parching' of the spelt before it was pounded to release the grains, the crop being accidentally burnt and therefore discarded. Quern stone fragments identified by stone specialist Fiona Roe are evidence of the next stage in the process – milling. Most querns from Shapwick Roman sites are fashioned from Mendip Old Red Sandstone from the Beacon Hill quarry near Shepton Mallet. Other lithologies include greensand from Pen Pits on the borders of Dorset, Somerset and Wiltshire and a quern of igneous stone found at *Sladwick* whose geological origin is Hestercombe, near Taunton.[76]

Pulling back from this archaeological detail, the Roman countryside at Shapwick was clearly a patchwork of land uses and agricultural activities. The spreads of Roman pottery collected by Shapwick fieldwalkers are remarkably even, implying control over patterns of refuse disposal and land use. They are not at all the kinds of distinctive 'haloes' of pottery that might be expected had some sort of infield–outfield system been in operation and manuring had taken place with greater intensity close to settlements. That said, we do not know in detail which areas were cultivated when, what fields might relate to the different settlements we have identified, or even if some sort of crop rotation was practised. Much of this material is concentrated between the 10m and 60m contours, suggesting that this band of land is likely to have been the arable core right along the Polden flank. On the other hand, it is precisely the absence of pottery that suggests a continuous block of pasture on the north side of the Nidons in the area of modern Coppice Gate Farm. This is not far from the Nidons villa, which we have already suggested may have had a large stable block for horses. Other isolated fields can be singled out across the parish and closely match those indicated as pasture in the eighteenth and nineteenth centuries. In the south of the parish, Loxley Wood seems to have been considerably more extensive than it is today and was probably actively managed. Charcoal recovered from Roman layers demonstrates the presence locally of oak, ash, blackthorn and the hawthorn/*Sorbus* group, all of which were used as domestic fuels. Taken together, the fieldwork evidence seems in tune with the broader picture obtained from pollen studies.[77]

Our excavations and geophysics also picked up traces of the rural infrastructure of lanes and fields. Some Roman field boundaries were found to be sizeable, that north of *Sladwick* in Field 0024 being 1.75m wide and perhaps 0.80m in depth, presumably with a hedge running beside it. Roman tracks tended to be simple, with lightly metalled surfaces like that excavated at *Buddle/Bassecastel* (Field 2700); they have single or double ditches and sometimes followed earlier alignments. Other, better-frequented routes were more significant: that running through the middle of the settlement at *Blacklands* had a solid capping up to 0.30m thick and stone-covered drains alongside, and was more substantial, in fact, than the Poldens road. Unfortunately we have very little understanding of the matrix of fields, tracks, roads and settlements and how they connected with each other or the wider world. Given that the response of the archaeology to aerial photography is generally quite poor across the parish, a helpful way forward, as we have already discussed in Chapter 3, is to measure the prevailing orientations of boundaries observed on historical maps. This exercise shows a discrete set of boundaries aligned at 105° (and at right angles to that) mostly in the west of the parish, corresponding with the later Iron Age and Roman settlements at *Abchester* and *Borgh/Chestell* but also including similar alignments to the east of the village near *Sladwick* and the Nidons villa. We argued in Chapter 3 for an advanced stage of land clearance in later prehistory but there may also have been a slight realignment of some field boundaries during the later Iron Age and Roman periods as settlements increased in number and size. Obviously this has important implications for the dating of parts of the surviving modern landscape, but at this stage it is best treated as no more than an invitation for more systematic study of field boundary patterns over a wider area.

In this chapter we have begun, in a small way, to reveal the nature of Roman life and settlement on the Poldens and to show how archaeologists reach their conclusions about the communities that once existed there. Through a suite of settlements and artefacts we have seen how archaeology provides direct evidence for the presence of blacksmiths, carters, farriers, thatchers, shearers and weavers, ditch diggers, woodsmen, ploughmen and labourers. Skills were also available in construction: there were middlemen selling products such as building stone, slate and ceramic tiles, craftsmen to lay floors and carpenters to raise timber buildings. To these we should add the bakers and butchers, estate administrators and landowners. Just like Shapwick farmers today, these people understood their local conditions, knew the weather and the soils underfoot. Unseasonable weather, fine harvests, rising prices – these were the topics of everyday conversation for those living in the countryside: which is to say, most of the inhabitants of *Britannia*. Much of this farming knowledge and practice was the product of long tradition, but there was also transformation in people's lives. Conquest had stimulated a market economy with novel products and services and now fed a growing population with new material wealth through a changing infrastructure. All that, however, was about to change.

CHAPTER FIVE

Postholes and People

From the End of the Roman Empire to the Early Middle Ages, *c*.AD 350–*c*.AD 800

All around lay crumbling ruins – walls of stone, red tiles and mounds of building rubble that were too hummocky to plough. Iseult knew well enough that people had been buried there. It was old ground and she respected that. Away to one side stood the old king's hall, smoke blowing away from the reed thatch and out over the spring. It would be warm in there, she thought, out of the blustering wind that came in across the bog. Her husband, Lyfing, and the other families scattered in the farms across the hillside had been out since first light driving their lambs and sheep to the reeve of the new abbey at Glaston. They would be pleased to be home tonight.

Hers was a world of tales. Her grandfather, Cynlas, had told her how, many years before even he was born, storytellers spoke of ships from the east taking slaves in exchange for jars with exotic oil, potent red alcohol and other mysteries, but there was no sign of them now. Hardly any pottery was in use at all; there were better ways of storing, cooking and serving food using metal vessels and wooden barrels. No-one thought it worth the effort to prepare the clay, shape the pots and manage the kilns. Iseult's mother said food boiled in clay pots tasted muddy, others that it brought bad luck.

The future seemed so uncertain. The elders in particular complained that the old system of law and order had broken down. They told of a mythical lifestyle of mighty banquets and indolent days of bathing and leisure that had gone for good. The farmers, though, were glad not to have to pay so much tax and keep so many soldiers and officials hanging around. There were new laws now. Only a week ago Lyfing had taken the food renders to the royal hall at the far end of the ridgeway. The renowned King Ine of Wessex, whom they had seen hunting crane out in the marsh with his band of thegns, seemed to be making sure that everyone was treated fairly; though to be born a Saxon was to be worth more than to be born a Briton. At least her children would not suffer from the slur of being British; they were both christened with Saxon names – Lyfing after his father and Ingeld after the king's brother.

Strange matters were afoot, things she did not understand. Only yesterday, as they gathered around the fire in the centre of the hall, there had been talk of the holy men who lived with so little out on the inaccessible islands in the marshes. It was said that they had done well out of the new church. In exchange for their lonely life, Ine and his eccentric bishop Aldhelm had had them moved into the new monastery being built at Glaston. Its position at the foot of the hill made it more accessible and, in return, they would be expected to look after the spiritual welfare of the people on the surrounding estates. At least the monks wouldn't starve now, quite the opposite. They had been given a lot of land, including the estate of Pouholt. Iseult wondered why they needed the land at all; they seemed to relish being poor, and what were they going to do with all the produce from it? Perhaps it would go to support the Irish priests and pilgrims who still passed through the area, travelling between Ireland and the continent. Many carried relics of obscure holy men, toe bones and bits of skull, that were said to have holy healing powers. Cynlas had once told Iseult how one of them, a holy woman called Brigid, had become an anchoress on an island at Glaston that people now called Bekeria or 'little Ireland'.

Iseult's world of *c*.AD 700 is perhaps the most difficult to reconstruct. She was probably a descendent of the same (but more-Romanised) people who were around in the fourth century and could doubtless have traced her ancestry back into prehistory. We would call her 'British' (Brythonic), a native of the island and a descendant of those who lived under Roman authority, as opposed to 'English' and therefore with some Anglo-Saxon ancestry, like her husband. Her parent's language was almost certainly Celtic,[1] though Iseult may well have spoken English at home, and she was probably a Christian. Excavations at Wells have suggested possible Christian continuity from the late Roman mausoleum to the Anglo-Saxon cathedral.[2] The burials referred to here are at *Sladwick*. Iseult's grandfather spoke truthfully of tablewares that were imported from the East Mediterranean and Tunisia in the first half of the sixth century and these wares may have been exchanged locally for metals or their ores or quite possibly slaves, as we suggest here. We hear about British slaves from the Byzantine historian Procopius of Caesarea. The evidence for the early church at Glastonbury has been discussed by Philip Rahtz.[3] By the reign of King Ine of Wessex (AD 688–726) most of Somerset was probably fully under Anglo-Saxon political domination and Ine certainly built, or perhaps rebuilt, a church at Glastonbury at the Abbey site. Certain clauses in the Laws of Ine, which date to AD 694–9, seem to make reference to Britons just like Iseult.[4]

Shapwick in 'late antiquity'

This chapter discusses Shapwick in the 400 years between the end of the Roman period and around AD 800, by which time Shapwick lands belonged to the Abbey at Glastonbury. The principal problem in this period, in this part of Britain at least, is the recognition of archaeological sites when their structural remains are so slight and distinctive artefacts so elusive.[5] Local Roman towns, Bath and Ilchester among them, were either abandoned or occupation in them changed its character so dramatically that we no longer recognise it so easily in the archaeological record.[6] Even villas such as Lopen and Ilchester Mead, where new mosaics were still being laid after AD 350,[7] had no long-term future. Many similar sites were either demolished or abandoned, possibly as a result of raiding, while temples, after a period of development in the fourth century, disappear too in the succeeding centuries.[8] Well before the conventional end date of Britain as a Roman territory in *c*.AD 409, 'Romanitas' had already ended; Somerset had ceased to form a part of any 'Roman world system'.[9]

Turning now to the evidence from Shapwick, what can we see? Surely the four metalwork and coin hoards found on Shapwick Heath are a sign of these disrupted times. They form part of a cluster in the West Country during the period AD 395–410 (Figure 5.1).[10] Of the three hoards discovered in the 1930s, two are earthenware beakers containing silver coins while the third is a pewter canister with bronze coins

inside. All were found within a few metres of each other and it could reasonably be conjectured that they were deposited by the same person or family, though quite possibly on separate occasions. Other finds of bronze bowls have also been recovered and, while the Shapwick Project was underway, another discovery was unearthed by local resident Sir David Allen with his rotavator, in low-lying pasture to the north of the village. This collection consisted of seven Roman vessels including dishes, a pedestelled bowl and two small cups.[11] If nothing else, this rich concentration of valuables is testament to the success of the commercial ventures and personal wealth of local farmers and to the social stress they perceived during the last years of the fourth century and into the first decades of the fifth century.

As we discovered in Chapter 4, hoarding had long been a feature of Roman Britain, but it was only at the end of the fourth century that such deposits came to include suites of multiple objects such as coins and sets of complete metal items. The threat was clearly powerful and urgent, perhaps a matter of life or death. The likely causes of this were economic breakdown, a lack of goods and coinage in circulation, a financial system that had ceased to operate and a chaotic political situation. Though it does seem curious that there is no evidence for the defence of settlements, we can speculate that law and order had broken down too, leaving Poldens farmers in fear for their future, divided among themselves and exposed to Saxon

Figure 5.1. Shapwick metalwork hoards. One of the 1930s hoards was found in 1936 by James Crane, a peat digger. It consisted of a pewter cup capped by two dishes; inside the cup was a beaker containing 120 late-fourth-century silver coins.

raiding.[12] If we are looking for a crude modern analogy then the local re-emergence of cultural differences following the withdrawal of colonial powers in the Balkans might be one parallel.[13] The fact that so many Shapwick hoarders never returned to collect their valuables seems to speak eloquently enough of

their fate,[14] though other interpretations are possible; as we saw in Chapter 3, at least some hoards may have been religious offerings, perhaps in the hope of salvation from the social and economic collapse that their owners were witnessing around them. Was the wetland a sacred place? And, if so, to what extent was there continuity of practice from late prehistory?

Of the nine Roman sites discussed in Chapter 4 all were receiving fewer pottery finewares in the first half of the fourth century,[15] but not one can be *proved* to have been occupied beyond *c*.AD 360–370. Shapwick sites have a notably lower share of the fineware pottery market from the Oxfordshire and New Forest industries than many other sites in the region, such as Catsgore, Bradley Hill and Kenn Moor, while later Roman shell-tempered wares are notably absent. Indeed, some of the Roman field boundaries we excavated at *Borgh/Chestell* and north of *Sladwick* (Field 6987) were already filled in by the middle of the fourth century AD, which implies that they were no longer maintained. On the face of it, the case for severe disruption of settlement looks convincing. However, we need to be careful how we go about our interpretations. Does an absence of evidence really provide convincing evidence of absence? It may be that finewares failed to reach Shapwick simply because the supply routes that had previously supplied Samian, amphoras and other imports were not now so accessible.[16] Rather than suffering a dropping-off of population and demand, Shapwick may now have lain towards the edge of pottery distributions such as Roman shell-tempered wares. On this basis there might be greater continuity of settlement than the pottery evidence allows for, so perhaps occupation persisted but left behind fewer visible traces for the archaeologist to detect. If Roman pottery was recycled, for example, and pressed into longer periods of service, or if material culture changed little, or if pottery was not in use at all and wood had been substituted, then we might easily mis-read the evidence. Similarly, coins may have circulated for longer. Arguing in this way, the pendulum of the debate can be swung back again towards some form of continuity. While as archaeologists we might observe a change in material culture from the mid-fourth century, by other measures of continuity, in land tenure or administration, for example, the 'end of Roman Britain' might have been a process that extended well into the fifth century.

Entering a sub-Roman world

For much of the period AD 400–700 Somerset lay well beyond Anglo-Saxon influence and culture. Pagan Anglo-Saxon burials[17] and characteristic early Anglo-Saxon buildings such as sunken-floored buildings, or *grubenhauser*,[18] are barely represented in the county's archaeological record. Somerset lies in a sort of 'no-man's land'. In the east of Britain there are fifth-century Anglo-Saxon sites which are well studied, well excavated and reasonably well dated.[19] Meanwhile, in the far west, there are many more sites and settlements that have been identified by excavation and dated by imported Mediterranean pottery (Figure 5.2). But in between, in the western half of England and outside early Anglo-Saxon settlement, our knowledge of fifth-century 'British' occupation remains poor or non-existent.[20] Roger White argues that the Roman province of *Britannia Prima*, which included along its eastern border the later counties of Dorset, Somerset, Gloucestershire, Worcestershire, Herefordshire, Shropshire and Cheshire, remained essentially 'Roman' longer than anywhere further to the east – on into the sixth and seventh centuries AD.[21] New forms of governance and power must have taken hold almost as soon as the Poldens were free of Roman rule, one clear response to this being the refurbishment of Iron Age hillforts such as nearby South Cadbury and Cadbury Congresbury from the late fifth century onwards.[22] Presumably Durotrigian towns such as *Lindinis* (Ilchester) could no longer be defended and a renewal of activity at hillforts and other elite sites by local war lords relates to the eventual emergence of kingship. The forging of the identities of new kingdoms is implied by the sixth-century writer Gildas: 'Britain has kings, but they are tyrants'.[23] In turn, this new pattern would then be swept away by the expansion of Anglo-Saxon kingdoms late in the sixth and seventh centuries AD. It is in this context that we should see the origin of the legends of King Arthur (though they may go back into prehistory), as a post-Roman or late Roman commander defending his British kingdom against incursions from the east.

Finding out what happened on the Poldens during this time is no easy matter. The lifeblood of archaeological chronology in the historic periods is pottery, but, as we saw above, potters and other craftsmen no longer operated in this part of Britain and would not do so again for many centuries. Coins, too, had ceased to be minted and even imported coins were in short supply. Yet there *were* people living in the landscape, and there were cows to be milked, sheep to be sheared and pigs to be fattened. Radiocarbon dates for several sites across the region (see Figure 5.2) show that they *were* occupied: Yarlington, for example, into the fifth and sixth centuries and South Petherton and Peasedown St John in the sixth and seventh centuries, while the Stoneage Barton cemetery near Bishops Lydeard has produced a date in the seventh century.[24] The evidence is admittedly slight but it is there, as we shall see below for the field at Shapwick called *Sladwick*. Whoever these 'sub-Roman' people were – and we have suggested in our story at the start of this chapter that they were mostly descendents of the Romano-British people who had lived on the Poldens for many generations – our guess is that their material world consisted partly of reused objects made before *c.*AD 400 and partly of newly manufactured ones that have not survived because they were made of perishable materials. Although the old villa lands were now under new control, the types of objects in circulation make local communities almost invisible to us.[25]

There has been much discussion about exactly when the Anglo-Saxons 'took over' the West Country. In 1960 the landscape historian William Hoskins wrote a seminal paper looking at records of battles and trying to make sense of an 'advance' by the kingdom of Wessex westwards into Devon.[26] Archaeologists Philip Rahtz and Peter Fowler, at about the same time as the historian John Morris, emphasised particularly the significance of the battle of Dyrham in AD 577, when Bath (and its region?) were taken over. The battle of *Peonnan* (?Penselwood in south-east Somerset) in AD 658 perhaps marked the real 'takeover' of what is now the county of Somerset;[27] afterwards the British are said to have been driven back to the line of the river Parrett,[28] and most scholars would probably still agree that the Saxons were politically and militarily dominant in Somerset by the end of the seventh

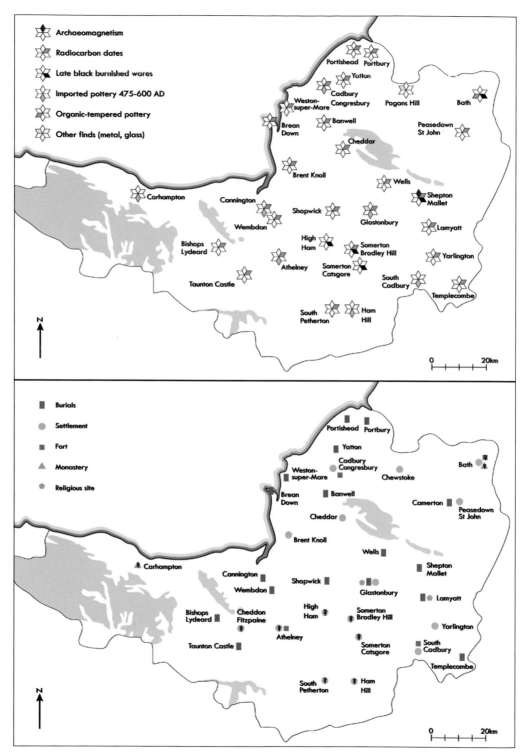

Figure 5.2. Two maps illustrating firm evidence for occupation in AD *400–700 in Somerset. Above: a county map illustrating six means of dating from radiocarbon to finds of imported fifth- and sixth-century pottery such as amphoras and fine red-slipped wares. This pottery seems to represent traded goods between Britain and the eastern Roman Empire in two phases of importation between* AD *475–525 (products from the north-eastern Mediterranean) and* AD *525–550 (products from the Carthage area of North Africa), though there is also a small amount of pottery from western Gaul from the sixth century which continues to arrive until the seventh century. The map below illustrates the types of sites identified to date and their even scatter across the county.*

century.[29] The first charter for Glastonbury Abbey is from AD 670, during the reign of Cenwalh,[30] and by this date the 'Anglo-Saxon zone' certainly extended to the west of Shapwick. Nevertheless, it remains true that identifiable Anglo-Saxon material culture of fifth- to seventh-century date is rare across Somerset, and burial and settlement evidence is very ephemeral indeed.[31] The absence of recognisable Saxon burials is, of course, mostly the result of the conversion to Christianity that had taken place by the mid-seventh century, before Somerset was drawn into the Anglo-Saxon world. For the most part, grave goods cease to be present in Christian burials, and at that point it becomes much more difficult to identify Anglo-Saxon burials, though radiocarbon dating is now helping to expose a truer picture (see Figure 5.2).

A great estate of *Pouholt*

In the kind of non-commercial society that is assumed to have existed over much of Britain and Ireland in the period between *c.*AD 400 and *c.*AD 700 agricultural produce probably circulated in the form of tribute, land rents and renders according to traditional social obligations between lords and their tenants.[32] One hypothesis that has proved especially attractive is the organisation of early medieval England (and elsewhere) into a series of large royal estates, sometimes called 'multiple estates'.[33] There has been some criticism of this model,[34] but the kernel of the concept is of immense value in landscape studies because it provides a spatial and economic context that can be identified convincingly in the archaeological and historical record. In 1985 a graphic version of the model (see Figure 1.5A) attempted to amalgamate a 'central place', settlements, land use, place names, Church organisation and land units into a single diagram. This has been widely quoted in the last twenty years and provides a useful starting point for our thinking about Somerset during this period.

We can surmise that many such estates existed in Somerset in the early medieval period, perhaps as many as thirty in this one county alone.[35] Those centred on Bath, Brent, Bruton, Chew, Chewton, Crewkerne and Martock are reasonably well-defined examples and, in the Shapwick area, estates centred on Cheddar–Axbridge, Wedmore, Sowy, North Petherton and Somerton almost certainly existed too.

The assumption is that the lands of these estates were in royal hands, although they are usually recorded for the first time only when they are granted away to ecclesiastical landowners – bishops or abbots – following the foundation of monasteries (in this area) from the seventh century onwards. For example, according to Stephen Morland, not far away to the east and abutting the northern edge of Shapwick were the scattered lands attached to Glastonbury Abbey known as the 'Twelve Hides'.[36] These twelve tax-free hides, which are listed in Domesday Book, consisted of land at Glastonbury as well as at Meare and Panborough – in other words, they defined an area around Glastonbury extending westwards into the moor and marsh.[37] Whatever else this was (a vill, a liberty or a hundred, or a collection of islands in the marsh), it is likely to have been an estate representing the earliest endowment (possibly pre-Saxon) of lands for the support of the Abbey.

There was probably also a royal estate or multiple estate arrangement in the Shapwick area in the period AD 400 to 800, and it was Nick Corcos who first suggested the existence of a large multiple estate centred on the Poldens called *Pouholt*. Other early forms of the name are *Pouelt*, *Poelt* and *Poholt*. The first element is uncertain, but is perhaps Old Welsh;[38] the second is OE *holt* – a 'wood'. The present form, 'Polden', with OE *dun* – a 'hill' – is first recorded in 1231, so the later name means a 'wooded hill'. Like many estate names in the south-west in the early medieval period, therefore, *Pouholt* is not a settlement name but refers to a topographical feature. This estate would have included Shapwick, a 'sheep farm', as one of its pastoral components – perhaps a processing point for flocks right across the Polden flank.[39]

In 1999 a preliminary attempt was made to map this estate but, inevitably, the story is rather more difficult to disentangle than we had originally thought.[40] It is important to resolve this, however, because, as we shall see later, the solution greatly affects our interpretation of the archaeology examined by the Project, particularly in *Old Church* (Field 4016). The sort of evidence required to demonstrate the existence of a large cohesive estate in the early medieval period must be gathered from a variety of sources. This includes charters or land grants,[41] the structure of later medieval administrative units called hundreds at, for example, the time of the Domesday survey and place-name evidence. In the case of Shapwick we are fortunate in several ways. Somerset is particularly well endowed with charters, being one of only a handful of counties where substantial numbers have survived from the early medieval period. The Shapwick area boasts a group of early charters that must include the later area of the ancient parish. The reason for these remarkable survivals is the vast archive built up by the monks of Glastonbury Abbey from the late seventh century to the Dissolution of the monastery in 1539, a large proportion of which has survived through to the present day.

Lesley Abrams has discussed a handful of eighth-century transactions involving the *Pouholt* estate.[42] First, there is a multiple grant by King Ine of Wessex of twenty hides of land at *Pouelt* to Abbot Berwald of Glastonbury Abbey in AD 705/6. Following the interpretation offered by Stephen Morland, Abrams suggests that this area of land represents the later Shapwick and Moorlinch parishes.[43] Second, a grant of land at *Pouholt*, regarded as authentic and of sixty hides, was made in AD 729 by King Aethelheard to Abbot Coengils. This is thought to include the land of the former dependencies of Shapwick to the west of the later parish (Catcott, Edington, Chilton Polden, probably Cossington, Woolavington and Sutton Mallet) as well as Walton parish, with its sub-units of Ashcott, Pedwell and Compton Dundon.[44] Third, in AD 754 King Sigeberht is said to have sold twenty-two hides of land at *Pouholt* for fifty (gold) solidi to Abbot Tyccea; this probably includes the later parishes of Bawdrip and Stawell.[45] Finally, there is a record (which is not dated) of a sale of a further six hides of land for fifty solidi by King Sigeberht to the abbot of Glastonbury. This is presumably also *Pouholt*, and Lesley Abrams suggests it should be identified with Puriton, at the western end of the Polden Hills.[46]

Figure 5.3 shows this process of accumulation of territory by the newly founded Anglo-Saxon monastery at Glastonbury as various kings of Wessex granted away their lands on the Polden ridge with successive charters.[47] Since all the land was being granted to the monastery at Glastonbury (Box 5.1) by the kings of Wessex, perhaps we should not see this so much as the break-up of a great estate into smaller units, allocated to numerous owners of lesser status, but rather as the transfer of a large block of land from one major landowner (the king) to another (the

monastery), even though the negotiations unwind over a period of fifty years. In this context, both Street and Butleigh are omitted and Lesley Abrams suggests that the manor of Shapwick may have been remembered as the centre of this ancient estate.[48]

Other interpretations of this sequence of grants are possible, however (Figure 5.4A). One that we would favour sees the first 'chipping-away' of the royal *Pouholt* estate as a grant of land at Leigh in Street (referred to as *Lantocai*) that must at some stage have been given to Bishop Haedde or a predecessor before he gave it to Glastonbury in AD 677×681.[49] The *lan* element of this early name has led Teresa Hall to suggest that Leigh could represent the original pre-Saxon monastic centre of which the Tor at Glastonbury formed an outlying hermitage. This land was confiscated by the bishop and then regranted when the new monastic regime was set up at Glastonbury itself.[50] Thereafter, returning to the eighth-century transactions discussed by Abrams, the sequence may have been: twenty hides in AD 705/6, possibly at Butleigh, though the charter is suspect;[51] sixty hides in AD 729 in one large central block of land, including Shapwick with Moorlinch, Walton and other members;[52] twenty-two hides in AD 754×756, perhaps Butleigh for the first time (or again in confirmation);[53] six hides in AD 754×756[54] at the western end of *Pouholt*, perhaps at Puriton (six hides at Domesday) or a combination of Cossington (three hides) and Stawell (two and a half hides) which is otherwise unaccounted for;[55] five hides in AD 762 at 'Compton', perhaps Compton or Dundon, for which there is no other charter;[56] and twenty *mansiones* in AD 801 at Butleigh,[57] which may be a grant or a confirmation.[58] By AD 854 part of Puriton was apparently held by Glastonbury Abbey, as it was granted exemption from all secular dues on three hides there,[59] but the land was in royal hands again by 1086 according to the Domesday record, when it was held by Queen Edith, Edward the Confessor's queen.

Despite these caveats, most scholars believe that the *Pouholt* estate broadly equates to the Polden Hills and that it comprised all the places shown on Figure 5.4A.[60] This includes land units from Puriton in the west, at the end of the ridge, eastwards to at least Walton and probably as far as Street and Compton Dundon.[61] This Polden 'spur' from Puriton to Butleigh (where it perhaps bordered the royal estates of Bruton and Somerton) would have formed

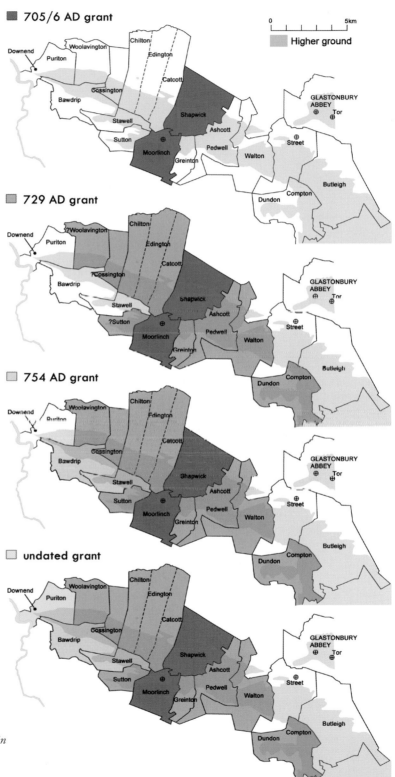

Figure 5.3. Reconstruction of the Pouholt estate, showing the different blocks of land being granted away in four phases, beginning with Shapwick and Moorlinch in AD 705/6 and ending with Puriton at the west end of the Poldens.

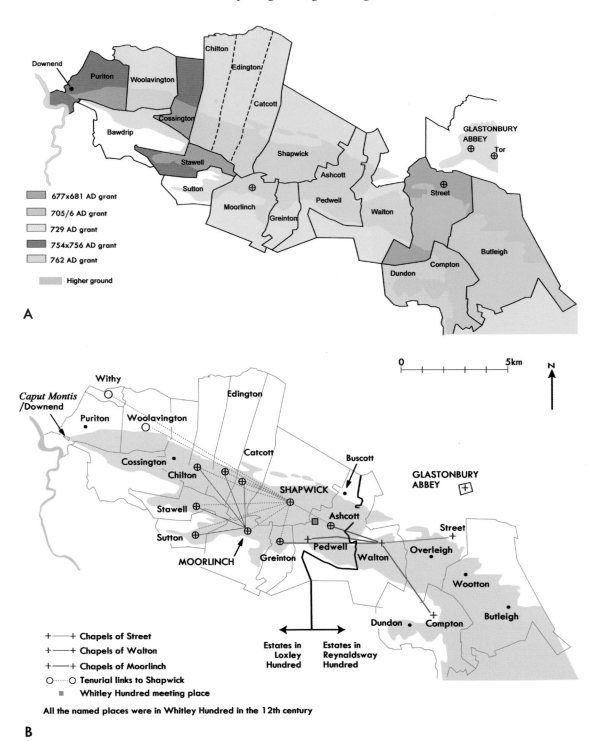

Figure 5.4. A: a reinterpretation of the sequence of grants to Glastonbury Abbey in the seventh and eighth centuries AD. This version stresses the inclusion of lands at the eastern end of the Poldens. B: a map of Whitley Hundred with ecclesiastical and tenurial links between different estates in the later medieval period.

a natural entity for taxation and service, bearing in mind that topographically it is almost a peninsula hemmed in by rivers and fens.[62] The origins of this estate, and others like it, may lie in the Roman period or even before,[63] but this is impossible to prove no matter how likely it might seem to us.

Whatever its earlier origins, by AD 650–700 this Polden estate was royal land and the probable setting for the folkloric tale of the murder of St Indracht and his friends while King Ine was stationed nearby (see Chapter 1). And we may surmise that the land had been in the hands of a British chieftain or minor king for 200 years or more before that. It was then gradually granted away to endow the monastery at Glastonbury in the eighth century, while, at the same time, the abbot and monks were purchasing other areas to enhance the land unit. Taken together, these transactions and gifts would have created a sizeable new monastic estate. No doubt the Wessex kings saw this as a sound investment for their own spiritual welfare and that of the kingdom but the acquisition of large areas of land also marked a great change in the attitude and lifestyle of the monks: no longer were they austere, fasting hermits on their islands in the Levels; henceforth they would become a more organised, centralised and probably better-fed community sustained by their own great agricultural estates (see Story, above).

Later hundredal arrangements and Pouholt

Since our contemporary documentation for the early medieval period is so limited, clues to help decipher earlier estates must also be looked for in the later history of the Polden Hills. Elsewhere in the country the definition of later medieval administrative divisions within a shire, usually called 'hundreds' in this part of England, has proved helpful in this respect because these units are thought to preserve relict features that reflect earlier arrangements.

In the later Middle Ages virtually all of the Polden Hills, our original *Pouholt* estate, was included in Whitley Hundred, which is named after Whitley Wood in Walton, a few miles east of Shapwick.[64] On the Poldens this hundred encompassed land on the northern slope from Woolavington through Cossington, Chilton Polden, Edington, Catcott, Shapwick, Ashcott and Walton, as well as land on the southern slope at Stawell, Sutton, Moorlinch and

Greinton, and territory further east at Street, Butleigh and Compton Dundon (Figure 5.4B). As already mentioned, Puriton, at the west end of the ridge, was a royal estate in 1066 and held by the Church of Rome (that is, by the Pope) in 1086, but it too is assumed to have been part of the earlier estate. This list reads almost exactly as the land units thought to have made up the *Pouholt* multiple estate and mapped in Figure 5.4A.[65] As Robert Dunning has pointed out, however, Whitley Hundred was probably created in the later twelfth century out of two earlier units: Loxley and Reynaldsway or Reynoldsway (sometimes called Ringoldsway) Hundreds. The first of these, Loxley, took its name from the wood high on the Polden ridge at the southern edge of Shapwick, while the second is named after Reynold's Way, on the west side of Butleigh wood. These were the sites where the hundredal meetings actually took place, though they are quite possibly earlier places of assembly.[66] This Loxley site cannot have been far from the later *Whitelegh* gallows, the *Furchdonne* as it was referred to in the 1325 survey of Ashcott, so judgement and punishment were meted out at two sites not far distant from each other on the high ground at the southern edge of the later parish.

It looks, therefore, as if the earlier unit, *Pouholt*, was split into two at some stage *before* the compilation of Domesday Book in 1086, perhaps for administrative convenience, and then recombined again by 1200. While this split was in place the Loxley Hundred must have covered the western end of the Poldens while Reynaldsway covered the eastern end, arrangements that may reflect older territorial and ecclesiastical units. In detail, Loxley Hundred seems to have included those estates looking to Moorlinch as their mother church and to Shapwick as their administrative centre, that is, Catcott, Edington, Chilton Polden, Stawell and Sutton Mallet.[67] As we have seen, Walton seems to have had, at some time, the dependent chapels at Ashcott, Pedwell, Greinton and Compton Dundon, though Walton itself was a chapelry of Street. Perhaps Street (or *Lantocai*, as it was known) was then the ecclesiastical focus for the eastern end, with Walton becoming the administrative focus only later on.

So, through a careful reading of available documents, it seems likely that the *Pouholt* estate stretched from the western end of the Poldens at least as far eastwards as Shapwick. That would be a reasonable

BOX 5.1

Christianity in Wessex and Glastonbury Abbey before AD 800

Tradition has it that there was a British monastery at Glastonbury and Philip Rahtz's excavations on Glastonbury Tor may well have uncovered a small eremetic monastery there. But there should have been a larger central monastery somewhere in the vicinity to which the hermit sites out on the Levels were loosely attached. Was this at Glastonbury? Although there is Roman pottery from the area of the Abbey there does not appear to be any archaeological evidence to suggest that there was a British monastery on the present site[b1] and the Tor was perhaps too small to have been the main monastery. There is a clue from one of the Saxon charters in Glastonbury's cartulary which hints that the earlier monastery may have been at Street. Bishop Haedde (AD 670–706) granted land at *Lantocai* (identified as Leigh-in-Street) and at Meare to Abbot Haemgils of Glastonbury Abbey. This is interesting in two respects: the name *Lantocai* derives from the British element *lan* for an enclosure (usually around a church), in this case dedicated to St Kay or Kea, and this implies that there was a British monastery at Street; and land that had been attached to a British monastery was being given away by the bishop rather than the king. It is tempting to read into this that Bishop Haedde had taken the old British monastery into his own hands so as to close it down because it was considered heretical. Only after the new Saxon monastery was founded at Glastonbury did the bishop grant the land at Street back. The new Anglo-Saxon monastery was situated on a more easily accessible site at the foot of the Tor and laid out in a large rectilinear enclosure. As well as monks, there would have been priests who went out to preach in the surrounding countryside, but they would have lived in the monastery itself. The bishop would undoubtedly have encouraged such a reorganisation because he aligned himself with the Church at Rome and therefore would have favoured the model of the monastery as a community.

The original land grant of Glastonbury Abbey is said to have been the legendary twelve hides which included Glastonbury itself, part of West Pennard, Meare and the islands out in the marshes to the west of Glastonbury. Most of this land was far from ideal for a monastic community that would be expected to provide for its own members, as opposed to one that lived frugally on the donations of surrounding populations, so it is likely that the grant of the 'twelve hides' was a confirmation of lands owned by the original British monastery at Street. Thereafter, from about the beginning of the eighth century, Glastonbury rapidly acquired several large estates, including Shapwick in *Pouholt*, Brent and Pilton, setting it on the road to being the largest landowning monastery in the country at the time of Domesday.

Glastonbury Abbey before the Norman Conquest did not look at all as it did at the time of its Dissolution in 1539, nor indeed like the picturesque ruin it is today. It is likely that the enclosure around the Abbey, the monastic precinct, was not as extensive as it came to be in the later Middle Ages (Figure B.5.1). A ditch, with a bank to the west, was found by archaeologists under the north transept and the chapter house of the later Abbey church and has been dated to the late seventh/early eighth century by radiocarbon dating. The rest of the pre-Conquest circuit, however, is less certain; on the basis of topographical parallels elsewhere in southern England there may have been an earlier, smaller, playing-card-shaped precinct with a triangular marketplace and the church of St Benedict or Benignus lying immediately to the west. The bounds of the monastery may well have been modified more than once, perhaps with a major phase of renovation during the time of Abbot Dunstan in the tenth century. Inside the precinct, traces of several early churches have been found in an east–west alignment across the enclosure (see Box 6.1). Of domestic buildings we know little.

Patronage from monasteries such as Glastonbury attracted specialist crafts such as metalworking, leather and vellum-making, and glass production; these were not merely isolated retreats with limited links to the laity. Indeed, they were actively involved in laying out settlements to accommodate their workers and servants.[b2] The fixed nature of religious communities, in contrast to the peripatetic nature of the royal household, meant that goods had to be moved *to them* for consumption, rather than, as had been the case previously, the communities visiting the sites of production as consumers.[b3] Several minsters, including the older established monasteries, were certainly accompanied by features characteristic of early urban development[b4] and an early marketplace has been suggested immediately to the west of the Abbey adjacent to St Benedict's.[b5] It is noticeable how a number of early medieval monasteries have 'marketplaces' attached to their precincts. Some of these are irregular or triangular (as at Glastonbury), and they stand in contrast to the late medieval rectangular

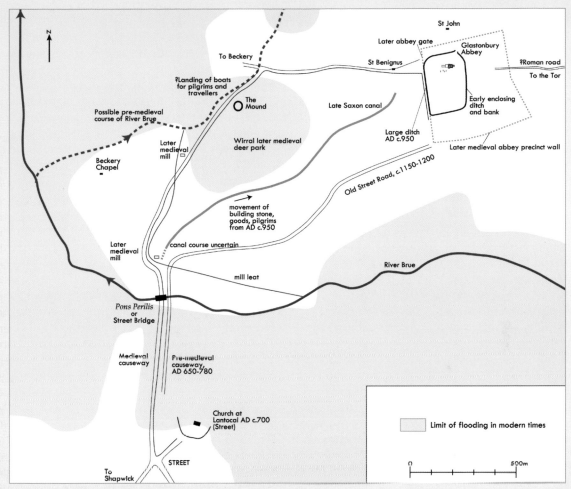

Figure B.5.1. Glastonbury Abbey in the late eighth century. The site lies on a peninsula with wetland on three sides. Parts of the circuit of the early precinct boundary are confirmed by excavation and have been dated to the seventh century; other parts are suggested by local topography. This vallum monasterii *consisted of a ditch and palisaded bank, which probably extended as far west as St Benedict's church. Other features in the surrounding landscape include the pre-Conquest causeway across the floodplain of the river Brue, now dated to AD 650–780; Beckery Chapel, a small monastic site on the edge of the Glastonbury island which was founded by the seventh century; the Mound, where travellers may have alighted in boats to make their way to the abbey, and the canal, for which a tenth-century date has been postulated and which may have terminated close to a Saxon marketplace.*

marketplaces that represent additions or replannings. Examples of these later phases of development can be seen at Ely, Peterborough and Bury St Edmunds, as well as at Glastonbury, where the long straight street past St John's Church was probably the main late medieval market street. In acting as an integral part of the local trade infrastructure the monastery at Glastonbury might therefore have fulfilled several 'proto-urban' roles and been engaged in many of the functions typical of other towns of the period, but without the dense population and built-up areas.[b6] This probably remained the case until the addition of markets, mints and fortified *burhs* that produced so many new urban centres in Somerset in the late ninth and early tenth centuries.[b7] As far as events at Shapwick are concerned, Glastonbury was only 8km distant as the crow flies, 11km along the Polden ridge, and was thus easily accessible for a return journey within the day.[b8] For the people of Shapwick the route eastwards along the Poldens to the monastery was well travelled and it is no surprise that radiocarbon dates obtained for the construction of the causeway across the flood plain of the river Brue between Street and Glastonbury should centre on the eighth century AD, at a time when the Abbey was expanding its interests and estates.[b9]

assumption. But, on the basis of this later evidence concerning the Hundreds of Loxley and Reynaldsway, the estate might once have covered ground even further east that included Walton and Street, and perhaps even as far as the 'root' of the Polden peninsula at Compton Dundon. Quite how far east *Pouholt* extended remains uncertain, but the most easterly parish later to be associated with Whitley Hundred is Butleigh.[68] More importantly, given that one of the hundredal meeting places is Loxley and that most of the woodland bearing that name probably lay within Shapwick parish, this emphasises the point that Shapwick was an important central place on the Glastonbury estate on the Polden Hills by the eleventh century.

The caput and the minster of the Pouholt estate

Having set out the geographical extent of the *Pouholt* estate, a further question to resolve is where its administrative centre, head manor or *caput* lay. The first place to look for clues is in local place-names, which might be expected to reflect the importance of this *caput* and therefore to be of a particular type.[69] On examining the list of known early estate centres of Somerset, such as Bruton, Cannington, Chewton, Petherton (North and South), Taunton and Williton,[70] it becomes clear that each of these names incorporates two distinctive elements. The first is a major topographical feature of the region, usually a river (for example, the river Tone in Taunton or the river Willet in Williton), and the second is '-tun' – perhaps to be translated as 'royal vill or farm', or estate centre. On this basis the name for the *caput* of the royal Polden estate might be expected to contain an element which refers to the hills (as it is not a riverine estate) combined with the element 'tun'. Something like 'Pouholt tun' or 'Polden tun' is plausible, a name that might emerge as a modern name like Poulton, Poldenton or Poldinton, or even Poldington.

Sadly, no record exists for a name anything like that anywhere on the Poldens, but Lesley Abrams suggests that it might be significant that the monks of Glastonbury filed their documentation for *Pouelt* under Shapwick in the Middle Ages.[71] This surely implies a link in their minds between the two. But what sort of link might that have been? The monks' filing system might reflect only Shapwick's

contemporary importance, or perhaps Shapwick was the first portion of the old royal estate to be received by Glastonbury and thus it became *their* estate centre. There are certainly hints from later arrangements that might indicate some administrative dependencies on Shapwick. The *Nomina Villarum* of 1316, for example, describes Ashcott, Greinton, Moorlinch, Stawell, Sutton (Mallet), Edington, Catcott and Chilton (Polden) as hamlets of Shapwick; and we know from other documents that Withy was a detached part of Shapwick and that the nearby Woolavington was also a dependency (Figure 5.4B).[72]

To our mind, however, the case for Shapwick being the original centre of the *Pouholt* royal estate is shaky. In the first place, a *caput* would not normally have a place-name like Shapwick, 'sheep farm' – which implies a rather lowly settlement. It also seems inherently unlikely that the royal *caput* of the *Pouholt* estate would have been included within the initial portion of land granted away to Glastonbury. When the estate started to break up in the late seventh or early eighth century we would expect peripheral bits to be nibbled off the main estate and granted away first before the core area of the original estate was finally disposed of. This is logical because if the land including the estate centre was given away first then the rump of the remaining estate would still have needed an administrative centre from which to operate, requiring a new royal estate centre to be founded, which makes very little sense. As we shall see, this principle is especially critical to our discussion because if Shapwick *was* the first part of the larger estate to be granted away, as Abrams suggests in her interpretation, then it is unlikely to have been the centre of the earlier royal estate.

Finally, we might expect the *caput* of the *Pouholt* estate to have acquired the first substantial church in the area, built as a 'mother' or 'minster church'. Here, too, Shapwick's candidacy looks uncertain. In the late seventh or early eighth century there was a royal initiative in Wessex to establish a network of minster churches staffed by groups of priests: one at the centre of each royal estate. Over the following 200–300 years more churches were founded, usually by noblemen, but sometimes by monastic owners too. These new churches were initially subservient to the minster church, but gradually became the parish churches we know today as they gained the right to perform pastoral care for the people in the part of the royal estate in which they were situated. It is sometimes possible to work out which church in an area was the minster because of the number of chapels dependent upon it.[73]

In fact, for the western part of the Poldens it is Moorlinch that has the best credentials as a mother church. In the ecclesiastical arrangements of the later Middle Ages the chapels at Catcott, Edington, Chilton Polden, Stawell and Sutton Mallet were all dependencies upon this church.[74] But there may be more to the Moorlinch story. The church there is strikingly situated on a prominent rounded high knoll projecting from the south side of the Polden Hills (Figure 5.5); unlike many other minster churches of Somerset and Dorset, which are on fairly level, low-lying sites, it overlooks vast areas of the Somerset Levels to the south.[75] This leads us to speculate that Moorlinch may be a residual 'British' church on the royal estate: in other words, one that pre dated the Anglo-Saxon political domination of this region in the last quarter of the seventh century. This might further suggest that the church at Shapwick was founded by Glastonbury *after* the monastery had been granted the land there.

Taken together, this somewhat contradictory evidence of ancient status indicates that, on the one hand, Shapwick was the head manor of the Poldens and, on the other, that Moorlinch was the mother church of part of the western Poldens. Nick Corcos has argued for some sort of joint arrangement between Moorlinch and Shapwick churches[76] along the lines demonstrated by historian Steve Bassett for Beckford and Overbury in south Worcestershire.[77] There, Beckford was the original minster and Overbury was set up as another mother church within the estate when the ownership was divided. It is not really necessary, however, to argue for such a complex and unusual arrangement between the Polden churches. A solution that fits the evidence equally well is that Moorlinch was the original church for the pre-Saxon *Pouholt* estate. As such it is possible that it may already have had the pastoral care for the *Pouholt* estate by the time it was given to Glastonbury. According to this version of events, Shapwick church would have been founded *after* the estate was granted to Glastonbury

and then later acquired its own chapel at Ashcott. The confusing and contradictory indications of status are therefore explained by changing patterns of tenurial and ecclesiastical allegiance as the old *Pouholt* estate was transferred into the hands of Glastonbury Abbey.

In her model of the beginnings of church organisation in the West Country Teresa Hall has argued that, when earlier British centres were taken over in the Saxon 'conquest', old centres were sometimes replaced by new sites in very different topographical settings.[78] The earlier British churches usually lost their status and became chapels or dependencies of the newly founded Saxon minsters. The best examples of this are Sherborne Castle (*Lanprobus*)/Sherborne and Street (*Lantocai*)/Glastonbury, where earlier British church sites, on knolls or islands, often with rounded perimeter enclosures, were replaced by more regularly laid out rectilinear sites on flat lowlands beside rivers. Similarly, Moorlinch might be interpreted as a pre-Saxon British centre for the Polden area, possibly even a hill top monastery, with dependencies or hermitages within the early estate out on the numerous islands out in the Levels.[79] All this might then have been replaced in the Anglo-Saxon period, from around AD 700 onwards, by a new centre for the monastic estate which was placed at *Old Church* in Shapwick,[80] although Glastonbury seems to have been content to let Moorlinch keep its earlier status as mother church rather than downgrade it to a chapel of the newly founded church at Shapwick.

Returning now to arrangements on the royal *Pouholt* estate, Teresa Hall and Frank Thorn have both suggested that the *caput* would probably have been on the land that was retained longest in royal ownership. According to our interpretation that site must be at Puriton. If the site of the *caput* does not lie under the present village there, an alternative is the hamlet of Downend in the same parish, where a small fortified promontory overlooks a former great meander in the course of the river Parrett (Figure 5.6).[81] In the twelfth century this location, which lay next to a poorly sited motte-and-bailey castle at the western end of the Poldens, was chosen for the failed medieval new town of Caput Montis and there was some kind of landing quay or small port here on the south side of the hill alongside the river Parrett.[82] No recent archaeological work has taken place here,[83] but if we

Figure 5.5. Moorlinch. A: the village from the air, looking north-east; the church is on a projecting spur overlooking Sedgemoor to the south of the Polden hills. B: the church has a late thirteenth-century tower but the site is probably that of an earlier mother church, possibly a 'British' church on a royal estate.

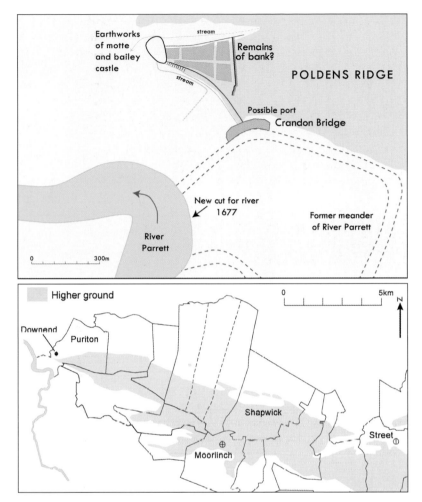

Figure 5.6. The hamlet of Downend sits on a westward-projecting promontory with steep slopes to the south. This is the site of the failed medieval borough of Caput Montis, which was probably established in the twelfth century. It consists of a castle, housing plots, a possible chapel and a port to the south-east. Evaluation trenches in advance of residential development have produced evidence for twelfth- to thirteenth-century occupation and small-scale metal-working. The port was still relevant to life at Shapwick in the sixteenth century, when tiles for the chancel roof were collected here, but the port was soon eclipsed by Bridgwater, further upstream.

are right what might be expected is a royal 'palace' like those investigated near Malmesbury or at Cheddar.[84] A site like this would have been used intermittently by the visiting king and his retinue and, at the very least, there would have been accommodation there for the steward, who administered the royal estate on behalf of the king while he was absent elsewhere. We surmise that there would have been one or more halls with hearths and areas for sleeping, cooking and eating, and that there were probably storage buildings too, perhaps a bakery and brewery, possibly even a separate kitchen. There may also have been buildings for private accommodation together with barns and stables, all constructed of timber, wattlework and thatch.[85] According to this interpretation, Shapwick would have been just one component of a wider estate of which Downend or Puriton was the *caput*; only when Glastonbury finally acquired *Pouholt* was Shapwick elevated to become the centre of the new monastic holding.

We can summarise these complex arguments as follows. First, there was a large royal estate (called something like *Pouholt*) on the Polden hills by the late seventh–early eighth century. The Saxon takeover of Somerset probably occurred around AD 650, so there was clearly a period of anything up to eighty years when the Polden area was in Saxon royal hands before it came to Glastonbury Abbey. This unit may well have originated as a Roman estate or a post-Roman British estate, although there is no secure evidence for this. The boundaries of *Pouholt* are disputed, but we have reconstructed them to include all the land from Butleigh in the east to Puriton in the west, defined as it is by marshes and rivers – the river Brue to the north and the river Cary to the south.

Second, within this royal estate there would have been a *caput* or centre at least adequate for a steward, but probably for a royal residence or palace. It is not clear where this was. The place-name evidence is uninformative, as is the abundant charter evidence. In spite of the archaeological evidence from *Old Church* at Shapwick (to be discussed below), and some weak indications that favour other locations, we present Downend in Puriton as the best candidate. Few examples of this type of site have been excavated, so we are unsure about what buildings were typical or whether anything would survive to be found. Unfortunately much of Downend has been cut away by quarrying and the construction of the railway and the M5 motorway. To the east of the site, however, and in an alignment that effectively cuts off the end of the peninsula, there is a large bank running from the cliff edge in the south to the stream in the north. This might represent a defence for the *caput* enclosure, perhaps one that was based on the pre-existing Iron Age hillfort or promontory enclosure.

Finally, the British Church in Somerset was probably reformed after the Saxon takeover of the area in the late seventh century. Pre-existing centres such as Moorlinch and Street (*Lantocai*) should perhaps be regarded as British monasteries, with dependent cells or hermitages located on the islands and out in the countryside around. This arrangement was then entirely disrupted by the foundation of a system of minster churches by the kings of Wessex (one of which was Glastonbury Abbey itself), although, as we have seen, the earlier importance of some churches, such

as Moorlinch, was still reflected in the dependency of surrounding chapels recorded in the later Middle Ages. New estate churches, of which Shapwick was probably one, were then founded from around AD 700 onwards, along with the promotion of new estate centres, by Glastonbury. One of these new centres can probably be identified as the site partially excavated at *Old Church* (see below).

Settlements

The reconstruction of the administrative and ecclesiastical linkages between places on the Poldens in the early medieval period is crucial to our understanding of the archaeological record. In Chapter 1 we explained how the general model used by archaeologists and historians across the country involves the replacement of a predominantly dispersed pattern of early medieval settlement by one of villages in which most of the local community was grouped together in one place. A particular problem for us, therefore, was to identify where this scatter of early medieval farmsteads or hamlets lay within the estate of *Pouholt*, or at least that part of *Pouholt* that became the later Shapwick parish – a problem made all the more difficult by the lack of pottery and other artefacts generally collected during fieldwork. To try to overcome this limitation a strategy evolved at Shapwick based on the identification of so-called 'habitative' field names, principally those extracted from medieval surveys (see Box 5.2 for method). These are field names with place-name elements such as *wic* and *worth* that are normally attached to settlements rather than fields.[86] The geographical locations of these names in the fields were identified from maps and documents before fieldwalking, geophysical surveying and geochemical sampling took place wherever possible (Figure 5.7). Excavation formed only a minor component of our campaign.

Henry

To the west of the modern village lie the fields called *Henry*, an unusual name that can be traced back to *Enworthie* furlong in the 1515 survey and earlier still to *Emmyngewurth* in 1312–13. This name is probably derived from the OE personal name Hemming and can be explained as his worth or farm.[87] On maps

Figure 5.7. The early medieval landscape, fifth to ninth century. As far as possible the spellings of the furlong names are taken from the 1515 survey. They have been located according to the 'new' medieval map constructed from that survey. Broadwood is taken from the tithe map of 1839. Purycrofte, in the West field, remains unlocated. Key 'habitative' field names are coloured pink.

of the 1760s the fields were called *Ennery* or *Innery*, an abbreviated form of the earlier name. It is not unusual in Somerset for names ending 'worthy' (and sometimes 'withy') to end up being spelled on maps as they were presumably pronounced in vernacular speech, with the end-element '-ery'. On Exmoor, *Pinkery Pond*, from *Pinkworthy*, and *Sweetworthy*, shortened to *Sweetery*, are other examples.[88]

Various scholars have discussed the possible meaning of the place-name element *worth*.[89] It seems to refer to a 'settlement or homestead', but one that

was enclosed, so the idea of a hedged or embanked farmstead comes to mind. Here, a field or furlong name indicating an enclosed farm in what was later to become the open-field strips of the West Field suggests several possibilities. Not only does the enclosed nature of the site signify a landscape different in appearance from that of the open fields but such a name must surely pre-date their development. Any such enclosed farmsteads must have been dismantled when open-field farming was introduced in the parish, whenever that was.

Figure 5.8. Excavations at Sladwick. A: removing the rubble over the top of the late Roman building. B: view looking north across the rubble collapse with the reused hearth visible and the east wall of the dwelling on the right (east). The limestone nearest the hearth has shattered in the heat. One of the post-Roman postholes is marked by the three upright packing stones up against the wall between the hearth and the ranging pole. The fill of this posthole contained adult human bone. Other human and animal remains were found buried in among the rubble.

Attempts through fieldwork to locate an early settlement site for *Henry* began, logically enough, by examining all those fields that bore the name in the past. These lie grouped to the west of Manor Farm, to the west of the village. Gradiometer scanning across Field 7951, to the north of this block in the area probably known as *Estopenwell* in 1515, showed a low level of response, but more detailed survey suggested no more than very weak linear trends that were not judged to be archaeologically significant. This helped to narrow the area of search to the fields south and west of Manor Farm, where phosphorus concentrations and patches of enhanced magnetic susceptibility around the farm buildings initially raised hopes. After further analysis these results also had to be dismissed; they were far more likely to be associated with more recent farming activities.[90] Ideally, our search would have continued in a similar vein but here we hit a snag. During the lifetime of the Project no further work was permitted here, precisely in the area suggested to be the core of *Enworthie*, with its associated furlong names of *Langenworthie* and *Shortenworthie* immediately to the west. *Henry* would have to remain an enigma.

Sladwick

Another intriguing field name, this time one that does survive on later maps, is *Sladewyke* (Field 1303)

(located on Figure 5.7). As we saw in Chapter 4, the derivation of this name seems to be '*wic* on marshy ground' or 'in the valley'.[91] The field today is low-lying, so the name is apt. Just like that in *Shapwick*, the OE element *wic* derives from 'buildings' or 'a farm',[92] and so this place can reasonably be expected to be another former habitation site, possibly a 'dependent' or 'dairy farm'.[93] An important discovery here was a previously unsuspected rectangular late Roman building (see Chapter 4) which had burnt down in the mid-fourth century (certainly after AD 325).[94] However, the story did not end there. There were clearly people around using the site in the post-Roman centuries. The outside walls may have been pushed over after the fire – the north and south walls in a southerly direction, and the east and west walls in a westerly direction. Rubble was then cleared and dumped to one side. Postholes in and alongside the Roman walls suggested that a windbreak or timber wall had been erected in the south-east corner; even the original hearth of the building may have been reused (Figure 5.8). Among the plant remains retrieved from the ashes were sedges that suggest the peat may have been burnt as fuel, though fen sedge in particular can also be used as a thatching material.[95] In all likelihood the Roman dwelling had been partially refurbished in some rudimentary fashion and, although its occupation was not at all sophisticated in its architecture or material culture, it could nonetheless have been made comfortable. Whether or not this was reoccupation of an abandoned building or merely the much reduced circumstances of its last occupants is not known.

A surprise was the discovery of human remains of one or two individuals and a complete sheep skull incorporated into the fill of one of the postholes and inserted in the rubble of the building. A radiocarbon date from one of the human ribs gave a date of AD 430–640 at 96.4 per cent probability or AD 530–620 at 67 per cent probability.[96] The sheep skull gave similar dates. While we are perhaps used to thinking of early medieval funerary monuments in terms of burial mounds and cemeteries, it is not unknown for burials to be inserted into the rubble of earlier Roman buildings,[97] perhaps because the site was revered or remembered, for simple expediency or to avoid taking up better agricultural land for burial, as has sometimes been argued. Given that an older monument was in this case appropriated for reuse, perhaps it is not too fanciful to think that *Sladwick* was regarded as the burial place or residence of ancestors; it certainly would have been more visible as a low mound in the sixth or seventh century than it is today and the use of masonry would have set it apart. Burial here may have been intended to stake a claim to territory through the emphasis of links with the memory of a Roman past. While it is possible that the burials at *Sladwick* were of 'incoming' Anglo-Saxons, it is more plausible at this date that they were members of the native post-Roman British population, in which case the burials may be a continuation of an infrequent Romano-British practice possibly associated with cults of the dead (see Chapter 4).[98] Either way, the radiocarbon date provides solid evidence that the Shapwick landscape was farmed and inhabited.

Greazy, Buddle and Bassecastel

In the middle of the former East Field there is another group of habitative furlong names whose likely extent can be approximated from our reconstruction of the medieval map for 1515 (located on Figure 5.7). The first name of interest is *Grasshaie* in 1515, *Greazy* in 1839, which probably derives from OE *gaers* – 'grass', with *ge haeg* – 'an enclosure'. Nearby there is also *Buddle Orchard* (Field 0011), which was *Buddel* in 1515 and may derive from OE *bothl*, a

'building', 'hall' or 'dwelling'.[99] To the south, a third name mentioned in the 1515 survey is *Bassecastell*. This name might derive from the ME *castel* (from French) meaning 'castle', or possibly it might be OE for a 'village' or 'settlement'.[100] It could also be OE *caestel*, a 'stone heap', though this survives elsewhere in the 1515 survey as *Chestell* which makes that interpretation less likely. Whatever their origin, this group of names again suggests enclosures and a variety of other structures in an area that was later incorporated into the medieval open fields.

Old Church

To the east of this interesting cluster of names in 1515 lies *Oldechurche*, the site of the earlier church. This field (4016) registered the largest concentration of tenth-century pottery sherds in the whole parish and, with its various phases of occupation, it may well have been inhabited continuously throughout the early medieval period. As we have already seen in this chapter, early administrative and ecclesiastical arrangements imply that *Old Church* might have been the centre of the later monastic estate on the Poldens, a focal place, and that there was a church here from at least the eighth century.

Excavations at the site of the medieval church in *Old Church* were intended only to evaluate the condition of the below-ground remains and assess any plough damage; the earliest development on the site was not examined in any detail. In its latest phase in the early fourteenth century the church comprised a three-cell building with a nave, crossing tower and chancel, but there was evidence for more than one phase of construction. In particular, excavation revealed a gap between the east end of the crossing tower and the chancel (clearly visible in Figure 5.9A and B). The later chancel has a stepped west wall, strongly implying that it was once the exterior wall of a separate building. It may have been some sort of small chapel or oratory, to which a crossing and nave were added later,[101] though even this, we think, is unlikely to be the oldest phase of the church, which must surely have been constructed of wood. The choice of location, here among the ruins of the Roman villa, is surely not accidental. The reuse of Roman structures such as forts, villas and towns is a well-established feature of British and Anglo-

BOX 5.2

Field names and a 'new' medieval map

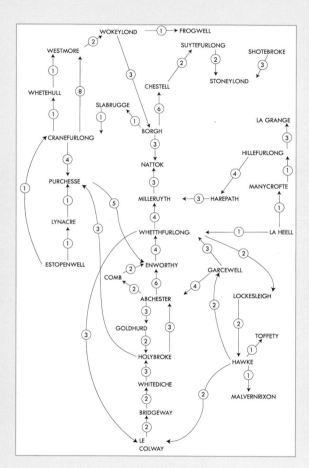

Once we had decided to use field names as a tool to locate early medieval settlements the next step was to pick them out on one of Shapwick's historic maps. This exercise would provide targets for geophysics, shovel-pitting and excavation. Unfortunately, the earliest map for the parish with a complete set of field names is the tithe map of 1839. While there are some potentially interesting names listed on the accompanying apportionment, field names are notoriously fickle, and we were unsure just how far their locations had shifted after enclosure (see Chapters 8 and 9). The ideal, we knew, would be to have in front of us a medieval map to work from and so we resolved to create a detailed reconstruction of the locations of all the medieval furlongs; in effect, we would create a new 'medieval' map of our own. The year selected was 1515, the date at which a thorough survey of lands – a terrier – was drawn up for Abbot Beere of Glastonbury.[b10]

There were two essential prerequisites for this work. The first was a fully accessible version of the 1515 document; this was produced by Michael Costen and revised by Martin Ecclestone.[b11] The survey begins with a brief description of the bounds of the manor and then goes on to a list of incomes and expenditure for the meadow, pasture, quarry,

Figure B.5.2. Flow diagram showing the most common sequence of furlongs in the 1515 lists in the West Field.

Saxon planning, particularly in the south-west of England.

We can envisage several models for the origin of this church.[102] Once it had acquired the *Pouholt* estate it is likely that Glastonbury Abbey would have provided a church for its estate centre at *Old Church*, perhaps to complement the former British church at Moorlinch, which acted as the mother church for other chapels and settlements on the Poldens. Another possibility is that the Shapwick church was built only in the tenth century and provided for

people on the immediate estate, but it is worth noting that William of Malmesbury, writing in the twelfth century, includes both Moorlinch and Shapwick in a list of important churches that were dependent on Glastonbury and exempt from the visitation of the local bishops (of Wells).[103] Even if we may doubt the date of AD 729 that William attributed to such an arrangement, it does show that in the later Middle Ages the church at Shapwick was regarded as being of higher status than many of the churches on other Glastonbury estates and that it was already thought windmill and so on. The bulk of the text, and the most useful part for our purposes, is a list of forty-four tenants in order of seniority and the land they held, furlong by furlong. The second prerequisite was a full sequence of historic maps transcribed at a standardised scale (see Chapter 2). Equipped with these, the 1515 survey was then carefully dissected for any details it might contain. It soon became clear that the medieval 'clerk' had recorded the names of the furlongs for each tenant in a roughly clockwise fashion around the parish, beginning with the East Field by Northbrook. It was almost as if he had a mental map of the parish in his head that he was using to refer to individual parcels and holdings. Within these fields there were almost circular groupings of references, tenant by tenant, as the clerk recorded the holdings.

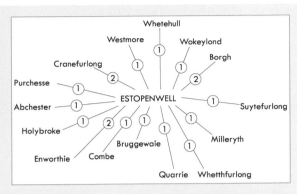

Figure B.5.3. Example of the location diagrams for West Field, showing the number of times each furlong is recorded next to the others.

Crucially, several furlong names had survived to be recorded on later maps and surveys, so some pieces of the jigsaw could be fixed quite quickly, at least to within 100m or so of their true location.[b12]

Those familiar with solving crossword puzzles or sudoku will be familiar with some of the techniques we used. One approach, attempted by Teresa Hall, was to compute the number of times each individual furlong name occurred in the 1515 lists next to each of the others. This produced a kind of 'flow diagram' that gave a spatial impression of where each furlong lay in relation to its most frequently occurring neighbour (Figure B.5.2). An alternative approach was to construct a 'wind rose' diagram with unlocated furlongs at the centre and, placed around them, with the number of instances noted, all the other furlongs next to which it occurred in the lists (Figure B.5.3). This took us only so far, but fortunately the 1515 survey also indicates the number of strips in a furlong and their acreages. These were now added together by Teresa Hall and Martin Ecclestone to reveal the relative areas of the medieval furlongs, which could then be compared against modern maps.[b13] Some modern fields had changed little from their 1515 equivalents; *Whitediche*, for example, had 8.75 acres in 1515 and now has 8.87.

Figures B.5.4 and B.5.5 shows the results of this process for the West Field in 1839 and again in 1515, based on our reconstruction from the medieval survey. Several names are immediately recognisable on both maps – *Coleway*, for example – while others have changed a little – such as *Garcewell* to *Gazwell* (Gaswell Lane still

of as being of some antiquity by the twelfth century. Taken together with the archaeological evidence, this leads us to favour an earlier eighth-century date for its foundation.

Moving away now from the remains of the church, but still focusing our attention within *Old Church*, we come to one of the most exciting discoveries of the work at Shapwick. Excavation in 1999 revealed the remains of a timber building, probably of seventh- or eighth-century date, to the north-east of the spring (Figure 5.10A). This consisted of thirty-six postholes

dug to support vertical timbers, probably of oak, which formed the outline of a trapezoid-shaped building 16.5m long and 7m wide at the east end (Figure 5.11). Later features had destroyed much of the ground plan, so any reconstruction above ground must be conjectural. What we can say, however, is that the building was constructed of paired timber uprights[104] at intervals of 0.6–0.8m, probably with panels of horizontal timbers secured between them.[105] No evidence of these existed in the ground, but the posts in the north-west corner of the building appear

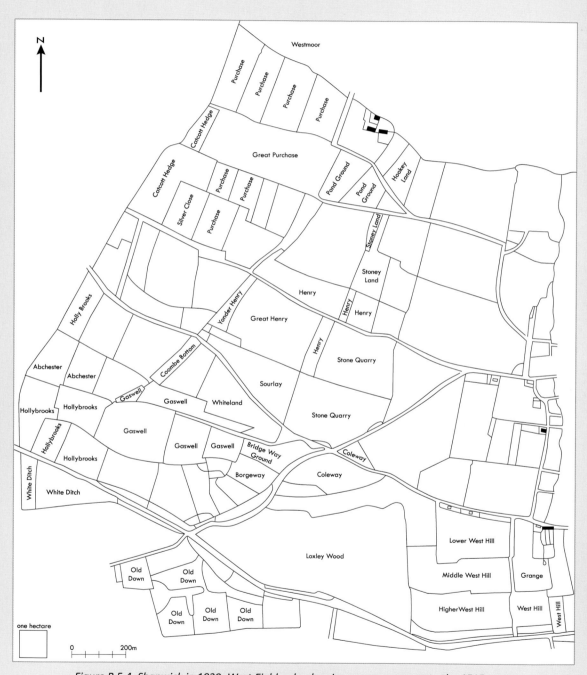

Figure B.5.4. Shapwick in 1839. West Field only, showing names common to the 1515 survey.

exists today). The group of *Enworthie* names in the middle of the West Field in 1515 that had become *Henry* by 1839 is clearly identifiable (see main text) and this is one of the habitative field names that seems to refer to settlements, farmsteads or buildings that pre-date the laying out of the open fields. Other names of archaeological interest here include *Abchester*, from *ceaster*, a 'fort', a site that is associated with Roman remains (see Chapter 4). Armed with our 'new' 1515 map, each of these field names would now be pursued in a series of more detailed archaeological investigations.

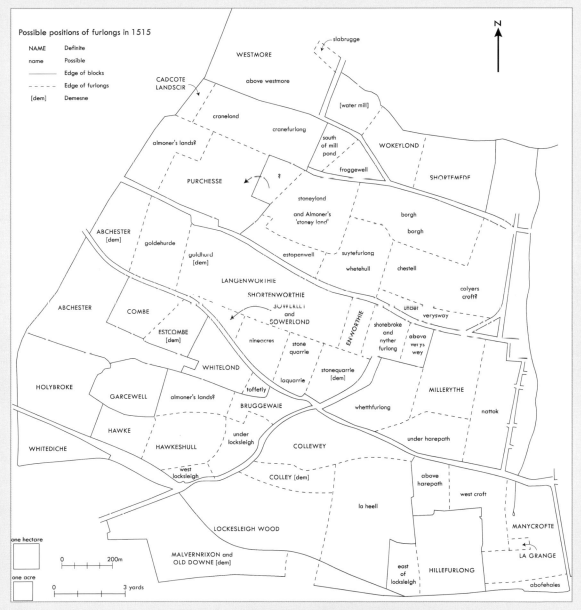

Figure B.5.5. Shapwick in 1515. Possible positions of furlongs.

Figure 5.9. Early structural phases at St Andrew's church in Old Church. A: a view down the 'join' between the structural units which made up the later medieval church. On the right the chancel wall has a stepped plinth and clearly pre-dates the crossing tower on the left. The top of the wall is 0.70m wide and the base is 0.95m wide. B: view looking east down onto the plinth. Note the construction technique used for the walls, with a rough core and a selection of larger, straight-edged stones for the outer faces.

Figure 5.10. A: excavations in Old Church north-east of the spring, here looking east over the excavated timber hall. The flue of the overlying limekiln (R98) is clearly visible to the right of the ranging pole. In the distance the bedrock is exposed. The full plan can be found at Figure 5.11. B: the drip gully around east end of the hall under excavation.

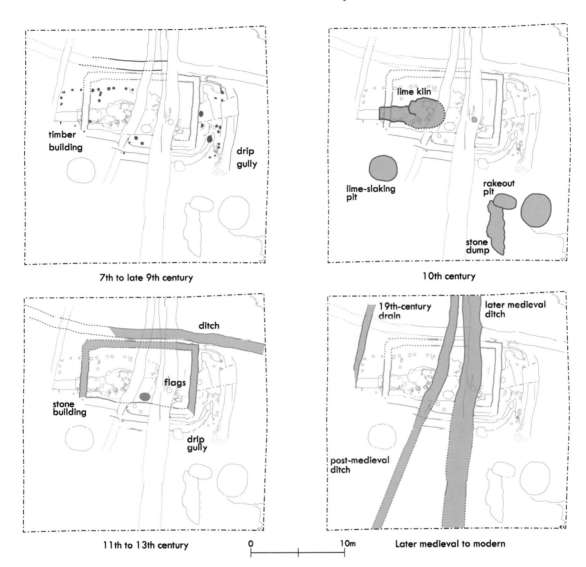

7th to late 9th century

10th century

11th to 13th century

Later medieval to modern

Figure 5.11. Phasing of the various structures in Old Church north-east of the spring between the seventh century and the nineteenth century. Notice how the early timber building is overlain first by the lime kilns and then by the later medieval stone building before, finally, all these are cut through by later ditches.

to have supported north–south horizontal panels, and there was also some wall daub, which might suggest a wattle-and-daub fill between the posts. Since the postholes were not deep this suggests that the timbers were themselves fairly short, implying low walls that would have been capped with wall plates in order to spread the weight of the roof. Some sort of cruck construction may possibly have been

used, but none of the surviving postholes suggests anything as substantial. More likely, the uprights were held in place by tie beams that supported the rafters, perhaps with additional strength provided by internal posts such as R99 and R200.[106] There is no archaeological evidence at all for roofing material, suggesting something perishable, such as wooden shingles or the heavy thatch shown in Victor Ambrus's

Figure 5.12. Reconstruction by Victor Ambrus of the timber building of seventh- or eighth-century date to the north-east of the spring in Old Church. The only features to have survived from such an imposing structure are the postholes for the walls and the encircling drainage gully (see Figures 5.10 and 5.11). The interior hearth was probably removed by the later digging of ditches.

reconstruction (Figure 5.12). No entrances were located, and at this date they may not necessarily have been situated centrally in the long walls; nor was there any evidence for aisles, though an internal partition was added about 4m from the western end of the building at a later date.[107] The building's function is unclear: if it had been a barn for grain storage we might have expected some cereal grains to have dropped down into one of the many postholes, but we did not find any. Had it been a hall, on the other hand, a central hearth would have been present for heating and cooking (see Story, above),[108] but if this ever existed then it would have been entirely removed by later activity on the site.

There are nine radiocarbon dates from the timber postholes here. Together, these give us a likely date for the building of AD 610–720,[109] with an 86 per cent probability of construction before AD 705/6. At the other end of its life, the building must have been out of use by the time a limekiln cut through its floor

plan around AD 910–1060 (see Chapter 6),[110] and the end of the wooden building is estimated to be at AD 810–980. On that basis this seems to be a seventh- or eighth-century hall which could have been in use until the ninth or possibly early tenth century. The precise life cycle of the building, however, is not easily estimated given the extended chronology suggested by the small number of radiocarbon dates and bearing in mind that the building could have been abandoned or dismantled some time before the limekiln was constructed. Even so, there is a possibility that this building actually pre-dates the acquisition of the estate by the monastery at Glastonbury and that it stood on King Ine's royal estate of *Pouholt*. If that is so – and the degrees of probability inherent in the radiocarbon dates do not allow us to be absolutely sure – then this building belongs to only a handful of known 'British' halls in the west.[111] Some of these do indeed have structural affinities with Shapwick, such as its slightly curved end walls, internal subdivisions and the drip gullies seen being excavated in Figure 5.10B,[112] but, as we have already seen, the historical evidence cannot easily support such a conclusion. Once more the dimensions of the hall are not as impressive as might be expected. One hall at Yeavering in Northumberland was 25m × 12m, and recent work at Sutton Courtenay in Berkshire uncovered a hall 30m long by 10m wide, both far more substantial structures than the one suggested by the plan recovered at *Old Church*.[113] On the basis of the accumulated historical and archaeological evidence, therefore, we believe it to be more likely that this structure was built *after* the estate had passed to Glastonbury Abbey in AD 705/6, in which case the building could have been used by a reeve or steward when visiting this part of the Glastonbury estate. In either case, the hall probably endured for at least a century as an administrative centre for the Abbey, and perhaps considerably longer, in which case there is likely to have been considerable repair and rebuilding. The range of dates for the postholes could suggest this. There must have been other buildings close by too, at the very least barns and farm buildings, and quite possibly also the bishop's hall mentioned at the 'vill' of *Poelt*, which may have been located here rather than at Greinton, to which place it was later attributed.[114]

Worthie and others

The name *Worthie* does not occur in any of the historic map sources but, according to our reconstruction of the furlong names in the open fields in 1515 (see Figure B.5.2), it lay in the East Field immediately east of *Bassecastel*. In 1327 there are also references to *Nutherworthe* and *Overworthe* – presumably places above and below *Worthie*, that is to say, situated to north and south. The *worth* name in this context suggests that there was once an enclosed farm here, though there is nothing in the fieldwalking data to verify archaeology of any period in that particular field, even if *Old Church* is immediately to the north-west.[115] Meanwhile, the field names *Abofehaies*, *Ludecrofte*, *Manycrofte* and the unlocated *Purycrofte* sound like references to enclosures, perhaps indicating some sort of subdivided hedged landscape. Given that these farmsteads and enclosures cannot have existed when the open-field system was in

operation, this reinforces the notion that these field names are relics of something earlier, evidence of a very different kind of landscape in the post-Roman period. It follows, therefore, that there must have been a significant reorganisation of settlement and field systems in Shapwick at some point in the early medieval period.

Taken together, our reconstruction of the parish in the period AD 400 to 800 (see Figure 5.7) suggests that there were three centres of settlement in the middle of the northward-facing slope of the Poldens. The picture is admittedly patchy but, first, there seems to have been a centre of settlement in the western part between the Holy Brook and the Shoot Brook, a conclusion based on the numerous variations of the name *Worthie* and its later corruption to *Henry* rather than on any confirmed archaeology. We envisage a small farm here or perhaps a hamlet consisting of a number of timber houses and outbuildings. Second, there is *Sladwick*, much lower down the slope, almost on the edge of the fen and near to the prolific springs at *Mazewell*, though exactly how this site was being used is debatable. It appears to have been short-lived, a temporary adaptation of a late Roman ruin. Thirdly, there is a significant cluster of names around *Old Church*. This might indicate a single large area of occupation, a dispersed scatter of several smaller sites, perhaps shifting over time, or only a very few sites whose influence, in the form of the later extent of furlong names, became disproportionate to their true significance. And, of course, somewhere nearby was another, presumably quite small, settlement called 'Shapwick'. The location of the earlier settlement of Shapwick – the 'sheep *wic*' – remains elusive, even after all the research for this project. Our fieldwork confirms that it is most unlikely to lie beneath the present village, though the name could relate to the Roman site at the north end of the village whose chronology remains uncertain (see Chapter 4). Or, of course, it could be identified with *Borgh/Chestell*, the extensive complex to the east of Manor Farm (see Figure 4.8). Our preference, however, is for the site at *Old Church*, for which we have contemporary archaeological and dating evidence but no plausible early documented name. This, we think, was Shapwick.

While it is only in the case of *Old Church* that we have any inkling of what the buildings on these early medieval sites might have looked like, it is now at least possible to produce a general map of post-Roman settlements for the parish and to begin to appreciate some of their characteristics. None are far from either surface water supplies or pre-existing Roman sites, for example. More precisely, those sites with habitative elements embedded in their names all lie close to known sites with late Roman pottery, whereas the earlier Roman sites, such as that to the north of Shapwick House or at the Nidons villa, do not seem to have been remembered by the people who later applied the habitative names. The early medieval settlement pattern is therefore a relict pattern of late Romano-British farms and villas, something that surely suggests some general continuity of occupation and land use. Indeed, in those parts of the country where pottery and diagnostic artefacts are non-existent or otherwise difficult to distinguish, late Roman sites with a spatial association with Anglo-Saxon (OE) place-name elements indicating habitation might be a fruitful guide to earlier (AD 450–650) and middle Saxon (AD 650–850) settlement sites.

The developing landscape

In Chapter 1 we learned how, until quite recently, historians and scholars regarded the countryside of the fifth and sixth centuries AD as a wild place that had reverted to its natural state after the Roman period. As late- and post-Roman agricultural activity declined, so it was thought that the arable fields were abandoned and woodland inexorably regenerated.[116] Nowadays, we do not accept such a dramatic collapse in the centuries after the Roman period. The expected decline in pollen from crops and grassland and an increase in tree and shrub pollen as woodland spread at the expense of arable farmland has simply not been recognised by environmental scientists.[117] A recent survey of radiocarbon-dated pollen sequences for Britain concluded that the period stretching from the fifth to the ninth century was not generally one of agricultural stagnation in Britain; indeed, the survey showed that woodland clearance, along with agricultural activity, actually increased in some areas.[118]

Confirming this picture more locally is not without its problems. While in the west of the county there was little change in vegetation between the fourth and the sixth centuries, only in parts of the Somerset Levels did the peat that preserves the pollen continue to accumulate in the early medieval period. In addition, many deposits have had their upper layers truncated by later cutting for fuel, while others have become desiccated or disturbed during reclamation and cultivation. Fortunately, the Somerset Levels Project (see Box 1.1) undertook a great deal of palaeo-environmental fieldwork. Much of this research centres on the prehistoric period (and mainly the earlier prehistoric periods), but some information relating to post-Roman times has been retrieved.[119] For our purposes, the pollen diagram for Meare Heath, just to the north of Shapwick, is especially informative.[120] This shows that the clearance of woods on the dry land, which had begun in the late Iron Age, continued all through the Roman period and well beyond to at least a date between AD 550 and 690, when the sequence is curtailed.[121]

While we must accept that the Meare Heath sequence captures data from only a small catchment a little way from the Shapwick upland, the implications are that there was probably little change in the overall balance of woodland and farmland in the centuries after AD 400. We should not expect a great increase in woodland cover even if there might have been some conversion of arable to pasture, particularly where the clays were heaviest.[122] Some sites like *Sladwick*, we know, were abandoned, but this process of shifting settlement is entirely typical of what had gone before. Beyond the farmsteads there was probably a mixture of arable and pasture, with meadow on the lower-lying land and woodland and pasture on the hills as well as lower down closer to the Levels edge. There is pollen evidence to indicate that the wetland was beginning to dry out, but while cattle and other livestock could graze for some months of the year in certain areas there was still fishing and fowling to be had elsewhere. It is assumed that there would have been an 'infield' next to each of the settlements that was permanently cropped and heavily manured with farmyard refuse, with an extensive 'outfield' beyond, which would occasionally be broken up and brought into cultivation as necessary. In order for each of the farms to share in the different types of agricultural land use – arable, woodland, meadow and pasture – we envisage that the lands associated with each farm or group of farms may have run from the ridge of the Poldens northwards down towards the Levels.

Beyond these generalities, many questions remain. From the evidence gathered by the Project it would be rash to claim conclusively that an infield–outfield system existed in the period AD 400–800. Whereas elsewhere in the country, such as at Barnsley Park in Gloucestershire, dense scatters of pottery have been used to suggest this, Shapwick has no ceramics at this date to prove the case one way or the other.[123] As for any evidence for middle Saxon field layouts between the mid-seventh and ninth centuries, it is possible that the enclosed ground suggested by the *worthie* and the various *croft* names (see above) represents the introduction of new layouts, perhaps even compact blocks of demesne land newly enclosed by Glastonbury Abbey after the late seventh or early eighth centuries. But in the absence of further topographical or archaeological evidence this is speculative for the moment. There is no independent verification from Shapwick that might tell us when open fields and strip cultivation first came into being; as we shall see in Chapter 6, we argue only that large arable fields existed *by* the tenth century. Nor was our botanical work to prove helpful in pinpointing ancient hedgerows that might date from this period or before. As we mentioned in Chapter 2, we were keen to test the hypothesis, known as 'Hooper's Rule', that the composition of hedges might be a clue to their age. What we found instead was that many different factors can influence the present day composition of a given hedgerow. Having lived in Somerset for a number of years Mick had seen how farmers sometimes dug up seedlings or took cuttings of various woody species from nearby woodlands in order to repair gaps in hedgerows, a practice actually recorded at Shapwick in the early fourteenth century (see Chapter 7). It is also known that some 'ghost' hedges were established as woodland was being cleared away for conversion to arable or pasture. These 'woodland relic hedges' therefore start out with a high number of woody species. The initial composition of more recent hedges could also be influenced by such factors as the availability of well-stocked nurseries of 'quicksets' (hawthorn saplings) at the time of the enclosure of the field.[124] As anticipated, Hooper's Rule did not appear to apply with any consistency across the parish. Indeed, from other surveys undertaken across the country, including several others in Somerset,[125] the consensus now is that the method

is more effective in some parts of the country than others, but the general thrust appears to be correct: the older a hedgerow is, the more woody species are likely to be present. Whether or not an accurate date of planting can be calculated using Hooper's method is far more doubtful and, certainly, we could not use the technique to distinguish with any precision between field boundaries of prehistoric, Roman or early medieval date.

Logically, however, some use must have been made of prehistoric and Roman field boundaries and we suspect significant physical continuities with earlier field layouts even if cropping practices and tenure had evolved. Our excavations in *Buddle/Bassecastel* (Field 2700) are proof that parts of the enclosed rectilinear arrangement of fields on the later maps of the post-enclosure landscape were conditioned by the layout of furlong boundaries around strips in the open fields (see Figure B.3.4).[126] These reflect, in part, the open, ditched versions of rectilinear Roman and prehistoric land divisions that originated from the division and allocation of land on the fertile northern slopes of the Poldens some way back in the second millennium BC (see Chapter 3). While we do not say that *all* modern field boundaries are prehistoric in origin – that is plainly not the case; even some of the Roman hedges and ditches clearly seen in our geophysics plots bear no relation to their modern counterparts – we know that some are and the orientation of many other more recent ones must be influenced by them. In addition, many of the roads and tracks running east–west along the Polden slope were probably already in use at this period. Some certainly pre-date the current village, whose plan appears to be adjusted to fit a pre-existing network of communication routes (see Chapter 5). Though the settlement pattern might have changed, there are still elements of the post-Roman landscape that are familiar to us today.

No useful assemblages of early medieval plant macrofossils provide insight into the uses of the fields at Shapwick. It is safe to assume that varieties of wheat, barley and oats were grown, probably along with peas and beans, and the usual range of domesticated animals would have been present: cattle as a main meat source, for milk products, for hides and for traction; sheep for meat, skins and clips of wool; and pigs for meat. If the economy in the early medieval period was close to subsistence level, as it probably was, farmers are likely to have kept a mix of stock for different purposes. As we explained in Chapter 1, however, some degree of economic specialisation might also be expected in the outlying vills over which the *caput* or 'central place' of the multiple estate had control. In both the Roman and later medieval periods, for which we have good faunal evidence, sheep seem to have been the most important livestock at Shapwick, followed by cattle, with little evidence of pigs.[127] The place-name indicates as much. Among the activities that might have taken place here are the culling of surplus or diseased animals, the fattening up of others for meat and the deliberate management of ewes for milk and wethers, or castrated males, for their fleeces. All this remains to be tested through archaeological evidence, however, though it might be demonstrated one day if we were ever able to accumulate enough information to enable fine-grained comparisons between the economic functions of different parts of the same multiple estate (sheep, horse breeding, cereal growing, and so on).

Thinking back to the wider administrative and tenurial context for Shapwick at this period, we described earlier how it lay within the large royal estate of *Pouholt* that was centred on a *caput*, possibly located at Downend in Puriton parish. This estate is envisaged to have been largely self-sufficient, at least in terms of its main foodstuffs and other commodities. Agricultural produce from the various units of the estate (of which Shapwick would be one – the sheep *wic*) would have been used to support the tenants on the estate through a process of renders to the royal officials at the *caput*, with some of the goods being redistributed back to the farmers. We hear of renders of butter, cheeses, hens, eggs, ale, honey, lambs and much else from the documents at this time.[128] When the king and his attendants were in residence the food renders from the estate were also used to feed them. The interesting point about such an economy of renders and redistribution is that it needs neither coinage as a means of exchange nor recognised markets through which transactions can take place. Neither does it require an elaborate communications network in order to move goods about. Kings such as Ine and his retinue simply travelled about from royal estate to royal estate, eating each clean of foodstuffs before moving on. For these purposes the former Roman communications network of the road along the Polden ridgeway, together with lanes along the slope parallel with it, would have been adequate for movement across the estate and between the *caput* to the west and its related settlements. There is no evidence of imported foreign goods, at least not from sites within the *Pouholt* estate, and there is no evidence of a regional trade, such as in the later types of black burnished pottery from Dorset.[129] Any bulky goods, such as stone and constructional timber, of which there is some evidence from the buildings at *Old Church*, might have been obtained locally, or else they could have been moved by water.[130]

As we have stressed throughout this chapter, part of the problem when writing about this period in this region is that the archaeology is far more ephemeral than it is for both the preceding Roman period and the succeeding late Saxon and later medieval periods. The distinctive elements of a market economy – coins and mass-produced artefacts such as pottery, for example – were circulating in ever-decreasing quantities. Coins cease to be manufactured after about AD 400 and are not issued again until around 400 years later, and pottery appears not to have been produced between about AD 400 and the renewal of production in the ninth or tenth century.[131] It is difficult to imagine a society that functioned without the use of fired ceramic pottery vessels. After all, not far away, in other parts of Wessex, there is organic-tempered pottery from several sites in Wiltshire[132] and from places such as Wareham and Wimborne in Dorset.[133] People on the *Pouholt* estate may have returned to using vessels made of wood, leather and basketwork, unless possibly archaeologists have just not recognised or accurately dated some of the late Roman or even later Anglo-Saxon pottery that has turned up on archaeological excavations.[134] Without objects such as pottery and coins (not to mention the lack of permanent building materials) it is all the easier for archaeologists to file away undated burials, features and contexts as being prehistoric or Roman in date. This problem becomes especially critical in the next chapter, when we investigate the origins of the village of Shapwick.

CHAPTER SIX

A Village Moment?

Shapwick Before the Norman Conquest, *c.*AD 800–1100

'Hu gaeþ hit?' ['how goes it?']. The voice came out of nowhere.

Aelfric started, his cold hands grappling with the slimy willow basket, and the eel hive slipped back into the water. Squinting into the early morning spring light, he could just make out a man on horseback wending his way towards him. The farmer recognised the new reeve, Wulfric. He had seen the man only yesterday, watching intently while he and a handful of others from Enworthy were out ploughing the infield around their houses and sowing with wheat, barley and beans.

'Hit gaeþ god' ['it goes good'], Aelfric replied grudgingly, cursing his ill luck. But Wulfric was well aware that the farmer did not want to talk, and that suited him fine. The man's field had been an untidy mess with odd patches of different crops all intermingled and it would have been more untidy still had it not been set within the banks and ditches of earlier fields. How old they might be no-one knew. In places there were terraces too, half a man in height, and the banks went off into the distant outfield, where the cattle and sheep grazed. Farmers like Aelfric usually had enough to feed themselves, which was all well and good, but there was only ever a small amount left over to render as food rent to the monks at Glastonbury. All this was about to change, as Wulfric knew only too well. Guiding his horse gingerly along the edge of the bog, he reflected on his good fortune now that his older brother Dunstan was abbot of Glastonbury and had entrusted him with the role of steward to the outlying estates.

At the Abbey he had made friends with a well-travelled old monk who often chatted to him about what was happening abroad, though it might as well have been on the moon as far as Wulfric was concerned. Only yesterday Dunstan and the old monk had greeted him in the guest hall. There was honey and bread on the table and they had all supped wine with their meal. There were few other warm places to sit at the Abbey, not now that all the new building works at King Ine's church and the monks' old cemetery were underway. Though he spoke only Latin to the old monk, Dunstan had explained in English some new ideas of his about running the estate. In August, once the harvest was in, several of the old fields by the boundary stream would be fenced in and gangs of men with pegs and string would lay out housing plots of different sizes. Timber was already being stockpiled from Loxley Wood and shortly after the harvest the first new houses would be ready. Aelfric and the other families would be moved out of Enworthy and the other hamlets together with all their belongings, animals and stores. The old houses would have to be dismantled and their timbers carted to the new plots where they could be used to build barns and byres. By the feast day of the Epiphany the old hamlets would be gone and all that would remain out in the new fields would be the mills, the old church and the hall next to it, where the abbot's business would continue to be conducted.

If only Wulfric could be persuaded of the benefits of these changes, said Dunstan, then it would be easier for him to persuade the Pouholt farmers that everything would be for the better. Wulfric kept his doubts to himself; the man fishing for eels, he knew full well, would get very little. The farmers didn't work the land as intensively as they could, it was true, but they were unlikely to go to all that trouble even if it did save their souls. Most of their houses were only hovels, but to them they were home. Then they would all grumble about the new food rents required by the Abbey, even if their accommodation was better. And would they really agree to everyone living together in one place – like one of those crowded, busy new towns? Wulfric doubted it. As for cooperation in the fields, even fathers and sons seem to spend most of their time bickering among their own flesh and blood about odd bits of fencing or crop. What Dunstan was suggesting was nothing less than a veritable army of peasants all living on top of one another and working together in one huge field of cereals. At least the moors would stay as before, thought the steward, and the fat eels would always be there to catch.

This story presents one interpretation of the origins of Shapwick village. Our Wulfric is based on Dunstan's brother, Wulfric, whom we know from the earliest *Life* was appointed by Dunstan as steward in charge of the monastery's scattered estates in the second half of the tenth century, when the events described here take place.[1] Dunstan became abbot of Glastonbury in around AD 940, soon after the miraculous escape of King Edmund at Cheddar, when the reins of the king's horse snapped at the very edge of the gorge, a divine sign that he should make amends with Dunstan, who had recently been expelled from the court.[2] In AD 959 Dunstan became archbishop of Canterbury. These and other stories are recounted in the *Life of Dunstan*, from which something of his character can be gleaned. Dunstan's structural additions to Ine's church are also described there, though we do not know if, as we imply, Dunstan had a sweet tooth. There are thirty-eight vineyards listed in Domesday Book, so it is quite possible that grape juice and wine were produced on Glastonbury's estates. Otherwise, the towns to which Wulfric refers were the *burhs* established in Wessex by Alfred, namely Axbridge, Bath, Langport, Lyng and Watchet, to which can be added other centres with mints and markets, many of them royal properties. The feast day of the Epiphany is held on 6 January.

In the last chapter we saw how, from the early eighth century, Glastonbury Abbey built up its estates along the Poldens and centred its operations there at Shapwick. This was largely achieved by the ninth century. The Abbey then continued to exploit and develop its lands over the next 300 years and beyond, though the monastic community probably faced considerable difficulties in the ninth and tenth centuries as a result of depredations by the Norsemen (Vikings/Scandinavians), who had landed at Portland in Dorset, killing the king's reeve there, and attacked the monastery on Holy Island (Lindisfarne in Northumbria) in the 790s. From that time onwards their presence was continually disruptive. In the late ninth and early tenth centuries the Vikings were particularly active along the Bristol Channel. By the time of Alfred, king of Wessex, at the end of the ninth century, the monastic way of life and much of its associated culture was dead in England;[3] so much so that monasteries had to be refounded by Alfred and his successors. A few decades later, in the tenth century, during the reign of King Edgar, three great churchmen, including Dunstan of Glastonbury (Box 6.1),[4] refounded Benedictine monasticism and re-established many of the monasteries that had been

destroyed.[5] The tenth century is therefore marked by this monastic reform, after which the abbeys began once again to acquire estates and lands from their secular neighbours.

It is against this disrupted regional background that one of the most important periods in the history of the parish was played out, with great changes taking place in the way in which settlement was organised, the types of building people lived in and the way they managed their farming. As the archaeological evidence will show, much that is familiar in the village and parish today had its origins here. This is the time when the foundations of the village and its field system were first laid down, when people were gathered together into larger consolidated communities and when they increasingly worked together in the fields. Relationships within and between families would inevitably have been close, not only because the settlements they lived in were not large but also because individuals needed to commit themselves personally to their share of the burden of the agricultural year. The frankpledge system of Anglo-Saxon England did much to consolidate these ties by imposing corporate responsibility for behaviour.[6]

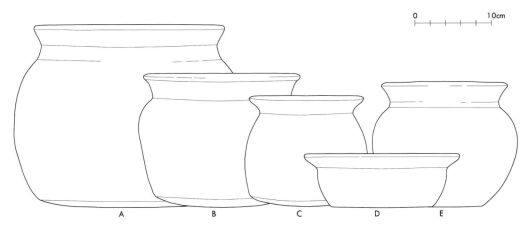

Figure 6.1. A range of medieval pottery recovered from Shapwick sites, late tenth–eleventh centuries, reconstructed by Alejandra Gutiérrez. All the forms here are jars with the exception of a bowl (D), and they would have had more than one function in the home, in cooking as well as storage. The jar labelled E is sooted from being placed close to the hearth, possibly on a trivet. The complete forms seen here are reconstructed from sherds excavated at Bridewell Lane (A, B, E), Old Church (C) and Lawn Farm (D). Nearly 800 fragments like these were recovered from Old Church (4016) and various excavations in the village.

Archaeological evidence for a village

It is not until around AD 900 that pottery in Somerset reappears in any noticeable volume in the archaeological record.[7] Although several slightly different fabrics were in circulation over the next two centuries, generally sherds are characteristically soapy to the touch, with wiped surfaces, glassy quartz inclusions and voids where limestone fragments have leached out of the fired clay. Against the brown background of a cultivated plough soil the dull shades of this pottery can be hard to pick out and even the most robust fragments are unlikely to survive for long when exposed to winter frosts or struck by the plough. As if to make identification more difficult, there is very little variation in pottery forms over the next 200 years. Only jars and bowls were used at this time (Figure 6.1) and although these were complemented in the Anglo-Saxon household by a wide range of containers made of leather and wood[8] these are perishable materials that survive only in exceptional circumstances.

As if this were not enough to contend with, how *do* you find out about the origins and development of a village when it is still occupied? It is hardly an acceptable research strategy to bulldoze all the buildings in a village in order to examine the archaeology underneath for signs of earlier occupation!

Rather, opportunities have to be taken wherever and whenever possible to look in gardens and vegetable patches for evidence of earlier activity. In order to establish a date for the origins of the modern village the main weapon in our armoury was the test pit (see Chapter 2), though larger excavations were also undertaken wherever possible and we took other opportunities where they presented themselves.

Among these opportunities were a series of watching briefs and excavations undertaken along the length of a new water pipeline that was being laid for the Poldens villages (see Figure 2.21A). This pipeline cut right through Shapwick Park to the south of the mansion, the largest area of open ground within the footprint of the modern village, and it produced some of our best evidence for late Saxon settlement. One ditch in particular attracted the attention of its excavators, Charlie and Nancy Hollinrake, at the time. Running more or less due north–south, it seemed to be a boundary that once separated two house plots in the later medieval and post-medieval village – 46 Chapmans Lane and 57 Brices Late Davidges Lane, as they are named on later maps (Figure 6.2). The interesting thing from our perspective was that the dating of the sherds from the ditch centred on the eleventh century. To investigate further, the excavation was extended to examine an adjacent stretch of the same ditch (Figure

BOX 6.1

Dunstan

Figure B.6.1. Dunstan kneeling before Christ in his 'classbook'.
Note the simple monastic habit and the tonsure.

There were three architects of Benedictine monastic reform in the tenth century. The first was Aethelwold (*c.* AD 904/9–984), who was made abbot of Abingdon in AD 954, where he reformed the Abbey and increased its endowments before becoming bishop of Winchester in AD 963. The second was Oswald, who attended the reformed Cluniac monastery of Fleury (now St Benoît-sur-Loire in central France) in the AD 950s before returning in AD 958 and being made bishop of Worcester in AD 961 and subsequently archbishop of York in AD 971. He died in AD 992. The third was Dunstan, who was born in Somerset, probably at Baltonsborough, around AD 909–910 or a little earlier. His parents were Horstan and Cynethryth and his family were wealthy, with land in the Glastonbury area. He was educated locally at the Abbey and had been ordained a priest by AD 939. Dunstan spent much of the AD 930s (when in his 20s) at the court of King Aethelstan and then the next decade in intense study at Glastonbury Abbey with Aethelwold. Many of his ideas about monastic reform and how to run a monastery were probably worked out at that time.

Sometime between AD 940 and 946, when he was in his mid-30s, Dunstan was appointed abbot at Glastonbury by King Edmund, though he still spent time at the royal court (Figure B.6.1). The period from then

6.3A) which this time produced twenty-three sherds from its fill. All bar one of these fragments were dated to the early–mid eleventh century, so the evidence pointed to this ditch being backfilled at that date. The incorporation of domestic pottery into the fill implies both that there was contemporary settlement in the immediate vicinity and that the boundaries between properties were *already* in place by that date. Other features of possible early medieval date in the same area included a post-pit with a packing of large stones, a narrow beam-slot[9] perhaps for a wooden structure and an undated stakehole.[10] Frustratingly, these could not be investigated further because of the restrictive width of the pipeline corridor.

The same pipeline also provided an opportunity to examine a major boundary on the west side of the Park. This proved to consist of two parallel ditches with a truncated central bank 2m in width.[11] The scale of these ditches was impressive: they were 6.5m wide and 0.8m deep on the western side and 4m wide and 1m deep on the east and certainly formed a substantial barrier that would have been at least 0.2m deeper when first dug. Given its placement and alignment this is likely to be the boundary that once separated the village from the open fields, quite possibly with a hedge planted on the central bank. It therefore defines the western side of the 'village envelope'. Although we cannot say precisely when these ditches were dug, until his exile at St Peter's at Ghent in Flanders (AD 956–957) is the most likely time during which he could have engineered changes on the Glastonbury Abbey estates at places such as Shapwick. That would have been in the mid AD 940s–mid 950s – probably AD 946–956 – when he was between 35 and 45 years old.[b1] Several architectural features commissioned by Dunstan at Glastonbury have also been identified during excavations there. The footings of his chapel dedicated to St John the Baptist, for example, were famously excavated by architect Frederick Bligh Bond in 1913 after he was guided to dig at the spot through the medium of automatic writing.[b2]

The overall impression of the pre-Conquest monastic precinct in Dunstan's time, one gained from the intermittent publication of excavations, is of a series of churches orientated along a single axis: a family of churches in which new buildings stood beside old.[b3] This axial planning is a typical arrangement on pre-Conquest monastic sites. These churches were St John the Baptist and St Mary to the west – the latter on the site of the reputed earliest wattle and daub church, the *Vetusta Ecclesia* of legend – then the main church of St Peter and St Paul in the centre, under the west end of the later Abbey, and possibly others further east. These structures were linked by a colonnaded atrium to the west and a chapel building over a crypt (called a *hypogeum*) to the east: there were 'porticus' or side chapels to north and south. There seems also to have been a cemetery with pillars marking important graves to the south and later a cloister (there by the tenth century), and there would have needed to have been a dormitory, refectory, kitchen and guest house too. From the west, from the direction of the Poldens, the main approach was along St Benedict's Street up to the west gatehouse of the Abbey, though a canal was also constructed, quite possibly in Dunstan's time (see Box 5.1 for the wider landscape setting). There may have been a market here, outside the Abbey precinct in some sort of 'proto' town, as happened at other large Benedictine centres.[b4] And it was quite possibly through such a market that commodities such as pottery found their way to outlying estates such as Shapwick.

In AD 958 Edgar, the king of Wessex, recalled Dunstan from abroad and appointed him bishop of London. Shortly afterwards he received his pallium from the Pope when he visited Rome in AD 960. He also held the see of Worcester in plurality. In AD 959 (when he was almost 50) he was made archbishop of Canterbury, a position he held for nearly thirty years until he died in 988, aged around 80. During this time, in AD 973, the Council of Winchester debated and agreed the *Regularis Concordia*, which was to form the basis for reformed Benedictinism in England. The tenth-century revival led to the foundation of many important monasteries and Dunstan was regarded as a saint as soon as he died. By the time of Cnut (1020×1022) he was venerated all over England as a scholar, author, scribe, artist and craftsman, being associated particularly with monastic crafts such as manuscript production and metalworking.

because they are likely to have been cleaned out more than once, judging by the pottery found in the basal fills it looks as if the ditch on the western side of the bank was already filled in by the twelfth century. The boundary alignment was still there to be mapped on the village plan of *c*.1764 and its location in the context of other late Saxon features can be seen on Figure 6.3B.

Other excavations also produced evidence for early medieval occupation. At the very north end of the village a scatter of late tenth- to early eleventh-century pottery[12] was recovered around Shapwick House mansion, together with a loomweight. These finds are all from later contexts but they are sufficient to suggest

occupation nearby in the pre-Conquest period. Although the relative fragility of late Saxon pottery fabrics has few advantages for the archaeologist, it does mean that sherds like these are unlikely to have travelled far from where they were first deposited. More early medieval pottery was recovered from excavation trenches further south in the village plan, at Bridewell Lane. The size of the assemblage, over 400 sherds in all, is enough to indicate strongly that people were active on the plot in the late tenth to early eleventh centuries. A William I penny dating to 1074–77 was also found here. Among the possible occupation features at this site were a narrow flat-bottomed gully, perhaps a beam-slot,[13] though it was

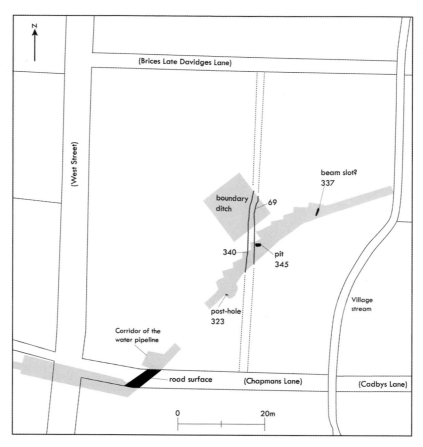

Figure 6.2. Early medieval features identified in excavation trenches within Shapwick Park. The corridor of the Wessex Water pipeline is outlined in grey with a square extension of excavations to the north. The alignments of lanes as they were in the mid-eighteenth century have been superimposed. For location see Figure 6.3.

devoid of finds; a patch of red-brown soil with charcoal inclusions within a shallow scoop that was interpreted as a possible hearth; and compacted clay surfaces containing late tenth- or early eleventh-century pottery (Figure 6.4). These kinds of features, which can be very difficult to recognise and interpret because they are so ephemeral, have been identified locally at other sites where late Saxon buildings are present, among them Lower Court Farm (Long Ashton), St Mary-le-Port Street (Bristol), Bristol Castle, Brent Knoll, Bickley, and Ash in Martock.[14]

Further south, at Lawn Farm, fieldwalking prior to housing development collected forty-one sherds of early medieval pottery, and the subsequent digging of foundations for housing produced yet more. A number of pits at the same spot were thought to have

been early medieval in date, but they contained too few artefacts to be sure. Most enigmatic of all was a series of narrow intercutting water channels at the base of a wider ditch (Figure 6.5A). These channels had closed ends and appeared to be joined so that water could spill over from one into another. At one end multiple stakeholes and postholes had been cut into the upper surface of the wider ditch (Figure 6.5B). We do not understand the purpose of this feature; the channels seem too regular and straight-sided to be the result of simple ditch maintenance, but perhaps they were for retting flax (too narrow?) or the fulling of woollens, in which case the stakeholes might be for tenters for drying or stretching. Other suggestions include the growing of watercress in the base of a freshwater channel and troughs for keeping

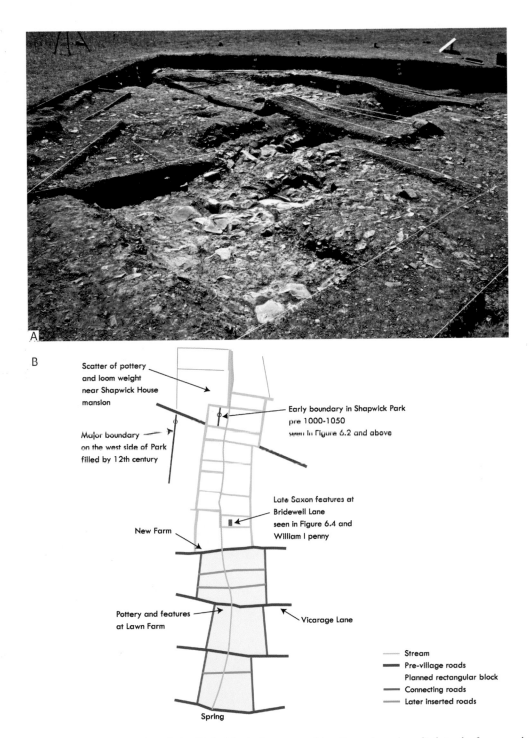

Figure 6.3. Excavations in Shapwick Park (Field 6767). A: the truncated late Saxon boundary ditch in the foreground, looking south-west. B: the village plan marked up with early boundary features.

Figure 6.4. Excavations north of Bridewell Lane revealed a flat-bottomed gully typical of features identified at other late Saxon sites (the location of this site is shown on Figure 6.3).

eels! Whatever their purpose, however, they are early features which were soon out of use: the water-borne silts at the base of the channels contained exclusively late tenth- to early eleventh-century pottery.[15]

Of all the excavations we undertook in the village, only those at Vicarage Lane, New Farm and at the spring site[16] did *not* produce late Saxon pottery fabrics of tenth-/eleventh-century date (see Figure 6.1). Vicarage Lane almost certainly lay outside the bounds of any early medieval settlement and, since only fifteen sherds of pottery in all were recovered at New Farm, the blank there is no surprise. The absence of material from the spring site is rather more puzzling, but this part of the village could have been a communal resource and not itself occupied.

Turning now to the evidence from our eighty-one test pits (see Chapter 2 for methodology), every 'block' along the full length of the village plan produced at least a handful of early medieval pottery (Figure 6.6). As might be expected, the quantities were never huge, with even the most productive test

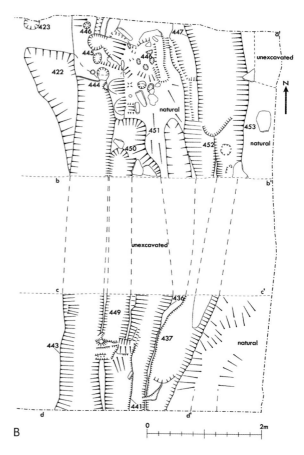

Figure 6.5. Puzzling water channels (A) excavated by Charles and Nancy Hollinrake at Lawn Farm Paddock. In plan (B), the inter-cutting channels sit in the base of a wider ditch. The adjacent surface had many stakeholes and postholes without any obvious arrangement. After some recutting the channels silted up by the thirteenth century. Their function is not understood.

Figure 6.6. Plan of the modern village superimposed with densities of early medieval pottery sherds recorded per cubic metre of excavated soil from each of the test pits.

pit producing only six sherds, although clusters were noted at Hill Farm, where sixteen sherds came from seven test pits, and at Forsters, where there were seven sherds from three test pits. Taken together, these results suggest that the whole of the core of the modern village – that is to say, all the spaces between the 'rungs' on its 'ladder-like' plan – were in use and occupied in the late Saxon period.[17] There is, crucially, no hint that one part of the village was occupied before any other. The village also appears to owe little to Roman antecedents. Our test pits from the village produced only three sherds of Roman pottery, and larger excavations yielded little more.[18] Then again, had the village been in existence in the fifth–tenth centuries, when, as we saw in the previous chapter, occupation was largely aceramic, we might have expected to see many more undated ditches and gullies in our open-area trenches. Instead we found few features of this type and no metal or bonework that might conceivably date to this period. On the other hand, we did find copious and widespread late Anglo-Saxon pottery, some 775 sherds in all, together with a scatter of possible occupation features.

Ideally we wished to *prove* not just that there was occupation in the late Anglo-Saxon period on the site of the modern village of Shapwick but also that the framework of roads and plots we see today was set out at that date. To that end we deliberately targeted not only boundary ditches but also some of the inter-communicating lanes within the village plan. But our ambitions were frustrated for three reasons. First, as we mentioned in Chapter 4 in our discussion of Roman sites, the stratigraphy was very shallow. Almost any later medieval and post-medieval activity would have endangered the survival of anything earlier. Second, there is a great deal of residual material from earlier periods, which complicates dating. Third, while the evidence from the excavations in Shapwick Park confirms that the layout of streets and lanes known from post-medieval maps *did* exist before the early thirteenth century, it cannot pinpoint its origins precisely. The nature of the local Lias bedrock, alas, is such that it makes excellent flat natural surfaces. This characteristic was made full use of at Shapwick, and dating worn rock surfaces is a near impossibility.[19] How long it took for the traffic to erode down the road surface into bedrock we do not know.

These setbacks aside, there is nothing from our fieldwork to suggest anything other than the existence of a late Anglo-Saxon settlement whose layout remained largely unchanged until the middle of the eighteenth century (see Chapter 8). The plan of this village was orientated north–south, with two streets (the verticals on the 'ladder') flanking fifteen plots that run down the centre (see Figure 6.3B), the plots being separated one from another by sixteen lanes (the 'rungs' on the ladder) that run east–west. This regular uniformity gives every impression of planning. The village might be classed as a well-defined row settlement in which, presumably, each plot contained timber domestic structures and a few agricultural buildings.[20] There are excavated parallels for this form from as far afield as Gasselte (Drenthe, Netherlands), to name one European example of the ninth to twelfth centuries.[21] Though the plan is unusual nationally, several similar examples have been identified in recent regional surveys of settlement forms, including the 'gridded cluster' settlement at Ingarsby in Leicestershire.[22]

Readers may be surprised to find that the question of settlement origins cannot be resolved more quickly by a close reading of the historical documents. Not so – settlement patterns were generally ignored in manorial surveys because clerks were more concerned with boundaries. The more varied business of manorial courts *can* produce incidental evidence, but there are very few thirteenth-century court rolls to help us. In fact, the first definitive documentary evidence for a village at Shapwick is as late as 1307, when seven villeins were fined for extending their field strips by up to two feet on the lane from Shapwick to the church, *via ducente de Schapwk ad ecclesiam*, as the scribe recorded their misdemeanour.[23] The village, we may safely conclude, must already have been in existence at that date since people were walking *from* the village eastwards to the church of St Andrew's in *Old Church*. Another possible clue to its antiquity comes from villagers' surnames, of which we know twenty-seven for 1239, thirty-three in 1260 and about seventy for the better-documented fourteenth century. Had the village been recently established those surnames might have reflected the earlier settlement pattern – for example, we might expect to see the surname 'Enworthy' – but instead all the locations referred to are places within the existing village or near the church,[24] such as (*atte* or *de*) *Fairswey, la Herepathe, la Purie* and *Fonte* in 1239.[25] So, documentary evidence does no more than hint that the modern village was there *by* 1239 and confirms its existence at the beginning of the fourteenth century. That said, we might anticipate some clue in the abundant documentation had there been any really dramatic change in settlement arrangements during the previous century.

Looking at the village plan

The village plan itself, as well as the archaeology and available documents, may be inspected for any evidence to elucidate the origins of the village. Here it at once becomes obvious that some of the east–west boundaries and roads that enter the village from the west emerge again in a straight line on its eastern side, almost as if the village itself were invisible. We realised then something that now seems obvious – the village had not been laid out in an abandoned or virgin landscape; rather, some of the east–west lanes had existed *before* the village came into being. This was later to be confirmed by excavation in Field 2700, which showed that one of the boundaries linking the village to the fields is indeed pre-Roman in date (see Figure B.3.4). That being so, the two north–south streets of the village plan seem, therefore, merely to provide linkages between a pre-existing set of east–west routes and boundaries.

Another noteworthy feature is the change in the centre of the village blocks as the village plan 'follows' the course of the stream: the watercourse, therefore, is the spine of the layout. When seen in plan the village looks rather less like a ladder, even a rickety one, and more like a set of badly stacked books on the verge of toppling over (to the east). Once more, not only is the village not perfectly rectilinear but the spines of those 'books' – that is, the parcels of land between the lanes and roads – are of differing thicknesses. This required further investigation.

Measuring the village

A very simple analysis of the properties in the village quickly suggests that a fixed measurement, or module, was used when laying out the basic structure. While this is expressed on Figure 6.7 in 100-foot units the reality is probably that the module was 20 feet. This length, called the 'rope' in Somerset, and presumably based originally on a real length of rope, was a measurement of distance from at least the fourteenth century and was used to calculate payments to peasants for the digging of ditches, the constructing of banks and other physical labours.[26] Beginning with the blocks *between* the east–west roads, there seems to have been one pre-village road (east–west) at the north end of the village that was removed when that area was replanned into small rectangular plots. Further south there were other pre-village lanes or at least boundaries – as many as six in all. The distances between these look to be consistent at 30 ropes (600 feet) for the southern three blocks and 60 or 65 ropes (1,200 or 1,300 feet, and therefore possibly twice the 30-rope unit) further north – though it could be argued that one large block of land, the northern half of the village, was laid out at 90 to 95 (but perhaps intended to be 100?) ropes long. On this basis alone, the village divides into two distinct parts – a southern half with blocks 30 ropes in length (600 feet) and a northern half comprising one large unit up to 100 ropes long (2,000 feet) with subdivisions.[27]

Within the northern and southern areas there is also a difference in the size of the plots recorded on the earliest maps. In the northern half the plots are five ropes wide (100 feet north–south), while the rest are twice this, at ten ropes wide (200 feet), so it looks as if the southern ones are double plots in many cases. This might suggest that the village plan was laid out with the following plot dimensions in mind: nine large plots in the south-east sector of the village, which are numbered in red on Figure 6.7 to the south on the east side of the stream. These may have measured 10 ropes wide and 15 ropes long originally (200 by 300 feet). Continuing north, there are then at least thirteen medium-sized properties in the northern area to the east of the stream that are 5 ropes wide and 15 ropes long (100 by 300 feet), while to the west of the stream in the south-west sector there are nine small properties, more irregular in size and shape than elsewhere, but mainly 10 by 10 ropes square (200 by 200 feet). Finally, there are thirteen plots in the north-west sector measuring 5 by 10 ropes (100 by 200 feet), though they are, again, somewhat irregularly shaped in places. The impact on the village plan of the later manor house and mansion (that is, Shapwick House) unhelpfully obscures the original detail at the northern end of the village.

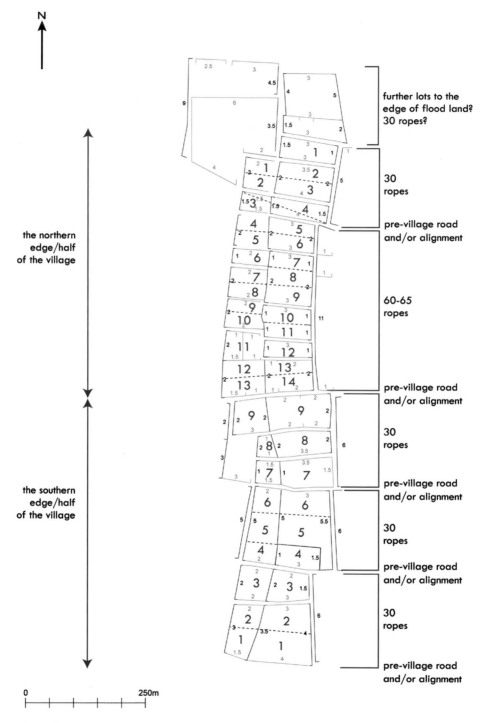

Figure 6.7. Modules of 100 feet measured across the mid-eighteenth-century plan of the village (in black for distances north–south, in grey for distances east–west). The consistency is striking and implies deliberate planning. The red numbers refer to the possible original number of plots in each sector of the village; nine in the south-east, at least thirteen in the north-east, nine in the south-west, and thirteen in the north-west (see p. 171).

Some models of development

The revelation that the village consists of blocks of land of varying but apparently consistent dimensions is intriguing. At first, before all the archaeological results from our test pits had been analysed, we played with the idea that these different-sized blocks might represent different phases in the formation of the village. Four models of development were proposed (Figure 6.8), the first of which suggested that the north end of the village was laid out initially, with expansion then taking place as crofts were added southwards, here shown as 'first' and 'second' phases. Since there was no way of knowing whether south came before north or vice versa, the opposite sequence could also be advocated, with an earlier manor at the south end of the village near the spring, and this became our second model. Additional appeal was lent to this second hypothesis by a cluster of field names at the southern end of the village – *West Croft* and *Manycrofte*, which are suggestive of early enclosure (see Chapter 5), together with *La Grange*, a name which might indicate a high-status site. These field names had been located for the first time on our 'new' medieval map of 1515 (Box 5.2). According to this second model the village would have developed towards the north, possibly culminating at the northern end of the village with the move of the Abbey's *curia* at the end of the thirteenth century or with the digging-out of the moat sometime earlier (see Chapter 7).

There is also the possibility that the differences in plot size we have noted might have been sensitive to something other than chronology. For example, they might reflect the kinship composition of households and thus vary according to age, marriage patterns, numbers in a household and so on. We also considered the idea that plot size might be influenced by the agricultural tasks performed there, such as dairying, cereal processing, orcharding or perhaps a craft such as ironworking, so that, say, dairy farmers took the larger plots. Such differences might be possible to detect archaeologically, but it is hard to test for them satisfactorily within a 'living' village where the total excavation of plots is utterly impractical. Finally, we felt that tenurial status might be a critical factor in determining the village layout[28] and so Model 3 assumes that the whole Shapwick plan

was developed at one time but that the differences in toft size reflect these tenurial distinctions. This idea was taken up by Nick Corcos, who went further to explain that one phase might be pre-Conquest and a second post-Conquest. Thus the northern block might represent a 'post-Conquest settlement of peasantry, in larger numbers, with smaller holdings and of a reduced social status as compared to their southern neighbours'.[29] Given the archaeological evidence presented above, which shows pre-Conquest activity across the full length of the village plan, we do not believe that this can be correct. The possibility of a link between the size of tofts and the social status of the tenants who occupied them, however, remains plausible.

Needless to say, there is no way of knowing the details of the social structure of tenants and tenancies for the tenth century but it *is* possible to gauge this for the later Middle Ages. Martin Ecclestone has compared the size of holdings with the tenants mentioned in the late medieval surveys (of 1189, 1239, 1260, 1325 and 1515) (Figure 6.9). Here holdings are listed as two-virgate (120 acres) one-and-a-half-virgate (90 acres), virgate (60 acres), half-virgate (30 acres), ferdeller (15 acres) and half-ferdeller (7½ acres), along with other smaller holdings of 5 acres and 2½ acres, with some cottagers who presumably had smaller plots. Around forty-four to forty-eight holdings are listed in all for each of the medieval surveys.[30] This figure compares remarkably well with the eighteen or so larger plots and the twenty-six to twenty-eight smaller plots identified on the ground in the village, which together total forty-four to forty-six plots. Likewise, Domesday Book for Shapwick also lists forty-two tenants, a number that includes six slaves, five freemen, fifteen villeins and sixteen bordars.[31]

When the measured plots at Shapwick are considered in relation to these documented holdings it seems a possibility that the peasants with between half and one and a half virgates (30–90 acres) might have held the larger plots at the southern end of the village, while the twenty-five to twenty-six tenants with smaller holdings of 15 acres or less took up plots further north. This does not work out entirely satisfactorily for all the surveys but, nevertheless, there does seem to be a real difference between those

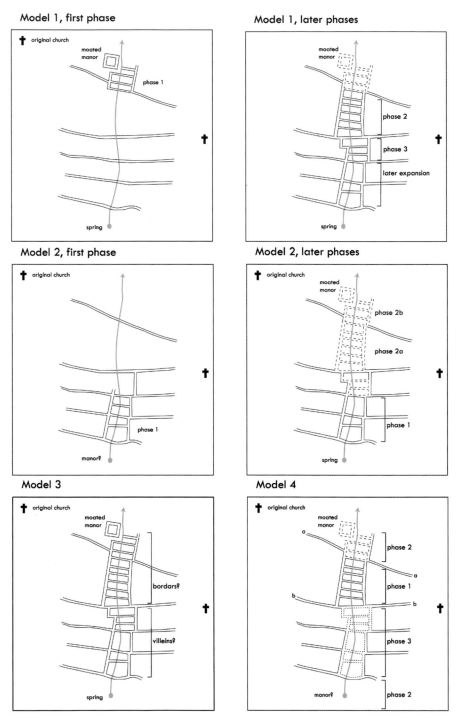

Figure 6.8. Four hypothetical models of development for the Shapwick village plan. The first two models presuppose that plot size and orientation change over time. Model 1 therefore proposes early development at the north end of the current village while Model 2 reverses that sequence. Model 3 suggests something altogether different: that the dimensions of the plots are related to social structure. Finally, Model 4 proposes that land ownership might be a major factor. Thus, an early block of village plots developed on land that may have formed part of the demesne land of the manor.

Holding	1189	1239	1260	1325	1515	1515 heriots
1½ virgates	2	1	1	1	-	-
Virgate	3	3	3	3	4	4
Half virgate	16	14	12	15	14	16
Ferdells	-	-	-	21	15	23
Half ferdells	-	-	-	1	2	2
'15 acres'	1	-	-	-	-	-
'7½ acres'	-	5	1	-	-	-
'5 acres'	26	20	25	-	-	-
'2½ acres'	-	1	-	-	-	-
Cottagers	-	-	-	7	1	1
Total number	48	44	42	48	36	46

* Including 111 acres of rented demesne lands

Figure 6.9. Descriptions of holdings by customary tenants in various surveys. Note that one tenant could have more than one holding and that the number of heriots in 1515 suggests that such tenants were mostly ferdellers.

tenants with more than 15 acres and those with less, and the number of peasants certainly relates closely to the number of plots available on the village plan.[32] Our conclusion is that there was indeed some sort of correlation between the status of tenants and the numbers of plots. If we are also able to accept the archaeological evidence that tells us that the village, more or less in its present form, was in existence by AD 1000, then this suggests that there was a remarkable and unexpected stability to the village plan over a 500-year period. Indeed, it would seem that the layout of Shapwick remained more or less static from the date that its original plan was set out in perhaps the tenth century right through to the maps of the eighteenth century – eight centuries in all.[33] This does not mean to say that population numbers were static over all that time (Box 7.1), only that more or fewer people were accommodated within the same broad plan.

A fourth and final model of village formation can be tentatively developed on the basis of land ownership (see Figure 6.8). During the late Saxon period all the land belonged to the Abbey, but if we focus on much later patterns of ownership it is striking how land belonging to the rectory estate in the eighteenth century includes a triangular block running from the rectory manor house in the middle of the village east towards the earlier St Andrew's church. This land includes much of the scatter of early pottery over the *Old Church, Greazy, Buddle*

and *Bassecastel* areas that have been pinpointed in Figure 5.7 as forming one of the early settlement, pre-village clusters in the parish. One explanation for this is that this block of land formed part of the demesne land of the manor before it was split and therefore might have been more intensively manured and thus received more early pottery. The western end of this area, meanwhile, because it was land under the Abbey's absolute control, may have formed the nucleus of the early village with settlement then being grafted on to the south and north. In favour of this interpretation is that the most regular ladder-like part of the village plan – the most assiduously stacked books, to follow our earlier analogy – is encompassed by this block of land, suggesting that it might indeed represent a deliberate planning exercise on a virgin site. Less regular expansion as the population grew could then explain the pattern of plots to the south. It might also help to explain why, when the church was moved in the fourteenth century, it was located in the middle of the village (rather than, for example, at a greenfield site alongside the built-up area of the village) and why later the Rectory 'manor' was developed here as well.

At first this fourth model appears to be ruled out because it suggests development of the village plan over several phases whereas the archaeology suggests otherwise. But this could be a misrepresentation of the evidence. The archaeological results demonstrate only that the village was in existence, in its entirety, *in* or *by* the tenth century. This does not rule out the possibility that phases of development took place within the tenth century itself or even *before* that date. Indeed, the idea of medieval settlement creation being multi-staged has been mooted before. In the East Midlands a recent survey of medieval settlement debated the two options of sudden upheaval or nucleation over many years and was unable to reach a firm conclusion.[34] In Northamptonshire, on the other hand, Tony Brown and Glenn Foard seem more certain. They believe that they have discovered evidence for several stages of development in nucleated settlements and envisage the desertion of dispersed settlements of Middle Saxon date and the process of manorialisation leading to 'the imposition of a regular open-field system over whole townships [fixing] the settlement pattern at whatever level of nucleation it had reached' by the ninth and tenth centuries. Regular planned village settlements then came into existence.[35] Such a model means that the nucleation of some settlements was *already* taking place in the seventh and eighth centuries, with a subsequent phase of replanning of both villages and their open fields some time later, in the ninth and tenth centuries. According to Brown and Foard, the creation of the open fields post-dates the initial nucleation of the settlement and is associated with the later phase of village replanning.

Such a model is not, of course, intended to be universal, but, taken at face value, the archaeological evidence from Shapwick could fit it perfectly well. The arguments against it are largely historical and tenurial. In the first place, we argued in Chapter 5 that the church *could* have been founded by the beginning of the eighth century in association with the transfer of land from royal hands to the monastery at Glastonbury. If this *was* the case then we might expect the church to be located somewhere within the footprint of the modern village which, by inference, would have grown around it. The fact that it was not strongly indicates that the village *did not exist* at that time. Second, it is hard to see how the officials of a decaying monastic system in the ninth century, which included Glastonbury Abbey, were in any position to replan settlements when they were already under pressure from Viking depredations. If they did

achieve it, however, and the village was indeed laid out as a series of enclosures[36] along a stream sometime earlier in the eighth or ninth centuries, it could be that the final plan of the village was only formalised later, possibly in the tenth century, following the refoundation of Glastonbury Abbey under Abbot Dunstan after AD 940. On balance, the tenth century seems to us to provide a much more propitious time and calmer circumstances in which the planning of villages and the development of open-field systems could be engineered.

To summarise these arguments drawn from our four models of village formation, the weight of archaeological and documentary evidence favours a date for the laying-out of the present village sometime after the eighth century but before the late tenth or early eleventh century. The creation of this new settlement at Shapwick would have put an end to the shifting pattern of settlement typical of later prehistory and the Roman period. Figure 6.10 is a reconstruction of the moment at which the old farmsteads were dismantled in preparation for the move. Dispersed dwellings would have been ploughed under and a primary settlement firmly locked in place, its farmyards made ready for the increased agricultural capacities that open-field arable farming would bring. Our Model 3 proposes that differences in plot size were inherent in the original village plan and that these reflect differences in tenurial status. The balance tips in favour of a tenth-century origin for the village because Shapwick was owned by a monastic landowner and this is the time of the monastic revival at Glastonbury Abbey, fostered by Dunstan. Although there is no documentary evidence to prove it, it is likely that his reforming message extended to a comprehensive rethinking of the management of the Abbey's estates and its sources of income. Dunstan was certainly familiar with settlement planning, as his endeavours at Glastonbury in terms of reorganising the shape of the monastic precinct and the buildings within it (Box 5.1) clearly show. At this time the Abbey was also busy extending its property locally and, like other landlords, the monks acted to maximise their income where they could.

There are still parts of the puzzle that cannot be solved. Why was Shapwick not laid out near or around the pre-existing church? Why choose another

Figure 6.10. Reconstruction by Victor Ambrus of the moment when the dispersed farmsteads were dismantled and the village of Shapwick came into being. We think this happened in the tenth century, possibly at the behest of Abbot Dunstan of Glastonbury sometime between AD 940/6 and 956/7.

location altogether? This is not an easy question to answer, but one reason might be that water resources were more plentiful at the new village site. Not only was there a prolific spring at the south end but, by directing its overflow stream down the slope and through the village, every housing plot was assured of direct access to fresh running water. This was as necessary for watering stock as it was for daily domestic life and industrial activities. It also cannot go unnoticed that the village has a central position in relation to its land unit, thereby providing ample space for the open-field system to be set out to the west and the east. This location maximises the well-ordered use of, and access to, valuable arable land in a way that a new village established at the church site could never have done. Given the journey times of peasants walking out to their holdings in the open fields, something we shall return to in Chapter 7 (see Figure 7.37) the most efficient place for their homes was between the two fields and midway up the slope of the Poldens. It may well have been this important

consideration – of easy and quick access to the open fields – that finally determined the position and site of the village. There is no doubt, however, that the new location also provided a visible and quite deliberate break with the past, lying as it does mid-way between possible former settlements at *Old Church/Buddle*, *Enworthy* and *Abchester*. There was no greater signal of control than the imposition of a nucleated settlement structure upon a scatter of previous (and probably individually organised) hamlets and farmsteads, and the new location was to favour all the abbot's tenants equally.

The pre-Conquest curia in Old Church

For at least part of the period AD 800–1100 the wooden building to the east of the church, described in Chapter 5, probably continued to stand. On the basis of the radiocarbon dates from charcoal recovered from its postholes and the date of the limekiln that evidently succeeded it on precisely the same spot (see Chapter 7), an estimated date for the

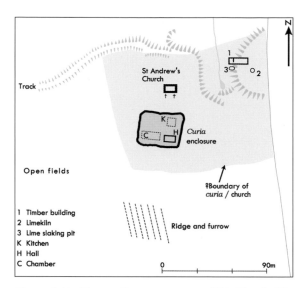

St Andrew's
Church

Track

K

C   H

*Curia
enclosure*

Open fields

?Boundary of
curia / church

1 Timber building
2 Limekiln
3 Lime slaking pit
K Kitchen
H Hall
C Chamber

Ridge and furrow

0   90m

Figure 6.11. The pre-Conquest curia in Old Church. This plan draws together information from excavation, geophysics and topographical survey.

end of use of the building can be calculated at cal AD 810–980.[37] It was probably at this time that a new *curia* site was established a little more than 100m away to the south-west, on the south side of the church. Exactly what form this new complex took is unfortunately masked by later activity on the same site (see Chapter 7), but there is sufficient evidence on the geophysics plot to indicate some details (Figure 6.11). In the south-east corner of the enclosure there is an unexcavated building, with the lines of its walls represented by substantial postholes. Without the benefit of further work, our best guess at what a *curia* might consist of would be a timber hall, possibly an aisled building, perhaps with a contiguous chamber, private apartments or *camera*.[38] Only excavation could confirm whether or not the round-cornered ditch around the *curia* is a primary feature of the site,[39] though it seems likely that it was, and there may well have been other buildings arranged around a courtyard, such as a gatehouse (either here or at the entry to the larger *curia*/church area), kitchens, dairy and a granary. No rubbish pits were identified and possibly the site was simply too constricted to use up space in this way.

Among several pre-Conquest finds recovered from

later contexts there is a fine strap end with an animal head terminal that dates to the tenth or eleventh centuries (Figure 6.12A). This was once attached to a belt or girdle for a horse or person. The finding of two keys implies a need for security for valuables, something which would be consistent with a *curia* at this location (Figure 6.12B and C). Finally, there was a bone dress pin fashioned from the fibula of a pig that came from unstratified layers not far from the seventh- or eighth-century timber building. This might have been used to secure an article of clothing (Figure 6.12D), though the dating of the object remains uncertain. While they are usually thought to be pre-Conquest in date, bone pins have also been recovered from twelfth- and even thirteenth-century phases on some excavations.

This *curia* site, with its ditches and huddle of timber buildings, was more than the symbolic heart of the Abbey's presence at Shapwick: it was the place at which taxes, dues and fines were paid, as well as the home of the bailiff or steward and therefore the administrative centre of the demesne estate. It was probably here, too, that the manor court was held, the villagers attending sessions and being bound by decisions presided over by the steward. The *curia* complex was more than merely a collection of buildings, therefore; it was in a sense the embodiment of the organisation of the manor.[40] Unlike many other places in southern England where the land was held by tenants or lessees, the manor of Shapwick was run directly by the Abbey and its officials and it was in their interests to invest in the construction of new buildings, something that might not have been the case at other places along the Poldens.

The church

Immediately north of the new *curia* lay St Andrew's church and we argued in Chapter 5 for its origins being long before the tenth century. We believe its construction at an earlier date explains why the church was *not* incorporated into the new village but, given that only one trench was dug across the foundations of the church, it is not easy to be definitive about the sequence of construction. Geophysical survey shows that it had a nave, chancel and central tower in its latest form (Figure 6.13) and this arrangement (though without the porch) may have already been

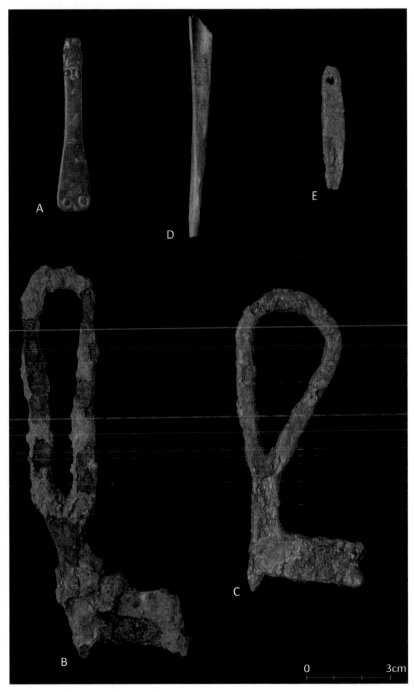

Figure 6.12. Early medieval artefacts from excavations in Old Church. A: strap end with animal head terminal with two rivet holes at the opposite end, tenth or eleventh century. Once attached to leather or textile strap to secure clothing. B: loop key, late Anglo-Saxon. C: loop key, late Anglo-Saxon. D: bone pin. A sharpened pig fibula, probably to secure clothing. E: lead plumb bob pierced for suspension.

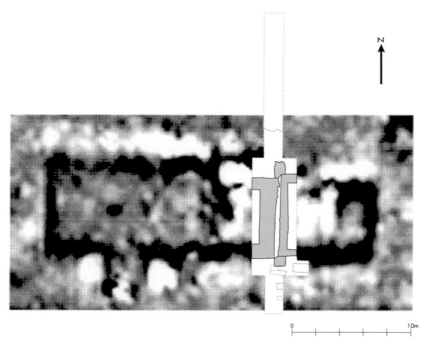

Figure 6.13. Excavated features of the medieval church superimposed on the geophysics plot. The eastern unit (the later chancel) is likely to be the earliest; excavation revealed a stepped plinth projecting externally (see Figure 5.9).

in existence by around 1100.[41] This church would have been the first substantial stone building in the parish since the Roman period and it was certainly accompanied by a graveyard by AD 900–1150,[42] as demonstrated by the calibrated radiocarbon date of a child's burial up against its south wall.[43] Presumably this cemetery was used by the people of the parish and manor at Shapwick and by its dependent chapelry of Ashcott.[44] People at Catcott and Chilton Polden, for example, would have buried their dead at Moorlinch, as the mother church, and, further east, Walton and Street churches would have had own burial grounds as well. It is also just possible that any wealthy peasants of Shapwick, perhaps the later freeholders of 1515, might have claimed burial at Glastonbury Abbey itself, though there is nothing to substantiate this.

Limekilns found near the church were probably fired to produce lime for a major phase of the church's construction. The first kiln, R38, was of a simple single flue type (Figure 6.14A), 3m in diameter at the top tapering to 1.82m at the base and just over 1m in depth, in which a hearth on the floor of a pit, piled with wood and broken up lumps of limestone, would have been lit.[45] Though the kiln was neither lined nor floored, the presence of daub suggests a clay superstructure[46] – the walls were baked red from firing – and earth and turf were perhaps used for insulation. A large kiln-pit such as this might have taken four to seven days to burn and a similar length of time to cool off. The pit would then have been dug out and the burnt lime unloaded from the top to avoid contamination from the wood ash beneath. This would have been done shortly after the lime had cooled and before it was exposed to any moisture that would kickstart the quick lime process. A possible stoking pit lay immediately alongside (Figure 6.14C). Whatever happened, limekiln R38 was clearly not a success, as most of the contents of the chamber had failed to burn thoroughly; quite possibly it was flooded and had to be abandoned.[47] Not long afterwards, on the basis that the edges of the kiln chamber were fresh and uneroded, the carcasses of

Figure 6.14. Limekiln R38 in Old Church, radiocarbon dated to the first half of the eleventh century. A: removal of a quarter of the fill of the firing chamber. B: excavation underway. C: the 'flue' half-sectioned.

dead animals were dumped into the cavity, and it was these bones that provided a date of *before* 1000–1050 for the kiln's last firing.

A second kiln, R98, lay only 16m away but had a completely different structure. Instead of the firing chamber being dug down into the bedrock, this kiln sat on top of the ground surface.[48] The diameter of the central chamber is a little larger than that of its neighbour (3.6m), but the main difference is its west-facing flue, 3.1m in length and 1.5m in external width (Figure 6.15A–B). The purpose of the flue, effectively a covered passage, was to draw hot air upwards into the kiln and out of the top. It also kept the fuel away from the charge, thereby ensuring a clean lime product. The radiocarbon date for the fuel in the firing chamber was 1020–1160,[49] a calibrated date that is consistent with one of the nearby postholes, which

gave a date of 1040–1220.[50] This posthole contained substantial stone packing and obviously once held an upright post, possibly to support part of the kiln superstructure or a windbreak.

Other features of this workshop included heaps of limestone, such as that seen to the west (left) of kiln R38 in Figure 6.14A. Some of this stone could have been robbed out of derelict Roman structures nearby or been freshly quarried, perhaps from ground later known as Quarry Field, to the north-east of Beerway Farm.[51] There was also a simple earth-dug pit for the mixing of slaked lime,[52] where lime and water would have been allowed to stand before other ingredients were added to make plaster and mortar (Figure 6.15C). It is reckoned that a fortnight is needed to create a perfect putty consistency, and the final product can be stored for several years if

Figure 6.15. Limekiln R98 in Old Church. Charcoal from here was radiocarbon dated to 1020–1160 (at 95 per cent confidence). A: looking east down the mouth of the flue that provided the draught for the kiln. The burnt orange clay of the kiln base is in the background. B: detail of the flue 'throat', showing charcoal deposits with sandstone and limestone blocks at the base of the flue wall; the superstructure may have been clay and wattle. Shuttering marks on the wall daub suggest a wooden mould was used to give it shape. Sandstone was probably favoured for construction because it reacted better to high thermal stresses above about 900°C. C: the lime slaking pit.

necessary.[53] Finally, kiln R98 was surrounded by ditches. These had originally been dug around the pre-existing timber hall, but they were made use of again to create a dry environment around the kiln and this may explain why this particular location was chosen. Quite possibly the workshop operated only during the summer months, five to twenty days being required for a single firing.

Lime-burning is known to have been practised in the early medieval period. There are Saxon references to lime and mortar and a twelfth-century reference to whitewashing with lime in York in the late seventh

century,[54] and several limekilns have been dated by association with nearby Anglo-Saxon churches.[55] The practice, however, did not become commonplace until after the Norman Conquest, when the development of more sophisticated types of smaller limekilns with air vents, rakeout and breather apertures, and stone facings all increased the flexibility of the use of the kiln.[56] Both of the excavated Shapwick examples belong to the larger, earlier variety. They make use of Roman technology and are therefore of particular interest because they pre-date the bulk of the documentary and archaeological evidence for lime-burning in the thirteenth and fourteenth centuries. Their discovery at Shapwick implies the presence of late Saxon quarrymen, masons and plasterers and an architect, to whom we should add carpenters and smiths as well as administrators, though not all of these would have had their workshops on site. A plumb bob recovered from the excavations may tie in with one or other of these episodes of construction (Figure 6.12E). Most important of all, the kilns imply construction on a large scale and at least two phases of lime-burning.[57] An obvious candidate for such a project would be St Andrew's church, only a few metres away to the west, or one or more of the buildings of the new *curia*.

To summarise, the archaeological evidence demonstrates that neither the *curia* nor the church of St Andrew were incorporated into the new village of Shapwick in the tenth century. Indeed, the fact that they were not and that major structural alterations at the church or *curia* were being undertaken within a generation or two of the village being established may be sending a significant message. After all, why would a church not be sited for the greatest convenience of its congregation? Did Glastonbury Abbey perceive some advantage in the physical separation of the *curia* with its church and the village? Or was it simply a question of funds, with the Abbey preferring to commit itself to major alterations and repairs rather than to an expensive stone building in the new village? Inertia may have been a factor, but also custom – the old church site was no doubt bestowed with many family associations over the (at least) 400 years of its existence. Suspicions and beliefs might also have played a role; the separation of the dead in the existing churchyard from any new church may have been seen as lessening their chances of eternal salvation. And whilst we know the land was later taken into cultivation when the church was eventually moved, this would not have happened right away, probably not for several generations, so there would have been no immediate economic advantage in terms of gaining more ground for cultivation, even if that were considered a priority.

It is possible, too, that villagers in the tenth century might not have wanted the dead in their midst. After all, in a pre-nucleated landscape the majority of people would have lived at a distance from the church and its burial ground. People were content to bury at a distance from their settlements, as at Cannington, for example, where a cemetery was in use near the hillfort up to *c.* AD 700, or at Henley Wood, where the fifth- to seventh-century cemetery lies away from the site of Congresbury hillfort.[58] When minsters were founded in the late seventh and early eighth centuries it is presumed that most people were then buried next to the church. Again, these dead were not in the midst of the ordinary people in their dispersed settlements; they were buried where a group of clerics were present to pray for them. Living with the dead may well have been an idea that took some getting used to, and it might have been only in the centuries following settlement nucleation, when local lords started to found churches for themselves and their tenants, that people came to accept it as normal.[59] A survey of ninety-two medieval villages in south-east Somerset revealed that 14 per cent of churches were outside their local population centre, so the situation at Shapwick is not as unusual as it may seem at first.[60] Winter or summer, rain or shine, for the next 400 years the villagers would have to walk the 500m eastwards to attend services, baptise their children and bury their dead.

Watermills

While there is no mention of a mill at Shapwick in Domesday Book in 1086, there might have been a number of early medieval watermills along the minor streams of the parish. We know of such smaller mills elsewhere in England from excavations at West Cotton, Raunds (Northants)[61] and Tamworth (Staffs),[62] for example. At Shapwick one particularly interesting cluster of Roman, early medieval and later medieval pottery has been identified in Fields 0387 and 9400, immediately to the south of Kent Farm and on either side of the 'Holy Brook'. This area, adjacent to the later medieval mill site at Kent mill, is called *Pond Field*. Nine unworked fragments of Mendip Old Red Sandstone, suitable for making querns, as well as a piece of Wedmore building stone, the same as that used in St Andrew's church, were collected from here. The possibility exists that this collection of stone is all that remains of a tenth- or eleventh-century or earlier watermill. Another concentration of stone, including a large quantity of Wedmore stone and Mendip Old

Red Sandstone and fragments of Ham stone and Hestercombe diorite,[63] was recovered in Field 8144 and this may be another, undated, mill site. Such watermills are likely to have been of the 'horizontal' or 'Norse' type, which leave little archaeological trace, though a large number are known from Ireland from the seventh century, where they are often associated with monastic holdings.[64] They consisted of little more than a timber shed positioned over a stream with paddles on a horizontal wheel that were pushed round by the force of the water and drove the mill stones in the upper half of the building (Figure 6.16). With no need for gearing or elaborate waterworks to channel the water onto the wheel, such a relatively simple technology could have been employed widely across the late Saxon landscape.

A new landscape

Fields and farming

Across the county, evidence for the origins of open-field agriculture from boundary clauses in Anglo-Saxon charters remains ambiguous,[65] and archaeology currently provides little detail for crops or for any marked change in their relative proportions.[66] Fortunately, we can at least get some sense of the extent of the late Saxon farming landscape at Shapwick by examining the distributions of pottery collected by fieldwalkers (Figure 6.17A). It is not unreasonable to assume that this material got into the fields alongs with manure and domestic debris and to suggest that it provides an indication of the area devoted to arable agriculture. What emerges is a rectangle of cultivated land symmetrical to the site of the new village covering about 234ha. If there were two fields of more or less equal size here, then the area under the plough in any one year would have been roughly 125ha, or 309 acres.[67] This area is bounded by higher land to the south of High Street and Lippitts Way, a marginal strip along the Catcott boundary and the area east of the Cats Drove stream (in the Northbrook area). To the north there seems to have been uncultivated marshland, while the sherd distribution also suggests that the Nidons were not cultivated and that there was uncleared woodland encircling this central cultivated core, especially to the south, where Loxley Wood remained later.

Several interesting points of debate emerge from

this, though admittedly discussion is not helped by the meagre volumes of later Anglo-Saxon pottery plotted on the distribution map. The first point is that some clustering is evident, particularly to the east of the village envelope, as if manuring had differed in its intensity across the parish. Had there been extensive cultivation in place, as there was by the fourteenth century in the 'common fields' of Shapwick, then perhaps we might have expected a more even spread of material than this. Possibly then there were subdivided 'open' fields in existence, but without the strict regulation we might associate with a 'common field' system. In fact, the distribution plot looks rather more like what we might expect had there been an infield–outfield system in operation. A second point to note is that not all of the pre-existing field boundaries can have been swept away. It is much more likely that some older fields were incorporated into the new layout shown on Figure 6.17A. Excavation at the core of the East Field in Field 2700 indicates as much, suggesting that some of the boundaries of furlong blocks in the open fields follow pre-existing alignments. Finally, the eastern edge of the distribution of early medieval pottery terminates more or less at the point where the field boundary alignments change from the 85° alignments in the centre of the parish and the East Field (highlighted in orange on Figure 6.17B) to the 97° alignments further to the east and in Ashcott parish (highlighted in blue). This might lead us to conclude that open fields were established in these peripheral areas rather later than they were in the centre of the parish. And if this is right, the pottery and the evidence from field boundaries suggest that there must have been an expansion in the open fields of Shapwick between *c.*1000 and *c.*1250. We shall return to this point in Chapter 7, but the main point to emphasise here is that the full development of the open-field system must have proceeded in stages, both in terms of its overall extent and its regulation. While there may have been wholesale reorganisation of the landscape in or by the tenth century, the patterns established at that time did not endure unaltered.

Pasture and woodland

There must have been pasture land both on the fallow of the open field when it was not in cultivation and down on the Levels when the peat was sufficiently

Figure 6.16. Thatched water mill at Huxter (A), one of several aligned along this stream on the Shetland mainland. B: interior showing millstones. The upper stone rotated on a spindle driven by the force of the water acting on the horizontal wheel below. Grain would have been stored in a wooden hopper above. The rectangular basin around the millstones is a 'flour bin', from which milled grain could be scooped into sacks. On the right is the 'sword' under which a wedge is inserted. This connected to the 'sole tree' which supported the weight of the spindle/millstone assembly and wheel. The sword allowed the whole assembly to be raised or lowered and could be used as a kind of clutch. Mills like this one, easy to construct and low in maintenance, may once have been ubiquitous before the Norman Conquest.

dry underfoot. Defining areas of woodland is more difficult, though a start can be made by assuming that those fields without late Saxon pottery in them on Figure 6.17A were not cultivated. Some support for this idea comes from later medieval 'woodland' names which sit around the boundaries of the parish map, from *Lockesleigh* in the south to *La Hurste* in the east, *Caterwode* in the north and *Broadwood* in the west (Figure 6.17A). The last two named woodlands might, however, be later medieval in origin; only the name *Loxley* is convincingly pre-Domesday. The 'ley' element of Loxley refers to OE *leah*, a word meaning

Figure 6.17. Evidence for fields and farming in the late Anglo-Saxon landscape. A: the distribution of early medieval pottery from fieldwalking, also showing the main Roman sites and early sixteenth-century woodland names. B: the orientations of field boundaries with excavation in Field 2700 highlighted. C: the distribution of wayfaring tree (Viburnum lantana) in hedgerows. D: the distribution of wild madder (Rubia peregrina) in hedgerows.

'wood' or 'clearing' that can be interpreted as 'an indicator of woodland which was in existence and regarded as ancient when English speakers arrived in any region'.[68] There are many examples of similar names near Shapwick; Whitley in Walton[69] is one, but there are also Butleigh and Butleigh Wootton to the east, as well as Leigh in Street.[70] In our region we might expect the common usage of Old English from the eighth century, so early medieval woodland was, it seems, considerably more extensive then than it is today. Some woodlands are likely to have been managed to produce timber for building and wood for rods and poles to make fencing and wattle, while other parts may have been wood pasture, where animals could graze and forage more freely.

To help pin down the extent of woodland at this period one additional source of evidence is open to us: the distribution of plant species in Shapwick's hedgerows. Figures 6.17C and D, for example, show the concentrations of wayfaring tree and wild madder across the parish. On the face of it, and without considering further the botanical habits of these two species at this stage, these distributions could be taken to confirm that Loxley, in the south-west of the parish, once extended all along the high ground on the southern boundary of the parish and that the open-field block later called Eastfield by Northbrook, in the east of the parish, was also originally more wooded, together with the Nidons and the margins of the Levels. The hedges with wayfaring tree and wild madder might therefore be 'ghosts', the vestigial remains of woodland habitats left behind when the intervening woodland was cleared. However, neither the field shapes nor the overall botanical structure of the local hedgerows suggest this to be the case and there is probably a more complex interplay of mechanisms at work. One possibility is that, if the woodlands were once larger than they are today, any hedges that abutted or lay close to them would be more likely to be colonised by 'woodland' species. This might happen in several ways, such as the slow colonisation of 'woodland' plants out from the woodland edges or the deposition of seeds in the droppings of woodland birds nesting in nearby hedgerows. Both these mechanisms might be a partial explanation for the distinctive distributions of species seen on Figures 6.17C and D. Another explanation, one that we will explore further in Chapter 9, is

that these distributions were artificially encouraged by local farmers who planted up their hedges with saplings from the local woodland at the time of enclosure. In addition, the distributions of hedgerow plants may have become more exaggerated if those species that are more sensitive to ground conditions did not survive. So, while the distributions of some plant species in the hedgerows and the area we have reconstructed as early open fields in the late Anglo-Saxon period seem to be mutually exclusive, it is still possible that both spatial patterns may in fact be related to something quite different – a combination of soil pH, moisture and microclimate.

We are left with a frustratingly partial picture of pre-Domesday land use, though one further observation should be made. As Figure 6.17A shows, at least five of the seven major Roman settlements that we identified in Chapter 4 lie outside the core of arable cultivation as defined by the tenth-century pottery scatters. The possible implication of this is that woodland may have regenerated in the extremities of the parish during the post-Roman period.[71] Whether or not this regeneration began in the fifth, sixth or seventh century cannot be accurately determined but, given the pollen evidence discussed in Chapter 5, our working hypothesis is that woodland regenerated later rather than earlier in this chronology and that it was then followed by renewed clearance as the open fields were extended in the period AD 900–1300.[72] This may be when inroads were made into the north side of Loxley Wood as assarting took place (see Figure B.3.4).

The only archaeological information we have about the Shapwick stock that grazed in these fields comes from the years immediately before the Norman Conquest of 1066. Excavations at *Old Church* recovered a remarkable assemblage of animal skeletons from the upper fills of the disused limekiln (R38, see above), including six of cattle, more than one of horse and two of pigs.[73] This assemblage, which is shown being sampled in Figure 6.14B, subsequently produced a radiocarbon date between AD 980 and 1160,[74] though on statistical grounds the bones are most likely to have been dumped here in the first decades of the new millennium between 1000 and 1050. There is little doubt that some of these bones were merely domestic refuse, the pigs being a case in point, but the intriguing feature of the cattle carcases is that they show no sign of cut marks, butchery or gnawing, so they were neither eaten nor left out to rot. Indeed, care was taken to dispose of them and some attempt may have been made to sterilise the environment by adding white lime and charcoal. The absence of younger animals is also striking; on the basis of wear to their mandible teeth the cattle can be aged between 3 and 10 years old and these were probably oxen that had served as draught animals. The best explanation is that some catastrophic event, such as 'murrain' – as the disease was referred to in medieval documents – caused their death. Murrain is best thought of as a generic term that referred to several different diseases as we would recognise them today, ranging from sheep scab to foot rot and 'foot and mouth', though one author believes that it could have been rinderpest.[75] Whatever it was, in this instance the disease devastated the local cattle population to the extent that nothing could be salvaged. Two later episodes of high cattle mortality are known on the Glastonbury Abbey estates, in 1258–59 and the early 1320s respectively,[76] while the *Anglo-Saxon Chronicle* records three episodes of disease among cattle in the years 1048, 1111 and 1131, all of which fall within the range of the radiocarbon dates for the Shapwick pit.[77] Unlike the bone assemblages that are usually available to faunal specialists for study, this one does not represent the remains of domestic consumption. Rather, these animals represent part of a live herd that under normal circumstances would have been slaughtered elsewhere on the Glastonbury estate.[78]

As quickly becomes clear, between the eighth and sixteenth centuries the Glastonbury connection was inescapable for Shapwick. Although in the late Saxon period there were other places nearby with markets, most obviously at Axbridge to the north and Langport to the south,[79] to reach either of these would have required the crossing of peat moors, something which may only have been conducted safely in the height of the driest summer. These and other further-flung Anglo-Saxon towns, such as Bath, Bruton, Frome, Ilchester and Taunton, had mints as well, but they were some distance from Shapwick and probably had little day-to-day impact on the village. On the other hand, the ridgeway along the Polden crest to Glastonbury and the lanes on the slope below, the *Veryswey* and the *Harepath*, were well trodden.

A wider context

It is widely thought that the large royal federative estates began to break up during the period between AD 800 and 1000 as smaller blocks of land were reallocated to thegns or tenants-in-chief on a more permanent basis.[80] These allocations were generally fixed at units of about five hides and comprised a range of agricultural resources such as woodland and grazing.[81] Many later parishes, with their villages and churches, and surrounded by their own open-field systems, may have emerged at this time, although this is difficult to demonstrate in detail for any one estate. Adequate documentary evidence is lacking for the tenth and eleventh centuries, and it is doubtful whether the process could be charted easily from what survives of the archaeology in the ground. For this reason it is necessary to set our findings into a more general historical context. Specifically, we need to understand a little more about the role and responsibilities of the Abbey's thegns and to assess the impact of wider demographic trends on what was happening in and around Shapwick.

On the first point, the great *Pouholt* estate had already been divided up into smaller units by the time of Domesday Book, though for the most part it was not administered or assessed using the particular individual parishes that we know today, as we might expect. The reason for this is that, before Dunstan's reformation of the monastery in the tenth century, Glastonbury appears to have housed a group of canons or priests and would have been more like a minster church than the later medieval monastery that is so familiar to us. The canons or priests probably held Glastonbury's lands in a prebendal type of system – in other words, the land was divided up between them to provide many individual incomes, rather than being held in common so that each might benefit equally from a shared income.[82] The grouping of the *Pouholt* manors as they are listed in Domesday Book therefore reflects this: a holding centred on Shapwick, comprising Sutton Mallet, Edington, Chilton Polden, Catcott and Woolavington; a holding centred on Walton, comprising Compton Dundon, Ashcott and Pedwell; and a holding at Butleigh.[83] These 'mini multiple estates', as we might like to think of them, exist only amongst the lands that Glastonbury acquired in the ninth century or earlier.[84] Each group of manors seems to comprise a block of demesne belonging to the Abbey together with one or more blocks of land held by thegns who provided military service in return.

Much of late Saxon society was organised in this way, with thegns holding their land directly from the king in return for military assistance when it was needed. These individuals would have lived in large halls on their estates with their military supporters and retainers[85] and through the eleventh century they increasingly settled their men on separate small estates (the later parishes) in a process called 'enfeoffment'. This explains the presence of the thegns who held land by the time of Domesday; it was their responsibility to provide the military service that the Abbey owed to the king. Accordingly, the monasteries set aside some of their lands to provide for their thegns[86] because even after the king had given away land on the royal estate to his retainers he would still normally expect all the renders due to him from that estate, along with the requisite military service.[87] Thus the portions of land granted to Glastonbury Abbey by the king in the disputed sequence of grants described in Chapter 5 would still have provided thegns[88] to serve as soldiers in the king's army, though the land would almost certainly have been exempt from other secular dues.[89] The food renders might go partly to support the thegns themselves, but mostly to the monks in the monastery. In compensation, the monastery would no doubt have been obliged to be hospitable to the king and his retinue whenever they visited.

By the time of Domesday we can identify the numbers of thegns settled on the *Pouholt* estate who were providing this military service. Sutton Mallet, Edington, Chilton Polden and Catcott were held in King Edward's time by fourteen different thegns, one of whom is named as Alwy, son of Banna. These individuals, Domesday tells us, 'could not be separated from the church', which shows that they were part of Glastonbury's provision of men for military service.[90] By 1086, however, virtually all of this land had been confiscated by William I, who then redistributed it again to his own knights. A good proportion of this Glastonbury land, including Sutton Mallet, Edington, Chilton Polden and Catcott, was duly passed to Roger of Courseulles (in Normandy).[91] Some of the remainder appears to have been confiscated outright; the count of

Mortain, William's half-brother,[92] is recorded as holding Kingstone, Stoke-sub-Hamdon and Draycot directly from the king, whereas all had previously been thegnland of the Abbey. The values given in Domesday Book show us how onerous this burden of military service was judged to be. The abbot's portion of the Shapwick estates was worth £12, Roger of Courseulles' portion was worth £19, while that of Alfred of Épaignes[93] (who held Woolavington) was worth £7. So, at Domesday, the total value of the Shapwick manors was £38, £12 of which belonged to the abbot directly and £26 of which went as income to his military tenants. Essentially the abbot retained under a third of the total value of this group of Polden manors,[94] but he saw to it that the monastery fulfilled its military obligations with as little involvement as possible.

Much of this early arrangement survived the Norman Conquest and later became formalised in the feudal system as land held in return for military service by knights, each unit of land being a 'knight's fee'.[95] Later still this service was commuted to a cash payment (or scutage) and these obligations were recorded in 1166 in the *Cartae Baronum*.[96] In certain cases, therefore, there is a relationship between the tenth-century thegn with his five-hide unit and the twelfth-century knight,[97] and ultimately their purpose was the same. Not only would the lord, in our case Glastonbury Abbey, have to muster the required number of armed men for the king, but status would be conferred on the tenant, be it a thegn or knight, as a minor lord of a small estate (later a manor or parish).[98] Eventually, some of these smaller units (the later parishes) were called after the thegn who had received them (or a Norman knight after the Conquest).[99] Men at the social level of thegns and knights were anxious to better themselves and to establish dynasties so that land, property and possessions could be passed to their successors. Acquiring small estates, the later parishes, was one mechanism of achieving this ambition.[100]

The second broad point we need to touch upon is demography. It is thought that the population was rising at this time and that there were, therefore, more mouths to feed.[101] This is not something which is easy to calculate with any accuracy; there are few measurable data that can be quantified. Increases in the volume of pre-Conquest pottery recovered by fieldwalkers, for example, may merely be symptomatic of its easier availability, while counting numbers of recorded settlements is hardly more reliable. A broad impression is gained only by combining several different sources of evidence, among them estimates of Roman population levels which can be contrasted against those assumed from Domesday Book, as well as charters, place-names, numismatic evidence, the development of proto-urban sites such as *burhs*, cemetery data and archaeology, all of which indicate a substantial expansion of settlement into new areas of the landscape from the later seventh century onwards. Given that the early medieval diet of this expanding population was predominantly cereal based (bread, pottage and ale),[102] armies of well-organised peasants were needed to tend the fields. This was not only because there were more mouths to feed but because a greater proportion of the population was no longer directly involved in food production and made their living instead from crafts, industry and commercial activity.[103]

The obvious difficulty with this assumption is that there is no simple match between population figures extracted from Domesday Book and those parts of the country with lots of villages. In a general sense, however, we think that the changes to settlement and field systems in the tenth century might have been stimulated as much by the need to produce more cereals in order to feed a growing rural and urban population as they were to support the non-productive military sector of thegns. By organising communities into nucleated settlements and by regulating the way in which farming was conducted in the open fields through manorial customs (see Chapter 7), crops could be produced in greater quantities. At critical months in the farming year the whole community could have become involved in activities such as ploughing and weeding, particularly during the harvest, when all the grain for future food supplies and for seed for the next sowing season had to be brought in as expeditiously as possible. While those at the lower end of the social scale must have suffered considerable disruption from the imposition of this new system they also gained secure tenure in return. The result was that enough of a surplus was created to support the non-productive military elite as well as those who lived in the towns and monasteries. Indeed, rural and urban populations were now mutually dependent upon each other – the exchange of goods, including agricultural produce,

was facilitated through the new markets and fairs being granted to the towns.

To summarise this sequence of events, we believe that the proliferation of smaller tenurial units under the sub-tenancy of various thegns goes hand-in-hand with the foundation of villages, open-field systems and village names.[104] A new estate might even be christened after its thegnly controller and later, of course, these holdings became parishes. In effect, what we are observing in this process is the delegation of control by large institutions such as Glastonbury Abbey to private individuals (we might think of them very loosely as 'country gentry') who then administered quite small areas of land for certain largely self-serving objectives, resulting in the invigoration of the rural economy. Though there was stability at the level of ownership, at least for the great ecclesiastical estates, beneath that level responsibilities were repeatedly devolved down to small independently managed holdings. Perhaps the most visible impact of this on today's countryside is the presence of a church in most rural settlements. Many of these churches were paid for by landholders for their own use and that of their tenants. We can see this in action with the foundation of churches at Edington, Chilton Polden and Sutton Mallet.

In the area of Shapwick exactly this kind of pattern of small units developed out of the partially fragmented *Pouholt* estate, probably over a relatively short period of time in the century or so before the Norman Conquest.[105] This much is suggested by a superficial examination of the parish boundaries on the northern flank of the Poldens, to the west of Shapwick. Here there appear to be five such smaller units that extend from the prehistoric or Roman road at the crest of the hill down onto the peat moor below. From east to west, these are Catcott, Edington, Chilton Polden, Cossington and Woolavington (Figure 6.18). Edington, in particular, has a north–south orientation, a central stream and east–west tracks that define compartments in the village.[106] But all betray signs of planning[107] and all were pre-Conquest holdings belonging to Glastonbury Abbey. Four of these five are also five-hide units,[108] each containing a single settlement somewhere close to the mid-point on the slope, and all have place-names ending with '-tun' or '-cot'. Bearing in mind what we have said about the role

SHAPWICK

COSSINGTON

EDINGTON

⊕ Parish church

0   300m

Figure 6.18. The village plans of Shapwick, Cossington and Edington in the nineteenth century, taken from early editions of OS maps. The ladder plans of Shapwick and Edington are very similar, as are north–south elements of the Cossington plan.

of the Abbey's thegns at this period, it is probable that these place-names still preserve the names of those who originally took control of these estates: thus Woolavington might relate to Hunlaf or Wiglaf; Cossington to Cusa; Edington to Eadwine or Eadwynn (a woman); and Catcott to Cada.[109] Since we know that these estates belonged to the Abbey, these men and women cannot have been owners; rather, we should see them as ambitious sub-tenants keen to improve their incomes.[110] If they *are* behind the restructuring of these land units then this transformation must have taken place between the beginning of the eighth century, when the royal estate of *Pouholt* was passed over to Glastonbury Abbey (see Chapter 5), and 1066, when the names of all these units are recorded.[111] There is some support for this chronology from the archaeological evidence, in as far as one of the central blocks of the

village plan at Edington seems to have been occupied from the later tenth century. This was followed by further planned expansion at the northern end of the village, perhaps in the eleventh or twelfth centuries, so the sequence here seems to be similar to that at Shapwick.[112] Michael Costen, in his examination of settlements on lands belonging to Glastonbury Abbey in the tenth century, has pointed to other possible planned villages at East Lydford, West Pennard, High Ham and Low Ham, as well as at Lamyatt and Hornblotton.[113]

Shapwick, needless to say, is somewhat exceptional because the parish is not the same regular, rectangular shape as either Edington or Chilton Polden. In fact, the later parish is approximately twice the size of the other early units. Could it be an amalgamation of two five-hide units? If that were the case one of these two units might have been centred on a settlement in the

BOX 6.2

Old auster tenements

Above all it is the juxtaposition of low-lying peat moor and Polden upland that gives central Somerset its special landscape quality. In terms of modern land classification and management we tend to define the historic landscape character of these topographical units very differently; lines on maps demarcate where one zone ends and another begins. In the historic past, however, their distinctive agricultural qualities were considered to be complementary. When the King's Sedgemoor, to the south of the Polden Hills, came to be drained and enclosed in the late eighteenth century land was allocated in the newly drained moor in relation to the number of tenements in each of the surrounding villages that had existing rights of common there (Figure B.6.2). These areas of common rights are referred to as 'austres' or 'austers'; thus Shapwick, which had 3.49 per cent of all auster tenements in the area, was allotted 3.43 per cent of the moor.[b5]

Old auster tenancy was an ancient right that is first documented in the fourteenth century, though it is assumed to be much older. It was widespread in Somerset, being recorded from Combe St Nicholas, on the border with north Devon, to the parishes of Winscombe in the north, Stogumber in the west and Wookey in

Figure B.6.2. King's Sedgemoor from the air, looking east. This area was enclosed and drained in 1795. The dark fields in the centre of the picture, either side of the Shapwick Right Drove, were allocated to tenants in Shapwick. On the right of the picture, the wide 'rhyne' or canalised watercourse is King's Sedgemoor Drain.

west of the parish, perhaps somewhere near *Enworthy*, and the other on the long-lived settlement in *Old Church*. If *each* of these places had been allocated a long thin strip of land, like the others, then the same territorial pattern would be repeated westwards along the Poldens all the way to Cossington, the stream

down the middle of Shapwick village becoming the boundary between the two units. There would now be an *Enworthy* parish in what is now the western part of Shapwick parish, perhaps with its own planned village along the Shoot Brook east of Manor Farm. This village would perhaps have been named after its the east. A survey of 1650 for the manor of Winscombe, in north Somerset, suggests that the properties with old auster rights were entitled to unlimited (unstinted) pasture over all the commons, greens, and wastes of the parish. This was a very valuable resource that enabled tenants to keep many more animals than their individual holdings could otherwise have supported. Widows could continue with these rights, though they came with obligations and responsibilities – a heriot of best goods was to be paid on the death of the tenants[b6] and there were banks, ditches and sluices to be maintained if flood water was to be kept off the low-lying land. Old austers were therefore one of a number of ancient privileges enjoyed by a relatively select group of villagers on the basis of their landholding and status.

The fact that Shapwick formerly had grazing rights in King's Sedgemoor, to the *south* of the Poldens, as did most of the other Polden villages, is a good indication that the *Pouholt* estate also had extensive rights in the same area. More significant for our purposes, however, in terms of mapping the spatial development of medieval settlement, is that old auster rights may have been granted to the original core properties in the village when the settlement was originally being planned and laid out. Other obligations, such as maintenance of the churchyard wall and gates, seem also to be attached to these older properties. It is thus of considerable interest to learn how this type of tenancy worked in Shapwick, where a combination of enclosure records for Sedgemoor and mid-eighteenth-century maps for the village demonstrates a cluster of five or six old auster tenements at the north end of the village (Figure B.6.3). Although this is almost certainly not the full number of properties involved it may provide some measure of support for the notion that the northern part of the village was established first. Further research on Somerset villages is needed to investigate the implications of this discovery more fully.

Figure B.6.3. The distribution of old auster tenements across the village.

thegn tenant in the late Anglo-Saxon period and in time it might have acquired its own parish church.[114] And, of course, there would probably also be a village next to the old church site in the eastern unit, just west of Beerway Farm.

But this is not what happened. There are, in fact, no personal names attached to settlements in the later parish of Shapwick. For some reason the fission of the earlier estate never proceeded to its logical end-point here. If there were ever two units originally they were combined and treated as a single entity when the parishes were laid out. Probably such a disproportionately sized unit of land reflects Shapwick's high status in the medieval period, with this large unit having been retained as the demesne part of the estate to be farmed directly by Glastonbury Abbey itself. It is even possible that the Shapwick unit was once somewhat larger, because some intermixing with the land of Ashcott on the eastern bounds of the parish is described in the 1515 survey,[115] implying that at some stage Ashcott and Shapwick were considered to be a single territorial unit,[116] and this arrangement is echoed in the fact that Ashcott was a dependent chapelry of Shapwick. The broader point to emphasise is that the fission of estates in this area was a continuous process and that, for example, Shapwick and Catcott were split from each other before Shapwick and Ashcott. Since Ashcott does not form part of the Domesday entry for Shapwick, however, even this took place before the end of the eleventh century.[117]

We have suggested in this chapter that some of the motives behind the creation of the nucleated village were social and economic, but, in a sense, we might go one step further and claim that the nucleated village is merely the by-product of another major change in the landscape at this period, and that is the establishment of open-field systems. The argument can be crystallised like this. The old multiple estates had a good deal of under-cultivated land (see Figure 1.5). One way to improve income and self-sufficiency at a time of rising population was to encourage higher yields through improved technology (that is, the plough), but a far greater impact could be had by fundamentally recasting the ways in which farmers laboured together in the fields, imposing greater cooperation and coordination in the agricultural cycle and the more efficient spatial arrangement of fields. For groups of tenants sharing plough-teams this would have made a lot more economic sense. By gathering all the people together to live in a single settlement this freed up more space and effectively created a new landscape canvas on which fields could be laid out. Thus village creation and the establishment of open fields may each be parts of one and the same process. Not so much a 'village moment' as a dramatic and sudden *landscape* transformation. There must have been a first season when whatever system that had operated before, perhaps fields worked individually

(in severalty) by tenant farmers, was replaced by new strips allocated to tenant farmers in furlong blocks in each open field, west and east,[118] when the old way of arable farming ceased and a new arrangement of open-field farming began.[119]

Domesday Book

In 1066 William of Normandy successfully invaded England and with his supporters took over the country, displacing the Anglo-Saxon landowners. At the very end of the period discussed in this chapter a great survey was undertaken to assess the value of estates and to ascertain to whom they were allocated. The Great or Exchequer Domesday Book was a product of the great Inquisition set in train by King William I after 'deep speak' at Gloucester during Christmas 1085.[120] The *Anglo-Saxon Chronicle* makes clear that this survey was unparalleled and the English of a later age gave it the name 'Domesday' in reference to the Book of Judgement. It seems likely that all the data collected were initially compiled into preparatory volumes; the version for south-west England survives in the Exeter Cathedral Library as Exeter Domesday (also known as Exon). This gives fuller and more authoritative information than Great Domesday, which seems to be an abbreviated assessment of the main items.[121] As well as Domesday Book for the south-western counties there are tax returns or geld rolls that record taxes, probably for 1084; these are also included in the Exeter or Exon Domesday. What can these great surveys tell us about the arrangement of the settlement and lands we have been describing?

The entry for Shapwick provides our first relatively detailed view of the community in its landscape. Domesday Book, of course, was not written for present-day scholars and it is sometimes difficult to grasp exactly what the information is telling us.[122] The Domesday entry for Shapwick cannot simply be equated with what was to become the parish of Shapwick. To begin with, Glastonbury Abbey treated most of its holdings on the western end of the Poldens as a single manorial estate, so that the Domesday entries for Sutton Mallet, Edington, Chilton Polden, Catcott and Woolavington are united as one under the heading of Shapwick. Moorlinch, which is not mentioned, was probably amalgamated as well. Most of these places were leased out to other landowners, who are listed in Exeter Domesday.[123] It was clearly convenient to record them like this in 1086, but possibly the roots of the division of the entries lie in a much earlier time, perhaps even as far back as when the church of Glastonbury was held by canons in the pre-Dunstan reformation period (see above).[124]

Even bearing in mind that the entry does include other places, the Shapwick estate was large and wealthy, taxed for thirty hides. In its entirety, this area was large enough to require forty plough-teams to prepare the arable land[125] and to add to this there was other land for an additional twenty plough-teams on which the abbots of Glastonbury had never paid tax. In all, 124 people are listed on the whole estate,[126] but this is unlikely to include everyone in the population, as Frank Thorn points out. Probably only heads of households were recorded. In addition, there is no mention of a supervisor (bailiff, reeve or steward), of wives, or of children, old people or a priest. We probably need to multiply the figure of 124 by three or four at least to get at the real size of the population living over this wider area.

For the purposes of the survey these heads of households and their families were regarded as part of the equipment of the estate. The entry goes on to detail the other resources – the animals and the different kinds of land use. Thus, in the Exon entry for Shapwick, there are two cob-horses, twenty-three cattle, eleven pigs and 100 sheep listed, together with fifty-seven acres of underwood, perhaps at Loxley, sixty acres of meadow and the same of pasture. The Levels do not appear to be assessed or included. Values are then given for the whole estate, the portion directly in Glastonbury's hands being worth considerably more than when Abbot Thurstan received it about ten years before, when it had been worth only £7.[127] So, it looks as if there had been considerable investment and development in the estate even in the twenty years since the Norman Conquest. Perhaps the figures indicate the further development of the field system, the clearance of remaining woodland around the core of the open fields and investment in the plots and tenements within the village.

Landscape archaeologist Steve Rippon has examined the relationship between the Domesday data and the emergence of villages and open fields at a broader county level.[128] He finds no correlations between the pattern of villages and the distribution of early medieval woodland or meadow, population density, numbers of plough-teams (and therefore arable) or any measure of economic development such as towns, mints or markets. Although conditions of topography, natural environment, land use, population and economic development similar to those at Shapwick can be found in other parts of the county, villages did not develop there. We find his observations and arguments convincing and this leads us to believe, like him, that some other factor must explain the distribution of villages. One possibility is the influence of lordship, but not all the Glastonbury manors recorded at Domesday had villages, and not all villages lie on the Abbey's manors. Once more, Rippon identifies a considerable variety of planning, even on Glastonbury estates, from the 'ladder' plan recognised at Shapwick through to the single row at nearby Meare. This diversity in village forms within the Abbey's ownership is another argument for the involvement of thegns and perhaps local communities in the decision-making process.

Domesday Book may be silent about the many changes that had taken place at Shapwick and elsewhere over the previous 200 years, but it is remarkably informative even though by this time the old multiple estates had been dismantled and had evolved into many separate manors, self-contained units run from their own centres. In this chapter we have proposed how, why and when the village of Shapwick came into existence as an integral part of this process. We believe this to have been a tenth-century event that is explained by a combination of factors including the break-up of multiple estates and their substitution by smaller, less diverse territories, the emergence of the thegnly class, the perceived greater economic benefit of a community-based approach to agriculture in the face of new technologies and, finally, the increasing pressures of arable production for a growing population. In the case of Shapwick it may be that one man, Abbot Dunstan of Glastonbury, either allowed village creation by new sub-lords or else pressed through the decision himself, together with the introduction of open-field farming. We shall perhaps never know the answer for certain.

CHAPTER SEVEN

Manor and Abbey

Schapewik in the Later Medieval Period, 1100–1539

Matilda atte Welle, middle-aged widow, sat alone and tired. Idly trapping a flea against her leg with her finger, she dropped it into the cess bucket. It was getting dark and, although it was spring, there was still no break in the weather. At least it was warm and comfortable under the straw thatch of her cob house, if rather smoky. She could rest easy – there would be no lambing for another fortnight yet. On the fire, built up from strips of peat from the moor and the kindling she had gleaned from the floor of the wood at Loxley, Matilda's cauldron-like cooking pot was 'seething' hard. It was brimful of cereal grains, onions, soaked peas and beans. A neighbour with bad breath, Thomas Whibbery, the one who complained of tooth-worm, had given her a few beef bones with scraps of meat on them, and her two growing sons would eat well tonight with the pottage, bread and some cider.

She didn't know how she was going to get by now that her husband, Adam, had passed on. The Abbot, the lord of the manor, would press her to remarry; a widow with a quarter-virgate of land was an attractive proposition to the many landless labourers that were about. Much as she wanted to carry on with the holding herself, Matilda would need to fulfil her obligations to the Abbot first – ploughing, haymaking and harvesting. Her holding of thirty strips was widely scattered in the two common fields and some of them took an age to walk to. Recently, in heavy rain, the cart had become mired in the thick clay soil and it had taken a whole hour just to arrive at her strip in Cranefurlong in the West Field, only for her to find it too wet to sow. She was exhausted when she finally returned but her luck changed the very next day when some long-forgotten coins were turned up by the plough. The Abbot had allowed her to keep one; 'always labouring for our betters', Matilda thought. The steward had joked that they would call the furlong 'Goldhorde' now. She would buy a few more sheep at the autumn fair in Glastonbury with the money, but until then the gold coin would stay strung around her neck for safety.

Still she felt low, even after a couple of draughts of the cider from a horn cup. She could not rely on the soil to keep throwing up coins! She had to put her faith in the Lord and hard work. Her sons would help; they were steady, healthy lads and one of them would probably inherit the holding one day (and they would get the heriot sorted out, she had promised). But she was clear in her own mind that they would also have to hire some labour. If they could buy in some help to fulfil their labour services for the Abbot then they could spend their own time working on their holding. Her husband had acquired a big-shouldered ox, 4 years old and trained up, which helped to make up the eight oxen of one of the village plough teams, but what Matilda really wanted was a cow. Then she could make cheese, not only for themselves, but to sell in her baskets at the weekly market outside the Abbey gate. 'I'll be needing another crock', she thought absentmindedly, 'and a wickerwork sieve, to separate the whey and press the curds'.

This story takes place in the thirteenth century. Though the recovery of Roman artefacts in the medieval period is an intriguing facet of the archaeological record at Shapwick, for her continuing prosperity Matilda would have relied on the transmission of land through the family, from father to son. 'Heriot' is best translated as a death duty; in this case, Shapwick peasantry were to give up either their best beast or their most valuable possession.

As tenants, they neither owned the land they farmed nor were they free to move between estates or to labour where or when they wished. Instead, they paid rent for their houses, provided unpaid labour service on the Abbey's lands and ground their corn at the Abbey's mill at Kent Farm. The village was a close-knit unit that provided subsistence for its occupants and a varying agricultural surplus that was extracted by the Abbey. This system was founded upon obligations and duties and depended upon cooperation between villagers.

Matilda's thrifty use of the donated meat scraps makes the point that cattle bones are not always the most accurate indicators of beef consumption. Bones like those given by Thomas were a nutritious addition to soups, stocks and heavier food such as pottage; the vegetables would have come from her own garden and the cider apples from her orchard. Dairy products such as cheese are one reason Matilda might have wanted a cow, but these were multi-functional animals that could produce calves, be milked and work a few acres; Matilda's quarter-virgate equates to about ten acres of arable land. Oral hygiene (confirmed by tooth loss in adult mandibles from the graveyard) rather than diet was more than likely the cause of her neighbour's bad breath.

In the later Middle Ages Shapwick was one of the thirty or so manors that made up the estate of Glastonbury Abbey, by this time one of the richest monastic houses in England. Particularly from the twelfth century onwards, developments in the village and its surrounding fields all become considerably clearer to the archaeologist and historian. As we will see in this chapter, this is partly because there is an abundance of pottery, metalwork and structural features, but also because the documentary detail is richer. Domesday Book, compiled in 1086, and a series of Glastonbury Abbey documents provide an increasingly vivid view of life in the parish; ordinary Shapwick people are named for the first time and the everyday life of medieval country folk begins to come into focus. At the end of our period the survey by Abbot Beere (1493–1524/5), compiled in 1515, gives not only a snapshot of each tenant and their holding in the village but also a picture of individual farming strips out in the fields.

The medieval village

Most of the families who lived in medieval Shapwick were tenants of the Abbey. The men folk, including boys from the age of 12, would have been stockmen, shepherds, ploughmen and labourers, handy at most tasks around the farm from ditch-digging to pig-killing. Their lives were governed by the farming year, from ploughing in winter and spring through cycles of harrowing, sowing and weeding to the busy harvest, carting corn, mowing meadows and making haystooks. Individual circumstances varied a

good deal. Whether 'virgator' or lowly 'cottar', social status was judged not solely on the basis of material possessions – for, as we shall see, these were few and far between – but on the size of the holdings of individuals and their obligations either in terms of services to the Abbey or the cash payments that replaced them during the course of the fourteenth century.[1] Landless men and male children who worked as paid labourers for the Abbot and his tenants, known as *garciones* ('lads'), were at the base of this social hierarchy, while at the top were the miller, blacksmith, priest, reeve and bailiff.[2] For all of these men (women and young children are less often mentioned by name) the monastery at Glastonbury was central to their daily lives, from the blacksmiths who forged the ironwork for the ploughs and shod the lord's 'affers' (working horses) to the four men who drove their carts to Baltonsborough, 12km (eight miles) away, to collect and carry firewood to the Abbey.[3] Even when they travelled together down the 'king's highway' to Pilton, it was to fence lengths of the pale of the Abbey's deer park there. Village and monastery were tightly bound.

Roads

Several of the modern lanes that criss-cross the medieval parish from east to west were ancient routes. As Figure 7.1 shows, the *Veryswey*, 'the road to the fair',[4] ran across the middle of the parish, taking the line of modern Northbrook Road through the village. It was gated, presumably to keep beasts from straying into vegetable patches.[5] The *Harepathewey* that led from Catcott to the *King's Highway called Riggeweye*[6]

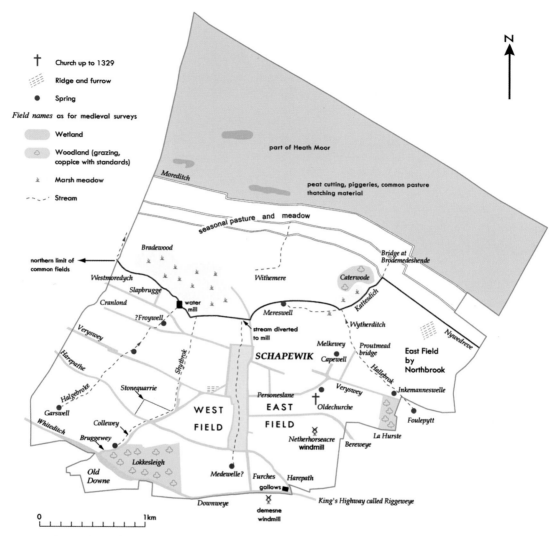

Figure 7.1. *The parish in the later Middle Ages (1100–1540), showing land use, roads, bridges and other places. Note the symmetry of village and fields.*

ran along the modern High Street/Lippetts Way. There were far fewer north–south routes, but a myriad of paths led out into the common fields: *Personeslane*,[7] the *Collewey*, *Bruggewey* and the *Greneweye* in the west, and the *Melkewey* and *Beerwey* in the East Field. Those referred to as 'droves' headed out northwards onto the pastures of the peat moor. *Nywedreve*, for example, the modern Buscott Lane, lay in the north-east of the parish. Where the droves crossed streams such as the *Kattesdych*, *Westmoredych* or *Wethyrdych* there were, by the early fourteenth century at least,

wooden bridges – the timber for which proved too much of a temptation for Nicholas Pury, who made off with it in April 1307. Repairs could be a charge on all tenants, and one they might be reluctant to pay, just as they were in the troubled years of the late fourteenth century, when the *Slapbrugge* was fallen and submerged.[8]

Viewed as medieval eyes could never have seen it, in plan or from the air, Shapwick's roads and lanes formed a basic grid of geometric regularity (Figure 7.2). Those houses that we know of, either

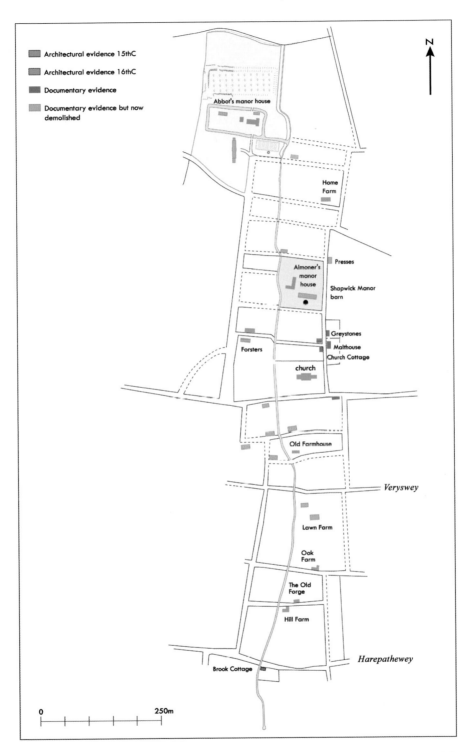

Figure 7.2. Shapwick village in the fifteenth and sixteenth centuries, showing buildings known to have existed from architectural or documentary evidence. Dwellings tend to be aligned along the horizontal 'rungs' of the ladder plan.

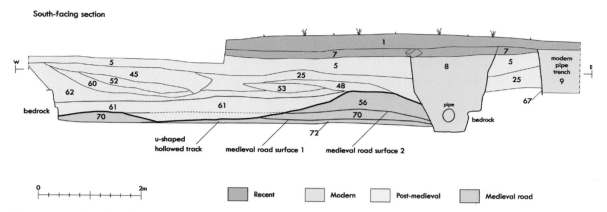

South-facing section

Figure 7.3. Archaeological section cut through the line of the medieval road behind (east of) the Old Bakery, showing repeated repairs and final infill in the early nineteenth century.

from documents or because they have been dated through their architecture, were built to face onto the interconnecting lanes. During the life of the Project we cut archaeological trenches across five of these lanes with the aim of dating their earliest phases of use and understanding how they had developed. These investigations showed how the bedrock initially provided convenient, smooth and horizontal surfaces before the roads became rutted (Figure 7.3). Even though these routes would have carried local traffic and not the merchants who plied the main *Riggeweye* past the gallows on the Polden crest, wear and tear were still considerable. Medieval West Street, for example, was eroded down into the bedrock in a hollow 7m wide, while on the other side of the village East Street sat in a trench 10m wide and 1.25m deep.[9] For villagers on foot the two streets must at times have more resembled streams than highways, and particularly so in a downpour. Matters were only made worse by the peasant farmers who shovelled out silt and dung to manure their gardens, paddocks and fields.[10]

Not until the mid-sixteenth century were English roads inspected and more regularly repaired, but until then the general practice at Shapwick was to dump stone, limestone cobbles and other loose materials readily to hand to level out the potholes. Only when surfaces became unacceptably worn and uneven were longer stretches levelled and relaid, a process that often shifted the road alignment to one side or

the other. If the evidence from Chapmans Lane and West Street is typical, major street repairs took place more or less simultaneously in the thirteenth century along Shapwick's inter-connected lanes, presumably at the instigation of the Abbey; this is a flourish of investment that seems to have coincided with the move of the *curia* into the village (see below).

Tofts

On either side of these lanes were drystone walls and ditches for drainage. Behind them lay houses, farms, yards, orchards and gardens; there is no evidence for a village green.[11] Properties were not defined in any sort of standardised way. Those on the western side of the High Street were separated from each other by a wide deep ditch[12] (Figure 7.4A), whereas the churchyard was bounded by a drystone wall.[13] Hill Farm had a banked boundary with a drystone wall along the top at one time, and a wooden fence at another (Figure 7.4B).[14] These differences probably reflect the needs of the stockman. Where a toft was adjacent to the common fields, for example, as was the case at the spring site,[15] a bank and external ditches had to be dug to keep stock out, rather than to keep beasts penned inside.

Medieval boundaries, of course, also provide evidence for divisions *between* tenants, so when they are filled in and the boundary ceases to provide any barrier to movement between adjacent plots this tells us that properties are getting larger. Conversely, where

Figure 7.4. A: excavations north of Bridewell Lane, looking north-west. Recording sections through the black fill of the east–west ditch. Finds indicate that this ditch was backfilled in the thirteenth/fourteenth century when two village plots were amalgamated into one. B: the base of a medieval boundary wall that ran down the east side of the plot at Hill Farm. C: circular rubbish pit of medieval date north of Bridewell Lane: one of several excavated on this site.

new boundaries were being created, subdivision was occurring. Either way, the village plan was dynamic in detail; it did not remain unchanged century after century.[16] This process was revealed in action north of Bridewell Lane, where a single property had been subdivided by the digging of a ditch down the middle. The local circumstances that led to this can only be guessed at, but, for example, an elderly couple might have given over part of their messuage to a son, who then built another house on the same plot in return for looking after the needs of his relatives. The new dwelling might have been divided from the old by a ditch, which was later filled in again when one or other of the houses fell vacant. Since the ditch at Bridewell Lane contained more than 500 sherds of thirteenth- to fourteenth-century date it must have been filled in either at that date or immediately afterwards, before any later material could be incorporated into the fill.[17] This date was probably significant in the life cycle of the tenant family who occupied the plot.

This is a well-documented situation elsewhere,[18] and Abbot Beere's survey of 1515 makes it clear that, at that time, several former tenements and houses lay abandoned and empty.[19] One croft in Shapwick contained a house decayed 'of old' – in other words, beyond living memory[20] – and, since only thirty-seven tenants are listed against the fifty tenant holdings recorded in 1325,[21] it is clear that some tenants were already holding more than one ancient property even by the early 1300s. Later in the same century the local population was again depleted by the Black Death (Box 7.1). In neighbouring Ashcott large arrears of rent income mounted up in 1349–50 because there was no one left to pay – the tenants had died 'in the time of pestilence'.[22] Across the estates of Glastonbury Abbey some 67 per cent of *garciones* (landless labourers) were able to obtain land in 1350, whereas for most normal years the figure was only about 5 per cent. This indicates that there must have been many empty properties at the time, as borne out by the court roll for Easter 1350, which shows an unusual number of properties being transferred.[23] In the late fourteenth and fifteenth centuries, therefore, deserted tenements provided opportunities for the wealthiest tenants to combine plots together,[24] and Shapwick might have looked a little like a shrunken or partly deserted settlement, with some dilapidated houses and overgrown gardens. This is the opposite of the earlier situation, when a rising population between the tenth and fourteenth centuries must have driven a tendency towards subdivision.[25]

Internal space within the medieval tofts was used in a variety of ways. Gardens are never mentioned except in relation to the *curia* site (see below), but every household must have grown its own produce for the pot. The vegetable basket might have included onions, garlic, leeks, cabbage, peas, spinach, beans, parsley and borage, with its cucumber-flavoured leaves; and doubtless there were apples, pears, cherries and plums too. Filbert (hazel) bushes and walnut trees would have provided nuts.[26] Of these, only apples and onions are mentioned by name in Shapwick documents because they were sold.[27] It was reckoned that six apple trees would supply a peasant family with enough cider for a year. Any surplus was probably exchanged between families, as it still is today in many villages, particularly in the Mediterranean – part and parcel of the network of favours that bound relatives, friends and neighbours together.

Abbot Beere's 1515 survey suggests that tofts typically contained a dwelling, small pieces of meadow or pasture and occasionally an orchard. Shapwick's demesne accounts for the thirteenth and fourteenth centuries[28] regularly mention cattle, pigs, geese, chickens and horses, for which there is also archaeological evidence in the form of animal bones and, in the case of horses, horseshoes.[29] Together with roaming dogs and cats all these creatures must have been very familiar, and the variety of farm animals and agricultural activity perhaps explains why some village plots, such as Hill Farm, were subdivided internally by ditches. Others, such as Lawn Farm, had roughly metalled surfaces of limestone cobbles, convenient dry hardstandings for a hayrick, cart or horse, or for chores such as chopping wood. There was rough cobbling, too, around the village spring, presumably a well-frequented communal area.

Several village tofts contained rubbish pits (Figure 7.4C), often conveniently sited close to buildings. A typical example from Lawn Farm paddock was 0.40m deep and about 2m in diameter. Similarly shallow, wide pits were being dug in the twelfth and thirteenth centuries at Bridewell Lane, where they were found to contain domestic waste that included animal and fish bones and broken pottery. Since medieval pottery is also found in the fields in great quantities, where it must have been spread after being swept up into manuring middens in the village farmyards, there was clearly more than one way to dispose of household rubbish. One pit excavated at 36 Holes Lane contained four almost intact globular jars, a possible colander and parts of at least three Ham Green jugs. There were more than 500 sherds of late twelfth- to early thirteenth-century vessels here in all, many sooted or with burnt bases.[30] This particular assemblage is suggestive of house clearance and it may be that pits were dug only at times when large quantities of, or especially unpleasant, domestic rubbish needed to be disposed of urgently.[31] All medieval populations, not just the inhabitants of Shapwick, would have been familiar with waste and its odour.

While each of the two 'manors' had large barns (see below), there may have been other less substantial agricultural buildings such as sties (for the pigs) and granaries elsewhere. To some extent, variations in status may have been reflected in the number and size of buildings present, as well as their construction methods.[32] What is slightly baffling in the case of Shapwick is that there is relatively little evidence for medieval construction of any sort; many tofts seem to have been sparsely developed.[33] This pattern of intensive and non-intensive land use within the tofts has also been recognised at nearby Edington, where abundant evidence of medieval occupation lies adjacent to other areas with apparently few dateable features and finds, and which may have been put down to livestock or horticulture.[34] There is, therefore, a contrast to be drawn, visually at least, between the macro-scale at which fields and village layout were structured, with a regulated spatial order, and the micro-scale, at which individual plots showed considerable diversity in their use of space. If we were to travel back in time and walk down a Shapwick lane in, say, 1400, we would not see identical plots to left and right. The placement of buildings would vary, as would boundary walls and gates, surfaces and farmyard animals. Any semblance of regularity would have been further broken down by trees and hedges at varying stages of maturity. Archaeological evidence, depicted in map form, often gives a far greater sense of regularity than ever would have been appreciated by the contemporary eye.

Houses

Historical records reveal almost nothing about the dwellings of the peasant community in the village but, fortunately, there is a later medieval house that is still standing and occupied. This building, known as 'Forsters', has the classic open hall plan with services

at one end and an inner room/chamber at the other (Figure 7.5). The service area may originally have been intended for storage and the preparation of food and the chamber for the keeping of personal items and for sleeping, while the hall was a multi-purpose space at the core of the house. In this case, in spite of the later insertion of a fireplace and a first storey, not only is most of the arch-braced roof in the hall preserved but even some of its medieval thatch (Figure 7.5C).[35] Blackened from the smoke that first rose more than five centuries ago from the hearth, the 'weathering coat' of thatch has been repaired many times, but the basal layer of strong-stemmed rivet wheat has lain undisturbed on the north side. Quite how old this thatch might be is harder to determine; there are currently difficulties in dating elm roofs using dendrochronology and no radiocarbon dates for the burnt thatch at Forsters have so far been submitted. The building itself is often cited as being of fifteenth-century date, but there is no reason why it cannot be a hundred years or more earlier and there are houses of similar plan in Somerset that date to the late thirteenth century.[36]

Forsters may well be representative of later medieval buildings in the rest of Shapwick between 1250 and 1500, at least for the middle stratum of peasants approaching yeoman standing. While not all houses in the village were of a uniform size, and many would have been much smaller, the principles of construction and the materials used at Forsters are probably typical. Straw thatch, for instance, would have been common and Ralph le Thechere, who lived in Shapwick in 1283, would not have lacked gainful employment.[37] Finer building stone was reserved for the manor houses and the church, so that in one sense all buildings of secular and religious authority were visually set apart. As for the interiors of buildings, it is also now generally agreed that the most common arrangement for the medieval peasant house between 1250 and 1500 was one of three bays divided into a hall (open to the roof) with one or two additional chambers, as at Forsters;[38] the introduction of stairs and upper rooms was probably a sixteenth-century trend. Unfortunately, supporting archaeological evidence from Shapwick for this claim is lacking. There was insufficient left of the fifteenth- to sixteenth-century building excavated at 36 Holes

BOX 7.1

Population

Different sources of evidence have to be pieced together to show how many people lived in Shapwick at any one time. With the exception of benchmarks such as Domesday Book and modern census data, which begin at the start of the nineteenth century, these will always be best guesses. Even when the density of archaeological sites is understood with reasonable confidence this is hard to translate into population levels, especially if we do not know for certain whether sites are contemporary with each other. For this reason we cannot be certain about the numbers of people on the Poldens in prehistory, though we would now see as many as twenty-five settlements here in the later Bronze Age. At times the juxtaposition of the pollen record and scatters of lithics indicates that the population was substantially lower, as in the later Mesolithic, later Neolithic and early Bronze Age (see Chapter 3). On the basis of greatly increased densities of settlement and multipliers of people per site, Shapwick may have had as many as 300 inhabitants in the Roman period (see Chapter 4) and rather fewer in the post-Roman centuries, but levels rose again before the Norman Conquest (see Chapter 6) to an estimated 200 people at Domesday.

Figure B.7.1 plots Shapwick population against national trends. This shows a substantial rise in the number of inhabitants through the twelfth and thirteenth centuries, although it is unclear whether this was steady growth or a sudden upsurge after the last two decades of the twelfth century, as some have suggested.[b1] Certainly there was a decline in the early 1300s that culminated nationally in the Great Famine of 1315–17. Diminishing agricultural profits, the lack of paid work and environmental factors such as epidemics or murrain years are just some of the possible reasons for the ensuing crisis,[b2] though Shapwick seems to have been unusual among the other Polden manors in not making a recovery before the arrival of the Black Death in the autumn of 1348. The death toll then was terrible. The court rolls for Glastonbury manors for 1348–49 intimate 30–60 per cent fatalities, the word 'mort' being written by the clerk next to the names of tax-paying labourers who had not survived the year. In real numbers this suggests a pre-Black Death population at Shapwick of around 250, which dropped in the later fourteenth century to just 100–150 and then rose again to about 190 by 1515.[b3] The archaeological evidence for the swooping curves on our graph is typically patchy. Since the modern churchyard was not investigated archaeologically we did not find grave pits and skeletal remains dated to the mid-fourteenth century. And the abandonment of fields for a season or longer would be difficult to recognise because our pottery dating is simply not tight enough. Sometimes we struggle to make the link between archaeology and the recorded events of the history books, though, as we have seen, the ditches filled in at Bridewell Lane do suggest that properties were amalgamated in the fourteenth century, when there were fewer people about.

For the post-medieval period a variety of estate or tithe documents and maps can be used to establish the number of houses and their tenants with reasonable accuracy. Although the returns of the Hearth Tax have not survived[b4] and the bishop of Bath and Wells did not respond to the ecclesiastical survey of Archbishop Compton in 1676,[b5] comparative population data can be taken from a useful list of Church Rates dated to 1660 that was later annotated with the names of tenants in 1750. Something can also be deduced from the numbers of baptisms and burials recorded in the parish registers after 1700. Burials reached crisis levels in 1722 and 1747, but the trend remains upwards until around 1830, when there was a notably high birth rate. The various census returns record that around 400–440 people lived in Shapwick in the nineteenth century, but there was continuous immigration into and emigration from the parish – people were very mobile and often did not stay long, particularly those in their teens and twenties. From the last quarter of the nineteenth century the population declined steeply for the next fifty years. In 1930, during a time of agricultural depression, numbers sank as low as 275, not all that different from 1309, but the population has risen again towards 500 today. Viewed over the long term, therefore, the picture is far from stable; the evidence stresses cyclical change rather than steady 'progress' towards the present day. Numbers at Shapwick hovered between 200 and 300 for much of the post-Roman period but disease also made drastic inroads and there were long periods of stagnation. During

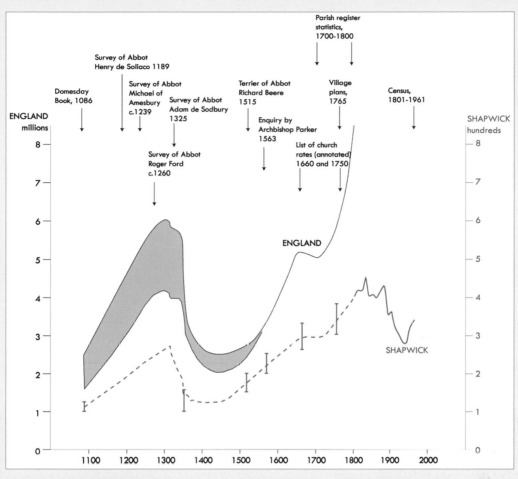

Figure B.7.1 Shapwick and national population from the Middle Ages to the present.

this period there were no major movements of population into the area (unless we count car commuters) and lengthy periods of restricted landownership have done little to attract employment, enterprise and growth.

Reflecting on this evidence as archaeologists, it seems a puzzle that so few actual skeletons have been found in the parish. If there was continuity of occupation in the parish from around 8000 BC onwards, even with only a small population, with generation gaps of around twenty-five years this represents some 400 generations of Shapwick people. If the population was only ever 200 or so on average in the parish area, this could still add up to some 80,000 people who have lived in Shapwick over the last 10,000 years – yet our excavations produced fewer than 100 individuals. Given that the local soil conditions seem to favour the survival of bone, the answer is probably, in part, that we did not target Shapwick's prehistoric burial monuments, such as the six early Bronze Age barrows, choosing to focus instead on structural complexes. In the Roman period cremation was probably favoured in the first and second centuries AD, if not for longer, and the two possible Roman cemetery sites in the parish were not targeted. Nor did we excavate extensively at medieval and later cemetery sites, or near the gallows at the junction of the Ridgeway (A39) and the road into Shapwick. It is also possible that people were buried outside the parish – for example, in the post-Roman period, when Moorlinch may have had an earlier and more important church – and we should remember that if the wetland was favoured for burial during the prehistoric past those deposits may have been cut away and burnt as fuel. Even so, the discrepancy is striking.

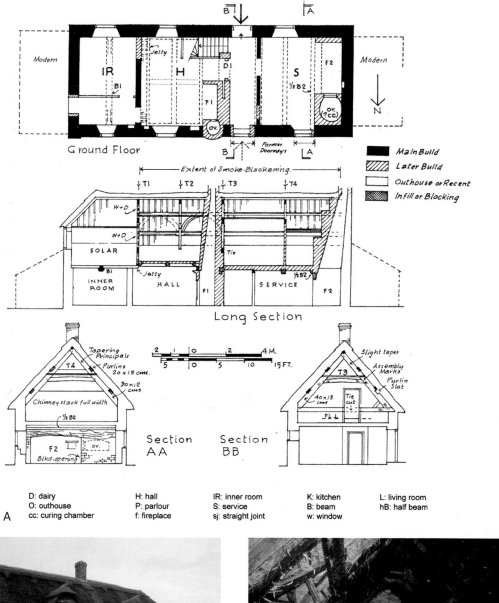

Figure 7.5. Forsters, the oldest of Shapwick's village houses. The plan of this hall house (A) has three rooms in a line, formerly with a central hall open to the thatch. The south-facing façade (B) includes the window into the service end on the left, the entrance to the cross passage, a window into the hall and, at the end, another into an inner room. The interior (C) shows the medieval roof with its smoked blackened truss and thatch.

Figure 7.6. Excavations at Shapwick Sports Hall revealed a hearth with dressed stone, part of a badly disturbed late medieval building. Alongside, the lower half of a pottery cistern was found inverted and pressed into the natural clays. As the photograph suggests, the stratigraphy here was very shallow; the top of an unexcavated well can be seen in the bottom right-hand corner.

Lane, for example, to show anything other than its hearth with dressed stone edging and a floor of large limestone slabs (Figure 7.6).[39] Where we excavated in the modern village post-medieval buildings probably lay on the same footprint as earlier structures, and where we excavated in the open spaces of Shapwick Park buildings had been thoroughly robbed for their construction materials and landscaped away.[40] We did find some evidence of other kinds of earthfast structures during our excavations, but these did not have hearths and may have been ancillary agricultural buildings. Three postholes, a beam-slot and a length of walling thought to be the corner of a possible eleventh- to thirteenth-century building were seen at 56 Brices Lane, where the pipeline trench ran through Shapwick Park,[41] and a modest twelfth-century building was examined at Bridewell Lane that measured about 9.75m long by 4.0m across (Figure 7.7A and B). Constructed of large posts set in individual pits, seen under excavation in Figure 7.7C and D, this may have been a small barn,[42] perhaps with an upper storey.

The survival of Forsters raises many questions.

It seems unlikely to have been unique and we must suspect that building stock of a similar age was demolished unrecorded in the eighteenth and nineteenth centuries. The dwellings of those lower in the social hierarchy may have been built of cob, though Lias walling is also possible given the presence of stone quarries in the parish. Roofs were perhaps supported by cruck trusses, as is the case in other parts of the county; timber-framed external walls are not so much a feature of vernacular architecture in this region.[43] Generally, we must imagine medieval houses that were long and low in their proportions, with thatched, half-hipped roofs with neither chimneys nor dormer windows. Since freestone was not available locally decorative door and window surrounds would not have been usual and, in the absence of glass, windows would have been kept small and shuttered to keep out the cold and unwelcome draughts. Inside, warmth and light would have come from the central open hearth, with thick smoke swirling towards the thatch. Those readers whose homes are heated by wood-burning stoves will know the feeling of a well-toasted face and a cold back,

Figure 7.7. Excavations north of Bridewell Lane. A: west end of a timber building of possible twelfth-century date. The contemporary ground surface had mostly been ploughed away. Associated finds included a broken 'pin beater' (with implications for weaving), pottery and a rare William I penny dated 1074–77. B: the plan of the building is defined by twenty post-pits (shaded in orange) around an internal space measuring 9.78m × 4m. C: the post-pits had darker soil and were packed with limestone to keep the posts upright. D: the posts themselves have been removed or rotted away. Each one was carefully sectioned and drawn.

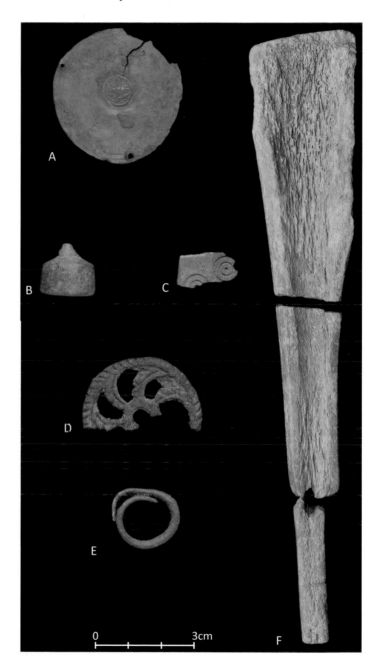

Figure 7.8. Finds from later medieval excavations in the village. A: balance or scale pan made from copper-alloy sheet with two remaining holes for suspension, possibly used to weigh coins. B: cylindrical lead weight c.25g. C: bone strip-mount with ring-and-dot pattern, probably to decorate a wooden box or even a comb. D: badge, probably a star design with eight wavy rays, beginning of the fifteenth century. E: finger ring, penannular with oval section, perhaps twelfth/thirteenth century. F: worked horse metacarpal, unfinished object or rough-out from which to cut dice or similar. All these finds are from north of Bridewell Lane with the exception of D (from Shapwick Sports Hall) and F (from north of Shapwick House).

and the experience of medieval interiors may have been somewhat similar. Perhaps the most noticeable feature to our eyes would be the sparse furnishings as indicated generally by wills and inventories. A table, stools and perhaps a chair or two might, in some houses, have been supplemented by a chest for storing finer bedding and cloths. One sliver of bone panel with a ring-and-dot motif (Figure 7.8C) is very likely to have decorated a wooden casket[44] and acts as a reminder that many household items would have been made of wood or basketry, which has not survived in the ground.

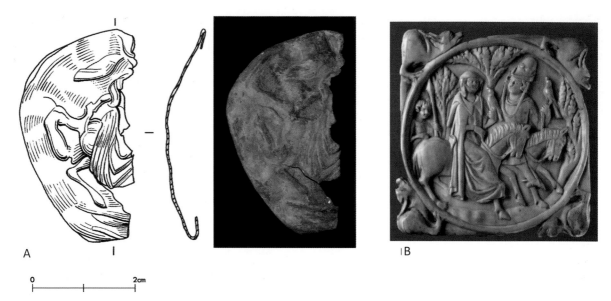

0   2cm

Figure 7.9. Mirror case from excavations north of Bridewell Lane, mid-thirteenth- to fourteenth-century date. A: the repoussé decoration suggests a women riding. B: among several parallels for this object is an ivory mirror case of about 1325–75 from Paris, 97mm diameter (© The Trustees of the British Museum). The image of a lady hawking symbolised the hunt for love and was associated with high status.

Possessions

We come closest to the medieval material world, perhaps, when we handle objects from the Middle Ages, and this is particularly true of those personal possessions that show signs of patina on their metal surfaces. Many of these are everyday items such as hairpins, buckles and the strap ends that reinforced leather belts, or the pendant mounts from which a knife or purse was suspended at the hip. These ordinary objects are reminders not only of the daily routines of lacing, strapping, belting and buckling but also of changing fashions in medieval dress. Lace ends, for example, which bound the ends of lengths of cloth, silk and leather so that they could be threaded through eyelets in clothing, became more popular after the fourteenth century as clothing came to be more tightly fitted to the body. Everything from dresses to codpieces required securing and laces were often the means to do that, tedious though their continual unpicking and tightening must have been.

Other items have a more personal story to tell. What anguished searching must have followed the loss of a finger ring at Bridewell Lane in the eleventh or twelfth centuries (Figure 7.8E)?[45] And what messages were intended by the wearing of a livery badge[46] depicting a star and crescent (Figure 7.8D)? Badges were popular accessories in the Middle Ages and made a show of religious, political and social allegiances. This one is apparently a sign of affiliation to a lesser livery instituted by Henry IV (1399–1413) at the beginning of his reign.[47] Possibly the wearer had a royal or Lancastrian connection: given that the object was inexpensively made from tin and lead and was very probably one of many from the same mould, the owner may have been a servant or someone who had taken part in Henry's campaigns against the rebel barons. Perhaps the badge was thrown away when it was no longer deemed to be to the owner's advantage.

Equally intriguing is a fragment of copper-alloy sheet from north of Bridewell Lane (Figure 7.9). This has been identified as a damaged mirror case of thirteenth- or fourteenth-century date, one of only twelve known from Britain with repoussé or raised decoration. Only the front legs of a horse and the outer garment of a woman can be picked out, but comparable examples, including ivory cases from mainland Europe, suggest the depiction of a lady hawking while riding side-saddle.[48] This symbol of the hunt, perhaps the hunt for love, implies a treasured token of romance, perhaps one exchanged between a courting couple. Since not everyone had access to the pleasures of medieval hunting its owner may have been of high status,[49] and this conclusion is consistent with another find of the same date from the same site, a flat balance scale pan with a central stamp with a stag motif (Figure 7.8A). Complete with two of its three original suspension holes, a scale pan such as this might have been used to weigh coins, precious stones or metals.[50] Whoever their original owners were, these finds are a reminder that the most sophisticated fashion accessories of the Middle Ages were not exclusive to urban areas or to 'high-status sites'.

All manner of activities is suggested by individual finds; a bone rough-out, probably a preparation for making dice, recalls the medieval addiction to games of chance (Figure 7.8F), while a cylindrical lead weight of sixteenth-century type suggests commerce (Figure 7.8B). It would be wrong, however, to think of the medieval Shapwick household as full of exotic trinkets. To modern eyes medieval peasants lived in austere surroundings; possessions were positively meagre.[51] The lack of keys, usually such common finds on excavations at medieval settlements,[52] suggests that few Shapwick homes harboured possessions of any great monetary value. Even agricultural tools were scarce, although many have simply not survived;[53] a heavily corroded iron scythe or sickle blade, recovered from Bridewell Lane,[54] is perhaps the only tangible evidence of the harvest, the focus of the agricultural year. It would have been used to cut the stalks of grain before they were bound together into sheaves, assembled into stooks, dried and carted away for storage, perhaps in Shapwick's Great Barn.

Among the artefacts recovered from our excavations, none are more curious than the small collection that appears to have been salvaged in the Middle Ages from local Roman sites (Figure 7.10).[55] Among these is a Y-shaped tool of red deer antler with an oblong hole driven through its middle, presumably to hold a short wooden shaft in order to allow its use as a hoe. The two 'points' or tines of the antler have been

shaped, cut to a point and then polished by frequent use in breaking up the soil.[56] It is easy to imagine a trophy like this being dug up, taken home, misused, broken and then discarded in a medieval pit. Other finds similarly 'out of context' include two pierced Roman coins, presumably suspended as pendants (see Story, above). Both of these fourth-century coins were recovered from late twelfth- to early thirteenth-century contexts at separate sites.[57]

We can be slightly surer of the background to these particular finds because of the underhand activities of one John Sherp. In 1348 Sherp took charge of the harvest at Shapwick but quickly found himself under the spotlight when his masters at the Abbey discovered that he had loaded two hay carts with stone and made off with them to his own house in Glastonbury. Sherp was clearly not a pleasant man; when John Buryman, one the abbot's servants, refused to cooperate Sherp beat him so badly that he was unable to work again.[58] What is especially striking about Sherp's misdemeanours is that the stone he took was robbed from *Abbelchestre* or *Abchester*, one of the Roman sites in the parish described in Chapter 4. In truth he was probably unlucky to have been caught because such activities were not at all unusual. Our excavations at *Sladwick*, another Roman site, also demonstrated clear evidence for stone robbing, the looters leaving tell-tale clues in the form of sherds of twelfth- to thirteenth-century pottery, perhaps evidence for a meal eaten as they picked through the rubble searching for decent stone.[59] Sherp and his like could have pocketed anything that looked promising, but they were selective. Roman brick and brooches were left behind in favour of objects such as coins and antler hoes. One could argue that these were merely thieves with a practical eye but some of the objects they salvaged may have had a more unusual purpose as protective amulets. Across early modern Europe old coins, fossils and prehistoric objects (usually flint arrowheads or axes) were believed to protect against thunder and lightning, and during storms they were possibly held in the hand while charms were recited. Perhaps the perforated coins were used in this way, as medallions to be worn around the neck.[60] There are plenty of examples of medieval coins that have been adapted as brooches, sometimes even gilded on one face,[61] and since they display cross ornamentation

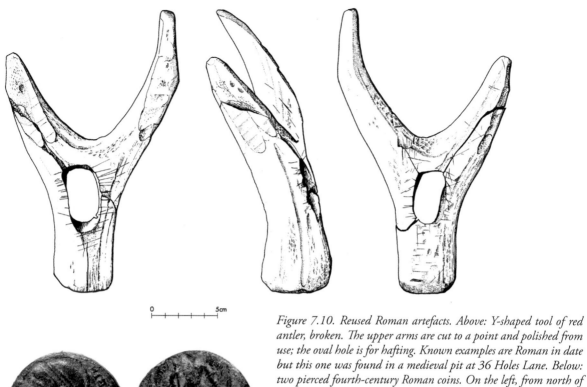

0   5cm

Figure 7.10. Reused Roman artefacts. Above: Y-shaped tool of red antler, broken. The upper arms are cut to a point and polished from use; the oval hole is for hafting. Known examples are Roman in date but this one was found in a medieval pit at 36 Holes Lane. Below: two pierced fourth-century Roman coins. On the left, from north of Bridewell Lane, Constantinopolis/Victory on prow, Lyons mint, AD 330–335. Obverse shows Constantinopolis laureate, helmeted and holding a sceptre with a globular end; reverse shows Victory standing on a prow with a long sceptre in the right hand and resting the left on a shield. On the right, from Old Church, Magnentius/Decentius in poor condition. Reverse: Victoriae dd nn aug et cae (or caes), AD 351–352.

they may have been valued for their religious symbolism. Those devoid of any obvious Christian meaning, like the Roman coins from Shapwick, may simply have conjured protective magic for the wearer or, alternatively, they might have been worn in imitation of knightly insignia or seals. Perhaps they even circulated as token coinage.

The bulk of the finds from the medieval village comprised domestic pottery: some 13,000 sherds in all, weighing over 71kg! Among this collection there is no evidence for industrial activity in the form of crucibles or distilling apparatus; indeed, there is little variation at all between assemblages from different households (Figure 7.11). Shapwick peasants had no

use either for the kind of northern French pottery found at Cheddar[62] or the fifteenth-century Spanish lustrewares purchased for use at the Abbey[63] – nearly all of the later medieval pottery we found was made at workshops in South or Central Somerset, perhaps at Glastonbury or Bridgwater,[64] though there were also products from Bristol (Ham Green) and the kilns at Laverstock, just outside Salisbury. These vessels would have been familiar household items, used to fetch water from the well and milk from the dairy, for washing hands and so on – medieval coarseware pots were the ubiquitous plastic containers of their day. Two sherds, however, stand out. They are fragments of 'face jugs' – vessels which mimic parts of the human face, in one case a stylised eye and nose and, in another, moulded eye ridges (Figure 7.12A).[65] There is a long tradition of anthropomorphic and zoomorphic decoration on medieval objects[66] and, in this case, the designs suggest a specific link between men (since the faces have beards) and drinking.[67]

Medieval pottery has a range of forms, fabrics, glazes (brown, green and transparent) and decoration (dot-and-ring impressions, rouletting, applied cordons) that enable the specialist to pinpoint its source – sometimes only roughly, sometimes down to specific kiln sites. In turn, this reveals something about the nature of buying and selling. From the twelfth to the fourteenth centuries there was a general proliferation of markets across the country, so that by the time of the Black Death there was a dense pattern of places licensed to hold weekly markets (and annual fairs) in every county. Not all of these places were of equal standing, the older the market the more significant the place and those in royal, episcopal and ecclesiastical hands were of particular importance. Glastonbury, the closest 'central place' for the people of Shapwick in the Middle Ages, had developed sufficiently to become a parliamentary borough by 1319.[68] At the same time, new towns with markets were being developed near Axbridge at Rackley, Lower Weare and Badgworth, at Downend on the river Parrett (see Chapter 5) and at Wells

Figure 7.11. Coarseware jar from an unlocated local workshop. The black sooting shows that this pot was placed in or near to the hearth, so that it had been used for cooking. The vessel was broken into numerous sherds when it was first found at Holes Lane (on the Shapwick Sports Hall site). The pot was stolen from a store room in (then) King Alfred's College, Winchester, in 1998.

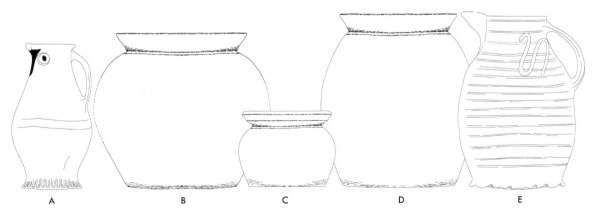

Figure 7.12. A selection of later medieval pottery recovered from excavations in the village, reconstructed by Alejandra Gutiérrez. A: face jug with applied decoration under dark green and purple glaze (from the moat bank at Shapwick House). B–D: three unglazed local coarseware jars for cooking and storage. E: green glazed Ham Green jug from Bristol with applied decoration in the shape of a snake over concentric grooves (from a medieval pit at Shapwick Sports Hall).

and Bridgwater. The last of these, which was easily accessible along the Polden ridge, must have become increasingly familiar to peasants at Shapwick after its foundation in 1200 as a market, borough and quay.

We do have to be slightly careful about assuming that all the pottery found at Shapwick was purchased locally. Pottery was sometimes given as gifts or in payment or bequeathed in dowries, and pots did travel in the baggage of estate owners and officials too.[69] Nevertheless, coarsewares had little value and it is very likely that most of the pottery owned by villagers was acquired at either Glastonbury or Bridgwater. The Abbey was probably the major customer at Glastonbury market and, judging by what happened elsewhere, buyers from the monastery may have had preferential treatment and been able to reserve items before the day's trading got underway.[70] Shapwick villagers would not, however, have enjoyed any special privileges: they were merely tenants of the Abbey who hawked their honey, wax, eggs, apples, poultry and vegetables. These markets lay at distances of only 9km and 12km respectively, and the villagers would have been able sell and buy produce and then return home before nightfall with their larger and more delicate items packed away in straw on the back of carts.[71] Cash from these sales helped out with rents and taxes and sometimes even generated a small surplus.[72] Farthings, halfpennies and pennies recovered from three different sites confirm both the ownership and the use of coins by peasants, who needed them for everyday transactions. The farthing from *Old Church* might have bought a loaf of bread, while the halfpenny from Bridewell Lane might have been enough for a chicken, but it is perhaps significant that all five medieval coins happen to be thirteenth century in date, precisely the time when the amount of cash needed for rents, taxes and church dues was on the increase. As Glastonbury and Bridgwater became more fully developed so there were further opportunities for involvement in the cash economy, a situation that may be contrasted with the position before 1100, when the community at Shapwick was relatively more isolated.

Peasant diet

The medieval peasant diet of lowland England was based on cereals.[73] Barley was brewed for ale, a high-calorie drink, and other cereals were used to make bread and pottage – a sort of thick soup. To the latter would have been added peas or beans, the other produce of the open fields, and some sort of onion or brassica. This concoction would have been eaten with bread (*companagium*).[74] Given that cheese and bread could be cut with a knife, a universal tool found at almost every site dug in the village, few medieval households needed anything more than a wooden spoon and a large globular pot in which to heat and soften their pottage (see Figure 7.11). Soot patterns on the exterior surfaces of these cooking pots demonstrate that they were sometimes placed on tripods, sometimes directly on the embers of the fire and, in the case of those with blackening on only one face, close to the heat rather than immediately on top of it. It is easy to imagine a pottage of meat, vegetables and cereals simmering away, but a certain amount of experience would have been needed to prevent the food burning or the pot cracking and to maintain a more or less constant temperature. Nor was all peasant food so simply prepared. Soot noted in a band around the upper half of their external surfaces shows that some pots must have been placed inside others rather like a 'bain marie'. The contents could then be steamed or heated more gently; milk sweetened with local honey is just one possible recipe that might have been prepared in this way. Other beverages, such as ale and cider, were served from glazed jugs, while trenchers of bread or wood have not survived.

Faunal evidence adds a little more detail. Mutton, beef, pork and all their many by-products were familiar to Shapwick villagers, perhaps increasingly so after the mid-fourteenth century, but neither game nor poultry seem to have made up any significant part of the 'peasant' diet, though rooks may have been taken for pies. Excavations at Bridewell Lane produced two partial sheep skeletons from a gully (Figure 7.13): the head and the feet of two first-year lambs. A dish of sheep's head and trotters is the most likely interpretation, though our faunal specialist, Louisa Gidney, also notes a tradition of hanging carcasses in yew trees to repel flies in warm weather.[75] Bones like these need not always equate to large quantities of meat; bones have long been a basic ingredient of soups, stock and pottage, as well as a source of marrow. The staples of the peasant diet

Figure 7.13. Horned skull of a young sheep, probably female and aged about one year at death. This individual probably died in the spring, when its carcase was skinned, the head and feet being buried perhaps after the carcase had been salvaged. Alternatively, the animal may have been poached and the evidence buried secretively, or this may be the remains of a dish of sheep's head and trotters.

were: bacon, salted or possibly smoked; air-dried sausage; eggs (which were also part of the rent); and dairy produce such as cheese.[76] To this list should be added different types of grain, pulses and legumes, which were transformed into pottage, and *maslin*, the gritty everyday bread of the poor made from wheat mixed with rye or, more probably at Shapwick, with barley or beans.[77]

Fish also supplemented the carbohydrate-based diet (Figure 7.14). Among the fish bone from excavations along Bridewell Lane, eel dominated (80 per cent by bone count), but there were also small quantities of freshwater species such as perch, stickleback and possibly pike. Some of these fish might have been netted locally, while the herring may well have been cured rather than eaten fresh. Although large quantities of marine fish were being consumed at this date in nearby Langport,[78] and neither coastal markets nor freshwater wetlands were very far distant, fresh fish was evidently a rarity. This absence might be considered particularly surprising given the proximity of the Meare Pool and Glastonbury Abbey's fishponds

there, but that catch was destined for the monastery's table and the tenants probably made do with netting along the drainage ditches or rhynes that criss-crossed the wetland.[79]

Overall, the medieval peasant diet at Shapwick was low in saturated fats and high in fibre. It was, when we throw in plentiful apples (and cider) and occasional luxuries suggested by the peach stones from Bridewell Lane, and add the outdoor exercise of tilling fields and digging ditches, apparently something of a nutritionist's paradise. This is not, however, an entirely truthful picture. While Shapwick peasants were unlikely to succumb to high cholesterol, they would sometimes have lacked vitamins (particularly A, C and D), particularly if they avoided fish and apples, and their diet could be both low in calories and subject to seasonal variations, especially when harvests were uncertain. Hunger was not unknown; in 1333–34, for example, the abbot gave the impoverished tenants nine quarters of beans.[80] A useful source of protein, the beans would either have been dried and ground down to bulk up wheatmeal in bread or added to

Figure 7.14. Some 1,020 fragments of fish remains were recovered from excavations at Shapwick. In the later medieval period eels were the most common species, with low numbers of freshwater fish such as pike and perch. Herring bones indicate supply from coastal markets, probably as cured rather than fresh fish.

pottages. A more detailed panorama of health and disease, such as vitamin C deficiencies, might be gauged from a larger sample of medieval skeletal material than we obtained.

The *curias*

In order to manage its estates Glastonbury Abbey needed local bases to act as administrative centres, the day-to-day running of which was delegated to local lay officials. The key posts were those of the bailiff, reeve and steward.[81] Thus, Thomas Bodden was the bailiff 'of the manor' in 1515 when Abbot Beere's terrier was drawn up, and he might be thought of as the equivalent of a senior farm manager, who journeyed around the Glastonbury manors in his care. He would have made payments and collected them as well as keeping a close eye on John Whybbery, who was named as the manor's reeve that year.[82] It was John's task, sometimes with a *berebritt* or granger to help him, to manage livestock and disease, collect dues

and rent, check up on property and draw up lists of repairs, arrange the sale of timber and wood and set out the accounts when the agricultural year ended at Michaelmas on 29 September.[83] Not all postholders were entirely competent,[84] but, nevertheless, we might like to imagine John and his like at a table by the fire in a room in the abbot's hall on an early October day dictating Shapwick accounts to a clerk under the supervision of the bailiff. Rental income, fines and sales of grain and animals had all to be set against the wages (and probably the accommodation costs) of the manor's *famuli*, the three or four employees who did whatever work was necessary after the tenants had completed their compulsory labour services, such as ploughing, mowing and harvesting. There was also expenditure on new livestock, seed from other manors[85] and structural repairs to be considered; all this before the paperwork went before the Abbey's keen-eyed auditors for approval. Lastly, in addition to the bailiff and the reeve, there was the steward. He acted as a more general administrator, holding manor courts, inspecting manors, attending fairs and sometimes authorising expenditure. There was only one steward for all the Glastonbury estates, so this was a highly responsible and professional post and its incumbent would have come from a good family with all the gentry connections that implies. Of course, stewards and bailiffs alike stood to profit from their positions and they would have had many contacts at the Abbey, not only with the abbot but also with other monks in administrative offices such as the cellarer, who was particularly involved in finances and food stocks.

Since the reeve had his own dwelling he would not have lived at the *curia*, though he would have been a frequent visitor to its door. His immediate supervisor, the bailiff, may well have held lands elsewhere, but at the beginning of the fourteenth century he was responsible for a geographical area that included Ashcott, Greinton, Street and Butleigh, and he would have needed somewhere to stay. The steward, too, since his role covered all thirty-two of the Abbey's manors, would not always have been able to return home at night. In that sense the Shapwick *curia* was unlike a lay manor; there was no lord of the manor in residence, and it acted more like an inn and venue for formal administrative tasks. The use of the term 'court' in the fourteenth century highlights a judicial function too, and this entailed visits from senior monastic officials, among them the abbot and his retinue. Archaeologically, we might expect the kind of well-appointed domestic and agricultural buildings that could be found on any wealthy secular estate in the Middle Ages, with appropriately sized spaces for the stabling of horses, entertainment, eating and business, as well as day-to-day farming operations. Conventual buildings would not be expected, though there was a chapel.[86]

During the later Middle Ages the location of the *curia* at Shapwick was shifted. From as early as the eighth century, and quite possibly even before that time, the *curia* stood in what we call today *Old Church*, immediately west of Beerway Farm. It was established there before the creation of the present village and we suggested in Chapter 5 that it originally formed one element in a dispersed pattern of settlement. The *curia* then endured in its original location for several centuries after the village

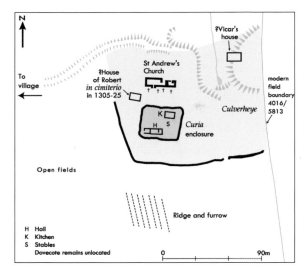

Figure 7.15. Later medieval buildings in Old Church including the curia enclosure, church and other buildings near the spring. As interpreted from geophysics results and excavation. This figure may be compared with Figure 6.11 to see how the site developed.

came into being but eventually, at the end of the thirteenth century, it too was incorporated into the village plan. The circumstances are discussed below. During the Shapwick Project we had the opportunity to investigate both these sites archaeologically, and we refer to them below as the old *curia* (?eighth century–*c*.1285) and the new *curia* (*c*.1285–1539). Relocation at the end of the thirteenth century left the church of St Andrew virtually alone in the East Field for the next fifty years or so, but eventually, in 1331, a new church was consecrated in the centre of the village. Only after this date were agricultural and administrative bases, parish church and village to be found all in one place.

The old curia complex

The old *curia* lay out in the centre of the former East Field, immediately south of the church of St Andrew, within a walled and ditched enclosure of about 1,050m² (Figure 7.15). The main structural detail recovered by excavation relates to the final phases of occupation in the late twelfth and thirteenth centuries.[87] By that time the principal structure was a rectangular stone building with a flagged floor and a door in the north wall (Figure 7.16A–C). The full plan of this building was not uncovered, but results from geophysics and excavation suggest that it measured around 13–15m by 5.8m internally and consisted of three plastered rooms, with the smallest, at the east end, having a clay hearth.

The stone floor, the hearth and the volume of pottery and other finds all point to this being a domestic residence rather than something like a stable. However, the plan seems too long and narrow to be a building block with a first-floor hall and the walls would, in any case, be too insubstantial to support an upper chamber (Figure 7.16D). A reconstruction of it as a three-unit single-storey structure fits much better with the archaeological evidence, in which case the excavated building may be interpreted as a classic later medieval domestic plan, with service rooms, an unaisled open hall and an inner chamber, not unlike Forsters. The excavated east room might be the services, used mainly for storage, while the inner chamber would lie beyond the partially excavated hall. The hall itself would have been a flexible space, laid out for meals when larger groups were present, but cleared again for administrative paperwork and for sleeping.[88]

This house did not stand alone; geophysics reveals at least one other structure. Rectangular in plan, this building was also constructed of stone and, since it is associated with enhanced magnetism probably from burning, the obvious interpretation is that this is a detached kitchen. And it is the diet of those who fed here, as deduced from the analysis of the animal bones they left behind, that most clearly underlines the status of the site.[89] Meat consumption was dominated by sheep, cattle and pig, whole carcasses (minus the head) being eaten, with a preference for beef that was less than 4 years old at slaughter, the occasional milk-fed lamb and tender young chicken. Fish included herring, perch, eel and possibly Dover sole,[90] the latter probably originating from the Bristol Channel. Most suggestive is the procurement of wild venison (red and roe deer), a characteristic of high-status sites such as castles and manorial complexes. Game such as hare, duck (wild and domestic), woodcock, teal, thrush and rook were also provided for the table and,

since there must have been large flocks of wild birds over-wintering on the Levels, all these birds could have been netted locally or targeted by falconers.[91] Attitudes towards animals were not sentimental[92] and the squabs, uniquely recorded here among all the medieval contexts at Shapwick, may have been plucked in their hundreds from the nearby dovecote. Such details provide a novel angle on the lives of the Abbey officials, clerics and court, who would expect to be well fed when they made their periodic excursions to Shapwick.[93]

The direct connection with Glastonbury Abbey probably facilitated access to stone from the quarries at Ham, Doulting and Wedmore as well as to some of the more unusual objects recovered from the old *curia*, such as a blue phyllite whetstone or honestone that may have originated in Norway (Figure 7.17F).[94] These fine-grained stones were used to sharpen knives and were easily lost, even though, as in this case, they were sometimes drilled through to suspend them around the neck or from the belt. Valuables like these, modest though they may seem, may also explain why so many of the buildings were kept locked. In contrast to the village sites security was clearly a high priority, judging by the number of keys and hasps found (Figure 7.17C–E). Metalwork from the site also suggests that horses were present – an iron prick spur, a six-pointed spur rowel and a bridle bit all came from the plough soil (Figure 7.17A and B) and documents report that horses were pastured near the old *curia* at *La Culverheye* between 1313 and 1315,[95] surely a long-standing practice. Horse meat was distributed as 'kennel food' and the dogs made off with the bones as far as the boundary ditch on the eastern side of the churchyard, from where they were excavated. And when the dogs died, they too were sometimes fed to their kennel mates. Given the potential for scavenging under these circumstances, it is surprising that no rat bones were recovered, though both mice and vole species were present. Perhaps the buzzard, whose remains were also retrieved during the excavation,[96] kept the numbers of rats down. Whatever the case, the faunal remains are a reminder that the excavated stone buildings cannot have stood alone; there must have been stables and kennels within the enclosure, and perhaps other outbuildings as well.

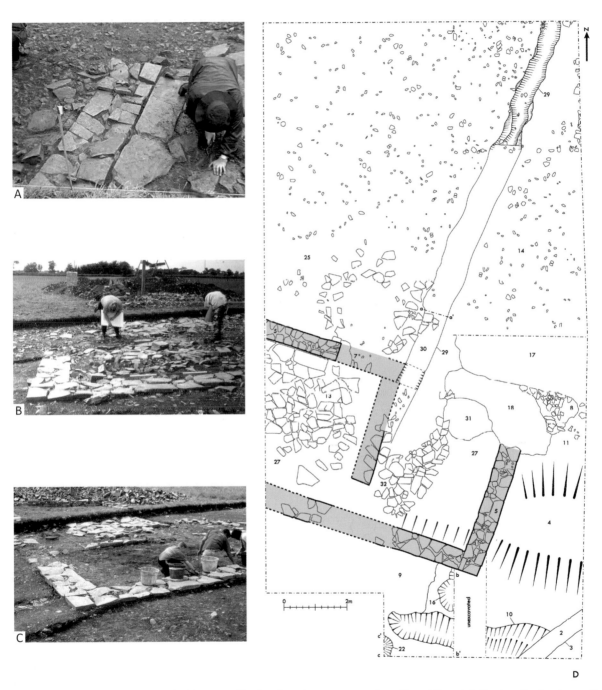

Figure 7.16. The medieval curia building in Old Church under excavation. A: walls and Lias slab flooring. B: drawing walls and partially robbed flooring. C: trowelling beneath the flooring at the east end of the building. D: the excavation plan of the east end of the main curia building: a substantial rectangular building with at least two rooms, probably three.

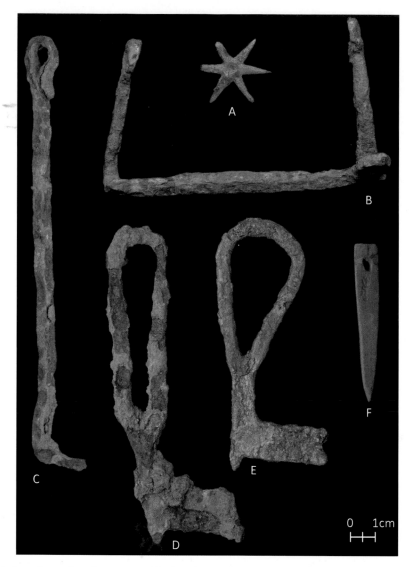

Figure 7.17. Finds from the medieval curia in Old Church. A: star rowel with six points, thirteenth century or later, part of the horse spur which sat at the back of the ankle. B: bridle bit, in this case a curb bit with a rigid mouthpiece with looped and hooked cheeks, with eleventh-century parallels. C: key with looped handle. D: key with elongated loop. E: key with pear-shaped loop: all three late Anglo-Saxon to Norman in date. F: whetstone.

The church and churchyard

Right from the start of the project it was known that an early church dedicated to St Andrew had stood to the east of the village.[97] This site is referred to as *Oldechurche* in the 1515 survey, by which time it was being ploughed over as part of the common field,[98] but the church seems never to have been forgotten by local inhabitants (see Chapter 1) and is still marked on Ordnance Survey maps. Aerial photographs, geophysics and excavation demonstrate that, in its final form at the beginning of the fourteenth century, it was composed of three axial units: a nave with a

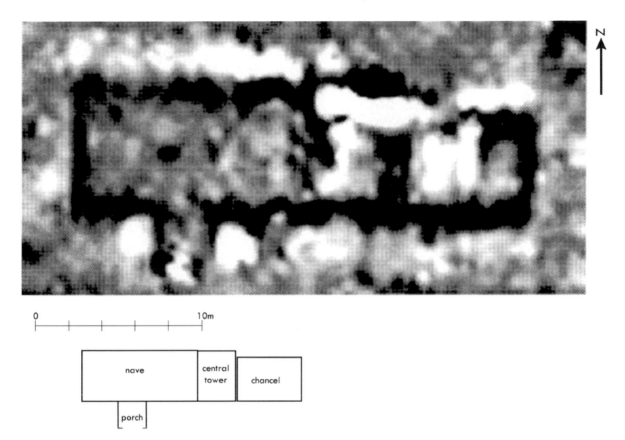

0   10m

| nave | central tower | chancel |

porch

Figure 7.18. Geophysics results for St Andrew's church in Old Church (see Figure 7.21).

south porch, a central tower and a chancel (Figure 7.18).[99] Three-unit plans like this survive elsewhere in the county (Figure 7.19)[100] as well as at the nearby fourteenth-century church of St Mary's in the village of Shapwick (Figure 7.19D). No window glass, flooring materials or architectural fragments were recovered during its excavation,[101] so not much can be said about the decorative detail except to say that slate, stone tile and glazed clay roof tile covered the roof while on the crest perched at least one globular green-glazed ceramic finial, a product of the kilns at Ham Green near Bristol (Figure 7.20A).

During a very limited investigation of the churchyard (Figure 7.21A) three graves were found to be delimited by Lias blocks that had been carefully placed in the shape of a tapering coffin. The head and foot of these graves were marked by stones set

vertically, and these would have protruded above the ground surface (Figure 7.21B foreground). Whether the mourners wished to make a modest grave look like a more expensive memorial, or whether the unworked slabs were placed onto the grave when the ground began to sink, we do not know.[102] Burial at Shapwick in the later medieval period seems to have been a simple affair for most,[103] though a stone grave-cover (Figure 7.21C) engraved with a straight-arm cross with circular trefoil terminals was also uncovered. This is similar to thirteenth-century examples from Wells Cathedral, even if not as accomplished in its execution,[104] and the likelihood is that it was carved locally. As we saw in Chapter 2, for many centuries the parish was the site of quarries for limestone slabs of Blue Lias. Indeed, Abbot Beere's 1515 terrier helpfully reports that in the West Field 'there is a quarry of

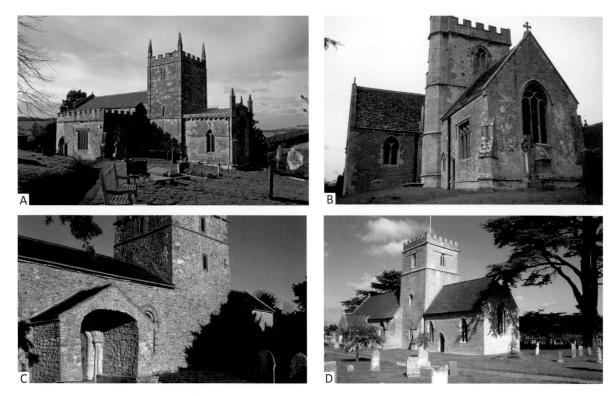

Figure 7.19. Three architectural parallels in Somerset for St Andrew's church, Shapwick, all with nave, central tower and chancel. A: St Peter's at Englishcombe, where the tower and part of the chancel are Norman. B: All Saints at Lullington; the lower part of the central tower is Norman. C: St Mary's at Christon is Norman and late Victorian in date (note the Norman south doorway). D: St Mary's at Shapwick.

"lyas" from which the quarry-stone was made and sculpted for the tomb of the Venerable Father, Abbot Nicholas Frome, which stands in the nave of the church [that is, the abbey church] in Glastonbury.' Our work on historic maps suggests that the 'lyas' quarry being referred to is *stonequarrie* and *laquarrie*, which the 1515 survey recorded as lying in the middle of the West Field (see Figure 7.1).

Much of the human bone recovered by excavators and fieldwalkers near the medieval church was fragmentary and had doubtless been disturbed by the cutting-through of bodies when new graves were dug as well as by medieval and more recent ploughing. Nonetheless, individuals of 12–14 years, 15 years and 19 years of age were identified, together with other adults – a total of fifteen in all.[105] The sample is not large enough to provide meaningful population

statistics but the average age of adult males excavated at nearby Beckery Chapel, Glastonbury, for example, was just 33 years, so the age range should not surprise us.[106] Also among the Shapwick individuals were two adults with degenerative joint disease, a roughening of joint surfaces commonly found in knees, feet and hips. These may well have been painful conditions, though, in the absence of antibiotics, a juvenile with an infection of the wrist would doubtless have been of greater immediate concern to his/her family. Far more common, however, was evidence for poor dental hygiene (see Story, above). One adult had lost teeth before death, while a 19-year-old suffered from calculus and periodontal disease. Calculus is dental plaque that is characteristic of a high protein or high carbohydrate diet,[107] but it can lead to gum irritation and affect the bone, as it did in this individual. Dental

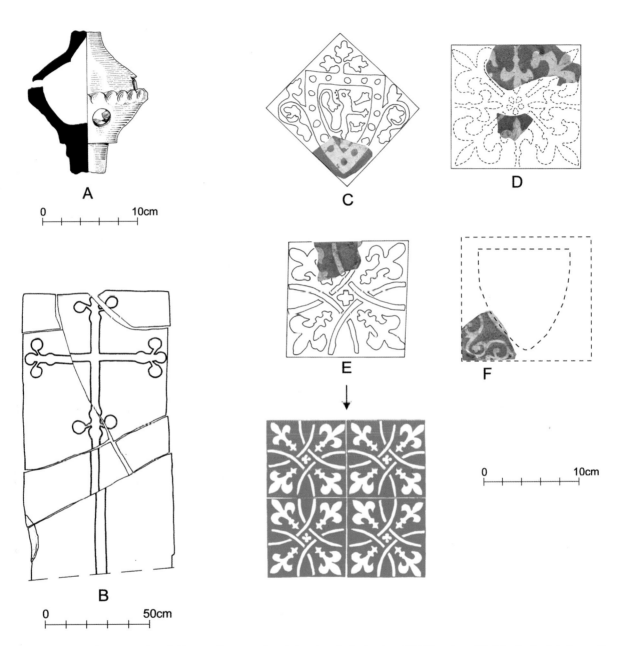

Figure 7.20. Finds associated with Shapwick's two medieval churches: St Andrew's in Old Church and St Mary's. A: globular roof finial from St Andrew's, with cordon and perforations, rod beneath to insert into socketed ridge tile; a Ham Green product, from near Bristol. B: grave cover from St Andrew's, incised Blue Lias, broken, probably late thirteenth century. C–E: inlaid floor tiles of the thirteenth and fourteenth centuries recovered from excavations either side of Bridewell Lane adjacent to St Mary's church with reconstructed panel of E below. F: floor tile probably from the chapel at Shapwick curia, later Shapwick House.

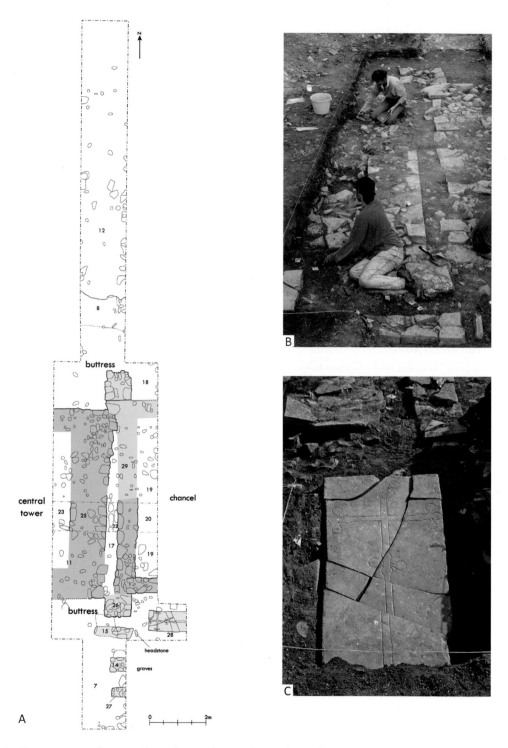

Figure 7.21. Excavation trench cut north–south over the top of St Andrew's church in Old Church. A: the trench revealed the junction between two structural units, the join between them (number 17) being obscured behind two buttresses (26 and 18). To the left (west) is the central tower (23), to the right (east) a separate and earlier stone church/chapel (20). B: excavation in progress. Note the grave revealed at the feet of the kneeling digger (number 15 on plan A). The structural junction is already clear. C: the incised Blue Lias grave-cover close to the south wall of the chancel. The fractures are caused by the weight of agricultural machinery passing above.

conditions such as this were not easily shifted with a medieval toothpick.

The exact size and shape of the churchyard cannot easily be inferred. High resolution magnetometer survey over the site suggests anomalies to the north and south of the church that might be graves, while excavation and fieldwalking indicate that the cemetery bounds lie no more than 20–30m away from the church.[108] In whatever way the limits of the burial ground were marked on the ground, it did not show up during geophysical survey and goes unmentioned in historical documents. It is possible that there was a hedge, fence or line of posts rather than a wall. The earthwork bank 30m west of the church, which has always been thought of as the churchyard boundary, proved to be a late feature in the site's history (Figure 7.22A).[109] It is reasonable to suppose that this is the same ditch referred to in the account rolls for 1313–14 when payment was made for a length of wall, a gate and ditch and, intriguingly, for collecting plants for the hedge to enclose *la Culverheye* and *la Wythyber*.[110]

Other buildings

Among the other buildings close to the church and *curia* enclosure was a stone building that stood north-east of the spring on the footprint of the earlier timber hall (see Chapter 5). This building measured 6.2m wide and 11m long internally and had walls 0.64–0.76m wide. Figure 7.22B shows its construction technique, which used mortared but undressed Blue Lias slabs for the walls and flags for the floor. Outside, at the east end, there was a shallow drip gully parallel with the gable end to help drain away the rainwater.[111] On the basis of the radiocarbon dates for the underlying limekiln (see Chapter 6) this building must have been constructed after AD 1050–1350 and was already out of use when a ditch containing twelfth- to thirteenth-century pottery was cut through its middle.

The purpose of this building is still a mystery, though we think it might be a house used by clergy attached to the nearby church. There are only a few archaeological finds, including a possible medieval pin shank and the blade from a knife, but otherwise there was little of the domestic material that might be expected of a permanently occupied dwelling. The 1230 agreement between the bishop and the Abbey, however, may provide a significant clue. It mentions

not only the church but also its 'ancient house and other appurtenances, incomes and offerings'; once more, the document states that the existing vicar (John) and his successors were to have the property.[112] Later, in 1269, the vicar was removed from Shapwick to Ashcott and thereafter granted the abbot 'his principal house in Shapwick in which previously the vicars of Shapwick used to live'.[113] This phrase seems to refer to the same vicarage provided in 1230, which from 1269 would now be owned by the abbot. Important evidence for the location of the vicarage is then provided by much later post-medieval maps which show that half an acre on the eastern side of the field belonged to the post-Reformation rectory manor. Since the lands of this later manor were essentially the same as those held by the Abbey's almoner, and our trench was in this location, this might plausibly tie the excavated stone building to the 'ancient house' of 1230. Furthermore, since the stone building must surely be a direct replacement for the timber hall on whose footprint it lies, a case can then be made that both were used by a priest before the vicars moved into the village. If this was the house of Shapwick's pre- and post-Conquest clergy then it is a rare and early example that has been found.[114]

To the west of the church lay another later medieval stone building that had been ploughed away almost completely (Figure 7.22C). Finds of pottery suggest that this building was occupied in the thirteenth century, though little can be said about its function. Robert *in cimiterio*, sometimes called Robert *atte Churcheye* (in the 1327 Exchequer Lay Subsidy, for example), is recorded in the 1306–25 court rolls and, although his surname is not an entirely reliable guide, Robert may well have had a dwelling near Shapwick church. The large quantities of calcareous sandstone recovered from Field 4016 during excavation and fieldwalking could derive from this and other lost buildings, such as the dovecote 'next to the church' which was being repointed in 1314–15, or so the demesne accounts tell us.[115]

Taken together, all this evidence paints a picture of bustling activity at *Old Church* (Figure 7.23), with a church, the essential focus for the local community, standing right next to the administrative heart of the manor – a complex of domestic buildings, stables and kennels within its own ditched enclosure. But there were other structures here too, perhaps a vicarage, if

Figure 7.22. Excavations in Old Church. A: the fourteenth-century boundary to the churchyard. This ditch had been cut and recut on several occasions but was only finally backfilled after the later seventeenth century. B: the stone foundations of a thirteenth-century stone building to the south and west of St Andrew's church in Old Church, almost entirely removed by ploughing. The moderate abundance of later medieval tablewares suggests a domestic function. C: The east end of the eleventh-century stone building near the spring site in Old Church. The foundations survived to one or two courses but were cut through by later ditches, one of which is seen immediately to the right of the ranging pole.

Figure 7.23. Reconstruction by Victor Ambrus of Old Church in around 1250. In the foreground is the ditched platform enclosing the curia buildings, including a dovecote, stables, a detached kitchen and hall. Behind is St Andrew's church with its central tower. Other buildings are shown round about.

our identification is correct, and at least one other domestic building and a dovecote. Between these stone buildings lay a graveyard, which was examined archaeologically only in a very limited way, and the spring that presumably watered the horses and other farm animals. We should not imagine a lonely church in a field to which villagers trudged for their religious services on Sundays, to receive confession and communion and to attend baptisms, marriages and funerals. When they arrived at their church the villagers saw for themselves the familiar juxtaposition of religious and secular authority represented by church and *curia* buildings, all cheek-by-jowl with their departed.

The new *curia* at Shapwick House (Hotel)

The changing appearance of the demesne manor house on Glastonbury Abbey's Shapwick estate can be brought to life by combining several different sources. A good place to begin is a detailed entry in the Abbey's accounts for the year 1333–34 that lists the locks for the hall, chambers for the abbot, monks and clerks, a pantry, a buttery and two cellars for wine and cider (all these perhaps housed in the same structure), plus an ox-house (where working horses might also have been stabled), a barn, a granary (for storing grain), a harvest office, a meat store, a postern towards the pasture (some sort of gatehouse) and a dovecote.[116] Apparently even the pigeons required securing for their own good; as we have already seen, they were kept for their meat as much as for their droppings, which were used as fertiliser. Among other buildings in the list are a kitchen, a chapel with an adjacent house (whose lock was repaired in 1311), a cider press (near the stables), bakery, stables and a pinfold for holding animals that had wandered unsupervised into the common fields.[117]

Figure 7.24. Excavations on the north side of Shapwick House. A: a medieval building, perhaps a bakery, whose clay floor was reddened by intense burning. A later waste pipe has removed part of the original floor. B: the walls of the building being cleaned by Phil Marter.

There is more limited physical evidence for these fourteenth-century buildings than there is for their later fifteenth-century successors. We speculate that the residential buildings listed in the 1333–34 account probably underlie the present mansion, with services such as the kitchen not far away; many of the agricultural buildings, we think, would have been further to the west, perhaps near the present converted stables. The medieval dovecote may have stood close to the site of its post-medieval equivalent, which is still there today. It was built in 1314–15, when sundry payments were made to men for 'digging the stone', as well as to a limeburner, a mason and a carpenter to make the door (with its hooks, hinges and key),

and for paving, pointing and whitewashing. The thirty-two *flaks pro stayring* are likely to be steps for the potence, the wooden ladder that provided access to the nesting boxes.[118] Only one building from this fourteenth-century complex was uncovered during our excavations: the west end of a burnt-out and dismantled building that was probably the bakery (Figure 7.24).[119] It must have had an oven and been rather vulnerable to fire after it was reroofed with oak tie beams and straw in 1333.[120] Several hundred grains of what was probably rivet wheat were recovered from the clay floor of the building[121] – a partially cleaned crop, perhaps, or the remains of burnt thatch of the sort identified at Forsters. Charcoal of oak and elm

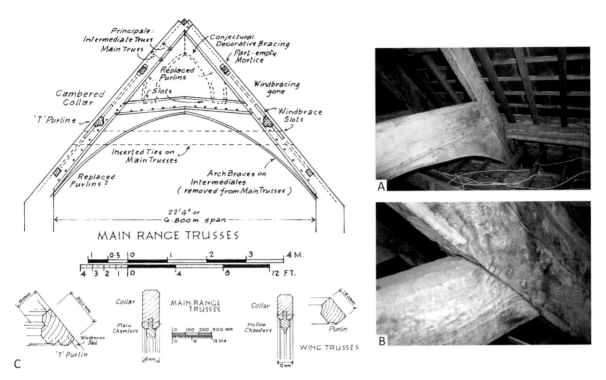

Figure 7.25. The timbers of the medieval roof (1489) over the hall range and east wing at Shapwick House. A: the roof comprised heavy arch-braced trusses with two tiers of wind-bracing (missing) in a decorative scallop pattern. B: an unusual feature of the roof is the carpenter's assembly marks for the trusses. Plumb and level marks are also present, some marked in ochre. C: this cross-section shows how the medieval roof was fitted together.

found here might have originated as structural timbers or just possibly could be the remains of the pair of plough harness poles, the trough or even the ladders that were listed in 1333–34.[122] Hurdles for sheep and the withy baskets, also mentioned in the account, may be the origin of roundwood identified, but kindling of hawthorn, blackthorn and willow would also have been stockpiled. Finally, two fragments of medieval tile, one of which has scrolls in the corner and a central shield of unknown design (see Figure 7.20F), probably come from the floor of the chapel, which, as we also learn, had a roof of lead and wooden shingles, so it may have been a separate building.

Better evidence survives for the later buildings in this manorial complex and their recognition is something of a detective story in its own right. The house seems never to have been examined by architectural historians before our Project began and it had been assumed for a long time, certainly as far

back as the time of Collinson writing in 1791, that Shapwick House was built or rebuilt in the sixteenth or seventeenth centuries. So, when members of the Somerset Vernacular Buildings Research Group began their survey of the building they certainly did not expect to find hitherto unrecorded medieval oak timber trusses 9.5m (thirty-two feet) up in the roof and wings of the house (Figure 7.25).[123] Some of these trusses were found to bear their original assembly marks as well as painted plumb and level lines used during construction.[124] As more detailed investigation proceeded, so measured plans and elevations revealed that the roof had been part of a first-floor hall with a large storeroom below (Figure 7.26). Coring of the timbers by Dan Miles produced a felling date for the oak trees soon after the spring of 1489 (Figure 2.23B).[125] By good fortune, one of the trusses had been erected 'green' – possibly a last-minute addition – and had enough sapwood to establish a firm date.

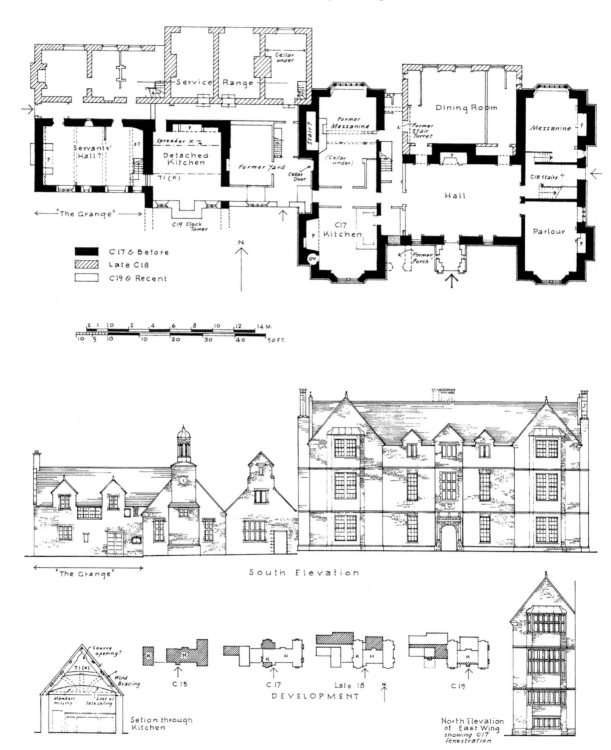

Figure 7.26. Shapwick House, plan, south elevation and structural phasing. The sequence shows how the medieval first-floor hall and kitchen evolved into the structure we see today.

Figure 7.27 is a reconstruction of how the upper hall might have looked when completed. Shallow slots indicated where wooden tracery had been pegged to the underside of the principal rafters, so the roof had been designed to impress.

Quite unexpectedly then, masked behind the nineteenth-century façade of Shapwick House (Hotel) lay an architectural jewel – the hidden core of a fifteenth-century manorial complex. Late medieval first-floor halls of this kind are extremely rare; Ashbury Manor (Berkshire) and Norwood Park (Somerset) are two surviving fifteenth-century houses each with Glastonbury Abbey involvement, as is nearby Meare Manor Farm, an earlier fourteenth-century house which, like the other two, was used by the abbot himself as a domestic residence (Figure 7.28). Its medieval function may have been part administrative, part social. Abbots John, Geoffrey Fromond and Adam of Sodbury all stayed at Shapwick in 1291, 1313 and 1324 while they dealt with local business at nearby Butleigh and Street and they did not travel alone; the accounts specifically mention chambers for monks and clerks. Other than some impressive cooking, however, the archaeology of these episodic visits is enigmatic. One further find from the moat, a contemporary late fifteenth- or sixteenth-century coin weight that bears the figure of the Archangel Michael spearing the dragon, is of a kind used to test whether gold coins called 'angels' fell below their permitted legal weight. Finding it here suggests the kinds of accounting practices we might expect of senior officials (Figure 7.29).

Immediately adjacent to and to the west of the first-floor hall lay a detached kitchen (Figure 7.30); smoke-blackened timbers in the roof produced a dendrochronological date of spring 1428 for the felling of the timber.[126] Only a single truss of the original roof remains, but this is sufficient to show that it was once wind-braced and probably had a louvre or vent to allow the smoke to escape from the roof. This timber therefore pre-dates the main hall by around sixty years and the building must have been constructed originally to serve an earlier hall, quite possibly on the same spot. We do not know whether kitchen and hall were physically connected, as they are today; quite possibly there was some sort of pentice that protected the servants and plates of food from the weather. Equally uncertain is the layout of the

Figure 7.27. Shapwick House. Reconstruction by Jane Penoyre of the first-floor hall based on a survey of the existing roof timbers. The roof, with its closely spaced trusses, arch braces and decorative windbraces, is typical of the period. The positions of the missing windbraces are reconstructed from surviving mortices. The room looks a little bare, but lacks textiles, painted wall hangings and possibly panelling as well as colourful objects such as pottery. Furniture was simple, though perhaps the abbot had his own chair as a symbol of his authority.

rest of the complex. In 1515 another survey lists a hall, chamber, storeroom, kitchen, stable, garden and barton, all inside 'la mote'. We assume the 'stable', 'garden' and 'barton' remained near the later stables block and that the 'barton', or farmyard, would have included a granary and other agricultural buildings such as the cider press and bakery mentioned in 1325. By this date, however, the main barn stood outside the circuit of the moat (see below).

The moat

The existence of the moat mentioned in Abbot Beere's terrier of 1515[127] was confirmed when a trench for a new electricity cable was dug to the north of Shapwick

Figure 7.28. Meare Manor Farm, an early fourteenth-century summer residence of the abbots of Glastonbury. Though earlier in date, this house also has a first-floor hall like Shapwick House. Notice the low ground floor and the blocked tall windows on the upper floor. The upper room was entered from an external stair and the interior was probably divided into two in order to create a hall with an adjacent heated inner chamber (Emery 2006, 591). The Shapwick building would have had internal stair access.

Figure 7.29. Coin weights tested the authenticity and proper weight of a coin. This one, with the figure of St Michael, is for a half angel. Late fifteenth or sixteenth century (1470–1604). Though the image is worn, the wings, body and head of the archangel can be made out, as well as his sword or spear; at his feet is the dragon. The scene is taken from a passage in the Apocalypse (Revelation 12: 7–9) and symbolises the battle between Good and Evil.

House hotel.[128] Faint traces of subsidence and infill were then identified as earthworks in the surrounding lawns and flowerbeds[129] and a major excavation was undertaken across its alignment.[130] This verified at least one small part of the whole ditch circuit but left the full plan uncertain. Figure 7.30 is therefore based on a total area for the moat platform of 7,865 square yards (6,576m²), 0.66ha or one and two-thirds acres, taken from Beere's survey and assumes that the statute acre was used in the clerk's calculations. Since James Bond's topographical survey suggests a north–south width of 55m for the moat platform, this gives an east–west measurement of about 120m. An apparent conflict with the earlier survey of July 1325 which reports 'the court with barton contains 2 acres' (0.81ha)[131] is resolved if a moat 4.5m wide is included in the measurements.

Excavation demonstrated that the area of the *curia* had been occupied as early as the late tenth–early eleventh centuries and that the moat itself might have been dug as early as 1200 (Figure 7.31). For some time it was difficult to see a context for the digging of such a substantial moat when the *curia* itself was elsewhere at that time (near the church of St Andrew in the East Field). It made so little sense,

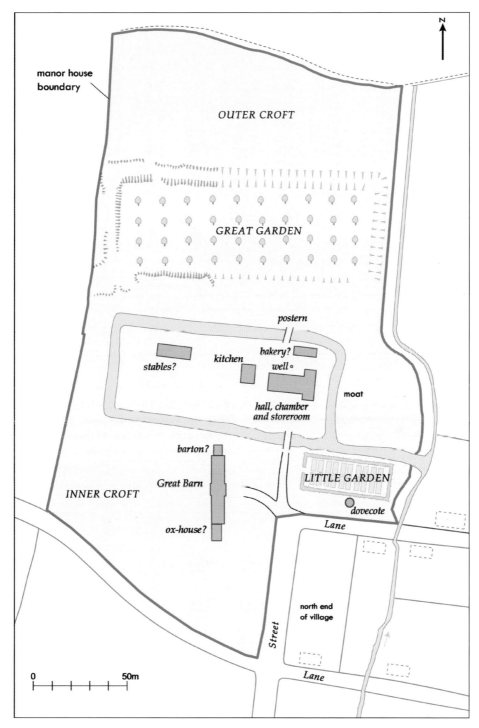

Figure 7.30. Reconstructed layout of Glastonbury Abbey's manor house or curia on the site of the later Shapwick House in c.1500. The terms in italics are those translated from medieval documents. Some buildings within the moat are documented but their locations are uncertain.

in fact, that we repeatedly returned to question the archaeological evidence. More recently, however, revisiting a statement originally made by Collinson in 1791, it seems that the origins of the moat might lie with earlier tenants. A clue to their identity is suggested by the acquisition in 1285 of the substantial estate of the freehold tenant Walter de Shapwick by John of Taunton, abbot of Glastonbury (1274–91).[132] Walter was almost certainly the wealthiest of the Abbey's tenants in Shapwick,[133] with lands that had been in his family since 1129, and it was probably they who were responsible for the digging out of the moat in around 1200. Walter himself must have been a significant local figure as he was active at the Glastonbury courts, witnessing a wide variety of legal agreements ranging from the transfer of the office of butler in 1262 to a transfer of land in Glastonbury in Northload Street.[134] He himself donated a reed bed in Withy to the church of St Andrew (Shapwick) in about 1245, the rent from which was to provide a light before the Lady Altar. Towards the end of Walter's life, in 1285 and possibly on his deathbed, he then granted away all his holdings in Withy to Glastonbury Abbey.[135] These documents were drawn up and witnessed at Shapwick and it could well be that Abbot John was sitting at Walter's bedside as he lay dying. It seems that Walter did not have any heirs and, following his death, his widow, Isabella, quitclaimed all his lands in Shapwick, Withies and Chilton on Polden to Abbot John in exchange for lands and a court at Leigh in Street where she was to live until her own death in 1296.[136] This was quite a coup for the monastery, and Edward I granted the Abbot a licence in mortmain[137] to permit him to acquire the messuage and three 'carucates' of land.

Much has been written about possible motives for the digging of moats like the one at Shapwick. Over and above its advantages, among them the provision of light defence and fishponds, and the benefits of lowering the water table around the buildings constructed on the platform, it seems that moats appealed to a less practical but eminently human desire for display and status. Landscape archaeologist James Bond has called them 'the double garage of the thirteenth century'[138] – a symbol of status, the moat being designed to look like defences to anyone approaching the manor house and the island. Some 5,300 moated sites are known across England and Wales and the chronology proposed for Shapwick fits with the national picture, which suggests that a few moats were dug in the late twelfth century, the peak in construction following between the mid-thirteenth and mid-fourteenth centuries, with far fewer being created thereafter.[139] Only after Walter's death and the donation of his fashionable moated home to the abbot in 1285 was the old *curia* in the East Field finally abandoned once and for all and its administrative functions brought into the village to the Abbey's newly acquired site.[140]

In the fourteenth century and later, therefore, the principal group of residential and agricultural buildings belonging to Glastonbury Abbey stood within the circuit of a U-shaped moat that stretched some distance west of the current Shapwick House.[141] The banks of this moat were a tangle of plants typical of disturbed waste ground, such as bramble and common nettle, which were periodically cleared. The waterlogged silts (Figure 7.31C) had preserved unworked wood including elm, hawthorn and willow/poplar, as well as a sliced root bole of elm complete with axe marks and hazel roundwood whose two side branches had been hacked off with an axe or billhook.[142] Significant pollen percentages for ash, elder and elm indicate overhanging trees or perhaps a mixed hedge close by; the latter is thought more likely on the basis of the land snails present.[143] Waterlogged macrofossils of elder, fruit stones of sloe/bullace, thorns and pollen from *Rosaceae* (the rose family), and pollen from ivy and other 'hedgerow herbs', all paint a consistent picture. Heather Tinsley, who undertook the pollen analysis, describes a mixed hedge of ash, elm, elder, rose and ivy, probably with vetch, hop and bittersweet climbing over woody plants and with cow parsley, hogweed, deadnettles and woundwort, with its spikes of pinkish flowers, growing at the base of the hedge. While low frequencies of pollen from other trees were detected (alder, hazel, oak and willow, for example), the impression generally is of an open landscape around about.[144]

Several strands of evidence combine to show that the moat must have contained water, though never a flowing current. Small mammal bones were virtually absent, confirmation that conditions were simply too wet. The thick grey-black clays at the base of the moat contained plant macrofossils such as watercress as well as aquatic beetles and the kinds of mollusc

Figure 7.31. Excavations across the medieval moat. A: excavation underway viewed from the roof of Shapwick House. Planks and scaffolding for safety. B: the excavated moat. Note the darker waterlogged silts and clays with water at the base. C: two sets of environmental samples were taken: a monolith of sediment for palynological sampling, and a column of samples at 50mm intervals for botanical, entomological and molluscan analysis, which Kerry Ely is extracting here. D: the cleaned east-facing section: grey waterlogged silts at the bottom and light brown silt clays above, capped by dark brown garden soils.

Figure 7.32. A second section across the moat north of Shapwick House. This trench cut through the moat at an oblique angle. The ranging pole is in the base of the moat, which has not been completely excavated. The two stubs of walling may be a revetment to take the timbers of a bridge. Among the stone dumped into this part of the moat in the mid-seventeenth century were fragments of an octagonal stone chimney shaft, a stone mullion, a door jamb and an arched window, all of which came from an earlier building of fifteenth-century date.

that might be found in shallow puddles or pools.[145] All this suggests stagnant, shallow, discoloured water, never more than half a metre deep, perhaps with a growth of duckweed and yellow marsh marigold on the banks in the summer, succeeded in later years by aquatic plants such as watercress as the moat slowly silted up. Since the vegetation was never able to colonise the moat fully the circuit must occasionally have been drained and cleaned out, at least partially so, and it was probably one of these maintenance

parties who left behind tell-tale signs of the clearance of undergrowth along the banks.

At 6m the moat around the new *curia* was too wide to be casually hopped across, and some kind of bridge would have been needed. One logical point of access lies on the south side of Shapwick House, now beneath the tarmac but somewhere close to the medieval porch at the end of the hall. Quite possibly there was more than one crossing. That much is hinted at by documentary references to *porta bertoni et duas portas cur' et uno posterne ad curtillag* ('gates for the barton, and two for the *curia* and curtilage') in the demesne accounts for 1313 and a 'postern towards the pasture' in 1333/34.[146] One of the excavation trenches across the moat on the north side of the *curia* did reveal columns of worked Lias stone (Figure 7.32), possibly sleeper walls that could have carried low wooden trestles for a simple railed bridge.[147] Evidence for woodworking, in the form of elm and oak woodchips, oak bark from the trimming and dressing of split planks and an elm piece axed to a chisel point[148] may be the by-products of bridge construction or on-the-spot repairs.

The contents of the encircling moat also provide some insights into activities at the new *curia*. Among the charred plants were cereals, primarily probably rivet wheat[149] but also barley, with some cultivated pulses and non-edible vetches or clovers. Presumably the vetches originated as weeds in an arable crop and it may be that this is all that is left of an old thatch or perhaps soiled animal bedding. Barley straw may also have been fed to animals being fattened for the table, hence the relatively high values of cereal pollen in the same contexts. Some or all of this refuse, together with a dung beetle and a fungal feeder, may have been tipped into the moat from stables not far away.[150] All manner of other life also made its way into the sediments: whipworm eggs (*Trichuris*) indicate faecal contamination, for which the drain of the 'abbot's chamber' mentioned in 1330 may well have been responsible,[151] while pollen of Ericaceae (heath plants) and spores of *Sphagnum* (known to have been used as toilet paper) could have reached the moat in sweepings of peat stacked for fuel. The moat was apparently too hard to resist as a convenient dumping ground. Domestic food waste was also scraped into fires and the ashes then dumped into the ditch,[152] while larger, more inviting scraps of horse meat were fought over by dogs that left behind their tell-tale gnawings on the bones. There were even several dog bones from the moat, including that of a puppy that may have drowned or, more probably, *been* drowned in the muddy water.

There are several hints from the archaeological evidence that those who dined at the moated site enjoyed a more refined diet than their village neighbours. True, they discarded the waste from plates of beef, pork and young lamb but they also ate rabbit, hare, venison (fallow deer), fish and oysters as well as chicken, goose and duck.[153] Even peafowl were present and, in a remarkable tie-in with the documentary evidence for this site, these large, brilliantly feathered birds also feature in the early fourteenth-century account rolls. Valued for their ornamental appearance, peacocks were displayed at the table with plumage intact. Archaeologically, they tend to be found at wealthier sites, including religious houses.[154] Viewed from a national perspective, the evidence seems to suggest that more birds, wild ones in particular, were eaten in the later Middle Ages,[155] and that certainly fits the pattern seen here. A gaggle of geese picking at the grass between the apple trees in the village would have made noisy neighbours but a welcome seasonal addition to the diet. And given that egg rents were a recognised form of 'currency' at Shapwick and across medieval Britain, most villagers must have kept chickens at the least, any surplus birds doubtless making their way onto the tables of the abbot and his court.[156] The ducks, however, were probably snared on the Levels rather than raised domestically.

Animal bones alone cannot tell us about the quantities of food served, the spices ground for added flavour, the balance of meat and fish or individual preferences at the table,[157] but they do at least – especially treats such as game – emphasise greater variety in the lordly diet.[158] At least two of the animals consumed at the *curia* were relatively recent novelties. The rabbit had been introduced into Britain only in the late twelfth century and was viewed enthusiastically by medieval diners. Likewise, the fallow deer appears for the first time in archaeological deposits of the mid-eleventh and twelfth centuries as part of the aristocratic diet.[159] The venison on the abbot's table at Shapwick would, given the Glastonbury connection, very probably have been hunted in a local deer park, possibly at Pilton.[160] Their

consumption here makes an unavoidable statement about the status of the household, especially since the food was presented in such grand surroundings. Unfortunately, the archaeology only hints at what that dining experience would have been like: the textiles have rotted, knives been sheathed away, and any objects of value removed and recycled. The only artefacts to survive are those for which no further use could be found, such as broken pitchers.

The Great Barn

A barn is first mentioned hereabouts in 1274, when its roof (and that of the ox-house) required repair after a *ventus validus*, a gale. Payments in 1311 for clearing and levelling an upper floor suggest an interior loft of some sort and a tiler was paid to repair the roof and repoint the *summitate*, the upper part. This first barn was therefore tiled and not thatched in 1333[161] and it was probably here that John le Irrische and William le King 'stacked' in 1325, manoeuvring the bundles of wheat sheaves being stored there in the dry after the harvest.[162] Quite where this barn was located is not known but, given its inclusion in the 1333–34 accounts (see above), it may well have stood on the moat platform.

The late medieval Shapwick barn depicted by Bonnor to the south of the moat in the late eighteenth century is probably a fourteenth-century successor.[163] His view shows five buttresses either side of the porch, a roof regularly coursed with either slates or stone tiles, and a cupola at its crest (Figure 7.33A). The latter is undoubtedly an addition, whereas the central cart porch depicted on the village map in *c*.1764 as projecting from the central bay had evidently been removed in the intervening twenty-five years. Using the buttresses as a guide, and assuming from the evidence of surviving barns a bay width of about 3.4m, this barn would have been about 38m long and between 6.2m and 8.4m wide.[164] To span this width, base-crucks with upper principals are likely; they are common to all surviving examples[165] and essential if a roof weighing around 125 tons was to be adequately supported.[166]

This is a considerable structure, therefore, though not one of the enormous barns such as those at Abbotsbury in Dorset, Beaulieu in Hampshire or Bradford on Avon (Wilts).[167] Of the fifteen barns known to have existed on the medieval estates

Figure 7.33. A: Shapwick barn in 1791, extracted and enlarged from Thomas Bonnor's view of Shapwick House. B: the surviving monastic barn at Glastonbury. Note the buttresses, the porch and the slate roof. The arms of Abbot Bere date the structure to around 1500. C: Shapwick Great Barn wall and exterior yard surface. Coursed rubble was used for walling at Shapwick, a particular feature of construction being the use of a green binding clay and limestone plaques which had been jammed vertically into the clay to prevent moisture seeping back under the wall. Among the finds were many nails, used to secure the slate roof, and a whittle-tang knife with a circular bolster of post-medieval date.

of Glastonbury Abbey, only those at Doulting, Glastonbury (now part of the Somerset Rural Life Museum), Pilton and West Bradley still survive today (Figure 7.33B).[168] They are often referred to as 'tithe barns' in the belief that their function was to store the produce rendered by the tenants as tithes, that tenth of their crops due to the Church.[169] Most, however, would better be regarded as warehouses where produce from the demesne farm could be stored either for use on the Glastonbury estate or until it was sold on. It was from this barn that William Cole, a Shapwick labourer, stole in June 1595 'three partes of a pecke of wheate' belonging to Thomas Walton, who held the manor at that time.[170] Although he pleaded guilty, William was still whipped for his crime. Earlier, the barn had been securely locked, a reflection of the tremendous value of its contents.[171] A *furnus*, or oven, recorded between 1366 and 1375, was probably in use nearby to dry damp grain or to malt at low temperatures so it is no surprise that charred wheat grains, peas and weed seeds were discovered trampled into the floor of the barn (Figure 7.33C).[172]

Gardens and precinct

Fourteenth-century accounts for Glastonbury Abbey itself reveal that there was a 'Great' and a 'Little' garden there. At times these seem to have been no more than paddocks where horses or sheep grazed in among apple and pear trees, while at others they were mown for hay or cultivated with onions, leeks, beans, garlic and dyeing and fibre-producing plants such as flax.[173] Later there is mention of a flower garden too. Something similar probably existed at the Shapwick *curia*. We know that a gardener was employed from 1300 and, from a combination of archaeological, architectural, topographical (Box 7.2) and historical sources, something can be reconstructed of the physical environment.

There were four enclosures around the *curia* buildings, two of which, described as the 'great' and 'little' gardens, covered five and a half acres in 1325.[174] The larger of the two produced between five and a half and eight quarters of apples (between 850 and 1,250 medium-sized apples each year) and its herbage was rented out; the smaller garden may have supplied herbs and medicinal plants as well as vegetables for the kitchen.[175] There were also two other 'crofts' that were sufficiently well manured to be cultivated every year. Figure 7.30 proposes their locations within the manorial precinct in a manner that seems consistent with the 1325 survey and other contemporary account rolls. The total area within the proposed boundary is 12.9 statute acres, close to the 1325 total of 13.75 acres. Within this block of land the 'outer croft' was normally sown with beans, which were well suited to the heavier land at the northern end of the site. This crop could have been dried as an ingredient for pottages or fed to the horses, pigs and pigeons.[176] The southern boundary of this 'outer croft' coincides with a prominent earthwork identified by James Bond (see Figure B.7.2). Immediately to the south lay the 'great garden', which may have been enclosed in some way, but we exclude the small moated site to the north-west of Shapwick House,[177] which on balance seems more likely to be part of a sixteenth- or seventeenth-century garden design (see Chapter 8). Finally, south of the moat was the 'inner croft', measuring three and a half acres and last recorded in 1333–34,[178] and the 'little garden', which equates to a smaller parcel of land to the east of West Street near the existing dovecote. Its layout in Figure 7.30 is based on those of gardens of a similar date.

A satisfyingly complete impression of the new *curia*, with its moat and gardens, can therefore be drawn together from documents and archaeological fieldwork, though the reason why Glastonbury Abbey wished to bring their administrative headquarters into the village in the last quarter of the thirteenth century goes unstated. Perhaps there was a lack of space at the old *curia*, or perhaps the condition of the buildings in the East Field left something to be desired, but these explanations ring hollow. It is more likely that the monastery wished to exercise more control over its resources, to involve itself as directly as possible in the production of cereals and wool for market and thereby to increase its surpluses for a greater cash income. The Abbey may well have wished to accomplish the move into the village somewhat earlier, but did not find it easy to regain its lands once they had been leased to men such as Walter.[179] Perhaps the move was accompanied by a redefinition of labour services and, on the Glastonbury estates, we know that the labour force was enhanced during the thirteenth century by demands for the same amount of service for half the area of land.[180] Our suggestion is that the move of the *curia* into the village of Shapwick was a physical expression of the age of demesne farming, a sign of strengthening local management at a time of worsening conditions for the local peasantry. It seems significant to us that the new *curia* stood at the northern end of West Street, at the head of the village. Spatial manifestations of social order, the most visible symbols of feudal relations, regulation and wealth in a medieval rural community, were etched into the village plan.

The almoner's 'manor'

Parts of the estates of the larger and wealthier monastic houses were often allocated to senior officials within the Abbey. In Glastonbury's case, different abbots over the centuries kept their own houses, to which they escaped periodically. In the sixteenth century Sharpham Park House was built for this purpose by Abbot Richard Beere,[181] and it was to Sharpham that Abbot Richard Whiting was taken for interrogation at the Dissolution in 1539 before his removal to the Tower of London and subsequent trial.[182] At nearby Shapwick it was not only the abbot who had property but also the almoner, the official at the Abbey responsible for dispensing alms to the poor.[183] This came about in 1230, when the Abbey decided to raise more income and took the step of appropriating the rectory of Shapwick church.[184] The income of the church was then split into two unequal amounts; the smaller would in future go to support the vicar,[185] while the larger was apportioned to the almoner. Thereafter the almoner acted as rector and took formal responsibility for the chancel in the church and for additional expenses such as the purchase of vestments and books for services. In return he received some of the offerings and dues from the church along with most of the tithes,[186] and it is for this reason that his manor is referred to as the 'rectorial manor'.[187] Part of the almoner's estate was rented from the Shapwick main manor. According to the 1260 survey this amounted to two freehold virgates and seventeen and a half acres of land in villeinage, in all about 100 acres, for which he paid a total rent of 18s 1½d;[188] by the early sixteenth century that area had tripled to 300 acres.[189] Other than tithes and crops, the almoner

BOX 7.2

The earthworks of Shapwick Park

Among the many remarkable contributions made to the Shapwick Project is an extremely detailed example of the art of earthwork survey undertaken by landscape archaeologist James Bond around Shapwick House (Figure B.7.2). We choose to highlight this technique in particular because archaeology is too often associated with excavation and some fail to appreciate the value of earthwork recording, which has rather fallen out of fashion against geophysics and other forms of remote survey. This example shows how the skill of hachure drawing can still be used to the greatest effect.

Field 6086, to the north-west of Shapwick House, contains some features of recent origin, including numerous hummocks and hollows that may mark the positions of grubbed-out apple trees. Of greater interest is a prominent platform which is clearly defined by a shallow trench on three sides. This ditch cannot ever have held water and it seems too far north to be one of the hollow-ways of the medieval village. A likely explanation is that these are the remnants of formal gardens of medieval date and, as we have seen, the 1325 survey does mention a garden of five and a half acres attached to the *curia* (see Figure 7.30). Other medieval features were also recorded by James in the lawns north, east and south of Shapwick House (Field 6477), where he was able to trace the line of a moat around three sides of the house. Although the north-east corner of the moated platform and a length of some 28m along its northern side were clearly visible his survey could find no evidence for causeways, bridges or a gatehouse.

The south-east corner of the moat was approached from the east by a short, broad linear depression aligned at an angle of about 20° to the modern drive. This may have been a leat linking the moat with the stream to the east, though it seems unnecessarily wide for that purpose, and it appears to be more or less in line with the northernmost of the village's east–west lanes, named as 'Jeanes Lane' on the eighteenth-century maps. If this is correct, then the north-western corner of the later medieval street system had evidently been lost before the middle of the eighteenth century. James even suggested from his survey that the south-eastern corner of the moat actually intersects this hollow-way, implying that the part of the road west of the stream may have been abandoned *before* the moat itself was constructed. Beyond the eastern limits of the moat James also picked out a narrow band of low ridge and furrow preserved at the very easternmost edge of the lawn near the modern overflow car park. This must pre-date the new curia precinct after 1285 (Figure 7.30).

Field 6767, between the two ha-has south of Shapwick House, was the most difficult area to understand since none of the features observed within it bore any clear relationship to anything in the parcels to north or south. The earthworks here were much confused by recent disturbances, including archaeological trenches and the Wessex Water pipeline. There was no clear evidence on the ground of either the barn drawn by Bonnor (see Figure 7.33A) or the later medieval dovecote. Field 6152, on the other hand, contains some impressive earthworks, including a cambered hollow-way about 10m wide, the 'West Street' marked on old maps. Several other lanes could be seen at right angles to this, the line of 'Godfrys Lane' coinciding precisely with the eastern part of the southern ha-ha separating parcel 6767 from parcel 6152. The part of this field between West Street and the stream, therefore, appears to contain four later medieval crofts, two bounded by lanes on either side, while the two between Bartlets or Poles Lane and Clarks Lane seem to have been separated only by a ditched boundary. Of the vanished dwellings identified on mid-eighteenth-century maps, not one could be located with confidence, though, perversely, two possible buildings that can be postulated from the field evidence fail to appear on any of the eighteenth-century maps. One is a small but prominent rectangular platform with two tree-pits on the top, located immediately south of the Clarks Lane junction with West Street. Possibly this building was removed at an earlier period.

The task of earthwork interpretation has been compared with guessing the contents of a package without unwrapping it. In the case of Shapwick the field evidence is especially well complemented by a good series of maps, aerial photographs, pictorial illustrations and other written records: the cartographic sources in particular provide invaluable information on roads and buildings that have fallen out of use since the eighteenth century, and in some cases this evidence can clearly be related to the earthworks recorded on the ground.[b6]

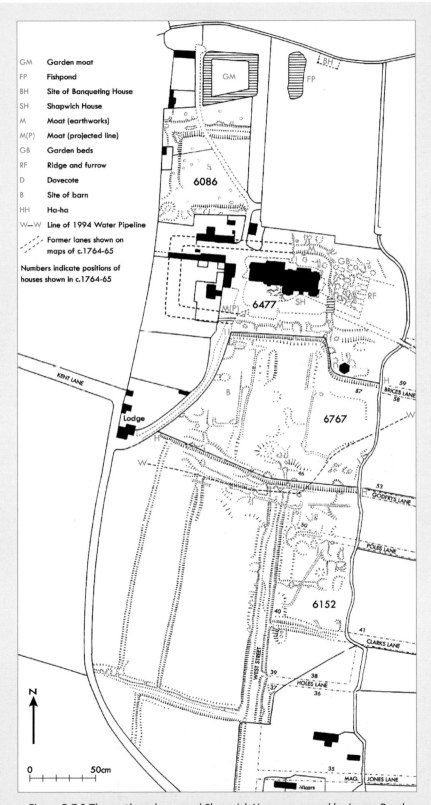

Figure B.7.2 The earthworks around Shapwick House, surveyed by James Bond.

also earned income from property. In 1257–58 his annual accounts show that he collected 30s 6d from his Shapwick tenants and 82s 6d from Glastonbury tenants, a not inconsiderable sum.[190] The vicar, on the other hand, although it was he who ministered to the parish, had to get by more frugally on the income from some glebe land and certain lesser tithes.[191]

Quite when the almoner first constructed a house in Shapwick village remains unresolved. The later rectorial manor house lies in the northern half of the village[192] and although no large-scale excavation was possible there, eight test pits dug in the grounds did produce occasional finds of eleventh- to thirteenth-century pottery, together with some features[193] sufficient to indicate domestic activity. From the thirteenth century this was quite possibly no more than a complex of agricultural buildings run by a bailiff who managed the lands and tenants on behalf of the almoner. There probably never was a large house at this site until the sixteenth century, and the 1515 survey is silent on the matter. In 1540, however, an account of 'Fryer Robert Gylde, Almoner' mentions a house as being let out to Agnes, wife of John Frye the Bailiff, who surely managed the demesne land for the almoner at Shapwick.[194] In the records of the Court of Augmentations, which considered the distribution of monastic property at the time of the Dissolution, the site is described as 'a hall, four chambers and a buttery, a kechyn, a bruhowse and a maltehowse above, and a howse to put hee [hay] in'.[195] Several early sixteenth-century features do still survive among the standing buildings, among them the arch for the inner door of the porch, but the floor plan of the original building where Agnes once lived cannot be reconstructed with confidence;[196] the house was comprehensively remodelled a century later (see Chapter 8).

The earliest building on the site today is the dovecote, a circular structure with a low doorway and a cupola on the roof (Figure 7.34A). The conical roof was rebuilt quite recently and Figure 7.34B shows the rafters rising from the wall plate to meet the circular frame that supports the octagonal lantern with its apertures on each face for the birds. Clearly seen in this photograph are the dovetail joints on the oak timber wall plate, which may be of some antiquity; much of the rest of the roof is nineteenth century.[197] Inside there are fourteen tiers with thirty-seven nests in each, making a total of 426 nestholes

in all, perhaps housing for about 1,000 birds (Figure 7.34C).[198] Unfortunately there is little to indicate a firm date of construction, though the first certain documentary reference to a dovecote on the almoner's estate is dated 1446 and there is no reason to doubt the present structure's medieval credentials.[199] The hay barn alongside, however, has not survived, although in dry summers its outline can be easily be traced as parchmarks on the lawns. First mentioned in 1540,[200] it was probably demolished when Down House was gentrified in the early nineteenth century – the same fate that befell the Great Barn nearby at Shapwick House (see Chapter 9).

The new church

Although the remodelling of church architecture was widespread in the Middle Ages, it is unusual to know so precisely the circumstances of a new construction, as we do at Shapwick. Sometime prior to 1329 a petition was filed for a new church to be built within the bounds of the village; then, in January 1329, Ralph of Shrewsbury, bishop of Bath and Wells, in his role as diocesan authority, responded to the abbot of Glastonbury[201] voicing his agreement. 'The church of Shapwick', he writes, 'is situated at a great distance from its village, on account of which it is agreed both church and parishioners suffer considerable inconvenience.'[202] When the bishop attended the consecration of the new church in September 1331 he cannot have failed to notice that the new dedication to St Mary mirrored that for Glastonbury Abbey. This was a clear reference to the ownership of the manor and probably reflected the monastery's role as principal sponsors of the building; certainly the speed of the work implies well-coordinated finance such as only the Abbey could muster. As it turned out, the parishioners were fortunate to get the new church completed before 1348. The outbreak of plague in that year stalled many other building programmes, sometimes by as much as fifty years or more.

The present church seems to have taken a maximum of about thirty months to construct, and a little can be deduced of its original structural detail. Accounts for Withy in 1330–31 state that one acre of reeds was given for roofing the *campanilis*, the bell-tower or belfry of the new church, while the chancel and nave were probably tiled with slate.[203]

Figure 7.34. Shapwick Manor dovecote. A: the exterior with pigeons aloft and the mansion behind. B: the dovecote under repair, showing dovetail joints in the wall plate. C: the interior with nesting boxes.

Inlaid medieval tiles recovered from our excavations immediately to the north once formed part of the original floor of the church and must have been discarded at the time of its restoration in the 1860s (see Figure 7.20C–E). The fabrics, dimensions and decorative motifs of these tiles are characteristic of a well-known tilery which supplied the Abbey after the 1280s, so the tiles were a direct result of the Glastonbury connection with its outlying estates and can be found at several other sites in the region, such as Glastonbury Tor, the Beckery chapel and the Abbey itself, as well as further afield. Apart from the introduction of seventeenth-century memorials and fixtures and fittings and new fenestration, the basic fabric of the medieval church has changed little[204] and, since we also have the plan of St Andrew from the geophysical survey, Alex Turner was able create a 3D model of the existing church and compare the two (Figure 7.35). This exercise shows that the new church was similar in plan but somewhat larger. That extra space would have allowed for the reordering of seating, greater flexibility for processions and improved views to images and the high altar. Some

parts of the medieval liturgy, such as baptism, required families and godparents to gather around the font and so simply required more room.[205] That said, to build a central tower like this, rather than one at the west end of the church, was already an antiquated idea in the fourteenth century. The appearance of St Mary's may therefore have deliberately echoed its predecessor in order to ease any local concerns about the move into the village. Perhaps the parishioners did not want a new church at all, in spite of what the authorities claimed on their behalf, or perhaps the division of responsibility between the parishioners (for the nave) and the rector (for the chancel) hampered any stylistic innovation and so led to a more conservative design. The early decades of the fourteenth century were not times of plenty (Box 7.1).

Outside, in the graveyard, responsibility for the upkeep of the perimeter wall was apportioned to different farmsteads. Shared maintenance is a feature of a number of settlements in Somerset,[206] and in this case communal commitment was indicated by stones that were carved with initials or numbers set into the wall, one of which still survives (Figure 7.36A).[207]

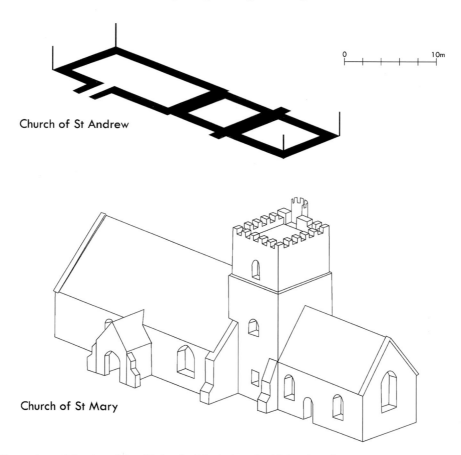

Figure 7.35. Comparison of the plan of the old church of St Andrew (Field 4016) with a simplified reconstruction of the present church of St Mary.

An eighteenth-century plan of the village[208] indicates those tenements with this obligation to repair, all of which lie within the village 'footprint', just as we might anticipate given the nineteenth-century date of most of Shapwick's outlying farms (Figure 7.36B). This was either a new obligation imposed following the move of the church into the village in the fourteenth century or one that reflected a previous arrangement at the earlier church site. The fact that only certain core properties bore this imposition must imply that the latter was the case. One unsolved problem, however, is quite how the graveyard came to be accommodated within the existing village plan in the first place. If we are right and the village was founded in the tenth century then, 400 years later, we

would surely expect the village to be fully occupied with farmsteads, even if population numbers were struggling, as the documentary evidence seems to suggest. Unless there was a green in the centre of the plan – a suggestion first advanced by geographer Brian Roberts, but one for which there is no evidence[209] – an opportunity must have been seized to clear a space amidst the farm buildings.

There are a number of implications to this idea. First, the present churchyard should preserve the outline of one or more tofts in the village plan. Second, *under* the church and the graveyard should be the remains of one or more farmsteads dating between the tenth and the fourteenth centuries. In fact, when the dimensions of the churchyard are compared with adjacent spaces in the village on the eighteenth-century plans (for example, on Figure 7.2), it does look as if the space it occupies is the equivalent of two tofts.[210] Whatever buildings once stood here,[211] a significant reordering of space was certainly undertaken to relocate the church right at the heart of the village community. Moving the church, ostensibly at the behest of the laity, brought religious devotion into the heart of Shapwick village after around 400 years during which the church had always been spatially isolated from its community. This new location now placed the church at the geographical centre and visual core of the village, next to the crossroads. Since the new church also had a bell-tower, the noise of the bells must have been more clearly heard within the village, regularising the working day, calling the villagers to services, advising of births and deaths and ringing out the festivities of the Christian year. No longer could the church be accused of being 'distant' and 'inconvenient', to use Bishop Ralph's own words.

Back at the site of the old church of St Andrew, what remained? Our excavations showed that the graves of friends and family were left behind, but did the superstructure itself disintegrate or was it dismantled? It is extremely hard to say. The lack of building stone, even the roughed-out Lias blocks from which the foundations were built, hints that much was taken away, perhaps even for the new church in the village. Likewise, no window glass or architectural fragments in Ham Hill or Dundry stone were left behind. Yet if the building materials were systematically recycled we might not expect to find the large quantities of roofing slate, the stone roof tile and the broken ceramic finial that we did recover. Perhaps the church was left standing for some time,

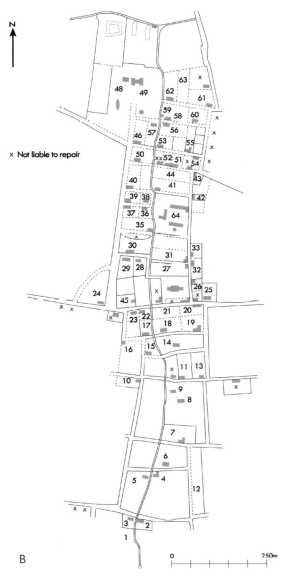

Figure 7.36. Obligations for the upkeep of the churchyard wall. A: stone carved with initials. B: village plan showing those tenements with obligations. This information is taken from an eighteenth-century map entitled 'A Plan of the Houses and Cotes etc. in Shapwick lyable to repair the church yard Wall with the measure in Feet and inches of each Plot of Church yard wall belonging to each House or Cote; NB Those which are Numbered are only lyable to repair Church yard Wall; Those which are lettered x are Not lyable' (SRO DD/SG 13 c.1765, though catalogued as c.1731).

until parts of the roof began to fail, at which point everything of value was then salvaged, though there is no evidence in the present church of, say, an earlier font, pulpit or screen. The field name *oldechurche* first appears in 1367, little more than a generation after St Mary's was completed, but by this date the conversion from sacred space to arable field was already complete. Brusque and businesslike though this might seem to us, the change was perhaps seen rather differently at the time. The medieval graveyard at St Andrew's had always been a multi-functional space, with dovecotes, enclosures, grazing animals and houses close by. Medieval people were used to seeing churchyards as spaces for the holding of markets and fairs and for games playing, so the encroachment of the plough may not have seemed so alarming.

A later medieval landscape

Arable fields

By the time of Abbot Adam of Sodbury's survey in 1325 Shapwick had developed a common-field system that might be described as typical of a band of 'planned countryside' stretching across England from Durham in the north-east of England through the Midlands and across Wessex. Either side of the village were two large arable fields, East and West, more or less of the same size and each subdivided into furlongs and these into bundles of strips (Figure 7.37).[212] Grain accounts for 1311–12 to 1314–15, 1330–31 and 1333–34 for the demesne arable show that the same furlongs and acreage were being sown in alternate years, so the whole of each common field was rotated biannually.[213] This symmetry and regularity is characteristic of common-field systems.

The West Field stretched out from the village to the western boundary of the parish with Catcott, and from Kent Farm and the watermill up to the woodland at Loxley on the upper slopes. By 1515 there were about seventy furlongs here, each with a varying number of strips. The East Field was divided by the *Hallebrok*, today's Cats Drove stream, into a northern section called East Field by Northbrook and a southern section called East Field by Southbrook. The former had about twenty furlongs, the latter about forty-five. The common fields were thus roughly similar in area and numbers of furlongs, though by no

means mirror images. Little archaeological evidence survives in the form of ridge and furrow to help with a more detailed reconstruction, although earthworks do survive at Beggars Bush Copse, at Ice House Copse and in the grounds of Shapwick House, as well as immediately west of the village, and there is often some clue to orientation on geophysical surveys, post-medieval maps and later field boundaries. On this basis, for example, the predominant pattern in the West Field and East Field by Southbrook is known to be north–south strips within a rectilinear pattern of furlong blocks.

Figure 7.37 makes use of the details available in the 1515 survey to plot the lands and strips of one of Shapwick's later medieval tenants, John Pytt. John's messuage, curtilage and garden were situated in the south-west quadrant of the village and from here he would have set out to tend his strips in the arable fields. Although he is listed only as a ferdeller, the status of a tenant and the size of their holding were not at all related by the sixteenth century and John actually held over forty acres of arable as well as meadow and pasture held in severalty (that is, held individually rather than in common), including rough pieces of land on the banks of streams and along the green lanes, such as *harepathway* in East Field. The scattering of John's strips shows just how far a tenant would have to travel to work their land. This doubtless took many hours out of the week, but it by no means represents all of his journeying. John would also have had access to pasture on the Moor to the north and an interest in pasture in Loxley Wood over the winter, not to mention the regular visits he would have made to the manor court, church and mills, as well as to the markets at Bridgwater and Glastonbury. What emerges from this map of John's daily activities is the sense that medieval peasants were constantly on the move along networks of lanes and paths, greeting each other as they passed through the village as well as at key locations out in the fields, such as *Proutmead* and *Slape* bridges. It also emphasises just how much of any tenant's time was invested in agricultural tasks and the need to react promptly if any part of the infrastructure was placed at risk. Thus the court rolls show time and again an urgency to keep Shapwick's watercourses clear and flowing so as to prevent flooding and waterlogging. John Buryman

Figure 7.37. The holding of John Pytt, ferdeller, in 1515. Pytt's land and strips were widely scattered across both arable fields and he also had access to pasture on the Levels or moors and to Loxley Wood. The figure indicates possible routes taken by Pytt as he made his way across the parish from his home in the village.

– probably the very same man who was beaten by stone robber John Sherp in 1348 (see above) – was found guilty of obstructing the *Medewell* in 1368 and then failed to clear its watercourse again seven years later. Sometimes a team of men was ordered out to help, as they were in 1358 when the *Westmordich* was obstructed. No less important was the cutting of new

ditches to improve drainage into upland streams such as the *Shytbrok* (now the Shoot Brook past Manor Farm) in 1311. There was also significant interest in improving the soils, just as agricultural treatises of the day recommended.[214] The sheer quantity of medieval pottery collected by eagle-eyed fieldwalkers, most notably across an inner core of furlongs to either side of the village, is witness to the labour of Shapwick villagers month-by-month, year-after-year, carting manure out to the common fields. The cycles of the agriculture year, reinforced through rituals of Church and calendar, formed the ever-persistent rhythm of life in the community.[215]

By 1325 there was about 500 acres of demesne arable: lands cultivated exclusively for the benefit of the Glastonbury Abbey 'home farm' and on which the tenants gave free labour. The demesne occupied much of the best land in the parish, on the Nidons for example, but there was also a further 800 acres of tenants' customary land and rented demesne arable, together with perhaps 200 acres of the almoner's land, making a total of 1,500 acres in all.[216] Exactly how this land was farmed did change over time. At the end of the twelfth century, for example, the Abbey began to manage its demesne more directly, reducing the number of sheep in favour of arable crops.[217] For much of the later Middle Ages the Abbey exploited Shapwick as a wheat producer, as it did the neighbouring manors of Ashcott, Greinton, High Ham, Street and Walton. When the Abbey's auditors came to calculate the value of each manor in 1311–12, Shapwick was ranked thirteenth of the thirty-five listed; in terms of grain supplied to Glastonbury it ranked fourth. Wheat, sown in the winter, was the staple for bread production, and the most valuable cereal.[218] In 1311–12, 91 per cent of Shapwick's wheat crop went to Glastonbury, a percentage typical of those manors located nearer to the Abbey.[219] Oats and barley, the crop that gives its name to the medieval *Bereweye* and modern *Beerway* (OE *bere*, barley + *weg*, road), both spring-sown crops, were used mainly for fodder and feed and in the brewing of ale respectively.[220]

Palaeobotanical research confirms this broad sketch,[221] wheat being the most common cereal in our excavated samples, followed by barley and then oats, which were well suited to the parish's heavier soils. At Shapwick it would appear that both hexaploid bread wheat and a tetraploid species, probably rivet wheat rather than macaroni wheat, were grown for consumption, brewing and thatching (see above). Rivet wheat, a species that has not been grown commercially in Britain since the late nineteenth century, was noted for the excellence of its bread flour.

Rye, though widespread across southern England, seems not to have been a very important crop in this part of Somerset. Brassicas (cabbage or mustard) were also identified, as well as legume seeds, probably a vetch, peas and Celtic (field) beans. Glastonbury records show that the Sedgemoor manors were the main source of these crops,[222] though doubtless they were also cultivated in village plots and gardens as an essential ingredient for pottage or cattle fodder.[223] Flax, too, was sometimes grown by tenants in their own plots and gardens.[224] In 1368 Philip Shorel and John Cokeman were evidently retting or soaking their flax 'in the water used by oxen' which they were under orders to drain.[225] The flax fibres would have been processed, spun and then woven and, since the retting process produces a foul smell, the two men chose a suitable spot far away from the village out near *Caterwode* (see below).

What would Shapwick's common fields have looked like? The cultivated furlongs with their strips had no hedges, and they were probably separated one from another by baulks and headlands. We have argued that a proportion of these boundaries still persist as hedgerows and ditches today and, on the basis of our excavations, some medieval fields may also have had a more terraced appearance, with slight lynchets demarcating cultivated areas and tracks (see Figure 7.38).[226] It is perhaps difficult for us to envisage the Shapwick landscape as consisting of large unhedged areas, some fully cropped, others open prairies for animals grazing on weeds and stubble. Sheep, kept principally for their fleeces, were especially valued for their manure, and several flocks, possibly confined within temporary hurdle fences, would have grazed out on the fallow, including a demesne flock that followed the Abbey's shepherds between monastic manors.[227] An observant time traveller would perhaps be struck by two features of this medieval countryside. First, far more of the parish land was accessible in the Middle Ages than it has been at any time since. Second, Shapwick's fields undoubtedly supported a far richer flora than they do today. Among the arable weeds buried in the innermost roofing thatch at Forsters were the bright blue cornflower, yellow-flowering charlock and the pretty but poisonous purple corncockle, the latter anciently introduced to Britain from Europe, probably as a grain contaminant. Plant macrofossils identified from the bulk soil samples taken from excavations include sorrel and the mayweed-like stinking chamomile,[228] as well as other early introductions such as the grass darnel (also known as 'tares')[229] and thorow-wax, with its yellowish-white flowers.[230] Many of these species were to become much rarer with the invention of the seed-drill at the beginning of the eighteenth century; cornflower would be a rare sight in an English field today. We also found that eyebright (or possibly the closely related species red bartsia) and yellow rattle, with its dry capsules of seeds that rattle in the wind in late summer, flourished on Shapwick pastures and meadowlands.

This account of Shapwick's fields gave the impression that land use was static throughout the medieval period, but that was far from the case. Although the field systems described in Chapter 6 in the later Anglo-Saxon period were also 'open fields', we have no evidence that they were so tightly regulated with, for example, strict rotations of fallow. This sort of 'common field' arrangement may have developed later. It is also the case that the cultivated area described in 1325 and then mapped in detail for 1515 is a significant extension of the later Anglo-Saxon layout. By examining in detail the pottery scatters collected by fieldwalkers, and operating on the assumption that pottery found in the fields arrived there largely by virtue of its being incorporated in farm manure, it is possible to gauge roughly when individual modern fields were first cultivated. This exercise shows that the common fields expanded first at the fringes and then, by the end of the thirteenth century, the Nidons were cultivated together with fields to the north of *Hallebrok* (Cats Drove stream). This seems to agree with what little we can glean from the documentary record. The Nidons, for example, formed a major part of the demesne arable in 1260, but there is no earlier documentary evidence. Elsewhere, at Milton Podimore, another Glastonbury estate, Harold Fox demonstrated how a two-field arrangement was replaced by three fields in 1333,[231] so Shapwick was in no way unique in seeing bold alterations to its agricultural practices. It is well established that the layouts of medieval field systems could be changed[232] and an increase in output of the kind we are suggesting at Shapwick might be linked

Figure 7.38. Section through a lynchet between Bassecastel and Brimfurlong in the medieval East Field. The ranging pole lies on the limestone bedrock. The curving bank of a headland can be seen in the section, but it has been truncated and become flat-topped as a result of modern ploughing. Field boundaries like this are of considerable interest in any landscape study but are rarely examined by archaeologists.

either to population rise in the twelfth century or to the decreasing fertility of land in the immediate vicinity of the village. Either or perhaps both would be strong motives for increasing the size of the open fields and for regulating their cultivation more tightly. Another possibility is that these changes were related to management practice. For much of the twelfth century the Abbey's demesne land was 'farmed out' and the Abbey's food requirements were supplied by 'food-farms', of which there were two at Shapwick.[233] By the end of that century, however, a more direct 'in hand' system of exploitation was in operation and an extended field system may have been more efficient.[234]

Enclosure was also underway. By 1515 about 60

Figure 7.39. Loxley Wood seen from the air, looking east along the north edge of the wood. The snow in the lee of the wood highlights later field drains and possible assarts, the piecemeal clearance of the woodland which creates the zigzagged edge seen here.

per cent of the upland part of the parish had already been enclosed and much of it converted to pasture. The hedging of newly consolidated plots proceeded apace as field strips were sold or voluntarily exchanged and then amalgamated. The names of many field parcels betray their origins as strips or furlongs, pasture is spoken of as 'newly enclosed' and, on at least one occasion, an arable holding in scattered strips was erased in the records and replaced by a single furlong name.[235] New boundaries like these could sometimes cut across more ancient alignments, though more usually they mirrored the pre-existing pattern of strips.[236] The impression is one of enclosure steadily nibbling away at the peripheries of the common fields while most tenants retained a more or less

equal division of arable land between the East and West fields and continued to farm communally along traditional lines. Leasing and enclosure presumably provided Glastonbury Abbey with a profitable solution to the financial crises they faced in demesne farming and the fact that there was effectively only one owner, the Abbey, helped to ease the changes through at Shapwick.

Woodlands

The only surviving 'ancient' woodland in the parish is Loxley, the earlier *Lokkesleigh* (Figure 7.39).[237] The shape of this wood probably changed slightly during the medieval period, which would explain its uneven northern boundary: it was cut into from the Shapwick side to enclose newly cultivated ground at *Collewey* (for location see Figure B.5.5). This may have happened during a period of rising population in the thirteenth century, or possibly earlier, and the name *Collewey*, meaning 'charcoal road', hints at the activities underway in the vicinity. Several ancient woodland indicator species still grow here, including pendulous sedge, wood sorrel and primrose,[238] and the boundaries of the wood as we know them today were already established by the time Abbot Beere's clerks traced them in 1515 (see Box 8.2 for detail).[239]

Given its many internal woodbanks, we might expect *Loxley* to have been subdivided and managed as 'coppice with standards',[240] not least if underwood was being cropped to make charcoal for industrial and domestic use. That does not seem to have been the case, however, at least in the fourteenth century. The 1325 survey of Shapwick manor mentions fifty acres of pasture in the wood, held in severalty between 2 February (the feast of Purification) and 1 August (Lammas) each year and used exclusively for pasturing the lord's cattle during the spring and early summer; over the winter the wood pasture would have been accessible to all the tenants. In that same year John in the Herepathe 'felled and trimmed timber in the lord's wood', and this implies that the wood was in fact managed for timber rather than for coppice or underwood. Shapwick villagers probably relied almost wholly on local peat for their fuel, although wood for the fire and for fencing may also have been gathered from smaller woodlands.

In the fourteenth century two other woods are

recorded in Shapwick, both of them down towards the Levels' edge. We know little of *Bradewood*, the 'wide wood', except that it lay north-west of Kent Farm next to the boundary with Catcott, where the field name is persistent until the nineteenth century. In 1325 there was also an eight-acre 'spinney' at *Caterwode* with underwood and herbage[241] from which, in 1367, Lawrence Whittok stole three oaks, presumably saplings, valued at 2s.[242] The extent of this woodland is difficult to gauge, although three of the *Catswood* fields on the tithe map are situated at the east end of the Nidon ridge, on its north side, while the remaining field is on the southern side, separated from Henhills Copse by the Catsditch.[243] A survey of the trees in the present woodland at Henhills Copse showed that the oak trees that grow there today are only up to 1 m in girth. None are older than 150–200 years, though a further ecological survey, this time of the vascular plants, did produce a moderate number of ancient woodland indicator species, rather more than might be expected for a recent secondary woodland.[244] The explanation, the botanical team believe, is that ancient woodland species have survived in adjacent hedgerows and subsequently recolonised the site. The unusual number of saproxylic invertebrate species (those dependent on dead or decaying wood) in a hedgerow immediately north-west of Henhills adds further support to this idea (for methodology see Chapter 2). Botanical and field-name evidence, therefore, coincide in suggesting that medieval *Caterwood* was adjacent to the site of modern Henhills. Sadly, the only clue to *Caterwood*'s management is Whittok's thieving, which suggests timber; but perhaps it was from here that the villagers gathered the hazelnuts we found in our archaeological samples.[245]

The Levels

The 1,000 acres of wetland moors in the north of the parish provided a multitude of natural resources for the villagers of medieval Shapwick. Among the most important of these was common grazing 'as far as the east part that is at la Yoo [the Yeo]', as the 1515 Beere survey confirms.[246] The herd of cows to be found at Withy[247] was not at all unusual; at nearby Walton in 1312 thirty-five tenants owned the twenty-six cows grazing on the moor. Plough oxen would also have been grass-fed, though they would have eaten hay

to see them through the winter months, as did the horses, unless there was enough grass out on the drier pastures of the peat moor in a mild winter.

Patches of scrub woodland on the Levels were also exploited for fuel and Beere's survey of 1515 states that tenants of the manor could dig peat turves legally for their own use providing they filled up their holes immediately. Other products occurring naturally in the wetland included the water reed, one of the most durable of thatching materials, which was not only used as the main 'coatwork' for the new church at Shapwick in 1330–31 (see above) but is specifically mentioned in John of Glastonbury's mid-fourteenth-century account of the history of Glastonbury Abbey.[248] It is possible that water levels in reed beds were drained away for ease of cutting in the winter time and they must have been harvested in rotation if a constant supply was required. Traditionally, the ridge of a water reed roof was made with sedge because of its additional flexibility, and macrofossils of spike rush and sedges from our excavations on dry land sites may be either the remains of roofing material or were possibly dug up with the turf and accidentally preserved when they were charred on the hearth.[249] Rushes, too, grew locally. In 1325 the eleven acres of rushes growing at Withy were valued at 2s per acre[250] and the field name *Broderixon* in 1515 means 'land growing with rushes'. They were sometimes used in plaiting and weaving, as well as a floor covering inside houses – which may explain how coins and rings came to be lost there. Rush thatching is also said to endure the British weather longer than the wheat straws used, for example, at Forsters. Finally, 'withies', willow stems flexed to make baskets and fencing, were a constant of the local economy. The 'withyditch' is mentioned in the thirteenth century and in 1333–34 a withy basket could be found stored away in the granary at the new *curia*.[251] Large wicker baskets used to trap fish, known locally as 'puttes', may be the source of the willow charcoal identified at this site,[252] though willow was also woven to make wattlework and cut to burn on fires. The almoner's withy or osier beds at *Lez Alrodds*, mentioned in the description of the bounds of the manor in Abbot Beere's terrier in 1515, should be imagined as an area of willow trees coppiced for their stems[253] and, even if there was no wicker 'industry' as such in the medieval period, many households must have taken advantage of the ready supply of natural materials. The harvesting of reeds, rushes and withies, together with the grazing of animals on the moors, surely explains the occasional finds of medieval pottery far out in the Levels.

While much of the expanse of peat moor remained as seasonally flooded fen during the Middle Ages, there is some evidence from fieldwalking to suggest that parts of the Levels nearest to the Nidons began to be reclaimed. Today there are three 'rhynes', or drainage ditches, that run parallel to each other and the upland edge: the Russett Rhyne, the Land Rhyne and, furthest out on the peat moor, the Moreditch (Figure 7.1). The earliest pottery we found by the Moreditch is of thirteenth- to fifteenth-century date, which might logically imply that land there was occasionally cultivated. Documents indicate that the *Moredich* was in existence by 1368,[254] which suggests a significant encroachment on the Levels in a band 500–750m wide, similar to the reclamation progressing to the north around the islands at Meare, Westhay and Godney.[255] Quite possibly the deteriorating quality of older arable lands may account for this investment.

Mills

A watermill was first brought into operation at Shapwick sometime between 1086 and 1189 as one of eight built on Glastonbury manors during that period.[256] This is, as far as we can tell, the same one documented throughout the Middle Ages.[257] In 1357 John de Kent was said to have allowed both his hall and the mill to fall down, but it must have been restored to working order because it was still turning in 1515. Given the name of the tenant in the early fourteenth century this watermill is likely to have been located at what later became Kent Farm, to the north-east of the village (Figure 7.1), and an analysis of the topography suggests as much – a number of streams converge here, including the *Halgebroke* (or Holy Brook), the *Shytbrok* (or Shoot Brook), and the watercourse that runs through the village that was possibly called *Medewell*. All these seem to have been diverted into a canalised channel that ran from the north end of the village westwards to Kent Farm. This elaborate water management scheme combines

the small volumes of water from each of the individual streams into a single leat, an artificial waterway that ran along the contour.[258]

Very little is known about the watermill itself. A mill pond is specifically referred to in 1515[259] and there are slight traces on the ground today of what may be a small pond to the north of the farmhouse, perhaps with an undershot wheel attached to a mill on its south or west side.[260] Fragments of Mendip Old Red Sandstone, suitable as millstones, were recovered from an adjacent field.[261] Beyond the mill the overflow or mill race was diverted northwards into Mill Brook. The whole system would have required considerable surveying and bears all the hallmarks of the sort of scheme an abbey such as Glastonbury would have been involved with in or around the twelfth century. A similar engineering project can be seen at Winscombe, in north Somerset,[262] where, as at Shapwick, there is also little documentation.

The open windy country of the Somerset Levels is also ideal for running a windmill (Figure 7.40) and there are plenty of ridges on which to site them. A windmill on the Poldens at Shapwick, *molendinum ventricum*, is first mentioned in the 1325 survey, where it is valued at 40s per annum.[263] This windmill was probably erected at a relatively early date, sometime between 1316 and 1325, and would have been one of a dozen or so on the Glastonbury Abbey estates.[264] In 1330 an entry in the *compotus* rolls notes that 'half an acre of demesne land in *Netherhorseacre* (in East Field) was not sown this year, because Walter Pieres used it for the mound of the new mill' (see Figure 7.1).[265] Walter Pieres was a virgator, and may have been the reeve at the time. Since the 1333–34 accounts refer to a single windmill the 1325 and 1330 references must be to the same structure, though there is no trace of anything at that location today, where strips in the common field were evidently decommissioned to make space; the earthen mound piled up to weigh down its foundation timbers was just as easily removed again. A demesne windmill is also listed in Abbot Beere's survey of 1515[266] and again in the Minister's accounts of 1538–39, when it was held by Thomas Gunwyn.[267] This windmill probably stood on the south side of the ridgeway road, where there was a windmill in 1675 that survived until around 1762, and even as a mound until the 1970s.[268]

One of the key messages to emerge from this discussion of mills and indeed of Shapwick generally in the Middle Ages is the strength of the link with Glastonbury. The Abbey stood to benefit from these investments in mill construction at Shapwick not because they were needed to process grain for the monastery but because peasants were required by manorial custom to grind their corn there. The tolls imposed on grinding provided a steady income, as they did for many of the larger Benedictine houses, and so a mill could either be rented out at a profit or run by a directly employed miller for a wage plus a share of the produce. That there were no medieval quern fragments from our excavations in the village might be taken to indicate the degree to which Glastonbury reinforced its privileges. But the influence of the Abbey can be found not just in mill construction; in the village there was a new church with its graveyard after 1331 and the principal groups of buildings were the main abbot's manor, or *curia*, at the north end of the village and the almoner's house and farm with its barn and dovecote. As far as the eye could see land and buildings belonged to the monastery. The northern part of the parish was fenland and moor, not as yet reclaimed but exploited for rough grazing and its wetland and woodland resources. Peat was dug for fuel, while improvement and drainage may have already begun along the northern margins of the upland. Further upslope, the landscape was dominated by the two large common fields subdivided into furlong blocks and variable numbers of strips. The cultivated field was a patchwork of cereals, beans and peas, with the fallow field set aside as rough stubble grazing. Outside the limits of the common field system, in the south-west

Figure 7.40. A detail from a wall painting of St Christopher in the church of St Mary Magdalene, Ditcheat (Somerset), first revealed in 1931. It shows a postmill with a gabled and weatherboarded body which appears to be of two storeys. The painting (and the plaster beneath) is heavily restored but may be faithful to the fifteenth-century original.

corner of the parish, lay the main woodland at Loxley, while along the Nidons there was demesne pasture and arable. Much of the land was already enclosed by hedges in a foretaste of what was to come.

CHAPTER EIGHT

After the Dissolution

Post-Medieval Shapwick, 1539–1750

August 1556, Shapwick
William Walton, formerly under-steward of Glastonbury Abbey lands, has recently purchased the manor of Shapwick from Sir William Petre, a courtier and Secretary of State. But he stands accused of sending his men to assault a local woman, Joan Cronne, in a dispute over the lease of a hay meadow and now awaits the decision of the Court of Star Chamber …

The horseman was standing quietly in the road when William Walton came out of church.

'God's nails, here so soon. What news?' Walton, red-faced and fat, moved closer, nervous now. He fiddled noisily with the jettons in his hand, snapping them together. It was the lawyer, Poultney.

'I ride direct from Glaston, sir. There is news from London.'

'What have they decided?' Walton pressed. 'I am innocent?'

'Ay.' Poultney lowered his voice, drawing his cloak about him. 'All went according to plan. They say that you were not here and that the widow Cronne had no rights in the meadow. But sir –' he was whispering now '– that beating was a stupid thing. Your men all but took her life. "Of devilish evil mind", she called you before the Justice, and had it not been for vicar Barrett, things may not have turned out so well.'

Walton stared hard, his mouth tightening. 'Barrett was paid well enough for his time in court.'

Poultney hesitated. 'It is my opinion, sir, that you would be well advised to be rid of Petre's land while you can. You should profit from what you have, sir, before things worsen for you. Sell to your cousin Thomas while he shows interest. Destroy your papers. You know as well as I that those sales of abbey land at under value will not hold if the truth is out.'

'Pox on it. I will do no such thing.' Walton was raising his voice now and other churchgoers turned to stare at the rider. 'God's death. Shapwick was to be mine, the King's Commissioner said as much when the Abbey went down. Now the monks' papers flutter like butterflies, the lead is gone from the roof, stripped by the Augmentations men these past fifteen year and the abbot is scraped and hung from his own gate. Is that not enough?'

'You lose your way, sir.' Poultney looked directly at him now. 'You think too much on the old religion.'

Walton looked away across the valley where the morning mists hung low and white across the moor. 'Damn widow Cronne and damn cousin Thomas. They both deserve a sore thrashing. I will send a message to Ham. If Thomas will agree to me staying in the house, I will sell, though God's blood I sweated hard enough at the Abbot's books to have what should be mine. Parcels, dates, prices, I wrote it all out, year in, year out. Abbot Richard loved me well enough and I stood in good credit with him. But I tire now of the doubts and insults of Cronne and the others.' Walton seemed suddenly exhausted by the effort of speech. 'Go, brother Poultney, your work here is at an end.'

The lawyer smiled and turned his horse back up the village street. He expected no thanks from the likes of Walton and got none.

Behind him, the squire watched him go. 'Come, Mistress Blane.' He pointed his ringed finger at his housekeeper who stood hovering at the gate holding young Rich, his son, by the hand. 'Take the chest with the old papers from my study. Hide it in the stable. Understand?'

Walton looked down at the child. 'He is to have them. Whatever becomes of me and this place.'

Both Poultney and Blane are fictional characters. But William Walton did escape without conviction at the Court of Star Chamber over his brutal dealings with Joan Crone.[1] He kept all the manorial documents relating to Shapwick and did indeed leave them to his son, Richard, who probably destroyed them. Richard did not inherit and instead the estate passed to a Thomas Walton of Low Ham, possibly a distant relation, whose will of 1611 survives.[2] Young Richard led a colourful life of dubious land dealings and was twice in breach of the peace in London, on one occasion killing a man in Charing Cross Street. Illustrating the speed with which fortunes and reputations could be established in the late sixteenth century, one of Richard's sons was enrolled at Trinity College, Oxford, and proceeded to the Middle Temple in 1584. With no little irony, given the profit extracted by the Walton family from the Abbey's former estates, the son was named Dunstan.

From the spring of 1537 the larger monasteries were induced to surrender their lands, properties and goods to the Crown as English medieval monasticism drew to an end. One by one, Muchelney, Hinton Charterhouse, Bruton, Montacute and the other monastic houses of the county acquiesced to Thomas Cromwell's commissioners.[3] Then, during the autumn months of 1539, Glastonbury, at first declared 'the goodliest house of that sort that ever we have seen', came again under intense scrutiny.[4] A cache of incriminating books citing arguments against the king's divorce from Catherine of Aragon was allegedly found hidden in Abbot Richard Whiting's study. Shortly afterwards, money and plate were discovered in walls and vaults and the abbot quickly found himself in the Tower.[5] Already sick and weak and by now accused of embezzlement as well as opposition to royal supremacy, the abbot would implicate no others and on 15 November he was executed on Glastonbury Tor with two of his monks. Hanged, drawn, quartered and beheaded, sections of his body were placed on display at Bath, Bridgwater, Ilchester and Wells. His head was fixed above the Abbey gate.

The extraordinary image of Whiting's final journey down the Polden ridge to Bridgwater, through many of the parishes over which he and his predecessors had held sway for 800 years, is one that must surely have provoked astonishment in Shapwick. Their landlord gone, the events of late 1539 now heralded a time of upheaval and uncertainty. After the dissolution of the Abbey the ownership of Glastonbury lands was to switch from an ancient, bureaucratic, conservative, ecclesiastical corporation to a new breed of ambitious gentry. Shapwick would pass through many different hands over the course of the next three generations before its administration settled down again during the course of the seventeenth century. Once that happened, its new secular owners took every opportunity to make the investments in their houses and grounds that can still be picked out in the appearance of the village today. Other changes, rather less visible to modern onlookers, touched the everyday lives of people. For the fifty or so families in mid-sixteenth-century Shapwick, new theological teachings doubtless left some with strong feelings, others merely confused.[6] Almost every aspect of life must have seemed in flux, so that twice in the seventeenth century political beliefs were to be questioned, first during the Civil War and then again during the Monmouth rebellion in 1685 (see Chapter 1). Even the dependable routines of farming were to be transformed as the enclosure of fields gathered pace.

The archaeologist still has an important role to play in understanding these post-medieval changes and why they occurred, particularly when unravelling developments in architecture and material wealth. To work effectively on this period, however, archaeologists must join forces with historians. In our case, Joe Bettey and Nick Corcos analysed the wealth of sixteenth-century and later documentation, unravelling the complexities of ownership and landscape change.[7]

The village

In spite of the transfer of land to new owners there was no dramatic transformation in the basic distribution of settlement across the parish. The village continued to comprise its two tenurial units, by now referred to as manors, with as many as thirty smaller farms and the windmill on the hill. As yet there were no farms out in the fields, and the only people who lived outside the village were the miller and his family, at the watermill at what is now Kent Farm.

Roads

The layout of the village during this period can be reconstructed with some confidence from mid-eighteenth-century estate maps (see Chapter 2) which show the pattern of lanes and properties. The principal elements of the plan are illustrated on Figure 8.1 and can be seen on the accompanying aerial photograph. Most of the post-medieval lanes shown here had earlier precursors; only West Street, where it was investigated at New Farm, had a wholly different alignment later on.[8] The medieval road here seems to have been shifted to the west when 'Palmers or Callows House and Orchard' was converted into a farm about 1784 (Figure 8.2).[9] By this time the old road was well rutted and the daily traffic of carts and horses had worked away a dished hollow. Minor modifications aside, the earlier grid of lanes and plots remained stable, the endless rounds of repair continuing as before, holes being plugged with clay and whatever filler came to hand. Sometimes particularly heavy wear did demand a more considered response, so that a stone culvert of Lias slabs was constructed along the south side of Brices Lane, probably to ease drainage at an awkward spot in the road close to 'Davidges', the home farm.[10] Most obviously, the approach to Shapwick House was greatly improved.[11] Here West Street was widened by dumps of spoil and rubble and then recobbled to create a camber 7m wide (Figure 8.3). Later still the road was to be widened further (see Chapter 9). A curious feature of this and the other road surfaces examined as part of the Project was the range of finds we recovered, which included everything from the bowl of a glass goblet, clay pipes and a copper alloy spoon bowl to an ivory comb of sixteenth- or seventeenth-century date (see Figure

8.10L). From West Street there was even a decorated ivory handle from a fork, presumably thrown out with the washing-up water into the road or somehow incorporated into the patchings.

Properties and plots

Alongside Shapwick's lanes and streets were drystone walls with wooden gates leading into properties (Figure 8.4A). Inside there were yards, some metalled, like that at 36 Holes Lane,[12] others criss-crossed by stone drains and culverts, as at New Farm (Figure 8.4B).[13] Large areas were also put down to orchards and the growing of vegetables, with tree holes being excavated in several plots (Figure 8.4C). Ditches and hedges demarcated these different land uses north of Bridewell Lane[14] and kept livestock apart, among them the 'heifer mylche', the young milking cow belonging to husbandman Anthony Palmer in 1592[15] and William Clarke's 'grey nagg' in 1657.[16] Oxen and horses were a common sight in the village, as the many shoes recovered by fieldwalkers remind us (see Figure 8.11E–H), whether dragging the harrow, carrying sacks of wheat or pulling Palmer's 'newe wayne'. Some Shapwick residents owned more than one wagon like this,[17] so villages plots were far from empty unused spaces. Elsewhere, we found evidence of a seventeenth-century earth closet at Bridewell Lane, an insubstantial timber building of the same date at 57 Brices Lane, and many pits for domestic rubbish.[18] Only the metalworking residues from 46 Chapmans Lane[19] and West Street[20] suggest anything other than agricultural activities – in this case, a local smithy.

Many houses from the sixteenth to eighteenth centuries still stand in the village and these are of two main types.[21] The cross- or through-passage type with hall and kitchen was heated by fireplaces and included an unheated inner chamber for sleeping. This type of house, with three rooms in a line, can be seen in its sixteenth-century form at Home Farm and 22/24 Bridewell Lane (Figure 8.5A and B), while the former Post Office and Stores, known as Church Farm at this time, dates from a century later (Figure 8.5C).[22] The basic arrangement of interior spaces in these buildings is similar to the earlier Forsters (see Chapter 7), the major differences being that these newer houses were ceiled with chimneys,[23] which had

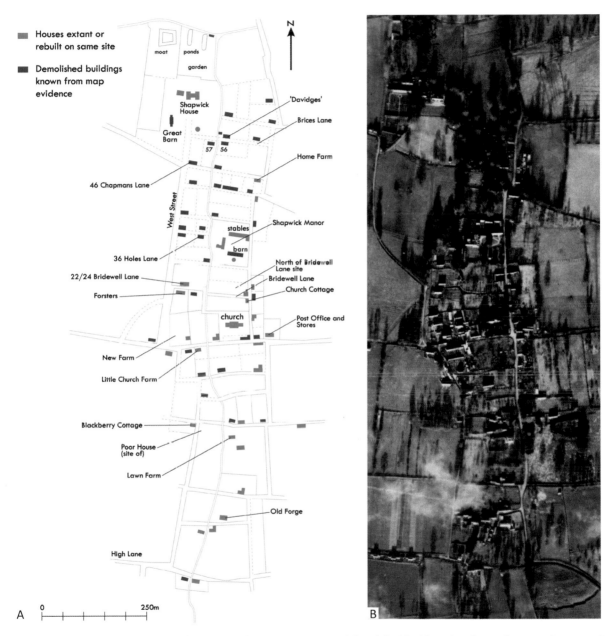

Figure 8.1. A: Shapwick village in the seventeenth century. Extant and demolished buildings based on tithe map of 1839 and estate maps of c.1765. B: the village in 1947 seen from the air by the RAF. Notice important changes such as the park created south of Shapwick House with its 'bypass' to the west, and the houses along High Lane.

Figure 8.2. Road cobbling in an evaluation trench at New Farm. The road, 4.40 m wide, was rutted and slightly dished. The excavation here was directed by Dick Broomhead.

replaced the open hearth in the medieval hall. The chimney stack might back onto a through-passage at the 'low end' of the hall, as at Home Farm, or it might be sited at the 'high end' of the hall, as it was at the Post Office and Stores.[24] The occupants were probably prosperous yeomen who farmed more than enough land to support their families: 'wealthy and substantiall men though none the best bredd', as one contemporary writer snobbishly referred to them.[25]

More limited accommodation for the less well-off husbandman or cottager was provided by dwellings with two rooms: a kitchen and a parlour separated by a cross passage. The Old Forge, a sixteenth-century

structure, is one of these (Figure 8.5D) and also one of two houses in the village with very thick walls,[26] which are probably constructed of cob faced with stone. Many buildings across Britain are built of clay and earth in this way, among the advantages being the cheap cost and excellent insulating qualities of their building materials. In plan these modest houses are more symmetrical in appearance than the three-room units of their prosperous neighbours, though a 'reading' of their façades sometimes reveals more complex architectural histories. Church Cottage and Blackberry Cottage, for instance, probably started out as three-room houses (Figure 8.5E and F) but then had one room shaved off at some point in their history. In the case of Blackberry Cottage, its east gable was rebuilt in the nineteenth century.

Both the two post-medieval houses partially excavated in Shapwick Park conform to a cross-passage plan with two or three rooms in a line (Figure 8.6). At 56 Brices Lane a short-lived seventeenth-century stone building was superseded by another farmhouse on the same foundations before this too was swept away. At Chapmans Lane, excavation in Plot 46 revealed a simple two- or three-roomed house with an outshot[27] to the north. The rooms of this house were small, only 2m wall-to-wall, with a floor of worn irregular Lias flagstones. The cross passage in this case was 1.4m wide. Among the demolition rubble was a hinge pivot for a door (see Figure 8.11B), an oxshoe and a fragment of cast iron guttering and bracket, as well as the clay pipes and pottery that must have been in use at the time of the building's abandonment in *c*.1765.

All these buildings are examples of vernacular architecture: simple, well-built structures, sometimes modified from durable later medieval forerunners. They are very much 'of the region' in terms of their building materials, and their design responded to the needs of local people. Most are built directly on the bedrock or levelled subsoils, and Lias limestone stone walls, mortar from limekilns using the local limestone, stone-flagged floors and roofs of thatch were the norm. Some bricks may have been produced locally from the seventeenth century onwards[28] but, for the most part, medieval traditions of building and materials such as the use of clay ridge tiles endured into the seventeenth century. Structural timbers,

Figure 8.3. Excavations along the line of West Street in Shapwick Park. A: looking north with Shapwick House behind. Notice the raised camber of the road. B: the 7 m-wide road with its wayside ditch to the east. Occasional repairs were evident.

which included elm, oak, beech and ash, were probably obtained from local sources, while roofing slate may have been quarried around Luxborough in the Brendon Hills.[29]

Fat slivers of plain plaster were a frequent find on our excavations, some complete with their original limewash finish, but not all houses were plain; at least one house boasted a more decorative interior. In the solar at Forsters there is a moulded frieze on the wall in a meandering floral pattern with stylised flowers, a style loosely derived from Renaissance Italy (Figure 8.7B). There are also two plasterwork

fleur-de-lis above the window and door and a third above the solar doorway flanked by the initials TRB and the date 1712 (Figure 8.7A). Here the medieval heraldic symbol has become more floral, with the central lobe split open to reveal the seeds within. The initials may refer to Thomas Bartlet and his wife; the house was described in a survey of 1754 as 'Bartlet's house, smiths shop and orchard'. The south-west of England is especially rich in decorative plasterwork like this on ceilings, overmantels and friezes,[30] and the specific design seen at Forsters can also be seen at two other houses in the county, The Gables in Stoke-sub-

Figure 8.4. Excavated features within village plots. A: the walls and 'kerb' at 36 Holes Lane (Shapwick Sports Hall) B: flat stones covering a drainage culvert at New Farm. C: the tree holes of an orchard being sectioned south of Bridewell Lane.

Hamdon and Wyndhams in Marston Magna. Both of these are considered to be early to mid-seventeenth century in date, so if the Forsters frieze really is 1712, as it claims to be, then the moulds were already old-fashioned.

Interior colour and variety would also have been supplied by objects and furnishings. To take one example, in 1660 Margery Higdon probably lived in a house that once occupied the site of Lawn Farm.[31] According to her will her home was full of

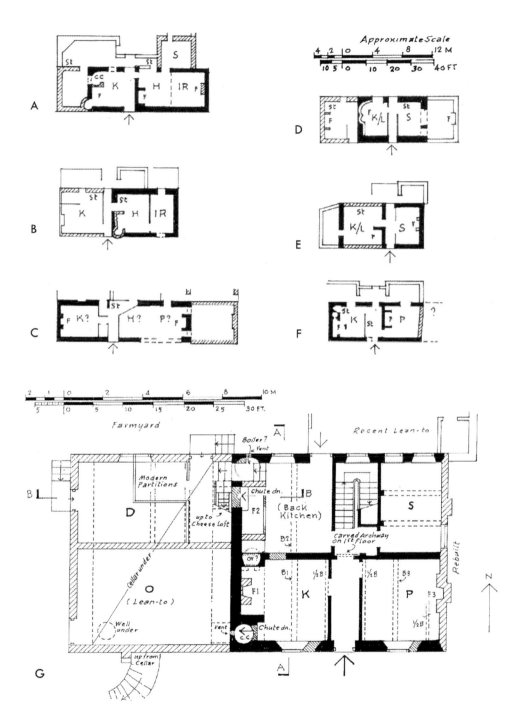

Figure 8.5. Post-medieval house plans. Three-room plans at Home Farm (A), 22–24 Bridewell Lane (B) and the Post Office and Stores (C), with more limited accommodation at the Old Forge (D), Church Cottage (E) and Blackberry Cottage (F). The double pile farmhouse (G) is New Farmhouse.

Figure 8.6. Excavation of two post-medieval buildings along the line of the Poldens pipeline; both sites directed by Charles and Nancy Hollinrake. A: sleeper walls exposed at 56 Brices Lane. B: flagged floor and walls at 46 Chapmans Lane; the cross passage is marked by the parallel ranging rods.

interesting textiles, including 'holland sheets', a fine kind of linen first made in Holland,[32] 'flaxen sheets', a pillow embroidered with 'black and silk',[33] a bolster tie, table cloths, a bedstead with bolster, a coverlet sheet and blanket and a feather bed with its bolster and yellow coverlet. Margery seems to have had an eye for clothing too – her family may well have been tailors – and she singles out her 'one new petticoat never yet worn', a 'french green waistcoat', a cloak, her 'best hat', a 'stammel peticoat'[34] and a riding coat. Goods like these, valuable enough to be passed from generation to generation, were not available to everyone in the village, and they illustrate that the homes of Shapwick's seventeenth-century 'middling

sort' were neither colourless nor plain,[35] especially when we add in the detail of carpentry and fixtures and fittings to these finishes and decoration.

Finally, a slightly later innovation in housing, but still within our period, was the more substantial 'double-pile farmhouse'. Houses of this type generally have a solid and imposing façade with four rooms behind in a symmetrical square plan. Early eighteenth-century examples typically have their front and rear ranges separately roofed, as if two houses were glued together through the middle. Inside not only was there more space but, with fireplaces in all rooms, comfort was greatly improved too. New Farmhouse in Shapwick conforms perfectly to this standard plan (see Figure 8.5G), with a living room and parlour at the front, the kitchen and dairy or scullery to the rear and the first floor mimicking the four spaces below. This arrangement affords far greater privacy than did the old cross-passage plan in which 'deeper', more private spaces, such as chambers or bedrooms, could be reached only by walking through intervening rooms. New Farmhouse may have been built by Captain Thomas Silver, who died in 1709, or by his son John. The Silvers might well have thought of their home as a small gentry house; indeed, John described himself as a 'gent' in his will of 1715.[36] Father and son would have guided privileged visitors from the front door through the hallway and into well-decorated and furnished rooms at the front of the house, avoiding the more functional service spaces towards the rear. In a sense, the house itself contains a hierarchy of rooms embedded with clues to social order and etiquette and it conforms to an architectural grammar relating to conceptions of public and private space that was by now very different from that of the medieval period.

Possessions

Three-quarters of the pottery found in Shapwick households in the period 1550–1750 came from local workshops.[37] A wide range of slipwares[38] and sgraffitos[39] (Figure 8.8) was fired in the kilns at Donyatt near Ilchester,[40] though a significant proportion of Shapwick sherds have a soft micaceous fabric that may indicate a different source, perhaps Bridgwater.[41] All of these products would have been bought at local markets and fairs or from carters

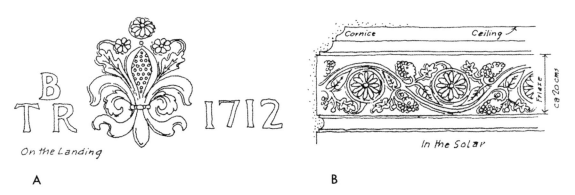

Figure 8.7. Plasterwork at Forsters. A: large fleur-de-lis over the dormer window at Forsters with the initials TRB (probably Thomas Bartlet) and the date 1712. B: floral meander pattern in plaster in the solar at Forsters, also eighteenth century.

Figure 8.8. A range of post-medieval pottery from Shapwick, reconstructed by Alejandra Gutiérrez. Mainly South Somerset wares, possibly produced at Donyatt, including sgraffito and slipwares of various kinds. Those reconstructed here are dishes, one-handled jars, bowls with thumb-applied cordons, pancheons and cups. Other products from North Devon, London and Bristol/Staffordshire were also recovered.

who travelled from village to village. Studies of the hundreds of seventeenth-century transactions between buyers and sellers recorded by beadles or toll collectors at Taunton and Castle Combe fairs demonstrate that most traders came from within a 15km radius[42] and, since there was as yet no route across the Levels to the north, Shapwick tended to look for its economic links along the topographical axis of the Poldens. This was still an agricultural community with poor communications. Mendip, home to coal and lead miners, was an effective barrier

to the north, and the county's roads were often in poor condition. Bath to Taunton was a two and a half day ride on a sturdy nag.[43]

That said, pottery did arrive from further afield, though little of it probably travelled overland.[44] For instance, the distinctive slipwares that make up nearly 14 per cent of all pottery in Shapwick at this time were produced in both Bristol and Staffordshire at the end of the seventeenth and eighteenth centuries.[45] The commonest forms are shallow dishes or 'flatwares' whose curved profiles were achieved by pressing the clay into a concave mould, the rims then being indented for a 'pie crust' effect. Even the most minute fragments of these dishes are readily identified by their characteristic buff-coloured fabric and feathered brown and white slips under an amber glaze, and there are also hollow wares such as cups and chamber pots with very similar kinds of decoration. It is likely that these were acquired as sets. Other pottery that probably also came from Bristol includes English tin-glazed wares, mostly dishes and bowls decorated in blue, and the five sherds of Anglo-Netherlands tin-glaze pottery[46] or so-called 'delftware'. These dishes, with their fine fabrics covered by opaque white tin glaze on the interior and transparent lead glaze on the exterior, were produced at workshops such as Brislington and Temple Back during the second half of the seventeenth century, and their manufacture continued near Bristol into the first half of the eighteenth century.[47] Though the final result was markedly inferior, the aim was to imitate heavy porcelain which, at the time, was being imported at great expense from mainland Europe or from the Orient.

The presence of delftware shows that some homes in the village could afford better-quality table wares and it is perhaps no surprise that there should be a correspondence between sites at which these sherds appear and those properties registered as having a higher value in a 1750 survey.[48] Still, it is surprising just how widespread their use had become, and this point is reinforced by an assemblage from north of Bridewell Lane[49] which includes not only Delft cups and a teapot but also Chinese porcelain tea bowls decorated in blue. Tea-drinking was still an expensive habit at the end of the seventeenth century and the Bridewell pottery group indicates that 'refined' behaviour was by no means exclusive to the two manors.[50] Quite possibly this and other pottery made its way to Shapwick via Bridgwater, which was, by this date, Somerset's major port with links to Ireland and mainland Europe. From here barges trafficked up the river Parrett as far as Langport and along the river Tone to Taunton. Both Staffordshire Blackware mugs and jugs and gravel-tempered vessels from north Devon[51] may have taken this route too. The latter seem to have cornered the local market for large heavy pancheons or open bowls with flared walls; they

remained competitively priced precisely because sea routes were cheaper than travel over land.

Of the vessels that were certainly imported from abroad before 1750, the majority arrived from the Rhineland.[52] Mass-produced Frechen stoneware bottles and tankards with their 'tiger glazes' were recovered right across the village,[53] but the most abundant of all the Shapwick imports during this period were the Westerwald jugs and mugs with their characteristic blue incised and moulded decoration and gunmetal-grey fabrics.[54] Unlike the Delftwares they did not craze and chip easily, and they were more easily cleaned too. The Shapwick vessels may have been redistributed through London or arrived direct at more local ports such as Exeter, where, for example, as many as 10,000–30,000 stoneware pots arrived in 1718, 1723 and 1738.[55]

Glass drinking vessels were not at all common in Shapwick homes before the later nineteenth century.[56] Excavation and fieldwalking finds include only occasional fragments of beakers, goblets and, more unusually, an eighteenth-century 'posset' from north of Bridewell Lane from which a mix of hot spiced ale and curdled milk would have been sipped. There was also a fragment of late sixteenth- or early seventeenth-century flask from the Great Barn site (see Chapter 7), as well as two jars and several phials for medicines or other liquids. Most of the glass fragments, however, are from wine bottles, and so reflect the growing popularity of imported wine (Figure 8.9). These bottles occur in a range of forms, including the 'onion' or 'bladder' shape that was popular between about 1680 and 1725. Designed to be refilled directly from the barrel, these decanters, as we should perhaps more accurately think of them, commonly carried the owner's crest or initials on a pad of glass which was applied to the shoulder; one such fragment from Shapwick is dated 1705.[57] The bulbous shape of the bottle – though it had the benefit of being difficult to knock over at the table – meant that the wine could not be racked for storage and it was probably the discovery that some wine could be improved by being left in the bottle that led to the development of the cylindrical shape we see today.

Among the commonest post-medieval finds are fragments of clay tobacco pipes. More than 2,500 were recovered in all, the very earliest from between the early

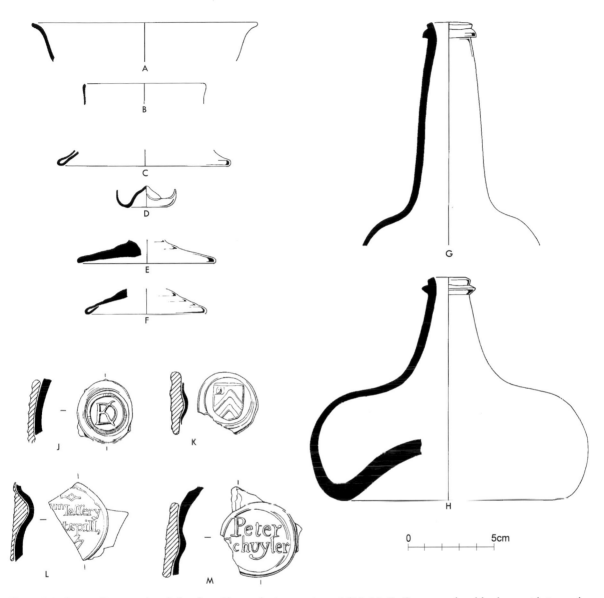

Figure 8.9. Range of post-medieval glass from Shapwick. A: green jar, c.1650–80. B–C: green pedestal beakers, mid-sixteenth to mid-seventeenth century. D: green cylindrical phial, late seventeenth to early eighteenth century. E: clear goblet, eighteenth to early nineteenth century. F: clear goblet, eighteenth century. G: green cylindrical wine bottle, eighteenth century. H: green bladder wine bottle, early eighteenth century. J: wine bottle seal [D K], eighteenth century. K: wine bottle seal, late seventeenth to early eighteenth century. L: wine bottle seal, mid–late eighteenth century. M: wine bottle seal [PETER SCHUYLER], early eighteenth century.

1570s, when tobacco smoking was first introduced to Britain and about 1620.[58] Thereafter, as the tax on tobacco was reduced and the numbers of centres of pipe manufacture rose to serve a new demand, villagers became more careless and regularly dropped their pipes in farmyards and fields. The first pipes seen in the village are likely to have been made in London and Bristol, but among the names and initials of makers on seventeenth-century examples those of Jeffry Hunt and John Burrow are the most common.[59] Hunt was from Norton St Philip, in north-east Somerset, while Burrow was probably a local man – his pipes seem to be distributed in the area between Taunton and Wells. Other pipes came from workshops at Chard, Chilcompton and Leigh-on-Mendip. Eighteenth-century makers are less easy to track down,[60] but one was probably William Champion of Shepton Mallet, while others came from Bristol.

It is much more difficult to say who might have been puffing at these pipes. Smokers would have acquired them filled with tobacco either at a local grocer or, as was more likely, at a local tavern or inn. What was on offer there was determined by which maker's cart had last replenished the shelves. Since the customer paid for the tobacco, the pipe was disposed of wherever it was convenient to do so – not necessarily in the smoker's own backyard. Bearing this in mind, one truly exceptional clay pipe was recovered in the collection from the water pipeline through Shapwick Park. The sherd is too small to illustrate but it was part of a large finely burnished bowl with a heel stamped three times with a central *fleur-de-lis* flanked by schematic hands or 'gauntlets'. The Gauntlett family were renowned clay pipe makers from Amesbury in Wiltshire and this example can be dated to 1640–70. Whether it was made for the tenant at 56 Brices Lane, known to be the Young or Youngs family in 1660,[61] is uncertain. This was an extremely expensive product, perhaps twenty-five times the price of an ordinary one, and it probably belonged to a smoker from the ranks of the gentry or nobility. Perhaps its owner was Sir Henry Rolle himself (see below). Whatever the case, the pipe serves as a reminder that post-medieval Shapwick now enjoyed a more varied network of social and economic contacts both locally and further afield. While Anthony Palmer left money to the poor in 'Batheforde' in his will in 1592,[62] the vicar, John Powell, had sisters and land in north Wales in 1608.[63] Reinforced by easier travel and the popularity of letter writing, these kinds of family concerns and links must lie behind the life histories of many of the artefacts we found on our excavations.

Among the other artefacts present in Shapwick's post-medieval homes were cutlery handles, most of which are probably from knives or spoons (Figure 8.10A–C). Even by the mid-eighteenth century forks were uncommon in England,[64] and seem to be associated with the more elaborate table settings that were a feature of the period. Other objects include a range of buttons, a cufflink, copper alloy and iron buckles and a purse bar to which a bag or pouch would have been sewn (Figure 8.10D–K). None of these were made in the village but they represent a general trend towards greater numbers of personal possessions, even if they are a wildly distorted picture of material culture at this period. Not only is the sample small and random but it omits everything that has not survived the rigours of the archaeological record, such as leather or cloth, objects of value that might have been passed on as heirlooms and, of course, anything at all that could be profitably recycled. This last point is well illustrated by the will of 1651 of William Champion, gentleman of Shapwick, who desired 30*s* 'to be added' to another silver bowl 'to make it a tankard' which was then to be marked with his initials and those of his wife.[65] The tankard was to go to his daughter Jane and then on to her children. There is very little listed in William's will – despite his substantial means – which would have found its way into the archaeologist's finds tray. Even though several lower denomination coins and a German jetton (1586–1630) were recovered by the Project,[66] William's gold ring, ewers, six silver spoons, mazer dish (probably a silver-mounted wooden bowl), books and furniture would be unlikely excavation finds.

A greater surprise, perhaps, is the lack of evidence for agricultural tasks, but then again few occupations required specialist tools and some artefacts, particularly knives, were multi-functional. A whetstone like the one illustrated in Figure 8.11J would have kept them sharp. A cylindrical lead weight also suggests some retail activity (Figure 8.11K), and there were thimbles for sewing or spinning, scissors and iron hooks for suspension (Figure 8.11A). There was also part of a grinding stone from Bridewell Lane, as well as two whetstones and several pattens – the metal parts of overshoes that were used to raise the foot above the mud and dirt (Figure 8.11C–D). The total finds haul is not large, certainly, but there are

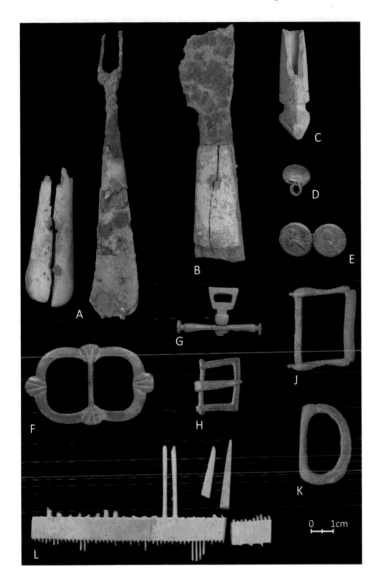

Figure 8.10. Post-medieval artefacts from Shapwick excavations. A: fork, two-tined with ivory handle. B: knife, iron tang with bone handle. C: handle, ivory with incised lines and notching. D: hemispherical cast button. E: cufflink decorated with a bust and illegible inscription. F: double looped buckle. G: purse bar with suspension hole and swivelling loop. H: double looped buckle, broken. J: single looped buckle, rectangular with bolster sides, pin missing. K: copper-alloy buckle of D-form, pin missing. L: ivory comb, double-sided with flat section. Some of the buckles shown here may be horse equipment rather than dress accessories.

at least glimpses of farming, tailoring or leather work and metalworking, while from the documentary perspective woodworking, brick-making, butchering, fishing, dairying, milling, baking, the quarrying of stone, lime-burning, malting, distilling and cider-making can all be added to the list of activities that took place in Shapwick.

How, then, should we imagine the experience of visiting an 'average' Shapwick household between the mid-sixteenth and mid-eighteenth centuries: the house of a substantial husbandman, yeoman or prospering craftsman? In many cases the front door opened onto a passage, rather than directly into a room. These passages had flagged floors and limewashed walls, so the immediate impression was perhaps cleanliness, a cool temperature, local materials and simplicity. Turning to the left and entering the kitchen, there might be a fireplace in the end wall burning with wood or perhaps coal, and a metal cauldron suspended from a hook and chain. Among the vessels in Margery Dowsey's will of 1638 were three brass pots, a brass pan and two

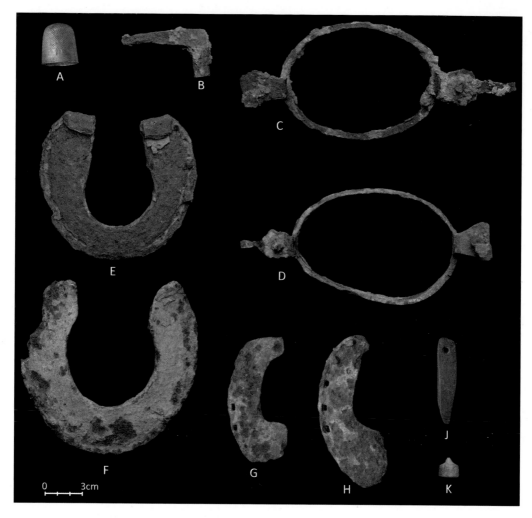

Figure 8.11. Agricultural and everyday objects from post-medieval Shapwick. A: sewing thimble with band inscribed 'GFH'. B: hinge pivot for door or window. C–D: iron pattens. E–F: horseshoes. G–H: oxshoes. J: worn whetstone, perforated, black stone (phyllite or slate). K: lead weight (c.25g) with suspension loop.

'caldrons' of brass, one 'little', the other larger,[67] that she wished to have distributed among her grandchildren, and a 'lead' – possibly a lead tray for cider-making.[68] Another house, that of Thomas Lacy in 1640, contained two 'crocks', but it is not clear what these were. Their values in other inventories from the south-west of England suggests that they too were probably metal pots.[69]

While ceramic cooking pots or globular jars may by now have been consigned to the medieval past,

meat and vegetable stews were not, at least until the long slow boiling of food came to be replaced by faster methods of cooking in the saucepans of the eighteenth century. On the open shelves, most of the pottery was local, of red fabrics decorated with slips and sgraffito. By the end of the eighteenth century these were complemented by the rich yellow browns of the Bristol/Staffordshire slipwares, both flatwares and delicate hollow wares. The heavyweights of the kitchen were the green-glazed North Devon wares.

These make up 95 out of every 100 pottery sherds recovered for this period. The dominant colours were therefore browns, yellows and greens, with splashes of blues and purples supplied by English and Anglo-Netherlands tin-glazes, and dark browns and glistening blacks by Cistercian wares and Staffordshire Blackwares, along with the mottled salt glaze of Raeren stonewares. Within this range of colours and textures, the cobalt blue and manganese purple of the perfectly moulded Westerwald drinking vessels must surely have stood out. In addition, many homes also used pewter dishes and plates; Thomas Lacy left eight pewter dishes in his will in 1640,[70] while Margery Higdon left three in 1660.[71] Pewter tableware had probably been around for more than 100 years but became common only in the later sixteenth century; in less prosperous households there would still have been wooden vessels and trenchers on the table.[72] In fact, a time-traveller from the fifteenth century would find much that was familiar, though cooking was no longer restricted to the hall. For a twenty-first-century time-traveller, on the other hand, the surprise might lie in the familiar multi-functional nature of the seventeenth-century kitchen, which was not just for cooking but also for baking, brewing[73] and storage, as well as just plain sitting.

Turning back now into the passage and crossing into the hall, we step into the general living room. Here there was certainly another fireplace, with stone jambs and timber lintels, a clock, a mirror or perhaps a painting or print by the mid-eighteenth century, possibly a shelf or cupboard too with the best tablewares on view, the German stonewares, a Staffordshire Blackware tankard, a brass candlestick, a Bible and a few other books too. William Champion had a 'spewse chest' (spice or spruce chest?) in his hall in 1651.[74] Since there was a fireplace, we are perhaps too easily seduced by the conventional image of a woman sewing by the window, her husband asleep in the chair by the fire.[75] But this need not have been a silent place, and there were certainly musical instruments in some houses. In 1623 Stephen Dowsey, a Shapwick yeoman, left a 'payre of verginalls' to his daughter;[76] a virginal is a square legless spinet or harpsichord that was often, though evidently not exclusively, found in larger country houses during the sixteenth and seventeenth centuries.[77]

Beyond, in the 'inner room', there would have been a bed, sometimes referred to as 'furnished', and a chest or perhaps, by the mid-eighteenth century, a chest of drawers to store clothes and accessories such as belts and buckles, coats with buttons, and so on. The 'coverleds' given by Stephen Dowsey to his daughters, one 'collared blacke and yellowe', the other 'yellowe and redd', were counterpanes that might have been found in such a chest. Some homes had more than one; Margery Dowsey's will of 1638 mentions 'the mens trunk' as well as 'the chest that is papered inside', the latter perhaps containing a pair of sheets and blankets or her 'best cloak and gown'. Even the 'paire of bootes' left by Thomas Lacy to Thomas Flower in 1640 might have been found in the inner room, though they might equally well have been upstairs, where the lowering of the ceiling in the hall below had created extra space for bedchambers and storage. In all kinds of ways the medieval house plan had altered beyond recognition; rooms were now more numerous and there were more private spaces with designated uses to replace the multi-functional spaces of old.[78] Thus we encounter a 'buttery' in some houses for storing foodstuffs and pots, while the 'parlour' was becoming a room for sitting and dining.[79] These changing functions can be seen 'in action' in the house of Thomas Prewe, a yeoman, who made his will in Shapwick in 1630.[80] It is very likely that Thomas lived at the former Post Office and Stores, a seventeenth-century building that has in part survived through to the present day.[81] Unusually, this means that Thomas's will can be combined with what is known of the plan and architecture of his house to provide a 'walk through' of rooms, objects and furniture.

Figure 8.12 shows that Thomas's house was a farmhouse with traditional long proportions and three rooms in a line. Notwithstanding some changes to the interior of the house, notably the removal of the hall chimney and stack and some eighteenth- and nineteenth-century additions, the original plan as Thomas would have known it is still clearly legible. In the kitchen, for example, was 'the brass pot which was my wife's before she was married', 'one bason of brass', 'a paire of iron andirons' and 'the great iron spit'[82] on which heavier joints of meat would have been turned. The brass pans, platters

my best clock
the great iron spit
pair of iron andirons
my best bedstead
the tableboard with the forme and wainscot and
a chair
the great chest

cupboard
with the tableboard formes
and chair

OUTSIDE
best yoke with iron henges
two ewes and lambs
two ewes and lambs
my best waine and iron bound wheeles
my second best waine and iron wheeles

KITCHEN   HALL   PARLOUR

?   ?   ?

my best bed furnished

second best brass pan
two porringers
two platters

bedstead with the bed and
all the furniture belonging to the same

my best brass pan
two platters
the second best and one porringer
the best the brass pott
one bason of brass

Figure 8.12. Above: Thomas Prewe's house in the seventeenth century, as deduced from standing building recording, and populated with the objects described in his will of 1630. The objects listed above the plan were present when Thomas wrote his will; those listed below the plan (with the dotted locational arrows) are not specifically located. Below: Thomas Prewe's house as it looks today. At the time of the Shapwick Project in the 1990s Thomas's house had become the Post Office and Store, but it is now a house once again. The arrow indicates the main doorway on the plan above. There is now a two-storey extension at the back of the farmhouse and another at the east (right) end which were added in the eighteenth and nineteenth centuries. This transformed the house from three rooms-in-a-line to a double-pile plan.

and porringers are examples of the novel cooking and tablewares available at this time. Among the items in the hall were a cupboard, 'tableboard formes' (that is, trestles) and a chair. Further along, rather than an unheated 'inner room' like the one at Home Farm, this house had a parlour with a chimney that contained Thomas's best bedstead and a great chest with clothes and linen inside.[83] 'The chair now standing in the parlour' Thomas gave to his wife; chairs were on the increase in houses during this period, while benches were in decline.[84] Evidently Thomas's parlour was a kind of bed-sitting room, perhaps one reserved for guests.[85] While this not unusual for its day, a hundred years later the parlour would have been a place exclusively for sitting and dining, not sleeping. Among Thomas's other possessions, which sadly the appraisers did not locate for us precisely, there is a 'best clock', so he obviously had more than one. Clocks were rare at this date[86] and suggest time measurement, routines and the need for punctuality – new working habits. Somewhere there was also a 'tableboard with the forme and wainscot', again implying that the table top was detachable from the frame, just as it had been in medieval furniture. Thomas seems to have been bedridden when he dictated his will, because he refers explicitly to the bed 'which I now lie on', but where that bed was is not clear. Possibly he was upstairs, though the appraisers did not pry too much there.

Diet

Although it tends to be durable objects that receive the attentions of archaeologists, most expenditure in Shapwick households would have been on food. Unfortunately, none of the excavation trenches that investigated the houses and plots of Shapwick's post-medieval residents recovered significant faunal assemblages. The largest and best-dated, from 46 Chapmans Lane,[87] produced just 202 bones.[88] Here sheep/goat, cattle and then pig contributed most to the diet, though rabbit, chicken and goose[89] were also found, as were the remains of eel, herring[90] and a few oysters.[91] While the eels were presumably locally caught,[92] fishing boats plied the Bristol Channel from Minehead to Bristol and the herring probably came to Shapwick already processed, perhaps salted.

According to Mrs Beeton, half an ox head should make sufficient soup for sixteen persons,[93] and some of the Chapmans Lane bones may have been bought for stock or even their marrow, perhaps from Butcher White, who is recorded in 1765 as living in a house (now demolished) at the corner of Northbrook Road.[94] Just as in the Middle Ages, bread continued to be a vital part of the diet and might accompany peas, beans, cheese and meat, including bacon. Both wheat and barley, the latter perhaps for brewing, were also identified from Chapmans Lane. There was certainly a 'beer-house' somewhere in Shapwick, which was run by Betty Collings in the early eighteenth century.[95] Beer, rather than ale, was by now commonly available and it is likely that Betty had her own equipment and brewed the beer herself.[96]

The archaeological sequence is insufficient to develop a detailed understanding of post-medieval diet in the village. However, some purses must certainly have stretched considerably further than others. The mid-eighteenth-century diet of 'Doctor Young', who lived in a now-demolished house along Poles Lane, or Captain Silver at New Farmhouse, whom we have already met, probably differed quite substantially from that of widow Johnson at Little Church Farm.[97] Shapwick residents embraced a full social spectrum, from peers and gentry (see below) to people who, according to their wills at least, thought of themselves as gents or gentlemen, yeomen, husbandmen, widows, clergymen and servants.[98] The difference between these socio-economic groups is perhaps best expressed as follows: while gentry did not have to work for a living, the 'middling sort' of gentlemen and yeomen (who might have been farmers or craftsmen) worked independently and may have been employers, whereas labourers, who did not routinely make a will, worked for others.[99] As the archaeological, architectural and documentary records all make plain, these distinctions would have been apparent through income and in material culture, housing and diet.[100]

The church

The mid-sixteenth century would have been a time of tremendous uncertainty. Not only did the villagers of Shapwick have a new landlord now that the monasteries were dissolved but the interior of the building at the heart of their community, the parish church, was transformed to become more austere and less cluttered as Protestantism gained favour. Sadly, there is no direct evidence in Shapwick church for this period of the village's history and no late medieval surveys of church goods to tell us what might have been lost. If there were wall paintings, statues of saints and apostles, wooden screens and side altars in chapels, there is no evidence of them now.[101] Only the medieval font, pulpit (if the church had one) and the benches would have continued in use, to be replaced later on. We do not know of any acts of iconoclasm – the deliberate destruction of religious images – although elsewhere between 1547 and 1553 images, statues and roods were removed, surplus plate sold, mass books and breviaries abolished, wall paintings whitewashed over and statue niches blocked up.[102] Significantly, perhaps, the present set of church plate is dated 1746; any medieval chalices or vessels may have been destroyed a century or two earlier.

One important source of evidence for those with an interest in the church reforms of the sixteenth century is the account books kept by the churchwardens, but unfortunately these have not survived for Shapwick prior to 1712. Thereafter, there are snippets of tantalising detail, such as the hanging of a new 'great bell' in 1723, now replaced, and the purchase of Cornish slate for the roof repairs in 1730.[103] Significantly, the bell ringers were paid and provided with beer and cider for ringing on 5 November and on Oak-apple day, 29 May, to commemorate the restoration of Charles II in 1660. In honour of the king hiding in an oak tree after his defeat at the Battle of Worcester in 1651, the custom was to wear sprigs of oak leaves in lapels or hats, and the day was marked with special church services, bonfires and bells in many villages.[104] Just occasionally we do learn something more of the interior of the church. It is evident from one entry of 1718, for example, that there was a 'singing loft', a gallery capacious enough to hold both village musicians and a choir. This stood in the western half of the nave. In 1723, meanwhile, a new ceiling was inserted, the walls replastered and the whole interior painted in a deep hue of 'London blue'.

The pre-eminence of the Church of England is typical of a village dominated by one or two powerful gentry families who were anxious for their tenants to follow religious orthodoxy. Even if Quakers did congregate in their homes for worship (Box 8.1) there were no nonconformist chapels in or anywhere near Shapwick at this time[105] and numbers were never sufficient to warrant a meeting house. No doubt most of the people in the parish thought of themselves as practising Christians and walked to church at least once a week on Sundays. They would have been christened at the font, married at the altar and buried in the cemetery, and, by the seventeenth century at least, they expressed their Protestant beliefs with conviction through their wills. Once inside the church for the service, pews were allotted by the churchwardens according to the social status of the parishioners; benches for the poorest being erected further from the altar at the west end of the nave. When a carpenter, Thomas Stone, was called to repair the seats and pews[106] we learn that they were covered with 'matting', at least 90 yards being bought for that purpose in 1750. Evidently the social ranking of seating was observed with some interest by parishioners, so that when Edward Caddy constructed a very large pew entirely for himself 'to the great Incroachment and detarment of the Parish church in generall', twenty-four villagers clubbed together to sign a petition of protest. The Church in the eighteenth century could be a divisive place, but when the church plate came around at the end of the service the parishioners gave generously, especially when their money was destined for distressed Protestants in other European countries[107] or they were persuaded of the merits of distant causes during the sermon. Enthusiastic support was given to the repair of the church at New Shoreham in Sussex in 1715 and to those who had suffered by fire at Ottery St Mary in Devon the following year. Nor were charities closer to home ignored, as the beneficiaries of the twenty-three surviving wills from this period amply demonstrate. Then it was the poor of Shapwick[108] and the cathedral at Wells that were uppermost in villagers' minds.[109]

The Poor House

While some became more prosperous during this period, as is clearly evident from their investments in houses and domestic goods, others lived in abject poverty. A remarkable number of poor unfortunate people passed through Shapwick, pausing only to demand some relief from the churchwardens whose job it was to help.[110] Among those who came and went was 'a woman with six children', who was given a shilling to depart in 1713, and, rather less probably, an 'Olde Antient wounded Seaman that was Cast away'. This shipwrecked sailor and his wife and children were also persuaded on their way with a shilling, though a 'great bellyed woman' received only half that in 1720. These sums of money, miserable though they were, were generated from Poor Rates that were imposed on properties in the village. In 1712 by far the highest rate was paid by John Rolle, grandson of Sir Henry, who lived at Shapwick House. He paid 18s each year,[111] though the maximum paid by the other parishioners was only 2s, this income being supplemented by rents from church lands at Withy and in Shapwick that amounted to 17s per annum. With this money the churchwardens, who were drawn from a pool of farm tenants and so knew the parish and its people well, were also expected to look after the building fabric of the church and its churchyard as well as everything from the bread and wine for infrequent communion services to paying one man for 'whipping out the doges out of the church' and another for keeping down vermin. The latter was generously interpreted and included sparrows, hedgehogs, foxes, 'polecats' and badgers. In 1717, William Waite presented no less than 318 sparrows and was duly paid at the going rate of 2d a dozen.

In discharging a duty towards the poor, aged and destitute there was always a balance to be struck between minimising the number who required support by moving them on to the next parish and helping those who were genuinely local and in need of financial contributions, gifts of fuel, clothing or medical attention. For a pauper to receive aid from a parish he or she had to be settled there and this judgment fell to the Overseers of the Poor. Naturally enough, given their eagerness to disown potentially costly cases, underhand tactics were sometimes employed and the matter could finish up in court. In the 1630s the case of John Parker's child pitted Shapwick against Glastonbury. The latter complained

to the midsummer sessions of the Quarter Sessions in 1631 that Parker's orphaned child had been living in Shapwick, where his father had settled, but that the Shapwick overseers had brought the child to Glastonbury (where it had been born) and left it on the church doorstep. After hearing from several witnesses, two JPs decided that the child ought to be settled in Shapwick and, though the villagers did appeal, the decision stood.[112] Here the Overseers were effectively being called upon to act as moral guardians and in this role they regularly intervened to enforce paternal responsibilities. When Margaret Champion accused Thomas Higdon, a tailor from Shapwick, of being the father of her 'base-born child' in 1615, he was ordered by the Quarter Sessions to pay sixpence weekly to the Overseers so that the money could be used for the maintenance and education of the child; and, lest the responsibility not be shared, Margaret was ordered to do the same.[113] Nor was Thomas alone in his alleged behaviour. In 1616 Thomas Chinn, at one time the Shapwick miller, was ordered to pay 10d weekly as 'reputed' father of two children born to Cicelly Lyte of Somerton.[114] By securing payment through the court a long-standing financial burden on the parish was avoided.

More onerous still was a duty to run the village Poor House,[115] where the old and infirm were taken care of and destitute but able-bodied adults and orphaned children were set to work. Traces of the Poor House were found in 1997 during preparation for new housing at Lawn Farm.[116] The full plan was not recovered (Figure 8.13) but the building marked on mid-eighteenth-century maps seems most likely to be a smaller two-room house like The Old Forge (see Figure 8.5D). It certainly had a flagged floor and was surrounded by a ditch and possibly a hedge that was replaced by a drystone wall in the later seventeenth century. Particularly striking is the finds assemblage from this site. The pottery is indistinguishable from any other of the post-medieval dwellings in the village and includes a collection of stoneware mugs, trailed slipware plates, dishes and bowls and a sgraffito bowl. Records from the Minehead (Somerset) Poor House in the eighteenth century reveal a diet of cheese, greens, potatoes and broths of boiled water, oatmeal and

BOX 8.1

Nonconformity and popular superstition

While the majority of villagers attended church on a regular basis and Sunday services were a fixed point in the weekly timetable, there is also evidence for religious nonconformity in the village. Between the 1590s and 1641 four families were reported as 'popish recusants',[b1] persons who refused to acknowledge the supremacy of the monarch as head of the Church in England. Though Catholicism had undergone a significant revival under Mary (1553–1558), thirty years on this small Shapwick community may well have found themselves not only marginalised but also persecuted. In nearby Cossington, for example, Catholics absented themselves from church. Various risings and plots during the 1570s and 1580s linked Catholics with treasonable offences and foreign alliances that endangered the life of the monarch and the future of Protestant England.[b2] Though the majority did not present any real threat to the safety of the realm, loyalty to Rome was identified with disloyalty to queen and country.[b3]

A hundred years later, in 1689, the house of William Ames in Shapwick was licensed as a place of worship for Quakers. We do not know where this was, though a Giles Ames was living at Church(yard) Farm, immediately west of the parish church, in 1660. If a relationship can be confirmed between Giles and William – and they were quite possibly father and son – then William Ames's community of Friends must have worshipped in an early seventeenth-century building that still stands. In the mid-seventeenth century there was a burial ground for Quakers just over the parish boundary in Catcott.[b4] In 1690 the Polden Hill Meeting was moved from Sutton Mallet to Shapwick and Greinton, which were used alternately. By this time there had been a Quaker community in Shapwick for some years. William Stone, miller of Shapwick, is recorded as a Quaker in 1676 and in 1690 there is testimony against William for marrying a non-Quaker in a ceremony in a church.[b5] William, or perhaps his carpenter father John, lived at 2–4 Northbrook Road, not a great distance from Church(yard) Farm; he is referred to as 'Quaker Stone' on the 1765 survey and map.[b6]

We do not know if the presence of a small Quaker congregation in the village was disruptive. Quakers saw no reason to attend church and respected neither church authority nor the church service, so they were easily perceived as a danger to community norms. A Quaker from Edington was arrested in 1665, as were several others at Greinton, for non-payment of tithes. Most obviously, Quakers did not comply with the social practices of the day: they did not greet people with a 'good morrow', for example, and this was thought uncivil (Figure B.8.1). Their distinctive vocabulary also marked them out, the use of words such as 'saint' being avoided (including for place-names), the days of the week being numbered rather than named ('first', 'second' and so on), with March being the 'first month'. Titles were also shunned and, more generally, they used as few words as possible to communicate. Quaker dress, too, was demure; no fashionable lace or buttons were worn, while the hat became a symbol of their faith, with wearers refusing to raise them to acknowledge others and keeping them on even when in church. Their demeanour was widely thought strange; they walked slowly and stiffly, limiting their gestures to a minimum. 'Sober' and 'serious' are words often used to describe their deportment[b7] and it is easy to imagine how, with such notable differences in speech, dress and bearing, Shapwick Quakers associated largely with their own community. In 1765 William Ames was a tenant in a house that had previously

meat, and doubtless it was for these kinds of simple but sustaining foods that the dishes and bowls were needed. The stoneware mugs would have held tea, beer or milk[117] and, like the other crockery, were probably donated, which explains the similarity of the assemblage to others across the village and the

absence of any matching vessels. No personal items such as dress accessories were recovered; they would have been few in any case.

These unfortunates, many of whom perhaps spent only a few days in Shapwick, put us directly in touch with individual human tragedies and the economics been occupied by John Stone, so perhaps this suggests some social segregation at that time.[b8] On the other hand, many historians now take the view that local communities were much more accepting of religious diversity than had previously been believed.

Even among the church-going Protestants of the village, religious faith did not satisfy all their questions about the world around them; many popular superstitions were attached to the unpredictable and inexplicable.[b9] Witches and 'cunning-folk' or wizards serviced every need, from summoning fairies to healing the sick and bewitched.[b10] Among the possible archaeological manifestations of this are witch bottles, dried cats, shoes and written charms, all to be found concealed inside houses, and the adoption of old coins, fossils and prehistoric objects to cultivate their protective magic. An almost complete fifteenth- or sixteenth-century cistern found buried upside down near a hearth in a demolished house in Shapwick Park[b11] was suggested as possibly having a 'ritual function' by the excavator.[b12] More convincingly, symbols were scratched into Shapwick fireplace lintels, attic staircase doorways and roof timbers, possibly in the seventeenth century, to ward off evil spirits that were thought to descend from

Figure B.8.1. *Quakers as depicted in contemporary texts, here the frontispiece of Benjamin Keach's War with the Devil (1676). On the left the caption reads 'The youth in his converted state' and beneath 'Narrow is the way that leads to life'; on the right 'in his naturall state' and beneath 'Broad is the way'.*

Figure B.8.2. *'Witch marks' recorded at Shapwick House and Oak Farmhouse.*

above (Figure B.8.2). These symbols include a six-pointed star, a Christian four-pointed star, inscribed hearts and what has been identified as the astrological letter 'zain', all of which were believed to offer supernatural protection from evil at vulnerable points of entry into rooms and buildings.[b13] The early modern household was a battleground between forces for good and disorder, hidden forces that, if not held at bay, might affect anything from health and sexual potency to butter-making.

of mere survival. Yet illness was not confined to the poor. There is a touching entry in the will of 1692 of Henry Bull,[118] the owner of Shapwick Manor, concerning his daughter Elizabeth, who he says is 'infirm in body and not having the use and benefit of her speech and therefore wholly unfit for marriage'.

Fortunately, in this case, Henry was a wealthy man and able to provide for Elizabeth: 'I desire that all possible care may be taken that she be well used and maintained according to her birth and quality.' Not all were so lucky.

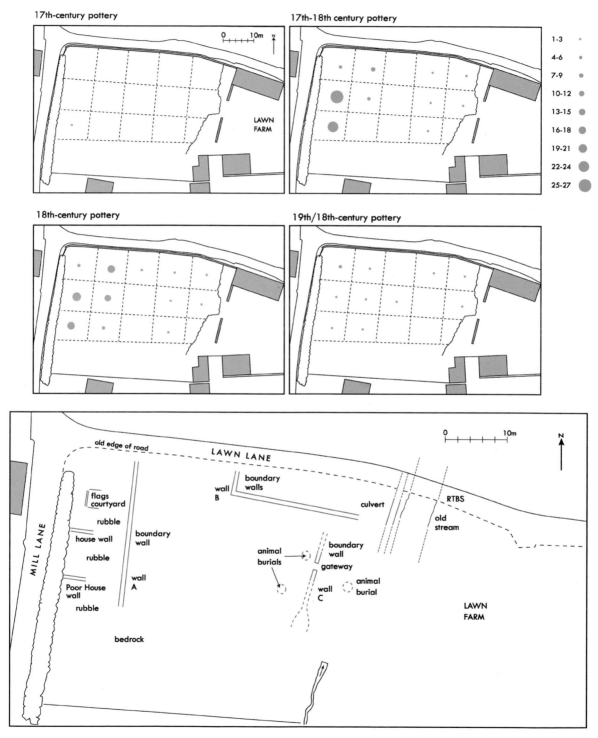

Figure 8.13. Surface collection of pottery and observation of other post-medieval features during watching briefs by Charles and Nancy Hollinrake on new housing development at Lawn Farm Paddock. The Poor House lay on the western edge of the plot at the junction of Mill Lane and Lawn Lane.

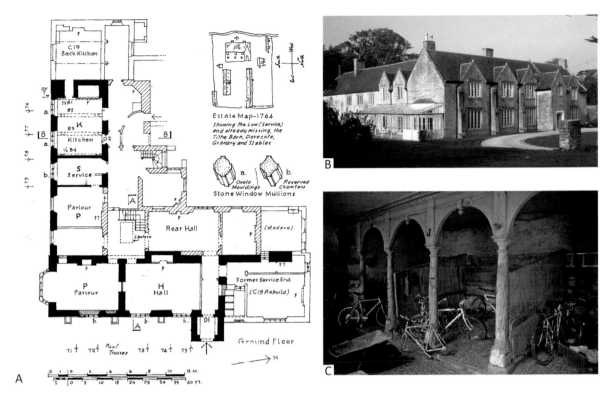

Figure 8.14. Shapwick Manor, home of the Bull family: a two-storey Jacobean building over-built in the nineteenth century in the Gothic style. A: the L-shaped plan. B: south and east façades. C: the late seventeenth-century stables with cobbled floor and timber arcaded screen in front of the stalls.

The post-Dissolution manor houses

When Glastonbury Abbey was suppressed in 1539 its lands throughout Somerset were sold and resold as speculative owners sought to profit from property transactions (see Story, above). The manors at Shapwick also changed hands many times before a period of relative stability at the beginning of the seventeenth century.[119]

Shapwick Manor

Shapwick Manor, formerly allocated to the almoner of the abbey as the rectory manor, was acquired by the Bull family of Wells in 1619.[120] Like the Rolle family, nearby at Shapwick House, the Bulls were 'new county men'. They had no well-established ancestry before the Dissolution and gained their status largely at the expense of the fate of the monasteries.[121] Their gentility was, effectively, purchased; and though they

were not nobility they might be described as 'rising gentry'. Where the Rolles' wealth was consolidated from the practice of law and influence at Westminster, barrister William Bull was a Justice of the Peace[122] and, as such, one of those who 'governed' the county.

As we discovered in Chapter 7, documentary and architectural evidence suggest that there was a sixteenth-century building on the rectory manor site. The whole complex was then remodelled in the seventeenth century, probably by William Bull. What remains today is largely a Jacobean building, heavily over-built in the nineteenth century (Figure 8.14A and B). The main building consisted of three rooms in a line with a cross passage and lateral fireplaces in all rooms along the west wall.[123] Characteristic dating features include the 'reserved chamfer' mouldings of the early seventeenth century and the depressed four-centre arch that today serves as the outer doorway to the porch. At some time in the early eighteenth century the former service room to the north of the porch was torn down, and this is the building whose plan is shown on the 1796 map.[124] Throughout these changes some medieval features were retained, including the early to mid-sixteenth-century kitchen at the west end of the wing.

The same blend of old and new was continued outside the main building. The medieval dovecote and barn remained, but a stable block was added in the later seventeenth century; this still survives to the north of the house, complete with its original stalls, cobbled floor, wooden Tuscan columns and mullioned and transomed windows (Figure 8.14C). Doubtless it was here that Henry stabled the 'four coach mares' for his 'best coach' that he left to his wife in his will of 1692,[125] though perhaps the family also enjoyed field sports such as hunting deer and foxes.[126] By 1750 this manor house was well on the way to being transformed from a working farm to a gentry house with surrounding ornamental grounds, but that change would not be fully completed until later in the century (see Chapter 9).

The real excitement about this phase of the building's life is that a detailed inventory exists of the house of Henry Bull for 1692 which provides good descriptions of rooms and furnishings, a complement to Thomas Prewe's humbler dwelling described above.[127] Henry Bull had inherited 'a plentiful personal estate', according to his father William, who died aged 81 in 1676,[128] and it had been his grandfather, also William (died 1622), who purchased Shapwick from the Perceval family in 1613.[129] Henry was a successful barrister at the Middle Temple and an MP for Bridgwater, as well as a country gentleman and farmer, and though he did not live long to enjoy the house after his father's death, the family had by then accumulated many possessions. Figure 8.15 maps the objects and furnishings described in each of the rooms of Henry's house onto the ground- and first-floor plans, as reconstructed on the basis of what is understood of the standing building.

Only durable goods appear in the inventory so the picture is not entirely complete.[130] Nevertheless, the hall sounds like a far more sparsely furnished and formal space than the 'great' and 'little parlour' and was perhaps used more for receiving guests and business matters than it was for relaxation. No dining room is mentioned by name but the number of chairs

in the 'great parlour' suggests that it fulfilled that function. The 'Turkey wrought chairs' listed both in that room and next door were fashionable items of furniture of the day: chairs upholstered in 'Turkey work' of tapestry canvas with a knotted stitch, usually in floral designs.[131] Upstairs, the best bedrooms were clearly comfortable, while the books in Henry's study were valued at £40, twice the value of his pictures but just half that of his linen. The inventory also lists a huge amount of cash kept in the house – £1,020, the equivalent of nearly £90,000 today – but most of this is explained in Henry's will by an entry for 150 'broad 20s pieces of old gold' which were left 'rapt up in papers' with directions for his wife.[132] From this description the coins may be confidently identified as gold unites of Charles I or perhaps early Charles II. For perspective, a labourer might have been earning £15 a year.[133]

No excavations were carried out at Shapwick Manor but some test pits were dug. Among the finds was a sherd of French Beauvais jug of seventeenth-century date,[134] possibly imported through one of the south coast ports such as Exeter. There were also fragments of at least three onion or bladder wine bottles of late seventeenth- or early eighteenth-century date.[135] Though they were more common later, wine bottles of this date would have been restricted to higher-status households. At the table they would have complemented the three dozen pewter dishes and six dozen pewter plates, together with the £120 of silver plate that was also registered in Bull's inventory.[136] Undoubtedly this was a wealthy family, weighed down by concerns for their standing in society. This much is clear from Henry Bull's will in which he speaks directly to his unmarried daughter Elianor. 'I advise her', he said, 'to be very careful in her choice of a sober, honest and discreet man for a husband, suitable to her own birth, breeding quality and fortune, and in no respect inferior to her'. Obviously he did not entirely trust her, asking that 'she take the advice and consent of her mother and other good friends in a business of so great weight and moment'.[137]

Shapwick House

At Shapwick House similar changes were taking place but on a grander scale.[138] Here a fashionable mansion was created within the shell of the fifteenth-century structure by remodelling the house on an H-plan with

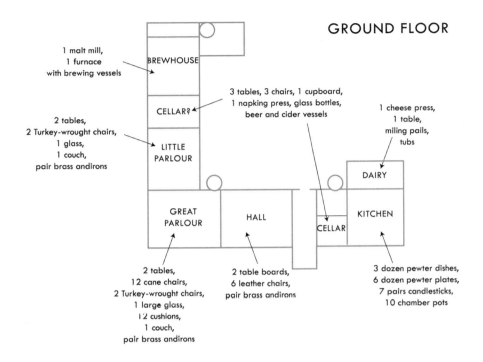

GROUND FLOOR

1 malt mill,
1 furnace
with brewing vessels

BREWHOUSE

3 tables, 3 chairs, 1 cupboard,
1 napking press, glass bottles,
beer and cider vessels

CELLAR?

1 cheese press,
1 table,
miling pails,
tubs

DAIRY

2 tables,
2 Turkey-wrought chairs,
1 glass,
1 couch,
pair brass andirons

LITTLE
PARLOUR

KITCHEN

GREAT
PARLOUR

HALL

CELLAR

2 tables,
12 cane chairs,
2 Turkey-wrought chairs,
1 large glass,
12 cushions,
1 couch,
pair brass andirons

2 table boards,
6 leather chairs,
pair brass andirons

3 dozen pewter dishes,
6 dozen pewter plates,
7 pairs candlesticks,
10 chamber pots

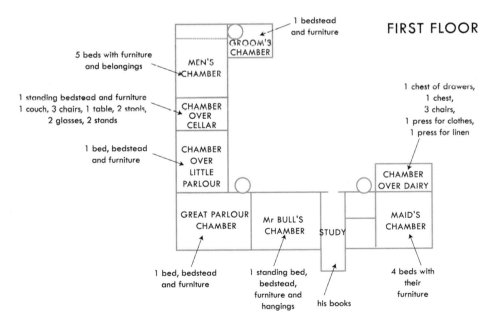

1 bedstead
and furniture

FIRST FLOOR

GROOM'S
CHAMBER

5 beds with furniture
and belongings

MEN'S
CHAMBER

1 chest of drawers,
1 chest,
3 chairs,
1 press for clothes,
1 press for linen

1 standing bedstead and furniture
1 couch, 3 chairs, 1 table, 2 stools,
2 glasses, 2 stands

CHAMBER
OVER
CELLAR

1 bed, bedstead
and furniture

CHAMBER
OVER
LITTLE
PARLOUR

CHAMBER
OVER DAIRY

GREAT PARLOUR
CHAMBER

Mr BULL'S
CHAMBER

STUDY

MAID'S
CHAMBER

1 bed, bedstead
and furniture

1 standing bed,
bedstead,
furniture and
hangings

his books

4 beds with
their
furniture

Figure 8.15. Reconstructed plan of Shapwick Manor in the late seventeenth century, with rooms and objects as described in Henry Bull's inventory of 1692. All these goods were valued at £505 10s 0d, which was only half the value of his cereals, 158 cattle (including 20 plough oxen), 70 sheep, 17 horses, 3 asses and 12 pigs.

Figure 8.16. Enlarged detail from Bonnor's 1791 print showing the Jacobean front of Shapwick House. The window for the long gallery can be seen on the eastern (right) gable end. The porch is no longer in the same position today and here marks the low end of the medieval hall range. Smoke rises from the former detached kitchen to the west (left).

three storeys.[139] Abandoning the original medieval design of the first-floor hall, floor levels were now adjusted, a new long gallery inserted, windows refenestrated and the kitchen facilities brought into the house. In addition, the old detached kitchen was converted into a bakehouse or brewhouse and a new building was added to the west, probably to be used as a servants' hall. The result was at once more convenient and fashionable, if radical. The long gallery, for example, now ran from one end of the house to the other and had to be inserted into a third storey beneath the roof, which may itself have been dismantled and raised. This probably explains both why the sequence of carpenters' marks on the medieval roof trusses is no longer consecutive and when the decorative windbraces were dispensed with. A flat ceiling now hid the old medieval timbers, natural light entering through two new windows in the gable ends and a new oriel bay three storeys high. This dramatic rearrangement of the accommodation turned a draughty, impersonal medieval house into a comfortable and private secular home suitable for a gentry family in a new age (Figure 8.16).

All these seventeenth-century changes to the house and its surroundings (see below) can be linked to the ownership of either the Burrell family or the Rolles. Abraham Burrell, the owner from 1622 to 1640,[140] may have been responsible, as two key stylistic details, the long gallery and the use of ovolo mouldings, do

suggest an early to mid-seventeenth-century date. These features can be found in other Somerset houses, such as Poundisford Park (*c.*1550), Barrington Court (*c.*1570) and North Cadbury Court (1589, and which is very comparable), and are typical of elite houses of the mid-seventeenth century (Figure 8.17).[141] However, ovolo windows remained popular well into the later seventeenth century, so extending the possible date of the changes into the ownership of the Rolle family. Indeed, the work at the mansion is traditionally ascribed[142] to Sir Henry Rolle (1589–1656), a wealthy London lawyer who became Lord Chief Justice under the Commonwealth, then the second-highest judge of the realm after the Lord Chancellor, and, in 1654, Commissioner of the Exchequer (Figure 8.18). He resigned in 1655 and died a year later.[143] If indeed it was Rolle who was responsible then the work in the house was carried out in a conservative manner. Interestingly, he was described by his contemporaries as 'by nature penurious; and his wife made him worse', so perhaps that explains his reluctance.[144] Whoever commissioned the work, it was an enormous undertaking that left the owner with an up-to-date mansion and plaster ceilings that hid all trace of the medieval shell beneath.

While 'moats' were incorporated into gardens of the sixteenth and seventeenth centuries, it was not by this time fashionable to have a ditch of stagnant water encircling the house and many were filled in

Figure 8.17. Elizabethan houses in Somerset, all with projecting wings on an E plan, three-storey porches and characteristic mullioned and transomed bay windows. A: Montacute House (c.1590), east-facing elevation of three storeys, symmetrical H-plan with long gallery. B: Barrington Court (c.1570), south front, also Ham Hill stone, twisted chimneys C: Fairfield House, Stogursey (1589), originally with additional storey, large mullion and transomed windows. D: North Cadbury Court (1589), three storeys, also with long gallery beneath a formerly open roof.

and their existence forgotten, as at Acton Court in Gloucestershire in the mid-1550s.[145] By the same date the medieval moat at Shapwick was choked with silt but still damp with murky water. One of the excavation trenches[146] revealed a substantial stone-built 'dam' crossing the moat at right angles (Figure 8.19), a feature which continues to puzzle us. It was clearly intended to obstruct water flow because some care had been taken to insert thin plates of Lias between the joints to prevent any leakage from side to side, so perhaps its purpose was to stop any further accumulation of sediment in the section of moat that lay beyond. Alternatively, perhaps it was intended to

Figure 8.18. Portrait of lawyer Henry Rolle (1589–1656), who was possibly responsible for the many changes made to Shapwick House in the mid-seventeenth century. This included adjustments to the floor levels and the insertion of new windows and a long gallery which hid the medieval roof timbers.

Figure 8.19. Excavations across the moat at Shapwick House revealed this seventeenth-century 'dam'. To the left (east) the footings of a later box drain are visible.

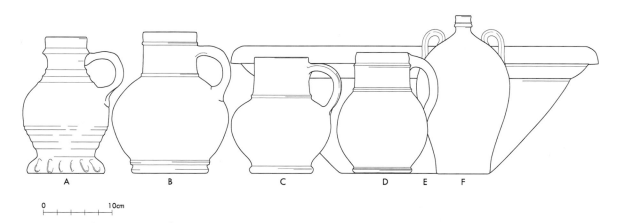

Figure 8.20. Selection of imported post-medieval pottery from excavations around Shapwick House. A: Frechen stoneware. B: Raeren stoneware. C: Malling jug from the Low Countries. D: Beauvais jug. E: Verwood pancheon from Dorset. F: Merida-type from Portugal.

stabilise the new ground surface when the process of infilling the moat began soon afterwards. Only further excavation could resolve the problem.

Fortunately for the archaeologist, among the rubble used to backfill the moat was a good deal of detritus from previous owners. The pottery includes the familiar range of types and forms, dominated by local wares. The range of imports, however, is somewhat wider than that excavated from villagers' homes. Together with German stonewares from Raeren, Frechen and Westerwald, there were two fragments of a jar from Portugal,[147] a second sherd of French Beauvais jug and two more of a distinctive tin-glazed vessel (Figure 8.20).[148] This 'Malling' jug was made in the Low Countries in the second half of the sixteenth century, though similarly stippled vessels were made in England in the next century. The Shapwick fragments are from a small globular jug about 150mm high, whose exterior is stippled in turquoise, brown, yellow, blue and black. Chemical analysis, carried out as part of a programme of work at the British Museum, showed this particular example to have come from a workshop in Antwerp. It is a rare find. Only twenty-three such vessels are known from the south-west of England, all bar one being from ports,[149] and the inference is that such a restricted distribution must be linked to wealthy households.

Excavations around Shapwick House also produced some of the highest-quality glass vessels of post-medieval date. Two of the four potash pedestal beakers of mid-sixteenth- to mid-seventeenth-century date would have been expensive items in their day. Equally exceptional, at least when compared against what was available in other Shapwick households, is a knob in crizzled (finely cracked) lead glass from a goblet or wineglass dating between 1670 and 1700. There was also part of a seventeenth-century alembic, used for distilling medicinal or domestic solutes from flowers (such as rosewater) and to make alcohol, as well as many fragments of wine bottles. By contrast, the metal assemblage is insubstantial and unremarkable: an illegible Nuremberg jetton dated c.1550–1630, perhaps used as a reckoning counter, three wire loop fasteners or eyelets from seventeenth-century contexts in the moat fills, a lead bullet, a window latch and some hooks. There was also a quern fragment of Upper Greensand stone, a reminder that this was a working agricultural environment.

More striking is evidence for the occupants' rich diet, particularly game. Bones of red deer, fallow deer, duck, pigeon, a wader, rabbit and hare were all recovered.[150] Goose bones might be from a farmyard bird and a rook/crow could be either have been a natural mortality or deliberately trapped, perhaps for a pie filling.[151] Notably, red and fallow deer bones are confined to excavations around Shapwick House, the majority coming from seventeenth-century contexts there. The red deer could have been from an emparked herd and the fallow deer almost certainly were, but since there was insufficient space for that near the mansion in the seventeenth century the Burrell or

Rolle households either hunted elsewhere or received the venison as a gift.[152] One of the antler fragments was chopped from the skull rather than shed, perhaps to be shaved for culinary use as a gelling agent for flavoursome rosewater or ginger jellies, or simply as a medicine to treat diarrhoea. Meat at the table, particularly the venison, implies wealth and status, while the presence of at least three species of marine fish, conger eel, the humble herring and possibly cod, proves that the owners of the manor house had access to fresh, salted or smoked products from coastal markets.[153] These were large specimens too, the eel being over 1.5m in length and the cod at least a metre. Perhaps they were served boiled with an anchovy and oyster sauce, a traditional recipe of the day. From the moat also came significant numbers of marine molluscs, including the shells of mussels, cockles, limpets and a great number of oysters. Many of these had been damaged during opening and several shells could be matched back again into their original pairs, hinting that they had been discarded directly into the moat. Perhaps the whittle tang knives (a type of knife where part of the blade fits into a hole in the handle) we found were used to prise the oysters open.

Clearly, at Shapwick House mansion there was lavish expenditure on food for the household and its guests. An almost contemporary account for Robert Cecil's expenditure at Cranborne in 1613 includes capons, brawn, lambs, pheasants, partridges, turkeys, woodcocks, pike, salmon, carp and cheeses.[154] None of these foods would have been out of place at Shapwick House. It is more of a struggle to assess the furnishings of the house in Henry Rolle's day and afterwards. Henry's will, dated November 1656,[155] makes no specific mention of either his house or land at Shapwick, only his 'baylie' (bailiff), one Thomas Hayward. Although he was buried in the village, towards the end of his life Henry was clearly living in Black and White Court at the Old Bailey in London, so his son, Francis, was probably already in residence at Shapwick House. Thirty years later, the focus of investment for Francis was on his home in Hampshire but it does sound as if he maintained more than a foothold at Shapwick. His will of 1686 speaks of the 'great stock of cattle and sheep and other things' there, not to mention 'the household stuff and furniture of my house at Shapwick, together with the

Figure 8.21. Reconstruction by Victor Ambrus of the gardens north of Shapwick House in the seventeenth century. Note the ponds, topiary and raised paths with the banqueting house in the background and the low-lying Levels beyond.

pictures, books and other things in the said house' that he left in the hands of his wife (and cousin) Dame Priscilla.[156] Many of the late seventeenth-century finds at Shapwick House may therefore be related to Francis or to his dissolute son Henry who had married without his father's consent. In turn, it was one of Henry's three sons, Samuel, the great-grandson of Sir Henry, who had his initials – SR 1727 – carved into the mantelpiece in the entrance hall.

The gardens and pavilion at Shapwick House
The remodelling of Shapwick House in the mid-seventeenth century was accompanied by a transformation of its gardens. The Rolle family had a special interest in horticulture which they indulged principally at their Hampshire residence at East Tytherley, near Stockbridge. When Francis Rolle died in 1686 his widow revealed that he had spent £15,000 on the house and grounds there, the equivalent of well over a million pounds today.[157] Far less lavish sums

were spent at Shapwick. Nevertheless, on the north side of the house there was a garden or walled lawn, then a terrace and beyond that a banqueting house with two ornamental ponds. Figure 8.21 reconstructs this scene with a raised gravel path and bedding running between the ponds.[158] Similar layouts are common in gardens developed in the sixteenth and seventeenth centuries, their formality and symmetry being influenced by the Dutch designs that became especially popular after the accession of William of Orange in 1689.[159] Gardens at Low Ham, Halswell Park and Nettlecombe were similarly inspired.[160] Water features often figured in these Tudor and Stuart gardens and the existing small moat to the north-west of the mansion was probably also incorporated (Figure 8.22).[161] Poet and author Gervase Markham specified just such a plan for a garden,[162] which may have been the blueprint for, or a drawing of, the surviving garden at Tackley in Oxfordshire.

Another standard feature of elaborate gardens such

Figure 8.22. *The water-filled 6m-wide moat to the north of Shapwick House. Though today well hidden, it may originally have been part of the post-medieval garden design. There is no trace today of any buildings on the island it encloses.*

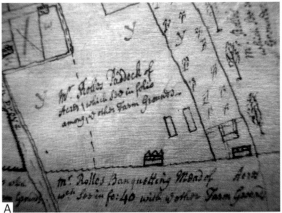

Figure 8.23. *The banqueting house north of Shapwick House. A: detail of map of c.1754 showing moat, two ponds and the banqueting house (SRO DD/SG 36 c/206). B: Claude Nattes' depiction of the banqueting house in 1787, painted from the south end of Icehouse Copse; on the distant horizon is the windmill which blew down in 1836, causing the death of the miller (see Chapter 10).*

as those at Nonsuch Palace or Wimbledon House (Surrey) was the banqueting house.[163] More often than not found at some distance from the main house, the 'garden pavilion', as they are sometimes called, was a stopping-off point for refreshments and rest on a walk or carriage ride around the estate. 'Mr Rolles Banqueting Mead', as it features on mid-eighteenth-century maps, is located much closer to the mansion but, to judge from pottery and clay pipes excavated there, it must have served a similar purpose.[164] With so many servants and visitors in constant attention, the banqueting house doubtless provided some much-appreciated privacy. The building itself is depicted as two storey with three gables (Figure 8.23A), but a slightly later watercolour of 1787 by John Claude Nattes, now in the village hall, shows it to be more modest later (Figure 8.23B). All that could be made out during excavation was the rubble cores of its walls, any ashlar facing having been removed and recycled elsewhere.

Views to, from and around the house were of great significance in this new garden design. Looking north from Shapwick House there was now a grand vista over symmetrical terracing and planting, ponds and paths, one which was appreciable from the upper floors, particularly from the long gallery. By the mid-eighteenth century the west side of this vista was bordered with planting, not so much a 'wilderness' area but more of an avenue that ran parallel to the main axial vista and out towards the garden moat. Other views could be enjoyed either from the banqueting house or from the raised Italianate terrace, both of which gave pleasing prospects towards Mendip. Few visitors would have entered the village from the north before the turnpike came through at the beginning of the nineteenth century, so this side of the house was secluded. Though there were also garden features to the south, among them an ornamental pond (Figure 8.24A) and a new dovecote (Figure 8.24B and C), the view in that direction was dominated by the active village scene of West Street, with its farmhouses and plots.

Figure 8.24. Post-medieval features around Shapwick House. A: ornamental pond south of the house, here being recorded after excavation; the backfill included fragments of an ovolo-moulded window frame of late sixteenth- or early seventeenth-century date, gable coping and a plinth, all of Doulting stone, though one paving slab was of Beer stone (Devon). All these came from the remodelling of the south façade of the house in the early nineteenth century. B: the dovecote. Keith Wilkinson far right, Chris Gerrard next to him. C: the interior of the dovecote at Shapwick House, with its 1,092 nestholes. This is probably the building shown on mid-eighteenth-century maps (e.g. Figure 2.2).

Perhaps it was partly for this reason that the owners of Shapwick House made use of other locations, ones that lay far from the comforts of the main house, for outdoor eating and entertainment.[165] A set of earthworks in Henhills Copse, a little over a kilometre away, probably represent traces of one of their 'pleasure grounds'. The earthworks there (Figure 8.25A) comprise a rectangular pond 60m long and 20m wide – only a fraction smaller than a modern Olympic swimming pool – as well as several grassy terraces and perhaps buildings, all enclosed by a bank. By the time the eighteenth-century maps of the parish were being surveyed Shapwick House was linked to this complex by an elm-lined avenue that ran first

northwards and then along the Nidons (Figure 8.25B). Like the banqueting house, this was a romantic and private destination, hidden away in trees in this case, where owners and their guests could enjoy some peace away from the bustle of the house (see Story, Chapter 9). More symbolically, the avenues traversed most of the parish, creating a kind of informal 'outer park' and silently demonstrating the Rolle family's control over the land through which they passed.

This shift in the scale of garden design is significant. Several elements of landscape, at some distance from each other, were here being purposely linked together by geometric lines of movement and new views drawn *through* the working countryside. After the turbulence

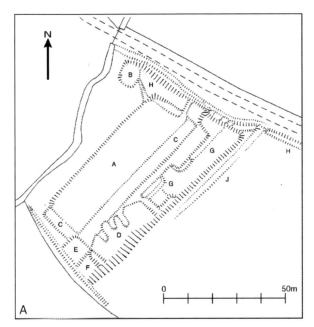

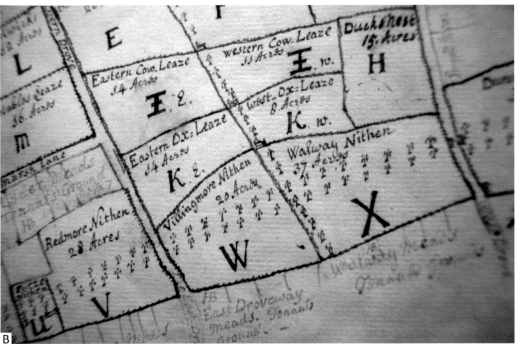

Figure 8.25. A landscape of pleasure. A: the earthworks at Henhills Copse with ponds (A, B), terraces (C, E, F), platform (D), boundary bank (G), later banks (H) and tracks (J). B: the avenue of elms running east–west across the Nidons or 'Nithens' in 1754. Part of one of nine folios showing enclosed areas of the parish (SRO DD/SG 36), north towards bottom of map.

of the Civil War such a visual statement exhibited a certain self-confidence and belief in a secure future. Elsewhere across England such developments often marked the beginning of grand landscaping schemes in which vast areas of fields were turned over to grass within private parkland. But here at Shapwick

there were additional complications that would have frustrated any such plans. Ownership of the land was split between two manors and many parts of the common-field system were still farmed by tenants. Though the Rolle family may have had the finances to achieve it, neither owner, of either manor, ever acquired enough control to turn the whole parish over to a 'designed landscape'; divided tenurial arrangements militated against such a development.[166]

A post-medieval landscape

Fields and farming

In the countryside around the village the medieval landscape of furlongs and strips was gradually metamorphosing into something quite different, visually, socially and economically: a new agricultural regime worked within hedged fields and managed for profit.[167] This process had begun in the Middle Ages and was already well advanced in the parish by 1550. As Nick Corcos has noted,[168] the process of enclosure at Shapwick encountered few obstacles and, although it might also be argued that vociferous protest was hardly embedded in the culture of the place after centuries of Glastonbury Abbey ownership, there is every sign that the process of enclosure was locally initiated, and clearly with no little enthusiasm. Enclosure and the subsequent leasing of land provided landowners with a ready solution to unprofitable farming practices that had tended to stifle initiatives such as the intensification of cropping, the introduction of new crops, control over animal breeding and sometimes even quite simple decisions concerning changes in land use. In short, enclosure was considered to be a step that would make farming both more efficient and more profitable.

As we saw in Chapter 7, the major landowner at Shapwick was among the first to withdraw from the existing open-field arrangement, though many others saw the benefits too.[169] Protests so often voiced loudly about the loss of pasturing rights in the common fields were not heard here. Quite possibly this was because pasture was already abundant on the neighbouring peat moors, at least at certain times in the year, and drainage there continued to improve conditions underfoot. Once more, tenants elsewhere in southern England were often tied into tithe payments on their produce and could not easily wriggle free of their obligations. At Shapwick, on the other hand, tithes had been converted to cash before 1539 and this eased the way to the transfer of tenurial responsibilities. Of course, there was no clamouring multitude of landowners at Shapwick to obfuscate the process either and the body of smallholders was not large.

From the evidence contained in the Shapwick manor court rolls for the seventeenth century it is clear that enclosure was brought about by agreement between tenants, a process that landscape historians refer to as 'piecemeal enclosure'. Land in dispersed parcels was first exchanged to create cohesive blocks and then enclosed, and land use switched afterwards if appropriate. In the seventeenth century this changeover was mainly from arable to pasture and field names such as 'New meads' (new meadow) in 1643 reflect precisely this process in action.[170] In theory, licences to enclose could be granted only by the lord of the manor through the manorial courts, but this ruling was widely abused, including by the lord of the manor himself. Evidently tenants decided for themselves how to repartition their acreages, an important shift in the decision-making process away from the community towards the individual.[171] Though some were written down, most agreements were private and circumvented official channels, so they are hard to trace. The first we hear of them is when there was a violation of a local bylaw, usually the obstruction of common paths by planting hedges across them, digging ditches or diverting watercourses. Attempts thereafter to reinforce customary regulations were largely ineffectual[172] and some tenants were routinely called before the court for breaches of conduct but simply ignored the outcome.

Where exchanges did find their way into the court rolls it was usually to ensure that there was proof of title. We read, for example, of tenants who combined half-acre parcels into larger blocks of two to three acres by exchange, enclosing them out of the common fields and then switching their uses from arable cultivation to pasture. William Cooke did precisely this in October 1623 when he exchanged two acres of arable in the West Field and one under grass in East Field for three acres of Hollybrooke Close in West Field in the south-western corner of the parish.[173] William was one among many who by now saw enclosure as a commonly accepted local practice, manor court sessions having taken on something of the demeanour of a card game in which different field combinations were acquired and then exchanged between players. In fact, so complex had these transactions become that it was not uncommon for pieces of land to be administratively mislaid in the process.

East Field
by Northbrook

0   1km

Figure 8.26. A composite map of the parish in the mid-eighteenth century drawn from nineteen different maps (1754–62). Notice the surviving strip pattern in what remained of the common fields at this date. The Levels remain unenclosed.

Figure 8.26 is a composite of nineteen maps dating to the mid-eighteenth century, the end of the period considered in this chapter. The Levels were still unenclosed, though the moors were hardly the blank wilderness the map implies. There would have been fishing and fowling, angling and netting, for which the retrieval of the bones of eels and ducks from our excavations provides archaeological confirmation, as well as the digging of peat and the gathering of wood for fuel and thatching materials as before.[174] And while a field name such as 'New door corner', which first appears in 1751, implies a way out onto

newly enclosed land,[175] Somerset was far slower than East Anglia in engineering new schemes of fen drainage. Before the Levels were fully enclosed and drained later in the eighteenth century (see Chapter 9) traditional activities still continued here, though to some extent the longer-distance movement of livestock from manor to manor and from winter to summer pastures must have been disrupted once the monastic estate was broken up.[176] Meanwhile, on the upland, the strip pattern of the remaining common fields is plain to see in parts of the West and East Fields, particularly in the centre–south of the parish and in the north-east in East Field by Northbrook. Over the rest of the parish there was a rectilinear pattern of strips and enclosure hedges: evidence that the process of enclosure was complete. Many of these new boundaries faithfully follow the edges of blocks of former strips, the exchange and consolidation of strips giving individual farmers cohesive holdings for the first time. This often resulted in small linear fields with curved boundaries that reflect the 'S-shaped' alignments of the individual strips in the former open fields. Our ecological team found that these older boundaries could often be identified by the number of saproxylic invertebrates present in the modern hedgerow, particularly beetle and fly ancient woodland indicator species (see Chapter 2 for method).

The hedges that were newly created during the process of enclosure in the later medieval and post-medieval periods were composed of a variety of native woodland and shrub species. Analysis of the modern hedgerows reveals the presence of alder, ash, blackthorn, buckthorn, dogwood, elder, field maple, guelder rose, hawthorn, hazel, oak, spindle, wayfaring tree and wild privet, most of which could either be cut for fuel or harvested for their fruit. Elm standards, too, seem to have been unusually common, particularly close to the village, and although this particular species does have an invasive tendency, it is also possible that many were planted intentionally. Certainly, the species list is long and varied and not all these plants were robbed out of existing woodland as perhaps we might expect. Wild madder, for example, is not at all frequent in the local woodlands and, in any case, does not make an especially effective hedging plant, yet it is found in hedgerows in the north-east corner of the parish and all along its southern edge. Probably several different mechanisms account for the presence of these different species and some plantings, of course, might be later additions to already established hedgerows. The shift to an enclosed landscape was far from sudden, however. Not only did agreement to enclose take time to negotiate, but hedge plants had also to be acquired and then some took time to become established. A hawthorn hedge takes about five years to thicken sufficiently to be an effective barrier to stock; before that time, certainly with modern stock densities, sheep will find their

out with ease. There was therefore no 'moment' at which common rights were extinguished. Actions were uncoordinated and some parcels of the old open fields of Shapwick continued to function just as they had done previously, with customary tenants holding a roughly equal share of arable land in the two open fields.

Something can be deduced about the crops in the Shapwick fields from the highly productive sampling programme on post-medieval deposits at 46 Chapmans Lane. This single village plot produced large volumes of charred macrofossils, mostly wheat, oats and barley, together with small amounts of chaff. As with the medieval samples discussed in Chapter 5, both bread wheat and macaroni/bread wheats were present. There was, however, no trace of the expected increase in the variety of foodstuffs, such as root vegetables, flax or hemp and rapeseed, though it must be admitted that root and bulb crops are hard to detect archaeologically because they are harvested before the seed sets.[177] While it is noticeable that some of the weed species noted from earlier centuries are no longer present, thorow wax, cleavers and charlock among them, many others clearly were. This tends to suggest that, in this assemblage at least, the innovations of early agricultural mechanisation had made limited headway.[178] Quite possibly the majority of farmers were still essentially subsistence producers who had made little movement towards more specialised and commercial farming. The main 'crop' grown in the newly enclosed fields, as indicated by the documents, was grass.

Woodlands

Just as enclosure spelled the end of common rights in the fields around the village, so a parallel process was underway in the woodlands. During the medieval period, as we saw in Chapter 7, Shapwick's only significant woodland at Loxley was common pasture for cattle over the autumn and winter while from February to late August this access was denied and the wood was privately managed. As part of this wood-pasture arrangement, some of the villagers' stock would have grazed there, including perhaps Anthony Palmer's yoke of oxen, 'Peake' and 'Star', another ox named 'Wighte' and two 'heifer yerelinge' that he left in his will of 1592.[179] Anthony's fourteen sheep, on the other hand, were probably pastured in one of Shapwick's newly enclosed fields.

Not long after Anthony's death, however, the apparent equilibrium of this arrangement was disrupted when the two manors fell into dispute after the Rolles at Shapwick House sought forcibly to exclude other users from Loxley (Box 8.2). By the end of the eighteenth century the Rolles had achieved their aim and Loxley Wood was devoted exclusively to the growing of timber. This new management regime has a clear signature in the archaeological record. Rowena Gale's analysis of the charcoal from deposits excavated in Shapwick Park for eighteenth-century contexts shows that chunks of elm heartwood, oak heartwood, ash, beech and willow/poplar were being burnt, some of which could well have come from managed woodland such as Loxley. Other species, such as hawthorn, maple and hazel, might well have been stripped out from the many miles of newly created hedges – using them as a sort of linear coppice. This idea was first suggested by ecologist Oliver Rackham as the source of fuel for the Donyatt potteries and may well have been a more widespread practice.[180]

Industry

On mid-eighteenth-century maps a windmill is shown by the roadside on the hilltop above the village.[181] Its sails had probably continued to turn throughout this period, millers Jones and Stone being recorded as living in the village in the mid-eighteenth century.[182] We have no clues as to how often the structure had been repaired, but the windmill may well have been nearing the end of its life because it was resited only a few years later (see Chapter 9). Of the watermill at Kent Farm nothing is known, but there may have been a successor to the medieval site located at the end of the stable range there.[183]

Among the 'extractive' industries some stone quarrying presumably continued, if only to supply building stone for the houses and walls being replaced in the village.[184] There was lime-burning too, a logical by-product from the quarrying, and a kiln is shown to the south of the later Beerway Farm site on a map of 1785–87.[185] Lime for mortar, lime plaster for the outside of buildings and limewash for interior walls would have been in constant demand as houses were

built and upgraded all through the seventeenth, eighteenth and nineteenth centuries. There is also some evidence for experimentation in brick-making at Shapwick as early as the seventeenth century. The earliest securely dated bricks in a sizeable collection of some 11,559 brick and tile fragments, 143kg in all, came from the excavations near Shapwick House. Unlike later bricks they are primitively moulded and have a soft external fabric. These bricks are the forerunners to later production at clamp sites near Brickhills Copse and Brickyard Farm[186] and were probably used for internal partitions. During fieldwalking fragments of fired clay were noted in a number of fields along the edge of the Levels and they may result from the firing of bricks in temporary clamps in fields where clay could be dug.

By the early eighteenth century many of the processes that were to lead to the present appearance of the village and its landscape were underway. In a long period of transition, medieval was being reshaped to become modern. As we have seen in this chapter, the archaeological signature of these changes is especially clear to see at Shapwick in terms of household possessions and the arrival of tobacco and the implications these have for domestic and overseas trade, and through investments in what might broadly be categorised as 'display' at the two post-Dissolution manor houses, which is particularly visible in architecture and through our analysis of diet. Although the Reformation must have led to the loss of medieval church decoration and fixtures and fittings, specific acts of iconoclasm are hidden in this case by the nature of the historical record, though dissenting voices do occasionally speak to us. Across the village, however, rebuilding in the traditional vernacular style was evidently well advanced and the former open fields were rapidly being enclosed. Many land exchanges were routinely initiated by tenant farmers who agreed among themselves who was to farm what and then planted up new hedge boundaries. The Levels themselves remained largely undrained and the present-day nature reserves in the wetlands in the north of the parish give a good impression of what this landscape must have looked like – a mixture of bog, scrubby woodland, shrubs and open areas of poor wet grazing.

BOX 8.2

Loxley Wood

Much useful information about past land management is gleaned by historians from legal disputes, when evidence was gathered and written down by opposing parties. Such is the case for a long-running disagreement that lasted for well over 100 years, from the seventeenth to the mid-eighteenth century, while the two manors battled over their rights in Loxley Wood.[b14] The background is as follows. During the later Middle Ages all the land at Loxley was open to common grazing for more than half the year, a practice that continued up until 1729 or 1730, when the tenants of the Rolle family, with the connivance of their landlord, joined together to dig a ditch across the wood from north to south, thereby separating the wood into two unequal parts to serve the tenants of each of the two manors (Figure B.8.3). This ditch, referred to as 'the fence made athwart Loxley', can still be seen running through the trees and is marked 'A' on the figure. Once they had finished, the Rolle tenants erected a gate and kept it locked 'whereby the cattle of Mr Bull's tenants were and still are hindered from depasturing in the part of Loxley so enclosed in ... which is full two parts of three of it in quantity and is by much the more valuable part of this place for depasturing cattle'. Among the ditch diggers was one John Grinter, whose evidence was abbreviated to state 'that it was all fresh ground where such ditch was made and no appearance of any ditch or fence was there before. That before such ditch was made the whole of Loxley was one piece, and no ditch or fence to separate or divide one part of it from another'. All agreed that the common right had applied to the entirety of Loxley;[b15] indeed, a contemporary map marks 'the commoners ancient way into Loxley', though whether this was a post-Dissolution invention or whether the tenants of the 'rectory' manor had really been commoners in the Middle Ages is not established.

It is clear that the management of the wood was being changed from wood pasture, where tenants had the right to graze animals on the grass between the trees, a sort of wooded common, to a place in which trees were grown for timber and perhaps shrubs for coppice and underwood, and from where animals would now be excluded. The ditches and gates put in by Rolle's men at Loxley achieved just that and put an end to multiple land use in favour of private property. This was not, however, the end of the story. Our woodland survey shows that yews, a tree species that is poisonous to cattle, were planted. Twenty-five years later the right of way to Loxley Wood through Loxley Close, a field at the north-east corner of the wood, was blocked off by the Rolles, so that even the third of the wood still available to Bull/Strangways tenants was denied to them.[b16] These acts seem almost pernicious but they certainly achieved their aim; by 1791 Loxley Wood was being described as 'a large wood of fine timber',[b17] implying that all rights of pasture and access were by now extinguished. Curiously, in spite of their direct involvement in the matter, it is hard to see any benefit in this for Shapwick's tenants at all. One map of *c.*1754 refers to Loxley Close as a field where 'tenants are yet permitted to put their cattle, and as is supposed by way of compensation for ye encroachment upon the west part of Loxley, tho' it is 7 times less in value and quantity'. So perhaps this is the answer: the interested parties were given Loxley Close in informal compensation. More difficult still is to fathom why the Strangways family gave in to such bullying tactics, though long-running family illness may have left them in no mood to retaliate.

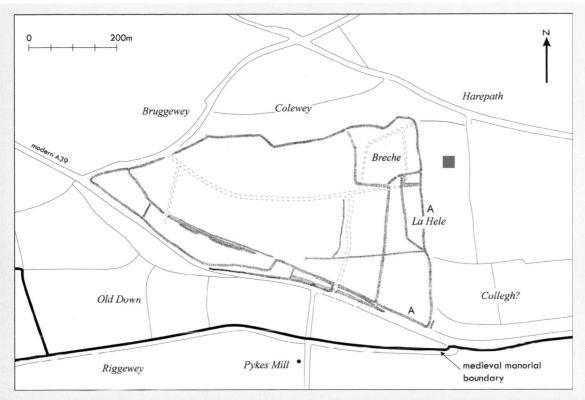

Figure B.8.3. Loxley Wood showing earthworks, medieval enclosures named in 1325 and 1515, mapped eighteenth-century features (from SRO DD/SG 15) and the manorial boundary. Ancient woodland indicator species are today present in the middle of the wood, while the irregular boundaries on the north side are typical of medieval encroachment by arable or 'assarts' (see also Figure 7.39). The boundary bank disputed in the eighteenth century is probably 'A'.

Many landowners were busy with their woods and plantations at this time. Woodland was just one more resource to be exploited commercially, not least for game, but it was also loaded with social significance. Timber was, and is, an investment for the long term, so planting saplings reflects confidence in the future, a belief that there will still be successors in the family home to take the profits many years hence. Even the tree cover itself is suggestive;[b18] oak for ship-building was the patriotic choice, and the hungry shipyards could not be fed from ancient coppiced woods like Loxley. As time went by so conifers became the popular choice for Shapwick woodlands, not only because they were faster growing and more immediately profitable but because they reiterated this continuing statement of ownership, in this case at the southern extreme of the Rolle estate.

CHAPTER NINE

Make Way for Tomorrow

Shapwick Yesterday and Today

'Miss Sophia! Miss Anna Maria! Come to the carriage and help me with the young masters John and James. Mrs Templer will be expecting us to be back at Shapwick House for afternoon tea. We had best prepare to leave now.'

'Oh! Do we have to go now, Nanny? It's my first day down at Shapwick this holiday and Aunt Jane said we might stay all afternoon,' said Anna Maria fretfully.

'No, no, we must go, cousin,' insisted Sophia. 'Don't you remember that George is coming back tonight? I haven't seen him for weeks and weeks; this is the first time he's been home since he went up to Oxford.'

'Oh, yes. I'd forgotten,' said Anna Maria, looking embarrassed. 'Do you think he will recognise me? I haven't seen him in over two years. Now I'm thirteen and Aunt Jane said I had grown a full two inches since she last saw me. It's a pity that Thomas Henry isn't here to see him. Do you think my brother has arrived in India yet? He was so looking forward to visiting all the places that Uncle George tells us about.' She paused thoughtfully and then remarked, 'I do hope Master George isn't going to pull my hair this time.'

Sophia laughed and pulled a face. 'No, he is hardly likely to do that. He has grown very pompous of late, and hardly speaks to us "children" at all. But I think you were always his favourite, Anna! Come, let's get the boys into the barouche. We won't be able to drive along the Nidon avenue today, the ground is too wet, and it always takes longer past the Bathing House and Beerways.'

The young cousins climbed into the carriage whilst the footman gathered the remains of their picnic into a large basket that he hoisted up next to him. Twenty minutes later the carriage pulled onto the long winding drive, past the old barn, across the ha-ha and up to the front of Shapwick House.

The ensemble made its way into the hall, and Nanny tried to marshal them upstairs to the nursery to make them presentable before tea time. They usually took tea in the nursery but today they would be joining their mother in the drawing room.

The sound of horses' hooves brought the children rushing back down to the hall, and, as they tore down the last few stairs, Mr Templer and his 18-year-old son, Master George, entered the front doors, opened wide by the footman. George stood gravely to one side whilst his father roughly embraced his children and pinched his niece Anna Maria on the cheek. 'My word, you all look well today. Have you been out in the park?'

'No, Father,' replied Sophia, 'we have been over to Henhills to see the fish in the pond and we had a picnic lunch in the cocoa house.'

'Well, that's splendid. Now say hello to your brother George. He has come down from Oxford especially to see you, Anna Maria,' teased her uncle, bringing the colour to both their cheeks. Anna Maria dropped a curtsey to Master George and held out her hand. She had gone to a lot of trouble with her dress and even put on little lace gloves. She didn't want him to think her a child.

George took her hand with an air of studied civility and bowed his head. 'Miss Anna Maria! Have we met before? I don't remember ever having been introduced to such a lovely young lady.'

Anna Maria's reserve broke and she giggled, which was the signal for George to whisk her up into the air and swirl her around. 'No, no. You ought not to do that anymore. I am far too grown up for that now,' she scolded, 'You will crease my gown. Put me down at once.'

There was much happy talk and laughter as the group made their way into the drawing room. Mrs Templer, who was sitting near the fire, was a renowned beauty. Putting down the creamware jug, she gracefully held out her hand to her eldest son. 'Welcome, George. It is such a comfort to see you looking so well.'

'Hello, Mater. You look radiant as ever. Is that a new gown – from Bath, I expect? It's very becoming.'

Mrs Templer laughed. 'He's lost none of his charm since he's been away, has he? I'll ring for more tea now.'

Sometime later the children were just preparing to go upstairs with their nurse when a loud knocking at the front door disturbed the leave-taking. The noise abated and the Templer family looked anxiously towards the door of the drawing room, which was flung open as neighbour Henry Strangways entered in a distraught state, clutching a copy of the Gentleman's Magazine.

'Madam, Sir.' He bowed. 'I must speak with you now, George, in private,' he said breathlessly.

'We will go immediately into my study. Come,' Mr Templer ushered him out of the door.

'It is bad news indeed, George. I have it here. I have just this minute read it. An appalling business … tragic, tragic … How are we to break the news?'

'Calm yourself, Thomas. What has happened? Let me see what you have there.'

Henry Strangways handed the latest copy of the Gentleman's Magazine to George Templer. The news was devastating and would affect all of them deeply.

The Bengal correspondent reported that on 7 October 1800 the East India Company ship *Kent* had been taken in the Bay of Bengal by a French privateer under one Robert Surcouf. Eleven English lost their lives, including Anna Maria's 16-year-old brother, Thomas Graham, who had reportedly gone up on deck to see the action. Thomas Graham had been brought up at Shapwick House by his Aunt Jane and was presumably on his way out to see his relatives in India. Some years later, Anna Maria, at the age of 20, married the Reverend George Templer, shortly after he took up the curacy of Shapwick church. A memorial with an urn finial to Henry Strangways' father Thomas can still be found there.

Thatched roofs, dirt roads and an almost complete absence of traffic: this would have been the scene that greeted the Shapwick visitor in the second half of the eighteenth century. But during the next 250 years the appearance of the village and the life of its inhabitants were to be altered in significant ways. Landscaping and the creation of parkland, particularly around Shapwick House, but also, to a lesser extent, at Shapwick Manor, led to a major recasting of the village plan that continued well into the nineteenth century. These changes remind us how, until relatively recently, ownership of the soil was the unique basis of prestige and authority, and the extent to which the life of tenants was dictated by their landlords. Most notably, there was to be an almost total rebuilding of the cottages and other dwellings in the village and a good many new houses were constructed. Many of the houses that still stand in the village today were either built or extensively modified at this time, although in recent years there has been some further building, in addition to the conversion of derelict farm buildings and the infilling of many orchards and paddocks.

Meanwhile, out in the fields beyond the village, the current pattern of farmsteads was also established during this period. The great open fields with their furlongs and strips, which had probably existed in some form for almost a thousand years, were completely enclosed and many of the field boundaries, hedges and woodlands to be seen today were first planted. Within the space of a single lifespan the Levels were finally drained and the east–west line of communication along the Poldens, which had been dominant since at least Roman times, was now supplemented by an important north–south route that traversed the Levels to Westhay and beyond. The parish also gained both a canal and a railway line that connected Shapwick to towns and cities for the first time, and ultimately to every corner of the country. The wider social and political context of our story becomes increasingly central as Britain acquired its worldwide empire and an international industrialised economy.

These latest episodes of our rural past were firmly on our research agenda and during the course of the Project we made a conscious effort to bring our archaeological and historical 'toolkit' to bear on more recent sites. We examined pottery, clay pipes and glass with as much rigour as prehistoric flints, recognising that even the near-contemporary lives and everyday activities of Shapwick's villagers cannot be told entirely through written records. Along the way we discovered for ourselves the real excitement of working on the archaeology of this period, partly through the melding together of written and physical evidence, partly in the more direct personal linkages with the houses and landscapes we see around us today.

The village

Lanes and streets

There was considerable disruption to Shapwick's lanes and streets first in the late eighteenth century, when Shapwick Park was created (see below), and then again in the early nineteenth century, when a turnpike route was made through the village. Although most minor lanes and tracks continued to be maintained by the parish, turnpikes were a means of improving long-distance routes by levying tolls on their users. The future income from the road was effectively mortgaged to provide the necessary investment to pay for better road surfaces in gravel, stone and anything else that was needed to create a faster route for horses, people and goods.

Figure 9.1 shows the route of the turnpike through the village. Previously the north–south traveller had made do with a series of straight lengths of road fitted in between the east–west routes along the Poldens. Now this route was made more direct by smoothing

out corners near Home Farm and, from the parish church southwards, cutting a new stretch of road nearly 400m long. The evidence for this realignment can still be seen today. Odd corners of grass at the sides of the modern asphalt betray the line of the medieval route and several modern houses have cracked façades where their foundations are gently subsiding into the infill of the hollow-way. In 1999 a short stretch of earthwork in the garden of the Old Bakery was still plainly visible and, when excavated, proved to be the worn depression of the old road filled with clay, limestone and domestic rubbish.[1] Some houses were also affected by the new route. The cottages at 2 and 4 Northbrook Road are the remains of an earlier house and outbuilding[2] which was actually cut in half by the new road. Immediately to the south, the Schoolhouse, otherwise 3 and 5 Main Road, was 'turned' to face west by constructing a two-storey extension block immediately next to the new Main Road. Meanwhile, at the south end of the village, where travellers once struggled up the hill towards the old windmill, a new, gentler route, better suited to horse-drawn vehicles at a downhill canter, now wound its way up to the 'Great Road on the Hill'.

These changes were all complete by the time the tithe map was drawn in 1839 and it is reasonable to assume that they took place in the late 1820s and the early years of the 1830s. The body responsible was the Wedmore Turnpike Trust, which, between 1827 and 1874, maintained this section of road as part of its longer turnpike. Leaving the village of Shipham on the Mendip Hills to the north, where this route joined the modern A38 above Churchill Rocks, the road crossed the Axe valley and then ran through Wedmore and Shapwick up to the present A39 trunk road on the Poldens. Both the modern trunk roads at either end of the new turnpike were themselves important eighteenth-century routes. The later A38 was improved by the Bristol Trust in 1749, while the road along the Poldens became a turnpike under the auspices of the Bridgwater Trust (1730–1870) ten years later.[3] One of its milestones still survives at the south-east corner of Loxley Wood, but perhaps the most obvious reminder are the many cottages built by the Trust to house their 'keepers'. Several toll houses, which once displayed and collected tolls from the passing traffic, can still be seen along the Wedmore

Figure 9.1. Changes in the north–south route through the village at the beginning of the nineteenth century. This figure compares maps from 1764 and 1885 and shows how the main road through the village was straightened. Where once the major routes had run east–west, they now became north–south. New housing reflected this axis in the alignments of their frontages while the Park at the north end of the village was 'bypassed' to the west.

Trust route at Shipham, Clewer and Westhay (Figure 9.2). There was once a tollhouse, too, near Moorgate Farm on the edge of the Levels, overlooking the route northwards;[4] its site produced a concentration of nineteenth-century domestic debris when it was fieldwalked. No doubt the tollhouse looked similar to those that still survive – single storey with a polygonal front facing the road, as illustrated here by Victor Ambrus (Figure 9.3). Given that no brick fragments were found, the Shapwick example was probably built of local Lias, with a red tile roof.

If, as a result of the turnpike 'improvements', some housing was demolished and the sizes and shapes of some village plots had to be slightly adjusted, these were relatively small-scale changes in comparison to the longer-term impacts. In effect the orientation of the entire village was now 'turned' through 90° so that, where once almost all the houses were strung out along the 'rungs' of the ladder pattern of the village, Shapwick's plan now took on a more linear appearance, with houses and farms facing east and west onto what had become a 'main' road. By 1885, housing had already begun to be constructed along this new north–south axis. A second, even more important novelty was that there was now a direct route northwards. Even at the time of the Day and Masters map of 1782 there was still no way across the Brue valley, a marsh labelled then as 'Burtle Moor and Heath' stretching from Woolavington in the west to Glastonbury in the east.[5] Now, with the benefit of the turnpike, journeys to Wedmore and onwards to Cheddar were more comfortable and faster. For the first time Shapwick became well connected through a comprehensive network of roads to all the main market towns in the region – Bridgwater to the west, Glastonbury and Wells to the east, Bristol, Axbridge, Cheddar and Wedmore to the north and Taunton to the south-west. Bridgwater particularly appears to have been the destination of choice, as it was for Joseph Sully in 1827, who was returning from the market there when he was thrown from the 'light cart' with two others and 'expired without groan or struggle' aged 101.[6]

Most turnpike trusts, including the Wedmore Trust, ceased to function between 1873 and 1878. Responsibility for roads then passed to a Highways Board and, after the Local Government Act of 1888,

county councils took up the baton. Though there were many later improvements, such as asphalt and signposting for the motor-car in the 1930s, these are minor adjustments when compared to the decisions taken by the turnpike trustees; it was they who were bold enough to break the mould of the medieval transport network.

Village plots

The late eighteenth and early nineteenth centuries saw an important phase of new investment in agricultural buildings, at least for those farms belonging to the Shapwick Manor estate.[7] A major contribution to this reorganisation was the non-renewal of life leaseholds on village farmsteads and their replacement with short-term tenancies, so-called 'rack rents'. At the same time, whereas the larger agricultural buildings such as barns had previously stood cheek-by-jowl with the mansions at Shapwick House and Shapwick Manor while farming was held 'in hand', that constraint was now lifted as demesne land began to be released. The effect was to create larger farming units elsewhere and give impetus to the construction of more specialised and efficient agricultural buildings.[8] Home Farm, at the northern end of the village, was equipped with a stable block for plough and cart horses together with a threshing barn, cattle yard and cowsheds for its mixed beef/dairy enterprise. The layout of Church and New Farms (Figure 9.4), on the other hand, suggests a greater emphasis on milk production with some subsidiary beef; arable here would have been dedicated largely to the growing of fodder. Hill, Little Church, Old (or King's) and Bowerings Farms all seem also to have been dairy units, so the sight of herds ambling through the village on their way to and from milking would have passed entirely without comment.[9]

For the archaeologist, working mostly below ground level, this investment is immediately visible in the reorganisation of boundaries and drains and new surfaces such as the cobbled yards for the dairy unit at Lawn Farm.[10] Evidence for the animals themselves is harder to come by except where some disaster befell the stockman. The litter of four- to six-month-old pigs buried near the village spring, for example, was presumably not easily disposed of. They must have been diseased because they had not been

Figure 9.2. Tollhouses at Shipham (A), Clewer (B) and Westhay (C) along the turnpike operated by the Wedmore Trust. The tollhouse across the road from Moorgate Farm must have been similar in appearance.

Figure 9.3. Reconstruction by Victor Ambrus of the early nineteenth century toll house at Shapwick, based on surviving examples. The census reveals that the toll keeper was more often than not a woman and she is seen here blocking the road in front of her toll cottage.

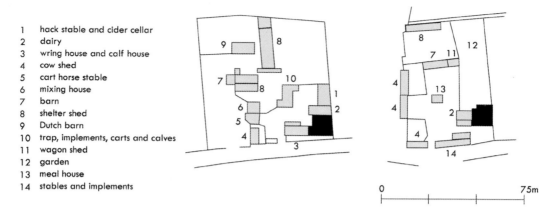

1 hack stable and cider cellar
2 dairy
3 wring house and calf house
4 cow shed
5 cart horse stable
6 mixing house
7 barn
8 shelter shed
9 Dutch barn
10 trap, implements, carts and calves
11 wagon shed
12 garden
13 meal house
14 stables and implements

Figure 9.4. Layout of Church(yard) Farm (left) and New Farm (right). These farms are more efficiently laid out than their predecessors and their buildings have dedicated functions, in this case with an emphasis on milk production with some subsidiary arable.

butchered[11] and their minimal tooth wear suggests that they had been fed in a sty. Farmyard animals would evidently have been present on most properties and pigs, in particular, were often a complement to cheese-making, and encouraged at least one novel architectural adaption at New Farm (Figure 9.5).[12]

The pigs certainly would have enjoyed the apples from Shapwick's orchards, of which we found plentiful evidence. At 27 Durstons Lane and north of Bridewell Lane several tree holes were excavated: sub-circular shallow pits with rootlet holes all around the rim, filled with loose Lias stones and soil (for locations see Figure 9.1). One had a stakehole alongside.[13] The local custom, so eighteenth-century agricultural writers inform us, was to plant orchard trees every thirty feet or so with the intention of 'rooting up every other tree (when) fifteen or twenty years old',[14] but there was little from our excavations to suggest such regular spacings. Cider cellars, however, were identified by the standing buildings team at Church Farm, Hill Farm, Home and New Farm and it is here that the apple juice would have been stored in casks after it has been pressed from the apples and filtered. The cellars were cool enough to allow the cider to ferment slowly through the winter months.[15]

Gardens themselves had little space to spare, as we found to the rear of the Old Bakery. There were postholes here for former fence lines, rubble and mortar hardstanding, perhaps for a wagon house, with a track leading to it (Figure 9.6), various generations

of drains and, as might be expected, garden beds with paths. Although most gardens must have had privies, few had wells; perhaps the Lias slab bedrock was just too hard to cut through. People relied on the spring, the village stream and rainwater off the roofs of buildings. The most striking thing about sites of this date, however, is the sheer quantity of domestic rubbish they generated; some green spaces around properties were evidently considered ideal for the disposal of unwanted waste and excavators regularly encountered large shallow pits filled with early nineteenth-century pottery, nails, brick, tile and mortar.[16] Unsightly material was obviously buried and then disguised by spreading the excavated subsoils about. Domestic rubbish, meanwhile, seems to have been incorporated into manure piles and then either carted out into the fields, where our teams retrieved it again during fieldwalking, or else mulched onto garden beds nearer the house. At the Old Bakery the soils contained a hotchpotch of discarded objects: buckles, a harness mount, a bottle marble, wine bottles and a good selection of clay pipes. There was also coal, cinders and undiagnostic slags in great quantities, remnants of the daily ritual of sweepings from the baker's ovens and fireplace grates.[17] Finally, several generations of 'faithful companions' had been buried out in yards and back gardens, as is still sometimes the custom today. At the Old Bakery, one of these animals was a dog with pronounced abscess-like lesions on its legs, which

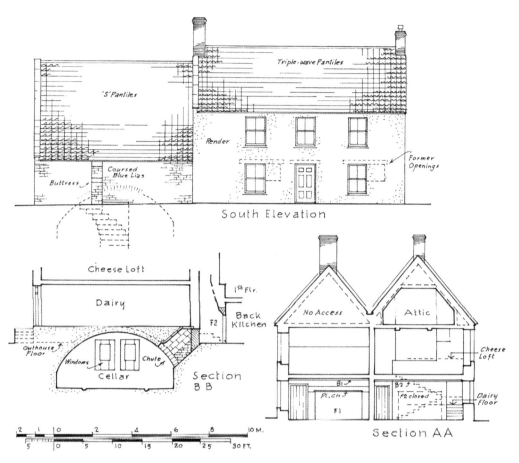

Figure 9.5. An unusual cellar at New Farm, probably for curing pork. The cellar was equipped with a furnace for heating water, chutes for efficient movement of the pig carcasses, hooks for hanging and good ventilation as well as a smoking chamber for hams and bacon.

Figure 9.6. Excavations at the Old Bakery. Late nineteenth-century metalling to rear of the garden.

Figure 9.7. Reconstruction of the Old Bakery in the later nineteenth century, by Victor Ambrus. Note the chained dog.

had probably spent much of its life chained up. The absence of damage to the dog's left tibia suggests that the dog may have had a preferred direction to circle (Figure 9.7).[18]

Housing
Farmhouses in the village

In all there were nine farms within the village during this period (Figure 9.8), together with the same number outside (see below). These housed families, their servants and sometimes workers who made a living from agriculture. Unlike the farm buildings, the preference as far as the houses were concerned was to extend, remodel and reface existing dwellings rather than to build entirely afresh. At New Farmhouse, a double-pile house of the early eighteenth century, a service block was added in the 1780s and the east gable wall rebuilt in the nineteenth century. The motive in this case was to convert an existing house into a farmhouse. Many farmhouses exhibit evidence for a continuous campaign of repair and improvement. For example, Home Farmhouse (Figure 9.9) is a house of late sixteenth-century origins with a two-storey wing added in the mid-seventeenth century. Then, during

the eighteenth century, the whole roof was raised and the interior comprehensively remodelled; good eighteenth-century joinery survives in the hall and wing. The farmhouse least affected seems to have been Bowerings, a seventeenth-century build, though even here a dairy was appended to the service end.

Other houses

Not all Shapwick villagers lived in farmhouses and many earlier dwellings persisted with only minor alteration. Some were extended, such as Forsters, the late fifteenth-century survival, where a blacksmith's shop was now added, or 50 Station Road, an eighteenth-century cottage that was extended in the early nineteenth century and later divided in two.[19] Following the trend seen in farmhouses, roofs were also raised and elevations refronted. Numbers 22 and 24 Bridewell Lane are examples of this, as is Church Cottage.

New builds were of varying plan. Among the more compact dwellings was 2 Timberyard (Figure 9.10A), constructed in the early nineteenth century in virtually identical fashion to its neighbour at number 4 with only one fireplace, a kitchen/living room and

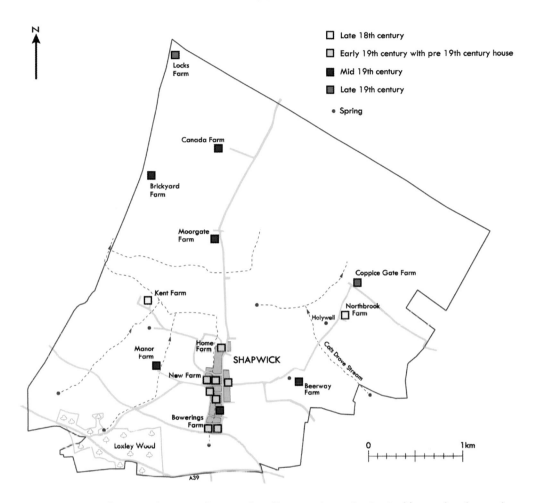

Figure 9.8. Locations of nineteenth-century farms in the village, together with other buildings referred to in the text.

an unheated service room on the ground floor. Quite a number of similar cottages were erected during the nineteenth century, though more often than not they have one-room frontages and a service room behind, the living space being at the front of the building. Kiln and Knapp Cottages are one such pair (Figure 9.10B), the Old Bakery (despite appearances) another, and 1–9 Church Road is a terrace of five identical cottages whose entrances also open directly onto the kitchen/living room.[20] A group of four pairs had also been constructed along the High Street by the time of the 1839 tithe map, probably to accommodate those families who had been displaced when Shapwick Park was created (see below). At least some of those made

homeless may have been forced into sharing existing housing stock. Multiple occupancy was common in the nineteenth century in rural areas, resulting in overcrowding that seems unbelievable today. The 1841 census reveals no fewer than twenty individuals at Brook Cottage, a house with only one heated room, seventeen people at 2–4 Northbrook Road, thirteen at Keeper's Cottage and nine at Forsters. Vagaries of the census data aside, houses with five occupants or fewer were very much in the minority.[21]

Among the new houses with more generous proportions and better heating was Little Lawn, a rebuilding of a house on the same spot in the late eighteenth century (Figure 9.10C). This house was

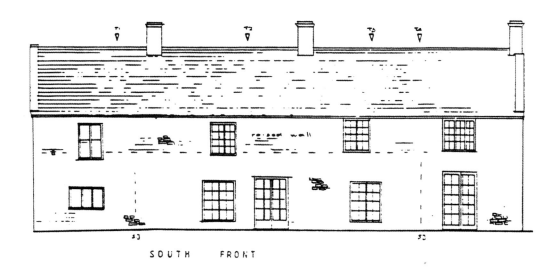

SOUTH FRONT

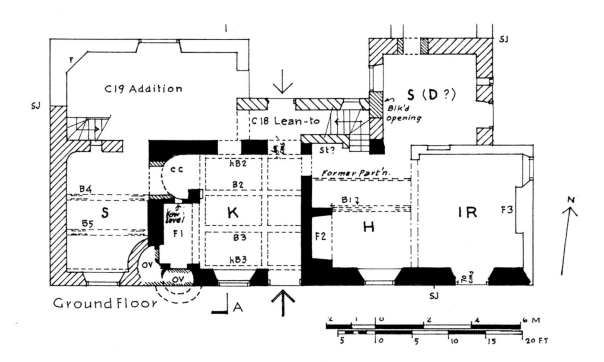

Figure 9.9. Home Farmhouse, at the north end of the village. South front and phased plan. This house was originally a traditional three-room plan of late sixteenth-century date. A two-storey wing was added in the next century and much of the interior was remodelled in the eighteenth century. The house exhibits a complete sequence of changes over 300 years.

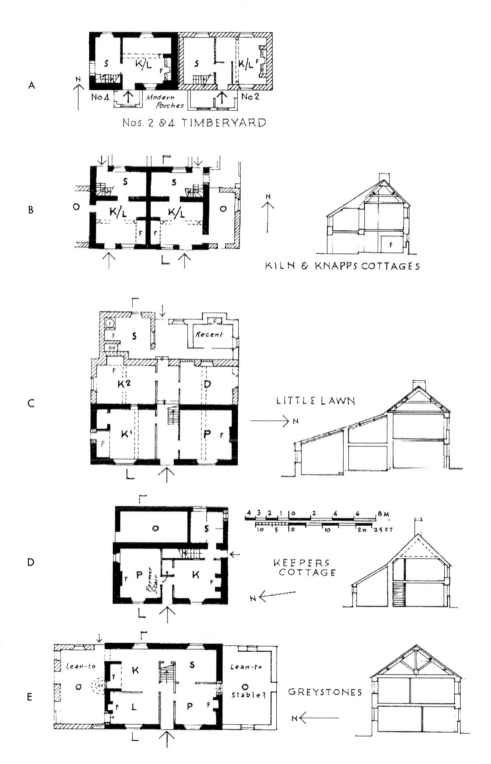

Figure 9.10. Plans of nineteenth-century buildings at Shapwick, including compact houses at Timberyard (A) and Kiln and Knapp Cottages (B) and those with more generous proportions at Little Lawn (C) Keepers (D) and Greystones (E).

originally one room deep with two fireplaces but a lean-to extension was then added, probably for commercial baking since the house was occupied by miller William Jones and his family. Keeper's Cottage, an early nineteenth-century build, is similar in plan (Figure 9.10D), though here the lean-to at the rear was integral to the design. The double-pile plan of Greystones was evidently constructed after the 1839 tithe map was drawn up (Figure 9.10E). Lawn House is also mid-nineteenth century in date and is probably a substantial rebuild by Shapwick's major landowner George Warry, who was living there in the 1841 census. The Vicarage is late nineteenth century in origin but was largely rebuilt in 1926 after a disastrous fire six years earlier during which a horse-drawn fire engine from Glastonbury was delayed on the icy roads.[22]

Until the late eighteenth century, then, the appearance of the village largely reflected traditional methods and materials: thatch, West Country slate[23] and Lias roof tiles were still the norm, despite the proximity of the many brickworks around Bridgwater. This began to change only when the housing in the village was upgraded. Wall levels were raised and sometimes refaced to give greater height to houses and so increase comfort in upstairs rooms. As a result the angle of the roof became shallower and thatch came to be replaced with pantiles. Welsh slate also began to appear on the roofs of some of the larger nineteenth-century houses, such as the Vicarage, while windows were modernised with sashes and casements. A uniform visual character now came to dominate the village, one that might be considered typical of 'improving' landlords in the late eighteenth and early nineteenth centuries.[24]

Possessions and diet

Whereas most families in the later Middle Ages had very few material possessions, by the late eighteenth century the situation was quite different. Households now contained pottery in abundance in a myriad of styles and forms that could be used for individual place settings at the table and specialist functions in the kitchen. In part these changes were fuelled by new social rituals such as tea- and coffee-drinking, so that, in affluent houses, the serving and drinking of beverages became almost ceremonial in tone, with strict rules of refined social behaviour.[25] The

cultivation of the appearance of politeness and civility necessitated a greater diversity of utensils, ceramics and containers as well as genteel dress and fine tablecloths, at least for those who could afford it.

These trends are quickly seen in diluted form in the collection of late eighteenth- and nineteenth-century ceramics from the village. Excavations at one typical plot in Bridewell Lane[26] produced a tortoiseshell dish and tea-pot, a printed creamware bowl, a painted creamware mug and bowl, a rouletted creamware plate and an oval serving dish (Figure 9.11). Together with these finewares there were also plain creamware mugs, plates, bowls and serving dishes, a navy blue earthenware teapot, plain and decorated pearlwares (hand-painted, printed and sponged), a factory-made slipware mug, plain and decorated porcelain, Nottingham-style stoneware mugs, a press-moulded stoneware dish and a plain red-ware mug. This collection can be dated with confidence to the period from around 1750 to around 1830. What is immediately striking is not only the sheer quantity of material, but also just how many are dearer products that come from Bristol or Staffordshire, rather than cheaper versions from nearby Donyatt. Many can be matched up into sets. Although Bridewell Lane was not among the highest valued properties in the village,[27] tea-drinking here was evidently the norm. Creamware, with its fine pale body and transparent glaze, was in use even in the very poorest households.

Unfortunately, very few groups of early modern artefacts can be linked with confidence to particular plots or named tenant families. The reason for this is that rubbish was no longer buried in pits in backyards; almost all 'modern' pottery was recovered from garden soils and levelling layers. From the Old Bakery[28] there were nineteenth-century printed and moulded pearlwares, bone china, modern lustrewares and a range of pancheons, storage jars and ink bottles that must relate to the use of the building (Figure 9.12), as must the seventy-six bottles and oven tiles.[29] The pancheons or large bowls were perhaps for mixing dough. One jam jar has a black printed inscription that reads [ORANG]E ME[RMALADE] LONDO[N]. Bones found on the site indicate a varied diet: hake, ling, beef, veal, mutton and pork.[30] Despite their busy routine the baker and his family clearly enjoyed a comfortable standard of living and the pottery they used at the table reflected links

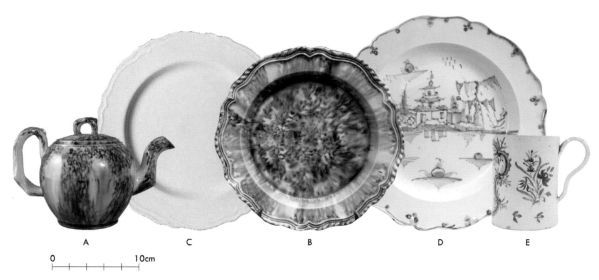

Figure 9.11. Late eighteenth-century pottery from excavations at Bridewell Lane includes decorated creamwares similar to those illustrated here: a tortoiseshell tea-pot (A) and dish (B), moulded creamware dish (C), hand-painted creamware dish (D) and a polychrome creamware mug (E).

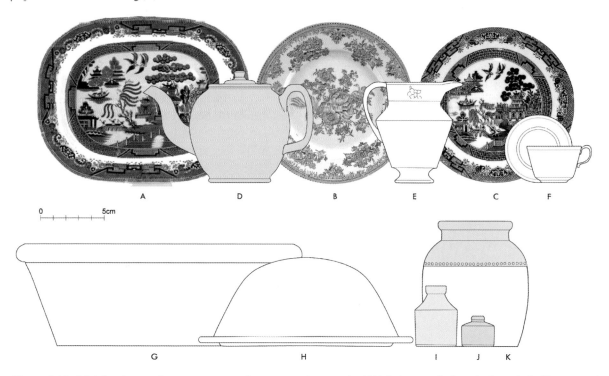

Figure 9.12. Mainly nineteenth-century pottery from excavations at the Old Bakery, including A, B and C: blue-printed pearlwares, a serving dish and two plates, late eighteenth–early nineteenth century. D: Rockingham-type teapot, all over brown glaze. E: lustreware jug, all over lustre with blue band at neck and moulded polychrome decoration. F: plain bone china with gilded lines. G: pancheon, internal brown glaze, South Somerset industrially made ware. H: bowl with internal brown glaze, South Somerset industrially made ware. I: cylindrical bottle Bristol-type glazed stoneware. J: ink bottle, brown stoneware. K: Bristol-type stoneware jar. Vessels D–K are all nineteenth century in date.

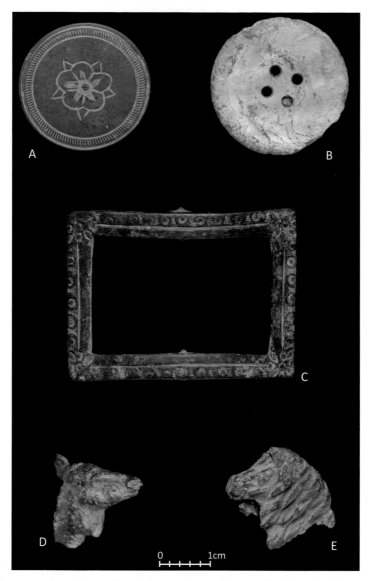

Figure 9.13. Nineteenth-century objects from village houses. A: button disc incised with petalled flower motif. B: button, mother of pearl on thin sheet metal backing. C: double-looped buckle, the central baluster bar is missing. D: lead toy, head of a donkey. E: lead toy, head of a sheep, possibly from a farmyard or Noah's Ark set.

with manufacturers all over Britain, not only from Bridgwater and Bristol but also from north Devon, Nottinghamshire, Derbyshire and even Sunderland, in the north-east. Similarly, the nineteenth-century clay pipes found at Shapwick, the workshops for which can sometimes be located with great accuracy, reveal products arriving from makers in Shepton

Mallet, Taunton and as far afield as Liverpool. One of the makers whose wares are represented at Shapwick in the middle of the century are the Ring family of Bristol who, as well as exporting to the Americas, managed to reach rural areas such as Shapwick through shopkeepers in the port of Bridgwater.[31] Retailers in local towns presented opportunities to

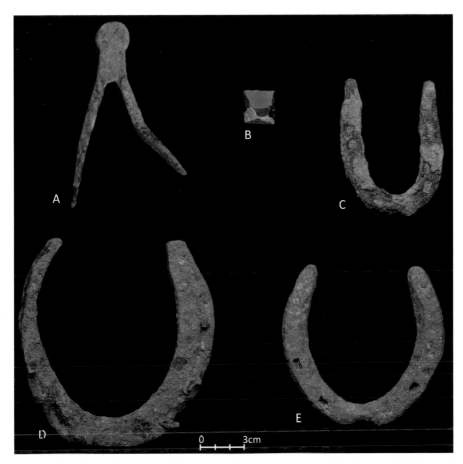

Figure 9.14. Agricultural and everyday objects of the nineteenth century. A: pair of dividers, possibly for use by a carpenter. B: gun flint. C: mule/donkey shoe with feathered heel and toe clip. D: horseshoe with side clips and differential arms. E: horseshoe with toe clip and bevelled section.

purchase all kinds of products for the home, from lead glass goblets to wine bottles.

A great range of finds of nineteenth-century date were recovered. These include dress accessories such as buttons and shoe buckles (Figure 9.13A–C), children's toys such as a pipeclay figurine, possibly made in Germany,[32] and two lead animals from a child's farmyard set or Noah's ark (Figure 9.13D–E). Among the agricultural items was a pair of dividers (Figure 9.14A), perhaps for use by a local carpenter, and many shoes for horses and donkeys/mules (Figure 9.14C–E). There were also four gunflints, three of them found by fieldwalkers. These are the distinctively wedge-shaped flints used to produce a spark when struck against steel so as to ignite the charge that fired

a flintlock gun (Figure 9.14B). The date suggested for these particular flints is from after 1770 up to the 1840s.[33] Other casual losses included coins: a George II Irish halfpenny, a George III halfpenny and a penny, three Victorian halfpennies and three Victorian pennies.[34]

If there is little among this metalwork to hint at greater affluence among the ordinary village residents, the same must be said for diet. The animal stock farmed in the eighteenth and nineteenth centuries went unchanged from earlier centuries. Sheep bones outnumber cattle and pig together, and there are more cattle than pig, although the pattern does vary across the village.[35] These variations may be more of a reflection of the bones present in our small sample sizes than what was really happening.[36] There is no reason to suppose that good tables were not kept in many village houses and this rather dull butcher's list might easily equate to tasty ham rashers, potatoes fried in cream, buttered toast and eggs for breakfast and sometimes beef-steak for lunch, followed by home-brewed beer and smoking, then tea and cards, with a supper of bread and cheese before bed. These dishes are all locally documented[37] and even the poorest households could muster pea soup, herring and potatoes, boiled peas, a basin of gruel, bacon and potatoes and suppers of tea with bread and butter, all of which are described at the trial of murderess Sarah Freeman.[38] Disregarding for a moment her addition of fatal dosages of arsenic, many of these dishes were fresher and more seasonal than most diets are today. Like many villagers, the nineteenth-century baker's family kept poultry, presumably to provide a steady supply of eggs for their cakes, but they also ate rabbits and probably bred them in hutches. In turn this seems to have attracted rats, a species almost unknown from other post-medieval sites in Shapwick.[39] High society with showy banquets this was not, but then neither did Shapwick's Victorians suffer like the urban factory worker.

Occupations

On a couple of occasions the suite of archaeological finds recovered from an excavated site was unusually distinctive, sufficiently so as to suggest the occupation of its tenant. The marmalade jars and bottles from the Old Bakery are one example, but altogether more unusual were the faunal remains from north of Bridewell Lane. Among these the bones of a roe deer, a fox, duck and moles, together with a gunflint, from which it might be deduced that this was the house of a gamekeeper who kept a gibbet for the vermin, or perhaps of a local poacher.[40] Otherwise, to learn more about skills and trades we have to rely on a combination of documents and maps, in this case the 1839 tithe map coupled with the 1841 census. Together they can be used to create a kind of social 'map' of the village for the mid-nineteenth century (Figure 9.15). As the map indicates, a stroll up the High Street in 1841 from north to south would take the inquisitive stranger past a series of cottages occupied by resident agricultural labourers, by the home of a plumber and up to several farms clustered near the church. A gardener lived at Church

Cottage and there was clearly a range of employment available in construction for Shapwick's five masons, four carpenters and plumber. Crafts are represented by a tailor who lived at Forsters, shoemakers and a basket maker and the food trades by two millers and a butcher. The census data also demonstrate that the vast majority of Shapwick inhabitants were born in the village, with a only smattering coming from surrounding villages such as Curry Rivel, Greinton, Street and West Coker and a very few from adjacent counties. Most exotic in 1851 were the schoolmistress, born in Calcutta (modern Kolkata), and the vicar, Thomas Mason, who was born in Bengal;[41] they were among a handful of professional people living in the village.

Figure 9.16 lists the trades of villagers ten years later in 1851 when, as might be expected, farming is again the dominant occupation. Each farm employed between one and eight people, variously described as 'boys', 'labourers' and 'women', and they would have been stockmen and dairymaids. Just over half the working males in Shapwick were involved with agriculture, while most of the women worked in domestic service and would have undertaken additional tasks in the home, such as cheesemaking, washing, cooking and curing, as well as finding seasonal employment at haymaking and the harvest. Many houses took in others, often a house servant, a farm boy or a labourer with a direct connection of employment, although several houses also allowed lodgers, who were usually farm labourers. One of those who gave evidence at the trial of Sarah Freeman was a typical lodger, John Wake. He lived in Sarah's house together with her husband, Henry, and her illegitimate child James. There were therefore four people in the house (at nearby Pedwell) and, though he was not a relative, John gave evidence to the effect that he slept in the same bed as James, who was at the time 6 or 7 years old. The sharing of rooms and beds was not considered unusual in any way.[42] After 1861, when the census allows us to establish consistently which families were linked to which farms, we find that neither farm labourers nor tenants stayed in the village for long: mostly for terms of less than ten years. Labourers were often forced to move on in search of work and even tenant farmers routinely left their holdings when their leases came up. There was no great desire to remain and long-term stability of tenants was rare.[43]

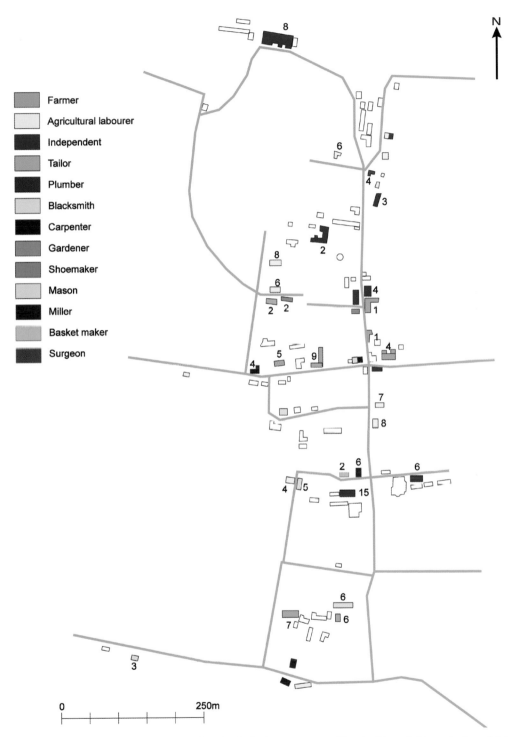

Figure 9.15. A 'social' map of the village in around 1841. Only the occupations of heads of households are indicated. Most of those living in the village were listed either as farmers or agricultural labourers, though a range of other employment was available. The numbers indicate the total number of householders present on the day of the census.

	Males		Females	
Farming	farm labourer	58	dairywoman	1
	farm boy	8		
	farmer	7		
	farm servant	5		
	farm bailiff	1		
	farmer's assistant	1		
	farmer's workman	1		
Domestic service	gardener	3	house servant	15
	footman	2	nurse	5
	gamekeeper	1	cook	2
	groom	1	housemaid	2
	house servant	1	housekeeper	1
			kitchenmaid	1
Skilled trades	carpenter	7	dressmaker	5
	shoemaker	7	basketmaker	1
	stone mason	6	needlewoman	1
	baker	2	tailoress	1
	blacksmith	2	shoemistress	1
	butcher	2		
	plumber	2		
	sawyer	2		
	tailor	2		
	brick and tile maker	1		
	glazier	1		
	miller	1		
	thatcher	1		
Professional	barrister	1	schoolmistress	2
	landed proprietor	1	governess	1
	vicar	1		
Retailers	turf merchant	2		
	shopkeeper	1		
Other	labourer	6	gatekeeper	1
			laundress	1
Retired, etc.	pauper	3	pauper	2
	Chelsea pensioner	2		
	farmer (former)	1		
	surgeon (ret)	1		
Children	scholar	32	scholar	37
	infant under 6, not 'scholar'	16	infant under 6, not 'scholar'	15
Given no occupation		15		102
TOTAL		207		197

Figure 9.16. Trades and occupations in 1851, derived from census data. The variety of trades listed is impressive; the village would have been almost self-sufficient in its needs for anything from glazing windows to mending a hole in the roof.

The church

The body of Shapwick church was restored in 1861 by the Victorian architect George Gilbert Scott, who went on to supervise several similar projects in the county.[44] Scott gave the chancel a new roof and restored the nave, reputedly reusing some of the original fifteenth-century timber there. Any old box or bench pews would have been done away with at that time – certainly, tombstones in the nave and elsewhere were removed – and fittings such as the font, lectern and reredos renewed. The mid-nineteenth-century stained glass, too, probably dates to Scott's time.[45]

During excavations of the adjacent plot to the north of the church (see Figure 8.4C) fragments of thirteenth- to fourteenth-century floor tiles (see Figure 7.20C–E) and 1,455 pieces of roofing slate were discovered. They had probably been dumped over the churchyard wall by Scott's workmen.[46] Buttresses were also added to the tower at this time and the original pinnacles and balustrade were replaced by a parapet.

The restoration of Shapwick church was part of a widespread movement in the nineteenth century; many church buildings were in a poor state of repair and the increased wealth of the time could result in drastic structural alterations to or even rebuildings of medieval churches. One contemporary visitor to St Mary's thought the church had been left 'without beauty or interest' after Scott's intervention,[47] but, then again, the condition of the church in the 1850s is unknown to us. While early prospects do not show much dilapidation, there was obviously a mood for change and the restoration was paid for by public subscription. It is significant that, while the Warry family made a handsome donation, it was the Strangways who paid for the restoration of the chancel, which included a new altar rail of Australian oak shipped over in 1861, presumably by Henry Bull Templer Strangways (see below). This responsibility for a specific part of the body of the church stemmed from the medieval division of the two estates, the abbot's (Shapwick House, now Warry) and the rector's (Shapwick Manor, now Strangways); the latter dictated what could and could not be done in the chancel. The two landowning families were constantly in dispute over church matters.[48] In his diaries the vicar recounted that after one sermon on the forgiveness of injuries, probably sometime in the 1860s, Strangways and Warry left their seats and met halfway, under the tower, shook hands and knelt together at the altar. People wept. In a spirit of reconciliation, lawsuits were withdrawn on the Monday, but by the following Saturday one family had already brought an action against the other for illegal trespass, and so the feud continued.

Just as there were three classes on the Victorian railways, so the social hierarchy of the village was mapped out on a weekly basis in church. As we have seen, the majority of the villagers were farm labourers, domestic servants and those in crafts and trade such as shoemakers, gardeners, masons, cordwainers, carpenters, dressmakers and so on. Middle-class villagers were few but might have included some of the farmers who employed servants. The upper classes could be found only in the two manor houses; they were the owners of much of the parish land and the grandest mansions with the largest households, and had established positions in county society. Because of their many disputes, the Warrys made a point of sitting in the nave while the Strangways sat in the chancel,[49] but, other than this peculiarity, the church seating plan reflected a deeply embedded sense of social hierarchy, in which each person was conscious of their own station[50] and each social class shared common values.

In the eighteenth and nineteenth centuries there is no evidence of nonconformity in the parish, just as might be expected from a 'closed village' – so there are no Methodist, Baptist or other chapels. Presumably, and especially given the control and paternalism exercised by the two landowners and the conservative nature of this rural agricultural society, the entire population went to the Church of England parish church. Otherwise they would have needed to go outside the parish to a place of nonconformist worship. Locally, the earliest of these were at Pedwell in Ashcott (Wesleyan, opened 1827), Bawdrip (Congregational, 1830) and Glastonbury (Congregational, 1814), all at some distance, especially on foot.[51] Drinkers had to travel very nearly as far; there has never been a public house or an alehouse in the village,[52] though there was a public house at the railway station in the nineteenth century down on the northern edge of the parish, called the Griffin's Head Inn in the 1871 census.[53] Before that time there was clearly no benefit to Shapwick squires in encouraging such amenities for their tenants.

The Poor House

As we discovered in Chapter 8, after the Reformation parishes were obliged to discharge their duties towards the poor, aged and destitute in the form of money and accommodation funded from the Poor Rates. Although there was every incentive for lords of manors to minimise the number and likelihood of people needing relief, there were always some individuals who could not support themselves. Surviving books kept by the Overseers of the Poor for the period 1745–65 reveal some sad stories and

Figure 9.17. The remains of Shapwick Poor House after the soil was stripped for modern housing in Lawn Farm Paddock (A), and its replacement after 1834 – the workhouse at Northgate in Bridgwater (B). Many people died there from dysentery and typhus brought on by the poor diet. Shapwick occupants could not expect to return to the village, even for burial.

the pressures that eventually led to the breakdown of the system.[54]

The Overseers continued to make regular monthly payments to a dozen or so deserving families in the village, with occasional contributions to others in times of special hardship. Spurious claims had become a particular concern, and to overcome this in 1752 the poor were made to wear badges with the initials PS (for 'Pauper Shapwick') so that they could be readily identified. To keep the costs down every effort was insisted upon to avoid fraudulent claims. In 1756 the parish paid for one family to be escorted away by two guards to Broadhembury in Devon. Likewise, however, Shapwick was obliged to accept families brought forcibly from other parishes and counties. The Bishop family from Calne in Wiltshire arrived under just such circumstances in 1754 and had thereafter to be provided with accommodation, furniture and fuel. Given that one of the responsibilities of the Overseers was to set the able-bodied to work, after a year a loom, wool and thread were handed over in the hope that the Bishops would begin to support themselves by weaving. Quite probably, this family occupied the village Poor House for a time (Figure 9.17A).[55] Local coarsewares and

plain lead-glazed pottery were recovered from the site, together with better-quality tablewares including creamwares, pearlwares and porcelain, continuing evidence of donations from other householders. Those who spent time in the Poor House would have had little they could call their own.

All kinds of tangled circumstances could cause the Overseers to spring to the aid of people in the parish. In May 1756 Mary Reeves, an unmarried woman, was found to be pregnant and therefore a likely burden in the foreseeable future. Under questioning in Bridgwater, Mary soon revealed that John Chard of Butleigh was the father. Chard was duly apprehended, a marriage licence obtained and the two were married in Butleigh church in front of paid witnesses. Even the bell ringers were paid and a ring bought at the expense of the parish. Another case, that of Mary Jones, was well known to the Overseers. She occupied a house on the site of what is now Oak Villa[56] and between 1748 and 1752 was regularly in receipt of money and clothing. The parish paid for bread, butter and fuel to keep her fed and warm through the winter, as well as someone to attend to her while she was sick. Eventually, in April 1755, after some three years of 'treatment', a doctor was paid for in Wells and by

Figure 9.18. After the passing of the 1870 Education Act a new school was built at Shapwick. The building next door was converted for the 30-year-old schoolmistress from Bristol. Some sixty-two 'scholars' over the age of 5 are recorded in the 1871 census out of a total village population of around 412, bearing in mind that some were away from home when the census called and others were visiting.

the beginning of the following year Mary was back in Shapwick happily cured. Unfortunately, her good health rather backfired on the Overseers because by May 1756 she was found to be pregnant. She then managed to extract a further 6s 6d from the Overseers before she would reveal the name of the father. Unfortunately the man was never located and the baby died, the parish paying for the child's coffin.[57]

The Overseers' Books reveal a parish with, in effect, its own local government and ethics committee, managed by local officers and dominated by two major landowning families who were themselves part of the county system of justice and authority. Although paupers are still recorded in the census data of 1871[58] the Poor House at Shapwick eventually went out of use after the 1834 Poor Law Amendment Act was passed and parish arrangements were replaced by very large, purpose-built Union workhouses serving a group of parishes. Shapwick parish belonged to the Bridgwater Union,[59] which included the Polden parishes and a wide area around Bridgwater across to the Quantocks. By 1839 the workhouse itself, at Northgate in Bridgwater, was already the centre of a scandal involving the poor treatment of the inmates (Figure 9.17B).[60] Needless to say, the workhouse system not only mixed together the infirm, the aged,

children and the unemployed, it also cut the inmates off from their home parish. This was in marked contrast to the village Poor House, where the inmates remained in their own community. The devastation and alienation of such a system can well be imagined and was still remembered with horror as late as the mid-twentieth century.[61]

Schooling

In the early nineteenth century some provision was made for the basic education of boys and girls in various houses and cottages in the village. One of the parish's three day schools was founded in 1819 and partly provided for by Anna Maria Templer, the wife of the Revd George Templer (see Story, above) (Box 9.2). It was typical of country gentry and clergy, those who either inherited or had achieved a social position, to be active in good works and when a parochial school (an Anglican National School) was built near New Farm in 1840, it was supported by Isabella Warry.[62] National Schools had been set up in 1811 as an educational society of the Church of England.[63] After the passing of the 1870 Education Act a new school was built at Shapwick, with an earlier building, 3 and 5 Main Road, being converted to a schoolmistress's house next door (Figure 9.18).[64]

BOX 9.1

Denys Rolle (1720–1797)

Figure B.9.1. Denys Rolle (1720–1797), by Sir Thomas Hudson. One of a series of portraits to be found until recently at Great Torrington Town Hall in the Rolle/ Clinton collection.

Deep in the woods on the banks of the St John river in Putnam county, Florida, not far from the modern town of Palatka, is a small plaque that marks the site of Rollestown, an English colony of the 1760s founded by Denys Rolle, owner of the Shapwick House estate from 1779 to 1786/7 (Figure B.9.1). The plaque is a reminder of a forgotten episode from the days of Empire, the unhappy story of the British province of East Florida.[b1]

Denys first embarked on the nine-week voyage to his colony in June 1764 with fourteen people. On his arrival at Charlestown six colonists made off. There was some suggestion that Rolle had kidnapped them in the first place, as many were London vagrants and debtors, but the rest of the party continued on to the former Spanish seaport at St Augustine, where they were received by governor Grant. Rolle's original intention had been to make his way further west, but he found the intervening country inhabited by Muscogee or Creek Indians with whom 'no conference had been held' (Figure B.9.2). He opted instead for the comparative safety of settling near Picolata fort where a sergeant and eight men were stationed, but immediately met with setbacks. His provisions and tools were lost in his boat, soldiers from Picolata carried off a smith and his wife and two gentlemen were 'enticed with the dissipation of Augustine'. Rolle himself wounded a bear and had encounters with rattlesnakes, while the local Indians hunted at his request and brought him presents of venison, honey, bear meat and buffalo tongue in return for entertainment over rum and 'a bottle of port wine'. Meanwhile Rolle's little band cleared 'inclosures' for corn, rice, citrus fruits and cotton and kept their own poultry, cows and horses, as well as developing a turpentine extraction enterprise. Their misfortunes continued, however, for in spite of the arrival of a second shipload of settlers in July 1765 and a third chartered in September 1766, Rolle's relations with governor Grant were clearly tense and he writes with feeling of the obstructions 'given by the jealousy and designs of the evil-minded'.[b2]

Rolle's intention was not only to be there in person to help establish his 'plantation', as he called it, but also to organise voyages from south-west England and to publicise the advantages of East Florida. In his advertisement he stressed the benefits of the climate that was 'betwixt the scorching heat of the tropicks, and the pinching cold of the northern latitudes', and offered financial inducements.[b3] Those with fifty guineas to spare would have a town lot for a house and garden and a plot of five acres nearby for a small 'quit-rent'. In spite of these attractions, it would prove to be an uphill struggle to fill the entire 20,000 acres he had been allotted with 200 'protestant white inhabitants' within ten years, let alone with men and women who knew so little of farming.

In 1774 a passing traveller was able to record only the overseer, the blacksmith and their families in residence, something he attributed to the ever-present threat of Indian raids.

East Florida was one of the two principal acquisitions made by Great Britain at the Peace of Paris in 1763, the other being Canada. Rolle was therefore quick to see the opportunities, though he never profited from his venture at Rollestown (or Charlotta/Charlotia, as it was first known in honour of the Queen consort, wife of George III). After twenty years in British hands Florida was returned to the Spanish and Rolle's possessions were lost forever. He sought financial compensation but never received all that he felt he deserved. He did, however, establish two settlements on Great Exuma, about 300 miles south-east of the coastal United States in the Bahamas, at Rolleville and Rolletown. As one of four major landowners on the islands, with 1,975 acres, Denys's plan was to clear the ground for cotton to supply the mills of northern England. By 1800, however, mismanagement and disease had blighted the enterprise. In 1842, four years after the abolition of slavery, his descendent John Rolle ordered that the family's land should be sold. Slaves were given plots of land if they took his name, and there are still many families with the Rolle name living there today.

Figure B.9.2. The Muscogee Indians, whom Denys Rolle encountered in his Florida adventures.

Though we cannot be absolutely sure, it was very probably Denys's financial position after his Florida adventures that necessitated the sale of Shapwick House. Nevertheless, even his short spell as owner had already made quite an impact on local archaeology and architecture. Denys was very involved in drainage plans for the Brue valley and, given that his favourite pastime was 'husbandry' and that his personal library contained many volumes on practical farming methods, the 'seeding' of pasture and meadow with metal slags could well have been done at his suggestion. He was also responsible for building Shapwick's first outlying farm – at Northbrook in about 1780 – not to mention the emparkment of the northern part of the village. These broad sweeps of landscape change and 'improvement' were perhaps influenced by the colonial experience of working with a blank landscape 'canvas'.

Regarded as a 'great talker', Denys was also something of an eccentric. According to his obituary he would dress as a peasant to work in his own fields and in this disguise would direct enquirers to his own house. He also took a great interest in the personal affairs of his tenants and was judged to be 'generous to his tenantry, indulgent to his servants and, above all, extensively benevolent to the poor'.[b4] One find from our fieldwalking in October 1994, a large marine mollusc known as the 'money cowrie', may have some connection to him. There is good archaeological evidence to confirm that enslaved Africans took cowries across the Atlantic with them, perhaps worn as jewellery or attached to clothing.[b5] Denys is known to have had 104 slaves in Florida and perhaps more in the Bahamas. Does Denys provide an unlikely link between the cowrie shell, Africa, the New World and Shapwick? Might he have returned from one of his Florida voyages with the shell? There is certainly a direct Rolle connection with the shell's findspot on the eastern side of Station Road; his tenants lived in the four cottages that once stood there, of which 50 Station Road is the only survivor today.

In 1903 there were ninety pupils, making it one of the larger schools on the Poldens in its day, and we found archaeological evidence of this during our fieldwalking in the form of lost or discarded slate writing pencils.[65] Doubtless Shapwick's police constable in 1871, Edward Davies, was kept busy ensuring the attendance and safety of the children, though Shapwick life was not entirely innocent, as we have seen in the case of Sarah Freeman. All kinds of minor criminality are recorded in local newspapers, from the stealing of wheat to assault, and even convicts on the run.[66]

The manor houses

Shapwick House

Important changes were made both to the outward appearance and the internal arrangement of Shapwick House in the late eighteenth century. The least successful of these was a new dining room that still fills the space between the projecting wings on the north side of the house (Figure 9.19A). Denys Rolle, the owner of the estate between 1779 and 1787 (Box 9.1), may well have been responsible for this ugly square brick structure, just as he was for some of the service buildings at the west end of the main house and for the elegant main stair in the west wing.[67] More drastic was a series of changes made in the early part of the nineteenth century, quite possibly commissioned by either Edmund Hill of Middlesex between 1805 and 1809/10 or by his relative the Revd Elias Taylor, the owner of the house for the next seventeen years and to whose memory there is a small window in the parish church. During these works the later medieval porch was taken down, Henry Rolle's seventeenth-century oriel window and all the south-facing windows were removed, and the chimneys and parts of the roof were modified and releaded, the roofers leaving behind their own testimonies (Figure 9.19B). By comparing the Bonnor print of 1790 to the building as it stands today (Figure 9.20) it becomes clear just how substantial these renovations were. The whole of the south front was refaced and made symmetrical and the earlier south-facing windows were replaced by sashes.

It is only by patiently reconstructing the biographies of owners, reading their wills and obituaries and building up family trees and time lines that any understanding can be gained of the patterns of investment seen inside grand houses like Shapwick House. Denys Rolle, for example, certainly spent money but his broader financial position was precarious and he was soon forced to sell. George Templer, on the other hand, owner of the estate between 1787 and 1805 (Box 9.2), invested in the park rather than the house until his money too ran out. There then followed another burst of investment from the Hill/Taylors, again largely at the mansion and focusing particularly on its external appearance, but there was a lull between the death of Elias Taylor in 1827 and the date at which his widow Sarah finally moved to Cheltenham, sometime between 1846 and 1849.[68] It was at this point that George Warry, who had been living at Lawn House,[69] took possession (Figure 9.21) and it was he who joined the service buildings to the west of the house for the added convenience of his large number of servants and remodelled the old detached kitchen (see Chapter 7) to incorporate an octagonal bell cupola and a new clock, dated 1865. These were all loosely designed according to the romantic Gothick style of the day and therefore in line with the restoration of the church. Warry continued to live at Shapwick House until his death in 1883 and, although the estate was sold to Samuel Vestey in 1943 (see Chapter 2) and the house became a convalescent home during the Second World War, the property was to remain with Warry's descendents until the 1950s.[70]

Wills, even nineteenth-century ones, which tend to lack detail, can provide some insight into how Shapwick House worked as a household. Sarah Taylor's will of 1846, for example, mentions horses and carriages (in the plural) as well as linen, 'wearing apparel, trinkets and personal ornaments'. Sadly, these objects have not been left behind for archaeologists to find, though there are others that may indicate something of Sarah's quality of life. A fragment of a delicate lead glass beaker, the opaque white globe from an oil lamp and a single drop from a crystal chandelier came from our excavations near the house.[71] Jars of prize-winning marmalade, a fish drainer and a sugar bowl recovered from the infilled ornamental pond north of the house could well have been in use on Sarah's table. The bowl, hand-painted in blue, reflects the fashion for European scenes on pearlwares that was developing in the period 1810–1830. Other finds include the ivory handle of a fork or knife and

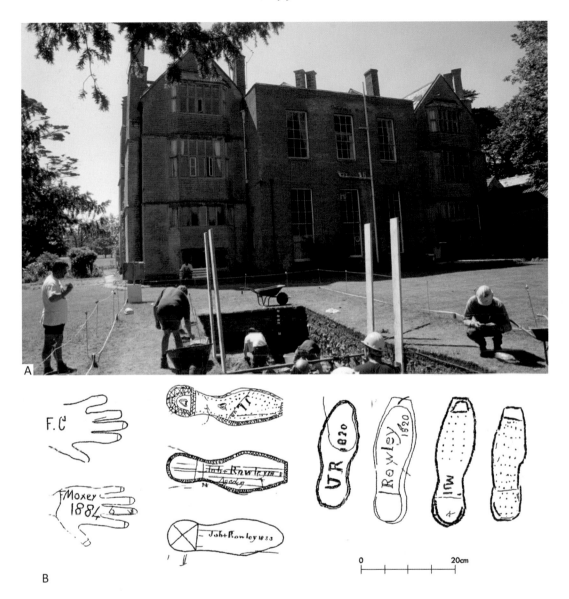

Figure 9.19. Improvements at Shapwick House by Denys Rolle. A: the brick kitchen to which George Warry so objected B: shoe and hand graffiti scratched into the lead above the kitchen. The earliest dates to 1820 and is signed 'Rowley' – probably local man George Rowley, who is listed as a mason in the 1841 census. Marks like these are vulnerable to the theft or replacement of roof leading on older houses.

a toothbrush handle made of bone (Figure 9.22). The high proportion of finewares reveals the distinctive lifestyle enjoyed at this high end of the social scale, with its sociable dining and tea-drinking in elegant surroundings.[72] By the 1820s Sarah's household was already disposing of sets of decorated tableware that had

first been brought to market only forty years earlier.[73]

In the nineteenth century one of the most obvious social divides in the village was between those who employed domestic servants and those who did not. In her will Sarah rewarded her two servants and a maid for their longstanding service with sums of between

Octogonal bell cupola

Chimneys in groups of three placed symmetrically on the two wings

17th century transom and mullion windows retained where they are not so visible

Refaced south front

New windows

Mullioned windows replaced by sashes

Dormer windows for new bedrooms converted from long gallery

Clock dated 1865 on gable end of shortened medieval kitchen

New Elizabethan-style porch in the centre of the facade, replacing the medieval porch which lay to the left and the oriel window which lay to the right. Access now to the middle of the hall

Figure 9.20. Shapwick House today, illustrating changes since Bonnor recorded the building before 1791.

£20 and £40. Her coachman, Richard Hill, had died a few years earlier.[74] When the census came to call at Shapwick House in 1841, Sarah had a household of eight installed there, among whom would have been a cook. Her equipment would have included copper pans for boiling and making sauces, brass and copper baking pans and sheets, and locally made bowls, pancheons and jars, some of which we found evidence for on our excavations.[75] George Warry, on the other hand, maintained a rather larger household. By 1851, when he was in residence, his wife, five daughters and son were accompanied by a governess from Hull, a cook, a nurse, an under-nurse, a housemaid, a kitchen maid, a footman and a groom.[76] In a large house such as this just carrying the coal, filling the oil lamps, cleaning boots, clothes and furnishings and polishing the Shapwick House livery, not to mention cooking and serving food, required at least one servant on average for each member of the family. Not all houses in the village were so attentively served, however. In 1871 the larger farms employed a more modest staff, often with their own 'domestic' or 'general' servant as well as 'farm servants' in some cases, while the vicar was well looked after by his 'parlor' maid, house maid and kitchen maid. Living in the rather more cramped circumstances of the vicarage, these four would have had to manage their own version of the upstairs/downstairs divide.

Figure 9.21. George Warry (1795–1883). Although he inherited Shapwick House and its estates at the age of 32, Warry took possession of the house only when he was in his early 50s after Sarah Taylor, widow of the Revd Elias Taylor, moved out. Until that time he built and lived at Lawn House with his family. Warry had active interests in the law and agriculture as well as being a knowledgeable local historian. His impact on the Shapwick landscape lies in the construction of new farmsteads, the planting of woodlands for timber and pressing the interests of the railway. He was clearly strong-minded too, as his constant feuding with the Strangways family indicates.

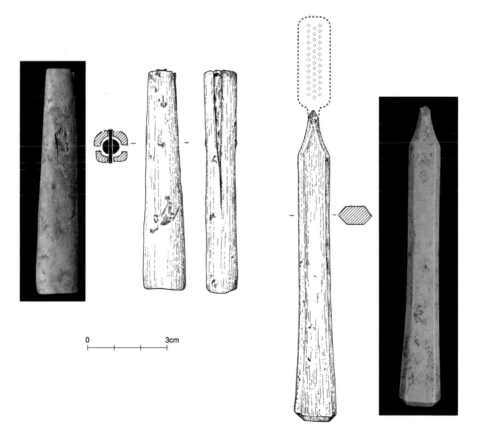

Figure 9.22 A range of nineteenth-century artefacts from excavations at and near Shapwick House. Left: an ivory handle for cutlery, hollow in the top half to accommodate the tang. Right: the handle of a bone toothbrush.

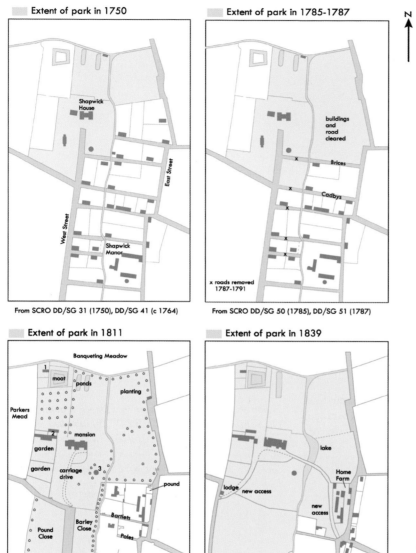

Figure 9.23 The making of Shapwick Park. Four annotated maps, which draw on eighteenth- and nineteenth-century originals, illustrate developments from 1750 to 1839 (from SRO DD/SG 31, 41, 50, 51, 53 and A/BEO 1/3).

Shapwick Park

Perhaps the most significant change to the village landscape began in the second half of the eighteenth century, when the geometric gardens to the north of Shapwick House began to be replaced in importance by the parkland to the south. Figure 9.23 makes use of historic maps, earthwork surveys and excavation to show what happened between 1750 and 1839. These alterations entailed a great deal of upheaval; the village layout had to be altered, roads blocked up, dwellings demolished, earlier garden features removed or covered, ha-has dug, pastures established, ornamental trees and a perimeter belt planted up and, finally, a bypass road constructed to skirt the parkland with a newly built lodge to monitor access.[77] Such a dramatic impact was only made possible by Shapwick's particular economic and social circumstances in which property ownership was so restricted.

The work involved in and costs of creating this new park were staggered over several phases by a succession of owners. The map sequence shows that seven houses were demolished nearest the mansion between 1750 and 1785, together with five more that lined the main road.[78] On the west side of the village stream, the removal of the two houses nearest the mansion now permitted visitors to enter either along Cadbys Lane from the east and then sweep round to the north towards the house or to arrive from the south down West Street.

The dates for this initial phase of work can probably be refined to between the late 1770s and c.1785.[79] But demolition was not the full story. Pottery found during excavation of Glastonbury Abbey's Great Barn in Shapwick suggests that this building was adapted to function as a dairy late in its life. Furthermore, structures that had accreted at either end were removed, the size of the entrance was reduced and a cupola was added to the crest of the roof.[80] This clearing of open spaces around the mansion and the prettying of views towards its south façade were completed under the ownership of the Rolle family. The most likely candidate is John Rolle Walter (Figure 9.24). He had inherited in 1730, but spent a good deal of time on the family's Devon estates and abroad. As one of the sitters for Baroque artist Pompeo Batoni, one of the great Italian painters of the second half of the eighteenth century, John was certainly absent in Rome for a while in the 1750s on his Grand Tour.[81] He died in 1779 but thirty years before it was his youngest brother Denys who held courts at Shapwick and it was he who finally sold the manor to George Templer in 1786/7.[82] Even though he was away for long stretches of time, philanthropist Denys was therefore probably the instigator of the changes and the fine cedar trees planted on the south side of the mansion are likely to be his doing, as is the planting scheme around the perimeter of the park first shown on the 1811 map (Box 9.1).

It is from this Rolle phase of demolition that

Figure 9.24. John Rolle Walter by Pompeo Batoni, c.1753. Oil on canvas. Rolle Walter (1712–1779) inherited Shapwick House and its estate in 1730, though it is more likely that he lived at Stevenstone in Devon. He was an MP for Exeter 1754–1776 and Recorder of Great Torrington for forty years after 1739. He was probably the owner when the idea to create a new park was first discussed, although his youngest brother, Denys, seems to have taken responsibility for the Somerset estate and it was he who finally sold the manor to George Templer in 1786/7. For the privileged traveller on tour through Europe, Batoni was the portrait painter of choice in Rome. In 2008 this work was purchased for the Royal Albert Memorial Museum in Exeter.

Shapwick's most remarkable find comes – a composite object that combines a Bronze Age blade with a medieval socket and holder. The bronze socket is early twelfth century (Figure 9.25) and originally an ecclesiastical piece designed to hold a cross vertically, perhaps on an altar. On stylistic parallels it is believed to have been made in Ireland[83] and, functionally at least, it mirrors the great processional cross of Cong which is dated by inscription to 1127–36, though

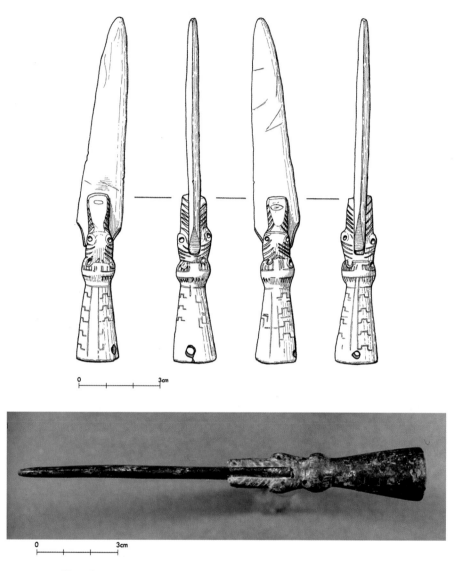

Figure 9.25. A curio, possibly a letter opener, undated but probably seventeenth or eighteenth century and certainly lost by c.1765. The socket is twelfth century and originated in Ireland as a cross holder, but the blade is Bronze Age, so this object has two components manufactured thousands of years apart. The Rolle family had the wealth and contacts to acquire such an object and it is possible that both halves were found locally. Glastonbury Abbey, the owners of Shapwick House in the later Middle Ages, had many Irish links, as emphasised in, for example, the story of St Indracht.

that piece is altogether more ambitious in scale. The moulded profile and style of the animal masks and the stepped decoration on the tubular socket all occur on the portable shrine of St Manchan, another product of the Shannon school of metalworking. The cross head, now lost, would have been clamped between the 'jaws' of the two animal masks, but at some stage in its life this has been substituted for a reworked Bronze Age blade. Perhaps the exotic combination was intended to be used as a letter opener or admired as some sort of *curio*. How the medieval components of it came to Shapwick we do not know, but the Glastonbury connection, with its links to Irish saints such as Indracht, provides a plausible context. Perhaps the cross once stood on a later medieval altar at Shapwick House or belonged to the church that was demolished in the fourteenth century? Whatever the truth behind its strange biography, it must have been acquired or rediscovered much later. Possibly it had a place in a cabinet of curiosities in the mid-seventeenth century and stayed in the Rolle family until it was lost or disposed of a century later. From what we know of the character of Denys Rolle it certainly might have appealed to him. The find itself was made 100m from Shapwick House at the base of a ditch infilled during demolition and landscaping in preparation for creating the park.[84]

After 1786/7 George Templar enthusiastically set about the task of clearance begun by Denys Rolle (Box 9.2) Even if Rolle had never thought so expansively of creating a parkland to the south of his mansion, Templer certainly did. His ambition was to create a far larger park, though that necessitated the demolition of the village houses between West Street and the village stream. On the map of *c.*1785 the streets and numbered plots on this block of land appear to be scratched out (Figure 9.26) and, since the Bonnor prospect of 1791 shows nothing there, the houses must have been removed between these two dates. Figure 9.23 shows Templar's expansion to the south and west by 1811, including the carriage drive illustrated by Bonnor (see Figure 2.5) that shows up so clearly on geophysics and as parchmarks on aerial photographs (Figure 9.27). Quite where the displaced tenants went we do not know, but they may well have been accommodated in existing houses, in the new cottages on High Street, at Gamekeeper's or Island Cottage, or hidden away to the north of Shapwick House overlooking the moors,[85] or perhaps they moved away from the village altogether. At least nine tenanted houses were removed in this operation and for a short period West Street became the main approach to Templar's residence from the south.[86] Perhaps to celebrate quieter times and the end of what must have been five years of disruption, Templer now employed Claude Nattes in 1787 to paint watercolour prospects of his estate (see Chapter 2)

Figure 9.26. Coloured map of around 1785 (SRO DD/ SG/50). Shapwick House and the Great Barn are shown only schematically, but the church, village stream and the 'ladder' pattern of roads are clear. Sometime after this date, but before 1791 when Bonnor drew the mansion, the five east–west lanes within the new park and to the right (W) of the stream were scratched out on this copy (from the south they were Holes, Turfhouse, Poles, Cadbys and Brices late Davidges lanes). Someone was clearly updating the map as time went by. North is towards the bottom of this map.

and Thomas Bonnor to capture the house and its expanding park.

Bonnor shows us a view across the parkland towards the south façade of Shapwick House past horses and grazing sheep (see Figure 2.5). The portly gentleman glimpsed through the trees walking his dog on a lead is presumably George Templer himself, the

BOX 9.2

The Templers

One family intimately involved with Shapwick life from the late eighteenth to the mid-nineteenth century was the Templers. Their involvement with the village begins with George J. E. Templer (of Shapwick House), who was born in 1755 at Rotherhithe, Kent. He was the fourth son of James Templer who, shortly before his death in 1782, completed the building of Stover House at Teigngrace in south Devon. In 1736 James was apprenticed to an 'architectural carpenter' in Exeter but within two to three years he had 'run away' to join a vessel at Plymouth bound for Madras. He had already made his fortune in India by the age of 22 or 23, but returned to England where he was involved in the construction of the dockyard at Chatham. In about 1760 he and his partners were awarded the contract to build a new dockyard in Plymouth, which necessitated his residing in Devon, where he first rented and then bought Stoford Lodge and the manor of Teigngrace. Stover House was completed in 1780, two years before James died from drinking contaminated mineral water.[b6]

George's oldest brother, also James Templer, inherited the 80,000 acre estate and at his own expense built the Stover Canal from Kingsteignton to Teignmouth, which was used to ship clay to Staffordshire for fine earthenwares. Stover House was lost to the family in the next generation, when George Templer of Stover, a better sportsman than businessman, was forced to sell the estate to the Duke of Somerset. This George Templer (nephew of our George J. E. Templer) opened Haytor Quarry and constructed a granite-slab railway from the quarry to the Stover Canal to ship out the granite, which was used in the construction of, among other things, London Bridge and the British Museum.[b7] He died in a hunting accident in 1843.

Like his father, George J. E. Templer of Shapwick also made his career in the colonies, becoming an East India Company Civil Servant based in Calcutta. He is mentioned in charges against Warren Hastings, the Governor-General of Bengal in 1774–85, who also had estates in Somerset. George was a commissioner for grain, and in another instance, in January 1777, at the age of 22, he is mentioned as a contractor for feeding the company's elephants. In the latter case, we learn that Warren Hastings had accepted Templer's tender, even though it was not the lowest offer and differed in its essentials from what was asked for in the advertisement. Hastings went on to extend his contract from three to five years without going out to tender again, and accepted new conditions proposed by Templer, 'by which the Company were very considerable losers'. This was one of a number of misdemeanours cited against Warren Hastings in the House of Commons in 1786 following his retirement and of which he was acquitted.[b8]

All this had no adverse affect on George, who went on to make a considerable fortune in Calcutta and founded the London and Middlesex Bank. On his return to England in 1786/7, at the age of 31, George purchased Shapwick Manor from Denys Rolle.[b9] Rolle's main estate in Devon (at Bickton) lay very near to Stover House, so it is likely that the two men knew each other before the sale. George became MP for Honiton for the years 1790–96, but he never made a speech in the House of Commons. Shapwick House remained in Templer's hands until 1805, when he sold it on to Edmund Hill for the sum of £60,000. This was not George's only Somerset estate. He had also purchased the nearby manor of Cossington in 1792, selling it again in 1806, a year after he had disposed of Shapwick.[b10] It seems likely that these sales were necessitated by losses incurred in banking. In 1817 he was forced to return to India, only to find the role of the East India Company quite changed.[b11] He died there of fever in 1819, aged 64. Jane Templer, his wife, returned to England and lived on to the age of 86. She died at Shute near Exeter in Devon, presumably cared for by her daughter's family.[b12]

While in India, George had met and married Jane Paul in 1781 (Figure B.9.3). She was six years his junior, one of two daughters of Henry Paul of West Monkton, Somerset, and later bore him three sons and a daughter. An oil portrait of Jane when she was 31, painted by the French court painter Jean Laurent Mosnier (1743–1808), was exhibited at the Royal Academy in 1792 and is entitled 'Portrait of Mrs Templer of Shapwick'. It was offered at auction in 2007. We also know that Jane had a sister, Ann, who was also thought to be a great beauty; she married Thomas Graham of Kinross. They had two daughters and a son who was lost at sea in a pirate attack in 1800 on his way to India. This son, Thomas Henry Graham, was brought up by his aunt at Shapwick Manor when his family were out in India[b13] and it must be supposed that the two daughters were frequent visitors there also, as one of them went on to marry her cousin, George Henry Templer (see Story, above).

The engraving by Bonnor of Shapwick House with its barn that appears in John Collinson's history of Somerset was probably commissioned by George Templer, presumably after he had bought the property in 1786/7 but before Collinson published in 1791 (see Chapter 2). In addition to this engraving George Templer also commissioned a set of watercolours by John Claude Nattes, which were done in 1787. These were given to the village in 1947 when Mrs Warry left Shapwick House. Four paintings survive, but it is more than likely that there were others of Shapwick House itself. George Templer was also involved in commissioning maps, in particular 'A plan of the Turf Moor' in 1782 and 'A plan of the Manor of Shapwick' in 1787, both by Thomas Jones.[b14] His most important contribution was perhaps in continuing the work of emparkment begun by Denys Rolle.

George Henry Templer, born in 1782 in Calcutta, was the first of George and Jane Templer's children. From the age of about 4 or 5 he was brought up in Shapwick House, where his three younger siblings were born. At the age of 18 he went to Merton College, Oxford, obtaining the degrees of BA in 1804 and MA in 1808. When his father sold Shapwick House in 1805 he retained the advowson of Shapwick Church, presumably because his son was counting on being appointed to the living. He duly was, following his ordination in 1806. In 1811 George Henry

Figure B.9.3. Portrait of Jane Paul, later Mrs Templer of Shapwick, by the French court painter Jean Laurent Mosnier (1743–1808), exhibited at the Royal Academy in 1792.

became a prebendary of Wells Cathedral, taking up the Canonry of Combe (St Nicholas) the Ninth. He also held the rectory of Thornford in Dorset from 1810 and had inherited Cossington Manor from his father. In 1807 he married his cousin Anna Maria Graham at Shapwick Church. They had one daughter, Sophia Jane Templer, born in 1808. An entry in the list of marriages in St Mary's Church, Shapwick, records her marriage to Henry Bull Strangways on 22 September 1830.

The 1841 Census records that Jane was living with her son George Henry at Shapwick, presumably in the Old Vicarage, otherwise known as the 'parsonage house'. They had three female servants, Mary Brown, Louisa Bryant and Sarah Herald. Jane's will, which survives, was also made at Shapwick in June 1840.[b15] In it Jane left £3,000 to her youngest son, Reverend James Ackland Templar, to invest on behalf of Anna Maria Templer, the wife of her eldest son, the Reverend George Henry Templer, as well as money to her grand-daughter, who had married an employee of the 'honourable East India Company's Civil Service Bengal', her other son John William Templer, who was employed by the same company, and her five grandchildren. In a codicil to her will made in the year of her death in 1847 she specifically makes mention of her 'household goods and furniture, wine and other liquors', which she left to James. Jane was not long outlived by her eldest son George Henry Templer. In his will of May 1849, in which he describes himself as the clerk and vicar of Shapwick cum Ashcott, he left everything to his wife, Anna Maria.

The Templer story in the late eighteenth and first half of the nineteenth centuries is intimately linked with the British Empire in India, first in construction (James), then through the East India Company (his son George J. E. and grandson John William). Together they spanned over 100 years of involvement in the East, from the age of trade to the full emergence of imperial ambitions. The Company was finally dissolved in 1858.

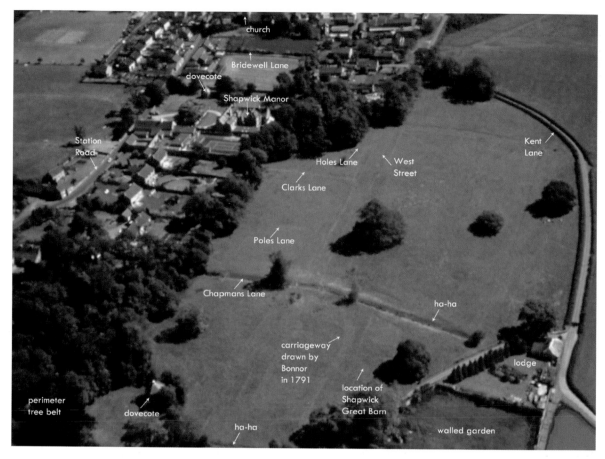

Figure 9.27. An annotated aerial view of parchmarks in Shapwick Park, looking south.

patron to whom the plate is adroitly dedicated. There are no village houses to be seen, no hint of agricultural activity, only the Great Barn, the carriage drive and the mansion itself. It is, of course, a snapshot of what was a continuing programme of works. Glastonbury Abbey's Great Barn appears to have been demolished in the early 1790s, shortly after Bonner packed up his easel, and it was around this time that the south front of the house was refaced, rubble from the old facing being used to fill in the ornamental rectangular pond in front of the house.[87] Unseen in the Bonnor view, the banqueting house to the north of Shapwick House was also taken down a few years later, around 1800, when one of the two ornamental ponds there was filled in with the demolition rubble.

As we have seen, the next owner of Shapwick

House was Edmund Hill, to whom Templer sold out after nineteen years in 1805, probably bankrupted by his banking losses (Box 9.2). In 1809–10, after only a few years in possession, Hill passed the property to his nearest relative, Elias Taylor, who died in 1827, and the property was then inherited by Taylor's nephew, George Warry, although Elias's widow Sarah continued to live in the house. The archaeological evidence suggests that much of the clearance work around the house was completed by 1815 but several additions may date from Hill or Taylor's time. These include the diversion of Kent Lane to provide a new 'bypass' together with the lodge that now guards the entrance to the park on the west side,[88] as well as the digging of two ha-has and the planting of trees and shelter belts (see Figure 9.23). At some point the stream to the east of the house was also dammed to create a small ornamental pond or lake and a drive was cut through to give access to the main village street, where a Home Farm was established around a core of earlier buildings.[89] During the course of the late eighteenth and nineteenth centuries both Bartlets and Poles Lane to the east of the stream were also closed off; they were now *cul de sacs* that served no particular purpose.

We need not look far for other examples of emparkment in action. On the west Somerset coast, at West Quantoxhead, tenants' houses along the main driveway to the manor house gradually dwindled away between 1761 and 1860 and local roads were also diverted in order to extend the parkland.[90] Unlike at Shapwick, the church at West Quantoxhead also lay within the bounds of the park, which prolonged the process further and eventually entailed its rebuilding in the 1850s. Many similar reorganisations of village housing took place around the country in response to changing fashions in landscape and garden design, so the Shapwick story is not in itself unusual.[91] Formal and geometric layouts had begun to be replaced with open, sinuous, more 'naturalistic' landscapes at least a generation before the first houses were demolished around Shapwick House in the 1760s so, in that sense, the existing gardens would already have seemed dated.[92] Shapwick Park never had any summerhouses, grottoes, pavilions or Gothick cottages; the fashion for these in the 1740s had already passed. In any case a succession of no less than six Rolle family owners in the forty years before 1730, one of whom committed suicide, another of whom filed for bankruptcy, and half of whom had no children, was hardly a stable foundation on which to plan ahead, and when John Rolle Walter inherited he was, as we have seen, elsewhere engaged. Once completed by Templer, however, the new park made a strong statement, excluding villagers from the grounds of Shapwick House, emphasising differences of class, controlling the space around the house, altering patterns of circulation across the village and severing the ties with individual properties that some families had tenanted for generations.[93] Elements of 'designed' landscape also spread out into the wider landscape. Clumps of trees were planted at particular points in the views out from the house and on prominent hills around.

These can be seen from the time of the tithe map (1839) onwards, where they are usually labelled as 'plantation'. Private 'rides' included destinations such as the 'Holywell', a saline spring near Northbrook Farm, where a small pump room and bath were constructed around 1820 (see story). In the mid-nineteenth century the quality of the water here was evidently of some commercial interest 'and found to resemble the Harrogate water'.[94]

Shapwick Manor – Down House

Throughout the late eighteenth and the nineteenth centuries the second of Shapwick's main houses, Shapwick Manor,[95] was occupied by the Strangways family.[96] Like Shapwick House, this mansion was also heavily modified in the early nineteenth century, most probably by Henry Bull Strangways. He remodelled the main range in the fashionable Gothick style with plaster archways internally, gabled dormers and buttresses externally.[97] This archaic form of architecture added solidity to the impression of a 'country house'. He also had the service end north of the porch rebuilt and extensions added to the rear of the wing (Figure 9.28A, and see Figure 8.14A for plan).

There were also improvements outside. To the east of the house, on the other side of the road, cottages were demolished and ornamental tree plantings now framed the vista towards Glastonbury Tor. As at Shapwick House adjacent roads were closed off for added privacy and it seems very likely indeed that the two manors were able to collude here in achieving this aim.[98] Although the dovecote and seventeenth-century stable block were retained, all traces of the farmyard, including the large barn and granary, were swept away; earlier cobbling was rediscovered beneath the grass lawns by our test pits (Figure 9.28B).[99] To add a touch of elegance to the front of the house a fine Jacobean garden screen, obtained from elsewhere, was set up there with balusters, obelisks and a pedimented archway (Figure 9.28C).

The Strangways household was far more modest in scale than that of the neighbouring Warrys.[100] The 1871 census records Henry Strangways, 'magistrate and landowner', in the house with his wife Harriet and daughter Cordelia together with three domestic servants and an elderly visitor from London.[101] When

Figure 9.28. Shapwick Manor or Down House, residence of the Strangways family. A: aerial photograph of Shapwick Manor from the south. In the immediate foreground is Field 7722, where our excavations took place north of Bridewell Lane. B: earlier cobbling was buried to create new lawns and vistas. C: the Jacobean garden screen. Given that this screen does not figure on mid-eighteenth-century maps, it must have been brought in from another house and re-erected here.

the census officials knocked at the door the family was doubtless waiting anxiously for news from Australia where their son, also Henry, who had been premier and attorney-general of South Australia until the previous year, was now on the point of resigning from Parliament and returning home.[102] Four years later, in June 1875, Henry Bull Templer Strangways was to read a paper to the Royal Colonial Institute that was published in their proceedings. It reviewed the progress of Britain's colonial empire from 1835. He might easily have taken Shapwick as his theme, for over the space of 100 years the two major landowning families in the village had made and lost their fortunes on the three continents of America, Australia and India.

An early modern landscape

Field and farming
By about 1750 just eight or so 'islands', or about 475 acres in all, of the later medieval open fields remained (Figure 9.29).[103] Each 'island' operated as a miniature open field with the usual strips and scattered holdings and its own system of rotation and cropping. Over the next few decades this system continued to decay, larger blocks fragmenting into smaller ones and taking with them some of the most familiar names in the Shapwick landscape. 'Northbrook Field' now fell out of use, though the name was taken up by Northbrook Farm, Shapwick's first purpose-built ring-fence farm to stand outside the village (see below). Some of the new names merely indicated the acreages of the new enclosures, such as *Seven Acres* in Eastfield by North Brook or *Nine Acres*, *Ten Acres* and *Six Acres* in West Field; others, such as *The Croft*, *Home Ground* (3 of these), *Quarryfield* (twice) and *Rabbit Run* are common enough across southern England. For a time it must have been very confusing for people finding their way around the new landscape with so many new and uninformative names.

This continuing pattern of disintegration can be followed through a series of minutely detailed eighteenth-century field books and estate maps that show the feverish over-writings as land exchanges were propelled along by high grain prices during the Napoleonic Wars.[104] For several reasons, however, the enclosure process in the parish was not easily driven to

its logical conclusion and, as the eighteenth century drew to a close, a few patches of open-field arable still clung on.[105] Full enclosure was probably achieved only in the second decade of the nineteenth century, so that by 1839 the tithe map shows a parish that is completely enclosed with two farms outside the village – Northbrook and Kent. For further farms to be established the act of enclosure in itself was not enough; ownership, too, had to be consolidated into meaningful blocks of land. For a brief while longer the village still provided the optimal location for the farmer because it gave the most convenient access to scattered holdings across the parish,[106] so that while this advantage persisted, landowners continued to invest in the farm buildings within the village (see above).

Enclosure was not simply a question of hedging new fields, however. Land use was also evolving. In 1839 there was 3,588 acres of land in the parish, of which only 576 acres (16 per cent) was arable. The remainder, apart from 127 acres of woodland, was meadow and pasture (80 per cent overall). This can be contrasted with the scene 300 years earlier in 1515, when, of 1,844 acres, 32 per cent was pastoral and 66 per cent arable. Enclosure had facilitated such a marked switch from a largely arable economy to a pastoral one that in 1872 cheese production was claimed to be the staple of the parish.[107] Beyond these changes to land use, enclosure also encouraged agricultural 'improvement' in various ways. The manuring of fields was now undertaken more assiduously, for one thing, and fieldwalking results provided ample evidence for this in the massive increase in volumes of pottery, broken brick, tile and slates being distributed by farmers across their ploughed fields during manuring. Another problem for the farmer was drainage. Shapwick soils quickly become sticky and claggy after rain, and by the twentieth century every field in the 'upland' part of the parish had probably been under-drained in some way or other. Our excavations across the parish regularly hit upon clay drainage pipes and fieldwalking invariably produced vast quantities of broken red clay drainage pipes that had been struck by the plough.[108] Most of these pipes were probably produced in the Bridgwater brick fields though a few may have been made in Shapwick, such as the local bricks used at

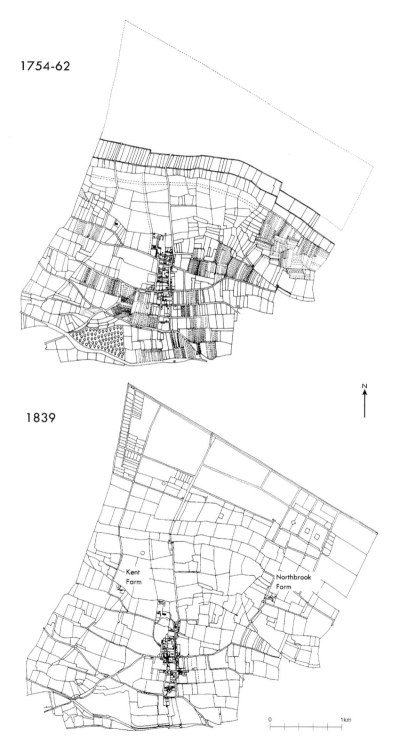

Figure 9.29. The advance of enclosure. Above: a composite mid-eighteenth-century map based on nineteen originals dated 1754–62. Notice the strip patterns to east and west of the village and the unenclosed peat moor to the north. Below: Shapwick in 1839 with completely enclosed fields near the village and the beginnings of enclosure in the north. Woodlands are not distinguished here.

Northbrook Farm (see below).[109] The digging of miles of trenches and the laying of thousands of drainage pipes must have been a familiar scene to the people of Shapwick over several centuries[110] and many air photographs show the lines of field drains, as did our geophysical surveys. Much of this effort was put into improving pasture rather than arable, something that is supported by the types of farm buildings being constructed and confirmed by the analysis of late eighteenth-century plant macrofossil assemblages.[111] All the samples consisted mainly of wheat, oats and barley, with many of the crop weeds noted for earlier periods, such as fat hen, sorrel and stinking chamomile, still present. There is little evidence for 'improvement' to be seen here.

The Levels also witnessed important changes. As we have seen in previous chapters, only modest efforts had been made locally to drain the vast area of fen in the northern third of the parish during the Roman period and the Middle Ages. The Brue valley to the north of Shapwick was not drained and exploited in the Roman period as the Axe valley was and it was not one of the areas first tackled by farmers in the medieval period, like the Parrett valley near Sowy, to the south.[112] But in the late eighteenth century more serious drainage and reclamation works were attempted and the drainage of the whole of the Brue valley was completed between 1780 and 1790 so that, in 1784, the enclosure of 1,015 acres of the peat land allowed cultivation to replace pasture.[113] This success, however, was short-lived. The soils quickly became exhausted and the fields returned to pasture. Setback followed setback. In 1794 the whole of the Brue valley was flooded and in 1797 teams of men were again out digging rhynes to remove the surface water in order to reclaim the heaths of raised peat bogs in Shapwick, Ashcott and Street. A year later, a breach in the sea wall at Huntspill flooded the whole area, including Shapwick. Drainage and flooding cycles were not finally sorted out until after 1829, when the South Drain was widened and deepened to take the Glastonbury Canal (see below).

There is, therefore, an important contrast to be drawn between the processes of enclosure as they unfolded across the different topographies of the parish. Enclosure on the upland was achieved primarily in piecemeal fashion, by stages. That is to say, tenants agreed between themselves that they would exchange strips and create larger blocks of land and then remove a field from communal use. This unfolded over many generations; it had begun before the mid-fourteenth century (see Chapter 7) and took 500 years to wind to a conclusion. Many such agreements were, as we have seen, strictly illegal, in that they did not pass through the local manorial courts. On the peat land, on the other hand, enclosure was about reclamation rather than the consolidation of property and the whole process took only a matter of years because landownership rested in only a few hands.[114] A formal arrangement, in this case the Shapwick Enclosure Bill of 1777, could be drawn up relatively speedily given that the idea was enthusiastically promoted by both of Shapwick's major landowners, Denys Rolle and Elizabeth Strangways,[115] as a means of making more productive use of 'under-used' land. Greater productivity meant higher income, which Rolle in particular was in need of.

Although customary rights, such as the digging of peat for fuel, were now to be extinguished,[116] the only serious protest against enclosure was to come from outside the parish, when Messrs Burgum and Pulsford, as lords of the manor of Glastonbury, claimed right of common in the Heath Moor. Burgum's attempts to cultivate support from the ranks of villagers, however, came to nought and when Pulsford withdrew Burgum was left to protest alone in vain.[117] One reason that might explain the lack of reaction from the villagers, other than their understandable nervousness at upsetting their landlords, was that they stood to gain something from the process. Every tenant, including landless cottagers, received land in compensation for the enclosure of the Moor, a gesture that may be the origin of Shapwick's 'field gardens' or allotments out to the east of the village (Field 4200).[118] Their location was first identified by fieldwalkers who collected vast quantities of nineteenth- and early twentieth-century finds from the northern half of the field (Figure 9.30). This extraordinary density of material, whose boundaries are so clearly delimited, can only be the result of the extremely intensive manuring of vegetables over many seasons. Typically under schemes of this sort the land was let from a farmer at a wholesale price by a local association and then planted out by 'field-garden tenants', the value of the vegetables far

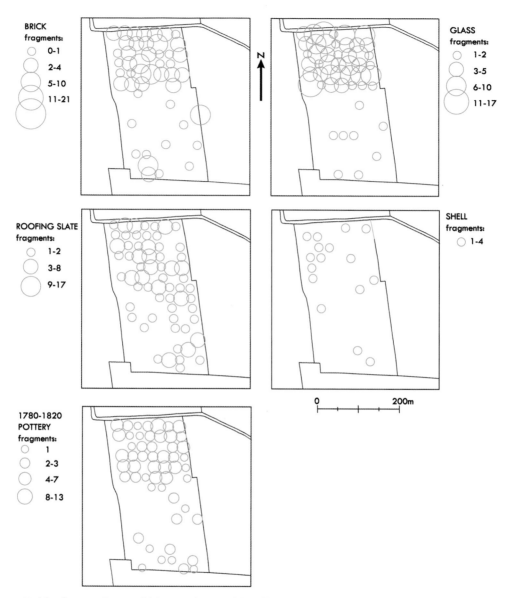

Figure 9.30. Fieldwalking results in Field 4200 to the east of the village. Some of the highest densities of material were recovered from the 'field gardens' here. The strong clustering of material in the northern half of the field indicates a lost east–west boundary.

outweighing the rent. At the same time, of course, the landowner benefited from the improvement to his soils while salving his social conscience about the condition of local labourers.[119]

The impact of the enclosure process on the landscape was profound. For one thing, it marked the beginning of large-scale restrictions on land access. Such matters had been largely immaterial when the

open fields were operating and every headland of every furlong was a line of access, particularly in fallow years. Even the immediately post-enclosure countryside was laced with footpaths that linked all the farms with the village and local roads (Figure 9.31). This network, so well illustrated on early Ordnance Survey maps, is far denser than the designated rights of way of modern times and shows

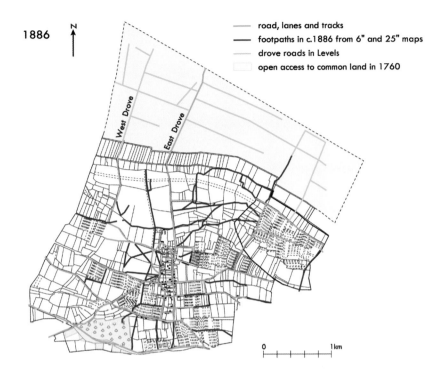

1886

road, lanes and tracks
footpaths in c.1886 from 6" and 25" maps
drove roads in Levels
open access to common land in 1760

West Drove

East Drove

0   1km

1970-72

public road and lanes
public rights of way as shown on
1:25000 Explorer Map 141 (1997)
cycle way along old railway

0   1km

Figure 9.31. Rights of way in the parish. Above: 1886 footpaths as shown on 6-inch and 25-inch maps. Below: 1970s rights of way as shown on 1:25,000 Explorer 141 (1997).

just how much less accessible the countryside has become. Enclosure inevitably involved the planting of hedges and the digging of ditches which redefined routes and the movement of people and animals, a process that can occasionally be followed in some detail. Thus, in May 1749 John Walter was presented before the court for illegally fencing a piece of land at *Crosse* in Shapwick's West Field. He had probably taken a yard or two of land that was not rightfully his. Walter then returned to face the court in May 1752 for illegally planting trees on the same piece of land; it seems that he was trying to establish a permanent hedge line and a stockproof barrier.[120]

Exactly what species Walter planted we cannot now know, as the hedge he planted cannot be identified on the ground, but he may have simply taken whatever was to hand – cuttings from nearby hedges, plants stripped from the woodland – just as his ancestors had done (Figure 9.32),[121] or he may have opted for a restricted selection of elm, hawthorn and blackthorn, as was the tendency after the eighteenth century. As we discovered from our botanical survey, there is no simple equation between the age of a hedge and the number of species present. A detailed study of thirty hedgerows at Shapwick ranging in date between the later Middle Ages and the later eighteenth century failed to produce any meaningful correlation at all between their age and the average number of woody species present per 30m length. In fact, some of the most recent boundaries were also found to be the most varied in composition, with an average of 9.6 species. This may be telling us that the selection of plants used for hedging by Walter and his like was surprisingly varied, but it is also a warning. With one exception all the hedgerows believed to represent early enclosure appear in the bottom half of the list when it is ranked; there is actually a reverse correlation between age and the recorded numbers of woody species which may be the result of aggressive colonisation by species such as elm and blackthorn. As every gardener knows, not every plant will take well. In the intervening decades the composition of the hedge will inevitably have been affected by the type of soil, microclimate, management techniques, the differing success of species in colonising the hedge and the proximity of the hedge to other seed banks. All of these factors will promote the development of

the flora and, ultimately, the range of species present to be recorded by the botanist.

Enclosure had an effect on local wildlife too. Hedges favoured the rabbit, the blackbird and the robin over the hare, lapwing and skylark,[122] while out on the Levels better drainage and ditching had the effect of lowering the water table so that marshy grassland and mires became grassland and scrub. One archaeological feature of this lowland landscape was a duck decoy pond, one of forty-five that once existed on the Somerset Levels, a region with plenty of migratory wildfowl in autumn and winter as well as locally bred birds (Figure 9.33).[123] The Shapwick example consisted of a square central pond with four netted arms or 'pipes' coming off it, at the end of which a selection of trapped birds were taken for the table. No records of the working of this particular decoy have survived but it would have been a valuable asset – more than 2,000 ducks per year were taken at a nearby decoy at Compton Dundon.[124] The key shift in land use on the Levels, however, was the more vigorous exploitation of the peat. This did provide a little permanent employment in the village, and a 'turff cutter' is recorded in the 1851 census,[125] but far larger numbers, including women and children, were employed in the summer in cutting and stacking square 'bricks' of peat to dry in 'mumps' (Figure 9.34). From the late 1860s machinery began to be introduced and continued to operate profitably right through to the mid-twentieth century. The peat was compressed as horse bedding and dipped in fuel to make firelighters; only later did the profitable horticultural market for peat emerge.[126]

Both the final enclosure of the common fields and the reclamation of the Levels for farming were instigated by Denys Rolle (Box 9.1). A subscriber to *The Annals of Agriculture*, Denys had an appetite for improvement and wrote disapprovingly of the wastes of Exmoor and Dartmoor. At Sarsden in Oxfordshire, despite opposition from locals, he enclosed more than 4,000 acres of common and wasteland.[127] In many ways the process he encouraged at Shapwick was a complete reversal of what took place when the common fields were first created in the early medieval period (see Chapter 6). Then, hedges and hedgebanks were removed and any enclosing ditches filled in to be replaced by the open landscapes of common fields,

Figure 9.32. Reconstruction by Victor Ambrus of hedge planting for new enclosures. The saplings may have been taken from nearby woodland.

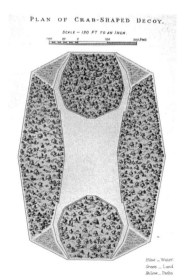

Figure 9.33. The duck decoy pond in Decoy Pool Wood, east of Canada Farm, was crab-shaped, like the idealised example illustrated (left). Having enticed the birds with a small fox-like dog, the decoyman, who hides behind the screens, then emerges to scare the ducks into flight up the netted pipe where they are collected (middle). A modern example with nets and screens in place at Boarstall, Bucks (right). The illustrations are taken from Payne-Gallwey 1886.

Figure 9.34. 'Turf' cutters at work on the Moors. One man cuts turves and lifts them up onto a board. Another man forks the turves onto a barrow which is then wheeled over to the turf stacks or 'mumps'. Below: women turn the turves for drying.

with their unenclosed furlongs and strips. Now, in the eighteenth and nineteenth centuries, hedges, banks and ditches were reintroduced as the open landscape was again subdivided into smaller fields and allocated to individual tenant farmers.

Farmsteads outside the village

In 1750 all eight of Shapwick's farms still lay within the village envelope, with the exception of Kent Farm, the site of the medieval watermill. A century and a half later, the late Victorian parish could boast one additional farm in the village (Lawn Farm) but no less than eight new farmsteads outside. After a thousand years of living compactly in a single village, powerful new forces were now at work that propelled the dispersal of the community. The enclosure of what had been communally worked open fields coupled with the taking-in of land from the peat moor had triggered the construction of new farmsteads and the reallocation of blocks of land to individual tenant farmers.[128]

The process began in the mid-eighteenth century with Northbrook Farm. Denys Rolle of Shapwick House built this elegant brick-built farm in the Georgian style in about 1780,[129] taking the name from the former common field in which the farm now stood (Figure 9.35A). The classical symmetry of the front elevation, capped by its steep pediment and large

finial, was all rather ostentatious for the tenant farmer who was to live in it and perhaps Rolle intended it for someone in his immediate family.[130] The brickwork, such a contrast to other stone farmhouses locally, obviously caught Claude Nattes's eye and he produced a watercolour of Northbrook Farm in 1787 as it was glimpsed through a stand of elms (Figure 9.35B). Nattes also painted Kent Farm on the same visit, and here too the architectural evidence suggests investment. As with the creation of Shapwick Park, Denys Rolle may have been the instigator but it was George Templer who commissioned paintings and commemorated Rolle's vision.

For the next burst of investment we have to wait until after 1827, when Elias Taylor had died and George Warry inherited. Possibly even Warry would have done rather less at the outlying farms had he been in residence at Shapwick House but, as it was, Sarah Taylor, Elias's widow, was still living there. Instead, he turned his mind to farming and between 1839 and 1875 five farmsteads were built on virgin sites away from the village. The two most significant complexes are those that flank the village to east and west, at Beerway Farm and Manor Farm respectively.[131] They have similar architectural styles and were carefully laid out to allow them to work efficiently (Figure 9.36A). Other farms then followed at Canada in 1855, at (the now ruined) Brickyard out

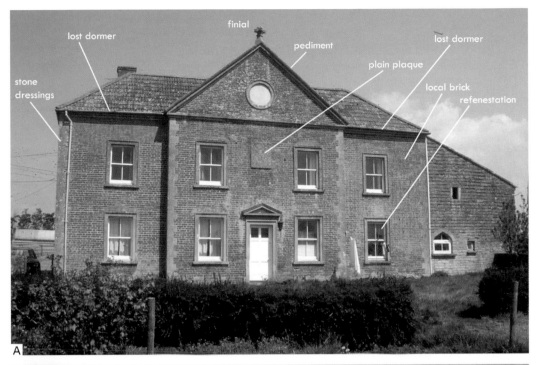

Figure 9.35. Northbrook Farm. A: the classical brick façade as it is today, with some of the key features indicated. Behind there are three rooms along the front, with a kitchen and dairy to the rear in two projecting wings. Described as 'a farmhouse lately new built in brick' in 1785 and probably commissioned by Denys Rolle. B: the watercolour of the house by John Claude Nattes in 1787.

on the moor (Figure 9.36B) and at Moorgate, though all these were on a smaller scale.[132] Finally, in the late nineteenth century, possibly still under George Warry's supervision or perhaps that of his son George Deedes Warry,[133] Coppice Gate Farm was developed from two semi-detached cottages. Within the space of a century, with the addition of the turnpike cottage on the toll road and the new buildings associated with the railway, Shapwick had ceased to be just a tight cluster of farmsteads and cottages surrounded by a sea of open agricultural land stretching out to the parish boundary. Some people, at least, now lived a more isolated existence out in the fields and had to walk a considerable distance to find the facilities the village had to offer.

As far as we know, George Warry did not record his motives for extending the number of farmsteads under his control. Manor and Beerway Farms, judging from the type and arrangement of buildings there, had stable blocks for plough and cart horses, threshing barns with adjacent cattle yards and cowsheds with collecting yards. They were mixed farms of arable, beef and milk. Moorgate, on the other hand, closer to the pasture of the peat moor, was exclusively a dairy unit.[134] More difficult to fathom is the purpose of Brickyard and Canada Farms. They have few of the buildings required for either stock or dairying, and milk production out on the Levels would have been limited to the warmer months of the year; at other times the stock may have been allowed to roam widely over the drier parts of the moor. Nevertheless, in spite of their isolation and limited potential, both farms were fully occupied. The census of 1871 found no less than seven members of the Sugg family living at Brickyard; Thomas's occupation is listed as a 'farmer of 47 acres', his wife Jane's as 'dairy and domestic duties'. For a while, perhaps, it might have seemed as if there were greater possibilities for enterprise at these remote sites, if not for brick-making then for arable, not least because of the opportunities presented by the canal and railway. In 1850 agricultural writer Acland was evidently impressed on Mr Warry's 'fine turnips and magnificent rape', and Mr Strangways's 'great improvements' down on the Turbary Moor. From the perspective of an optimistic Victorian such as George Warry, living through a peak in confidence in the new industrial economy, even if his farming

ventures were speculative, the level of investment was actually modest when it was compared to the rental income to be had.[135] With this regular money in hand he could set about realising other projects around Shapwick House and in the village.

Woodlands

From the mid-eighteenth century Loxley had become a private wood managed for the lord of the main manor at Shapwick House. The other small areas of woodland in the parish today were all planted up following enclosure, including Icehouse Copse, Purchase Copse, Hawke's Hills and Limekiln Plantation in the west of the parish and in the eastern half Furze Nidon Copse, Henhills Copse, Beggars Bush Copse, Brickhills Copse and Fifteen Acre Copse.[136] Most were probably developed as cover for game birds for shooting and several are still used today for that purpose, as the recovery of gun cartridges by fieldwalkers indicates. As discussed in Chapter 7, Beggars Bush Copse covers an area of ridge and furrow earthworks that must have once formed part of the common fields. Similar earthworks can also be found in Icehouse Copse, as well as the remains of a brick-built circular icehouse of probable nineteenth-century date (Figure 9.37).[137] The trees here may have been planted to provide more cover and cooling shade. The wood at Henhills, too, might have originated as a grove of trees to shelter the garden features there (see Story, above), though it also contains introduced plants such as garden privet and snowberry.

Industry

Since the mid-eighteenth century there have been three windmills in Shapwick.[138] Maps dated 1750 and 1754 still show a windmill standing on its medieval site on the ridge to the south of the village.[139] This spot is marked up on the next available map with 'the old windmill removed in 1762' and a new windmill appears to the east on, or very near, one of the mounds near the old telegraph station at the top of Shapwick Hill, now redeveloped as a housing estate.[140] A watercolour by Claude Nattes of 1787 shows a stone tower mill complete with its cap and sails (see Figure 8.23B).[141] It was this structure that blew down on 29 November 1836 in a great gale. The miller, William Jones, was fatally injured and

Figure 9.36. Nineteenth-century farm complexes in Shapwick parish. A: Beerway Farm, lying immediately east of Old Church. The original approach to this farm was probably from the south rather than through the farm buildings as it is today. Cider house, dairy and cheese loft are integral to the house with a sheltered verandah for cooling milk. The associated farm buildings, which include stables, barn and cowshed, are probably all dated around 1861. In 1871 the farm comprised 220 acres and, judging by the buildings, it was largely dedicated to milk and cheese production. Notice also the cropmarks to the south of the lane, which suggest that stone may have been stripped in shallow diggings. Many aerial photographs show dark, roughly rectangular areas like this in fields. B: Brickyard Farm as it is today.

Figure 9.37. Remains of the icehouse in Icehouse Copse on the Nidons. Icehouses preserved blocks of ice cut from lakes or ponds in the winter. The ice was stored in straw in underground cool chambers, with drains below to remove any melt water. The ice was useful in the kitchens for cooling and in food preparation, especially desserts.

his brother was also badly hurt.[142] A few years later the two plots of land are labelled as the 'old windmill ground' on the tithe map of 1839.

Almost immediately after this tragedy a new windmill was constructed a little way down the slope to the east.[143] A new location may have been required because of the new turnpike (see above); no windmill was permitted within 200 yards of the road (Figure 9.38A). Sadly, this mill too met with an unhappy end and it seems to have been left empty by the unlucky Jones family after a fire around 1856.[144] By the time of the first edition Ordnance Survey map of 1886 the site is shown only as a circle, unlabelled, so it was probably already abandoned; it certainly was by 1906 when it was marked as the 'old windmill'. Today there is a well-preserved earthen mound near the field boundary. On the west side a gap in the mound leads to a well-preserved interior of stonework up to one metre high; evidently, as indicated on the tithe map of 1839, this was a stone tower mill.

Over roughly 550 years Shapwick had had four windmills, all for the milling of grain. Gradually,

however, these were replaced by new technology. A steam mill for flour was built next to the stream in the High Street by 1839 and the adjacent mill house, built a little while later, survives as a three-storey stone building (Figure 9.38B). It once had a loft for storage, mill stones on the second floor and a lean-to engine shed to the north and there is still what remains of a pond to supply water to the boiler.[145] Even this innovation, however, could not survive the arrival of the railway, after which hard wheat from abroad could be milled into flour at ports and then distributed. The steam mill was converted into a saw mill between 1905 and 1909.

At the time of the production of the first edition 6-inch to the mile Ordnance Survey maps in the 1880s there were still a number of active quarries across the centre of the parish. Others may have existed for a short time while the surface stone was removed but then these were quickly backfilled, producing the 'block' cropmarks sometimes seen from the air in drier seasons,[146] for example in Figure 9.36A, and leading to the intense scatters of nineteenth-century

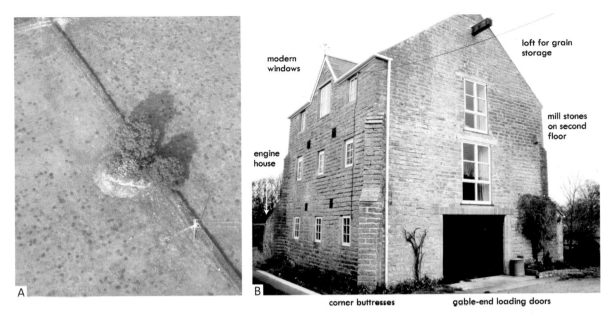

Figure 9.38. *Two later mills at Shapwick. A: aerial photograph of the nineteenth-century windmill, a replacement for the one drawn by Nattes. It was damaged by fire in 1856 and had ceased to be used by the late nineteenth century. B: the steam mill, built in the early nineteenth century and shown on the tithe map of 1839. A three storey stone building with a loft for grain, milling stones on the second floor, engine house to the north and a pond that supplied water to the boiler.*

roofing tile, slate and brick observed by fieldwalkers. Some of these quarries must have been opened up a long time previously – quarries are mentioned in the 1515 survey, as we have seen – and they are indicated too by field names in West Field on the tithe survey of 1839. Most of the stone extracted, particularly in the later period, would have been for walling in the houses and closes of the village and the construction of the new farms out in the fields.[147] Some would have been fired in the few limekilns in the parish, such as the ruined one on the road out of the village heading for Bridgwater. These kilns produced lime for the fields, but perhaps also mortar for building, lime plaster to coat the interiors of the houses and limewash for their exteriors.[148]

Among the industries new to the parish, a temporary brickyard is suggested at Brickhills Copse, named after brick clamps set up in the fields to supply local construction projects such as Northbrook Farm, which is not far away. Large numbers of fired-clay fragments were collected by fieldwalkers in an adjacent field[149] and many of these show signs

of primary burning and therefore a lack of kiln temperature control. A brick worker was probably locally contracted to work a source of local clay and in this respect it is intriguing that Edward Sealy, a well-known manufacturer of brick and tile from Bridgwater, was married to Mary Tylee at Shapwick in 1770. One may well ask how it is that Edward met Mary, and whether or not he was involved in a speculative brick-making venture in the parish with Denys Rolle, either then or later, perhaps at Northbrook or for the building of the brick dining room extension at Shapwick House.

Brickyard Farm, meanwhile, came into existence sometime between the date of the tithe map in 1839 and the census in 1871. Bricks were certainly manufactured here but the venture appears to have been experimental at best and the final product considered unsatisfactory.[150] There is certainly nothing to be seen at the site today. Semi-permanent buildings such as drying and moulding sheds would have left little trace in the landscape when removed, though it is possible that structures shown to the south and west of the farm in the mid-1880s had uses other than agricultural.[151] Quite possibly the aborted project was managed by one George Sharland, who appears as a brick and tile maker in the village census of 1851.

New lines of communication

The two great innovations of the late eighteenth- and nineteenth-century communications network were the canal and the railway. In 1825 proposals to build a canal from the sea near Highbridge to Glastonbury were already advanced and two years later an Act was obtained for its construction. It soon became clear, however, that the initial plan was impractical and in 1828 John Rennie, a civil engineer of national repute, recommended that the new line of the canal should adopt that of the South Drain dug out between 1801 and 1807 as part of the Brue Comprehensive Drainage Scheme.[152] At a depth of ten feet this was to be a deep canal, designed to take the forty- to sixty-ton coasters that plied the Bristol Channel. There was a single lock at Shapwick, three-quarters of a mile west of the later Shapwick railway station. This was supervised from The Lock Cottage (which no longer exists).[153]

Begun in 1829, the Highbridge to Glastonbury canal was finally opened on 15 August 1833, amid great celebrations (Figure 9.39). After a few modifications the new waterway proved a success for navigation as well as an additional outlet for flood waters.[154] Phelps, the Somerset historian, mentions that goods such as pottery, salt and coal from Manchester and Birmingham and iron from Newport and Cardiff were all brought up to Glastonbury, and in return elm timber, paving stones, corn, cheese and cider were taken out.[155] But maintaining the level of water in the canal eventually led to more, rather than less, flooding in the valley and the canal was eventually purchased by the railway company in 1848 at a price of £7,000.[156] The canal age was both late in coming to Shapwick and short-lived, unable to compete with the seductions of the 'express' train.

In 1852, the year after the Great Exhibition at Crystal Palace, the railway's new broad-gauge line began to be laid along the south bank of the canal from Highbridge most of the way to Glastonbury. Though railways were no longer a novelty and were still controversial for some, their advantages were well understood, particularly for the rapid distribution of consumer goods, such as milk, that were both perishable and bulky. The new line, which opened on 17 August 1854,[157] was called the Somerset Central Railway (SCR) and its chairman from 1855 to 1862 was none other than George Warry from Shapwick. The SCR later became part of the standard gauge Somerset and Dorset Railway, of which Warry served three stints as chairman (Figure 9.40).[158]

There was a local station with a level crossing and a signal box as well as an inn in Shapwick. These stood where the road north from the village crossed the railway and former canal, and the villagers shared in the excitement of their own railway service by renaming the main street Station Road. Doubtless this was Warry's idea. As far as is known, there was never any intention of making Shapwick a destination for workers' housing, stores or hotels, though the village might have expected to benefit from cheaper commodities and greater mobility, not to mention wider markets for its milk, timber and bricks. There were other recreational excitements to be had, too. In 1859 the line was extended east to Wells and the previous year holiday trains were already running to Burnham-on-Sea, from where the railway company laid on a paddle steamer to take its passengers to south Wales.[159]

The railway was the third in a series of infrastructural improvements in the period between 1750 and 1900, following the canal and, before that, the turnpikes. Together they not only brought more comfortable and faster travel for passengers, some of whom came to live in Shapwick from other parts of Britain, but also encouraged access to a range of new products. The sheer quantity of domestic rubbish we found on our excavations, from children's toys to shoe buckles, from factories far afield, shows the extent to which makers and traders could reach even the smallest rural communities. Where distribution networks were once local they were now far wider. In some respects Shapwick was now linked to the rest of the world, through the British Empire and its colonial links in the Rolles and Strangways families, the birthplaces of its schoolteachers and vicars and its altar rail of Australian oak. The same clay pipes discovered on excavations in Shapwick are also found in North

Figure 9.39. Celebrations at the opening of the Highbridge to Glastonbury canal in August 1833. The joy was short-lived and the canal was purchased by the railway fifteen years later and put out of business.

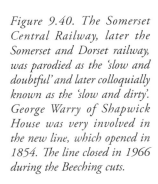

Figure 9.40. The Somerset Central Railway, later the Somerset and Dorset railway, was parodied as the 'slow and doubtful' and later colloquially known as the 'slow and dirty'. George Warry of Shapwick House was very involved in the new line, which opened in 1854. The line closed in 1966 during the Beeching cuts.

America. Yet, in so many other ways, as we have seen, this was a closed community with powerful, feuding patrons who spent money on Christian welfare at their local church and took a personal interest in schooling. But it was their investments in moulding their own miniature environments around their mansions that led to radical changes in the village plan and it was the tearing-down of houses and the blocking-up of roads during the process of emparkment between 1750 and around 1815 that surely had the greatest impact on the lives of their tenants. It was this that probably led to the construction of new houses, to rebuilding using new materials and also to overcrowding in some cases as dislodged tenants sought out new accommodation. The impact of national developments had a varying significance for different social classes. Yet while there was poverty and customary rights were diminished, including the erasure of the last vestiges of the open-field system, there were also specialised new agricultural buildings, eight new farmsteads outside the village, better drainage on the upland slopes and reclamation out on the wetland, and much else besides. Above all, although there were a variety of other crafts practised in the village, from construction to milling and basket making, life at Shapwick continued to revolve around agriculture.

The twentieth century

When the Shapwick Project began, virtually all of the farmland in the parish belonged to the Vestey family (see Chapter 1). Shapwick House, which was in separate ownership, had become a hotel,[160] while Shapwick Manor, the former Strangways residence, was purchased by the Vesteys in 1944 and afterwards leased out as a school for dyslexic pupils.[161] Momentarily at least, the new purchaser had once again reunited the parish into single ownership, just as it had been during the Middle Ages. Over the next four decades many houses in the village were sold off and, by the time the Project was ending, this pattern was being extended to farms and land. Several of the main farms were sold to their tenant farmers (Northbrook Farm to the Elliott family and Manor Farm to the Coombes family), a trend that seems likely to continue. In a few years' time landownership will no longer be a privilege shared

between the two manors, something that has been the norm at Shapwick since 1230; the traditional pattern will have been replaced entirely by individual farm-owners and private householders of cottages and houses, many of them newcomers who have brought a more integrated social mix.[162]

This upsurge in private ownership had its own impact on the village's twentieth-century development. No single landowner today has the economic will or authority to make sweeping changes to the settlement pattern such as those that took place in the eighteenth and nineteenth centuries. Indeed, at first glance, there is remarkably little difference between the village plan as mapped in 1904, on the left of Figure 9.41, and that of 1970–72, on the right. A closer look, however, reveals the multiplicity of changes. Inside houses there is now piped water, mains sewerage and electricity, all connected between 1920 and 1936.[163] Corresponding finds from our excavations and fieldwalking include Bakelite electric plugs, gutter and drain pipe casings, a curtain ring, chains for a bath plug, ballcocks, stopcocks and piping, not to mention discarded fire grates; all these are indicative of greater privacy and comfort in twentieth-century houses with interior bathrooms and central heating.[164] This, it appears, is the distinctive archaeology of the twentieth-century house, together with buttons, lead toy soldiers, a toy car, a brooch, a lapel badge, food waste in the form of ubiquitous aluminium ring-pulls, bottle tops, stoppers and plastic lids for sauce bottles – the everyday household losses and discards (Figure 9.42). Curiously, one of the most informative of archaeological sources – pottery – is actually quite rare, almost as rare as early medieval pottery; modern waste management has put a stop to the burying of waste on site and archaeologists of the future will have to look elsewhere for their clues.

Outside, farm buildings have been converted, garages for motor cars have replaced stables and outside privies, and the old orchards, so much a feature of medieval and later village life, have been infilled with new buildings;[165] there is also a small development of council housing to the south-east of the church. Infilling continued after 1988 when land was built over at Lawn Farm and along Mill Lane, Vicarage Lane, Church Lane and Bridewell Lane,[166] and the number of green spaces within the village

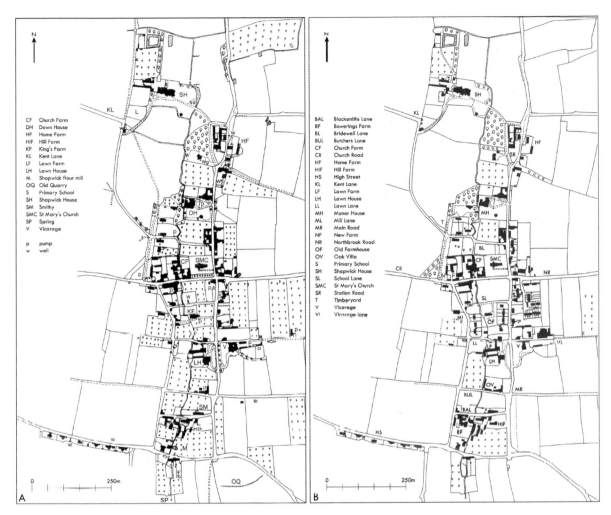

Figure 9.41. Plans of the village in 1904 (left) and 1970–72 (right). Notice the infilling at Oak Villa and near Church Farm, the changed footprint of the vicarage after it was rebuilt following a serious fire in 1920 and the new housing east of the school. The number of orchards has also declined over the course of the twentieth century, a process now being reversed in some parts of the county. Somerset is well known for cider production and has been for hundreds of years.

footprint is now far fewer than it has been at any time during the historic past. It was in acknowledgement of this that Lord Vestey gave the building that had been used as the village hall to the village.[167] Once again, the archaeology indicates a range of practical ways in which outdoor spaces have been used. A range of tools includes two hammer heads, two axeheads, saw blade fragments, garden rakes, spades, forks and billhooks; the industries of the gardener and the DIY enthusiast.

In 1935 Shapwick still boasted a blacksmith, a butcher, bakers, a grocer, a builder, an undertaker, carpenters and wheelwrights. Two World Wars left few obvious scars, at least on the physical fabric of the place,[168] and there are no pill boxes or other concrete or brick constructions in the parish from the 1940–45 period other than the communications centre that once stood to the south of the village.[169] Perhaps the most important transformation was a social one. For most of the twentieth century Shapwick retained its

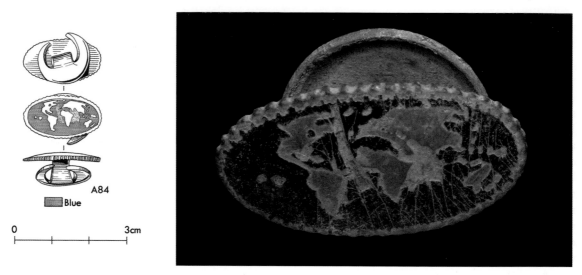

A84

Blue

0   3cm

Figure 9.42. A modern lapel badge depicting a world map, recovered by the fieldwalking team: an object which is emblematic of Shapwick's colonial contacts in the eighteenth and nineteenth centuries.

rigid social hierarchy, but today the traditional grip of the village squirearchy has evaporated entirely and although there are still a few who work as agricultural labourers on the local farms, most of the present residents of the village actually work outside the parish. Some drive down the ridgeway along the Poldens, now the A39 trunk road, for which there are plans for a dual carriageway, while others head for the old turnpike, which is still one of very few north–south routes in this part of the county. With their television sets and computers, village families can live in complete isolation from one another. Those who stay behind during the working day might be retired,[170] but few Shapwick residents are employed in the village now that the Post Office and village shop have closed. Where villagers once walked to work, mostly to manual occupations, professionals now drive. Members of staff even come from outside the village to work in the school at Shapwick Manor, where most of the children who attend (some of them boarders) are also from elsewhere – Anna Maria Templer would be disappointed to hear that the local children have attended the neighbouring village school at Catcott since Shapwick School closed in 1984.[171]

Outside the village, the peat-workings down on the Levels have long since been abandoned. Whereas peat was traditionally a fuel, latterly it was more profitably dried, milled and spread for soil improvement. In 1961 much of the Levels was designated a National Nature Reserve; in 1964 this was increased in size to 546 acres and the 90 acres of Canada Farm was made a Site of Special Scientific Interest.[172] Today little of the peat in local garden centres comes from Shapwick; there are more environmentally responsible substitutes and cheaper imports from Ireland and Russia. Those areas where peat has been extracted down to the underlying clay have become water-filled hollows, rich in wildfowl and wading birds, while other peat cuts are overgrown with scrub woodland, which is excellent cover for roe and fallow deer and other wildlife such as water voles. Change here is largely kept at bay. Looking to the future, much of the interest for the visitor in Shapwick may well be related to tourism and, if that is to be so, the results of the Shapwick Project should be a useful starting point from which to appreciate the human dimension of this part of central Somerset.

Today Shapwick Heath is a tranquil spot; all George Warry's ambitions for his railway came to nothing when the line closed in 1966 during the Beeching cuts. The railway hotel, bereft of regular custom, was demolished five years later.[173] But although the railway and its station have gone, many still remember the events of a foggy August morning in 1949 when there was a collision between a mixed train of the London, Midland and Scottish Railway (LMS)[174] and a narrow gauge peat train that had stalled on the level crossing. The derailed 0–6–0 LMS engine plunged down into the South Drain and buried itself in the peat. It took eight men eight days, working in eleven-hour shifts, to cut up the locomotive and tender into four pieces weighing a ton each and take them away. The engine itself could not be salvaged partly because it had sunk so far and partly because the adjacent ground was not solid enough for a crane capable of lifting it.[175] In 1980 it was reported that portions of the engine dug up by Wessex Water Authority during drainage work had been presented to the Somerset and Dorset Railway Museum Trust (Figure 9.43).[176]

Farming is no longer at the centre of village life. As recently as 1950 there were still many small farms in Shapwick, and one of the characteristics of the Poldens then was the sense of a shared life in contact with the land. Today only Bowerings Farm survives within the village itself, farmed by Eric Lockyer.[177] As fewer and fewer people have been needed to work the land, so the fields have become empty and farming has become disconnected. While some farming families retain a long association with the parish[178] not all have thrived. Two of Warry's speculative farms, Canada Farm and Brickyard Farm, the latter last mentioned as being occupied in 1931, are in ruins. Moorgate Farm lies empty and up for sale.[179] A map of the village with its tenant farmers and their holdings was prepared in 1954–5 on behalf of the Vestey estate,[180] a kind of mini-Domesday book of its own day and age. This shows that, fifty years ago, there were twenty-six tenants with more than five acres, though only nine of these held over 100 acres.[181] Only the largest of these holdings have survived as farming units[182] and by 1988 just seven farms still operated.[183] Farming families, in their late eighteenth- and nineteenth-century farmhouses, have lived through an age of mechanisation, ever more powerful farm machinery and the increasing use of fertilisers, not to mention the impact of subsidies and changing market demands. Much of the land is still

Figure 9.43 *The engine on the Somerset and Dorset railway after its collision with a peat train at a level crossing in Shapwick on a foggy August morning in 1949. In 1980 portions of the engine were dug up by Wessex Water Authority during drainage work and presented to the Somerset and Dorset Railway Museum Trust.*

pasture, many fields being on long leys – such as the field with the old church site, where the ground is ploughed and reseeded every five to seven years – but crops, too, have changed: maize is increasingly grown for fodder, and there is even some linseed and oilseed rape. It is here in the fields that the detritus of modern farming life continues to accumulate.[184] Fieldwalkers retrieved almost every imaginable part of a tractor or car that could come loose and fall, from spark plugs to windscreen wipers. There were also over 3,000 nails, ten spanners, three chisels, rasps, a punch, pliers, torch or headlight bulbs, crowbars, bucket handles, plastic tool handles of many different sorts, enough hinges, pivots, washers, nuts and bolts to run a stall at the market, caborundum whetstones, a farrier's knife, a bull leader, iron railings, 12-bore shotgun cartridge cases and plenty of barbed wire.

A slightly closer look at those fields shows that the 'enclosure landscape' completed in the early part of the nineteenth century has again been altered. Hedges have been grubbed up to create larger fields that now come closer in visual appearance to a later medieval open field; Dutch Elm disease has decimated the hedgerow timber that Denys Rolle would have known. There are still many links with the past, though. In 1987, when the Project began, Bert Hillburn, the estate foreman, continued to dig out Christmas trees for the tenants of the Vestey estate each year, an echo of an earlier time when the common rights of the tenants to graze animals and gather wood were relinquished and Loxley Wood became a private woodland. In recognition of his contribution, Limekiln Plantation was given by the Vestey estate to Bert in the 1990s. That same year the 21.25ha of Loxley were sold to the Woodland Trust, which has set about recreating it as a traditionally managed 'ancient' woodland by clearing it of conifers and opening up the canopy to encourage ground flora. For the first time since 1730 public access here is actively being encouraged.

Shapwick villagers are far more aware today than they have ever been about the development and evolution of their community and its landscape. When in 1990s the local authority for the area, Sedgemoor District Council, proposed a Conservation Area for the village, the boundary was fixed without any reference to the findings of this Project. Even when an extensive revision document was supplied by Mick to the Council with recommendations based on our research, still nothing was done. But more recently the villagers have had their own opportunity to submit a Village Design Statement document and this was subsequently published in 1999. This document does reflect many of the results of the Project and highlights some of the features found by people who worked with us over a decade and which have come to be seen as of value by many of the people in the village and, we hope, further afield. There is much in Shapwick today that would be unfamiliar even to a time-traveller from 1900 – structures of steel, concrete and corrugated iron, smooth roads, strange black and white cows in the fields, frighteningly quick cars, pylons and satellite dishes, the lack of shops or a smithy, the absence of horses and carriages, larger fields, overgrown hedgerows, the loss of flowery meadows and much more. He might be pleasantly surprised, though, on meeting a modern resident in the churchyard, to find out just how interested they seemed to be in him.

CHAPTER TEN

Wider Contexts

Accustomed as we are these days to the frenetic pace of environmental and social change within our own lifetimes, there is nothing unalterable about the English countryside. As we have discovered over the course of this project, the sickly sweet image of the rural landscape is far removed from reality. The Poldens, the hills on which the village of Shapwick sits, have evolved in many different ways over the past 12,000 years and the clues to those changes lie embedded in its landscape. In this book we have used many different techniques to tell the story of that transformation, relying for our narrative on the skills of the historian, the archaeologist, the human geographer, the standing buildings specialist and the practitioners of a variety of other disciplines ranging from chemistry to ecology.

The dynamism of change has been impressive. New boundaries have been etched, hedgerows planted, trees felled, farmsteads, settlements, inhabitants and their livestock have come and gone. If every generation reproduces every twenty-five years, then fewer than 500 generations have passed since early Mesolithic man trapped eels in the Brue valley. During that time change has sometimes been brusque, perpetrated within only a few years, and at other times it was been slower, noticeable only within a generation or two, but mostly it has been scarcely perceptible, unfolding over several centuries at a pace that the archaeologist can readily appreciate. We begin this chapter by examining the evolution of settlement and landscape at Shapwick according to three different scales: the long-term, the medium-term and the short-term. In the final section we reflect on the questions about village origins that first inspired this project.[1]

Over the long term

Settlement

The evolving pattern of settlement is most easily imagined as a twelve-minute black and white film with one minute dedicated to each thousand years of its history (Figure 10.1). If occupation across the parish were to be depicted as white lights of differing intensity, we would come away with a clear visual impression of how settlements have changed their locations, sizes and shapes in the past. Envisaged in this way, stripped of all detail, the first point to emphasise is that human activity in the parish did not suddenly begin in early prehistory and then intensify with a steady growth in population numbers according to any logical and discoverable formula. Instead, there are periods when human activity is more intensive and others when it seems barely perceptible. The latter is especially true of the later Mesolithic, the later Neolithic, the early Bronze Age and the early medieval periods. We do have to be careful that the weakness of human pulse in these earlier landscapes is not confused with our lack of ability to record it, and that fewer archaeological sites are not merely being registered because the material culture in use at the time has survived less well. With that caveat, however, the on–off flickering of human activity, with its episodes of presence and absence, does appear to be a genuine feature of the archaeological record for much of the human past. This recurrent pattern might be described as slow evolution, though one that is interrupted at unpredictable intervals by sudden transformative bursts. This creates a rising and falling cycle of human activity whose wavelength would have been beyond the appreciation of a single human being, beyond that even of several generations.

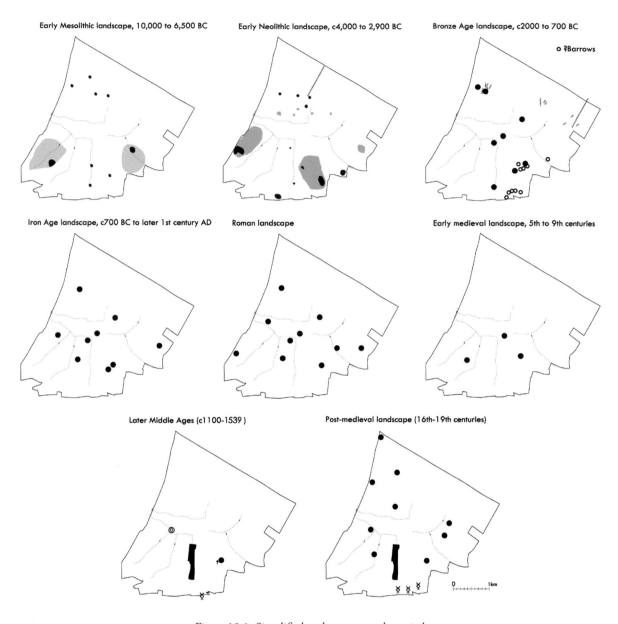

Figure 10.1. Simplified settlement maps by period.

A second surprise is that for much of prehistory and the Roman period settlement at Shapwick was dispersed, not clustered in one place as it is mostly today. For much of the duration of our film the lights remain tiny, bright, but far apart. This is because people lived together as families in farmsteads or in small groups in hamlets that were spread out across the landscape. Only when we reach the tenth century is there a dramatic change, just for the last minute of our twelve-minute cinematic presentation, when the population suddenly converges on one location on the map. As archaeologist John Hurst used to

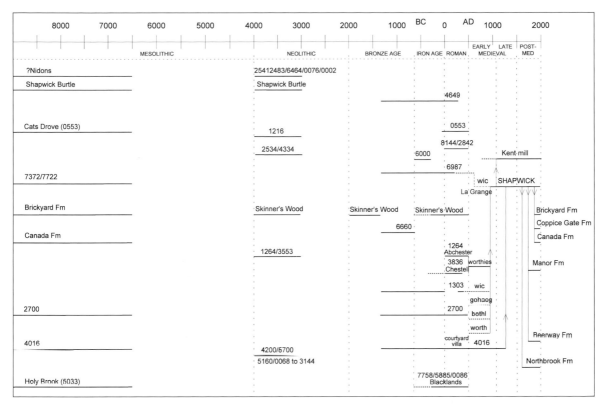

Figure 10.2. Chronological chart showing settlements and other centres of activity by period.

say of Wharram Percy in Yorkshire, the village is an 'aberration' when compared with the way settlement has traditionally been organised. This is only partly true of Shapwick because, as we have seen, there were Roman 'villages' in existence previously; what is unusual in the tenth century, however, is that life in a larger community was the *only* option, at least on the Poldens. It is precisely this restricted range of habitat that is aberrant; human societies in the past have generally not lived in this way, all grouped together in one place. Given that this 'habitat' was to a large extent conditioned by a set of imperatives (field systems, land ownership) that no longer apply, one wonders how the settlement pattern would continue to evolve in the future were legislative constraints to be relaxed.

Although the *form* of settlement may have changed, another feature of the evolving settlement

pattern that should be very clear from our film is that there have been persistent periods of relative stability when the same general locations have been preferred for settlement (Figure 10.2). It is true that some settlements appear and then vanish again, never to return; the Roman village at *Blacklands* is one of these (see Chapter 5). But this is not common. Instead, many places have extremely long histories of occupation, especially those close to water and on lighter soils, and, if we were to slow down the film and examine this trend a little more closely, there seems to be a constant shuffling – a jockeying for position over the same ground. The area in and around *Old Church* (4016), to take one example, includes scatters of material from the earlier Mesolithic right through to the fourteenth century, and then again from the mid-nineteenth century through to the present day. Its modern manifestation is Beerway Farm. Clear

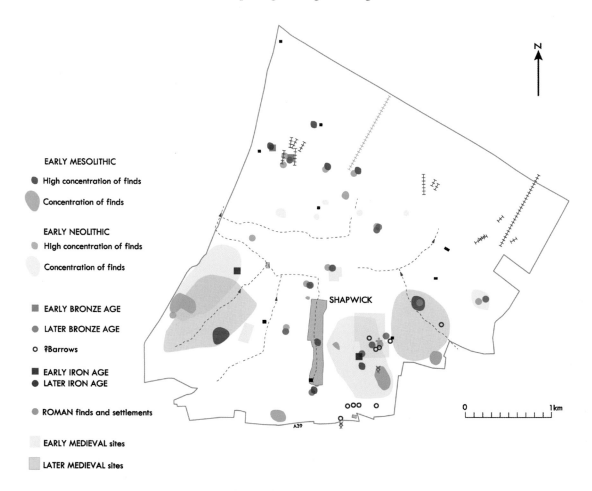

EARLY MESOLITHIC

● High concentration of finds

● Concentration of finds

EARLY NEOLITHIC

● High concentration of finds

● Concentration of finds

■ EARLY BRONZE AGE

● LATER BRONZE AGE

○ ?Barrows

■ EARLY IRON AGE
● LATER IRON AGE

● ROMAN finds and settlements

EARLY MEDIEVAL sites

LATER MEDIEVAL sites

SHAPWICK

Figure 10.3. Parish map showing all known archaeological sites.

preferences for specific locations such as this one can easily be picked out on Figure 10.3, which shows the complete map of all the archaeological sites discovered during the Project. While almost every square metre of the map shows some evidence of past land use or settlement, the lower and middle uplands in particular are densely smothered in archaeology, especially around the mid-slope 25–30m contour. On the higher slopes above 60m rather less activity is evident, but there is still early Neolithic occupation in Field 2534/4334 (Figure 3.9), the ridgeway route and the sites of the medieval gallows and a windmill.

In addition to resources such as water, a pervasive influence on settlement location has been the past

itself. To focus just on the post-Roman period, *Sladwick* (1303) was the site of a Roman masonry building and a small cemetery in the early medieval period, probably during the sixth century (see Chapter 6). This choice of location for burial may have been intended, quite deliberately, to forge a link with the ancestral past.[2] Likewise, *Old Church* (4016) is one of more than 250 sites across England at which Roman structures became the focus for a church in the early medieval period.[3] Rather than argue for the continuation of a local Roman Christian cult, we have suggested that the continuity of secular authority here for over 1,000 years from the Roman period until the late thirteenth century was itself a powerful attractor, the location of the medieval church being intimately linked to that authority in the Middle Ages. If this interpretation is correct, then the early medieval structures here were perhaps intended to revitalise that sense of power.

This same principle can be applied to buildings and even to objects. In Chapter 8 we discussed the similarities in plan between the now-vanished church of St Andrew and its fourteenth-century replacement of St Mary, the present church that stands in the centre of Shapwick (see Chapter 8). We do not believe this likeness to be coincidental; quite the opposite. Here, architecture is perhaps being deployed coercively, so that the message it carries reads 'not to worry, the future will be like the past, time is changeless, and we may be depended upon'. Although no individual architectural stonework elements such as doorways or windows were recycled during its construction (at least as far as we can tell), the borrowing of the design of an earlier building evokes, it seems to us, a sense of continuity. For Shapwick villagers of the Middle Ages the past was not dead: it was a living entity that they used to construct contemporary ideas and understandings. Nowhere is this more clearly seen than in the twelfth-century Irish socket and holder with its Bronze Age blade recovered from its late eighteenth-century context in Shapwick Park: recycled items from prehistory and the Middle Ages combined as one (see Chapter 9). Two pasts embedded in the life of a single object.

In one form or another, memory has been a recurring theme throughout this book. We see it most obviously today in place- and field names. Kent Farm, for example, is a long-serving name that has been in use from at least the first half of the fourteenth century. It captures a memory of a single medieval person, John Kent, and links him with a place in the landscape, in this case the watermill where he was once the miller. This example, and the many others like it, add time depth to the modern landscape.[4] In the same way Shapwick field names recall people, animals and birds, land use, long-harvested crops and even events, in the case of *Nuthergoldhurd*, recorded in 1313 (see Chapter 2) or the naming of Canada Farm (see Chapter 9). These are not merely casual signposts. In a world where so much of the transfer of knowledge was oral, they say 'this is the

place where …'. In so doing, they reflect what was significant to the individuals who did the naming and, in due course, those who came afterwards and remembered. Field names strengthen the community's emotional connection to the land; they are, in that sense, 'biographical' because they invite curiosity and questions as well as delivering information. A particular feature of Shapwick's landscape, and of those of many other parishes across Britain, is the extent to which modern field names reflect multiple layers of memory all telescoped together into a single map. As we have seen, some names have mutated over time to become almost a meaningless cipher. *Henry* and *Greazy*, echoes of early medieval habitation, are two such (see Chapter 5), and it is revealing how, in spite of a long tradition of furlong and field names being written down, these names have nevertheless continued to evolve in written custumals and later maps. This is because the transmission of field names from generation to generation and periodically to clerk or surveyor was still oral. At the same time, there have been times when field names were swept away with sudden force and replaced by something altogether new, not unlike a board rubber sweeping across the countryside and erasing all that lies in its path. This rewriting must have occurred when the open fields first came into being, but it has been a continuous process since, particularly during the process of enclosure between the fifteenth and early nineteenth centuries when new fields with different dimensions and shapes came into being (see Chapters 8 and 9). And yet, in spite of the apparent pervasiveness of this process, so many of the Shapwick names are ancient. There has never been much advantage to unnecessary change that confounds traditional nomenclatures and accounting systems and, for many centuries at Shapwick, farmers, reeves, stewards and bailiffs under the watchful eye of Glastonbury Abbey have remained the guardians of collective memory. Stable ownership has promoted continuity.

Environment

Of course, we could greatly enhance the scenery for our twelve-minute film by adding in what we know about Shapwick's vegetation and landscape history. This is not to be treated as mere background; it is much more than that, providing the essential

BOX 10.1

The essentials

Reflecting now, at the end of the project, on the essentials for this study, the first prerequisite must be a good set of maps. We were lucky at Shapwick that there were so many cartographic sources that pre-dated the tithe map of 1840; in all, fifteen early maps eventually became available, not only pre- and some post-enclosure maps of the parish but also maps of the village itself, many of them drawn before the emparking activity around the main manor house. Without these detailed maps, valuable information about major and minor changes in the pattern of fields in the parish and the details of the houses and plots in the village would have been lost to us.

A second prerequisite is a wide range of documents. While it is reasonable to expect most places and parishes to have an entry in Domesday Book, be listed in medieval lay subsidies and poll taxes and to be the subject of an abundance of post-medieval documents, a place for which there are Anglo-Saxon charters with bounds and extensive medieval documentation, including court and compotus rolls, extents and surveys, is likely to offer more success in the extraction of details such as place- and field names. A powerful bureaucratic landowner such as an abbey like Glastonbury or a bishopric will have usually commissioned detailed surveys and, because of the inherent conservatism of such institutions, the documents are likely to have survived. The same is less true for secular records, particularly for the Middle Ages, because changes of dynasties and the failure of male lines of inheritance frequently disrupted the compilation or retention of documents in major aristocratic families, with the possible exception of royalty.

Wide or total fieldwork coverage is also desirable if the results are to be meaningful, and modern landownership is therefore crucial to the success of any project (in England, at any rate, where permissions are required). We were able to build good relations with the Vesteys' land agent, Bill Robbins, and with most of the parish's half-dozen or so tenant farmers, and there is no doubt that the single ownership of most of the land in the parish was a tremendous advantage. Were we to begin again, the presence of a single owner or relatively few owners would probably influence our choice of study area and we might even consider some form of binding agreement or code of practice before starting out. While a certain amount can be achieved by walking lanes and public footpaths, in the end permission for work over the land must be given wholeheartedly if the research is to run smoothly. One reluctant farmer right in the middle of the area being investigated can inevitably lead to an awkward hole in the data.

Good public relations, too, are absolutely vital (Figure B.10.1). We needed access to all sorts of places during the course of the project. This included pasture, arable and woodland as well as gardens, lawns and vegetable patches. A project such as this *has* to fit its research into the cropping patterns and land management of the farms. Finding out where stock was and where it was going to be moved to; which areas had been or were about to be ploughed; when they had been power-harrowed and when sown: all these became weekly concerns

resources and the very topography on which humans settled. In Chapter 3 we described the early Mesolithic impacts on the early Holocene pine–hazel woodland that created a mixed, and partially cleared, deciduous woodland around 5720–5530 BC with a fringe of willow and alder on the peat edge. Following partial regeneration in the later Mesolithic (*c.*6500–4000 BC) and renewed efforts at upland clearance during

the Early Neolithic (*c.*4000–2900 BC) there was regeneration once again, and a major episode of clearance later in the Bronze Age (AD 900–500). Before this, the character of the landscape had been profoundly changed, not just by the actions of humans on the upland but by environmental changes to the lowland too. From this time onwards there was to be a more open landscape and by the later Iron Age most of the field survey team. Permission to excavate also had to be negotiated some time in advance and, most sensitive of all, gaining access to people's homes for the purposes of building survey can be a delicate process. All of these ventures demand partnerships and from the outset communication and cooperation with the local people in the village was made a high priority. In this respect, it would have helped enormously if we had had at least one project member resident in the village for the full duration of the project, though we did our best to make ourselves available and to disseminate our results as widely as possible.

The Shapwick Project produced a huge quantity of individual archaeological finds, mainly pottery, tile, flint, bone and so on. Not only was the sheer density of material far greater than we had anticipated but the number of sites was also unexpectedly high. This was especially the case for the prehistoric and the Roman periods, where of course we were operating in a relatively well-researched environment. With the bedrock being so shallow we had forecast a widespread but diffuse pattern of finds, rather than the tight and structured patterns that emerged. To exploit these datasets to the full any project needs finds and pottery specialists to identify the objects collected. We were lucky to be able to draw together just such a team of experts, but the problem in Somerset, as we have seen, is that there does not seem to be much pottery produced at all between about AD 400 and 900, just at the time when some of the most interesting developments were happening in the village and its landscape.

Elsewhere in England the existence of pottery products from well-developed pottery industries at Ipswich, Stamford and St Neots mean that quite clear phasing of sites can be suggested from the changing pottery styles and fabrics. We made great difficulties for ourselves by choosing to work in a part of the country with so little in the way of ceramic evidence to help us identify sites in the critical early medieval period. On the other hand, it was precisely the lack of information from pottery that encouraged us to innovate and to think about other ways and means, such as geophysics, soil geochemistry and the study of field names.

Figure B.10.1. Guiding visitors around the excavation trenches on an open day at Shapwick.

of the natural woodland in the study area had already been felled. It is a striking thought that the essential land-use distribution of the historic and modern landscape, the physical skeleton of the countryside, was already established by later prehistory.

During the Roman period the upland landscape appears to have been intensively cultivated, with pasture closer to the Levels (see Chapter 4). There

would have been an extensive network of tracks that ran between blocks of enclosed fields, some of whose boundaries were already in place well before the Roman conquest. Even by this date Loxley was probably already in existence as a discrete block of woodland that has been discontinuously managed ever since. We have proposed a reduction in arable after the end of the fourth century, with less intensive working of the land until around AD 1000, and with expanses of woodland on the lower slopes and around the later Loxley Wood. Though we cannot prove it, we think it likely that dispersed farmsteads maintained their own infields for crops and outfields where livestock would have grazed (see Chapter 5). Sheep in particular may have been important, giving the place its name – sheep-'wic'. After AD 1000, by which time the two open fields had been laid out, arable expanded once again, and there was a possible further extension of the cultivated area around AD 1200 into East Field by Northbrook (see Chapter 6) and outwards to the parish boundaries which may have been coincident with common field regulation. Thereafter, the essentials of the modern landscape were in place and striking changes that followed were not so much in the balance of woodland and arable as in the enclosure of fields and the way in which the land was divided up on the ground. In particular, the lengthy process of piecemeal and later parliamentary enclosure has been the most fundamental transformation in the visual character of the agricultural landscape since the fifteenth century. As for the settlement patterns, where we have observed reiterative imprints and cycles, in essence much the same is true of field systems. 'Enclosure' took place in later prehistory and intensified through the Roman period, 'de-enclosure' followed when the open fields were laid out and then 'enclosure' began again after the fifteenth century. Over recent decades the cycle has been reversed once again, as farmers have been induced to remove inconvenient hedgerows to create larger fields for homogenised industrial agriculture.

This sense that there are cycles of long-term change in the landscape is inescapable. Boundaries fall in and out of favour depending upon the way farming is organised; settlement sites flicker on and off, sometimes in an episodic manner, with long intervals of time between periods of occupation. Why should this be? In the very broadest terms these cycles can be attributed to the inter-relationship between population and land use, with rising numbers of people leading to pressure on ecological resources and, sometimes, their mismanagement.[5] This is not the whole story, however. The natural environment has also intervened, specifically in prehistory when sea-level changes altered the pattern of resources.

That said, it is always the same heartbeat that lies behind people's lives on the Poldens – farming. While it may be true that the parish's natural building resources of stone, lime, wood and withies have been variously exploited, it is the everyday needs of the farmer for fresh water, for drainage, for shelter, for less rain and for warmer winds that have honed decisions about the best places to live, plough and grow crops and vegetables. Year in, year out, there has been the ceaseless round of ploughing, planting, weeding and harvesting of arable crops and the management of flocks and herds of domesticated animals (Figure 10.4). Whatever else was happening here – and we have spent much time looking at settlement development, building types, quarrying and so on – a major theme that has dominated life in Shapwick for most of the last 5,000 years has been agriculture. This is why patterns of prehistoric and Roman land use have had such an influence on later field boundaries, even when a village with new arable and pastoral systems was brought into existence by the tenth century.[6] Of course, whether farming will continue to fashion the landscape is more uncertain; it may be that a new phase is on the horizon, one that is not primarily driven by food production but that cherishes different values such as conservation and access. If that proves to be so, we hope that the results of the Shapwick Project might have a part in that future.

In terms of the relationship between local communities and their farming environment, a peculiar characteristic of the Polden parishes is how they unite upland with lowland, high with low, dry with wet, 'tamed' with 'wild'. In this project we have tried to draw both halves of that equation together, to view the landscape holistically as one geographical context. These contrasts have given rise to widely differing attitudes that provide a good example of long-term processes in action. On the one hand, for much of history the wet fen resources have been a provider and an asset. In medieval times, for instance, wildfowl, eels and fish, building materials, fuel and summer pasture were routinely exploited (see Chapter 7). So powerful have been these attractions at certain points in the human past that when the symbiosis between dry upland and wetland was disrupted it could affect the whole register of human activity.

Figure 10.4. Agriculture through the ages at Shapwick. A: reaping the crops with sickles. Note that the women are cutting the crop while the man gathers it into sheaves. Image from the fourteenth-century Luttrell Psalter BL 42130, f.172v. B: modern tractor with twin wheels and power harrow behind.

Around 5200–4800 BC, when the reeds and sedges available to early Mesolithic man were submerged beneath a rising water table, this transformed an environment of opportunity into one of constraint, upsetting seasonal patterns of hunting and gathering and wiping markers of human communities from our pollen diagrams. For early Mesolithic man, the wetland and the estuary were life-giving, one of the richest environments of all.

On the other hand, what passed as an environmental

catastrophe for Mesolithic man was precisely what the 'improving' landlord wished for in the eighteenth century. By that date the wetland was loathed by some as a profitless bog, something to be struggled against and vanquished, to be drained and sucked dry. Denys Rolle, gazing out from the vantage point of his well-ordered gardens at Shapwick House in the early 1780s, musing over his recent adventures in Florida, regarded the wilderness of the Levels with disdain and from a suitable distance. For him the wetland held no deeper significance, except as a botanical hunting ground on his many walks. One bold scheme touted that it be got rid of once and for all by digging out the Poldens clay and spreading it onto the peat like creamy butter.[7] As Rolle saw it, the subsequent intake and enclosure of 'new' land would put paid to the irritations of customary rights such as the digging of peat for fuel and create at least some potential for profit. It is only more recently, with the rise of the conservation movement and increasing awareness of its archaeology and wildlife, that the peat has again become a valued treasure. The same might be said of woodland, another of the parish's natural resources, now that the Woodland Trust has taken over the ownership and management of Loxley Wood.

We should recognise, too, that the wetland was not merely an economic resource; in the past it was a *special place* too. In Chapter 3 we suggested that the prehistoric wetland was a biologically fertile place, alive and vital for life. At times the natural environment may have played its part in rituals that involved water, the trackways that orchestrated movement out across the bog and the deposition of objects as well as animal and human remains. Though a great deal of evidence may have been lost to later peat cutting, there is much in common here with other prehistoric 'ritual landscapes' such as those claimed at Flag Fen, Fiskerton in Lincolnshire and across the Fens.[8] And we see the intimacy of people and natural places once again in the late fourth century, when sets of complete metal objects such as coins and bowls were buried in the peat (see Chapter 5). At this period the range of objects and their burial places are monotonously repeated, and we readily interpret these deposits as reflecting the actions and anxieties of wealthy local families who preferred to bury their valuables, hoping for a better day. Shapwick hoards of this date include one of the largest hoards of Valentinianic coins from Britain and by far the largest hoard of denarii. But, as we saw in Chapter 4, these finds do raise questions. Why did their owners never return? Were the locations of their hoards forgotten, or were they never meant to be retrieved in the first place? To what extent might hoarding in the wetland reflect more ancient tradition, a ritual dimension developed as early as the Neolithic, when the wetland may have had some spiritual meaning, and continued

in the Bronze Age and later (see Chapter 3)? If all these activities *do* have something in common with each other, it is that they connect the wetland with a sense of liminality, of 'otherness' and the supernatural, of being 'outside the normal'. No one who has experienced the strange summer mists creeping over the moor or the swirling flocks of starlings in late autumn could doubt the natural wonder of the place. In this landscape water is elemental and the wetland and their trackways offer an opportunity to tread through it, over pools and bogs with their own distinctive vegetation and wildlife, to experience a more isolated environment.[9]

In the early Middle Ages Christian religious foci were to be found on the islands and peninsulas that rose above the Brue valley. Glastonbury Abbey had hermitages or 'holy foci' out on the local islands at Andersey, Godney, Martinsey and Beckery, within the 'Twelve Hides' that constituted its early heartland estate. Here again, perched on local landmarks and surrounded by water and bog, it was the isolation and remoteness of the wetland that were sought out, and by the eighth century AD causeways were again being constructed as Glastonbury Abbey expanded its territorial interests and infrastructure along the Poldens (see Box 5.1). While we cannot demonstrate an ongoing tradition of medieval votive deposits associated with the wetland because of the cutting-away of historic peats, we may suspect a specific symbolic connection between this landscape and the early monastery, with very familiar solutions to the problems of movement.

Even for later Christians the sensory and symbolic environment was far from restricted to the interior of the church. The fourteenth-century stream called *Halghebrok*, which had become 'hollybrook' by the seventeenth century, taken together with references to a 'Holy Well' near Northbrook Cottage from the late eighteenth century, are a reminder of the continuing importance of the natural environment and water, though by the later Middle Ages it was locations on the upland that were marked out and named. The traditional view would be that these, and other small-scale sacred sites along the Poldens, may once have been places of pagan veneration that were adopted after Christian conversion, though whether or not there is any continuity between Romano-

Celtic (or earlier) paganism and later folk beliefs is entirely unproven here; there is no known association between either of these sites and the murder of St Indracht (see Chapter 1) or indeed with any other person, ceremony or belief.[10] The 'Holy Well', even if it was claimed to have mildly sulphurous curative properties in the nineteenth century, has no earlier documentary credentials, unless the *Hallebrok* or *Hallbrook* mentioned in fourteenth-century court rolls, perhaps a second 'Holy Brook', is in some way associated. This watercourse runs immediately adjacent to the later well. Unfortunately, archaeology may not be helpful here; the brook has been scoured and the well was 'cleansed out' in the nineteenth century. Only the site of St Andrew's church, immediately adjacent to an important spring site with long prehistoric associations, currently offers a more convincing link with past practice, and is the one site in the parish to acquire buildings and an institutional status that ensured its survival. Even here, as we have seen, continuity of sacred ground is a difficult thing to prove with absolute confidence.

So what conclusions can we draw from this evidence about the symbolism of the natural environment? There is sufficient to suggest repeated use of the wetland parts of the parish for ritual purpose from the Neolithic to the late Roman period. For the early historic periods, the archaeological evidence has either been removed or remains unexplored, and we are left with fragmentary clues – but this is not confirmation that the wetland held no symbolic meaning. It is likely that it did. At the same time, evidence from the later Middle Ages for a holy well and a stream on the uplands of the parish, partial though it may be, reminds us that the prehistoric ritual landscape may not have been confined to the wetland and also that the natural environment could have enduring connotations into later periods. More ancient sacred traditions were assimilated rather than discontinued.

In the medium term

Medium-term change is as well appreciated in the historical record as it is through the lens of archaeology. A key theme in the Shapwick story, for example, is the intimate link between lordship

and landscape. During the last decades of the twentieth century Shapwick was largely owned by one family, the Vesteys (see Chapter 1), but this is not the first time in its history that there has been a single landowner here. Between the eighth and the sixteenth century Glastonbury Abbey took up that role. The close proximity of the Abbey to the village, the value of the lands it held 'in hand' there and the importance of Shapwick for the monastic economy as a whole all meant that the officials of the Abbey paid close attention to the organisation and running of its estate. These were no absentee landlords. The Abbey determined everything from the choice of field systems to the crops in the fields. Although the abbot himself may have been a remote figure, the monastery was the focus of administration. Most residents on the manor, it must be remembered, were its tenants or employees, all the land belonged to the Abbey and the manor court, the forum for dispute and justice, was held in the Abbey's name (see Chapter 7).

Later lordship is of interest too. Even after the Dissolution of Glastonbury Abbey in 1539 and the frenzy of land transactions that followed, Shapwick still had only two major estates. The owners of Shapwick House and Shapwick Manor were to become the dominant forces in the parish over the next 400 years. During the eighteenth and nineteenth centuries it was still they who owned the land, controlled tenant housing and created farms and a park. They exercised their social authority through their varied appointments as MPs or JPs, for instance, and their moral discipline through the provision of improving cultural facilities such as schools and the Poor House (see Chapter 9). Although Shapwick was never an estate or 'closed village', it displays many of the characteristics of one and operated very much like one. As a result, a pervasive feature of life here until the middle of the twentieth century was what might now be termed 'low social differentiation', something that has only begun to evolve over the last fifty years or so. Older residents say that they were well treated as tenants as long as they toed the line, and that they could rely on help in hard times. The landowners were philanthropic but the cost in terms of personal development was high. Although nineteenth-century census records show that there were crafts, trades and a few shopkeepers in the village, there is also a noticeable absence of private enterprise. There is little evidence of manufacturing or industrial activity, for example. Without being actively enforced for the most part, there have been specific rules of conduct and behaviour (seating in church, for example) which have, over many centuries, counter-balanced the ambitions of the individual.

The highly stratified nature of society is something that has long been recognised as a feature of the English village and, in the case of Shapwick, change was inhibited in several ways.[11] For one thing, the relative stability of population kept the numbers of labouring poor, craftsmen and yeomen roughly in proportion. This tended to minimise social difference and promoted a stronger sense of community consciousness among the villagers. In effect, the development of widely varying group identities was retarded. Second, the centripetal forces that drove villagers to act as a community – its agriculture, the church, the lack of nonconformists, the absence of an alehouse, the imposition of social discipline over sexual behaviour and much else besides – outweighed the forces for change. Third, Shapwick is perhaps unusual in some respects in having experienced such extraordinarily long periods of control by one or two families who themselves dictated everything from social composition to housing stock. Nevertheless, in spite of this, a more critical analysis of housing, artefacts and diet reveals a far from homogenous scene. As our studies of architecture and archaeology demonstrate, not all houses were the same, not everyone ate the same food, people dressed in different ways and sometimes, the obvious case being that of the local Quaker communities, they went so far as to deliberately emphasise their differences (see Chapter 8). The Shapwick 'stage' may have come with its own embedded conventions, but the villagers were independent actors in many other respects.

In the last two chapters of this book we have seen how developments at Shapwick after the Reformation began to reflect broader social and economic frameworks at national and international levels. This shift from medieval to modern, from localism towards wider cultural change, is repeatedly demonstrated in many different aspects of the archaeological, historical and architectural record.[12] For example, there is new and fashionable pottery made in matched sets in white to accompany new manners at the table, and mass-produced and standardised goods which, by the nineteenth century, were being carted up the straightened roads of the turnpike (1827–39), floated gently down the Glastonbury canal (1833) or sped along the Somerset Central railway (1854). The theatres in which this new world of consumption was played out were the Shapwick houses where social difference was expressed through education and manners. At the same time, as a counter-balance to this more autonomous behaviour, other basic features of pre-industrial Shapwick were left untouched. Forces for integration were ever persistent. For example, the single event that affected the appearance of the village more than any other was the upgrading of the housing stock during the late eighteenth and early nineteenth centuries. Nearly all the smaller tenanted houses in the village were 'improved' by their landlords, their walls being raised with new roofs at a lower pitch and pantiles substituted for the original thatch. At the same time the small windows of the earlier houses were replaced with more up-to-date sashes and casements, some houses being refaced entirely with new stone. Their greater height and the uniformity of their building materials gave a new, more gentrified character to the village that was very different from the previous village scene, with its houses of steep-pitched thatch. Even those houses that were not externally 'improved' were altered inside. Houses such as Forsters were given new floors, chimneys and internal partitions, while outside in the fields the processes of enclosure were proceeding apace: the erasure of medieval strips and furlongs, the draining of the Levels and the closing-off of common land for profit. All of this, houses and fields alike, was carefully inked onto the new estate maps that showed the order of the landscape and provided proof of property for men of authority. In the emerging of the modern world, the old hierarchies were left largely untouched.

Short-term change

At the other end of our timescale there were rapid changes as a result of political and cultural events far away. The village is drawn into the events of history books, such as the English Civil War and the Monmouth rebellion, through its traditions of folklore – but they are sometimes much more difficult to detect in the archaeological record. Viking incursions, the Norman Conquest, the Black Death: these are among the moments of historical significance that seem almost invisible. Needless to say, it is those events that have a clear impact on the social and economic fabric which *are* apparent to the archaeologist, among them the 'end of the Roman Empire' and the subsequent abandonment of farms and the hoarding of valuables (see Chapter 5); the reinvigoration of monastic landscapes in the tenth century that we suggest led to the creation of the village; the Dissolution of the Monasteries in the sixteenth century, with its opportunities for investment in newly acquired properties; the increased profits to be had from grain farming after the Napoleonic wars that stimulated the building of Shapwick's first ring fence farm at Northbrook in 1778 and the enclosure of the peat moor in 1784;[13] and the arrival of the canal and railway (see Chapter 9). Here we see national and international processes impinging on local life. No rural community is either self-contained or changeless, even in a parish such as Shapwick that has been characterised by dominant power structures for so many hundreds of years.

Settlement at home and abroad

In this final section of this book we return to one of its core themes: the origins of Shapwick village. Through archaeological fieldwork and a combination of other techniques drawn largely from architecture and history we have discovered that later medieval Shapwick was a place in which almost everyone lived together in a single compact village (see Chapter 7). With the exception of the occupants of the mill at Kent Farm and the old *curia* in *Old Church* (4016), inhabitants – such as Matilda atte Welle, who we met in the story at the beginning of Chapter 7 – did not live in isolated farms scattered about the landscape. Farming was organised along communal lines, so that Matilda and the other villagers cultivated holdings across two large fields, of which one lay fallow every year.

Since the early twentieth century scholars have realised that this arrangement of village and common

fields is typical of a strip of English countryside that runs diagonally from County Durham and North Yorkshire through the Midlands to central southern England. Outside the width of this diagonal strip settlements tend to be smaller and more dispersed, with more extensive areas of pasture and woodland. Within it, however, is a countryside that landscape historians refer to as 'champion' land, the 'Central Province' or the 'Midland system', none of them terribly satisfactory terms (Figure 10.5). Try going into a travel agent and booking a holiday in 'Central Province', and you will probably get a ticket to Nice! Nonetheless, very thorough mapping of the morphology of nineteenth-century rural settlements across England has highlighted the distinctive nature of settlement across this part of Britain, of which Shapwick seems to be typical.[14]

If we now rewind the distribution of settlement at Shapwick back 1,000 years to AD 250, it is apparent from our fieldwalking and excavation results for the Roman period that the inhabitants of the parish did not always live in one place (see Chapter 4). The Roman distribution map is quite different to that of today, with perhaps as many as ten settlements spread about at intervals across the Polden slope. In our discussion of this post-Roman picture in Chapter 5 we were able to suggest, largely on the basis of field names, together with some evidence from excavation at *Sladwick* (1303) and *Old Church* (4016), that there is some basic continuity in settlement locations from the Roman period (bearing in mind the sort of 'shuffling' described above) and also that the settlement pattern was still dispersed when it came to be named in Old English, perhaps in the eighth century.

These observations lead us to two basic conclusions. First, at some time in the past there has been a dramatic transformation in the settlement pattern at Shapwick. The long tradition of dispersed settlements that begins in prehistory, that is certainly present in the later Bronze Age and that continues through into the early Middle Ages is gone by the later Middle Ages. Second, we can pinpoint the date of this transition to sometime between AD 700 and 1250. It was in this period that the distinctive settlement pattern represented by the 'Central Province' emerged. The question is – can the 'moment' of nucleation be

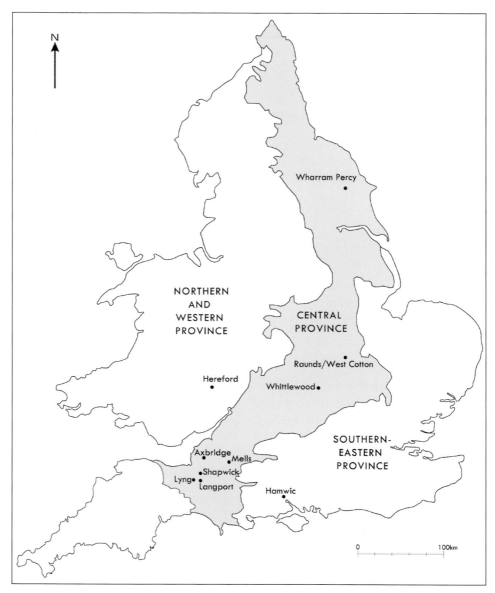

Figure 10.5 Regional variations in landscape character as defined by Roberts and Wrathmell (2002), with locations for places mentioned in the text (after Rippon 2008a, fig. 1.6).

refined down within that 550-year span? Archaeology and history provide some answers.

A question of dating
Refinement of these dates can be approached from both ends of our timescale, but it is easiest to begin

by working backwards from 1250 towards the turn of the first millennium. Sadly, medieval documents such as manorial surveys do not concern themselves with the sort of detail that archaeologists might find useful. As we discovered in Chapter 6, some of the most convincing evidence for the existence of the village comes from sources such as surnames, but even this does no more than indicate that the modern village was in existence by 1239. In spite of an exhaustive trawl through all the medieval documentation from the village, this seems to be the best we can do. However improbable we might find it that planned villages and their field systems were 'inserted' into the post-Conquest landscape, nothing in the historical record positively supports our conviction that the village was already old in the thirteenth century.

Fortunately, there is one more source of evidence at our disposal (Box 10.2) and this proves to be the crucial evidence on which the whole case turns – pottery, the lifeblood of so many archaeological projects. From our fieldwalking and our many interventions within the footprint of the village it appears that sherds dated to the tenth–eleventh centuries are to be found in the soils throughout the modern village and across the fields to east and west. This strongly suggests that the village *was* in existence at that time and therefore before 1066. Regrettably, the dating of this pottery is not as precise as it might be. At excavations of the Saxon palaces at Cheddar pottery of the same kind is dated to AD 945 on the basis of an associated coin, while pottery recovered from the postholes of the early medieval timber building at *Old Church* indicates a radiocarbon date of AD 810–980 (at 95 per cent probability). This at least provides a date range for the earliest use of this pottery. However, these late Anglo-Saxon fabrics show little change over time so, for the moment at least, no further refinement is possible.

Hedging our vocabulary carefully, on the basis of the pottery found the village of Shapwick may have been established around AD 950 or perhaps slightly later. This would make sense of the Domesday entry (see Chapter 2) and all the later documentary evidence. At Shapwick, radiocarbon samples recovered and dated for this Project have firmly demonstrated occupation in *Old Church*, while field names strongly suggest the presence of other sites, but there is no similar evidence which might demonstrate the existence of any village. Unlike other projects that have addressed similar questions, among them those at Raunds in Northamptonshire, Wharram Percy in Yorkshire and Whittlewood on the Buckinghamshire–Northamptonshire border (for locations see Figure 10.5), we have found nothing to suggest that the village of Shapwick grew out of a pre-existing settlement.

The planning of settlements on new sites was nothing new at the end of the first millennium AD in southern England. We are all familiar with the well-organised street-grid plans of Roman towns, and at Shapwick the regular linear layout of what appears to be a Roman rural settlement at *Blacklands* is strikingly reminiscent of the later medieval village. While there is nothing whatsoever to suggest that these particular Roman ruins were the prototype for the later planned settlement, classical concepts of geometry and order would have been familiar to anyone who spent time in monastic libraries. Engagement with different aspects of Roman civilisation, among them law and architecture, were well rehearsed in the seventh–eighth centuries and the twelfth century, for example. To create a 'grid-plan' settlement modelled on the symmetry of a Roman town perhaps represented *Romanitas* to the monks of Glastonbury. The contrast with the unplanned and unordered (hence barbaric) nature of earlier settlement would not have been lost on these classically educated men. At the same time there were already other types of settlements with regular street plans in existence. New coastal trading places, such as *Hamwic* near Southampton, called 'emporia' or '*wics*' by archaeologists, emerged in around AD 700, and they too show evidence of planning,[15] as do some ecclesiastical settlements of the seventh and eighth centuries, such as Hereford.[16] A larger group of defended forts or *burhs* developed later in response to the Viking threat and these were also logically ordered with regular street systems within their fortifications. No one in King Alfred's Wessex would have been more than 30 km from such a site, those closest to Shapwick being at Axbridge, Langport and Lyng.[17]

Bearing in mind, then, that the inhabitants of early medieval Shapwick and their landlords had already been familiar with the concept and layouts of regular planned settlements for many generations, it seems safe to pitch our search for village origins somewhere in the period after AD 700 and before *c.* AD 950. Sadly, the archaeological evidence lets us down here. Although earlier medieval phases of seventh- and eighth-century date were found in *Old*

BOX 10.2

Starting over again

There were certainly areas of weakness in our project.[b1] We found it difficult at times to reconcile the demands of full-time jobs elsewhere with the needs of the fieldwork at Shapwick. This could have been eased by having some employed staff to provide a permanent presence, even if only for one day a week. A project like this ideally needs a four-wheel-drive vehicle to negotiate muddy terrains and carry equipment and people. Accommodation, too, is essential, with the requisite power, heating and running water. We had these things some of the time but mostly we borrowed and begged.

We were pleased with the range of archaeological methods brought to bear at Shapwick and the sense of multidisciplinarity. Some of our techniques were innovative in this setting and have since been deployed on other projects, particularly test-pitting and shovel-pitting. We would have liked to have used these methods more, though shovel-pitting was not popular among our volunteers. Our understanding of the low density lithic spreads, for example, would have benefited from more intensive sampling, and, if we were to return, woodland and semi-permanent pasture would be obvious targets. Other techniques that we employed, like soils geochemistry, have inspired less interest. The difficulty here is partly the need for costly laboratory facilities and the slow speed at which samples can be taken, processed in the laboratory and translated into usable scaled plots of concentrations. In the way that we used the method it is undoubtedly too cumbersome a technique for direct application to commercial archaeology.

We were not after novelty merely for the sake of it. Tried and tested methods such as document transcription and analysis were as central to our reconstruction of the medieval *curia* sites as fieldwalking was for prehistoric and Roman landscapes. In many cases we adapted these techniques to address our own objectives. Fieldwalking, for example, was set up as much to examine past land use as to locate 'sites', while Michael Costen's interpretation of Shapwick field names was enhanced by the mapping of the 1515 survey that gave a better sense of their true location in the medieval landscape. However, if we were to return again then we would reconsider our approach to palaeo-environmental studies. Deep stratigraphy on rural sites and suitable sequences covering the last two millennia remained elusive but their identification would have made a huge contribution to our story, one out of all proportion to cost. Geophysics, too, might be used differently, as a prospection tool in its own right rather than merely to add detail to the layout of sites we had already identified using other techniques.

Ideally, a project of this type should have total geophysical, geochemical and LiDAR coverage as well as ongoing air survey, topographical survey and fieldwalking (Figure B.10.2). If we were setting up the project now a digital record would also be created based on Ordnance Survey grids and located with GPS. To this checklist should be added the many buildings that need to be examined, as well as botanical and geological studies. Indoors, a full assessment of all the available post-medieval and medieval documentation needs to be undertaken. We have no doubt that there was much more detail for the last thousand years in the medieval Glastonbury records and the post-medieval records of the Rolle, Templer and Warry families than we were able to handle, and it would have been desirable to have all this information to hand *before* the fieldwork began. Arguably, only when all this preliminary work is complete should small-scale excavations be conducted and only then should large-scale excavations even be contemplated. At the same time we must be careful not to over-manage a project into a fixed and linear research design. As many people have commented, painful though it was at times, one advantage of having so little funding for the fieldwork stages of the project was that we were less accountable to timetables and sponsors and this led us to experiment and follow our hunches. The ideal project design, we think, should have plenty of 'cycles' and 'loops' between tasks, not just straight lines and arrows, and there should be lots of opportunity for informal discussion and debate.

At Shapwick we did no set-piece, large-scale excavation. Indeed, the project was somewhat unusual in not starting with a big excavation and then moving out into the landscape later, as happened at Wharram

Figure B.10.2. Shapwick village, looking south up the Polden ridge with Shapwick House in the foreground. Though we spent a decade researching this landscape, there is still much to do.

Percy and Raunds.[b2] Nevertheless, several large-scale excavations could now be targeted very appropriately to follow on from all that has been done in the parish, and they would no doubt teach us a great deal. The full excavation of *Old Church*, which continues to be damaged by intermittent ploughing, is an obvious candidate, but so too is the complex of geophysical features recorded east of Manor Farm at *Borgh/Chestell*, some of which might represent the original 'Shapwick'. Smaller-scale excavations could also now be undertaken. We have drawn attention to several of the less disturbed flint scatters, prehistoric 'enclosures' identified from aerial photographs, the probable sites of early medieval watermills and much else besides. But we would not make all our excavation targets 'monuments' of this type; more sections of the kind we conducted in Field 2700 would have widened our understanding of how and when field boundaries came into existence and thus shed light on issues at the core of our agenda. For example, we were not able to resolve how open fields evolved from prehistoric and Roman layouts in the detail we would have liked.

Whether or not we have been successful in our venture is perhaps best judged by the inspiration it affords to others. If the reader finds this story of the people of Shapwick over several millennia stimulating, then that is one reward. If they are inspired to go out and use the methods we deployed, if they can develop these techniques further, adapt them to their own projects, that would be better still. As for Shapwick itself, after ten years in the field and ten years thinking about and writing up the results, many people will now undoubtedly think that Shapwick is 'done', that we 'understand' it and that those involved have, to a greater or lesser extent, 'achieved their objectives' and exhausted its potential. This is far from the truth. After nearly twenty years we are really only now in a position to begin!

Church (see Chapter 4), no pottery was associated with them. It would appear that pottery in pre-tenth-century Somerset was a scarce commodity. So, while we have radiocarbon dates from the fills of timber postholes in *Old Church* to suggest a timber building of seventh- or just possibly eighth-century date, and burials at *Sladwick* sometime in the sixth century, we are dependent largely on field names for a broader understanding of the settlement pattern. These field names suggest a landscape of scattered farmsteads or hamlets being named from the eighth century.

Against this rather hazy detail there is also the broad historical context to be considered. We should note, for example, how ownership switched from royal to monastic hands in the first half of the eighth century (see Chapter 5). Might this have been an opportune moment to establish a village at Shapwick? In fact, others have plausibly argued for the eighth century as a time of significant landscape change, and there is evidence to support this locally.[18] We have noted, for example, that the church of St Andrew in *Old Church* was probably established at that date and that there was a seventh- or eighth-century timber building nearby. Much was happening, too, in the surrounding countryside, including the construction of artificial watercourses and significant modifications to rivers, communication routes and land use in the Brue valley – all evidence of reorganisation on the part of the Abbey at exactly this period. That said, had the village existed at that time in its current location and form then the church at Shapwick would surely have been constructed within its envelope of houses and not out in the fields to the east. Likewise, we struggle to see a ninth-century date as plausible for the origins of the village; Glastonbury Abbey's administrative organisation and its finances were insufficiently developed. While in Chapter 5 we did explore the concept of a gradually nucleating settlement, and this remains a possibility that cannot be discounted on the basis of our archaeological evidence, the balance of probability is that the planned village we see today was established only in the tenth century. While we do not argue that the tenth century was the context for all village creation across England – in fact, we do not believe in a nationwide 'village moment' at all – this is the solution that makes best sense of the historical and archaeological clues for our particular case study.

Dunstan

If a tenth-century origin can be accepted for the village of Shapwick then a date sometime between AD 947 and 957 seems most likely on historical grounds because it was in this decade that Glastonbury Abbey was refounded under Abbot Dunstan (Box 6.1). Dunstan was one of three reformers who launched the Benedictine monastic revival, inspired by the great Burgundian abbey of Cluny that had been founded as a new Benedictine community in AD 909. Under the rule of St Hugh (1049–1109), the Abbey of Cluny was developing its estates at this time[19] and founding new villages as part of the process, as indeed were other newly reformed monasteries in Flanders and northern Gaul, among them those at Brogne, Ghent, Gorze and St Bertin. While there was no direct influence brought to bear by Cluny on activities at Glastonbury, one of its daughter houses, Fleury (St Benoît-sur-Loire) was home for a while to Oswald of Worcester, one of the other architects of Benedictine reform. It is worth bearing in mind, too, that Dunstan himself was later exiled to Flanders, having fallen out with the king, so he may well have already visited the new Benedictine houses there. All in all, Dunstan would have known about, and was almost certainly influenced by, these new monasteries in mainland Europe and there is some reason to believe that the foundation of villages and the reorganisation of peasant communities would have been known to him by the mid-tenth century. Indeed, far closer to home, in rural Northamptonshire, there is recently published evidence to suggest that settlements such as West Cotton were being newly planned and founded at almost exactly the same time as Shapwick, while others already in existence, such as Raunds, were being reorganised to incorporate a regular layout of plots.[20]

Motives

This leaves us to establish the motives behind Dunstan's initiative. Why would the Abbey want a village at Shapwick at all? We saw in Chapter 1 how a number of answers have been proposed to this question over the years. In the nineteenth century scholars leant heavily on ethnic explanations, but during the course of the twentieth century, with the emergence of historical geography and social and economic history, these views have been totally revised[21] and a number of new models have emerged.

Model 1 we might describe as economically driven. Its proponents, among them the agrarian historian Joan Thirsk, highlighted rising population as the main driver for change.[22] She envisaged the endless subdivision of land to cope with the pressure of increased production, coupling it with ever-expanding cultivation. Once sensible limits were reached and with pasture now all taken up by arable, the risks to local communities were considered intolerable. Grazing could only take place on the fallow if cultivators were sufficiently cooperative and rotations were introduced.[23] Among the positives of this model is the stress it places on the role of the *community* in the assessment of risk and management of the outcome. It is they who, in response to threats to their livelihood, reorganised themselves and cooperated to overcome their difficulties. This solution is thought to have spread as villages emulated the success of their neighbours and can also be extended to account for changes to settlement and field patterns well after the Norman Conquest.[24] However, critics of the model may wonder at the detail of the process. Was it really just *one* enterprising village that led the way where all the others followed? To what extent *could* villagers genuinely decide for themselves about the benefits of greater cooperation? And if the process *is* really one of emulation, why do we not see more evidence for some sort of 'core' area, where the idea was first hit upon, with a sub-circular peripheral zone in which the nucleated village and open fields were adopted as time went by?[25] It raises the question as to why Domesday population statistics and the national distribution of nucleated villages are not better correlated, as we might expect them to be if a rise in population had been the sole cause.

Rather than imagine these new arrangements unfolding democratically across the late Saxon and later medieval landscape of England, Model 2 stresses the role of the lord, the owner of the land, in the decision-making process. A rising population, for example, might lead to a ready solution imposed by strong or new leaders.[26] In the case of the Northamptonshire examples cited above, for example, planned settlement is envisaged as one aspect of a wider reorganisation of the landscape following the reconquest of Danelaw. But this 'top-down' model is also not without its critics. If agrarian knowledge and determined leadership is what was required it follows that there should be a clear link between certain landowners and the occurrence of villages. In the case of Shapwick and other Glastonbury manors strung out down the Poldens there *is* indeed some evidence for this. Several villages *do* have a planned look to them (see Chapter 6). But not all Glastonbury manors include settlements that were planned. Even some of the villages along the Poldens, such as Woolavington, have a more irregular look to them. Surveys of other pre-Conquest monastic estates, such as those for Ely Abbey in Cambridgeshire, reveal focused concentrations of planned villages. As landscape archaeologist Tom Williamson has pointed out, if there really was a uniform system of control in operation then this kind of private initiative would surely lead to patchy uptake right across England, perhaps on villages in the possession of certain wealthy monasteries. Given that what we actually see is a firm diagonal strip of nucleation stretching across the country,[27] the situation must be more complex.

Model 3 addresses the problem from a different angle. Re-examining the uptake of nucleation and open fields marked on the national atlas, Williamson has observed how strikingly similar the distribution is to the solid geology map of England. This cannot be denied and may reflect agricultural practice, ultimately influenced by the local terrain. In essence, Williamson's thesis for what he calls 'sheep-corn land' like that of Shapwick is that the soils were not especially well suited to long-term cultivation and therefore required intensive manuring, something that is indeed borne out by our fieldwork, which revealed high densities of later medieval pottery around the village. The introduction of strip farming was desirable precisely because it gave all farmers fairer opportunities on this better manured, more accessible land.[28] On heavier clay soils Williamson sees the matter slightly differently. Here, living together in one place was a matter of practical expediency because, so he argues, heavy and waterlogged soils required a rapid response by farmers to plough and harrow the fields when they were in a workable condition. Such speed and cooperation was best guaranteed when farmers lived close to each other in a single village.

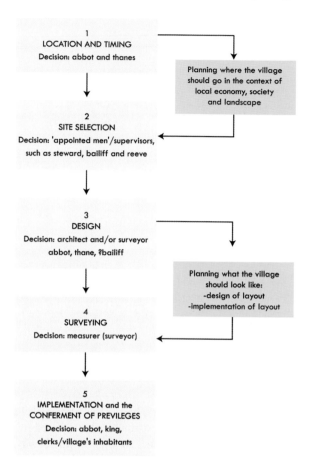

Figure 10.6. The five stages of village planning, adapted from an original by Keith Lilley (2005) for later medieval towns. No documentary records exist to prove that this was the process and it remains a speculative one. Who took the decisions is a matter for debate.

In addition, the nucleated village ensured that the demesne farmer had sufficient peasant labourers to cope with arduous seasonal tasks such as spring sowing and haymaking.[29]

With these models to hand, how do we see the Shapwick situation unfolding? Given what is now known of the distribution of habitative place-names across the parish and the lack of any solid information about the chronology or character of the *Enworthie* site to the west of the village, we think it likely that settlement began to agglomerate in the area of

Old Church by the mid-ninth century. A scatter of farmsteads might be imagined here, with the church and the Glastonbury Abbey *curia* spread over an area as large as 500 m by 400 m. This was not a planned settlement; rather, it had an 'organic' layout, but the farmers who lived there were mutually dependent upon each other's time and labour. In the fields around about the land was being divided into thinner and thinner strips, with shares of land close by and at a distance.[30] Then, at a stroke, the organisation of the whole community and its lands was recast in the mid-tenth century. The whole process is set out on Figure 10.6, a diagram that has been adapted from an original by Keith Lilley to explain the design of urban landscapes between the twelfth and the fourteenth centuries.[31] It has much to recommend it in our rural context too, not least because it emphasises the different steps in the process as well as the involvement of a range of decision makers.

The new site at Shapwick was close to a fresh water spring and stream with equal access not only to arable and meadow, and to the fuel and building materials available on the Levels, but also to the woodland at Loxley. At the same time, the creation of a new village also served to standardise holdings and tenant obligations and it was a unit with potential for further growth. If the farmers saw benefit in this, and if the Abbey recognised the potential for greater profit from its own demesne land, there may have been mutual agreement between all parties that reorganisation should take place. Maybe, as Lilley suggests for later medieval towns, it was a reflexive negotiation, with the steward acting for the lord's interest and a reeve representing the interests of the peasants; and perhaps the local thanes were very much involved too. Whatever the case, it seems likely to us that the abbot initiated the change and took the decision to create a new village *in principle*, but that he consulted others as to a suitable site. At this stage surely the voices of local landholders must have been heard regarding the suitability of the land, the quality of available water and so forth. Then, subsequently, there was the detail of design and planning to attend to. We do not know who oversaw this process and who took the ultimate decision on the alignment of roads and the dimensions of plots, but it would have required at least some elementary knowledge of geometry.

Was it the monks? Was a design ever committed to parchment? And who marked out the plan on the ground with ropes and pegs?[32]

What, then, motivated the creation of a planned village at Shapwick? In medieval feudal society families survived by supplying labour and the old depended upon the young for their support. There was a persistent pressure to have large families. Against a background of rising population and local knowledge of the modest fertility of Polden soils, 'thin limestone land' as it was referred to in the eighteenth century, there were certain benefits to be had for local farmers living in a village with an open-field system, such as a fairer distribution of land, both good and bad; greater facility to deploy more powerful agricultural technology in the form of a heavy plough with an iron share, a coulter 'knife' to guide direction and cut vertically and a mould board to turn the turves; and improved coordination of the agricultural community, particularly at certain points in the farming year. Other benefits may have included new housing, mutual support between households during childbirth, marriage and death, and the sharing of resources such as kindling and building materials. Perhaps there was peer pressure, too, to acquire greater material benefits, such as pottery or food on the table. For the Abbey there were obvious advantages too. The first was profit; greater efficiencies led to higher yields and the establishment of a village created a more central and readily marshalled labour force for work on demesne lands. The second was more subtle. The mapping of tenancies into a village plan, as happened at Shapwick, had the effect of documenting *on the ground*, through the spacing of roads, hedges and walls, the relationship between Abbey and its villeins, and between one tenant and his neighbour. Perhaps in some way this made the Abbey's human assets easier to account for and made rent easier to collect, but we think it more likely that the allocated spaces merely reflected social and economic status and responsibilities. The reluctance of the Church and Abbey's officials to move into the village core may also perhaps be read as a means of distinguishing roles, in this case some perceived need to maintain a distance between landlord and tenant.

We might like to think of the creation of the new village as a reaction to threats to people and their property, to human needs and wants.[33] But this was no sudden unanticipated event, such as an earthquake or another natural disaster; rather, it should be thought of as a series of intensifying pressures that were recognised as a risk and thus subsequently provoked a response from the medieval community. Although hazard or potential threat was present for most medieval settlements in one form or another, the scale of loss or economic vulnerability was perceived to be greater in some regions than in others, and for some properties on certain estates. Shapwick was one of these. Similar stresses of population growth in the modern world might be addressed through government action or foreign food aid, but in the Middle Ages only a limited number of potential solutions were available, namely to maximise the area under cultivation or to build up reserves of grain as an insurance against crop failure. In order to achieve a sustainable solution that maximised the possibilities of success the pattern of settlement was modified, and the presence of an effective local administration in this case in the form of Glastonbury Abbey was, we think, crucial to reaching this conclusion.

Did the monks have some fixed notion of the way a rural village *should* look? The plan at Shapwick is decidedly unusual. Once post-medieval modifications such the creation of Shapwick Park are stripped away (see Chapters 8 and 9), it is effectively a 'ladder plan' with a spinal watercourse and roads running parallel from east to west. Such a plan does not fit easily into the classification of village forms described by geographer Brian Roberts.[34] Although it does have all the characteristics of a planned village, such as regular, ordered tofts of repeated dimensions, symmetry with parallel roads and a clear orientation, Shapwick does not have a simple row plan[35] and it has no green. According to the Roberts classification it has more in common with an 'agglomerated village plan', a regular grid that was fortunate to escape the name 'Long Shapwick'. However, although Shapwick's morphology is unusual in a national context, it is not unusual locally. There are no fewer than six villages on the north-facing slope of the Poldens, on the same geology and soils, with similar plans,[36] although the villages of Bawdrip and Moorlinch on the south-facing flank are more irregular, Stawell is a regular two-row street plan and Sutton Mallet is a cluster of farms. In fact, none of these south-facing Polden villages are very similar either to each other or to those on the opposite side of the hill. This observation is important because it shows that Glastonbury Abbey did not impose one preferred settlement model on all their properties, possibly because any planning had to be mediated through the Abbey's sub-tenants and this led to certain amount of variation in practice, or possibly because the Abbey could only impose itself where it was directly involved in the management of the landscape. On that basis, the key to understanding village planning must be to unravel its social and economic context.

Whether or not we accept that village plans were decided upon by their tenants or landlords, or through a dialogue between the two, there must be some explanation as to why that *particular* plan was chosen. This is a topic that has not received much attention among archaeologists. One possibility is that the choice of layout was purely practical. The flow of the watercourses at Shapwick is from south to north downslope and the need for every family to have access to water might determine at least the orientation of the village and its elongated form. Likewise, the placement of dwellings on the 'rungs' of the settlement ladder, rather than along the 'uprights', arguably allowed domestic housing to be fitted in close to the water source. The spacing of the 'rungs', as argued in Chapter 6, may have had something to do with the differing status of villagers, or it may reflect a longer chronology of settlement formation. But is the general shape of the village merely determined by the terrain? There is an interesting fifteenth-century case at Mells in Somerset where the Glastonbury Abbot intended to lay out a number of new streets in the shape of a cross.[37] To this local example of a 'sacred design' should be added a long literature on the geometry and symbolism of later medieval town plans and cathedral buildings, including case studies of Benedictine monasteries (such as Glastonbury).[38] At one level, we might see in all planned settlements the desire of the planner to etch into it a statement about the relationship between tenants and between tenants and landlord. There is a simple code here that allows the visitor to read off status and community values. But might there be something deeper? Might villages such as Shapwick, which display such a regular

geometry, have deliberately echoed notions of Godly perfection in symmetry and proportion? The ratios of 2:1, 2:3 and 3:5 all appear in the plans of late twelfth-century 'new' towns in southern England, but they are also present at Shapwick, 200 years earlier.[39] Should we therefore see the plan of Shapwick as an image designed according to Christian aesthetic principles? While there seems little doubt of the importance of geometry in certain planning contexts in the later medieval period, it is much more controversial to suggest that these deeper psychologies had an impact on the planning of rural settlement, not least before the Norman Conquest. But the thought is worth bearing in mind, even if it is speculative. After all, the imaginative appeal of 'ladders' ascending up the Polden slope might have been striking to a ecclesiastical mind (Figure 10.7). In the Book of Genesis Jacob dreams of angels ascending and descending a ladder to heaven and the same literary device features in the teaching of St Augustine and the Rule of St Benedict. Members of the Order are described climbing to heaven on a twelve-runged ladder representing varying degrees of humility; at which point it should be remembered that Glastonbury was itself a Benedictine house. As a caveat, however, none of the six settlement plans on the Poldens are appreciable at ground level and they only become obvious from an aircraft and on a map, privileges that even the most affluent of medieval monks did not possess!

The Shapwick story in context

There is now plenty of research from other countries in Europe to show that planned settlement of the kind we see at Shapwick is not purely an English, nor even purely a north-west European, phenomenon. In Germany, for example, some linear settlements along the middle Rhine are thought to arise from Frankish colonisation in the eighth and ninth centuries.[40] Meanwhile, in the Dutch province of Drenthe, an excavated settlement at Gasselte comprises a series of farmsteads in large tofts laid out along the western edge of a road and, in the earliest of two phases, separated one from another by narrow paths. This plan dates between the ninth and twelfth centuries. The archaeologist Helena Hamerow has drawn these and other examples together in a review of settlement structure in north-west Europe in the early Middle Ages.[41] She concludes that there are sufficient regularities between excavated sites to identify the presence of 'row' (like Gasselte), 'grouped' and 'perpendicular' settlements, among others. The first of these categories, the 'row' settlements, she finds evidence for in southern Germany in the seventh and eighth centuries and in the Netherlands in the tenth century. The last category, the 'perpendicular' villages, Hamerow defines as farmsteads in a chequerboard layout. It is impossible to look at the evidence for these village plans, particularly excavated examples from Denmark and the Netherlands, without being reminded of Shapwick. To take just one example, excavations at Kootwijk in the central Netherlands revealed a Carolingian village of the early eighth century that was abandoned by the end of the tenth century. The village consists of eight blocks which contained one to three houses at any one time and were separated by a network of perpendicular trackways.

Nor was north-west Europe alone in being transformed in this way. Further south, *incastellamento* is the name given to the reorganisation of the Italian countryside and the reshaping of settlements around AD 1000 that resulted in the regrouping of dispersed populations in the shadow of castles.[42] The hilltop settlements that preceded *incastellamento* were often involved in the administration of monastic property and surviving texts make it clear that their purpose was to clear and consolidate lands and bring people together into a centralised location – a physical manifestation of social power but one with many advantages for the peasantry, who were able to sell their produce in newly established markets. The *incastellamento* concept has also been applied by French archaeologists to settlements in Islamic Spain[43] as well as to France itself.[44] As elsewhere in Europe, the precise timing of this change, in the absence of archaeological work, is not always obvious and the reasons for it are much debated. It is clear, however, that the purpose of *incastellamento* was not primarily security but the domination of a feudal population. Pierre Toubert, who first coined the term to describe the process in Lazio in Italy, envisaged bishops and abbots as the early and main promoters because the changes consolidated their holdings and maximised

Figure 10.7. Bath Abbey, south façade. One of the striking features of the architecture here is the ladders on which angels ascend to heaven. The motif is late fifteenth–early sixteenth century in date, admittedly far later than the origins of Shapwick, and said to have been inspired by the bishop's vision to rebuild the church. Is it possible that the 'ladder' image appealed to those who established Shapwick's plan?

effective exploitation. Moving east, to the southern Argolid in Greece, nucleated settlement has been linked there both with economic contraction and, in the case of the island of Melos, with colonial political and economic control.[45] In Spain, American historian

Thomas Glick describes a spatial reorganisation taking place in Catalonia 'with shocking speed and violence'.[46] Following civil war, the transition took just one generation between 1020 and 1060. Almost half of the 800 or so Catalan castles in existence in 1350 had been constructed by the end of the eleventh century. Further north and west, the transition from dispersed to nucleated settlement pattern may have followed the wave of Christian 'reconquest' over the course of the twelfth and thirteenth centuries.

Of course, not everyone in medieval Europe lived in a village with a church, castle or a green; in Brittany in France, in Galicia in north-west Spain and in much of the west of Britain settlement remained dispersed. There was considerable diversity in the form and economy of rural settlements, as is only to be expected. Nevertheless, as this whistle-stop tour of early medieval Europe illustrates, planned villages just like the one at Shapwick were present elsewhere as early as AD 750.[47] Given that there is such enormous variation in regional circumstances across Europe, what is it that all these areas have in common with each other? The first point to note is just how often periods of disruption and conflict seem to precede spatial reorganisations of settlement. This was true of Catalonia in the eleventh century, the north-east of England in the period 1050–1250, Northamptonshire following the return of Danelaw to English lordship in the early tenth century and, it might be argued, Glastonbury and monasticism, also in the early tenth century. Second, a common factor seems to be economics: an increase in population, in some cases involving migration of people, with consequential

stresses on resources. Greater tenurial control of living and labour conditions and the imposition of well-defined social roles are two means that landlords had at their disposal to combat this. Third, for the village settlement form to be preferred certain social and political conditions needed to be in place: namely, a society based upon an elite minority, tenants and taxation, rather than the sort of multiple estate model explained in Chapter 1.[48] The tensions that led to the creation of villages in the Middle Ages were indeed complex – an interaction of natural and social worlds in which the components were economic, social, political, environmental and geographical. The European landscape is full of clues, in terms of settlement patterns and changing agricultural practice, which illustrate this interaction at work.

This European perspective is helpful in providing a broader context for the changes seen at Shapwick. In this book we have argued consistently for the creation of a village in the tenth century, and we see the hand of Glastonbury Abbey and, in particular, Abbot Dunstan behind it, but we do not wish to argue that all villages were established at this time or under similar circumstances; we do not seek a single over-arching explanation.[49] Instead, settlement planning and the development of villages is a common response to a series of pressures that have occurred at different times across varied European landscapes. If we take the long-term view, this phenomenon is neither new nor restricted to the Middle Ages.[50] Planned settlements were around in the Roman period and they are still being constructed today. To some extent *all* villages are planned.

Notes

Notes to Chapter 1

1. Natural England (formerly English Nature) have a base just to the north of the parish at the Peat Moors Centre.
2. *Metro*, 30 March 2009.
3. 'British' in this context refers to the natives of the island in the 5th century AD: a mixture of Celtic and Roman culture. For concepts of nation and race in the nineteenth and early twentieth centuries see Floyd 2004. The key texts are *De Excidio Britanniae*, written by the monk Gildas in the mid-6th century (Winterbottom 1978), Bede's *Ecclesiastical History of the English-speaking People* of AD 731 (Colgrave and Mynors 1969) and a *c*. AD 890 compilation of later annals known as *The Anglo-Saxon Chronicle* (Whitelock *et al.* 1961). These were already available to historians such as William Stubbs and John Mitchell Kemble during the nineteenth century. Summaries appear in Thorpe (1845), Kemble (1849) and Stubbs (1874, 53–55). Many of their ideas were borrowed from German historians such as Jacob Grimm (J. W. Burrow 1981). The notion of Teutonic roots appealed to a Victorian sense of English racial superiority and secured a reassuringly ancient ancestry for England's institutions and laws (Burrow 1974). Not everyone agreed, however. Economic historian Frederic Seebohm (1890, 420–22), using his home town of Hitchin as a case study, sought to demonstrate the failures of what he termed 'communistic systems', by which he meant open-field systems. For Seebohm, a Quaker banker, the future lay in freedom of enterprise.
4. The English Place-Name Society was established in 1923. The earliest phase of Anglo-Saxon settlement was thought to be represented by those place-names in which *-ingas* had been combined with a personal name; Reading in Berkshire is one example. These places were followed by others with *-ingahām* names, such as Wokingham. *Cote* and *wick* names were thought to have been founded later, once the new population had become established and had begun to expand. Logically, these later names had to be subsidiary places. The final stage of 'colonisation' of the landscape was indicated by *field* and *hurst* names, as areas of woodland came to be cleared away for settlement and cultivation. This place-name chronology was united with the archaeological record in R. H. Hodgkin's *History of the Anglo-Saxons* (1935).
5. For example, relatively few places were thought to be recorded before the Norman Conquest because they were so sparse on the ground.
6. The first controlled excavations of 'Anglo-Saxon peasant houses' were undertaken by Edward Thurlow Leeds at Sutton Courtenay in Berkshire between 1921 and 1937 (Leeds 1947). Assistant Keeper and later Keeper at the Ashmolean Museum in Oxford between 1908 and 1945, Leeds had commented less than a decade earlier that 'not a single instance of an early Anglo-Saxon occupation area vouched for by the discovery of sherds or the like, such as litter the ground of any Roman site, has ever been brought to light in this country' (Leeds 1913, 15). In the event Leeds missed the evidence for timber buildings on the site.
7. Hoskins 1955.
8. Thorpe 1975.
9. See, for example, Dodgson 1966; Gelling 1974; Cox 1976. Even so-called 'secondary' place-names could not be trusted to reveal their date of origin; these were now conjectured to reflect the relative status of settlements.
10. The concluding volume of H. C. Darby's *Domesday Geography of England*, published in 1977, was influential in overturning earlier interpretations.
11. Whereas Romanist Robin Collingwood in 1929 had estimated between ½ and 1 million inhabitants of *Britannia* (Collingwood 1929), by 1977 Christopher Smith was placing that figure at between 4 and 6 million (further discussed in Salway's *Roman Britain* (1981, 542); Smith 1977).
12. For example, Rackham 1976.
13. Collingwood and Myres 1936, 325.
14. Sawyer 1979, 6.
15. Just as Seebohm had suspected. For example, Bill Ford working in Warwickshire (Ford 1979) and David Hall in Northamptonshire (1981; 1988). At Brixworth in Northamptonshire, Hall identified ten Anglo-Saxon settlements in a triangular area measuring roughly 2.5km by 2.5km where today there is a substantial central nucleated settlement (Hall and Martin 1979). For boundaries see Bonney 1972.
16. Catholme (Losco-Bradley and Kinsley 2002), Chalton

(Addyman and Leigh 1973), Cowdery's Down (Millett and James 1983), Mucking (Hamerow 1993) and West Stow (West 1985).

17. We must acknowledge here the very important role played by the Deserted Medieval Village Research Group (now the Medieval Settlement Research Group) since its formation in 1954, and particularly the contributions of John Hurst and Maurice Beresford and the excavations at the deserted medieval village of Wharram Percy in Yorkshire (eg. Beresford and Hurst 1990; Wrathmell 1996). Hurst was especially influential in the selection of sites for open area excavation by the Department of Environment during the 1970s (Gerrard 2009).

18. As early as 1966, June Sheppard, a lecturer in geography at the University of London working on a classification of settlement forms, suggested a planned layout for the village of Wheldrake in Yorkshire. She developed this idea in a series of articles about medieval village planning in the same county (Sheppard 1974; 1976) and at around the same time Durham University geographer Brian Roberts was also coming to the same conclusion from his work on other northern counties. Work by Roberts on village forms was to become particularly significant because it proposed nationally applicable terminologies, a 'language' of settlement, and went beyond mere classification of forms to examine, among other matters, their origins (Roberts 1977; 1987). Conzen's analysis of plan elements in medieval towns also led the way with work on Alnwick and then other towns (Conzen 1960; 1968). The idea of the planned village had evolved more generally following the example of Maurice Beresford's book *New Towns of the Middle Ages*, published in 1967. If towns could be planted on empty sites and laid out with regular rectilinear plans, why could not the same be true of villages?

19. 'Polyfocal' is Christopher Taylor's term (Taylor 1977).

20. Baker and Butlin 1973, 656; Fox 1981; Rowley 1981.

21. See Williamson (2003, 8–21) and Jones and Page (2006, 80–83) for useful summaries. These reasons were clearly stated at an important conference held at the Department for External Studies at the University of Oxford in January 1982 (Hooke 1985). In 1915 Harvard scholar Howard Levi Gray was the first to show that repeated division of property could create heavily subdivided fields as a result of inheritance (Gray 1915), while it was the Orwins in 1938 who highlighted the impact of the heavier mouldboard plough (Orwin and Orwin 1938).

22. Jones 1979.

23. Faith 1997, 15.

24. For eighth- or early ninth-century AD nucleation see Foard 1978; Hall 1981. For tenth century re-planning see Brown and Foard 1998.

25. Taylor 1983; Lewis *et al.* 1997. Joan Thirsk, the economic and social historian who pioneered the use of local manuscript sources in agrarian history, was among those who envisaged the *evolution* of open-field systems over a more extended period.

26. For other examples of interpretive historical archaeologies and a discussion see Wilkie 2009.

27. For Wharram Percy see, for example, Beresford and Hurst 1990; Stamper and Croft 2000. Other recent publications of deserted village sites include Caldecote (Herts; Beresford 2009). For discussion and context see Gerrard 2003. For impact of Shapwick methodologies more widely see Lewis 2007b.

28. For polite architecture see, for example, Airs 1975; Mercer 1975; for social change see Brooks and Barry 1994; for archaeology of the Reformation see Gaimster and Gilchrist 2003; for historical archaeology see Hicks and Beaudry 2006; for modern materialism see Mukerji 1983 or Shammas 1990.

29. Johnson 1996.

30. Thinking even then of a future project in Somerset, Mick suggested that 'in the east [of Somerset] a well-documented, surviving village should perhaps be selected' (Aston 1982).

31. These were the laying-out of new streets at Mells in the fifteenth century by Abbot Selwood of Glastonbury and a planned extension built over the open fields at Newton (Martock) a century earlier.

32. Rahtz 1971; Rahtz *et al.* 2000; Rahtz *et al.* 1992; Watts and Leach 1996.

33. Radford 1981; Rahtz and Watts 2003; Rodwell 2001; Alcock 1995; Barrett *et al.* 2000.

34. Aston and Burrow 1982; Rahtz 1991; Webster 2000.

35. Davey 2005.

36. Corcos 1982 (supervised by Harold Fox). Several other parishes were ruled out because of their more complex settlement patterns. For Cheddar and North Curry we were led to believe that several farmers would not cooperate. South Petherton was too far away for regular contact.

37. The term 'furlong' refers to a block of cultivated strips in a medieval open field.

38. The Vesteys established a family butchery business in Liverpool in the late nineteenth century, later expanding into South American beef products and creating their own shipping company, the Blue Star Line. In the mid-twentieth century the Vestey family were judged to be the 100th richest family in Britain since the Norman Conquest, worth over £7 billion. For many years they dominated the meat trade in Britain, developing the Dewhurst chain of butcher's shops

(disbanded in 1995). Lord Vestey has no connections at all with history or archaeology that we know of, though his family do have academic and philanthropic interests. They endowed the Vestey Professorship of Food Safety and Veterinary Public Health at the Royal Veterinary College at the University of London.

39. When Vestey land was sold off to tenants, two of the new purchasers made it increasingly difficult for us to gain access to their land.

40. Coles and Coles 1986.

41. The Abbot's Way is now dated to around 2500 BC.

42. Minnitt and Coles 1996.

43. A question mark hangs over the location of Indracht's supposed murder. The earliest version is that by John Seen of Glastonbury around 1342, who, according to Michael Lapidge (1993, 419–52), probably based his account on a now-lost twelfth-century *Vita S. Indracti*, a 'Life of St Indract', by William of Malmesbury. Another version, known as the Digby *passio* and probably based on a lost Old English account, dates to the very early twelfth century. This version changed certain details, shifting events to *Hywisc* or Huish Episcopi. Finally, the fifteenth-century antiquary William Worcestre confuses matters further, claiming 100 martyred companions and the existence of some sort of memorial stone at Shapwick, which he muddles with Shepton (Mallet). Askew (1521–46) and Cressy (1668) are still later versions. The Indracht legend was probably generated by Glastonbury Abbey no earlier than the second quarter of the eleventh century. The monastery seems particularly to have encouraged its Celtic associations (St Brigit, St Benignus and St Patrick). The John of Glastonbury and Digby versions can be studied side-by-side in Winterbottom and Thomson 2002, 369–81.

44. Lawrence 1973.

45. Some twenty-five fugitives are said to have been hung from a tree in the village. One of Monmouth's army saved himself by hiding in a chest and being covered with linen (Elworthy and Elworthy 1971, 62). He may well have thought the village a sympathetic haven given that Francis Rolle, Shapwick's major landowner, was a known Monmouth supporter and at that moment languishing in the Tower suspected of treasonable practices (Legg 1997). For a detailed account see Dunning 1984 or Jenner 2007. A set of four silver christening spoons found in the roof of Forsters are said to have been hidden there by the vicar at the time of the Rebellion.

46. This vicar was Churchill Julius (1847–1938), later bishop of Christchurch in New Zealand (1890–1925) and the first Anglican archbishop of that country (1922–5). The root of the quarrel concerned access to the keys to the chancel door of the church.

47. *The Times* 13–15 January, 20 January, 24 April 1845.

48. Examples are Hey (1974); Howell (1983); Wrightson and Levine (1995); Fleming (1998). This might also be thought of as 'micro-history', but that term is usually taken to mean a study developed around a particular episode or person. A good example would be the study of Montaillou, a Pyrenean village, whose villagers were accused of heresy in the fourteenth century (Le Roy Ladurie 1978). Other examples of micro-history are Ginzburg 1980; Davis 1983.

49. For a similar approach in a very different context, see Yentsch 1994.

50. For definitions and discussion see Aston and Rowley 1974; Aston 1985; Darvill *et al.* 1993.

51. Field surveys generally (Macready and Thompson 1985); Blenheim Park (Bond and Tiller 1987); Wharram Percy (Hayfield 1987); Berkshire Downs (Gaffney and Tingle 1989).

52. During the lifetime of this Project, further English landscape studies have been completed. Three of them, at Roystone Grange in Derbyshire (Hodges 1991), Overton and Fyfield near Avebury in Wiltshire (Fowler and Blackwell 1998; Fowler 2000) and in the Vale of the White Horse in Berkshire (Tingle 1991), have the chronological range of the Shapwick Project and emphasised their own landscape approaches. A fourth, at Clarendon Park in Wiltshire, co-directed by Chris between 1993 and 2005, applied some of the same techniques developed at Shapwick to a later medieval elite landscape (Beaumont James and Gerrard 2007).

53. East Hampshire (Shennan 1985); Chalton (Cunliffe 1972); Ambridge (Aldridge and Tregorran 1981). For more recent themes see, for example, Cosgrove and Daniels 1988; Newman 1999.

54. The Weld Estate project conducted in Dorset by Lawrence Keen perhaps came closest to our ambition, not least because of its strong botanical component (Keen and Carreck 1987).

55. Biferno valley (Barker 1995); Melos (Renfrew and Wagstaff 1982). The Melos publication even inspired Mick to track back over the study area adopted on that project and ponder the value of different sampling strategies for field survey. Other references are: Keos (Cherry *et al.* 1991), southern Argolid (Jameson *et al.* 1994) Boeotia (for example, Bintliff *et al.* 1999). As a result the Shapwick Project differs from the Whittlewood Project, for example, in its attention to material culture and structural archaeology.

56. For other *Annaliste* applications see Bintliff 1991; Astill and Davies 1997; Cunliffe 2000.

57. On one occasion we arranged for the children to fieldwalk a field over the site of the recently removed buildings at Home Farm at the north end of the village. We knew, of course, that there would be abundant post-medieval and recent finds and, sure enough, the

children collected bucketloads. Their taking home of the finds to wash and then dry in airing cupboards resulted in several complaints from parents 'concerned at the enthusiasm' of their offspring!

58. The doctoral theses were: Clive Bond (lithics from Shapwick and other projects; University of Winchester), Nick Corcos (landscape, archaeology and history; University of Bristol) and Andrew Jackson (archaeological soil analyses; University of Bristol). Dissertations at Masters and undergraduate levels on archaeological materials, laboratory work etc. numbered around thirty-five and included projects on soil geochemistry, woodland ecology and the impact of metal-detecting on finds recovery. We also hosted a day-school for the Medieval Settlement Research Group in 1996 and several on-site visits from universities other than our own, such as Exeter in 1997.

59. Some archaeologists were complicit in this, feeling that amateur or part-time involvement might jeopardise archaeology's professional integrity by claiming back the subject as a 'hobby' and therefore one not to be taken seriously. Similar concerns were raised about archaeology on television.

60. BNFL 1999, 38.

Boxes

b1. Coles and Coles 1986, 29.
b2. Jones 1986, 125.
b3. Shackley 1981, 72.
b4. Coles and Coles 1986, 32.
b5. Coles 1989a, 5–14.
b6. Jones 1986, 125.
b7. Hoskins 1959, 7. As a source of motivation for this kind of work, landscape historian William Hoskins (1959, 5) cited 'enlarging one's consciousness of the external world, and even … of the internal world'. Similarly, archaeologist Philip Rahtz (1985), speculating on what attracts people to the world of archaeology, cites intellectual curiosity and widening perspectives.
b8. Lowenthal 1985, 35–73.
b9. To quote one first-year student, 'expectations are always high and it feels great to be part of a team that is finding pieces of history. You can read books on the subject but you can't beat hands on experience' (BNFL 1999, 38).

Notes to Chapter 2

1. A useful complementary text here is Rippon 2004a. The fact that the Puxton Project (Rippon 2006), the Whittlewood Project (Jones and Page 2006) and Carenza Lewis' test-pitting project in the villages of eastern England (Lewis 2005; 2007a) have all been published *before* the final report of the Shapwick Project (Gerrard with Aston 2007) rather diminishes just how influential certain aspects of the Shapwick Project have been. In particular, extensive test-pitting, shovel-pitting, buildings survey and the use of geochemical/heavy metal testing in the soil were all methods that, though they did not originate at Shapwick, were intensively applied there for the first time in an integrated project centred on the medieval period. Other experiments, such as thermal soil recording, came to nothing.

2. West 1962; Macfarlane 1977; Harvey 1991; Friar 1991. The holdings of record offices are now sometimes searchable on line. Tiller (1992) is a little outdated, especially with the arrival of web resources, but still useful, as is Edwards (1993). A search of The National Archives (TNA, formed in 2003 from the Public Record Offices and the Historical Manuscripts Commission) may produce further documentary sources (<www.nationalarchives.gov.uk>) or check your local county Victoria County History volumes (for Shapwick, VCH 2004).

3. Corcos 1982; 2002; Costen 1991; 2007a; Abrams 1996.

4. Thorn 2008. Today, the basic unit of administration outside the main urban areas is the civil parish, which may include a village, several farms or hamlets and surrounding farmland. The area of this parish is usually more or less that depicted on nineteenth-century tithe maps (Blair 2005, 426; Tiller 1992; Tate 1951). The origins of most parishes lie in the tenth–twelfth centuries with the break-up of large areas of land served by minster churches and their granting to local lords, who built private churches for their tenant farmers. This ecclesiastical unit was often defined long before for economic and farming purposes, so parishes may reflect ancient territorial divisions.

5. We should not think of these 'slaves' as being segregated by gender or working in large gangs. These were people, anonymous to us now, who did not own land and were answerable to their owners; possibly they were the descendants of indigenous inhabitants subjugated in the seventh century with the 'arrival' of the Anglo-Saxons. By Domesday they range from 10 to 25 per cent of the recorded population by county. Their presence on an ecclesiastical estate is probably explained by the need to support monks resident at Glastonbury.

6. Watkin 1947; 1952; 1956. Dom Aelred Watkin, a monk of Downside Abbey and historian, edited *The Great Chartulary of Glastonbury Abbey*. This was a collection of all the documents entitling the abbey to hold its estates. For the working of monastic estates generally, see Knowles 1963.

7. Ecclestone 2007b. 'Hallmoots', or customary courts, were attended by tenants and representatives of the Abbey. Proceedings were concerned with the administrative and organisational detail of life and

work in the manor: everything from disputes between tenants, infringements of the rights and customs of the manor to transfers of property. A useful guide to manorial surveys, accounts and courts is Bailey 2002.

8. Such responsibilities are set out in the 'custumal' of 1234 and 1325.

9. Any reader therefore needs to know Latin (medieval not classical), palaeography and the abbreviations, and then what it all means! Two of the best-known economic historians of the twentieth century, Paul Vinogradoff and Michael 'Munia' Postan, both made use of the various medieval manorial surveys compiled by Glastonbury Abbey for its estates (for example, Postan 1952; 1956; 1973). A recent thesis by Michael Thompson (supervised by Harold Fox) examines the role of Glastonbury manors along the Poldens (Thompson 1997).

10. Bettey 2007a; VCH 2004. The latter provides a comprehensive summary of the successive owners of the Shapwick manors and disentangles the complicated relationships of Waltons, Burrells, Rolles, Dyers, Smythes, Spencers, Bulls and Strangways, along with the other families who acquired property in Shapwick.

11. Details of the various grants and sales of land during the sixteenth century are included in the series of *Calendars of Patent Rolls* and *Letters and Papers of Henry VIII*. Further evidence can be found in the extensive records of the Court of Augmentations, which was established to negotiate the disposal of former monastic land on behalf of the Crown. Fans of C. J. Samson's fictional sixteenth-century lawyer/detective Matthew Shardlake will be familiar with the Court's dealings.

12. To consider criminal cases such as murder. In the sixteenth century they also kept an eye on local administration of the Poor Law.

13. DRO 96M/- and SRO DD/SG respectively.

14. SRO DD/SG 15; Chapter 8, below.

15. SRO D/P/Shap/4/1/1.

16. SRO D/P/Shap/13/2/1.

17. Hill-Cottingham 2007.

18. For historic maps generally see Hindle 1988; for Ordnance Survey maps see Oliver 1993; for tithe maps see Kain and Oliver 1995. For early attempts at Shapwick mapping see Aston 1988, 74–5.

19. Land at Heath Moor, for example, was enclosed by act of parliament between 1777 and 1784, and details of the transformed landscape, covering 411 hectares (1,015 acres), and the laying-out of the parish boundary through the peat bog are provided by a preparatory map of 1777 and the enclosure plan of 1784. In 1782 George Templer had his own map drawn of his fields on the reclaimed land. Further information can be found on the large-scale map of the Brue Drainage scheme of 1806, which includes Shapwick.

20. Following the Tithe Commutation Act of 1836, the appointed commissioners ordered the drawing-up of maps to help negotiate land values. These maps, together with their registers, called 'awards', can be consulted at county record offices and remain a vital source of information for landscape historians because they show boundaries, houses, ownership, tenants, field names and land use.

21. There are ten maps of enclosed areas of 1754 (SRO DD/SG c206) and nine maps of post-1762 of areas of common field (SRO DD/SG 39 c206).

22. Such as Shapwick's duck decoy pond, created around 1850 and now destroyed by peat digging. For a handbook on drawing up village plans see Roberts 1990.

23. The county of Somerset does not have the benefit of a recent English Place-Name Society volume, though several general guides to place- and field names are available (eg. Field 1972).

24. The crane seems to have ceased breeding in Britain in the sixteenth century (Rackham 1987, 37), its remains being found at several archaeological sites, such as Glastonbury Lake Village in the Iron Age (Coles and Minnitt 1995, 195) and Anglo-Saxon Flixborough (Dobney *et al.* 2007). Fourteenth century cranes are depicted on the walls at Longthorpe Tower, near Peterborough (Stone 2006, 150) and were treated in historic times as noble and royal quarry. The grey heron is often confused with the crane in old records, however, and that may well be the case here (Holloway 1996). There was a Glastonbury Abbey heronry at Meare at the Dissolution (Rippon 2004).

25. Though this last may be a personal name rather than the 'hawk hill'.

26. The best general guides to field names are Field 1972; Smith 1956; Gelling and Cole 2000.

27. As well as Collinson, Bonnor also illustrated for Ralph Bigland (1791–2) and Richard Polwhele (1793–1806) (Clayton 2004). Stachey's best known work is *Observations on the Different Strata of Earths and Minerals* (1727).

28. Hardie 1967.

29. If Bonnor and Nattes were not a 'set' then it is improbable that Nattes did not paint the main house, not to mention other views of its gardens. What remains are merely a few farm views. Mick has assumed for some time that these views were removed by earlier owners and there is even a rumour that pictures went to Australia or New Zealand (see Chapter 9 for Australia connection). They may, however, be in a large unprovenanced collection such as that at the Victoria and Albert Museum. The existing Nattes prints given to the village by Mrs Warry around 1947 are on display in the village hall. To Bonnor and Nattes

we should add two views of the church, one by John Buckler (1770–1851), the other by Walter Wheatley (1775–1856), and there is also a sepia painting of Shapwick House in 1876 by 'MKW'. These later views are of less interest to our study.

30. Corcos pers. comm. This reference is very odd because the moat was filled 100 years previously. Either there was a local memory of its existence or parts of the circuit remained open.

31. Dunning 2004a.

32. Warner had a long life (1763–1857). His early interests were centred on Hampshire, where he wrote various guides, later moving to a ministership at Bath. His histories of Bath and Glastonbury are regarded as 'useful compilations' (Hicks 2004).

33. Richard Beere or Bere (*c*.1455–1525) seems to have had a particular interest in finances; not only did he order a detailed survey of his estates, he also lent money to gentry and merchants as well as having wider scholarly interests. He was a prodigious builder and several buildings still bear his initials and shield (Dunning 2004b).

34. Lishman *et al.* 1982.

35. Glastonbury sheet 296.

36. Hardy 1990; 1992.

37. In fields 5885 and 0024 (see frontispiece map).

38. Strange marks visible from the air in field 2400 proved to be areas of tufa deposits from various springs of Mazewell.

39. Rodwell 2001, 29; Badham 2005.

40. VCH 2004.

41. Marshall 1796, 199.

42. Lewis 1848.

43. Marshall 1796, 194.

44. Billingsley 1797.

45. Billingsley 1797, 56.

46. Acland and Sturge 1851, 89.

47. Among the monuments examined in this way were several possible prehistoric barrows, Shapwick's three windmills, the gallows site, ridge and furrow in Beggar's Bush Copse, the icehouse and the Holy Well and Bathing House near Northbrook Farm. For each of these there is documentary, map and earthwork evidence.

48. For an introduction to surveying techniques and interpretation see Bowden 1999, 43–96.

49. Wilkinson 2001 provides a good survey of possible approaches.

50. The 25m spacing was calculated to be the minimum diameter of artefact concentration we felt could be missed and still fulfil the objectives of the survey. It also struck a reasonable balance between time in the field and time spent processing the material. A higher rate of sampling, and thus larger assemblages of finds, would have stretched the capacity of the Project to cope.

51. At the time GPS units were beyond the pocket of most archaeologists and for most of the 1990s insufficiently accurate (Ainsworth and Thomason 2003; Howard 2007). If this Project were to be undertaken now, a GIS environment would be created from the outset, which would help to smooth integration and improve digital dialogue between contributors (Chapman 2006).

52. Including date walked, number and names of fieldwalkers, weather and soil conditions and name of farmer, together with a sketch map of the layout of the field, lines and stints.

53. Finds (but never metal objects) were washed carefully in water with a toothbrush and laid out on newspaper with the bag and waterproof label kept together with the finds. At this stage natural stones, plastic, etc were discarded.

54. Of course, some preliminary identifications were later refined by finds specialists. Overall, however, there were relatively few problems. The main concern was to keep up with the flow of boxes arriving from Somerset and maintain tight control over the paper and finds archives.

55. Much use was made of 'Abnormal densities above background scatter' or 'ADABS', a method of identifying high densities of finds developed by the *Ager Tarraconensis* survey in Spain (Carreté *et al.* 1995, 56). For method, see Gerrard 1997; Gerrard *et al.* 2007e.

56. The Whittlewood fieldwalkers covered 1000ha (2470 acres) (Jones and Page 2006, 24) while the Raunds Area Survey covered 3000ha (7410 acres) with a similar methodology using traverses 15m apart and divided into 20m lengths (Parry 2006).

57. The volume of material collected from Shapwick was high. In County Durham, for example, a very large fieldwalking project that walked three times the area covered at Shapwick with walkers placed at 10m intervals, double the intensity of the Shapwick Project, produced only 1,717 pottery sherds of all periods at an average density of 13.38 sherds per hectare, around 2 per cent of the Shapwick figure (Haselgrove *et al.* 1988). There are clearly significant regional differences in the acquisition and use of pottery, its disposal and the quality of its manufacture and/or in the processes that affect the pottery once it reaches the plough soil.

58. The Project did not make use of remote imaging from satellites, high altitude photography, thermal imaging, airborne radar or multi-spectral imaging, all of which were expensive and difficult to obtain when we began, but are now far more accessible and available at higher resolutions (David 2006, 2–8). These are methods, together with LiDAR, that future intensive surveys like Shapwick ignore at their peril and that are already yielding good results (for example, Powlesland 1997).

59. For aerial photography in archaeology see D. R. Wilson

2000; for specific applications to the historic landscape see Glasscock 1992.

60. Aston 1992. Three teams participated in the geophysics: Geophysical Surveys of Bradford, the Ancient Monuments Laboratory (English Heritage) and University of Winchester, the work being coordinated by Chris Gaffney, John Gater, Neil Linford and Alex Turner respectively.

61. David 1995; Gaffney and Gater 2003.

62. Had the whole parish been subjected to magnetic scanning more unexpected features would almost certainly have been revealed, but the lack of funding prevented this.

63. Tabor 2008.

64. Aston *et al.* 1998b; Heron 2001 provides a review.

65. Two students looked at *Old Church* (4016) in 1995 for their final-year project.

66. Jackson 2001; the thesis was supervised by Mike Martin and Mick.

67. To analyse for phosphate, a known signature of archaeological activity, there were additional procedures (Crowther 1997). To calculate 'loss on ignition', the remaining soil samples were left in a furnace set at 450°C for six hours and then reweighed, noting any weight loss of organic-carbon based material.

68. 1.4g per day per person. For a recent discussion see Guttmann *et al.* 2005.

69. Other processes, however, may complicate this picture. Wood ash from domestic hearths, for example, enriches the soil with the same heavy metals that naturally occur in plant tissue and, of course, animal dung may be used deliberately to fertilise the soil, a process that is strongly suggested by the scatters of archaeological artefacts collected by fieldwalkers at Shapwick.

70. Several other projects have since underlined the potential benefits: for example, Rippon *et al.* 2001.

71. Ideally what is needed is a machine that undertakes all the soil analyses, the geophysics, soil PhD and magnetic susceptibility and is all coordinated by GPS. During Andrew's research we were told that such a machine did in fact exist and that we could have it when it finished its current project, providing we fetched it ourselves. We readily agreed, we had a van. Where was it? Mars!

72. For the benefit of foreign readers, metal detecting in many countries of the world is illegal; even possession of a metal detector is frowned upon. In many European countries artefacts belong to the State rather than the landowner and an official permit is required to collect them. In Britain, by contrast, an unknown number of detectorists have operated freely across the country for the past thirty years, often without the permission of landowners. Goodness knows how much information has been lost, let alone the value of the finds. In many areas the landscape has been 'hoovered' clean of objects.

The Portable Antiquities Scheme, through which some metal-detected finds are now more routinely reported, had not yet begun in 1989.

73. N. Campbell 2000.

74. In one case at Shapwick the topsoil had been removed before house foundations were dug, only to be replaced with topsoil 'imported' from Cheddar when the houses were finished.

75. Gerrard *et al.* 2007a.

76. The Group had already surveyed the smaller manor house (the school) and produced scale plans and elevations, so Mick asked if they would agree to do the rest of the parish.

77. SVBRG 1996.

78. Books on building recording and interpretation include Johnson 1993 for innovative approaches; Alcock 1993 for a case study; Wade Martins 1991 for farm buildings; Barley 1961 for farmhouses; Brunskill 1971 for architectural features.

79. Hooper 1970; 1971.

80. Clements and Alexander 2007; 2009.

81. Knight 2007.

82. The 1325 survey states that there are fifty acres of pasture in *Lokkeslegh* worth 12s 6d a year.

83. Hayes 1985.

84. Bell 1990.

85. Hodges 1991, 55; though there was no sieving at Royston Grange.

86. Mithen 2000, 58.

87. Now Cotswold Archaeology.

88. Gerrard *et al.* 2007b.

89. Jones and Page 2006, 25–6.

90. For example, Lewis 2003; 2005; 2007b; Gardiner 2006.

91. For example, at Great Easton in Leicestershire in 2003 (Cooper and Priest 2003, 53–6). Test-pitting in the Shapwick model was also used in *Time Team* programmes at Nether Poppleton (Yorkshire), St Osyth (Essex) and Wicken, Northants.

92. Lovis 1976; Nance and Ball 1986.

93. Thorpe 2000; Earle 2004.

94. Tabor and Johnson 2000.

95. Thorpe and Gerrard 2007.

96. Assuming that the soil has been disturbed by ploughing to a depth of 0.20m and that artefacts are distributed evenly through the topsoil horizon, a 150-litre sample represents a 0.03 per cent sample of the 500,000 litres of topsoil (0.20×50×50m) in each 50×50m square.

97. For a general introduction to sampling for pollen and the interpretation of pollen diagrams see Wilkinson and Stevens 2003, 85–96. For Shapwick results specifically see Tinsley 2007 and Wilkinson 1998. The principle is that plants spread pollen that is deposited on the ground. In certain conditions it can last for thousands

of years. Via a count of the grain types a soil sample can provide a percentage ratio of plant types for a particular area and time and by examining several samples a relative chronology of changing pollen types can be built up. These basics are complicated by dispersal, survival and identification biases. For a review of palynological evidence for the post-Roman environment locally see Housley *et al.* 2007.

98. DoE 1990, para 21; for standards and guidance on field evaluation see IFA 2001.

99. To take one example, the evaluation of around 41m³ of stratigraphy at New Farm took five days, during which two trenches were machine-cut in shallow spits of approximately 200mm until either natural deposits or significant archaeological features were identified (Chapter 7, below). All archaeological deposits were then hand-cleaned, recorded, planned and photographed with standard written context records. By comparison, the manual excavation of double the equivalent volume and complexity of stratigraphy (83m³; trench 7722/B) at Bridewell Lane by about twenty-five Winchester students took twenty-five days (Chapter 7).

100. Broomhead 1997; Hollinrake and Hollinrake 1996; Hollinrake and Hollinrake 1997; Horton 1998.

101. Hollinrake and Hollinrake 1994; Chapter 8.

102. Webster 1992.

103. Brunning and Webster 2007.

104. Straker *et al.* 2007.

105. Radiocarbon dating defines the time that has elapsed since a particular organism died by calculating the amount of radioactive carbon 14 still present in a sample. For this and other dating techniques generally see Brothwell and Pollard 2001. Sadly, many general texts make use of prehistoric examples only.

106. For dendrochronology see Baillie (1995) and English Heritage 2004. The basic principle is that concentric rings in a tree trunk record the growing conditions over the life of a tree. Plentiful rainfall results in fat bands, drier years in thinner ones. Trees of different ages provide overlapping sequences of bands that slowly build into a longer chronology. When a sample is taken from a roof timber it is matched against the sequence and the final band laid down before the bark provides the season of felling. The date of felling and the date of construction may vary, and there are the added complications that roof timbers were regularly reused, sometimes in quite different buildings, while the sensitivity of different tree species and their patterns of timber growth vary. Oak provides a reliable sequence. For tree-ring dating on the prehistoric trackways see Morgan 1988.

107. When particles of iron in objects or clay melt and reform they line up on the magnetic pole. Fortunately for archaeologists, the magnetic pole has moved about during the past few thousand years and by knowing the position of the pole and the direction and inclination of the iron 'pointers', it is possible to date when the iron melted. It is the last firing of the kiln which is dated. In the case of the kiln in Field 4016 at Shapwick the collapsed clay superstructure of the kiln could not easily be differentiated from the horizontal kiln base, so several dates were clearly awry (English Heritage 2006 is an accessible guide).

108. Gerrard and Norcott 2000.

109. Unfortunately, neither the time nor the money was available to take our experiment further and our triumphs were quickly outclassed by glossier products.

110. The most comprehensive summary article is Aston and Gerrard 1999. Other topics covered are: Roman coins (Abdy *et al.* 2001), metalwork (Gerrard and Youngs 1997), pottery (Gerrard 1999), lithics (Bond 2003), soil analyses (Aston *et al.* 1998b) architectural survey (SVBRG 1996), sampling (Orton 2000), environmental archaeology (Wilkinson and Bond 2001). Different aspects of the Shapwick Project are also well cited by others (e.g. Taylor 2007).

111. Selkirk 1997.

112. Aston 1989; Aston 1990; Aston and Costen 1992; Aston and Costen 1993; Aston and Costen 1994; Aston and Gerrard 1995, Gerrard and Aston 1997; Aston *et al* 1998a.

Notes to Chapter 3

1. Wilkinson 1998.
2. Wilkinson and Bond 2001.
3. Coles 1989b.
4. Bell *et al.* 2002.
5. Bulleid and Jackson 1937; Coles 1989a.
6. Though there are far fewer flints at the west end. Thorpe and Gerrard 2007; John Coles pers. comm.
7. Wilkinson and Bond 2001, 61.
8. Coles 1989b, 19.
9. Bridewell Lane (7722) and at Hill Farm (7372); three of them are core rejuvenation flakes.
10. Woodman 1985.
11. Ingold 1996.
12. Cummings 2000.
13. Smith 1992, 15.
14. Wainwright 1960.
15. Heyworth and Kidson 1982; Rippon 1997, 41–44.
16. Smith 1992.
17. Brown 1986.
18. C. Bond 2007.
19. And with them went any opportunity for archaeologists to examine the crucial Mesolithic–Neolithic transition phase.

20. Coles 1989b.
21. Hillam *et al.* 1990.
22. Coles and Coles 1990. We are rightly impressed by the age and craftsmanship of the Sweet Track. It is worth remembering, however, that it may have been a typical construction and not at all noteworthy in Neolithic times.
23. Coles 1989b, 20.
24. In Fields 1264 and 3553. A gabbro is a coarse-grained igneous rock: Roe 2007. This axe may, of course, have been recycled as a handy raw material.
25. Richards 1992.
26. 6767/C and E.
27. Coles 1989b, 26.
28. For example, Whittle 1995; 1997. Although moving livestock to another area until after the harvest is a custom with a long history in the British landscape, cultivated fields and livestock are not incompatible, particularly if the latter are constrained within wattle enclosures.
29. Where only a generation ago we might have expected evidence for a comprehensive disruption of Mesolithic ways of life and its replacement with more sedentary lifestyles, we now see a fusion of cultural traditions and much longer term patterns of inheritance and continuity.
30. Coles and Orme 1984.
31. Coles 1989b, 23.
32. Coles and Coles 1986, 83–4.
33. Coles 1989b.
34. Edmonds 1995.
35. Tilley 1994. The 'Tronhulle' field-name may also refer to cranes (Boisseau and Yalden 1998; Louisa Gidney pers. comm.).
36. Lewis 2005.
37. Godwin 1960.
38. The Meare Heath trackway was excavated by Bulleid and Gray in the mid-twentieth century at two points in Shapwick parish in East Moors just south of South Drain and the old railway line and then more thoroughly by John and Bryony Coles from 1974 to 1977 after the site was threatened by peat digging (Coles and Coles 1986, 118, Fig. 28).
39. For pollen see Beckett 1978, 44–5; for dating see Orme 1982; Morgan 1978; 1982, 45.
40. Ellison 1982, 46.
41. Bradley 1990.
42. Coles 1989b.
43. Dewar and Godwin 1963.
44. Godwin 1960.
45. Godwin 1960.
46. Horner n.d. For 'bog butter' see Earwood 1997.
47. For example, pottery finds in the extreme north-west corner of the parish (HER 12058).

48. Bradley 1990.
49. There seems no inherent reason why the Somerset Levels should not have had bog bodies in the later prehistoric period. The key to preservation is now thought to be the sugar chemicals in the bog mosses that tan the tissues into leather. So far as we know, however, there are no records of bodies being found and reported, or folk memory of such.
50. Rippon 1997.
51. Cunliffe 2005, 282.
52. Gingell 1982.
53. Typical among these is the Iron Age and Roman settlement at 'Crockland' in Puriton, whose late Iron Age phase is assumed on the basis of a few sherds only.
54. Coles and Minnitt 1995.
55. Bailey *et al.* 1981.
56. Minnitt and Coles 1996.
57. Haselgrove 1997.

Boxes

b1. Edmonds 1995.
b2. Berstan *et al.* 2008.
b3. The jadeite axe was found during the excavation of the Sweet Track just to the south of the South Drain. A recent project across Europe – Programme Jade – has been researching into their origins and use and has recorded more than twenty examples from central and south-western England. The axe is now in the museum in Taunton on loan from the Department of Archaeology and Anthropology at the University of Cambridge
b4. Brunning 1993.
b5. Bond 2003.
b6. Pollard 2001.
b7. Fleming 1987; Yates 2007.
b8. For a summary of recent work and some examples see McOmish *et al.* 2002.

Notes to Chapter 4

1. Manning 1976. The precise sequence of campaigns in the South-West is far from proven.
2. For the latest research on the earlier Roman presence in Britain see Creighton 2001. For pre-conquest Roman imports see Hengistbury Head (Cunliffe 1987).
3. Though the fort at Charterhouse-on-Mendip dates from the late 40s AD, lead was mined before the conquest (Todd 2007).
4. Historic Environment Records (HERs) 10714 and 18033.
5. Langdon and Fowler 1971; Rippon 2008b. The other Roman 'port' on this estuary was at Combwich, to the north, now mainly under the modern village. There was also a landing site here in the later medieval period.

6. Scott 1993, 165–72.
7. For what is meant by 'Romanisation' see Mattingly 2006.
8. It is very difficult to prove absolutely that families continued to live generation after generation in the same spot. Even for the Roman period our dating evidence is not refined enough.
9. For example, the Somerset Levels Project collected Iron Age pottery alongside Roman finds in the northern part of Walton parish.
10. Rippon 1997; Leach 1982.
11. Dorchester (*Durnovaria*) was very probably the original civitas capital, but it seems that the Durotriges area was later split in two, with the northern half centred on Ilchester. An inscription from Hadrian's Wall mentions the civitas *Durotrigum Lendiniensis.*
12. Leech 1980.
13. The Shapwick Project has not been alone in this, see also work by Steve Rippon on Somerset and the Severn estuary (Rippon 1997; 2000), the South Cadbury Environs project (eg. Tabor 2002; 2004) and that undertaken by the University of Winchester on the Quantocks.
14. Here we use the commonly used architectural typology (Perring 2002).
15. The excavation at the Nidons villa was undertaken in September 1998 and again in August 1999, coordinated by Richard Brunning and Chris Webster of Somerset County Council.
16. Some of the responses may be caused by the outcropping limestone beneath the site but the overburden is also deeper here and the anomalies are less distinct. Correspondingly, the southern range lies at a shallower depth and is more at risk from plough damage, which accounts for the greater concentration of finds on the surface in this area.
17. The importance of household ancestry in determining the location of the site, here, at *Old Church* and at *Chestell/Borgh*, should not be ignored.
18. Many new plant varieties were introduced during the Roman period, including asparagus, carrot and celery.
19. Based on what is known of the chronologies of high-status Shapwick sites, it is even possible that *Borgh/Chestell* is the direct successor to the Nidons villa.
20. For a discussion of villa plans in the south-west see Branigan 1976.
21. Or perhaps the villa is facing 'away' from briquetage production sites on the western horizon? For a discussion of views from villas and a case study see Martins 2005, 75–84.
22. Hunting nets are mentioned in the Vindolanda tablets. The curious villa assemblage might be explained if the site has been cleaned out by metal detectorists.
23. Hobbs 2006, 34.
24. Minnitt 2001.
25. No trace of any receptacle was identified, but the shape of the hole indicates a leather or fabric container or basketry.
26. Hobbs 2006, 130–31.
27. Coin hoards in the West are further discussed by Isaac (1976) and Janes (2002, 103–14). Chris is grateful to Richard Abdy for discussions here.
28. Dressel 20.
29. Minnitt 2007a. The laboratory code for this radiocarbon date is SUERC-30961 (GU-22217).
30. Coal is routinely found at Roman sites (Dearne and Branigan 1995). Somerset sites benefited from the proximity of the south Wales and Somerset coalfields and must have taken advantage of cheap seaborne transport. The lack of coal from other Shapwick Roman excavations is a surprise: peat or wood-charcoal was presumably preferred.
31. Corcos 2002, 19.
32. For Brean Down see ApSimon 1965. For comparisons see Woodward and Leach 1993, table 20; Watts and Leach 1996; Rahtz *et al.* 1992, 243.
33. As an aside, this may suggest a hitherto unrecognised Roman military presence in the area. There are numerous places in Somerset where Roman forts or fortlets, or marching camps of the first century AD campaigns, could have been sited, including the Polden hills. However, this same brooch type is also found at *Abchester* and there are examples from Camerton, Catsgore, Charterhouse, Ham Hill and Ilchester (Bayley and Butcher 2004), several of which have no known military occupation. The type was probably copied. Leech (1982, 36) plausibly suggests that an occasional military or official presence is not unlikely in smaller settlements where taxes needed to be collected.
34. Minnitt 2007a.
35. Leech 1980, 335. Comments about Roman eating here are inspired by Cool 2006. Some apparent differences could be a reflection of the small sample sizes.
36. From what we know of other sites in the region a fusion of native and Roman deities is possible, as, for example, Sulis Minerva at Bath (Cunliffe and Davenport 1985). Other high-status rural sites with cult structures can be found at Littlecote in Wiltshire (to Bacchus), for example (Walters 1996). Corcos (2002, 26) points out the proximity of the sulphurous well at nearby Edington to a high status Romano-British site there.
37. Corcos 1982; the *Sladwyke* reference is Longleat 11246. For *wics* see Gelling 1997, 63–86; Coates 1999. Corcos 2002, 8–9, argues for them to be subsidiary or dependent places and that this status was understood by the Anglo-Saxons. The significance of Wiltshire *wics* has recently been examined by Draper 2006.

38. From Geophysical Surveys of Bradford.

39. On the basis of the smattering of sherds collected during fieldwalking we would not have known this site was there. The field lay outside the medieval open-field system.

40. Geologist Peter Hardy, who examined the slate, suggests that its source is likely to be the Somerset/Devon borders, around Luxborough in the Brendon Hills, or possibly Rooks Castle near Bridgwater or Delabole in north Cornwall.

41. Minnitt 2007a.

42. Miles 1984.

43. Wedlake 1958.

44. Leech 1981.

45. This lack of interest in overt display might suggest no need for that type of self-advertisement, possibly because this was a family of long social standing.

46. Hayward 1972.

47. There was also a single box flue tile from *Sladwick* but this could easily have been recycled.

48. This might explain the flourishing schools of mosaicists, a preference in the south-west for winged corridor villas with central, intra mural yards (Branigan 1976, 50–51), not to mention the number of Gallic deities in the region. See also Cunliffe 1993, 254.

49. Leech 1976.

50. Cunliffe 1993, 251.

51. For a recent discussion of these issues see Martins 2005.

52. Radford 1928.

53. Work at *Blacklands* was supervised by Chris Webster and Richard Brunning of Somerset County Council.

54. Timby 2007.

55. Stratified samples were analysed by Phil Clogg using X-ray fluorescence (Gerrard *et al.* 2007c).

56. Leech 1982.

57. Further Roman parallels cited by Leech (1982) include Pinford Lane at Castleton in Dorset. More recently the earthworks of several linear villages have been recorded within the Salisbury Plain Training Area, including those at Chapperton Down and Chisenbury Warren (McOmish *et al.* 2002, 98–104). The latter has a street that survives as a substantial terrace, a Late Iron Age origin and evidence for occupation shift and iron smelting. A useful, if dated, review article with further parallels is Leech 1976.

58. The polisher is made from Hangman Grit from the Quantock Hills, though it might have been retrieved as a beach pebble from the shores of the Severn Estuary (Roe 2007).

59. Minnitt 2007a.

60. Millett 1990, 184.

61. Leech 1982, 36–8; Millett 1990, 209–10.

62. For Wrington see Neale 1970. Corcos (2002, 28–33) argues for a 'regionally significant territorial entity' on the Poldens that was still recognisable when it was granted to Glastonbury in the early eighth century AD (see Chapter 5, below). For a summary of the continuity debate see Reynolds 2005.

63. AD 70–225 (SUERC-2979; 2935 repeat) and AD 20–210 (SUERC-2980).

64. Philpott 1991.

65. Comprising distal tibia, tarsals, metatarsal and phalanges. Sheep of the size and build of the modern North Ronaldsay may be envisaged.

66. Among recently published examples are Kingscote (Glos; Timby 1998, 275–6) and Roughground Farm, Lechlade (Glos; Allen *et al.* 1993). Examples from Somerset include Bradley Hill, (Somerton) (Leech 1981), Crandon Bridge (Bawdrip), Churchie Bushes (Bawdrip), Ilchester Mead, Ilchester and Catsgore (listed in Leech 1980, 338). At both Bradley Hill and Catsgore occupation debris sealed the floor slabs under which the infants were buried, but, notably, these are all late third to early fifth century in date and this has led to the suggestion that the practice was not adopted locally until the later Roman period. The Shapwick examples offer a more extended chronology.

67. Both reconstructed as a central tower with an ambulatory and annexes (Leech 1980).

68. HER 10008.

69. Rippon 1997, 67 and figure 18.

70. There was also a well-developed range of wooden agricultural equipment and tools that has not survived (Fowler 2002).

71. A biconical stone spindlewhorl from *Old Church* was made from White Lias, perhaps from the Radstock area, with ornamentation on the lower part of the concentric rings. Another was made of shale. The nearest suitable source of this material is the Kimmeridge area of Dorset, about 80km away, and this example had been lathe-turned to a truncated conical form. The spindlewhorls were threaded over a wooden rod, called a handspindle, and this provided momentum when rotated.

72. For pigs in the Roman diet see Cool 2006, 84.

73. *Contra* Branigan 1976, 79, who suggests specialised pig production locally.

74. Nothing of the original structure survived *in situ*, but many of the pieces had single surviving surfaces that were unvitrified and had been fired at a low temperature in oxidising conditions.

75. Straker *et al.* 2007. Weeds included both small-seeded, low-growing forms such as the mayweeds, climbers such as cleavers and large-seeded crop-height plants such as brome. For all of these weed species to be included, reapers at Shapwick must have cut the straw low to the ground, yet the straw nodes are largely absent from the sample so the straw itself must have been removed.

Sickles and reaping hooks were not found but they would have been kept sharp with the whetstones, smoothers, polishers and point sharpeners that were recovered from most Shapwick Roman sites.

76. Roe 2007.
77. The conclusion drawn from a study of a sample from Meare Heath for the Roman period was 'a mixture of woodland and open land … with cereal cultivation of dryland areas' (Beckett and Hibbert 1979, 98).

Boxes

b1. Minnitt 2001.
b2. Abdy *et al.* 2001.
b3. Gowland and Chamberlain 2002.
b4. Ucko 1969.
b5. Gowland 2001.
b6. Miles 1984, 15–16.
b7. Esmonde Cleary 2000, 139.
b8. Scott 1991.
b9. Leach 1982, 61–106.
b10. Chris Webster pers. comm.; Leach 2001.
b11. For example, Esmonde Cleary 2000.
b12. For example, Hill 1995.

Notes to Chapter 5

1. Some Germanic hybrid is also possible, as is late-spoken Latin. Poems and prose in Old Welsh, such as *Y Gododdin*, are arguably the closest we can get to the Brythonic language (but see Schrijver 2007). Old Welsh is not readily intelligible to a modern-day Welsh speaker, though some words are identical, such as *tir* for 'land', or similar, such as *did/dydd* for 'day'.
2. Rodwell 2001.
3. Rahtz and Watts 2003.
4. Wormald 1995, 977.
5. Both the preceding Roman period and the succeeding Middle Ages are far richer in material finds and structural remains, not to mention the extensive and detailed history derived from the mass of documentation available for the historic period. Also known as 'Anglo-Saxon' and 'Early Christian', this period is increasingly referred to as 'Late Antiquity' (Collins and Gerrard 2004), but it is also part of the 'early medieval' period, making the contrast with the period after 1100 (in effect, after the Norman Conquest of 1066 in England), which is seen as the 'late medieval period'. Two key texts are Webster and Brown 1997 and Higham 2007. Among those who support the notion of Late Antiquity most strongly are archaeologists in the west of Britain who see elements of continuity in Church and governance as well as socio-cultural links with the western Empire (Dark 1994a; 1994b).
6. For example, public buildings fall into disrepair or their use is changed (Mattingly 2006, 336–7).

7. HERs 15590, 53104.
8. Branigan 1977, 93–108; Leach 2001.
9. Faulkner 2002; Reece 2002.
10. There are other clusters in East Anglia and the north Thames region (Hobbs 2006, 55). In fact, there are nine hoards in all from Shapwick, and to this number should be added the 'Goldhurd' field name just to the east of the *Abchester* Roman site, and another possible example excavated at *Old Church*.
11. Minnitt 2001. For bowls see, for example, St George Gray 1939.
12. Documentary evidence for disruption includes naval activity against the Picts, Scots and Saxons; Constantine III declaring himself emperor in AD 407; and the withdrawal of Roman troops from the province, so that by AD 410 Britain was to fend for itself (Colgrave and Mynors 1969, *HE* 1.11–12). The *Anglo-Saxon Chronicle* mentions the burying of hoards in Britain in AD 418 by the Romans (Swanton 1996, 10–11). Archaeological evidence includes the construction of Saxon shore forts (Johnson 1976).
13. Laycock 2008, 140–44. Hoards of this period are a largely British phenomenon, with more than 80 per cent of silver hoards in the date range AD 388–410 occurring in Britain, where there seems to have been more of a power vacuum than on the Continent.
14. Another possibility is that the hoarders could not return because of seasonal flooding (Rippon 1997, 126) though this would not apply to the hoards in the upland area of the parish. This flooding episode is widely recognised around the Severn Estuary, where the Roman landscape is buried under a metre or more of silt. It is assumed that coastal and river defences eventually gave way and any reclaimed land became subject to seasonal flooding, as it had been in earlier times.
15. Oxfordshire wares, for example, accounted for 1 per cent at Shapwick compared with 7.1 per cent at Catsgore and 2.3 per cent at Kenn Moor, both in Somerset (Timby 2007).
16. For example, from the port at Crandon Bridge.
17. Geake 1997, 203, map 1; Lucy 2000, 2, fig. 1.1.
18. Rahtz 1976, 50, fig. 2.1; Tipper 2004.
19. Hills 1999 provides an excellent introduction to sites and debates.
20. Faulkner 2002, 75. We know from Gildas and Aldhelm that there was a post-Roman kingdom in the south-west called *Dumnonia*. Gildas tells us of a ruler called Constantine 'tyrant whelp of the filthy lioness of Dumnonia' (Winterbottom 1978, 29) whilst Aldhelm refers to it in one of his poems as *diram Domnoniam* ('nasty Devon'; Ehwald 1961, 524). He also refers to '*Cornubiam*' in the same verse, suggesting a recognised distinction by the late seventh century. It is possible

that these represented Devon and Cornwall by that date but we do not know their extent. *Dumnonia* may have been similar to the pre-Roman *Dumnonia* and may have included much, if not all, of Somerset.

21. White 2007. Essentially, Roger White's thesis amplifies and reinforces earlier discussions about post-Roman Somerset stretching back to 1972 (Rahtz and Fowler 1972). Ken Dark has hinted that there is decreasing Anglo-Saxon influence as one progresses westwards (Dark 1994b, vii, fig. 1, where his Area C 'The West Country' includes Dorset, Somerset and Gloucestershire).

22. Alcock 1995; Rahtz *et al.* 1992.

23. Winterbottom 1978, 29.

24. Respectively, HER 22758; Mary Alexander pers. comm.; Webster 2008.

25. Our excavations were not extensive enough to recognise the signs of architectural adaptions of Roman buildings such as the partitioning of rooms, as for example at Frocester in Gloucestershire (Price 2000).

26. Hoskins 1960.

27. Rahtz and Fowler 1972; Morris 1973.

28. Yorke 1995, 53.

29. The archaeology of the period AD 400–700 in Somerset was first reviewed by Philip Rahtz and Peter Fowler (1972). They drew attention to several cemeteries of east–west inhumations dating from this period, linear earthworks and occupied or reoccupied hillforts and hilltops (Burrow 1981) and a number of religious and/or monastic sites. The identification of additional sites has continued since 1972 (Dark 1994b). Today there is dispute about the precise nature of any 'advance' and the numbers of people involved. Current estimates from skeletal data suggest between one in every ten were 'immigrants' in the south-west (Härke 2002), while geneticist Stephen Oppenheimer reckons on one in every twenty or thirty, with a higher proportion in southern and eastern England (Oppenheimer 2006, 439).

30. Abrams 1996, 6, 28.

31. Meaney 1964, 218–19; Geake 1997, 203, map 1, 264, map 62; Lucy 2000, 2, fig. 1.1; Rahtz 1976, 50, fig. 2.1; Tipper 2004, 20, fig. 4.

32. Griffiths 2003, 77.

33. Jones 1979.

34. Gregson 1985; Hadley 1996; Blair 1991; Dark 1994a, 148–51.

35. Aston 1986, 51–7; Thorn 1987, 36.

36. Morland 1984.

37. 'Andersey' (the modern Nyland) is not included and was taxed. Other Glastonbury possessions nearby, such as Pennard, Pilton and Wootton to the east, lay outside this privileged area and, after the mid-tenth century, in other hundreds (Frank Thorn pers. comm.).

A hundred was a division of the shire, looked after by a reeve or constable who apprehended criminals. Very crudely, they are the equivalents of today's district councils. Hundreds go by other names in different parts of the country; in the north and east they were called 'wapentakes', for example. Teresa Hall (2000) has suggested for Dorset that the minster *parochiae* and the hundreds were based on earlier royal estates.

38. Oliver Padel (1985, 193) gives the element *pow*, meaning 'land or country'. In Old Cornish this is *pou*, in Welsh *pau* and in Old Breton *pou*. This seems possible and suggests 'wooded land or country'.

39. Corcos 1983. We refer to the name of the estate as *Pouholt* throughout, except where the name in a charter is directly quoted.

40. Aston and Gerrard 1999, 4.

41. Sawyer 1968.

42. Abrams 1991, 124–7; Abrams 1996, 204.

43. This is no. 371 in Finberg 1964, 112; and S248 – regarded as spurious by some. Although this is charter no. 371 in Finberg's list, it is now customary to refer to Saxon charters by the S number from the list compiled by Peter Sawyer in his 1968 corpus. The list is kept up to date and is at www.trin.cam.ac.uk/chartwww/esawyer.99/csawyer2.html.

44. Finberg 1964, no. 381, 115; S253; see also Grundy 1935, 114–16.

45. Finberg 1964, no. 387, 116; S1680. Frank Thorn suggests that if this charter contains genuine information, the twenty-two hides must represent a large estate or the sum of several smaller ones. Stawell is only two and a half hides in Domesday Book and Bawdrip two hides, the latter with no connection to Glastonbury. In addition, the location of Bawdrip hardly fits with the description 'wooded hill' (Frank Thorn pers. comm.).

46. Abrams 1996, 210 – see Finberg 1964, 116 within no. 387, no Sawyer number.

47. A similar sequence of events was happening at another Anglo-Saxon monastery founded at Muchelney, a little further south (Aston 2007a; 2009).

48. Abrams 1996, 207.

49. S1249; Finberg 1964, no. 357; Edwards 1988, 18–19; Abrams 1996, 153–4. When citing charter dates the accepted convention among historians is to express the possible date range within which the charter was produced in the form 677×681. Thus, in this case, this particular charter was written sometime in the four years between AD 677 and 681.

50. Hall 2003, 51.

51. S248; Finberg 1964, no. 371; Edwards 1988, 27–33; Abrams 1996, 204.

52. S253; Finberg 1964, no. 381; Edwards 1988, 40–41; Abrams 1996, 204.

53. S1680; Finberg 1964, no. 387; Edwards 1988, 63, 72; Abrams 1996, 204.

54. It must be in this date range as King Sigeberht reigned for only two years.

55. No S number; Finberg 1964, no. 393; Edwards 1988, 74; Abrams 1996, 210.

56. S1685; Finberg 1964, no. 393; Edwards 1988, 74; Abrams 1996, 210.

57. *Mansiones* are the equivalent of hides and are also referred to as *cassata*.

58. S270a; Finberg 1964, no. 401; Edwards 1988, 56–9; Abrams 1996, 76–7.

59. Frank Thorn pers. comm.; Finberg 1964, no. 408; Abrams 1996, 214.

60. Abrams 1996, 207–10; Corcos 1983.

61. This is *contra* Aston's map (fig. 2 in Aston and Gerrard 1999, which is based on Grundy 1935, 114–16, and is probably too restricted a version of the estate).

62. It looks like a 100-hide unit, since the Domesday Tax Returns for Loxley Hundred (47 hides) and Reynaldsway Hundred (59 hides) roughly equal that, and it is likely that the 'Sowy estate' (to the south-west of the Poldens), though evidently in Loxley Hundred in 1086, was not originally part of the 100 hides of *Pouholt* (Frank Thorn pers. comm.).

63. This point has often been made by, for example, Glanville Jones (1979), and Herbert Finberg for Withington in Gloucestershire, where he equates the parish with the Roman estate (Finberg 1964), and by June Sheppard (1979) for Marden in Herefordshire.

64. Dickinson 1889; VCH 2004; Michael Thompson has pointed out that the hundredal meeting house for the Whitley Hundred is mentioned in the medieval bounds of Ashcott immediately east of the village of Ashcott on the boundary with Walton (Thompson 1997).

65. Although Whitley Hundred also included odd estates elsewhere in Somerset, such as Milton Podimore, Holford, Wheathill, Blackford, Holton, Lattiford and Cary Fitzpaine – the unifying factor being later medieval ownership by Glastonbury Abbey (Dickinson 1889, 115–24) – we do not need to allow for these in our discussions of the early estate because these lands were almost certainly originally attached to their nearest royal estates in earlier times (see map in Thorn 1987, fig. 4.2). In the Exchequer Lay Subsidy Rolls for 1327 Whitley Hundred included the vills of Westonzoyland, Middlezoy and Othery, on Sowy 'island', to the south of the Poldens, arguably also a separate early estate.

66. VCH 2004, 9.

67. VCH 2004, 131.

68. Walton and Street are said, almost without doubt wrongly, to be hamlets of Butleigh in the *Nomina Villarum* of 1316 (a list of cities, boroughs, villages and hundreds with their lords compiled for Edward II); Dickinson 1889, 53. Beyond Butleigh to the east lay the great royal estate centred on Somerton.

69. Costen 1992a, 87–9; Hall 2000, 25–6.

70. Costen 1992a, 87–90.

71. To confuse matters, a reference to a 'vill called *Poelt*' is found in the margin of a post-Conquest Glastonbury document in reference to Greinton. Purporting to be a grant of privileges by Ine to Glastonbury (S250), it is in fact a post-Conquest forgery (Edwards 1988, 36–7; Abrams 1996, 132, 207).

72. Dickinson 1889, 53; VCH 2004, 213.

73. See Blair and Sharpe 1992; Blair 2005; Blair 1988.

74. VCH 2004, 131.

75. For instance, Congresbury, North and South Petherton and Taunton in Somerset, and Wimborne Minster, Charminster, Bere Regis and Gillingham in Dorset. In contrast to Moorlinch, the old church site at Shapwick was sited on gently sloping land, even though the building itself seems to have been positioned on a low mound.

76. Corcos 2002, 71–5. Both churches clearly have early origins; they are both listed in AD 725 (S250, though this document is thought to be a post-Conquest forgery) and again in 1191 (Watkin 1947, xxi). At that date Shapwick is one of the 'Seven Churches' that should be free of episcopal and archdiaconal jurisdiction, along with St John's Glastonbury, Meare, Street, Butleigh, Moorlinch and Sowy.

77. Bassett 1998, 22–3.

78. Hall 2000; 2003; 2009.

79. Aston 2003; 2007.

80. The sequence proposed here for the Poldens may not be unusual for Glastonbury estates. The Brent estate is similarly difficult to unravel; there, it is not possible to be certain whether South Brent or East Brent was the main church of the estate. This might be explained by their ownership by the Abbey. Most minster churches were very wealthy, leading to many of the characteristics that help us to recognise them – they tend to be big, high-status churches with lots of dependencies. However, because any financial benefits from the important churches on the Abbey's estates were being funnelled directly to Glastonbury, this group of minsters is less obvious. Exceptions, such as Pilton, were granted at a later stage and therefore had time to develop their wealth before Glastonbury acquired them. Although the Abbey had no policy on the status of its churches, it generally regarded them as income to be exploited to its own advantage (Teresa Hall pers. comm.).

81. Another possible candidate for the early estate centre is Chilton. This place-name might be 'cilda-tun', literally 'the children's tun' but more probably 'prince's tun' (Ekwall 1960, 104). Another less suggestive interpretation is the 'tun on the limestone hill' from

'cealc-tun' (Ekwall 1960, 105). The only 'directional' name that is known on the Poldens, Sutton – the 'southern tun' – lies to the south of Chilton, which may signal its earlier importance. Sutton is also south of Edington and Cossington, but not of Shapwick; it is also on the other side of the hill and would be south-central to the suggested outline of the early estate. Nothing of archaeological significance is known at either Chilton or Sutton.

82. Beresford 1967, 483–4.
83. Aston and Leech 1977, 39–41.
84. Hinchliffe 1986, 240–59; Rahtz 1979.
85. Excavations at Foxley (Wilts) revealed a timber hall with ancillary buildings (Hinchliffe 1986). At Flixborough (Lincs), where there was probably also a monastic component to the site, excavations produced evidence as well for industry and trade (Loveluck 2007; Loveluck and Atkinson 2007).
86. Aston 1994, 219–25; Costen 1992a; Costen 1993, 94–100.
87. Costen 1992a. The existence of the personal name in *Hemstitch* elsewhere in Shapwick strengthens this explanation.
88. Aston 1983, 94, 100.
89. Smith 1956, part 2, 273; Costen 1992a, 73; English 2002, 45–51.
90. We believe that the *Borgh/Chestell* name signifies an association with the Romano-British enclosure and possible villa site there (Chapter 4, above). We would readily agree, however, that this location requires more extensive examination before its credentials as a Middle Saxon site can be dismissed (Draper 2004).
91. Corcos 1982; Costen 1993, 92.
92. Smith 1970, 257; Coates 1999, 75–116; Draper 2002, 27–43.
93. Smith 1956, 257.
94. Gerrard *et al.* 2007d, 379.
95. Straker *et al.* 2007, 887.
96. SUERC-2938; Gerrard *et al.* 2007d, 386.
97. Percival 1976, 183.
98. Williams 1997, 2006, 181.
99. Smith 1956, 43–4.
100. Smith 1956, 81–2.
101. Alternatively, there may have been two contemporary buildings in a line represented by the chancel and nave that were later linked by a church tower, as has been suggested for Jarrow (Cramp 2005, 161, fig. 13.15). This must remain unsolved at present; the very small area examined makes any such interpretation highly speculative. For excavations see Gerrard 2007a.
102. Morris 1989; Blair 2005.
103. Stephenson 1989, 31.
104. As was building S at North Elmham Park, Norfolk (Wade-Martins 1980, 61).

105. As at Cowdery's Down, panel type B4; Millett and James 1983, 228.
106. This arrangement has been suggested for other early medieval structures, as at Congresbury (Rahtz *et al.* 1992, 193) and Dinas Powys (Alcock 1995, 31).
107. One of the partition posts was radiocarbon dated to AD 770–980 at 95 per cent probability (Gerrard 2007a, 419).
108. There is no detailed typology for early medieval timber buildings (Hamerow 2002, 46), but their ground plans are generally fairly predictable, consisting most often of a double square with opposing central doors in the long walls, and sometimes with internal partitions (James *et al.* 1984). Generally speaking, the plan of the Shapwick hall does not differ greatly from buildings at Cowdery's Down (C8) and Charlton (AZ1) in Hampshire.
109. 68 per cent probability or AD 540–760, 95 per cent probability (Marshall *et al.* 2007, 1190).
110. 68 per cent probability or AD 860–1100 at 95 per cent probability (Marshall *et al.* 2007, 1190).
111. These British halls are reviewed by Alcock (1995, 132–7). The Shapwick structure is too large for a church.
112. For example, buildings of fifth- to seventh-century date at Dinas Powys in south Wales had drip gullies very like our Shapwick example (Alcock 1963, 30–4) while another at Cadbury-Congresbury in north Somerset, dated to between the late fifth and end of the sixth centuries, was terraced into the slope and had a curved south end and a partition (Rahtz *et al.* 1992, 193, 195. This is structure 1 (9m × 3.4m).
113. See, for example, Yeavering and Sutton Courtney (Hope Taylor 1977; Wessex Archaeology 2010).
114. Abrams 1996, 132.
115. Smith 1956, 273; Costen 1992b, 73.
116. For general reviews of this see Turner 1981, 71; Rackham 1994; Dark 1996; Dark and Dark 1997, 143.
117. Bell 1989.
118. Dark 2000, 133. Environmental archaeologist Martin Bell also concluded that there was reduced agricultural activity associated with regeneration of woodland between the fifth and tenth centuries, but that much of it was in the seventh century, not in the immediate post-Roman period, when there was a switch from arable to pastoral farming (Bell 1989, 275).
119. For west Somerset see Rippon *et al.* 2006. A radiocarbon date from the tenth century AD has been retrieved from peat in Godney Moor that is similar to medieval peat surviving in the area of Athelney, to the south of the Polden Hills (Straker *et al.* 2002, 34). Nearby, at Glastonbury, the top of the peat at Wells Road was dated to cal AD 600–790 (95 per cent probability) (Jones 1999).

120. Beckett and Hibbert 1978, 88, fig. 53. For a useful review see Housley *et al.* 2007.
121. Dark 2000, 138.
122. Though the estate name *Pouholt* in the eighth century includes the element *holt* – the Old English for a wood (Ekwall 1960, 369–70).
123. Baker and Butlin 1973, 655. For Barnsley Park see Webster 1967. Peter Fowler remarks that whilst 'infield/outfield' may well have been a common way of farming in much of Britain in this period it is difficult to find documentary or archaeological evidence for it (Fowler 2002, 216).
124. Harvey 1974.
125. For example, Masters (1975) at Wrington. For a good introduction to hedgerows and history see Barnes and Williamson (2006).
126. Between *Bassecastel* and *Above Verysway*.
127. Elsewhere in England cattle and sheep were most important for meat, becoming more significant as time went on (Maltby 1981; Rackham 1994). Animals were slaughtered when they reached maturity: that is, when they were at maximum weight. Pigs are not well evidenced in the archaeological record though their use is documented – boned meat may provide an explanation. Excavations at Cheddar and Cadbury-Congresbury showed that cattle were always the most important animal and this can be interpreted as indicating 'an affluent society' (Rahtz 1979; Noddle 1992).
128. Jones 1979, 10, 17; Dyer 2002, 27–9.
129. Gerrard 2004, 68–9.
130. The Levels no doubt flooded each autumn and winter, only drying out in spring, as was the case in later periods.
131. Gerrard 2004; Rahtz 1979.
132. Eagles 2001, 206; confusingly, this pottery is often referred to as 'Anglo-Saxon'.
133. RCHM 1959, 130–32; Jope 1959, 138; Poulsen 1985, 81–5; sixth- to tenth-century pottery has been found at Bestwall, Wareham (Lilian Ladle pers. comm.).
134. One of us (MA) wonders whether some of the late Roman pottery goes on later than the fifth century (Gerrard 2004) and whether some of the ninth- and tenth-century pottery from, for example, Cheddar (Rahtz 1979) begins rather earlier. For a parallel argument, but for Greece, see Bintliff *et al.* 2007, 179.

Boxes

b1. Rahtz and Watts 2003, 32–5.
b2. Blair 2005, Chapter 5, 246 and 262–8. Glastonbury was producing glass in the ninth or tenth century, amongst other things (Harden 1971, 87). Material from many years of unpublished excavation is currently under review as part of an AHRC-funded research project directed by Roberta Gilchrist.
b3. Faith 1997, 15–16.
b4. Blair 2005, 330.
b5. Aston and Bond 1976, 75 fig. 14.
b6. Blair 2005, Chapter 5.
b7. Aston 1984; 1986, 58–63.
b8. Henry de Bracton, an eminent thirteenth-century lawyer, considered the maximum market journey to be 'six miles and a half and a third part of a half': that is, six and two-thirds miles or just over 10 km (Fox 1973, 75).
b9. Brunning 2010.
b10. BL, Egerton manuscript 3134.
b11. Costen 2007b.
b12. This process is described in more detail in Aston *et al.* 2007a.
b13. Ecclestone 2007e.

Notes to Chapter 6

1. Brooks 1992, 8. Following the Benedictine reformation the direct involvement of monks in their estates became much less common (Abrams 1996, 267).
2. Winterbottom and Thomson 2002.
3. Alfred was king AD 871–99. According to Asser, his biographer, he complained on his accession that not a single monk south of the Thames could understand divine services or translate from Latin into English (Keynes and Lapidge 1983, 125).
4. The others were Oswald of Worcester, later archbishop of York, and Aethelwold of Winchester and Abingdon.
5. Such as Peterborough and Ely: Knowles and Hadcock 1971.
6. Britnell 2001, 112–13. Frankpledge divided most of Anglo-Saxon England into tithings of ten households. Each of these groups of about thirty to fifty individuals monitored the conduct of its own constituent members and brought them before the court leet in the case of misdemeanour. Good introductions to the period are by Innes (2007) and Wickham (2009).
7. At Cheddar, not far from Shapwick on the edge of Mendip, Philip Rahtz could date no pottery securely before *c.* AD 930 (Rahtz 1979). Pottery is present rather earlier than this in other parts of Britain; for example, Ipswich Ware was widely traded in East Anglia between *c.* AD 650 and 850 (McCarthy and Brooks 1988).
8. Some of this pottery would have been used as cooking pots on an open fire – the predecessors of the large all-purpose cooking pots of the twelfth–thirteenth centuries – but other vessels might have been used for storage. They are multi-functional. The fabrics in question are AA1, AA2, AA4, AAN and U6S (Gutiérrez 2007a).
9. 0.25m wide and 0.25m deep (Gerrard 2007b).

10. None of these features contained any glazed pottery and on that basis must pre-date the thirteenth century, though the assemblage is not large.

11. PVP 122/135; Gerrard 2007b. Excavations along the length of the pipeline were directed by Charlie and Nancy Hollinrake.

12. Pottery fabrics AA1 and AA2 (Gerrard 2007c).

13. This measured 0.20m wide at the base and 0.20m deep.

14. Leech and Pearson 1986; Watts and Rahtz 1985, 78–80; Ponsford 1980; Young forthcoming; Ponsford 2003, 55.

15. Pottery fabric AA1; Gerrard 2007d.

16. Field 6660; Gerrard 2007d. The work at Lawn Farm was undertaken by Charles and Nancy Hollinrake.

17. Gerrard *et al.* 2007b. It could be argued that some of this pottery was manured into the fields, but the density of pottery recovered is greater than might be expected. The same distribution could also arise, at least theoretically, from the 'smearing' caused by large-scale movements of topsoil *between* village plots, but this seems highly implausible. For a review of manuring in prehistory and later see Guttmann *et al.* 2005.

18. Gerrard *et al.* 2007b. The largest excavated group was from north of Bridewell Lane, where thirteen sherds came from medieval and later contexts. Eleven sherds also came from the other side of the lane from Field 1000, eleven from trench 6767/A in Shapwick Park and seven from the pipeline.

19. Even on the largest excavated section across the roads, on West Street in Shapwick Park, all that can be said is that by the time that the thirteenth-century repairs came to be made the bedrock was already worn.

20. Several forms of early medieval settlement have now been defined in Europe by Helena Hamerow (Hamerow 2002, 54). These are: row settlements, grouped settlements, polyfocal settlements, perpendicular settlements and single farmsteads. Shapwick fits into the first category.

21. Hamerow 2002, 62–3.

22. Lewis *et al.* 1997, 123.

23. Longleat House MSS: Shapwick court rolls 1265–1408, LL 11252.

24. There is an *atte churchhey* in 1305, for example.

25. The latter is presumably a reference to the village spring.

26. Zupko 1985; Fox 1986. 'Ropes' as units of measurement for watercourses in Somerset have been discussed by Rippon 2006, 103.

27. Metric distances are largely unhelpful here. The total length of the settlement is 1083m.

28. For example, Campey 1989.

29. Corcos 2002, 173–4.

30. The range is 37–48.

31. Though these figures might include Moorlinch also.

32. The artefact assemblages show no discernible differences from one toft to the next, though the potential variation in such a restricted range of available artefacts is limited. Nor do social distinctions seem to be reflected in later medieval housing arrangements; three-room cross-passage farmhouses are evenly distributed and do not occur only at the southern end of the village where the plots are larger.

33. Some significant eighteenth- and nineteenth-century alterations to the village plan are considered in Chapter 9, below.

34. Lewis *et al.* 1997, 26–8.

35. Brown and Foard 1998, 91.

36. The equivalent of *hagas*, in fact. Nigel Baker and Richard Holt (2004, 175) use this term for (sub-) urban properties, the episcopal *haga* in Worcester being leased in AD 904 and subdivided into four blocks of land. Admittedly this is in an urban context, but the ecclesiastical involvement and the control and division of space might be equally applicable at rural Shapwick in the ninth or tenth century.

37. For excavations see Gerrard 2007a. Radiocarbon dates are at 95 per cent probability (Marshall *et al.* 2007).

38. For parallels see Goltho (Lincs; Beresford 1987, 74–5), Cheddar (Somerset; Rahtz 1979 with a reinterpretation by Blair 1996), or Faccombe Netherton (Hants; Fairbrother 1990, 70) where timber building 12 was replaced by a flint one, building 17.

39. At Faccombe, for example, the bank and ditch enclosing the site was a later addition. Both Goltho (Lincs) and West Cotton (Northants) have strikingly similar arrangements.

40. Gardiner 2007.

41. In Somerset similar plans can be seen at Butleigh and elsewhere (Figure 7.20).

42. At 95 per cent confidence; or cal AD 980–1030 at 68 per cent confidence (Marshall *et al.* 2007). For excavations see Gerrard 2007a.

43. This non-adult grave consisted of a simple coffin burial marked out by Lias blocks and stones at the head and foot. Children buried close to church walls are also known at St Guthlac's in Hereford (Shoesmith 1980) and at Raunds (Northants; Boddington 1996, 69), where they are said to demonstrate the emphasis placed upon the baptisms of infants at the time of the Norman Conquest.

44. Together with its dependency of Pedwell, just as it was for the victims of Shapwick's serial killer in the nineteenth century (Chapter 1, above).

45. Larger examples are known from Bedford Castle. Other examples are pit 71 at Southampton Castle (Oxley 1986, 63; Platt and Coleman-Smith 1975, vol. I, 205–6, 214). Kiln pits are also known from Roman sites (Dix 1982, 337).

46. As at limekiln JF 16 at Colchester, dated 1150–1250 (Crummy 1984, 87).

47. There has been some debate about the purpose of the adjacent pit. Possibly this was a rake-out pit, though no connecting aperture was discovered. Alternatively it may have been used to drain a flooded kiln. For further detail see Gerrard 2007a.

48. Parallels for this arrangement are also known, mainly from Roman limekilns, though there are medieval examples from North Elmham in Norfolk, for example (Wade-Martins 1980 B).

49. At 95 per cent confidence; OxA-11933 (Marshall *et al.* 2007).

50. At 95 per cent confidence; OxA-11932 (Marshall *et al.* 2007). Measurements for archaeo-magnetic dates failed to produce a result. Some samples were weakly magnetised so that the last burning event was not hot enough to re-align magnetic domains, others suffered from post-depositional disturbance, quite possibly the dismantling of the kiln superstructure (Linford and Martin 2000).

51. In 1839 there was a Higher and Lower Limekiln Field where Beerway Farm stands today, so there is a history of lime-burning hereabouts. An undated bank of stone found in trench 4016/D may be a dump of Lias blocks by the roadside awaiting breakage. The size of the burnt Lias fragments inside kiln R38 suggests that stones up to 100mm across were ideal, though the large surface kiln in 99/4016/R clearly required smaller stones, up to 30mm across. Reddened fragments of burnt Lias were also a frequent find from all the trenches in *Old Church*, the detritus of repeated firings.

52. Calcium hydroxide putty.

53. Dix 1982, 339.

54. Williams 1989, 4.

55. For example, Great Paxton in Cambridgeshire (Lethbridge and Tebbutt 1933–34).

56. Crummy 1984, 30.

57. The two dates of the kilns are not statistically consistent (Marshall *et al.* 2007).

58. Rahtz *et al.* 2000, 423; Watts and Leach 1996, 66–9.

59. Another reason may be that the Abbey feared that a new graveyard in the village might not accommodate the dead, whereas the existing site allowed ample space for enlargement.

60. Ellison 1983, as pointed out by Richard Morris (1989, 241–2).

61. Windell *et al.* 1990.

62. Rahtz and Meeson 1992; more of these small early water mills are turning up in excavations, as at Corbridge, Northumberland (Snape 2003), Ebbsfleet, Kent (Welch 2007) Worgret, Dorset (Maynard 1988, 77–98; Hinton 1992, 258–9) and Wellington, Herefordshire (Watts 2002, 72–82) For a comparative but much better-

preserved site at Nendrum in Ireland, see McErlean and Crothers (2007).

63. Diorite is a coarse-grained igneous rock. For stone objects see Roe 2007.

64. Rynne 1989, 20–31; 2000, 185–213. For mills generally see Holt 1988.

65. Costen 1991.

66. We assume wheat, barley, oats and rye, and varying quantities of peas and beans.

67. If we take Campbell's calculations (which are only a rough guide) of 1.5 acres per person per year to support an individual in arable food (B. M. S. Campbell 2000), then this area is estimated to have supported 206 people (Martin Ecclestone pers. comm.).

68. Gelling and Cole 2000, 237.

69. The Domesday spelling of Walton – Waltone – suggests that it is a 'w(e)aldtun' – a 'tun in a wood or a weald' rather than 'tun of the Britons or Welsh' (Ekwall 1960, 494–5).

70. Which comprised Overleigh, Middle Leigh and Lower Leigh. Baltonsborough, to the east, also produced a lot of wood and timber for Glastonbury Abbey in the later medieval period and must have been thickly wooded (Stacy 2001, 127; Collinson 1791, 2, 270).

71. This is rather different from what has been suggested from recent research, which seems to indicate little evidence for widespread large-scale regeneration of woodland in the post-Roman centuries (Bell 1989). The situation was clearly very variable at the local scale (Dark 2000, 152). For discussion on the botanical distributions we are very grateful to David Clements.

72. Climate change is probably not relevant here, though the ninth century may have been slightly warmer (Lamb 1982, 163).

73. Only a quarter of the contents of this pit was emptied because of fears, ungrounded as it turned out, that the bones might represent recent anthrax victims.

74. At 95 per cent confidence. Two cattle tibia provided dates of cal AD 990–1220 (GU-5898) and cal AD 890–1160 (GU-5899), both at 95 per cent confidence of cal AD 1021–1170 and cal AD 890–1160 at 68 per cent confidence. Since the bodies were deposited at the same time, with tendons attached, a weighted mean can be calculated and that is the one used here (Marshall *et al.* 2007).

75. Jordan 1996, 36; we are grateful to Martin Ecclestone for this reference.

76. Martin Ecclestone, pers. comm.

77. Garmondsway 1953, 167, 243, 261.

78. Documentary sources indicate that ten oxen were replaced annually, with about half going to Glastonbury for meat and the rest being sold on or dying of natural causes (Ecclestone 1996).

79. Aston 1986.

80. In Anglo-Saxon England a thegn (or thane) was a person of the highest rank, someone who later would be called noble or aristocratic (Lapidge *et al.* 2001, 443–4). Later the term was used for a small local landowner or tenant (Costen 1992a, 133).

81. Quite possibly these new territorial units reflected earlier single economic units worked by an individual community within the former great estate – areas of land with different types of land use suitable for varying aspects of a mixed farming system: arable, pasture, meadow, wood and waste.

82. Stacy 2001; Abrams 1996, 269–70. This is envisaged as being similar to the way that a cathedral's holdings (such as at Wells) was divided into prebends held by individual canons in the medieval period. In nearby Dorset, minsters such as Yetminster and Wimborne show signs of having had prebends (Hall 2000).

83. Other early holdings of Glastonbury appear in similar groupings – Pilton, comprising Shepton Mallett, Croscombe, North Wootton and Pylle; Ditcheat, comprising Hornblotton, Alhampton and Lamyatt; and Doulting, with Charlton.

84. We owe this suggestion to Teresa Hall.

85. Barlow 1988.

86. Poole 1954, 14–18; Costen 2007a.

87. Williams (1999, 40) points to the example of an eighth-century Kentish abbess who complained to St Boniface about the burden of the *servitium* she owed to the king. Land is occasionally granted away exempt from 'all matters of royal taxes and service and everything which is due to the royal vill' (S267, Beohtric 794 to his ealdorman Wigferth; Finberg 1964, 118–20; Williams 1999, 41). When this happens, it is explicitly stated that military service is not part of this exemption, 'except the military service which every *gesith* (*comes* or noblemen) is bound to discharge for the defence of the realm' (Finberg 1964, 118).

88. This would have been the case from as far back as when Glastonbury first acquired the land from the king.

89. Williams draws attention to the translation of 'miles' (the soldiers) as 'thegns' in Alfred's translation of Bede's *Historia Ecclesiastica*. This group of men are different from the *gesiths* (essentially noblemen) or *comes*, who had already done military service and received a reward of land where they could settle, marry and support a following of their own. The *comes* were, however, still obliged to serve their lords, bringing with them their own retinue. The dependent peasantry, though they did not owe military service as such, would have provisioned those who did and this could include bringing food to them on the battlefield. This is described by Bede, where, after capture, the nobleman Imma pretends to be a poor peasant bringing food to the 'milites' (Williams 1999, 37–9).

90. Thorn and Thorn 1980: DB 8,5; fol. 90a.

91. About seventy hides in all, just under half of the thegnland. Roger held around 100 estates in Somerset at Domesday.

92. Count Robert held more land than anyone other than the king in the south of England. He held eighty-six estates in Somerset at Domesday.

93. Epaignes is in the department of Eure in France. Alfred is sometimes dubbed 'Alfred of Spain', but this is a misnomer.

94. The abbot's income may have been slightly larger than this; he had ploughlands on which he did not pay tax. Additionally, the Abbey would have had rent from the thegns' manors as well.

95. Loyn 1970, 322–3; Britnell 2004, 531–3.

96. Warren 1973, 275–81.

97. John 1982, 212; Poole 1954, 14–18.

98. Warren 1987.

99. Thurloxton in Somerset is a good example. Thurloxton was probably originally part of the royal estate of North Petherton and seems to have been named after Reyner Tornach or Thurlac, the twelfth-century lord (VCH 1992, 318–19). The small manors that make up the Shrewton estate in Wiltshire are other well-documented examples (Aston 1985, 41).

100. Dyer 2002.

101. Costen 1992a.

102. Dyer 1989, 134; Dyer 1994, 77–99.

103. Towns that developed in Somerset at this time include Bridgwater (by 1200); Montacute (by 1102), Nether Stowey (by 1222), Dunster by 1197, Chard by 1206 and probably Taunton by 1197 (Beresford 1967, 483–6; Aston and Leech 1977).

104. Fleming 2003, 110–11.

105. Costen 1992a, 120.

106. The case for a distinctive group of 'grid plans' along the Poldens has been reiterated by Brian Roberts when examining the morphology of Somerset villages as a group, though we disagree with his assertion that they also each had a 'green' (Roberts 1987, 182–3).

107. As Nick Corcos correctly pointed out in 1983.

108. Woolavington, Chilton, Edington, Catcott and Sutton Mallet were all of five hides in Domesday Book in 1086 (and Puriton at six hides may originally have been so), while Stawell was two and a half and Cossington was three, each therefore probably being in origin half of a five-hide unit.

109. Ekwall 1960.

110. Restructuring their property portfolio, as we might call it today!

111. Note here that we are referring to the *names* of the settlements as recorded in Domesday Book – no inference is drawn about the *form* of settlement (Abrams 1996, 207–8; Corcos 1983; Costen 1992a, 118–19).

112. Hollinrake and Hollinrake 1994; 1998. Boundary ditches aligned on property divisions yielded animal bone that produced a late ninth- or tenth-century date (Brigers 2006; Rippon 2008a, 73).
113. Unfortunately, few of these planned villages have much in the way of archaeological evidence to help date them (though see Aston 1994, 222–5).
114. Perhaps at Moorlinch.
115. Costen 2007b.
116. Another explanation for the intermixing of holdings is that this area was not part of the early open fields, but might have been woodland or pasture shared between the two settlements. When the open fields of the two settlements expanded, this land was then shared between them, thus leaving the boundaries ill-defined and intermixed when the area was taken into cultivation.
117. Ashcott was part of the Walton group of estates.
118. In other words, a process of de-enclosure.
119. In many ways this was the reverse of the process of enclosure seen in later periods, when former common-field farming was superseded by land coming into individual ownership and management.
120. Or *descriptio*, as Domesday Book itself describes it: Thorn 2008, 1.
121. Thorn 2008.
122. We are grateful to Frank and Caroline Thorn for much discussion and advice on the Shapwick entry in Domesday Book. Thorn (2008) gives extra background as well as detailed discussion of Shapwick in 1086. For the unfamiliar reader, Finn (1973) is good introduction, if a little dated.
123. Other early Glastonbury estates are dealt with in a similar manner. Thus Walton included Compton Dundon, Ashcott and Pedwell; Pilton included Shepton Mallet, Croscombe, North Wootton and Pylle; and Ditcheat included Hornblotton, Alhampton and Lamyatt.
124. Above we have suggested that these manors are a reflection of the prebendal lands that belonged to the canons of the pre-Dunstan church of Glastonbury.
125. To put this into perspective, of the 891 estates in Domesday Book, 485 were of three hides or less and of these 273 were of less than one hide (Costen 1992a, 117).
126. Forty-six villeins or villagers, fifty-one bordars or smallholders, five *coliberti* or freedmen and twenty-two slaves altogether, of which in Shapwick itself there were fifteen villeins, sixteen bordars, five coliberti and six slaves.
127. Thurstan was Abbot of Glastonbury from 1077/8–1096; the Exon entry gives its earlier value.
128. Rippon 2008, especially 53–60.

Boxes
b1. Brooks 1992, 1–23; Lapidge 1999, 146–7.
b2. Hopkinson-Ball 2007.
b3. Taylor 1975, 158–60; Rahtz 1993.
b4. Such as Abingdon, Ely, Malmesbury and Peterborough (Aston and Bond 1976, 75).
b5. Williams 1970, 149; SRO: Strangways MSS Map 55; Enclosure Award 2 William White map of 1796 Q/RDe 116 part; King's Sedgemoor Somerset. The Commissioners' Award 1795, Shapwick, 165–72.
b6. SRO DD/CC 110733; we are grateful to Maria Forbes for drawing our attention to this particular document.

Notes to Chapter 7

1. Compared with manors elsewhere in England there were very few freeholders on the Glastonbury Abbey estate. In 1189 people are listed as holding a virgate, half a virgate or a number of acres (Stacy 2001, 140–43); in 1515 the survey records 'virgators', 'half-virgators', 'ferdellers', 'half-ferdellers' and 'cottagers'. These names relate to the size of holding, but by the sixteenth century holding size generally bore little relation to the measurements they were supposed to represent. A virgate was a quarter of a hide (nominally thought of as 120 acres, so thirty acres), but it could vary from as little as twenty acres to as much as fifty acres. Michael Thompson (1997, 81) suggests that most of Shapwick's virgators held forty to fifty acres, which would make the other holdings in Shapwick as follows: half-virgator at twenty to twenty-five acres; ferdeller at ten to twelve and a half acres; half-ferdeller at five to six and a quarter acres; while cottagers probably held about five acres. Presumably the larger acreages at 1515 result from more land being taken into cultivation over the centuries. More interesting, perhaps, is what the peasants would have called themselves, rather than the Latin terminology of clerks. A virgate was a 'yardland' – hence 'yardlanders' and 'half-yardlanders', and, as we have seen, 'ferdellers' and 'half-ferdellers'. Peasants with little land and a cottage were 'cottagers' (Homans 1941, 73–4; Bolton 1980, 18). Dyer (2002, 279–80) points out that a holding at or above fifteen acres was sufficient to feed the family and make a small profit; anyone with less would have had to supplement their income. The virgate seems originally to have been the standard peasant holding on the Glastonbury Abbey estates, but became subdivided (Stacy 2001, 28).
2. The manor's reeve was appointed for at least a year (beginning at Michaelmas) from among the tenants. An exemption could be bought.
3. Costen 2007f, 1057, and Stacy 2001, 140–43, contain further details of obligations. The virgators of Shapwick collected firewood from Baltonsborough in *c.*1260

(VCH 2006, 68; Ecclestone 2007d, 1055; Watkin 1952, 429–30).

4. ME *faire*, 'a fair' + *weg*, a road.

5. Ecclestone 2007a, 1075.

6. These terms are found in BL, Egerton Ms 3134, otherwise Beere's terrier of 1515. Spellings are variable, even in this one document. 'Harepath' is from *herepaed*, meaning 'military road or highway'; 'wey' derives from OE *weg*, a road; and 'Rigge' from OE *hrycg*, a ridge or long narrow hill (Smith 1956).

7. In 1260. ME *persones* is 'a beneficed clerk or priest' – a parson, in fact.

8. Ecclestone 2007a. The almoner also paid his share of these charges. His liability to repair *Proutmedes* bridge arose at thirteen courts between 1366 and 1369.

9. A paved road 1–2m wide was found at Wythemail (Northants; Hurst and Hurst 1969, 178), cart-tracks in the village of Wharram Percy (Yorks.) were 3m and 4m wide (Andrews and Milne 1979, 40, 53) and a small terrace-way by the churchyard 4–5m wide (Mays *et al.* 2007, 333), while at Raunds (Furnells in Northants) there was a 20m-wide trackway with boundary ditches (Audouy and Chapman 2009, 37, 44). The holloways at Barton Blount and Goltho were 12m wide and 1.5m deep (Beresford 1975, 46–7).

10. Rights of dung collection in medieval towns were sometimes contested, so valuable was the resource.

11. *Contra* Roberts 1987, 183.

12. Excavations north of Bridewell Lane (7722).

13. Excavations south of Bridewell Lane (1000).

14. Excavations at Hill Farm (7372).

15. Excavations at the spring site (6660).

16. Though the overall plan seems to have remained very stable: no new plots were laid out and no large areas abandoned. This was a lesson learnt at Wharram Percy.

17. Gerrard 2007d, 473.

18. Dyer 1986, 25.

19. BL Ms Egerton 3134; Costen 2007b.

20. Corcos 1982, 21.

21. These thirty-seven probably include numbers at Moorlinch.

22. Thompson 1997, 169.

23. Martin Ecclestone pers. comm.

24. And holdings – a process called 'engrossment'.

25. Corresponding changes to plot arrangements have been recognised at Wharram Percy (Yorks), West Whelpington (Northumberland) and Wythemail (Northants) (Lewis *et al.* 1997, 15).

26. Dyer 1994, 125.

27. In 1321–2 we hear of leeks, parsley, clary (a sage-like herb), cress, cabbage, cucumber, hyssop, spinach, borage and lettuce (Harvey 1981, 86).

28. There are twelve accounts between 1259 and 1334 (Ecclestone 2007c, 1072). The demesne was that part of the manor reserved as the lord's 'home farm', cultivated by a workforce of servile tenants. From the late fourteenth century the trend was to lease out this demesne, or even whole manors. The rest of the land was leased out to tenants of varying status.

29. For example, from Hill Farm (7372) (Viner 2007, 759). Both pigs and horses are mentioned in the Domesday entry for Shapwick (Costen 2007g, 1050). The manorial accounts tell us nothing about the tenants' own livestock.

30. Gutiérrez 2007a, 649.

31. Pits of this type are usually associated with urban living, but rubbish disposal practices clearly varied.

32. Dyer 1986, 26.

33. The evidence for this was found both north and south of Bridewell Lane. This is the classic appearance of most medieval garden plots, according to Dyer (1994a, 119).

34. Hollinrake and Hollinrake 1998.

35. Letts 1999, 57; Forsters is one of a small number of late medieval vernacular buildings with remnants of their original smoke-blackened thatch. For house plans see Gardiner 2000.

36. More than fifty buildings from the thirteenth to the fifteenth century have been dated by dendrochronology in the county. The earliest date to the 1270s and 1280s; the majority to the fourteenth and fifteenth centuries (McDermott 2006, 91). Two- and three-room houses may have been the norm in this area, with longhouses being more of a feature of Cornwall and Devon (Rippon and Croft 2008, 197).

37. Medieval carpenters and their clients were often conservative in their designs (Dyer 2006, 26). At Shapwick there was also a father and son called 'le helier' (thatcher) in the early fourteenth century. Kent Farm is still shown as thatched by Nattes in the late eighteenth century. Turf covering is possible for some houses.

38. Dyer 1994; Grenville 1997.

39. Gerrard 2007b, 510. Half a fifteenth- to sixteenth-century cistern was found upturned and pressed into the clay near the hearth. This vessel is almost complete bar the neck and rim – a beer-making experiment that went wrong, perhaps – and, once broken, it may have been reused as a stand (Gutiérrez 2007a, 649). The excavator suggested a ritual function (Webster 1992, 123).

40. At Eckweek, near Peasedown St John in the north-east of the county, one of the excavated farmsteads had three phases of construction between the mid–late tenth century and *c.*1250 (Young forthcoming). Stratigraphy of this complexity would be hard to interpret using the kinds of keyhole sampling strategies we employed.

41. Gerrard 2007b, 513; no floor levels were identified.
42. At North Elmham in Norfolk an excavated barn measured 5.6m × 3.8m (Wade-Martins 1980, fig. 141). Building 8 at Faccombe Netherton in Hampshire, dated to *c.* AD 981–1070, measured 7.85m × 5.03m and consisted of large posts set in individual pits 0.35m–0.46m deep. This was one of a number of buildings within the manorial enclosure (Fairbrother 1990, 107–9).
43. Though there are Somerset examples on the bishop of Winchester's estates (Penoyre 2005, 30).
44. From north of Bridewell Lane (7722). This may also be part of the side plate of a bone comb of eleventh- or twelfth-century date.
45. A medieval stirrup-shaped ring is also recorded by the Portable Antiquities Scheme (SOMDOR-3CD1A2). It is cast copper-alloy gilt and had lost its blue glass setting. Sadly, we do not know where the ring was found; nor has it been drawn (we are grateful to Eleanor Standley for this information).
46. From Shapwick Sports Hall.
47. Spencer 1990, fig. 239, cat. no. 180 from Salisbury; Steane 1993, 133. The best-known kind of medieval badge was manufactured for pilgrims and commonly worn on headgear or clothes. None are known from Shapwick.
48. Standley 2008.
49. Since mirrors could be bought at some popular pilgrim destinations, an alternative use could be that, when held in the air, they allowed a periscopic view of a shrine above the heads of fellow pilgrims, in the manner of an adjustable viewfinder on the back of a digital camera (Hinton 2005, 211). Perhaps mirrors like this could be bought at Glastonbury Abbey?
50. Though the excavation that produced these finds did not indicate a high-status diet (Gidney 2007, 900).
51. Documents tend to stress the differences between tenants in terms of their social status, whereas archaeology shows that material possessions were not always indicative of social condition.
52. At Wharram Percy security seems to have been of considerable importance, with plenty of evidence for locks and keys (Beresford and Hurst 1990, 39, 44).
53. For some peasants, cottagers, virgators and half-virgators, tools and agricultural equipment were supplied by the lord and would have been returned on the death of a tenant or the relinquishing of a tenancy (Hanawalt 1986, 46). Known equipment for cottagers in the late fourteenth century includes items such as a gallon brass pot, a brass pan or mashing vat, a barrel for ale, chests, trestle tables, chairs, a spinning wheel, a shovel, an axe, a harrow and a carder and comb (for flax). For virgators, a saddle and collar for a cart horse, a plough with coulter, share and yoke, a hoe, a shovel, an axe, a sieve, a flail, a hore harrow, a dungfork, a sheaf fork and a mattock may have been typical possessions.
54. Viner 2007, 759.
55. For further detail see Gutiérrez 2007a.
56. Examples are known from Britain and the Low Countries (MacGregor 1985, 178–9).
57. The coins were from excavations in *Old Church* (4016/Y) and Bridewell Lane (7722/B). Shapwick is not unique in this respect. Excavations at St Batholomew's hospital in Bristol also produced Roman coins, for example (Dawson 1998, 174).
58. Ecclestone 2007a, 1074.
59. There was also a concentration of medieval pottery from the villa site in Field 4649, perhaps from manuring, though it was suspiciously clustered.
60. Wilson 2000, 71, 427; Lightbown 1992. Flints were recovered from test pits and excavations in the village but none are diagnostic forms (Gerrard *et al.* 2007b, 247–8).
61. Egan and Pritchard 1991, 260–62; Richard Kelleher pers. comm.
62. Rahtz 1979, 351.
63. Kent 1997, 95–103.
64. 94 per cent, in fact (Gutiérrez 2007a). A single fragment of an Italo-Netherlandish ring-handled vase from a building at 56 Brices Lane (now Shapwick Park) is of fifteenth- to sixteenth-century date. The only examples known from the county are from Taunton, Cleeve Abbey and Glastonbury Abbey, and one wonders if this sherd did not originate at the moated site.
65. Gutiérrez 2007a.
66. Verhaeghe 1991.
67. Cumberpatch 2006. Hair on the head is not depicted.
68. Beresford and Finberg 1973, 156.
69. Le Patourel 1969.
70. Abby Antrobus pers. comm.; the Abbey may have ordered large consignments of pots for feast days.
71. Fox 1973, 75; Chisholm 1979, 104.
72. Dyer 2002, 164. Medieval markets were also important for dissemination of news. See Dyer 1998 for coins.
73. Dyer 1989, 157; 1994, 129.
74. Dyer 1994, 128–31; 1989, 151–8.
75. Gidney 2007.
76. Dyer 1989, 154.
77. Martin Ecclestone pers. comm.
78. Grant 1988.
79. Rippon 2004. There are also undated earthworks of fishponds at nearby Sharpham. Research has tended to indicate that, despite fishing in rivers and the construction of fishponds, most of the fish consumed in the Middle Ages was sea-fish, particularly herring but also cod, probably imported as dried slabs (Aston

1988; Dyer 1994, 101–11). That does not seem to have been the case at Shapwick.

80. Ecclestone 2007b, 36.

81. Dyer 2002, 122–3.

82. Costen 2007b.

83. The post of reeve was renewed annually, several previous postholders living in the village at any one time. In the 1260 survey, for example, Peter the Reeve held the position, but among the cottagers were Walter, William, Robert and John, each described as 'the old Reeve'.

84. William atte Berne, the Shapwick reeve in 1367, was fined for sowing the wheat too late, a consequence of allowing two ploughs to remain idle earlier in the year; three years later Henry Pryde thought nothing of driving his sheep and oxen onto better pasture that belonged to the abbot, deviously switching his master's beasts onto the common land (Ecclestone 2007a, 1075–6).

85. Seed was often bought from other manors because it was recognised that home-grown seed could be unsatisfactory in the long term.

86. At the Glastonbury manor at Hunstrete in 1310 there was a moat with a hall, a thatched solar chamber with garderobe, a kitchen, a bakery, another solar chamber next to the bridge and two further single storey chambers. A chapel, barn and thatched hayhouse lay outside the moat (BL, Egerton Ms 3321, f237). A survey of similar complexes by Bond (2004, 115–15) draws upon excavations at Evesham Abbey's house at Badby, Fountains Abbey's house at Cowton and Abingdon Abbey's grange at Dean Court, Cumnor (Allen 1994). Much of this archaeology is later.

87. In Trench Y; Gerrard 2007a, 435–41.

88. There is no central hearth (though it might lie in the unexcavated portion of the building) or evidence for a cross-passage screen either in the form of a scar across the floor or a second door on the south side of the hall opposite the entrance. These might have been expected. Only in the 1220s and 1230s were chamber blocks attached directly to the upper end of the hall as a matter of course (Blair 1993, 14–15) though several examples are known from the first half of the twelfth century, mostly from manorial sites of similar status to the Shapwick *curia*, such as Bishop's Waltham in Hampshire (Gardiner 2000, 170).

89. Gidney 2007.

90. For comparative archaeological data see Serjeantson and Woolgar 2006, 111–12.

91. Rather than having privileged access to the catch from the Glastonbury Abbey lake and fish-house at Meare or the Abbey's deer parks at nearby Sharpham, Wirrall, Norwood, Pilton and Mells (Bond 1998, 25–9), fishing and hunting probably took place on the Hethmore (Shapwick Heath), which is mentioned in 1515 as being 'hunted every year by the lord's tenants' (Costen 2007b, 1062). For wild birds see Thomas 2007.

92. The *Rule of Benedict* stated that monks should not eat the flesh of quadrupeds, so fish and fowl were always seen as acceptable food. However, by the thirteenth century other meats had been introduced into the diet using questionable arguments. Once more, since the Rule stated that such food should not be eaten in the refectory, it was eaten elsewhere – at the abbot's table and in the infirmary – though Advent and Lenten abstinences were still enforced (Harvey 1993, 40). This collection of food remains at *Old Church* might therefore represent the diet of clerics, or indeed the visiting court, which would have included secular officials, rather than monks.

93. Whereas documents stress the economic importance of *production* of oxen, and occasionally sheep, *for the Abbey*, the archaeological evidence from Trench Y shows the pattern of consumption *at Shapwick* itself, albeit for the privileged few. The manor dovecote at nearby Ashcott produced up to 360 squabs a year in the early fourteenth century (VCH 2004, 20).

94. Moore 1978, 68.

95. Longleat House MSS: Shapwick court rolls 1265–1408, LL 10656; Ecclestone 2007a, 1074.

96. In Field 4016, Trench Y.

97. St Andrew was one of the twelve apostles. Dedications to him are in use in the seventh–eighth centuries at Hexham, Rochester, Pegham and Oundle (Clayton 1990, 125–7). There was an altar of St Andrew in the north portico of St Dunstan's church at Glastonbury in 1096 when Abbot Thurstan, the first Norman abbot, was buried next to it (Carley 1985, 15). Wells cathedral is also dedicated to Andrew.

98. BL Ms Egerton 3134; Costen 2007b.

99. Mick argues that the church may have had north and south aisles; parchmarks on the aerial photographs could be interpreted in this way.

100. Pevsner 1958.

101. Trench 4016/C.

102. A similar type of burial occurs at Chicksands priory in Bedfordshire (Gilchrist and Sloane 2005, 189; Barney Sloane pers. comm.).

103. In contrast, stone-built cist graves for the timber and log coffins were found at Wells Cathedral (Rodwell 2001).

104. In the Lady Chapel-by-the-Cloister (Gittos and Gittos 2001, fig. 494).

105. Excavated material (4016/B and C) and 8 from fieldwalking (M. Lewis *et al.* 2007).

106. Daniell 1997, 133.

107. Roberts and Manchester 1995; for a list of medieval sites with individuals with these diseases see Roberts and Cox 2003, 260–62. At St Andrew's in York it is suggested

that a sick person had been provided with a special softer and perhaps more sugary diet that encouraged calculus to build up (Stroud and Kemp 1993, 247).

108. Away from the immediate vicinity of the church building only one other human bone was recovered from excavation, from a disturbed context in 4016/B. To this should be added the undated human bones reported as 'dug up' when the spring site was drained in 1820–30 (Anon. 1880). More tellingly, there was no human bone from trenches 4016/A to the west, 4016F and Y to the south, 4016/E, R and Z to the east and 4016/D to the north. In fieldwalking, only eight fragments of human bone were collected, all from grid squares close to the church site. The probable small size of the burial ground at the old church at Shapwick is another argument against this being a minster, since a major church with numerous dependent settlements would, over the centuries, receive a large number of burials.

109. Gerrard 2007a, 441–4; the ditch cuts through the middle of the stone building (possibly the former vicarage) and must therefore post-date its demolition.

110. Ecclestone 2007a, 1074; *culver* is a dialect word for 'dove' and probably refers to the field around the dovecote that stood near St Andrew's church.

111. Gerrard 2007a, 434–45.

112. Costen 2007c, 1052.

113. VCH 2004, 23; Costen 2007d, 1053. 'The house in Shapwick' in 1269 might also have been the chaplain's house before 1230 in Shapwick village (for which there is domestic pottery and some archaeological features), which would allow the almoner to retain the 'ancient house' of 1230 north-east of the spring and the land enclosing it.

114. A surviving example contemporary with the very latest phase of the Shapwick priest's house still survives not far away at Muchelney (Bond 2004, 238).

115. Ecclestone 2007c, 1073.

116. The 1325 survey describes the demesne manor house of Glastonbury Abbey's Shapwick estate as 'Court with barton [farmyard] contains 2 acres'. No moat is mentioned (Costen 2007f, 1056).

117. For comparison, the demolished late thirteenth- to fourteenth-century moated episcopal manor house at Blackford, Wedmore had stone floors and thirteenth- to fourteenth-century pottery (Rendell 1963). A recent resistivity survey shows two possible gatehouses and a complex of buildings including a possible chapel projecting from the east of the hall (Payne 2003, 116).

118. Ecclestone 2007c, 1073. Not included in this account is the 'grange', referred to in 1515, which probably lay at the southern end of the village. The same name also turns up on mid-eighteenth-century maps close to what

appears to be a turreted building, possibly a gatehouse, immediately east of Brook Cottage. The site was not investigated archaeologically, though clay tiles from nearby Hill Farm may be from here.

119. Trench 6477/A.

120. Ecclestone 2007c, 1073.

121. Straker *et al.* 2007.

122. Ecclestone 2007a, 1074.

123. Penoyre *et al.* 2007a, 279–85. Emery (2006, 593) concluded that 'nothing survives at … Shapwick', but this is not the case.

124. Details of this roof can be found in Miles 2007.

125. A dendrochronological date pinpoints the date of felling of the tree from which the structural timber was shaped and *not* the construction date of the building. Glastonbury Abbey, as experienced commissioners of building projects, invariably seasoned their timbers, but not here. For Meare Manor Farm see Emery 2006, 591–4. The timber for the Shapwick roof probably came from the Glastonbury Abbey estate, though Loxley Wood may have supplied oak timber. No study of the timber and wood resources of the Abbey in the Middle Ages ever seems to have been undertaken.

126. These timbers, too, were 'green' (Miles 2007). The Bonnor engraving of 1791 (Figure 2.5) shows that this kitchen once extended further to the south.

127. BL Ms Egerton 3134; Costen 2007b.

128. Trench 94/A; Gerrard 2007c, 543.

129. Bond 2007a, 116–18.

130. Trench 6477/F; Gerrard 2007c, 542–3.

131. Costen 2007b.

132. TNA C 143/8/17; VCH 2004, 167. Collinson (1791, 427) says that Walter's lands were purchased by the Abbey and 'built upon the demesnes there a large grange for the occasional reception of the abbots, and the transaction of publick business'.

133. Walter had three virgates of land including land at Withy. There is a preliminary study of Withy Manor (Hooper 1997).

134. Other documents include the *Ordination of Shapwick Vicarage* in 1269; an agreement between the vicar of Middlezoy and Glastonbury Abbey; a tithing agreement between Spaulesmede (or Burtle) Priory and Moorlinch; and various other transfers of land in Moorlinch, Greinton, Walton, Street and Brent (Watkin 1947, 37, 72, 120–21; Watkin 1952, 260, 270–71, 381, 407, 410, 411–12, 416–17, 418–20). Glastonbury records also record that Walter's grandfather held a messuage 'south of the church of St Benignus' in Glastonbury in 1215 (Watkin 1952, 323–4).

135. Watkin 1952, cxxxii, 376.

136. Watkin 1952, cxxxiii, 377–8; VCH 2006, 175.

137. In 1279 and 1290 Edward I passed the Statutes of Mortmain, which curbed the amount of land being

passed to the Church. The Abbot would have paid a fee for the acquisition of this land. Edward introduced this measure because, once land had been donated to the Church, the 'dead hand' (*morte main*) of the donor still controlled the use and ownership of the land and removed it from the obligation of paying inheritance tax, thus reducing the king's income.

138. James Bond pers. comm.

139. Le Patourel 1978a; 1978b. The distribution of moated sites thins out noticeably in the south-west: there are only twenty-three recorded examples in Somerset (Aberg 1978). Among other local moated sites investigated archaeologically are Rockingham Farm at Avonmouth (Locock 1997) and Pylle Manor House (Hollinrake and Hollinrake 1997).

140. This suggestion was made in VCH 2004, 167.

141. Gerrard 2007c, 542–3. Excavated moats rarely exceed 2m in depth, though they can be wider. Auguring at the episcopal manor house of the bishops of Wells at Court Farm, Wookey, confirms a moat 9m wide (Winstone 1998).

142. Brunning 2007.

143. The rounded snail (*Discus rotundatus*) and the glass-snail (*Aegopinella* sp.), for example, prefer the shade of woods and hedge-bottoms.

144. Like the worked ash, elm, willow/poplar, hazel, hawthorn and oak wood from the moat fills, dandelions, daisies, plantains, nettles, mugwort and teasel could all have grown on the edge of the moat or close to the stream as it runs through the village. The variety of sources for the plant remains is paralleled elsewhere, at Cowick in Yorkshire, for example (Greig 1986).

145. For example, the button ram's-horn snail (*Anisus leucostoma*), an aquatic species that lives in lowland rivers, canals and ditches.

146. Ecclestone 2007a, 1074.

147. Similar bridges of timber on piers of masonry can be found at Baconsthorpe Hall in Norfolk.

148. Brunning 2007; though the sample size hampers definitive interpretation.

149. Bread wheat is the commonest wheat found in medieval Britain. Rivet wheat and durum wheat are the same species but have different flour qualities and are impossible to distinguish archaeologically, which is why several types are bracketed together when describing them. Neither is grown in Britain today.

150. *Aphodius* sp. and *Mycetaea hirta* (Robinson 2007).

151. Ecclestone 2007c, 1072. Infection in humans can come from eating dry-stored goods such as pulses. Heavy infestations result in diarrhoea and other unpleasant symptoms; the parasites also infect cats and dogs.

152. Tinsley 2007, 852–7.

153. Gidney 2007; to this list can be added pigeon, since there was a medieval dovecote close by.

154. Serjeantson 2006, 142.

155. Serjeantson 2006, 145.

156. For example, in the 1515 Beere survey five or twenty-five hens' eggs are part of the standard sixteenth-century rent, paid at Easter.

157. Though these can now be investigated through isotope studies of human bone (Müldner and Richards 2005).

158. Game accounts for 10 per cent of the bone count in 6477/F, for example, though the overall number of bones recovered was not high.

159. Sykes 2006, 169.

160. The lack of native red deer species from this site, in contrast to the earlier pre-1285 *curia* in *Old Church*, probably reflects encroachment on their natural habitats. Allegations of the poaching of hares, rabbits, pheasants and partridges at Shapwick and round about can be found in *CPR 1354–1358*, when the abbot complained about the activities of two brothers from Stoke-sub-Hamdon.

161. For accounts see Ecclestone 2007c, 1073.

162. Costen 2007b, 1059.

163. With the exception of the barn of Doulting, all the surviving Glastonbury barns are fourteenth century. The trees for the roof of the Abbey barn at Glastonbury were felled between 1343 and 1361 (Bridge and Dunning 1981, 120).

164. Dimensions gauged from geophysical survey are helpful here (Gaffney *et al.* 2007, 225). The Shapwick barn is at the upper end of Bond's group of 'medium-sized' barns (up to 40m in length and 8–9m in width) and so compares with barns at Glastonbury itself and at Pilton and Doulting (Bond and Weller 1991, 83).

165. A system of two-tier cruck framing was used for the Abbey barn at Glastonbury.

166. Glastonbury is of seven bays and the roof weighs 11.43 tons per bay.

167. Bond 2001, 61.

168. Bond and Weller 1991, 61. Penny Stokes points to a fifth barn at Mells and there was probably one at Winscombe in north Somerset of which part may remain (Maria Forbes, pers. comm.).

169. In around 1200 all the tithes of the Glastonbury estates were appropriated to the sacristan's office by Bishop Savaric (Bond and Weller 1991, 63), and when Shapwick church became a vicarage in 1230 20s was paid to the sacristan in lieu of this. The great tithes were then attached to the Rectory manor belonging to the almoner while the lesser tithes went to support the vicar, who would probably have needed a small barn as he received tithe corn from nearly all of the crofts (VCH 2004, 177; Costen 2007b). The barn at the new *curia* would therefore not have been for tithe payments. Of Glastonbury's other manors, West Bradley might

have been a tithe barn, but the others were primarily intended to store the products of each demesne (presumably together with any tithe products).

170. Shorrocks 1998, 167.

171. Locks are recorded in 1333–4 (Ecclestone 2007a, 1074). Taking oats as an example, the four harvest years 1311–15 produced 305 quarters (or 180 quarters after subtracting 125 quarters for the necessary seed). In modern terms that translates as 49,000 litres or 23,800kg, to which should be added a further 145 quarters of oats stored temporarily from other manors. Of the total 325 quarters left after subtracting 125 quarters for seed (crops were grown from seed saved from the previous year's crop), 62 per cent was carted to the granary at Glastonbury, 31 per cent was malted and sent to Glastonbury and 5 per cent was given as fodder to the horses of visiting Abbey officials.

172. Straker *et al.* 2007, 879.

173. Keil 1960; Bond 1998, 36–7. In 1333–4 the Glastonbury garden had an orchard, a vineyard, herb garden, vegetables, possibly some flowerbeds and some pasture. Flowers may have been grown too, possibly to decorate chapels. A long list of medieval 'pot-herbs' at Westminster Abbey can be found in Harvey 1981, 78. The bishop of Winchester's medieval garden at Rimpton contained apples, pears and vines as well as flax, beans and peas. The apples were either sold or made into cider. The Rimpton enclosure was ditched and hedged (Hunt 1960).

174. Costen 2007b.

175. Ecclestone 2007c, 1073. See Bond and Iles 1991, 37–8, for further Somerset examples, including Glastonbury Abbey and estates. Numbers of apples are calculated roughly on the basis of 1 quarter = 12kg, and the observation that thirteen of the apples from Chris's apple tree weigh about a kilo.

176. Bond 2004, 51.

177. This second moat goes unmentioned in medieval and later records. However, many examples of adjacent moats are known, as at Chalgrove in Oxfordshire (Page *et al.* 2005).

178. Since the land south of the existing dovecote, to the south of Brices Lane, was the property of the 'Rectory Manor' in 1760, that area can confidently be excluded. In 1539, when William Walton junior held the demesne, the property outside the moat included a barn, oxhouse, carthouse, sheephouse and barton measuring 1.12 acres (TNA SC6/HenVIII/3163 m. 27), an area subsequently confirmed by a Patent Roll for 24 July 1554. This seems to coincide with the 'inner croft'. A sheephouse would have housed sheep through the winter.

179. The last lease on the Canterbury estates did not fall free until the 1290s.

180. Bolton 1980, 88–9.

181. Sharpham was rebuilt in the twentieth century reusing earlier material, including the coat of arms of Abbot Beere.

182. Carley 1985, 70, 73.

183. The almoner was a regular official of a Benedictine monastery; poor people, widows and cripples (or others with deformity or disability) were fed and clothed at the monastery under his direction (Knowles 1963, 483–4). The almoner also looked after pilgrims, poor travellers and the destitute by giving accommodation overnight, food (the leftovers from the refectory) and the monks' old clothing (Harvey 1993).

184. Costen 2007c.

185. Bishops insisted that an amount was set aside to support the local priest when monasteries took the income of their churches for their own use.

186. This income, known as the 'Great Tithe', was worth nearly £30 in 1446–7; some was received for meadowland but most was for grain (Ecclestone 2007b, 33).

187. The terminology is complicated. The almoner held a separate estate but, since his was really just another holding within the Shapwick manor of Glastonbury Abbey, it is not strictly correct to refer to two 'manors' at Shapwick before the Reformation, especially as the almoner did not hold a separate court. In post-Dissolution times the distinction is clearer, with two holdings persisting from 1540 to the 1940s – some 400 years.

188. BL Add. Ms 17450; Ecclestone 2007d. This is about £479 in today's money. Prior to 1971 and decimalisation there were pounds (£), shillings (s) and pence (d). There were 20s to the pound and each shilling was worth 12d. In the medieval period this system was used for accounting. Larger sums were expressed as marks, the equivalent of 13s 4d.

189. BL Ms Egerton 3134; Costen 2007b.

190. As a comparison, the wearing of silk and fur was considered aristocratic and a statute of 1337 restricted fur wearers to those with an income in excess of £100. The almoner's income from Shapwick was barely a tenth of that.

191. Sometimes referred to as 'Vicarial tithes'. Glebe land was set aside for the maintenance of the priest and could be sub-let.

192. Later Down House or Shapwick Manor, now Shapwick Senior School.

193. There was a posthole, a ground surface and a possible ditch or pit of later medieval date (Gerrard *et al.* 2007b, 259).

194. SRO DD/SG 9.

195. TNA E 315/420.

196. Penoyre *et al.* 2007a, 286–91.

197. Bond 2007b, 1137–43. This building was first noted

by Horne (1940, 14) and is said to have been thatched originally.

198. McCann and McCann 2003. Some of the lower nestholes have been blocked.

199. VCH 2004, 168 quoting Longleat House MSS, LL 10730.

200. VCH 2004, 168 quoting TNA E 315/420 f40v. There is some doubt about the identity and location of these barns. If the barn next to the house was to store hay then where did the almoner hold his tithes of grain? That may have been at 'la grange' at the south end of the village, where there was rectory property later on.

201. The bishop wrote from Barnes, which is curious. He kept a house in London in the Strand near the Bath Inn (Payne 2003, 126, 150–55).

202. Costen 2007d.

203. In the sixteenth century Thomas Lyde recalled that he had been hired to fetch tiles for the chancel roof 'at a place called Downe ende' (Gutiérrez 2007b, 809). Treborough slates may have been shipped to Downend from the Brendon Hills above Watchet. By 1730 the church was repaired with Cornish slate (Bettey 1998, 203). For floor tiles see Gutiérrez 2007b.

204. Of the *c.*8,000 surviving medieval parish churches in England today, some 6,000 were rebuilt or radically altered between the mid-fourteenth and early sixteenth centuries (Harper-Bill 1996).

205. Graves 2000; rising population was not the only motivation for increasing the size of the church.

206. For example, at Chew Magna (Aston 1985; Blair 2005).

207. Elsewhere in Somerset individual obligations could include maintenance of lengths of flood defence, as at Banwell.

208. SRO DD/SG 13 c1765.

209. Roberts 1987, 183, figure 9.6, shows a line of villages along the Poldens with rectangular grid plans with greens.

210. Nothing has been observed so far during alterations to the church or its graveyard.

211. In 1880 it was thought that Adam de Sodbury, abbot from 1322 to 1335, had rebuilt a church here at his own expense and that he then granted 'the use of his private Chapel to the parishioners' (Anon. 1880).

212. Abbot Adam's fourteenth-century world survived into the twentieth century at places such as Laxton in Nottinghamshire (Beckett 1989). For further Shapwick detail see Corcos 2007, 101–3.

213. The West Field was sown in odd years, the East Field in even years (Martin Ecclestone pers. comm.).

214. For example, Walter of Henley (Oschinsky 1971).

215. S. Wilson 2000.

216. The tenants' arable in 1325 is calculated on the basis of forty acres per virgate. In 1515 there were 1,240 acres of arable plus an unknown area belonging to the almoner

(BL Ms Egerton 3134; Costen 2007b), but some of this common field was arable that had been turned to pasture, and some of the arable (on the Nidons) was almost certainly not in the common fields. In total, the acreage of meadow and pasture was about half as much as the arable. We are very grateful to Martin Ecclestone for discussion about this.

217. Whereas 44 head of sheep were recorded in 1100–1135, there are none a century later. By 1331 they were beginning to return; in that year the demesne had 210 sheep and a shepherd was paid to keep 50 of his own sheep and 22 of the Lord's on demesne land; in the spring and summer of 1334, 160 sheep were pastured on *Raghemede*, *Benham* and *Cherlemede*.

218. Ecclestone 2007b.

219. By contrast, those manors distant from Glastonbury sold most of their wheat crop. For the seven manors with the greatest crop in 1311–12 (headed by Pilton), 74 per cent of the crop went to Glastonbury; for the seven leading producers more than 30km away (headed by Sturminster Newton), 68 per cent was sold.

220. Costen 2007e.

221. Straker *et al.* 2007.

222. For a map of grain sources on Glastonbury Abbey manors in 1361–2 see Bond 2004, fig. 12. The Shapwick assemblage is very similar to that from the medieval farmstead at Eckweek in north Somerset, which also included wheat, barley, rye, vetches, peas, field beans and possibly oats. There was little evidence of luxury plant foods there too, though hazelnuts were common in many samples (Carruthers 1995).

223. Unused vegetables and herbs tend to rot away. Charred arable crops such as wheat or barley and exotics such as fruit stones are often only the parts of the diet we can see.

224. Dyer 2002, 40, 167.

225. Ecclestone 2007a, 1075. Rippon 2005, 106, lists field names that imply flax retting.

226. The alignments of other former ditches and baulks are indicated by widely varying densities of medieval pottery, which must reflect differing manuring practice either side of a now-invisible boundary (Gerrard *et al.* 2007e, 156).

227. Bond (2004, 58) reckons that the Abbey had 6,000 sheep on its manors, about half of which grazed on the chalk downland of Wiltshire.

228. This weed was especially hated because the sap causes blistering of the skin.

229. When ground with wheat this can cause serious illness. Low levels of weeding may have been caused by a lack of available labour after the Black Death (De Moulins 2007).

230. This cornfield weed (*Bupleurum rotundifolium*) is now extinct in the county.

231. Fox 1986. Another, apparently less successful change from a two- to a three-field system was carried out around 1240 by Eynsham Abbey (also a Benedictine monastery) at South Stoke in Oxfordshire (Dyer 2002, 167). A three-field system was perhaps not favoured at Shapwick in the thirteenth and fourteenth centuries as a means of increasing production because this was a demesne farm.

232. Miller and Hatcher 1978, 90.

233. Ecclestone 2007b, 34.

234. Not until 1260 is there documentary evidence for the extent of the demesne, and in particular the area of arable land in the two common fields. Using the data on the sown acres in the accounts between 1258 and 1333, and the 1325 survey, it is clear that the total arable area in demesne declined slowly between 1260 and 1305, to around 600 acres, and then decreased more rapidly still to about 490 acres in 1330–33. The 'lost' acres were almost certainly leased to tenants; the 1325 survey records 77 acres held by eleven virgators, half-virgators and ferdellers, and about the same held by cottagers and non-residents. For arguments on declining arable cultivation in the twelfth century see Postan 1952.

235. Corcos 2007.

236. Barnes and Williamson 2006, 11–14.

237. Knight 2007. John Knight completed a study of Loxley Wood in 1998 for his MA in Landscape Archaeology at Bristol University.

238. BL Ms Egerton 3134; Costen 2007b.

239. *Carex pendula*, *Oxalis acetosella* and *Primula vulgaris*.

240. Rackham 1976, 78–9. Ecologist Oliver Rackham has shown that medieval and later woodland provided underwood – coppiced shrubs such as hazel that produced poles for fencing implements, house construction, charcoal and firewood – as well as timber, in the form of standard trees such as oak, used in construction.

241. Costen 2007e; 2007f.

242. Ecclestone 2007a, 1075.

243. These fields are named *Caterwood Grounds* and *Caterwood Nidons* with *Caterwood Meads* (SRO DD/SG c/206 c.1750).

244. Clements and Alexander 2007.

245. Straker *et al.* 2007.

246. Costen 2007b.

247. Ecclestone 2007b, 36. Withy, a detached part of Shapwick parish, bred cattle.

248. Carley 1985, 221.

249. *Eleocharis* sp. and *Carex* spp. respectively; Straker *et al.* 2007, 887.

250. Costen 2007f.

251. Ecclestone 2007a.

252. Rippon 2005, 105; Gale 2007, 892.

253. BL Ms Egerton 3134; Costen 2007b.

254. Or *Northings* or *Morerene* in 1515 (Costen 2007b).

255. Rippon 2005, 106.

256. The mill is mentioned in the survey of Henry of Sully of 1189 and was held by William the carpenter with half a virgate and five acres (Stacy 2001, 63, 141).

257. In 1230 'mills' are referred to in the plural (Costen 2007c); in 1260 the mill was held by Richard the miller (Ecclestone 2007d, 1055), in 1515 by William Lyde (BL Ms Egerton 3134; Costen 2007b; Ecclestone 2007a, 1076). Lucas (2006) calculates that in the thirteenth and fourteenth centuries up to 10 per cent of a monastery's total income might be derived from mills.

258. The level is 15m OD at the manor house, 11m OD at the mill site and 9m OD at the Catcott boundary.

259. Costen 2007b. There is a modern tradition of a watermill here, though the most recent remains relate to a cattle feed mill associated with the nineteenth-century farm buildings.

260. Given the shallow gradients and the irregular water supply, an undershot or breastshot wheel is the most practical proposition. There is insufficient fall in the ground to accommodate an overshot wheel fed by water falling from above.

261. Roe 2007, 783.

262. Like Shapwick, the manor at Winscombe was in the hands of Glastonbury Abbey from the late tenth century to around 1200, so this is the most likely period for its construction (Aston 2010).

263. Costen 2007f, 1057. A post mill is most likely. At Walton the Abbey's mill made use of timber boards, sail canvas and, of course, millstones (Bond 2004, 328).

264. The windmill is not mentioned in the account roll for 1314–15. According to one fourteenth-century chronicle, the Shapwick windmill was a contemporary of those erected by the Abbey at Winterbourne Monkton in Wiltshire and at Meare, near Shapwick (Keil 1964; Bond 1995). Windmills were cheaper to build than watermills but more expensive to maintain (Lucas 2006).

265. Ecclestone 2007c, 1073.

266. Costen 2007b, 1072.

267. When it was held by his widow Joan (TNA SC6/Hen VIII/3163 m27).

268. Aston 2007b, 109; see also Chapter 8, below. This mill (NGR 41873726) is shown on Ogilby's road map of 1675 (Plate 32) and on the tithe map of 1839, and can be seen on the 1940s RAF aerial photographs. Sadly, the mound seems to have been removed in the 1970s without any kind of record. Another windmill called 'Pykesmill' lay just outside Shapwick parish within the bounds of Moorlinch in 1515 (Costen and Ecclestone 2007).

Boxes
b1. Langdon and Masschaele 2006.
b2. Thompson 1998; Dyer 2010.
b3. The returns of the 1381 Poll Tax for Somerset have not survived (Martin Ecclestone pers. comm.).
b4. Except for a 1674 fragment.
b5. Whiteman 1986, 553.
b6. Bond 2007a.

Notes to Chapter 8
1. Bettey 2007b.
2. TNA PROB 11/117.
3. Bettey 1989.
4. Bernard 2005, 468.
5. Whiting may have refused to surrender; this led to the searches and, ultimately, to his condemnation by a jury of local men.
6. For the dramatic changes in the personal worship of ordinary people see Duffy (1992). The critical decade seems to have been in the 1560s, under Elizabeth I.
7. Their original analysis can be found in Bettey 2007a and Corcos 2007. For this volume there was a concerted effort to transcribe all available Shapwick wills; seventeen by Alejandra Gutiérrez, six by Nick Corcos. Further work has also been undertaken on secondary sources, as indeed it has for the volume as a whole.
8. Gerrard 2007d, 493.
9. SVBRG 1996, 100–101.
10. Gerrard 2007b, 522.
11. Gerrard 2007b, 530. During the seventeenth century two parish surveyors were nominated for six days a year to direct the repair of the highways of the parish. Where repairs were not made fines could be imposed by the Quarter Sessions.
12. Gerrard 2007b, 526.
13. Gerrard 2007d, 493.
14. Gerrard 2007d, 491.
15. TNA PROB/11/80.
16. TNA PROB 11/266.
17. The will of Thomas Prewe, yeoman, dated 1630, lists two 'waines' that had 'iron bound wheeles' as well as his 'best yoke with iron henges' (TNA PROB 11/158).
18. Gerrard 2007b, 521.
19. 6767/A.
20. 6152/E.
21. Penoyre 2005.
22. Penoyre *et al.* 2007a.
23. For which the archaeological evidence suggests the increasing use of coal as a fuel (Gerrard *et al.* 2007c, 832). For parallel observations on domestic architecture see Johnson (1993) in Suffolk and Alcock (1993) in Warwickshire.
24. Mercer (1975, 52) points out that this positioning of the chimney allowed the cross-passage to function as it had done in a medieval open hall. Many of the greatest houses of the Elizabethan and Jacobean age adopted this solution, with the chimney placed away from the entry.
25. Gerard 1633, 125.
26. The other is Old Farmhouse.
27. An outshot is an extension with a sloping 'cat-slide roof'.
28. Murless 2007.
29. Hardy and Gerrard 2007. This is the most likely source. Other possible outcrops that are geologically similar include Delabole in north Cornwall and Rook's Castle on the Quantock Hills near Bridgwater. Specimens from these quarries cannot be separated by eye.
30. As a recent survey has shown (Penoyre and Penoyre 1994).
31. TNA PROB 11/299.
32. In *Mill on the Floss*, by George Eliot, Mrs Tulliver is keeping her best Holland sheets to lay out her husband when he dies!
33. 'Blackwork', which is said to have originated in Spain, became popular in England in the sixteenth century on clothing and pillow covers.
34. 'Stammel' was a woollen cloth usually dyed red.
35. Given that Margery Higdon also left a 'holland sheet of seven yards' to her daughter and 'a pair of new cloth of five yards' to her grandchild she may have been involved in the textile industry in some way. The manufacture of cloth was an important source of employment at this time, especially in wool cloth production, centred on Bath and Frome, and the kersey-broadcloth industries in the south and west of the county (Mann 1971; Palmer and Neaverson 2005). 'Bridgwaters' and 'Tauntons' were household words in seventeenth-century England.
36. TNA PROB/11/551. The same Thomas Silver, d.1707, whose tombstone was moved from the aisle to the porch when the church was restored in 1861 (www.tutton.org/wedchrnt.html).
37. More precisely, 6,348 sherds of post-medieval pottery were recovered, weighing *c.*62kg, of which 75 per cent was 'Somerset wares'.
38. 'Slip' is clay diluted with water which is then 'trailed' or washed over the whole surface of the vessel ('all-over slip'). Lines of trailed slip can then be feathered, combed or marbled.
39. 'Sgraffito' is produced by covering a vessel with a slip and then scratching through it to reveal the fabric of the body of the pot.
40. Coleman-Smith and Pearson 1988.
41. The Bridgwater trading 'link' seems more pervasive during this period, as we shall see, but there are other possible candidates for this workshop, including Nether Stowey.

42. Gerrard 1987, 109–19.
43. London was scarcely less far, being a three-day ride.
44. A good introduction to post-medieval pottery is Draper 1984.
45. About 21 per cent of the total sherd count of pottery at this time.
46. So-called because the fabrics cannot be told apart by visual inspection alone.
47. The other West Country pottery was at Wincanton; see Archer 1997 generally.
48. In the mid-eighteenth century the stratified sherds appear in those properties valued at between £15 and £24, whereas 80 per cent of Shapwick houses were valued at £10 or less.
49. 7722/B.
50. There is some supporting evidence for this conclusion from wills and inventories (Overton *et al.* 2004).
51. From kilns at Barnstaple, Bideford and Fremington.
52. A small sherd of Italian marbled slipware was found at one of the excavations in Shapwick Park, 6152/E. This sherd may have originated at Shapwick House rather than in the village.
53. Raeren stonewares have a grey fabric and a distinctive mottled brown salt glaze, sometimes referred to as a 'tiger glaze'. The definitive guide to German stonewares is Gaimster 1997.
54. Fifty-three sherds; one fragment from fieldwalking may be a chamber pot.
55. Calculated from Gaimster 1997, 82–3.
56. Willmott 2007.
57. No link can be made between the names and initials recorded on the wine bottles and known late seventeenth- or eighteenth-century Shapwick families.
58. Lewcun 2007.
59. Though two of the Hunt pipes bear an incorrect spelling of his name and are clearly fakes, presumably because his products were seen as superior and worthy of a higher price.
60. This is because the flat heel, where the pipe was marked, was replaced by a pointed spur. Makers now identified themselves by cartouches on the side of the bowl or by marks on the pipe stem. These survive less well.
61. According to the Church Rates 1660; SRO DD/SG 16; Penoyre *et al.* 2007b.
62. TNA PROB/11/80.
63. TNA PROB 11/111.
64. Overton *et al.* 2004, 106.
65. TNA PROB 11/215.
66. These included a Charles I halfpenny (1675), Charles II farthing (1672–6), a William III sixpence and three halfpennies (1695–1700; 1695–8), a George II halfpenny (1738) and a George II/III halfpenny (1729–75).
67. TNA PROB 11/177.

68. The acid from the apples dissolved the lead and poisoning was one of the problems of cider drinking. According to West (1962, 123) a 'lead' could also be a measure of cheese (56 lb).
69. TNA PROB/11/186; Overton *et al.* 2004, 100.
70. TNA PROB/11/186.
71. TNA PROB 268/1587.
72. For additional references in wills and inventories see Gutiérrez 2007a, 666. Most Shapwick households would have used pewter or pottery plates by 1750.
73. William Champion mentions his 'great brewing pan' in his will of 1660 (PRO PROB 11/215).
74. TNA PROB 11/215.
75. Evidence from inventories elsewhere suggests that spinning lay within the woman's sphere (Overton *et al.* 2004, 78).
76. TNA PROB/11/144; often referred to as 'a pair of virginals' even when only one instrument was present.
77. Cliffe 1999, 161.
78. For further discussion see Johnson 1996.
79. In some seventeenth-century wills parlours were still bedchambers for guests, but at Shapwick House, a gentry home, the beds had gone from the parlour, which had by now become a 'reception room'.
80. TNA PROB 11/158.
81. This is deduced from his will, which mentions his son Thomas, who is very likely the Thomas recorded as living at the Post Office and Stores in the Church Rates in 1660.
82. TNA PROB 11/158.
83. Chests of drawers appear only around the middle of the seventeenth century, after Thomas's time.
84. Having one chair in the house, as Thomas had, is entirely in line with wills from Cornwall (Overton *et al.* 2004, 93).
85. Thomas was not alone in this arrangement. Margery Dowsey, who made her will in 1638, also kept her best bedstead in the parlour (TNA PROB 11/177).
86. Less than 1 per cent of Kent households in the first three decades of the seventeenth century had a clock, and none in Cornwall (Overton *et al.* 2004, 111).
87. 6767/A.
88. When sample sizes are so low, slight differences in results can skew the picture. Percentages are avoided here.
89. Gidney 2007.
90. Jaques 2007.
91. Light 2007.
92. Though Langport market was known for its eels and waterfowl, according to seventeenth-century antiquary Thomas Gerard (1633).
93. Beeton 1861, 84–8.
94. SRO DD/SG 13; Penoyre *et al.* 2007b.
95. Bettey 1987, 57–60; Bettey 2007b, 1085.

96. By the 1700s over 40 per cent of houses had 'furnaces' (Overton *et al.* 2004, 69).

97. Information on people and their homes is drawn from SRO DD/SG 13 (Penoyre *et al.* 2007b).

98. Bearing in mind that the goods of a wife belonged to her husband and only unmarried or widowed women are recorded, the two status groups omitted from this list are labourers and single women because there are no examples of their wills from Shapwick. Of course, both categories existed.

99. Wrightson 2000.

100. Some houses contained a lone individual while others had servants, and this household composition would have a bearing on the archaeological evidence. Nor can we assume that the same families continued to live in the same properties. The usual system at this period in Somerset was for leases to last for three lives under a nominal rent, but as the mid-eighteenth-century map evidence shows, many properties by that date had been occupied by at least two different families between 1660 and 1765. For example, Oak Villa was occupied by Francis Tillier (widow) in 1660, then by Parson Jones and by 1750 by Mary Jones (widow). During the first half of the eighteenth century fixed term leases created greater profit at higher rents and this encouraged the 'turn-over' of tenants that then further complicates the links between houses, archaeological finds and their owners.

101. Finch 2003.

102. Duffy 1992; Dunning (1976, 33) provides a documented example from the churchwardens' accounts at Yatton. Quite probably Shapwick, like most other churches in the county, did as it was requested to do.

103. Bettey 2007b, 1085. Three of the current six bell peal date to the first quarter of the eighteenth century.

104. Roud 2006, 275. There is also an entry in the Quarter Sessions Records concerning the conduct of Edward Lovell, 'minister of Shapwick and Ashcott', in May 1656, though the complaint is not specified.

105. There were, for example, Baptists in Somerton and Bridgwater in 1653 (Dunning 1976, 50).

106. The Stone family were evidently carpenters over several generations. John Stone is recorded as such in 1750 (SRO DD/SG 16; Penoyre *et al.* 2007b). His house no longer exists.

107. In 1716, for example, 17s 4d was raised 'for the reformed Episcopal church in great Poland and Polish Russia' (Bettey 2007c), the equivalent of around £66 in today's money.

108. Also mentioned are the 'poore of Batheforde' (1592) and, in two Bull family wills of 1677 and 1692, several local parishes too.

109. On three occasions. The church at Shapwick is mentioned twice, Woolavington church once.

110. From 1712 to 1765 (Bettey 2007a, 39).

111. The equivalent of nearly £69 today.

112. Barnes 1961, 59–60.

113. Bates 1907, 148–9.

114. Bates 1907, 214.

115. Munckton 1994. Poor Houses disappeared after the 1834 Poor Law Amendment Act when it became mandatory for parishes to form a union and build a workhouse (Chapter 9, below).

116. Gerrard 2007d, 486.

117. Bettey 1987, 65.

118. TNA PROB 11/410.

119. These complexities are fully described in Bettey 2007a.

120. VCH 2004, 168. To begin with the 'rectory manor' was leased from the Crown, first by John Berkeley of Bruton (who had been granted Bruton Priory after the Dissolution (Members of the Council 1894, xxxix), later by 1574 by Hugh (d.1581) and from 1581 by his brother Matthew (d.1583), members of the Smyth or Smythe family of (Long) Ashton Court. Their father, John, had been a Bristol merchant who invested his fortune in former monastic lands. Hugh was famously antisocial; Matthew a Middle Temple lawyer. Both were trouble-makers (Barnes 1961, 240) and in 1575 Hugh was brought before the Court of Exchequer for failing to maintain the chancel of Shapwick church (Bettey 2007a). The leasing arrangements are unclear; part of the estate including the house and tithes and a farm was leased to Andrew Dyer in 1573 and later by Richard Walton. Until 1599, when the Crown finally sold the estate, there were therefore three interested parties: the Crown as owner, the Berkeleys and Smyths as estate owners, and Dyer/Walton as lessees.

The freehold was acquired from the Crown by Sir John Spencer of London in 1599, possibly the infamous butcher/grazier of Warwickshire, ancestor of Lady Diana Spencer and the Lords Althorp of Northamptonshire, one of the post-Dissolution *nouveau riche*. By 1620 Shapwick Manor was in the hands of his son-in-law Lord William Compton, by that time the earl of Northampton, who then sold the manor to William Bull in 1619. The Bull papers (1623–90) may be found in the University of Bristol Special Collections (GB 0003 DM 155). They cover topics such as family illness and the Civil War. The estate stayed in the Bull family until 1751, when it passed by marriage to the Strangways family.

121. As had, for example, the Berkeleys, who bought Bruton Priory and some Glastonbury estates, or the Hoptons, purchasers of Witham Friary and other Glastonbury estates.

122. From 1629 to after 1640: Barnes 1961, 313. William Bull erected the fine memorial tablet in the church to his wife Jane.

123. Penoyre *et al.* 2007a, 288–91.
124. SRO DD/SG 41.
125. TNA PROB 11/410.
126. Cliffe 1999, 157.
127. SRO DD/SG4.
128. William Bull's will can be found at TNA PROB 11/353.
129. VCH 1992, 329.
130. For a review of inventories as sources, and their contents, Overton *et al.* 2004 provides a very useful commentary.
131. There is an oak chair in Turkey work upholstery, *c.*1645, in the Victoria and Albert Museum, London.
132. TNA PROB 11/410.
133. Unites were struck from the reign of James I until the mechanisation of minting in 1662, after which guineas appear. The term 'broad' refers to coins minted before this development (Richard Kelleher pers. comm.). For wages see Wrightson and Levine 1995, 41.
134. From test pit 95/10 (Gerrard *et al.* 2007b); other examples are known from Glastonbury Abbey (Kent 1997, 101–2).
135. From test pit 95/17 (Gerrard *et al.* 2007b).
136. At least some of these had probably belonged to his father William Bull, who, in his own will, left his son Henry 'my broad silver basin and ewer' and 'two silver flagons' and to his daughter-in-law, Henry's wife, 'two silver plates'.
137. TNA PROB 11/140.
138. Penoyre *et al.* 2007a, 285. The ownership of the manor after the Dissolution is complex. It passed first to the Crown and thereafter to Sir William Petre and later to the Walton family in 1554. Thomas Walton seems to have had possession from 1554 until 1576, though his step brother Richard occupied the house. Thomas's son, also a Thomas, then inherited, followed by his grandson Francis, who eventually conveyed the estate to Abraham Burrell in 1622 in order to pay his debts (VCH 2004, 166).
139. Monastic buildings were often modified. For example, houses might be converted from claustral buildings, as at Lacock in Wiltshire (Pevsner and Cherry 1975, 285), or from the monastic church, as at Buckland in Devon (Cherry and Pevsner 1989, 227). Far less information is available about the alteration of houses, manors and granges on monastic estates (Howard 2003; Doggett 2001).
140. In 1641 Burrell was almost as significant a landowner as the Bull and Rolle families; he was also a JP and his estate was assessed at £8, against £10 for the other two (VCH 2004, 172).
141. Others are Montacute House (*c.*1600), Barrow Court at Barrow Gurney (*c.*1610) and Fairfield House at Stogursey (1633).
142. Ascribed, for example, by Collinson (1791, 427), who says that 'upon the site of the old court-house of Abbot John de Taunton, Judge Rolle, about the year 1630, erected a large and handsome mansion'.
143. Henry Rolle (1589–1656). Father was Robert Rolle of Heanton Punchardon, Devon; mother, Joan. Matriculated Exeter College, Oxford, admitted Inner Temple 1608–9, called to the bar in 1618, recorder of Dorchester 1636, degree of serjeant-at-law 1640. Sat for Cornish seats of parliament 1614–29. Judge on King's Bench in Oct 1645, advanced to Chief Justice 1648. Refused to serve as one of the presiding judges at the trial of Charles I, probably because he considered the new court to lie outside the law and that all justice proceeded from the sovereign. After the execution of the king Rolle became Lord Chief Justice and a member of the Council of State 1648–9. Appointed Commissioner of the Exchequer in 1654. Buried at Shapwick. Spent his leisure time writing abridgments of his cases (Rolle 1668; 1675–6). Described in the introduction to one of his books as a person of 'profound judgment, singular prudence, great moderation, justice and integrity' (Rolle 1668). Henry Rolle's fortune came ultimately from his great-grandfather, George, a lawyer who had trafficked in monastic lands in Devon (Legg 1997).
144. Dick 1958, 106.
145. Rodwell and Bell 2004, 11, 140, 149.
146. 6477/F.
147. A Merida-type red micaceous ware jar. Only five other examples of Merida ware are known from the county (Gutiérrez 2007a, 628).
148. To this list might be added a sherd of Italian marbled slipware bowl from 6152/E, produced in northern Italy in the seventeenth century. The findspot is not far south of Shapwick House.
149. Gutiérrez 2007a, 628.
150. Numbers of rabbit bones were so high that Louisa Gidney (2007), in her report on the animal bones from Shapwick excavations, suggested there could have been an artificial rabbit warren to supply the mansion.
151. Crows do take hen and duck eggs. They would have been treated as a predator.
152. Perhaps from nearby Sharpham Park.
153. Fishing was a common coastal occupation west of the Parrett; Porlock was a herring port of note (Barnes 1961, 7).
154. Bettey 1987, 52; Cliffe 1999, 69–70.
155. TNA PROB 11/259.
156. TNA PROB/11/386. Dame Priscilla's will of 1708 also survives (TNA PROB 11/512). In our earlier account of the ownership of Shapwick House (Penoyre *et al.* 2007a, 285) we gave the impression that Francis's son, Henry, inherited later. Francis's will is very clear on this point: 'I have not by this my will taken notice of my

son Henry, the reason is because he has married without my consent, and his mother, to our great trouble, and the disparagement of his family. And since neglected to perform those easy commands in relation to his better education which I have laid upon him for his good. And therefore I do charge him upon my blessing, and by the words of a dying father, that he be obedient to his mother, and that he inhabit at such a place and keep such servants about him, as she direct.' We may conclude that there was a rift over Henry's marriage and possibly that he became resident at Shapwick under his mother's supervision. In the event widow Priscilla outlived her son Henry by sixteen years and by the time of her death in 1708 she no longer held Shapwick. The manor had passed to her grandson Francis, so the ownership of the manor skipped a generation. In all this it must be remembered that the family were traditionally Puritan. It was said that 'gaming at cards and dice have not been so much as tolerated in the family … for more than a full century of years'. On Francis's death in 1709 his brother John inherited, but shot himself in the grand salon of Tytherley Hall; his youngest brother Samuel died in 1729 of 'gout in his stomach' (Legg 1997). Thereafter the estate passed first to John Rolle and in 1750 to Denys, his youngest son (Chapter 9, below; Box 9.1).

157. Diarist and traveller Celia Fiennes noted of East Tytherley that 'Sir Francis Rowles has a fine House and Garden and Groves; one on the edge of the hill all in sight of the road looks finely of Scott and Norroway [Norway] firrs in rows looks very well' (Morris 1949, 75). The Elizabethan house was demolished in 1903 (Legg 1997), though the fine trees planted by Denys Rolle in 1787 still flourish.

158. Among the plant introductions at this period were the rhododendron and the pelargonium (Bond 1998, 64). The seventeenth-century planting scheme may well have featured topiary.

159. Though at Shapwick the ponds were more like medieval fishponds than the formal canals seen at Westbury Court (Glos), for example.

160. Aston 1978, 21; Bond 1998, 68–9.

161. Steane 1977. The existing moated site is an island of *c.*750sq m surrounded by a trapezoidal moat 6 m wide. The sides are revetted with drystone walling and modern concrete breeze blocks and the moat is full of water as a result of an abandoned trout fishing project.

162. Markham 1615, 183.

163. Strong 1979.

164. SRO DD/SG 36 c/206.

165. A well-documented example, dating from the early seventeenth century, is Somerleyton in Suffolk (Taigel and Williamson 1993, 39).

166. In recent years archaeologists and others have written a great deal about designed landscapes and garden schemes (Bettey 1993; Taigel and Williamson 1993; Williamson 1995; Taylor 1998). For Somerset in particular see Harvey 1981 and Bond 1998.

167. The process of enclosure and conversion to pasture was to accelerate through the eighteenth century and eventually resulted in the pattern of field boundaries seen on the nineteenth-century Ordnance Survey maps (Chapter 9, below). A useful summary of the debate on enclosure can be found in Johnson 1996, and a more descriptive account in Chapman and Seeliger 2001. The best recent account is Barnes and Williamson 2006. The major source for Shapwick is the Strangways collection in Somerset Record Office.

168. Corcos 2007.

169. The same might be said of the county as a whole. In the western half of the county enclosure was largely complete by the end of the sixteenth century, in the eastern part it was still in progress, though without much opposition. One of very few anti-enclosure protests was the destruction of a duck decoy pond in Kennmoor (Barnes 1961, 4). Since so much of the enclosure in Somerset was of waste, it rarely caused depopulation.

170. Costen 2007e, 1081. There were also, of course, meadows, hay being a valuable enough commodity to be stolen over the winter months, as Thomas Woodlow did in February 1655 (Bates 1912, 304).

171. Johnson 1996, 75.

172. Unsurprisingly, perhaps, since the lord of manor was himself regularly implicated.

173. Corcos 2007, 104.

174. Williams 1970, 25–38.

175. There is a reference to 'a door called Shapwick new door' in 1760 (Costen 2007e, 1081).

176. Rippon 2000, 220–40.

177. Straker *et al.* 2007, 887. Elsewhere this was a period of great innovation as farmers experimented with new crop varieties. Joan Thirsk records rapeseed, woad (dye), hops, madder (dye) and mulberries (for silk) (Thirsk 1997). There is no evidence for any of this at Shapwick.

178. We say this hesitantly because further analysis is needed of assemblages at different stages in the crop-cleaning process in order to be sure.

179. TNA PROB/11/80.

180. Rackham 1988, 3–8.

181. In Chapter 7 we discussed the possibility that this was also the medieval location for the windmill.

182. SRO DD/SG 16; Penoyre *et al.* 2007b.

183. Aston 2007b, 111.

184. Mining experience abounded in the county, with alabaster being extracted near Minehead, stone quarries

at Ham, Dundry and Doulting and lead-mining on Mendip which boomed in the first half of the seventeenth century.
185. SRO DD/SG/50 and 51.
186. Murless 2007.

Boxes
b1. VCH 2004, 179.
b2. For example, the Throckmorton Plot of 1583 was a plan to depose Elizabeth, while the Babington Conspiracy of 1586 was intended to substitute the queen for Mary. For Cossington see VCH 2004, 50.
b3. Coffey 2000, 86.
b4. SVBRG 1996, 55; VCH 2004, 33.
b5. Morland 1978, 15, 22, 31, 42, 69, 150, 210; VCH 2004, 179. It is odd that William chose to marry here, given that Quakers did not recognise church buildings as sacred spaces. The fact that he did so is perhaps an indication of the strength of social pressure locally.
b6. SRO DD/SG 13; Penoyre *et al.* 2007b.
b7. For Edington see VCH 2004, 62; for Greinton VCH 2004, 69; more generally Davies 2000, 59.
b8. Quakers were sometimes arrested for disturbing services and vilifying local ministers. Anti-Quaker literature suggested that no courtesy be shown to them and no welcome be given in the family home (Davies 2000, 27). For Somerset Quakers see Dunning 1976, 50–55.
b9. For witchcraft at this date see Scarre 1987.
b10. 'Cunning-folk' healed the effects of witchcraft as well as providing a number of services such as locating thieves. Davies (2003) provides numerous Somerset examples. For the archaeology of magic see Hoggard 2004 and Merrifield 1987.
b11. Gutiérrez 2007a, 649.
b12. Webster 1992, 123.
b13. Penoyre *et al.* 2007a, 318. We did not find evidence either for foundation deposits or for things hidden within the structure of buildings, though one does wonder about objects such as the four silver christening spoons found hidden in the roof at Forsters.
b14. Knight 1998, 207; 2007.
b15. This information is contained in legal papers prepared in 1754 for Thomas Strangways: SRO DD/SG 15. The case had not been raised previously because the previous owner of the 'rectory manor', Henry Bull, was mentally unwell at the time. He died in 1751.
b16. A draft letter from Thomas Strangways to John Melliar dated 1754 (SRO DD/SG 15) concerns the blocking of this right of way.
b17. Collinson 1791, 426.
b18. Cosgrove and Daniels 1988.

Notes to Chapter 9
1. Gerrard 2007d, 488–9.
2. Plot 20 on Church Lane, map SRO DD/SG 13.
3. Bentley and Murless 1985, 58–9. The Bristol Trust existed from 1726 to 1867 and invested in routes from Bristol southwards into Somerset.
4. Known as Toll Gate cottage in the census returns; the toll collector was most often a woman.
5. Ironically, the new route reinstated the north–south alignment of the Sweet Track after a nearly 6000-year absence (Chapter 3, above)!
6. Many references connect villagers to Bridgwater. The Tully reference is to an inquest on 2 May 1827. This was where murderer Sarah Freeman bought her poison and hair lotions, and it was from Bridgwater that Elizabeth Avery came to tend a sick person in Shapwick but then fell into the fire and was burnt to death (19 March 1823 inquest). As for the turnpike, we presume that the local landowners were financially involved, perhaps as trustees. This might have been either George Warry at Shapwick House, who inherited in 1827, or Henry Strangways at the rectory house, though all the land affected was Warry's.
7. That is to say, the Rolles, Templers, Taylors and Warrys. The two farms in the ownership of the Strangways family were Churchyard and Bowerings. The former had use of the buildings at the manor site. Both were upgraded later in the century.
8. Between the late eighteenth century and 1839, the date of the tithe map, New Farm rose from 38 to 544 acres, for example (Dallimore *et al.* 1994).
9. Even so, there is little evidence of cheeserooms or dairies at these farms today. Such rooms were usually within the farmhouse, often in the outshots, and have since been converted.
10. Gerrard 2007d, 486.
11. Gerrard 2007d, 484; Gidney 2007, 918. Other animal burials included several at Lawn Farm and a lamb in a ditch north of Bridewell Lane (Gidney 2007). In 1793 a gruesome inquest into the death of a nine-month-old baby from Shapwick recounted how the child's arm had been 'nearly eaten off by a sow'. The child later died (http://www.paulhyb.homecall.co.uk/inquests/INQ1793.HTM).
12. SVBRG 1996, 62–3.
13. Gerrard 2007d, 488.
14. Billingsley 1797, 221. Orchards might be kept by arrangement between tenant and landowner; sometimes the latter supplied the trees.
15. The cider was sometimes filtered a second time between Christmas and Lady Day. Bottling was done in April (Coulson 1898–9).
16. 6666/H; Gerrard 2007d, 484.
17. Gerrard 2007d, 495.

18. Gidney 2007, 918. The 1871 census records the baker as William Pitcher with a wife, Emma, daughters Eva and Kate and son Harry, who lived at the Old Bakery with Emma's mother, a cousin and a 19-year-old baker's apprentice called Sidney. William was perhaps the dog's owner. Several other animal burials were also noted at Lawn Farm (Gerrard 2007d, 486). During our excavation at the Old Bakery in 1999 we were contacted through our website by a doctor from Melbourne, Australia, who was related to the Shapwick bakers.

19. Another example is The Old Forge, a late sixteenth-century building, where a two-storey single room was added at the east end. The Post Office and Stores (known as Church Farm in the nineteenth century) gained a two-storey rear extension.

20. 7 Church Road combines two former cottages into a single dwelling.

21. These correlations are made by listing occupants on the 1839 tithe apportionment, linking the names with properties located on the tithe map and then looking for the same family names in 1841, where complete lists of occupants were provided for the census (but not their addresses).

22. Afterwards the vicar was taken in at Shapwick Manor and later at Manor Farm until the present vicarage was made ready. Houses built after the late nineteenth century were excluded from study for this Project.

23. Rather than Welsh slate, that seems to appear in the nineteenth century.

24. Penoyre *et al.* 2007a, 320.

25. Howard-Davis 2001, 211.

26. 7722/B.

27. Gutiérrez 2007a, 668.

28. Shapwick excavation site code OB/P.

29. Gutiérrez 2007a, 643; Willmott 2007; Murless 2007, 815.

30. Gidney 2007, 918–20; Jaques 2007, 927.

31. Lewcun 2007, 676.

32. Higgins 2007.

33. Bond 2007.

34. Minnitt 2007b.

35. At Bridewell Lane (7722/B) there were more cattle and fewer sheep and pigs, while north of Shapwick House (6987/A/B) there were more cattle.

36. Gidney 2007.

37. As described for nearby Mells in the nineteenth century; White 1990, 47–7.

38. In a poisoning case, the meals eaten by the victims had to be related in detail: *The Times*, 13, 14 and 20 January 1845.

39. Both rat-gnawed and rat bones were recovered.

40. 7722/B; Gerrard 2007d, 491.

41. In 1871 the census recorded only 24 individuals born outside Somerset among a total population of 404 villagers. These statistics seem wholly out of line with other parts of pre-industrial rural England. Kitch (1992) states that one person in two was married to someone born in a different community, citing examples of rural villages in which over 50 per cent of the population comprised newcomers. There was evidently less mobility in this more closed community.

42. *The Times*, 20 January 1845.

43. A comprehensive listing of families and farms can be found in Hill-Cottingham (2007, 1088). One farmer who did stay was William Biddlecombe, who was a tenant first at Church(yard) Farm and later next door at New Farm. Quite possibly he was a successful tenant farmer who was moved to a better property.

44. At St Mary Magdalene in Taunton (1862), Hatch Beauchamp (1867) and Orchardleigh (1879). George Gilbert Scott (1811–1878) was a key architect of the Gothick revival, hence his interest in later medieval buildings. He is best known for his design of the Albert Memorial and St Pancras Station in London.

45. Pevsner 1958, 287. The tombstone of Thomas Silver, d.1707, was moved from the aisle to the porch in 1861, for example (www.tutton.org/wedchrnt.html). There are also nine nineteenth-century monuments in the church. Elworthy and Elworthy (1971, 62) recounts that the windows were given ventilators that were kept closed!

46. Gerrard 2007d, 488. This material might derive from either the 1640 restoration or the Scott work of 1861, but more probably the latter.

47. Namely, the vicar Churchill Julius (Elworthy and Elworthy 1971, 63).

48. In brief, Strangways claimed control of the door and allowed the vicar a key for his own use. Warry argued that the vicar should maintain overall right of control and that Strangways was only entitled to a key to come and go. To press this claim, Warry offered to defray the costs to the vicar of any legal action that might arise in the ecclesiastical courts and then sought to compel the vicar to act by forbidding his tenants to contribute to the church plate. When the vicar did nothing, Warry instructed his tenants accordingly and the Strangways tenants, unwilling to bear the financial burden of church maintenance alone, then also refused to contribute. After negotiation with Churchill Julius, the new vicar, Strangways finally handed over his key saying 'You won't let Warry in, will you?' Julius then kept the door locked to both parties (Elworthy and Elworthy 1971, 231–2).

49. Elworthy and Elworthy 1971, 232.

50. Analyses of nineteenth-century social history can be found in Bédarida 1979, Briggs 1983 and many other volumes.

51. Stell 1991. The largest group of religious minorities was

the Protestant Dissenting churches, whose membership was drawn largely from tradesmen and artisans, only a few of whom resided in Shapwick.

52. Though lots of people brewed beer at home and some was sold.

53. The Railway Inn is first mentioned in 1883, became the Griffin Hotel in 1889 and 1894 and the Griffin public house by 1897, but was the Griffin's Head 1927–35. The owner for much of this period was one Theophillus Collins. Otherwise the nearest public houses were the Albion Inn above Pedwell, the King William Inn at Catcott, the Ring O'Bells and the Ashcott Inn at Ashcott, The Railway Inn at Ashcott Corner and the Bird in Hand at Westhay. These were all a considerable walk from the village. In contrast to Shapwick, there were 'six or seven' public houses in Ashcott in the mid-nineteenth century (Elworthy and Elworthy 1971, 63).

54. SRO D/P/Shap/13/2/1; these are studied in Bettey 2007c, 1086.

55. Gerrard 2007d, 486. Little is known of the structure, though by the mid-eighteenth century the enclosure ditch around the poor house had been filled in and replaced by a wall of local Lias stone.

56. SRO DD/SG16; SVBRG 1996, 107.

57. When the accounts end in 1765 Mary was still a regular charge on the parish rates.

58. When one aged 79 is described as 'an imbecile from birth' and presumably cared for within the family.

59. Youngs 1980, 671. The system failed owing to rising population and difficulties in identifying fraudulent applications for relief and in 'repatriating' the sick and homeless to parishes who did not wish to cover the expense, not to mention the financial pressures of a long European War and prolonged recession.

60. Built in 1836, demolished in 1980. Revelations of grave mismanagement at the Bridgwater Union workhouse were brought forward by John Bowen under the provocative title 'Is Killing in a Union Workhouse criminal if sanctioned by the Poor Law Commissioners?' (Buchanan 1987).

61. A list of available Poor Law Union records for Bridgwater can be found in Gibson and Rogers 1993, 41.

62. VCH 2004, 179.

63. By Andrew Bell and known as the *National Society for Promoting the Education of the Poor in the Principles of the Established Church*.

64. Now part of Millfield School.

65. The use of slates in schools is said to have been pioneered by Joseph Lancaster, a Quaker and founder of the British and Foreign School Society, in 1808.

66. These events took place in just two years, 1854 and 1856, and are recorded in the *Bridgwater Times*

(http://www.paulhyb.homecall.co.uk/index2.htm). The convict, George Rowley of Shapwick, had escaped from Wilton goal but was recaptured in Cheddar Wood. George Warry (1795–1883), as a barrister of the Chancery and Western Circuit and Chairman of Bridgwater County Justices, was a champion of county constabularies in the 1840s and 1850s.

67. Penoyre *et al.* 2007a, 285–6. In 1880 George Warry told a visiting party from the Somerset Archaeology and Natural History Society that the brick dining room, like the sash windows, were put in 'at the beginning of the present century' – i.e., around 1800 (Anon. 1880). As a lover of Gothick he clearly disapproved, complaining that his house had been 'sadly disfigured … with a view to entertainment and comfort, rather than out of respect to architectural taste', as he put it.

68. Sarah Taylor's original will and its two codicils (TNA PROB 11/2190) are clear on this point. She was still living at Shapwick House in March 1846, possibly with her nephew Charles Milles, but had moved to Cheltenham by February 1849, dying in 1854.

69. Lawn Farm is an imposing house of mid-nineteenth-century date that replaces two houses demolished on the same site.

70. VCH 2004, 166.

71. Willmott 2007.

72. 6987/B; Gutiérrez 2007a, 657.

73. For example, creamwares, hand-painted pearlwares, painted porcelain and bone china.

74. TNA PROB 11/1965. For the servants that is the equivalent of about £1,170 and £2,341 in today's money. Sarah had been a witness to Hill's will, 'proved' in July 1842.

75. Gutiérrez 2007a, 667.

76. By the time the children were older, in 1871, only a butler, footman, cook, a kitchen maid and two housemaids were required, though there was also a coachman in the lodge. Of these, Warry's butler was a Dorset man, his cook came from Devon and one of the housemaids was from Lincolnshire, the others being born in Somerset. Until recently, a coachman's livery button used by the Warry family at Shapwick House *c*.1880 was on loan at Somerset Record Office.

77. For today's archaeologist these changes create two magnificent opportunities. The first is that the switch of interest to the south of the mansion did much to preserve garden features to the north and it was there that earthwork survey, excavation and documentary study contributed so much towards the reconstruction of later medieval garden arrangements (Chapter 7, above). The second opportunity is provided by the new eighteenth-century parkland to the south of the mansion, which sealed beneath its turf the demolished remains of the medieval village and so gave us the

78. The streets affected were Jeanes Lane, Brice late Davidges Lane. At least five buildings lined these two streets together with a plot called the 'Vicar's Toft', while two others lie on Cadbys and Miller Jones Lane.

79. The very acts of surveying and measuring, drawing and naming are powerful means of inscribing property ownership onto the landscape (Johnson 1996, 91–2).

80. Gerrard 2007c; 2007e, 1001. Pottery from the barn includes dishes, cups, tankards, mugs and pancheons (Gutiérrez 2007a, 667).

81. Pompeo Batoni, 1708–1787. The National Portrait Gallery in London held an exhibition of Batoni's work in 2008. John Rolle (1712–1779), brother of Denys and William; he took the name Walter when he inherited his uncle's estates in Oxfordshire; MP for Exeter 1754–76 and Recorder of Great Torrington 1739–79.

82. See also VCH 2004, 166.

83. This unusual object is from 6767/A43; for further detail see Gerrard and Youngs 1997; 2007. It is not possible to identify the original bronze type (Stuart Needham pers. comm.).

84. MacGregor 1985; though George Templer also had an interest in artefacts. He purchased a 'fine old sword' from a resident near Sedgemoor who affirmed that the Duke of Monmouth left it at his ancestor's cottage when he fled. Templer sent it to the British Archaeological Association's meeting at Dorchester in August 1871 'for examination'.

85. SVBRG 1996, 68. Gamekeeper's, later Island, Cottage, was called 'the Kennels' in 1881 when it was occupied by a gamekeeper.

86. It may also have been at this time that the little curving short-cut that ran west out of the end of Bridewell Lane and onto Church Road was removed, though the logic is unclear. Quite possibly it merely fell out of use once emparkment had reduced southbound traffic on the west side of the village. Bond (2007a, 124) includes a plan.

87. Gerrard 2007c, 558; Penoyre *et al.* 2007c, 821.

88. The lodge on Kent Lane was constructed at some time between 1811 and 1839 (Gerrard 2007e, 1003).

89. Home Farm itself may be of sixteenth-/seventeenth-century origin. Estate development in the nineteenth century is less well researched than earlier periods (Williamson 2007, 11).

90. Aston 1985, 56; VCH 1985, 129–30.

91. For example, Nuneham Courtenay in Oxfordshire (Batey 1968; 1970), Milton Abbas in Dorset (RCHME 1970, 182–99; Taylor 1970, 175–7; Bettey 1993, 110–11) and Castle Howard, Yorkshire (Finch 2007), show that this process was happening around the country on large and small estates (Taigel and Williamson 1996).

92. The transition began with William Kent in the 1730s (Jacques 1983, 11) but is mainly associated with Lancelot (Capability) Brown (1750s–60s). The construction and form of the carriageway laid out from the south of the park to the front of the mansion reflected ideas about informality put forward in particular by Humphrey Repton in the late 1780s to 1800s (Bradney 2005).

93. Gerrard 2007e, 1004. The Rolle owners were: Henry (d.1692) and his sons, Francis (d.1709), John (suicide at East Tytherley 1727) and Samuel (d.1729). The estate then passed to a Devon cousin John (d.1730) and his son John Rolle Walter (d.1779).

94. Lewis 1848.

95. Known as Down House in the 1871 census.

96. Henry Bull d.1751; Elizabeth Strangways d.1766; Henry Strangways d.1805; Henry Bull Strangways d.1829; Henry Strangways d.1884; and Henry Bull Templer Strangways d.1920. There are eight boxes of family and estate papers in Somerset Record Office.

97. The arches are like those at Dillington House, Ilminster (Penoyre *et al.* 2007a, 286–91). The medieval revival influenced a broad spectrum of daily life from literature and painting to churches, railway stations and public buildings such as the New Palace of Westminster (Gerrard 2003, 30–34). For estate architecture see Williamson 2007.

98. These roads were Turf House Lane and Mag Jones Lane, closed between 1785 and 1839. The gate in the south wall with stone 'pineapple' decorations was probably blocked at the same time. Between these two lanes, the short length of Holes Lane may well have been stopped up too.

99. Gerrard *et al.* 2007b, 259.

100. Little is known of the house contents except a 'large silver waiter' that Henry Bull Strangways left in his will of 1829 (TNA PROB 11/1761), but the house was doubtless well furnished.

101. The 1851 census lists much the same household in residence, though with an additional daughter and son at home. The 1841 census found only two people present; the family were probably away.

102. Henry Bull Templar Strangways (1832–1920) visited Australia as a boy, then studied law and was called to the Bar in 1856. He returned to Adelaide in 1857 and was admitted to the South Australian Bar in 1861. He was elected to the House of Assembly for Encounter Bay in 1858–62 and member for West Torrens 1862–71. He was attorney-general in 1860–61, minister for

crown lands and immigration in 1861–5 and premier and attorney-general of South Australia in 1868–70. He initiated railway and overland telegraph projects in South Australia but resigned from parliament in February 1871 and returned to Shapwick.

103. Corcos 2007.

104. Williams 1970.

105. One theory is that, since most enclosure was for pasture, the enclosure of the Heath Moor after 1784 satisfied that need and so stalled the process in what remained of the open fields.

106. The difficulties here can readily be imagined. Waiting for all tenancies to fall vacant took time, especially when land had been let for a number of lives, usually three.

107. Corcos 1982, 93; Kelly's *Directories*.

108. Where fields have been converted from pasture to arable; occasionally other methods of drainage were encountered during excavations, such as Lias slab drains and culverts.

109. Murless 2007, 817. In 1846 Bridgwater manufacturers were advertising 'land draining tiles and pipes'.

110. Usually the pattern is 'herringbone', in which diagonal drains feather into a central drain. The costs of purchase and labour could be shared by landlord and tenant or advanced or borrowed under the terms of the 1849 Private Money Drainage Act. Nowhere in the parish can be assumed to be in the same condition of drainage as it was in the past. Parts of the common fields must have been much more boggy and marshy in the Middle Ages than they appear today, though ridge and furrow would have improved drainage. Without the benefit of more detailed augering and geomorphological mapping, we cannot be sure in detail.

111. Straker *et al.* 2007.

112. McDonnell 1979, 78, fig. 3; Williams 1970, 47–54.

113. The Shapwick Enclosure Bill was passed by parliament in 1777, but the award was not granted until 1784 (Williams 1970, 122, 131–40).

114. Apart from twenty-four acres of glebe land.

115. Widow of Thomas Strangways, whose memorial lies in the church.

116. There are many records of illegal peat digging from the mid-eighteenth century; the culprits included the vicar and twenty others in 1759 (VCH 2004, 175). Peat was also supplied to the poor.

117. Corcos 1982, 84. An account can be found in the 'Case for the Petitioners for Shapwick Inclosure Bill', May 1777 (SRO T/PH/fl c/2363).

118. Tenants received an amount of land proportionate to the size of their tenements, usually two to three acres. Landowner and benefactor Denys Rolle is known to have been keen on the idea of garden allotments for the poor.

119. Acland and Sturge (1851, 100) cite the lack of criminal convictions in parishes with 'field gardens' as part of their 'social value'.

120. SRO DD/SG 18; Corcos 1982, 86–7.

121. Barnes and Williamson 2006.

122. Chapman and Seeliger 2001, 140.

123. McDonnell 1984.

124. Payne-Gallwey 1886; Bettey 1988. The decoy appears to have been constructed in 1850 by William Chancellor (VCH 2004, 165). It was still in occasional use in 1885 but was abandoned by 1904. It is likely to have been dug away by local peat diggers in the 1930s (Minnitt 2007a, 729–31).

125. There was a 'Turfhouse Lane' on the mid-eighteenth-century maps immediately north of Shapwick Manor, now lost. In 1871 there were two 'turf merchants' in the village, one of whom lived with his son, a 'labourer at turf work'. Between 1889 and 1910 extensive turf peat moors of between 400 and 500 acres are recorded, of which eighty were being cut for turf.

126. Hewitt 1911, 355; VCH 2004, 174–5. There were also experiments to make 'portable peat coal', for which a model manufactory was erected at Shapwick Moor by Mr Alloway in 1872 (*The Times*, 22 October 1872).

127. Legg 1997.

128. Taylor 1983, 221; Roberts and Wrathmell 2002, 119.

129. A 1785 survey describes 'a farmhouse lately new built in brick' (SVBRG 1996, 66). At the end of the eighteenth century Denys Rolle thought classically, whereas George Warry, fifty years later, approved only of Gothick.

130. VCH 2004, 173; Penoyre *et al.* 2007a, 312–14. Corcos (1982, 80) suggests that Rolle may have built the farm for himself or for his immediate family, so grand is it.

131. Beerway is probably dated around 1861 (Dallimore 2005, 153), though an earlier cottage at Beerway is listed on the tithe apportionment of 1839. Beerway is unusual in that the farmhouse is at an extreme edge of the farmyard. The original intention was probably to have a carriage entrance on the south side of the house off the Ashcott Road. A barn at Manor Farm has a datestone which reads '1849 GW', for George Warry.

132. The 'Dominion of Canada' was formed on 1 July 1867, when three colonies united as a single nation. The name 'Canada' must have been adopted after that date. The farm is recorded on the 1871 census as a 'farmhouse' of eighty-two acres. Moorgate now appears rather isolated, but there was once a toll-house on the opposite side of the road.

133. George Warry died in 1883, George Deedes Warry in 1904.

134. SVBRG 1996. In 1871 Moorgate was lived in by one

Joseph Pursey, his wife and son, one domestic servant and a 'farm servant indoor'.

135. Farm rents also increased from an average of £0.66 per acre in 1784 to about £1.46 by 1879. At Beerway, for example, with 220 acres in 1871 two years' annual rent would have offset the cost of constructing the farmhouse (SVBRG 1996, 79).

136. There is a woodcutter in the 1851 census.

137. Another icehouse may exist in the garden of Island Cottage, just north of Shapwick House. There is an unexplained earthen mound in a similar location to that at nearby Montacute House.

138. Aston *et al.* 2007b, 109–10.

139. SRO DD/SG c/206 and c/206 36 respectively.

140. SRO DD/SG 39.

141. The cap on top of the tower rotated with the sails. Stone tower mills were much rarer than timber post mills, despite their durability (Langdon and Watts 2005, 697–718). Strangely, this mill is not shown on a map of around 1785 (SRO DD/SG 50 c1785), though it is depicted on Day and Masters's map of 1782 and is then shown on the series of early nineteenth-century maps of the parish.

142. Described in the *Taunton Courier* for 7 December 1836 under the strap line 'Great Gale on the Polden Hills'; see also Coulthard and Watts 1978, 58–9.

143. On the tithe map there is a drawing of a windmill in plot number 342a, on a completely new site.

144. VCH 2004, 175. In the 1851 census Betsy Jones is recorded as a widow while her two sons, Edward and William, aged 28 and 26, appear as millers.

145. VCH 2004, 175; SVBRG 1996, 74. William Paul Spearing ran the steam mill from 1889 to 1910, according to Kelly's *Directories*.

146. Aston 2007c, 182. Since the land itself was held by the parish's major landowners wage labourers may have extracted the limestone as and when there was demand; there is no evidence for quarries being leased out.

147. Though not the farmhouse at Northbrook.

148. Limekilns were being operated in 1902 by George Hitchcock, farmer, and in 1906 by Joseph Duckett, farmer.

149. Field 7142; the first-edition 1886 Ordnance Survey sheet shows a rectangular structure on the northern boundary of the copse.

150. Murless 2007, 817–18.

151. Shovel-pitting at Brickyard Farm produced some brick and tile, especially to the west of the surviving farm buildings (Thorpe and Gerrard 2007, 271).

152. Williams 1970, 222, 240. John Rennie (1761–1822) was the engineer on the Kennet and Avon Canal through Wiltshire and Berkshire (1794–1810), which included the locks at Devizes (Hadfield 1969, 88, 129).

153. Hadfield 1967, 78–81.

154. Body and Gallop 2001.

155. Phelps 1836.

156. The Bristol and Exeter Railway was opened as far as Highbridge in 1842. After an authorizing Act was passed, payment for the canal was made in 1850, the canal company being dissolved in 1851 (Hadfield 1967, 81).

157. The canal between Glastonbury and Shapwick bridge was closed on 1 July 1854 and the railway was opened a few weeks later, on 17 August (Williams 1970, 224).

158. Warry was chairman of the Somerset and Dorset railway in 1866, 1867 and 1871–3. In 1866 his son, George Deedes Warry, published a book on taxation and the railways entitled *The Law of Railway Rating*. His grandson, Bertram Arthur Warry, was in the Royal Engineers, also in connection with the railways.

159. In May 1877 an engine and four coaches ran off the line near Shapwick station. The train was lightly laden and the few passengers and officials 'escaped with a shaking' (*The Times*, 3 May 1877).

160. Shapwick House was lived in by Major Bertram Arthur Warry JP in 1919 but lay unoccupied from at least 1923 to 1935, probably longer. The house was a convalescent home in the Second World War. During the life of the Project its proprietors included Eddie Barrett (to 1999), Bernadette and Keith Gibson (1999–2006) and Dr Richard Stacey from 2006. It is now used mainly for weddings.

161. Henry Bull Templer Strangways died in 1920 and his only daughter in 1932. The estate then passed to her cousin Helen Sophia Vialls (who adopted the name Strangways) and it was she, and the trustees, who sold the estate to Lord Vestey. Helen continued to live in the house until her death in 1949 (VCH 2004, 166–8). Lord Vestey thereafter followed the Strangways as patron of the church.

162. This selling-off was much to the advantage of the Project (Chapter 1, above).

163. Electric light first came to the church in 1936; there is no gas (Peter Lamb, South Western Electricity Historical Society, pers. comm.).

164. All the metal finds in this section are discussed in Viner 2007.

165. For example, to the east of the School and east of King's Farm (later Old Farmhouse).

166. The least successful of these developments is at the Home Office Communication Depot on Shapwick Hill. This highly visible site was an inappropriate location for new housing, divorced as it was from the rest of the village up a narrow and very busy lane. Its location takes no cognisance of the way the village has developed historically.

167. With a new car park. The adjacent field is used for the

village fête and looks likely to be donated to the village as a sort of village green.

168. Shapwick is one of nine 'thankful' villages in Somerset. Of the thirty-two villagers who served in the First World War, none perished (www.fylde.demon.co.uk). Dame Muriel Joan Warry Marsham (1888–1972), daughter of William Warry, was awarded the OBE for her work in the First World War and later became chairman of the executive committee of the Girl Guides Association from 1938 to 1948. A booklet by Dora Watkins entitled 'Life was different then …' describes her childhood in the 1930s and 1940s in Shapwick.

169. The communications centre is HER 12349. Local knowledge also suggests that there was a searchlight or anti-aircraft battery in Beggar's Bush Copse, though nothing can be seen there today. There are local reports that a Wellington bomber crashed in a field near Kent Farm – probably in field 2488 (the western boundary with field 1400 was suggested) – but fieldwalking failed to find anything out of the ordinary. The story goes that the damaged aircraft was not allowed to land at Westonzoyland airfield as this would have required the landing lights on the aerodrome there to be illuminated. Instead the aircraft was diverted to Bristol, but then lost height and crashed, killing the crew.

170. The Old Age Pension was introduced in 1908.

171. The school closed in 1984 (VCH 2004, 179).

172. VCH 2004, 160.

173. Atthill 1967.

174. Engine Bulldog No 76 LMS 3260.

175. Atthill 1967, 129–30; 1970, 86. Sixty-five cylinders of oxygen and eighteen of acetylene were used in the cutting operation. The problem seems to have been that the peat companies working peat in the Brue valley and using narrow gauge lines to move their trucks of peat had to cross the main railway line between Highbridge and Glastonbury. The Eclipse Peat Company's workings on Shapwick Heath, for example, used horse-drawn trucks until around 1930 (VCH 2004, 164).

176. *Somerset and Dorset Railway Museum Trust Bulletin* 97, 1980.

177. The lands of New Farm were redistributed and the farmhouse sold in 1988. The same had happened to Hill Farm, Lawn Farm and Home Farm before the Project began. Church Farm was effectively decommissioned during the life of the Project when Stan Jenkins retired and all of its land was worked from Beerway Farm by his brother David.

178. For example, the Jenkins family at Beerway Farm. William Jenkins was farming there in 1902 while Frank Lockyer was at Moorgate in 1935. Farms were passed from father to son and the Vestey estate continued the policy of allowing a son to take over the lease of the farm if he had worked for a number of years alongside the father. Thus it was assumed that Manor Farm and Northbrook Farm (before they were sold) and Beerway Farm would be passed on to the next generation. Coppice Gate Farm was passed on to John Maidment when Arthur Maidment died, while the Project was underway. With the future of farming uncertain, this policy may be hard to maintain and further amalgamations and decommissionings seem inevitable. In a decade or so many Shapwick farms could have totally new owners.

179. Moorgate was still unoccupied in 2012.

180. The map was prepared by Jackson-Stops and Staff of Yeovil and kept by Bert Hillburn in Shapwick. It has been deposited in the Somerset County Record Office along with the paperwork associated with the Project.

181. Dallimore and Penoyre 1994.

182. In 1955 the tenants of the main farms were: Kent Farm (F. Lockyer) 305 acres, Manor Farm (W. G. Coombes) 246 acres, Beerway Farm (Mrs D. S. Jenkins) 216 acres, Home Farm (Mrs M. T. A. Tully) 189 acres, Northbrook (A. L. Hobbs) 208 acres, Hill Farm (J. Tully) 182 acres, New Farm (T. Harding) 196 acres, Littlechurch Farm (H. J. Barnett) only 6 acres, Old Farm (H. C. Stevens) 42 acres, part of Newlands Farm in Catcott parish (W. H. Williams) 54 acres, Moorgate Farm (M. H. Tratt) 97 acres, Canada Farm (G. A. and J. Brown) 175 acres, Brickyard Farm (H. J. Heal) 63 acres, Locks Farm (A. J. Whitcombe) 53 acres, Bowerings Farm (C. A. Jennings) 50 acres, part of Heath Farm in Ashcott (C. A. Jennings) 26 acres, Church Farm (no one listed) 148 acres, Coppice Gate Farm (A. Maidment) 74 acres, part of Buscott Farm in Ashcott (I. Banwell) 113 acres, part of Hill Farm in Ashcott (A. G. Hobbs) 146 acres and Butchers Shop and land (W. Durston) 52 acres.

183. These were, with their tenant farmers: Bowerings (Eric Lockyer) and Church Farm (Stan Jenkins) in the village, and Coppice Gate Farm (Arthur Maidment), Northbrook Farm (Graham Elliott), Beerway Farm (David Jenkins), Manor Farm (Jim Coombes) and Kent Farm (Pip Gibbons) out in the parish. New Farm (Norman Stevens) had recently been decommissioned when the Project began; the farmhouse had been sold to the tenant farmer and the land was about to be redistributed among the remaining six tenants. Farmers operate widely differing regimes. While David Jenkins has a large herd of cows and spends many hours each day milking, other farmers have few cattle and have abandoned their dairies. Pip Gibbons, at Kent Farm, has a very large acreage but hardly any animals. Most of his land is now ploughed, including much of the land held 'in hand' by the estate. He grows large quantities of potatoes, which are sorted and packed in large sheds

on the farm. By contrast, Eric Lockyer at Bowerings Farm has a prize flock of Texel sheep, so almost all of his land is down to pasture.

184. Viner 2007.

Boxes

b1. McFarlane 1994, 217–312; Mowat 1943. The exact site is disputed, but is thought to be at San Mateo. See also Bohnenberger 1925; Corse 1928.

b2. Rolle 1766.

b3. Stork 1766.

b4. Anon. 1797.

b5. Gerrard *et al.* 2007e, 175. Thousands of Indo-Pacific cowry shells were also shipped to Mexico in Manila galleons, for example, and then carried overland by mule trains (Smith 1996, 91).

b6. Templer n.d.

b7. Harris 1972, 77; Hadfield 1967, 118–21; Hoskins 1972, 156; Cherry and Pevsner 1989.

b8. Burke 1786, 171; Keay 1991.

b9. VCH 2004, 166.

b10. VCH 2004, 42–50. Although George sold the Cossington estate he had purchased the house, Cossington Manor, in 1803 with 150 acres and this he duly left to his son at his death in 1819. The Revd George Templer sold it again in 1828.

b11. Lawson 1993.

b12. Her daughter Sophia Anne Templer married Sir William Templer Pole (her cousin), who held Shute House near Axminster.

b13. The church monument at Shapwick, erected by his uncle George Templer beside the north door of the nave, implies that he attended the school of Westminster and the University of Glasgow, and that he was returning to 'the eager expectation, and the ardent hopes of an anxious father'. He seems to have been accompanied by one William Cator, who was also killed in the action and whose memorial is on the other side of the north door.

b14. Aston 2007d, 1089–92.

b15. TNA PROB 11/2060.

Notes to Chapter 10

1. This interplay of history operating at different timescales is behind *Annales* history, typified by the work of French historian Fernand Braudel and others. The Annaliste approach has been adopted by many of the most successful landscape surveys, including those in the Biferno Valley in Italy (Barker 1995) and in East Brittany (Astill and Davies 1997), and it is well suited to the exploration of themes such as the environment, farming and religion over long time-frames (Bintliff 2004; Bintliff *et al.* 2007, 180).

2. Cemeteries in masonry buildings such as that at

Sladwick make up the majority of known examples of this behaviour. Bell 2005, table 1, provides a list of sites and burials. There is particular concentration in the south-west. Somerset sites include Banwell (Winthill), Bradley Hill (Somerton), Brean Down, Henley Wood (Yatton), Somerton and Wells.

3. Morris and Roxan 1980. The case for true continuity has been most obviously argued for Rivenhall in Essex (Rodwell and Rodwell 1985; though see Millett 1987, 438, for a rejection of the Rodwells' sequence) and, locally, at Wells, where a Roman martyrium had a Saxon chapel built over it before the construction of St Mary's church (Rodwell 2001).

4. For memory see Scott 1990; Halbwachs 1992.

5. This explanation is inspired by Bintliff (2004), who observed very similar patterns in a completely different environment in Greece (Boeotia).

6. The Whittlewood Project also emphasised the influence of earlier field systems on medieval layouts (Jones and Page 2006, 228).

7. Billingsley 1797, 56. For recent views see Van de Noort and O'Sullivan 2007.

8. Pryor 1992; Parker Pearson and Field 2002; Yates and Bradley 2010.

9. The fen edge and watery settings seem to have had special significance at this period (Rogers 2007). For a study of perceptions of wetland over the long term in the Witham Valley (Lincs) see Stocker and Everson (2003).

10. As, for example, there is a St Aldhelm's well at Doulting.

11. Wrightson and Levine 1995, 174. For estate villages see Havinden 1999. 'Closure' is examined in Hinton 1999.

12. Johnson 1996.

13. Williams 1970.

14. Roberts and Wrathmell 2002, fig. 1.3. Because the open fields were later enclosed, often in geometric arrangements of fields, Oliver Rackham called it 'planned' as opposed to 'ancient' countryside.

15. Hodges 1982.

16. For Hereford see Shoesmith 1982, 88–94; also many minster settlements in Wessex (Hall 2000).

17. Though none of these has the layout of a grid plan such as Wallingford, Wareham, Oxford or Cricklade.

18. For example, Oosthuizen 2006; Rippon 2007.

19. Brooks 1992.

20. Knowles 1963; Bois 1992. It would be interesting to look for similar examples of village planning among the estates of the greater pre-Conquest monasteries such as Abingdon and Peterborough. Later examples include the village of Acklington in County Durham, which has been linked to the reorganising activities of Bishop Wacher in a single decade between 1071

and 1080 (Kapelle 1979, 189). Mells in Somerset is a documented example of the creation of part of a new village plan by Abbot Selwood of Glastonbury Abbey in the fifteenth century (Aston 1985). For West Cotton and Raunds in Northamptonshire see Chapman 2010, 240–47; Audouy and Chapman 2009.

21. These interpretations are described in greater detail by Williamson (2007).
22. Thirsk 1964.
23. Among them Carenza Lewis, Patrick Mitchell-Fox and Christopher Dyer in their study of villages in the East Midlands (Lewis *et al.* 1997).
24. Taylor 1983.
25. Though core areas for two-field systems are suggested by Roberts and Wrathmell, and reiterated by Rippon 2008a, 18, fig. 1.3.
26. Faith 1997.
27. Williamson 2003. This observation also stands for Model 1.
28. Earlier scholars such as the Orwins (1938) emphasised the importance of technology in the equation, arguing that new ploughing arrangements (rather like larger tractors today) needed fields of certain dimensions. The team of plough, oxen and ploughmen required sharing and cooperation to make them work smoothly. Elements of their model are incorporated in Model 3.
29. Williamson 2003.
30. Some later Saxon settlements, such as Yarnton, appear to have large enclosures around them rather like Roman settlements, not open fields (Hey 2004).
31. Lilley 2005, fig. 12.1. We have axed his Stage 5 – chartering – which is related to the conferment of privileges, though this does apply to some villages later on when they were granted markets.
32. The process of laying out new towns is illustrated in the first two chapters of Beresford (1967).
33. Smith and Petley 2009.
34. Roberts 1987. Long Lawford in Warwickshire, on his fig. 2.3 (b), comes closest. Shapwick can readily be picked out on fig. 9.6 and is mentioned in the text.

35. Like Long Load in Somerset, for example.
36. From west to east: Woolavington, Cossington, Chilton Polden, Edington, Catcott, Shapwick and Ashcott. See also important points made by Rippon (2008a, 89).
37. Only one, New Street, was completed (Bond 2004, 245–6).
38. For example Lilley 1998; 2004; Slater 1998.
39. Lilley 2005, 239. Van de Noort and O'Sullivan (2007, 86) contrast the orderliness and humanised natures of the dry land against the wilderness of the wetland. Was this deliberate on the part of Glastonbury Abbey?
40. Roberts (2008, 265–9) provides an English summary.
41. Hamerow 2002.
42. Toubert 1973; Moreland 1992.
43. Bazzana *et al.* 1988.
44. eg. Bourin-Derruau 1987.
45. Athanassopoulos 2004.
46. Glick 1995.
47. Twenty-five years ago French historian Robert Fossier suggested a chronology for *incastellamento*, beginning in northern Italy in the tenth century, in Provence before 950–1030, and in the Loire and Rhine valleys 100 years later (Fossier 1982).
48. Roberts 2008, 249.
49. The Whittlewood Project, an examination of settlements on the Buckinghamshire–Northamptonshire border, provides a fascinating comparison to our project. It was concluded there that some hamlets disappeared in the period AD 850–1000, while others grew to become villages (Jones and Page 2006, 101). There was clearly regional variation.
50. Christopher Taylor thinks that the planning of settlements was widespread and that, with close examination, most medieval villages display some aspects of it (pers. comm.).

Boxes

b1. Gerrard 2007f.
b2. Beresford and Hurst 1990; Parry 2006; Audouy and Chapman 2009.

Bibliography

Abdy, R., Brunning, R. and Webster, C. J. (2001) 'The discovery of a Roman villa at Shapwick and its Severan coin hoard of 9328 silver denarii', *J. Roman Archaeol.* 14(1), 358–72.

Aberg, F. A. ed. (1978) *Medieval Moated Sites*, CBA Research Report 17, London.

Abrams, L. (1991) 'A single sheet facsimile of a diploma of King Ine for Glastonbury', in L. Abrams and J. P. Carley (eds), *The Archaeology and History of Glastonbury Abbey*, Boydell Press, Woodbridge, 97–133.

Abrams, L. (1996) *Anglo-Saxon Glastonbury: Church and Endowment*, Boydell Press, Woodbridge.

Acland, T. D. and Sturge, W. (1851) *The Farming of Somersetshire*, John Murray, London.

Addyman, P. V. and Leigh, D. (1973) 'The Anglo-Saxon village at Chalton: second interim report', *Medieval Archaeol.* 17, 14–25.

Ainsworth, S. and Thomason, B. (2003) *Where on Earth are We? The Global Positioning System (GPS) in Archaeological Field Survey*, English Heritage Technical Paper, Swindon.

Airs, M. (1975) *The Making of the English Country House, 1500–1640*, Architectural Press, London.

Alcock, L. (1963) *Dinas Powys: An Iron Age, Dark Age and Early Medieval Settlement in Glamorgan*, University of Wales Press, Cardiff.

Alcock, L. (1995) *Cadbury Castle, Somerset: The Early Medieval Archaeology*, University of Wales Press, Cardiff.

Alcock, N. W. (1993) *People at Home: Living in a Warwickshire Village, 1500–1800*, Phillimore, Chichester.

Aldridge, J. and Tregorran, J. (1981) *Ambridge: An English Village Through the Ages*, Borchester Press (in association with Eyre Methuen), Borchester.

Allen, T. G. (1994) 'A medieval grange of Abingdon Abbey at Dean Court Farm, Cumnor, Oxon', *Oxonensia* 59, 219–447.

Allen, T. G., Darvill, T. C., Green, L. S. and Jones, M. U. (1993) *Excavations at Roughground Farm, Lechlade, Gloucestershire: A Prehistoric and Roman Landscape*, Thames Valley Landscapes: the Cotswolds Water Park I, Oxford.

Andrews, D. D. and Milne, G. eds (1979) *Wharram Volume 1: Domestic Settlement Areas 10 and 6*, SMA monograph 8, Leeds.

Anon. (1797) 'Obituary of remarkable persons …', *Gentleman's Magazine* LXVII, 617.

Anon. (1880) 'Excursion of the Society', *PSANHS* 26, 62–7.

ApSimon, A. M. (1965) 'The Roman temple, Brean Down, Somerset', *Proc. Univ. Bristol Spelaeol. Soc.* 10, 195–258.

Archer, M. (1997) *Delftware: The Tin-glazed Earthenware of the British Isles*, HMSO, London.

Askew, A. (1521–46) *The First Examinacion of Anne Askewe*, Nicholas Hill, London.

Astill, G. and Davies, W. (1997) *A Breton Landscape*, UCL Press, London.

Aston, M. (2003) 'Public worship and iconoclasm', in D. Gaimster and R. Gilchrist (eds), *The Archaeology of the Reformation 1480–1580*, Maney, Leeds, 9–28.

Aston, M. A. (1978) 'Gardens and earthworks at Hardington and Low Ham', *SANH* 122, 11–18.

Aston, M. A. (1982) 'Rural settlement in Somerset: some preliminary thoughts', in D. Hooke (ed.), *Medieval Villages*, Oxford University Committee for Archaeology monograph 5, Oxford, 81–100.

Aston, M. A. (1983) 'Deserted farmsteads on Exmoor and the Lay Subsidies of 1327 in West Somerset', *SANH* 127, 71–104.

Aston, M. A. (1984) 'The Towns of Somerset', in J. Haslam (ed.), *Anglo-Saxon Towns in Southern England*, Phillimore, Chichester, 167–201.

Aston, M. A. (1985) *Interpreting the Landscape: Landscape Archaeology and Local Studies*, Batsford, London.

Aston, M. A. (1986) 'Post-Roman central places in Somerset', in E. Grant (ed.), *Central Places, Archaeology and History*, Department of Archaeology and Prehistory, University of Sheffield, 49–77.

Aston, M. A. ed. (1988) *Aspects of the Medieval Landscape of Somerset: Contributions to the Landscape History of the County*, Somerset County Council, Taunton.

Aston, M. A. ed. (1989) *The Shapwick Project: A Topographical and Historical Study. The First Report*, University of Bristol, Bristol.

Aston, M. A. ed. (1990) *The Shapwick Project: A Topographical and Historical Study. The Second Report*, University of Bristol, Bristol.

Aston, M. A. (1992) 'The Shapwick Project: a study in need of remote sensing', in P. Spoerry (ed.), *Geoprospection in the Archaeological Landscape*, Oxbow Books monograph 18, Oxford, 141–54.

Aston, M. A. (1994) 'Medieval settlement studies in Somerset', in M. Aston and C. Lewis (eds), *The Medieval Landscape of Wessex*, Oxbow Books, Oxford, 219–37.

Aston, M. A. (2003) 'Early monasteries in Somerset – models and agendas', in M. R. Ecclestone, K. Gardner, N. Holbrook and A. Smith (eds), *The Land of the Dobunni*, Parchment, Oxford, 36–48.

Aston, M. A. (2007a) 'An archipelago in central Somerset: The origins of Muchelney Abbey', *SANH* 150, 63–71.

Aston, M. A. (2007b) 'Fieldchecking', in C. M. Gerrard with M. A. Aston, *The Shapwick Project, Somerset: A Rural Landscape Explored*, SMA monograph 25, Leeds, 109–13.

Aston, M. A. (2007c) 'Aerial photographs', in C. M. Gerrard with M. A. Aston, *The Shapwick Project, Somerset: A Rural Landscape Explored*, SMA monograph 25, Leeds, 177–83.

Aston, M. A. (2007d) 'Catalogue of Shapwick early maps and surveys', in C. M. Gerrard with M. A. Aston, *The Shapwick Project, Somerset: A Rural Landscape Explored*, SMA monograph 25, Leeds, 1089–92.

Aston, M. A. (2009) 'An early medieval estate in the Isle valley of south Somerset and the early endowments of Muchelney Abbey', *SANH* 152, 83–103.

Aston, M. A. (2010) 'Medieval settlements in Winscombe parish in North Somerset', *SANH* 153, 55–90.

Aston, M. A. and Bond, J. (1976) *The Landscape of Towns*, Dent, London.

Aston, M. A. and Burrow, I. (1982) 'The early Christian centres 600–1000 AD', in M. A. Aston and I. Burrow (eds), *The Archaeology of Somerset: A Review to 1500AD*, Somerset County Council, Taunton, 119–21.

Aston, M. A. and Costen, M. D. eds (1992) *The Shapwick Project: A Topographical and Historical Study. The Third Report*, University of Bristol, Bristol.

Aston, M. A. and Costen, M. D. eds (1993) *The Shapwick Project: A Topographical and Historical Study. The Fourth Report*, University of Bristol, Bristol.

Aston, M. A. and Costen, M. D. eds (1994) *The Shapwick Project: A Topographical and Historical Study. The Fifth Report*, University of Bristol, Bristol.

Aston, M. A. and Gerrard, C. M. eds (1995) *The Shapwick Project: An Archaeological, Historical and Topographical Study. The Sixth Report*, University of Bristol, Bristol.

Aston, M. A. and Gerrard, C. M. (1999) '"Unique, traditional and charming": the Shapwick Project, Somerset', *Antiq. J.* 79, 1–58.

Aston, M. A. and Leech, R. (1977) *Historic Towns in Somerset: Archaeology and Planning*, Committee for Rescue Archaeology in Avon, Gloucestershire and Somerset, Gloucester.

Aston, M. A. and Rowley, T. (1974) *Landscape Archaeology: An Introduction to Fieldwork Techniques on Post-Roman Landscapes*, David and Charles, Newton Abbot.

Aston, M. A., Hall, T. A. and Gerrard, C. M. eds (1998a) *The Shapwick Project: An Archaeological, Historical and Topographical Study. The Eighth Report*, University of Bristol, Bristol.

Aston, M. A., Martin, M. H. and Jackson, A. W. (1998b) 'The potential for heavy soil analysis on low status archaeological sites at Shapwick, Somerset', *Antiquity* 72, 838–47.

Aston, M. A., Costen, M. and Hall, T. (2007a) 'The later medieval furlongs of Shapwick: attempts at mapping the 1515 survey', in C. M. Gerrard with M. A. Aston, *The Shapwick Project, Somerset: A Rural Landscape Explored*, SMA monograph 25, Leeds, 74–101.

Aston, M. with contributions by G. Brown, M. Costen and D. McOmish (2007b) 'Fieldchecking', in C. Gerrard and M. Aston, *The Shapwick Project, Somerset: A Rural Landscape Explored*, SMA monograph 25, Leeds, 109–13.

Athanassopoulos, E. F. (2004) 'Historical archaeology of medieval Mediterranean landscapes', in E. L. Athanassopoulos and L. Wandsnider (eds), *Mediterranean Archaeological Landscapes: Current Issues*, University of Pennsylvania Museum, Philadelphia, 81–98.

Atthill, R. (1967) *The Somerset and Dorset Railway*, David and Charles, Newton Abbot.

Atthill, R. (1970) *Picture History of the Somerset and Dorset Railway*, David and Charles, Newton Abbot.

Audouy, M. and Chapman, A. (2009) *Raunds: The Origins and Growth of a Midland Village, AD 450–1500. Excavations in North Raunds, Northamptonshire 1977–87*, Oxbow Books, Oxford.

Avery, B. W. (1955) *The soils of the Glastonbury District of Somerset. Memoirs of the Soil Survey of Great Britain. Sheet 296*, HMSO, London.

Badham, S. (2005) 'Evidence for the minor funerary monument industry 1100–1500', in K. Giles and C. C. Dyer (eds), *Town and Country in the Middle Ages: Contrasts, Contacts and Interconnections, 1100–1500*, SMA monograph 22, Leeds, 165–95.

Bailey, G. N., Levine, M. A. and Rogers, S. J. Q. (1981) 'Animal remains, Meare Village West 1979', *SLP* 7, 38–44.

Bailey, M. (2002) *The English Manor c.1200–c.1500*, MUP, Manchester.

Baillie, M. G. L. (1995) *A Slice Through Time*, Batsford, London.

Baker, A. R. H. and Butlin, R. A. eds (1973) *Studies of Field Systems in the British Isles*, CUP, Cambridge.

Baker, N. and Holt, R. (2004) *Urban Growth and the Medieval Church*, Ashgate, Gloucester.

Barker, G. (1995) *A Mediterranean Valley: Landscape Archaeology and Annales History in the Biferno Valley*, Leicester University Press, London.

Barley, M. W. (1961) *The English Farmhouse and Cottage*, Routledge, London.

Barlow, F. (1988) *The Feudal Kingdom of England 1042–1216*, Longman, London.

Barnes, G. and Williamson, T. (2006) *Hedgerow History*, Windgather, Macclesfield.

Barnes, T. G. (1961) *Somerset, 1625–1640: A County's Government During the 'Personal Rule'*, OUP, Oxford.

Barrett, J., Freeman, P. W. M. and Woodward, A. (2000) *Cadbury Castle Somerset: The Later Prehistoric and Early Historic Archaeology*, English Heritage Archaeological Report 20, London.

Bassett, S. (1998) *The Origins of the Parishes of the Deerhurst Area*, Deerhurst Lecture 1997, Friends of Deerhurst Church, Bristol.

Bates, E. H. ed. (1907) *Quarter Sessions Records for the County of Somerset, Vol. 1, James I, 1607–1625*, Somerset Record Society 23, London.

Bates, E. H. ed. (1912) *Quarter Sessions Records for the County of Somerset, Vol. 3, Commonwealth, 1646–1660*, Somerset Record Society 28, London.

Batey, M. (1968) 'Nuneham Courtenay: an Oxfordshire 18th-century deserted village', *Oxoniensia* 33, 108–24.

Batey, M. (1970), *Nuneham Courtenay, Oxfordshire: A Short History and Description*, University Chest Estates Committee, Oxford.

Bayley, J. and Butcher, S. (2004) *Roman Brooches in Britain: A Technological and Typological Study Based on the Richborough Collection*, Reports of the Research Committee of the Society of Antiquaries 68, London.

Bazzana, A., Cressier, P. and Guichard, P. (1988) *Les châteaux ruraux d'Al-Andalus*, Casa de Velázquez, Madrid.

Beaumont James, T. and Gerrard, C. M. (2007) *Clarendon: Landscape of Kings*, Windgather Press, Macclesfield.

Beckett, J. (1989) *A History of Laxton: England's Last Open-Field Village*, Blackwell, Oxford.

Beckett, S. C. (1978) 'The environmental setting of the Meare Heath Track', *SLP* 4, 42–6.

Beckett, S. C. and Hibbert, F. A. (1978) 'The influence of man on the vegetation of the Somerset Levels – a summary', *SLP* 4, 86–90.

Beckett, S. C. and Hibbert, F. A. (1979) 'Vegetational change and the influence of prehistoric man in the Somerset Levels', *New Phytol.* 83, 577–600.

Bédarida, F. (1979) *A Social History of England 1851–1990*, Routledge, London.

Beeton, I. (1861) *The Book of Household Management*, S.O. Beeton, London.

Bell, M. (1989) 'Environmental archaeology as an index of continuity and change in the medieval landscape', in M. A. Aston, D. Austin and C. Dyer (eds), *The Rural Settlements of Medieval England*, Blackwell, Oxford, 269–86.

Bell, M. (1990) *Brean Down: Excavations 1983–1987*, English Heritage, London.

Bell, M., Allen, J. R. L., Buckley, S., Dark, P. and Haslett, S. K. (2002) *Goldcliff East Excavation, 2002: Interim Report*, University of Reading.

Bell, T. (2005) *The Religious Reuse of Roman Structures in Early Medieval England*, BAR British Series 390, Archaeopress, Oxford.

Bentley, J. B. and Murless, B. J. (1985) *Somerset Roads: The Legacy of the Turnpikes: Phase 1: Western Somerset*, Somerset Industrial Archaeological Society, Taunton.

Beresford, G. (1975) *The Medieval Clay-land Village: Excavations at Goltho and Barton Blount*, SMA monograph 6, Leeds.

Beresford, G. (1987) *Goltho: The Development of an Early Medieval Manor c850–1150*, English Heritage Archaeological Report 4, London.

Beresford, G. (2009) *Caldecote: The Development and Desertion of a Hertfordshire Village*, SMA monograph 28, Leeds.

Beresford, M. W. (1967) *New Towns of the Middle Ages: Town Plantation in England, Wales and Gascony*, Lutterworth Press, London.

Beresford, M. W. and Finberg, H. P. R. (1973) *English Medieval Boroughs: A Handlist*, David and Charles, Newton Abbot.

Beresford, M. W. and Hurst, J. (1990) *Wharram Percy Deserted Medieval Village*, Batsford/English Heritage, London.

Bernard, G. W. (2005) *The King's Reformation: Henry VIII and the Remaking of the English Church*, Yale University Press, London.

Berstan, R., Stott, A. W., Minnitt, S., Bronk Ramsey, C., Hedges, R. E. M. and Evershed, R. P. (2008) 'Direct dating of pottery from its organic residues: new precision using compound-specific carbon isotopes', *Antiquity* 82, 702–13.

Bettey, J. H. (1987) *Rural Life in Wessex 1500–1900*, Alan Sutton, Gloucester.

Bettey, J. H. (1988) 'The profitability of duck decoys', *Notes and Queries for Somerset and Dorset* 32, 712–14.

Bettey, J. H. (1989) *Suppression of the Monasteries in the West Country*, Alan Sutton, Gloucester.

Bettey, J. H. (1993) *Know the Landscape: Estates and the English Countryside*, Batsford, London.

Bettey, J. H. (1998) 'Shapwick parish records 1712–1765', in M. A. Aston, T. A. Hall and C. M. Gerrard (eds), *The Shapwick Project: An Archaeological, Historical and Topographical Study. The Eighth Report*, University of Bristol, Bristol, 203–5.

Bettey, J. H. (2007a) 'Documentary sources 1539–c1900', in C. M. Gerrard with M. A. Aston, *The Shapwick Project, Somerset: A Rural Landscape Explored*, SMA monograph 25, Leeds, 37–44.

Bettey, J. H. (2007b) 'William Walton of Shapwick: a Star Chamber complaint over his conduct', in C. M. Gerrard with M. A. Aston, *The Shapwick Project, Somerset: A Rural Landscape Explored*, SMA monograph 25, Leeds, 1084–5.

Bettey, J. H. (2007c) 'Shapwick parish records 1712–65', in C. M. Gerrard with M. A. Aston, *The Shapwick Project, Somerset: A Rural Landscape Explored*, SMA monograph 25, Leeds, 1085–6.

Bigland, R. (1791–2) *Historical, Monumental, and Genealogical Collections Relative to the County of Gloucester*, John Nichols, London.

Billingsley, J. (1797) *General View of the Agriculture of the County of Somerset, with Observations on the Means of its Improvement*, R. Cruttwell for the author, Bath.

Bintliff, J. ed. (1991) *The Annales School and Archaeology*, Leicester University Press, London.

Bintliff, J. (2004) 'Time, structure, and agency: the *Annales*, emergent complexity, and archaeology', in J. Bintliff (ed.), *A Companion to Archaeology*, Blackwell, Oxford, 174–94.

Bintliff, J., Howard, P. and Snodgrass, A. M. (1999) 'The hidden landscape of prehistoric Greece', *Journal of Mediterranean Archaeology* 12(2), 139–68.

Bintliff, J., Howard, P. and Snodgrass, A. M. (2007) *Testing the Hinterland: The Work of the Boeotia Survey (1989–1991) in the Southern Approaches to the City of Thespiai*, McDonald Institute monographs, Cambridge.

Blair, J. ed. (1988) *Minsters and Parish Churches: The Local Church in Transition 950–1200*, Oxford University Committee for Archaeology Monograph 17, Oxford.

Blair, J. (1991) *Early Medieval Surrey: Landholding, Church and Settlement before 1300*, Sutton, Stroud.

Blair, J. (1993) 'Hall and chamber: English domestic planning 1000–1250', in G. Meirion-Jones and M. Jones (eds), *Manorial Domestic Buildings in England and Northern France*, Society of Antiquaries of London 15, 1–21.

Blair, J. (1996) 'Palaces or minsters? Northampton and Cheddar reconsidered', *Anglo-Saxon England* 25, 97–121.

Blair, J. (2005) *The Church in Anglo-Saxon Society*, OUP, Oxford.

Blair, J. and Sharpe, R. eds (1992) *Pastoral Care Before the Parish*, Leicester University Press, Leicester.

BNFL (1999) 'The trench connection', *Alpha* 8, 37–8.

Boddington, A. (1996) *Raunds Furnells: The Anglo-Saxon Church and Churchyard*, English Heritage Archaeological Report 7, London.

Body, G. and Gallop, R. (2001) *The Glastonbury Canal*, Fiducia Press, Bristol.

Bohnenberger, C. (1925) 'The settlement of Charlotia (Rolles Town), 1765', *Florida Historical Society Quarterly* July 1925, 43–9.

Bois, G. (1992) *The Transformation of the Year One Thousand*, MUP, Manchester.

Boisseau, S. and Yalden, D. W. (1998) 'The former status of the Crane *Grus grus* in Britain', *Ibis* 140, 482–500.

Bolton, J. L. (1980) *The Medieval English Economy*, Dent, London.

Bond, C. (2003) 'The coming of the earlier Neolithic, pottery and people in the Somerset Levels', in A. M. Gibson (ed.), *Prehistoric Pottery: People, Pattern and Purpose*, BAR International Series 1156/Prehistoric Ceramic Research Group Occasional Publication 4, Oxford, 1–27.

Bond, C. (2007) 'Lithics', in C. M. Gerrard with M. A. Aston, *The Shapwick Project, Somerset: A Rural Landscape Explored*, SMA monograph 25, Leeds, 687–728.

Bond, C. J. (1995) *Medieval Windmills in South Western England*, Society for the Protection of Ancient Buildings, London.

Bond, C. J. (1998) *Somerset Parks and Gardens: A Landscape History*, Somerset Books, Tiverton.

Bond, C. J. (2001) 'Production and consumption of food and drink in the medieval monastery', in G. Keevill, M. A. Aston and T. Hall (eds), *Monastic Archaeology*, Oxbow Books, Oxford, 54–87.

Bond, C. J. (2004) *Monastic Landscapes*, Tempus, Stroud.

Bond, C. J. (2007a) 'Earthwork surveys', in C. M. Gerrard with M. A. Aston, *The Shapwick Project, Somerset: A Rural Landscape Explored*, SMA monograph 25, Leeds, 113–24.

Bond, C. J. (2007b) 'The dovecote at Shapwick Manor School', in C. M. Gerrard with M. A. Aston, *The Shapwick Project, Somerset: A Rural Landscape Explored*, SMA monograph 25, Leeds, 1137–42.

Bond, C. J. and Iles, R. (1991) 'Early gardens in Avon and Somerset', in A. E. Brown (ed.), *Garden Archaeology*, CBA Research Report 78, London, 37–8.

Bond, C. J. and Tiller, K. (1987) *Blenheim: Landscape for a Palace*, Sutton and Oxford University Dept for Continuing Education, Stroud.

Bond, C. J. and Weller, J. B. (1991) 'The Somerset barns of Glastonbury Abbey', in L. Abrams and J. P. Carley (eds), *The Archaeology and History of Glastonbury Abbey*, Boydell Press, Woodbridge, 57–87.

Bonney, D. (1972) 'Early boundaries in Wessex', in P. J. Fowler (ed.), *Archaeology and the Landscape: Essays for L. V. Grinsell*, J. Baker, London, 168–86.

Bourin-Derruau, M. (1987) *Villages médiévaux en Bas-Languedoc: genèse d'une sociabilité (X^e–XIVe siècle)*, Editions L'Harmattan, Paris.

Bowden, M. (1999) *Unravelling the Landscape: An Inquisitive Approach to Archaeology*, Stroud, Tempus.

Bradley, R. J. (1990) *The Passage of Arms: An Archaeological Analysis of Prehistoric Hoards and Votive Deposits*, CUP, Cambridge.

Bradney, J. (2005) 'The carriage-drive in Humphry Repton's landscapes', *Garden History* 33.1, 31–46.

Branigan, K. (1976) 'Villa settlement in the West Country', in K. Branigan and P. J. Fowler (eds), *The Roman West Country: Classical Culture and Celtic Society*, David and Charles, Newton Abbot, 120–42.

Branigan, K. (1977) *The Roman Villa in South-West England*, Moonraker Press, Bradford on Avon.

Bridge, M. and Dunning, R. W. (1981) 'The Abbey Barn, Glastonbury', *SANH* 125, 120.

Brigers, J. L. (2006) 'Report on an archaeological investigation: 'Little Haven', Church Road, Edington, Somerset', unpublished report.

Briggs, A. (1983) *A Social History of England*, Weidenfeld and Nicolson, London.

Britnell, R. (2001) 'Social bonds and economic change', in B. Harvey (ed.), *The Twelfth and Thirteenth Centuries 1066–c.1280*, OUP, Oxford, 101–33.

Britnell, R. (2004) *Britain and Ireland 1050–1530: Economy and Society*, OUP, Oxford.

Brooks, C. and Barry, J. eds (1994) *The Middling Sort of People: Culture, Society and Politics in England, 1550–1800*, Macmillan, Basingstoke.

Brooks, N. (1992) 'The career of St Dunstan', in N. Ramsay, M. Sparks and T. Tatton-Brown (eds), *St Dunstan: His Life, Times and Cult*, Boydell, Woodbridge, 1–23.

Broomhead, R. (1997) 'New Farm, Shapwick 1997: an archaeological evaluation for Mendip Construction Ltd', unpublished typescript report.

Brothwell, D. R. and Pollard, A. M. (2001) *Handbook of Archaeological Sciences*, John Wiley, Chichester and New York.

Brown, A. and Foard, G. (1998) 'The Saxon landscape: a regional perspective', in P. Everson and T. Williamson (eds), *The Archaeology of Landscape: Studies Presented to Christopher Taylor*, MUP, Manchester, 67–94.

Brown, A. G. (1986) 'Flint and chert small finds from the Somerset Levels. Part I: The Brue Valley', *SLP* 12, 12–27.

Brunning, R. (1993) 'Shapwick, ST 42053980', in C. J. Webster and R. A. Croft (eds), 'Somerset Archaeology 1993', *SANH* 137, 137.

Brunning, R. (2007) 'Wood', in C. M. Gerrard with M. A. Aston, *The Shapwick Project, Somerset: A Rural Landscape Explored*, SMA monograph 25, Leeds, 868–9.

Brunning, R. (2010) 'Taming the floodplain: river canalisation and causeway formation in the Middle Anglo-Saxon period at Glastonbury, Somerset', *Medieval Archaeol.* 54, 319–29.

Brunning, R. and Webster, C. (2007) 'Shapwick villa (Field 4649)', in C. M. Gerrard with M. A. Aston, *The Shapwick Project, Somerset: A Rural Landscape Explored*, SMA monograph 25, Leeds, 388–98.

Brunskill, R. W. (1971) *Illustrated Handbook of Vernacular Architecture*, Faber and Faber, London.

Buchanan, C. A. (1987) 'John Bowen and the Bridgwater scandal', *SANH* 131, 181–201.

Bulleid, A. and Jackson, J. W. (1937) 'The burtle sand beds of Somerset', *PSANHS* 83, 171–95.

Burke, E. (1786) *Article of Charge of High Crimes and Misdemeanors, Against Warren Hastings Esq. Late Governor General of Bengal: Presented to the House of Commons, on the 4th Day of April 1786*, Debrett, London.

Burrow, I. (1981) *Hillfort and Hill-top Settlement in Somerset in the First to Eighth Centuries AD*, BAR British Series 91, Oxford.

Burrow, J. W. (1974) '"The village community" and the uses of history in late nineteenth-century England', in N. McKendrick (ed.), *Historical Perspectives: Studies in English Thought and Society*, Europa publications, London, 255–84.

Burrow, J. W. (1981) *A Liberal Descent*, CUP, Cambridge.

Calendar of the Patent Rolls Preserved in the Public Record Office … Edward III … vol. 10 1354–1358 (1898–1916) HMSO, London.

Campbell, B. M. S. (2000) *English Seigniorial Agriculture 1250–1450*, Cambridge Studies in Historical Geography 31, CUP, Cambridge.

Campbell, N. (2000) 'Metal Detecting at Shapwick', unpublished BSc dissertation, King Alfred's College, Winchester.

Campey, L. H. (1989) 'Medieval village plans in county Durham: an analysis of reconstructed plans based on medieval documentary sources', *Northern Hist.* 25, 60–87.

Carley, J. P. (1985) *The Chronicle of Glastonbury Abbey: An Edition, Translation and Study of John of Glastonbury's* Cronica sive Antiquitates Glastoniensis Ecclesie, Boydell, Woodbridge.

Carreté, J. M., Keay, S. and Millett, M. (1995) *A Roman Provincial Capital and its Hinterland: The Survey of the Hinterland of Tarragona, Spain, 1985–1990, J. Roman Archaeol.* Supplementary Series 15, Michigan.

Carruthers, W. (1995) *Charred Plant Remains from the Medieval Farmstead at Eckweek, Avon*, Ancient Monuments Lab Rep 27/95.

Chapman, A. (2010) *West Cotton, Raunds: A Study of Medieval Settlement Dynamics AD 450–1450. Excavation of a Deserted Medieval Hamlet in Northamptonshire 1985–89*, Oxbow Books, Oxford.

Chapman, H. (2006) *Landscape Archaeology and GIS*, Tempus, Stroud.

Chapman, J. and Seeliger, S. (2001) *Enclosure, Environment and Landscape in Southern England*, Tempus, Stroud.

Cherry, B. and Pevsner, N. (1989) *Buildings of England: Devon*, Penguin, London.

Cherry, J. F., Davis, J. L. and Montzourani, E. (1991) *Landscape Archaeology as Long-term History: Northern Keos in Cycladic Islands from Earliest Settlement until Modern Times*, UCLA Institute of Archaeology, Los Angeles.

Chisholm, M. (1979) *Rural Settlement and Land Use: An Essay in Location*, Hutchinson, London.

Clayton, M. (1990) *The Cult of the Virgin Mary in Anglo-Saxon England*, CUP, Cambridge.

Clayton, T. (2004) 'Bonnor, Thomas (c.1743–1807×12)', *Oxford Dictionary of National Biography*, OUP, Oxford <http://www.oxforddnb.com/view/article/2854>, accessed 21 March 2012.

Clements, D. and Alexander, K. N. A. (2007) 'A comparative study of the invertebrate faunas of hedgerows of differing ages', in C. M. Gerrard with M. A. Aston, *The Shapwick Project, Somerset: A Rural Landscape Explored*, SMA monograph 25, Leeds, 332–41.

Clements, D. and Alexander, K. N. A. (2009) 'A comparative study of the invertebrate faunas of hedgerows of differing ages, with particular reference to indicators of ancient woodland and 'old growth', *Journal of Practical Ecology and Conservation* 8(2), 7–27.

Cliffe, J. T. (1999) *The World of the Country House in Seventeenth-century England*, Yale University Press, New Haven and London.

Coates, R. (1999) 'New light from old wicks: the progeny of Latin *vicus*', *Nomina* 22, 75–116.

Coffey, J. (2000) *Persecution and Toleration in Protestant England 1558–1689*, Pearson, London.

Coleman-Smith, R. and Pearson, T. (1988) *Excavations in the Donyatt Potteries*, Phillimore, Chichester.

Coles, B. J. and Coles, J. M. (1986) *Sweet Track to Glastonbury: The Somerset Levels in Prehistory*, Thames and Hudson, London.

Coles, J. M. (1982) 'Prehistory in the Somerset levels 4000–100BC', in M. A. Aston and I. Burrow (eds), *The Archaeology of Somerset*, Somerset County Council, Taunton, 29–41.

Coles, J. M. (1989a) 'The Somerset Levels Project 1973–1989', *SLP* 15, 5–14.

Coles, J. M. (1989b) 'Prehistoric settlement in the Somerset Levels', *SLP* 15, 14–33.

Coles, J. M. and Coles, B. J. (1990) 'Part II: the Sweet Track date', *Antiquity* 64, 216–20.

Coles, J. M. and Minnitt, S. (1995) *'Industrious and fairly civilized': The Glastonbury Lake Village*, Short Run Press, Somerset Levels Project and Somerset County Council Museums Service, Exeter.

Coles, J. M. and Orme, B. J. (1984) 'Ten excavations along the Sweet Track (3200 BC), *SLP* 10, 5–45.

Colgrave, B. and Mynors, R. A. B. eds (1969) *Bede's Ecclesiastical History of the English People*, OUP, Oxford.

Collingwood, R. G. (1929) 'Town and country in Roman Britain', *Antiquity* 3, 261–76.

Collingwood, R. G. and Myers, J. N. L. (1936) *Roman Britain and the English Settlements*, Clarendon Press, Oxford.

Collins, R. and Gerrard, J. (2004) *Debating Late Antiquity in Britain AD 300–700*, BAR British Series 365, Archaeopress, Oxford.

Collinson, J. (1791) *The History and Antiquities of the County of Somerset*, R. Cruttwell, Bath.

Conzen, M. R. G. (1960) *Alnwick, Northumberland: A Study in Town-plan Analysis*, Institute of British Geographers Publication 27, George Philip and Son, London.

Conzen, M. R. G. (1968) 'The use of town plans in the study of urban history', in H. J. Dyos (ed.), *The Study of Urban History*, Edward Arnold, London, 113–30.

Cool, H. E. M. (2006) *Eating and Drinking in Roman Britain*, CUP, Cambridge.

Cooper, N. and Priest, V. (2003) 'Sampling a medieval village in a day: the Big Dig Investigation at Great Easton, Leicestershire', *Medieval Set. Res. Group Annu. Rep.* 18, 53–6.

Corcos, N. (1982) 'Shapwick: the enclosure of a Somerset parish, 1515–1839', unpublished MA thesis, Department of English Local History, University of Leicester.

Corcos, N. (1983) 'Early estates on the Poldens and the origins of settlement at Shapwick', *SANH* 127, 47–54.

Corcos, N. (2002) *The Affinities and Antecedents of Medieval Settlement: Topographical Perspectives from Three of the Somerset Hundreds*, BAR British Series 337, Oxford.

Corcos, N. (2007) 'Enclosure at Shapwick: a brief history 1515–1839', in C. M. Gerrard with M. A. Aston, *The Shapwick Project, Somerset: A Rural Landscape Explored*, SMA monograph 25, Leeds, 101–7.

Corse, C. C. (1928) 'Denys Rolle and Rollestown, a pioneer for Utopia', *Florida Historical Society Quarterly* October 1928.

Cosgrove, B. and Daniels, S. (1988) *The Iconography of Landscape*, CUP, Cambridge.

Costen, M. D. (1991) 'Some evidence for new settlements and field systems in late Anglo-Saxon Somerset', in L. Abrams and J. P. Carley (eds), *The Archaeology and History of Glastonbury Abbey*, Boydell Press, Woodbridge, 39–55.

Costen, M. D. (1992a) *The Origins of Somerset*, MUP, Manchester.

Costen, M. D. (1992b) 'Huish and Worth: Old English survivals in a later landscape', in W. Filmer-Sankey (ed.), *Anglo-Saxon Studies in Archaeology and History 5*, Oxford University Committee for Archaeology, Oxford, 65–83.

Costen, M. D. (1993) 'Habitative field-names: a survey of the material for Shapwick', in M. Aston and M. D. Costen (eds), *The Shapwick Project: A Topographical and Historical Study. The Fourth Report*, University of Bristol, Bristol, 94–100.

Costen, M. D. (2007a) 'The early Middle Ages', in C. M. Gerrard with M. A. Aston, *The Shapwick Project, Somerset: A Rural Landscape Explored*, SMA monograph 25, Leeds, 26–31.

Costen, M. D. (2007b) 'Abbot Beere's terrier of 1515', in C. M. Gerrard with M. A. Aston, *The Shapwick Project, Somerset: A Rural Landscape Explored*, SMA monograph 25, Leeds, 1061–72.

Costen, M. D. (2007c) 'Documents relating to the old church at Shapwick', in C. M. Gerrard with M. A. Aston, *The Shapwick Project, Somerset: A Rural Landscape Explored*, SMA monograph 25, Leeds, 1051–3.

Costen, M. D. (2007d) 'Medieval surveys of Shapwick', in C. M. Gerrard with M. A. Aston, *The Shapwick Project, Somerset: A Rural Landscape Explored*, SMA monograph 25, Leeds, 1053–4.

Costen, M. D. (2007e) 'Field names of Shapwick', in C. M. Gerrard with M. A. Aston, *The Shapwick Project, Somerset: A Rural Landscape Explored*, SMA monograph 25, Leeds, 1078–84.

Costen, M. D. (2007f) 'A survey of the manor of Shapwick in 1325', in C. M. Gerrard with M. A. Aston, *The Shapwick Project, Somerset: A Rural Landscape Explored*, SMA monograph 25, Leeds, 1056–61.

Costen, M. D. (2007g) 'Early charters and Domesday Book for Shapwick', in C. M. Gerrard with M. A. Aston, *The Shapwick Project, Somerset: A Rural Landscape Explored*, SMA monograph 25, Leeds, 1049–51.

Costen, M. D. and Ecclestone, M. R. (2007) 'Abbot Beere's Terrier, BL Egerton 3134: the bounds of Shapwick', in C. M. Gerrard with M. A. Aston, *The Shapwick Project, Somerset: A Rural Landscape Explored*, SMA monograph 25, Leeds, 1097–100.

Coulson, H. J. W. (1898–9) 'On cider-making in Devonshire', *Journal of the Bath and West Society* VIII, 92–6.

Coulthard, A. J. and Watts, M. (1978) *Windmills of Somerset and the Men who Worked Them*, Research Publishing Co., London.

Cox, B. (1976) 'The place names of the earliest English Records', *Engl. Place-Name Soc. J.* 8, 12–66.

Cramp, R. (2005) *Wearmouth and Jarrow Monastic Sites*, English Heritage, Swindon.

Creighton, J. (2001) *Britannia: The Creation of a Roman Province*, Routledge, London.

Cressy, S. (1668) *The Church-history of Brittany from the Beginning of Christianity to the Norman Conquest under Roman Governours, British Kings, the English-Saxon Heptarchy, the English–Saxon (and Danish) Monarchy…*, Rouen.

Crossley, D. (1990) *Post-Medieval Archaeology in Britain*, Leicester University Press, London.

Crowther, J. (1997) 'Soil phosphate surveys: critical approaches to sampling, analysis and interpretation', *Archaeological Prospection* 4, 93–102.

Crummy, P. (1984) *Excavations at Lion Walk, Balkerne Lane and Middleborough, Colchester, Essex*, Colchester Archaeological Report 3, Colchester.

Cumberpatch, C. G. (2006) 'Face to face with medieval pottery: some observations on medieval anthropomorphic pottery in north-east England', *Assemblage* 9, <http://www.assemblage.group.shef.ac.uk/issue9/cumberpatch.html>, accessed 11 April 2012.

Cummings, V. (2000) 'Myth, memory and metaphor: the significance of place, space and the landscape in Mesolithic Pembrokeshire', in R. Young (ed.), *Mesolithic Lifeways: Current Research from Britain and Ireland*, Leicester Archaeology monographs 7, University of Leicester, Leicester, 87–95.

Cunliffe, B. and Davenport, P. (1985) *The Temple of Sulis Minerva at Bath: Volume 1. The Site*, Oxford University Committee for Archaeology Monograph 7, Oxford.

Cunliffe, B. W. (1972) 'Saxon and medieval settlement in the region of Chalton, Hampshire', *Medieval Archaeol.* XVI, 1–12.

Cunliffe, B. W. (1987) *Hengistbury Head, Dorset, vol 1: The Prehistoric and Roman Settlement 3500 BC–AD 500*, Oxford University Committee for Archaeology monograph 13, Oxford.

Cunliffe, B. W. (1993) *Wessex to AD 1000*, Longman, London.

Cunliffe, B. W. (2000) *The Danebury Environs Programme: The Prehistory of a Wessex Landscape. Vol 1: Introduction*, Oxford University Committee for Archaeology monograph 48, English Heritage and Oxford University Committee for Archaeology, Oxford.

Cunliffe, B. W. (2005) *Iron Age Communities in Britain*, Routledge, London.

Dallimore, J. J. (2005) 'Farm buildings and farmsteads', in J. Penoyre, *Traditional Houses of Somerset*, Somerset Books, Somerset County Council, 135–56.

Dallimore, J., Penoyre, J. and Penoyre, J. (and members of the Somerset and South Avon Vernacular Buildings Research Group) (1994) 'Shapwick houses and farms: a review of surveys made up to 1993', in M. A. Aston and M. D. Costen (eds), *The Shapwick Project: A Topographical and Historical Study. The Fifth Report*, University of Bristol, Dept of Continuing Education, 89–118.

Daniell, C. (1997) *Death and Burial in Medieval England, 1066–1550*, Routledge, London.

Darby, H. C. (1977) *Domesday Geography of England*, CUP, Cambridge.

Dark, K. (1994a) *Civitas to Kingdom: British Political Continuity 300–800*, Leicester University Press, London.

Dark, K. and Dark, P. (1997) *The Landscape of Roman Britain*, Sutton, Stroud.

Dark, K. R. (1994b) *Discovery by Design: The Identification of Secular Elite Settlements in Western Britain AD 400–700*, BAR British Series 237, Tempus Reparatum, Oxford.

Dark, P. (1996) 'Palaeoecological evidence for landscape continuity and change in Britain ca AD 400–800', in K. R. Dark (ed.), *External Contacts and the Economy of Late Roman and Post-Roman Britain*, Boydell, Woodbridge, 23–51.

Dark, P. (2000) *The Environment of Britain in the 1st Millennium AD*, Duckworth, London.

Darvill, T., Gerrard, C. M. and Startin, B. (1993) 'Identifying and protecting historic landscapes', *Antiquity* 67, 563–74.

Davey, J. E. (2005) *The Roman to Medieval Transition in the Region of South Cadbury Castle, Somerset*, BAR British Series 399, Archaeopress, Oxford.

David, A. (1995) *Geophysical Survey in Archaeological Field Evaluation*, English Heritage Research and Professional Services Guidelines No. 1, English Heritage, London.

David, A. (2006) 'Finding sites', in J. Balme and A. Paterson (eds), *Archaeology in Practice: A Student Guide to Archaeological Analyses*, Blackwell, Oxford.

Davies, A. (2000) *The Quakers in English Society 1655–1725*, Clarendon Press, Oxford.

Davis, N. Z. (1983) *The Return of Martin Guerre*, Harvard University Press, Cambridge, MA.

Davies, O. (2003) *Cunning-folk: Popular Magic in English History*, Hambledon and London, London.

Dawson, D. (1998) 'The coins', in R. Price and M. Ponsford, *St Batholomew's Hospital, Bristol*, CBA Research Report 10, York, 174–5.

De Moulins, D. (2007) 'The weeds from the thatch roofs of medieval cottages from the south of England', *Vegetation History and Archaeology* 16(5), 365–98.

Dearne, M. J. and Branigan, K. (1995) 'The use of coal in Roman Britain', *Antiq. J.* 75, 71–105.

Dewar, H. S. L. and Godwin, H. (1963) 'Archaeological discoveries in the raised bogs of the Somerset Levels, England', *Proc. Prehist. Soc.* 29, 17–49.

Dick, O. L. (1958) *Aubrey's Brief Lives*, Secker and Warburg, London.

Dickinson, F. H. (1889) *Kirby's Quest for Somerset*, Somerset Record Society vol. 3, Taunton.

Dix, B. (1982) 'The manufacture of lime and its uses in the western Roman provinces', *Oxford J. Archaeol.* 1(3), 331–45.

Dobney, K., Barrett, J. and Jaques, D. (2007) *Farmers, Monks and Aristocrats: The Environmental Archaeology of Anglo-Saxon Flixborough*, Oxbow Books, Oxford.

Dodgson, J. (1966) 'The significance of the distribution of the English place-name in -ingas, -inga- in south-east England', *Medieval Archaeol.* X, 1–29.

DoE (1990) *Planning Policy Guidance 16: Archaeology and Planning*, HMSO, London.

Doggett, N. (2001) 'The demolition and conversion of former monastic buildings in post-Dissolution Herefordshire', in G. Keevill, M. Aston and T. Hall (eds), *Monastic Archaeology*, Oxbow Books, Oxford, 165–74.

Draper, J. (1984) *Post-medieval Pottery, 1650–1800*, Shire, Aylesbury.

Draper, S. (2002) 'Old English *wic* and *walh*: Britons and Saxons in post-Roman Wiltshire', *Landscape Hist.* 24, 27–43.

Draper, S. (2004) 'Landscape, settlement and society: Wiltshire in the first millennium AD', unpublished PhD thesis, Archaeology Department, Durham University, Durham.

Draper, S. (2006) *Landscape Settlement and Society in Roman and Early Medieval Wiltshire*, BAR British Series 419, Archaeopress, Oxford.

Duffy, E. (1992) *The Stripping of the Altars: Traditional*

Religion in England, c.1400–c.1580, Yale University Press, New Haven.

Dunning, R. W. (1976) *Christianity in Somerset*, Somerset County Council, Taunton.

Dunning, R. W. (1984) *The Monmouth Rebellion: A Complete Guide to the Rebellion and Bloody Assizes*, Dovecote Press, Wimborne.

Dunning, R. W. (2004a) 'Collinson, John (1757–1793)', *Oxford Dictionary of National Biography*, OUP, Oxford <http://www.oxforddnb.com/view/article/5963>, accessed 21 March 2012.

Dunning, R. W. (2004b) 'Bere, Richard (c.1455–1525)', *Oxford Dictionary of National Biography*, OUP, Oxford <http://www.oxforddnb.com/view/article/2188>, accessed 21 March 2012.

Dyer, C. (1986) 'English peasant buildings in the later Middle Ages', *Medieval Archaeol.* 30, 19–45.

Dyer, C. (1989) *Standards of Living in the Later Middle Ages: Social Change in England c.1200–1520*, CUP, Cambridge.

Dyer, C. (1994) *Everyday Life in Medieval England*, Hambledon Press, London.

Dyer, C. (1998) 'Peasants and coins: the uses of money in the Middle Ages', *Brit. Numis. J.* 67, 31–47.

Dyer, C. (2002) *Making a Living in the Middle Ages: The People of Britain 850–1520*, Yale University Press, New Haven and London.

Dyer, C. (2006) 'Were late medieval English villages "self-contained"?' in C. Dyer (ed.), *The Self-contained Village? The Social History of Rural Communities 1250–1900*, Centre for English Local History, University of Leicester, University of Hertfordshire Press, Hatfield.

Dyer, C. (2010) 'The crisis of the early fourteenth century. Some material evidence from Britain', in D. Boisseuil, P. Chastang, L. Feller and J. Morsel (eds), *Écritures de l'espace social. Mélanges d'histoire médiévale offerts à Monique Bourin*, Sorbonne, Paris, 491–506.

Eagles, B. (2001) 'Anglo-Saxon presence and culture in Wiltshire AD c.450–c.675', in P. Ellis (ed.), *Roman Wiltshire and After: Papers in Honour of Ken Annable*, Wiltshire Archaeological and Natural History Society 1, Devizes, 199–233.

Earle, T. K. (2004) 'Culture matters in the Neolithic transition and emergence of hierarchy in Thy, Denmark: distinguished lecture', *American Anthropologist* 106, 111–25.

Earwood, C. (1997) 'Bog butter: a two thousand year history', *J. Irish Hist.* 8, 25–42.

Ecclestone, M. R. (1996) 'Dairy production on the Glastonbury Abbey demesnes 1258–1334', unpublished MA dissertation, University of Bristol.

Ecclestone, M. (2007a) 'Field names in the Shapwick court rolls', in C. Gerrard with M. Aston, *The Shapwick Project, Somerset: A Rural Landscape Explored*, SMA Monograph 25, Appendix 8, Leeds, 1074–7.

Ecclestone, M. (2007b) 'Later medieval documentary sources', in C. Gerrard with M. Aston, *The Shapwick Project, Somerset: A Rural Landscape Explored*, SMA Monograph 25, Leeds, 31–7.

Ecclestone, M. (2007c) 'The Shapwick demesne accounts', in C. Gerrard with M. Aston, *The Shapwick Project, Somerset: A Rural Landscape Explored*, SMA Monograph 25, Appendix 7, Leeds, 1072–3.

Ecclestone, M. (2007d) 'The Shapwick survey of c.1260', in C. Gerrard with M. Aston, *The Shapwick Project, Somerset: A Rural Landscape Explored*, SMA Monograph 25, Appendix 4, Leeds, 1054–5.

Ecclestone, M. (2007e) 'Using medieval surveys to locate furlongs', in C. Gerrard with M. Aston, *The Shapwick Project, Somerset: A Rural Landscape Explored*, SMA Monograph 25, Appendix 20, Leeds, 1100–102.

Edmonds, M. R. (1995) *Stone Tools and Society: Working Stone in Neolithic and Bronze Age Britain*, Batsford, London.

Edwards, H. (1988) *The Charters of the Early West Saxon Kingdom*, BAR British Series 198, Oxford.

Edwards, P. (1993) *Rural Life: Guide to Local Records*, Batsford, London.

Egan, G. and Pritchard, F. (1991) *Dress Accessories c.1150–c.1450*, Medieval Finds from Excavations in London 3, HMSO, London.

Ehwald, R. (1961) *Aldhelmi Opera, Monumenta Germaniae Historica*, Druckerei Hildebrand, Berlin.

Ekwall, E. (1960) *The Concise Oxford Dictionary of English Place-names*, Clarendon Press, Oxford.

Ellis, P. (1982) 'Excavations at Silver Street, Glastonbury, 1978', *SANH* 126, 17–38.

Ellison, A. (1982) 'Bronze Age Societies 2000–650 BC', in M. A. Aston and I. Burrow (eds), *The Archaeology of Somerset*, Somerset County Council, Taunton.

Ellison, A. (1983) *Medieval Villages in South-east Somerset*, Western Archaeological Trust Survey 6, Bristol.

Elworthy, G. and Elworthy, A. (1971) *A Power in the Land: Churchill Julius, 1847–1938*, Whitcombe and Tombs, Christchurch, New Zealand.

Emery, A. (2006) *Greater Medieval Houses of England and Wales, 1300–1500, Volume III. Southern England*, CUP, Cambridge.

English, J. (2002) '*Worths* in a landscape context', *Landscape Hist.* 24, 45–51.

English Heritage (2004) *Guidelines on Producing and Interpreting Dendrochronology Dates* <www.helm.org.uk/upload/pdf/Dendrochronology.pdf>, accessed 21 March 2012.

English Heritage (2006) *Archaeomagnetic Dating: Guidelines on Producing and Interpreting Archaeomagnetic Dates* <http://www.english-heritage.org.uk/publications/archaeomagnetic-dating-guidelines/>, accessed 21 March 2012.

Esmonde Cleary, S. (2000) 'Putting the dead in their place: burial location in Roman Britain', in J. Pearce, M. Millett and M. Struck (eds), *Burial, Society and Context in the Roman World*, Oxbow Books, Oxford, 127–42.

Fairbrother, J. R. (1990) *Faccombe Netherton: Excavations of a Saxon and Medieval Manorial Complex*, British Museum Occasional Paper 74, London.

Faith, R. (1997) *The English Peasantry and the Growth of Lordship*, Leicester University Press, London.

Faulkner, N. (2002) 'The debate about the end: a review of evidence and methods', *Archaeol. J.* 159, 59–76.

Field, J. (1972) *English Field Names: A Dictionary*, Alan Sutton, Gloucester.

Finberg, H. P. R. (1964) *The Early Charters of Wessex*, Leicester University Press, Leicester.

Finch, J. (2003) 'A reformation of meaning: commemoration and remembering the dead in the parish church, 1450–1640', in D. Gaimster and R. Gilchrist (eds), *The Archaeology of Reformation 1480–1580*, Society for Medieval Archaeology and Society for Post-Medieval Archeology, Maney, Leeds, 437–49.

Finch, J. (2007) 'Pallas, Flora and Ceres: landscape priorities and improvement on the Castle Howard estate, 1699–1880', in J. Finch and K. Giles (eds), *Estate Landscapes: Design, Improvement and Power in the Post-medieval Landscape*, Society for Post-Medieval Archaeology monograph 4, Boydell and Brewer, Woodbridge, 19–37.

Finn, R. W. (1973) *Domesday Book: A Guide*, Phillimore, London.

Fleming, A. (1987) 'Coaxial field systems: some questions of time and space', *Antiquity* 61, 188–202.

Fleming, A. (1998) *Swaledale: Valley of the Wild River*, Edinburgh University Press, Edinburgh.

Fleming, R. (2003) 'Lords and Labour', in W. Davies (ed.), *From the Vikings to the Normans*, OUP, Oxford, 107–32.

Floyd, R. (2004) '449 and all that: nineteenth- and twentieth-century interpretations of the "Anglo-Saxon invasion" of Britain', in H. Brocklehurst and R. Phillips (eds), *History, Nationhood and the Question of Britain*, Palgrave Macmillan, Basingstoke, 184–96.

Foard, G. (1978) 'Systematic fieldwalking and the investigation of Saxon settlement in Northamptonshire', *World Archaeol.* 9(3), 357–74.

Ford, W. J. (1979) 'Some settlement patterns in the central region of the Warwickshire Avon', in P. H. Sawyer (ed.), *English Medieval Settlement*, Edward Arnold, London, 143–63.

Fossier, R. (1982) *Enfance de l'Europe*, 2 vols, Presses Universitaires de France, Paris.

Fowler, P. J. (2000) *Landscape Plotted and Pieced: Landscape History and Local Archaeology in Fyfield and Overton, Wiltshire*, Society of Antiquaries, London.

Fowler, P. J. (2002) *Farming in the First Millennium AD*, CUP, Cambridge.

Fowler, P. J. and Blackwell, I. (1998) *The Land of Lettice Sweetapple: An English Countryside Explored*, Tempus, Stroud.

Fox, H. S. A. (1973) 'Going to town in 13th-century England', in A. R. H. Baker and J. B. Harley (eds), *Man Made the Land: Essays in English Historical Geography*, David and Charles, Newton Abbot, 69–78.

Fox, H. S. A. (1981) 'Approaches to the adoption of the Midland System', in T. Rowley (ed.), *The Origins of Open-field Agriculture*, Croom Helm, London, 64–111.

Fox, H. S. A. (1986) 'The alleged transformation from two-field to three-field systems in medieval England', *Econ. Hist. Rev.* 4, 2nd series 39, 526–48.

Friar, S. (1991) *The Batsford Companion to Local History*, Batsford, London.

Gaffney, C. F. and Gater, J. A. (2003) *Revealing the Buried Past: Geophysics for Archaeologists*, Tempus, Stroud.

Gaffney, V. and Tingle, M. (1989) *The Maddle Farm Project: An Integrated Survey of Prehistoric and Roman Landscapes on the Berkshire Downs*, BAR British Series 200, Oxford.

Gaffney, C. F., Gater, J. A. and Shiel, D. (2007) 'Geophysical survey Part 2', in C. M. Gerrard with M. A. Aston, *The Shapwick Project, Somerset: A Rural Landscape Explored*, SMA monograph 25, Leeds, 213–28.

Gaimster, D. (1997) *German Stoneware 1200–1900: Archaeology and Cultural History*, British Museum Press, London.

Gaimster, D. and Gilchrist, R. eds (2003) *he Archaeology of the Reformation 1480–1580*, SMA and SPMA monograph, Maney, Leeds.

Gale, R. (2007) 'Charcoal', in C. M. Gerrard with M. A. Aston, *The Shapwick Project, Somerset: A Rural Landscape Explored*, SMA monograph 25, Leeds, 889–94.

Gardiner, M. (2000) 'Vernacular buildings and the development of the later medieval domestic plan in England', *Medieval Archaeol.* XLIV, 159–80.

Gardiner, M. (2006) 'Review of medieval settlement research, 1996–2006', *Medieval Set. Res. Group Annu. Rep.* 21, 22–8.

Gardiner, M. (2007) 'The origins and persistence of manor houses in England', in M. Gardiner and S. Rippon (eds), *Medieval Landscapes*, Windgather, Macclesfield, 170–82.

Garmondsway, G. N. (1953) *The Anglo-Saxon Chronicle*, Dent, London.

Geake, H. (1997) *The Use of Grave Goods in Conversion-Period England, c600–c850*, BAR British Series 261, Archaeopress, Oxford.

Gelling, M. (1974) 'The chronology of English place-names', in T. Rowley (ed.), *Anglo-Saxon Settlement and Landscape*, BAR British Series 6, Oxford, 93–101.

Gelling, M. (1988; 2nd edn) *Signposts to the Past*, Phillimore, Chichester.

Gelling, M. and Cole, A. (2000) *The Landscape of Place-names*, Shaun Tyas, Stamford.

Gerard, T. (1633; 1900) *The Particular Description of Somerest, 1633*, E. H. Bates (ed.), Somerset Record Society 15, Frome.

Gerrard, C. M. (1987) 'Trade and settlement in medieval Somerset', unpublished PhD thesis, University of Bristol.

Gerrard, C. M. (1997) 'Misplaced faith? Medieval pottery and fieldwalking', *Medieval Ceram.* 21, 61–72.

Gerrard, C. M. (1999) 'A 'Malling' maiolica jug from Shapwick House, Somerset', in D. Gaimster (ed.), *Maiolica in the North: The Archaeology of Tin-glazed Earthenware in North-west Europe c.1500–1600*, British Museum Occasional Paper 12, London, 171–3.

Gerrard, C. M. (2003) *Medieval Archaeology: Understanding Traditions and Contemporary Approaches*, Routledge, London.

Gerrard, C. M. (2007a) 'Excavations at and near Church Field', in C. M. Gerrard with M. A. Aston, *The Shapwick Project, Somerset: A Rural Landscape Explored*, SMA monograph 25, Leeds, 405–47.

Gerrard, C. M. (2007b) 'Excavations in Shapwick Park 1992–7', in C. M. Gerrard with M. A. Aston, *The Shapwick Project, Somerset: A Rural Landscape Explored*, SMA monograph 25, Leeds, 503–36.

Gerrard, C. M. (2007c) 'Excavations in Shapwick House mansion 1993–97', in C. M. Gerrard with M. A. Aston, *The Shapwick Project, Somerset: A Rural Landscape Explored*, SMA monograph 25, Leeds, 537–62.

Gerrard, C. M. (2007d) 'Excavations in Shapwick village 1994–99', in C. M. Gerrard with M. A. Aston, *The Shapwick Project, Somerset: A Rural Landscape Explored*, SMA monograph 25, Leeds, 449–501.

Gerrard, C. M. (2007e) 'A rural landscape explored: people, settlement and land use at Shapwick from prehistory to the present day', in C. M. Gerrard with M. A. Aston, *The Shapwick Project, Somerset: A Rural Landscape Explored*, SMA monograph 25, Leeds, 937–1012.

Gerrard, C. M. (2007f) 'Methods and sampling strategies: an evaluation', in C. M. Gerrard with M. A. Aston, *The Shapwick Project, Somerset: A Rural Landscape Explored*, SMA monograph 25, Leeds, 349–53.

Gerrard, C. M. (2009) 'The study of the deserted medieval village: Caldecote in context', in G. Beresford, *Caldecote: The Development and Desertion of a Hertfordshire Village*, SMA monograph 28, Leeds, 1–20.

Gerrard, C. M. and Aston, M. A. eds (1997) *The Shapwick Project: An Archaeological, Historical and Topographical Study. The Seventh Report*, University of Bristol, Bristol.

Gerrard, C. M. with Aston, M. A. (2007) *The Shapwick Project, Somerset: A Rural Landscape Explored*, SMA monograph 25, Leeds.

Gerrard, C. M. and Norcott, D. (2000) 'Un mystère très British? Un village medieval dans le cyberspace', *Archéologia* 367, 46–54.

Gerrard, C. M. and Youngs, S. M. (1997) 'A bronze socketed mount and blade from Shapwick House, Somerset', *Medieval Archaeol.* 41, 210–14.

Gerrard, C. M. and Youngs, S. M. (2007) 'A bronze socketed mount and blade', in C. M. Gerrard with M. A. Aston, *The Shapwick Project, Somerset: A Rural Landscape Explored*, SMA monograph 25, Leeds, 761–3.

Gerrard, C. M. with Aston, M. A. and Hall, T. (2007a) 'Gardens survey and other surface collections', in C. M. Gerrard with M. A. Aston, *The Shapwick Project, Somerset: A Rural Landscape Explored*, SMA monograph 25, Leeds, 261–5.

Gerrard, C. M. with Aston, M. A., Costen, M. D. and Hall, T. (2007b) 'Hand-dug test-pits', in C. M. Gerrard with M. A. Aston, *The Shapwick Project, Somerset: A Rural Landscape Explored*, SMA monograph 25, Leeds, 244–61.

Gerrard, C. M. with Clogg, P. and Passmore, A. (2007c) 'Metalworking residues, coal and cinders', in C. M. Gerrard with M. A. Aston, *The Shapwick Project, Somerset: A Rural Landscape Explored*, SMA monograph 25, Leeds, 829–37.

Gerrard, C. M. with Brunning, R. and Webster, C. (2007d) 'Excavations in the outlying parish 1995–9', in C. M. Gerrard with M. A. Aston, *The Shapwick Project, Somerset: A Rural Landscape Explored*, SMA monograph 25, Leeds, 361–403.

Gerrard, C. M. with Aston, M. A., Gidney, L., Gutiérrez, A. and King, A. (2007e) 'Fieldwalking', in C. M. Gerrard with M. A. Aston, *The Shapwick Project, Somerset: A Rural Landscape Explored*, SMA monograph 25, Leeds, 124–77.

Gerrard, J. (2004) 'How late is late? Pottery and the fifth century in southwest Britain', in R. Collins and J. Gerrard (eds), *Debating Late Antiquity in Britain AD*

300–700, BAR British Series 365, Oxford, 65–75.

Gibson, J. and Rogers, C. (1993) *Poor Law Union Records Vol. 3 – South-West England, the Marches and Wales*, Federation of Family History Societies, Bury.

Gidney, L. J. (2007) 'Animal bone', in C. M. Gerrard with M. A. Aston, *The Shapwick Project, Somerset: A Rural Landscape Explored*, SMA monograph 25, Leeds, 895–922.

Gilchrist, R. and Sloane, B. (2005) *Requiem: The Medieval Monastic Cemetery in Britain*, Museum of London Archaeology Service, London.

Gingell, C. (1982) 'Excavation of an Iron Age enclosure at Groundwell, Blunsdon St Andrew, 1976–7', *Wiltshire Archaeol. Natur. Hist. Mag.* 76, 33–75.

Ginzburg, C. (1980) *The Cheese and the Worms: The Cosmos of a Sixteenth Century Miller*, John Hopkins University Press, Baltimore.

Gittos, B. and Gittos, M. (2001) 'Discussion and dating', in W. Rodwell (ed.), *Wells Cathedral: Excavations and Structural Studies 1978–93*, English Heritage Archaeological Report 21, London, 495–501.

Glasscock, R. ed. (1992) *Historic Landscapes from the Air*, CUP, Cambridge.

Glick, T. F. (1995) *From Muslim Fortress to Christian Castle: Social and Cultural Change in Medieval Spain*, MUP, Manchester.

Godwin, H. (1960) 'Prehistoric wooden trackways of the Somerset Levels: their construction, age and relation to climatic change', *Proc. Prehist. Soc.* 26, 1–36.

Gowland, R. L. (2001) 'Playing dead: implications of mortuary evidence for the social construction of childhood in Roman Britain', in G. Davies, A. Gardner and K. Lockyear (eds), *TRAC 2000, Proceedings of the Tenth Annual Theoretical Roman Archaeology Conference London 2000*, Oxbow Books, Oxford, 152–68.

Gowland, R. L. and Chamberlain, A. T. (2002) 'A Bayesian approach to ageing perinatal skeletal material from archaeological sites: implications for the evidence for infanticide in Roman Britain', *J. Archaeol. Sci.* 29, 677–85.

Grant, E. (1988) 'Marine and river fishing in medieval Somerset: fish bone evidence from Langport', in M. A. Aston (ed.), *Medieval Fish, Fisheries and Fishponds in England*, BAR British Series 182 (i–ii), BAR, Oxford, 409–16.

Graves, C. P. (2000) *The Form and Fabric of Belief: An Archaeology of the Lay Experience of Religion in Medieval Norfolk and Devon*, BAR British Series 311, Oxford.

Gray, H. L. (1915) *English Field Systems*, Harvard University Press, Cambridge, MA.

Gregson, N. (1985) 'The multiple estate model: some critical questions', *J. Hist. Geogr.* 11, 339–51.

Greig, J. R. A. (1986) 'The archaeobotany of the Cowick

medieval moat and some thoughts on moat studies', *Circaea* 4(1), 43.

Grenville, J. (1997) *Medieval Housing*, Leicester University Press, London.

Griffiths, D. (2003) 'Exchange, Trade and Urbanization', in W. Davies (ed.), *From the Vikings to the Normans*, OUP, Oxford, 73–104.

Grundy, G. B. (1935) *The Saxon Charters and Field Names of Somerset*, Somersetshire Archaeological and Natural History Society, Taunton.

Gutiérrez, A. (2007a) 'Medieval and later pottery', in C. M. Gerrard with M. A. Aston, *The Shapwick Project, Somerset: A Rural Landscape Explored*, SMA monograph 25, Leeds, 601–71.

Gutiérrez, A. (2007b) 'Medieval floor tiles', in C. M. Gerrard with M. A. Aston, *The Shapwick Project, Somerset: A Rural Landscape Explored*, SMA monograph 25, Leeds, 804–6.

Guttmann, E. B., Simpson, I. A. and Davidson, D. A. (2005) 'Manuring practices in antiquity: a review of the evidence', in D. N. Smith, M. B. Buckley and W. Smith (eds), *Fertile Ground: Papers in Honour of Susan Limbrey*, Oxbow Books, Oxford, 68–86.

Hadfield, C. (1967) *The Canals of South-West England*, David and Charles, Newton Abbot.

Hadfield, C. (1969) *The Canals of South and South East England*, David and Charles, Newton Abbot.

Hadley, D. (1996) 'Multiple estates and the origins of the manorial structure of northern Danelaw' *J. Hist. Geogr.* 22, 3–15.

Halbwachs, M. (1992) *On Collective Memory*, University of Chicago Press, Chicago.

Hall, D. (1981) 'The origins of open-field agriculture: the archaeological fieldwork evidence', in T. Rowley (ed.), *The Origins of Open-field Agriculture*, Croom Helm, London, 22–38.

Hall, D. (1988) 'The late Saxon countryside: villages and their fields', in D. Hooke (ed.), *Anglo-Saxon Settlements*, Blackwell, Oxford, 99–122.

Hall, D. and Martin, P. (1979) 'Brixworth, Northamptonshire – an intensive field survey', *J. Brit. Archaeol. Ass.* 132, 1–6.

Hall, T. (2000) *Minster Churches in the Dorset Landscape*, BAR British Series 304, Archaeopress, Oxford.

Hall, T. (2003) 'The reformation of the British Church in the West Country in the 7th century', in M. R. Ecclestone, K. Gardner, N. Holbrook and A. Smith (eds), *The Land of the Dobunni*, Parchment, Oxford, 49–55.

Hall, T. (2009) 'Identifying British Christian sites in western Wessex', in N. Edwards (ed.), *The Archaeology of the Early Medieval Celtic Churches: Proceedings of a*

Conference on *The Archaeology of the Early Medieval Celtic Churches, September 2004*, SMA Monograph, Maney, Leeds, 155–71.

Hamerow, H. (1993) *Excavations at Mucking. Volume 2: The Anglo-Saxon Settlement*, English Heritage, British Museum Press, London.

Hamerow, H. (2002) *Early Medieval Settlements: The Archaeology of Rural Communities in Northwest Europe 400–900*, OUP, Oxford.

Hanawalt, B. A. (1986) *The Ties that Bound: Peasant Families in Medieval England*, OUP, Oxford.

Harden, D. B. (1971) 'Ancient glass, III: post-Roman', *Archaeol. J.* 128, 78–117.

Hardie, M. (1967) *Painting in Britain II: The Romantic period*, Batsford, London.

Hardy, P. (1990) 'Geological survey', in M. A. Aston (ed.), *The Shapwick Project: A Topographical and Historical Study. The Second Report*, University of Bristol, Bristol, 59–67.

Hardy, P. (1992) 'Geological survey of the parish of Shapwick 1990/91', in M. A. Aston and M. D. Costen (eds), *The Shapwick Project: A Topographical and Historical Study. The Third Report*, University of Bristol, Bristol, 27–30.

Hardy, P. and Gerrard, C. M. (2007) 'Slate', in C. M. Gerrard with M. A. Aston, *The Shapwick Project, Somerset: A Rural Landscape Explored*, SMA monograph 25, Leeds, 819–21.

Härke, H. (2002) 'Kings and warriors: population and landscape from post-Roman to Norman Britain', in P. Slack and R. Ward (eds), *The Peopling of Britain: The Shaping of a Human Landscape. The Linacre Lectures*, OUP, Oxford, 145–75.

Harper-Bill, C. (1996) 'The English church and English religion after the Black Death', in M. Ormrod and P. Lindley (eds), *The Black Death in England*, Paul Watkins, Stamford, 79–124.

Harris, H. (1972) *Industrial Archaeology of Dartmoor*, David and Charles, Newton Abbot.

Harvey, B. (1993) *Living and Dying in England 1100–1540: The Monastic Experience*, Clarendon Press, Oxford.

Harvey, J. (1974) *Early Nurserymen*, Phillimore, Chichester.

Harvey, J. (1981) *Medieval Gardens*, Batsford, London.

Harvey, P. D. A. (1991) 'The documents of landscape history: snares and delusions', *Landscape Hist.* 13, 47–52.

Haselgrove, C. C. (1997) 'Iron Age brooch deposition and chronology', in A. Gwilt and C. C. Haselgrove (eds), *Reconstructing Iron Age Societies: New Approaches to the British Iron Age*, Oxbow Monograph 71, Oxford, 51–72.

Haselgrove, C. C., Ferrell, G. and Turnbull, P. (1988) *The Durham Archaeological Survey*, University of Durham Occasional Paper 2, Durham.

Havinden, M. (1999) *Estate Villages Revisited: A Second Up-dated Edition of a Study of the Oxfordshire (formerly Berkshire) Villages of Ardington and Lockinge*, Rural History Centre, University of Reading, Reading.

Hayes, P. (1985) 'The San Vicenzo Survey', in S. Macready and F. H. Thompson (eds), *Archaeological Field Survey in Britain and Abroad*, Society of Antiquaries, London, 129–35.

Hayfield, C. (1987) *Wharram: A Study of Settlement on the Yorkshire Wolds. Volume 5, An Archaeological Survey of the Parish of Wharram Percy, East Yorkshire*, BAR British Series 172, Oxford.

Hayward, L. C. (1972) 'The Roman villa at Lufton, near Yeovil', *SANH* 116, 78–85.

Heron, C. (2001) 'Geochemical prospecting', in D. R. Brothwell and A. M. Pollard (eds), *Handbook of Archaeological Sciences*, John Wiley, Chichester, 565–73.

Hewitt, E. M. (1911) 'Introduction: Industries', in W. Page (ed.), *The Victoria History of Somerset, Vol. 2*, Constable and Company, London, 353–62.

Hey, D. G. (1974) *An English Rural Community: Myddle under the Tudors and Stuarts*, Leicester University Press, Leicester.

Hey, G. (2004) *Yarnton: Saxon and Medieval Settlement and Landscape*, Oxford Archaeology, Oxford.

Heyworth, A. and Kidson, C. (1982) 'Sea-level changes in southwest England and in Wales', *Proc. Geol. Ass.* 93, 91–112.

Hicks, D. and Beaudry, M. eds (2006) *The Cambridge Companion to Historical Archaeology*, CUP, Cambridge.

Hicks, M. (2004) 'Warner, Richard (1763–1857)', *Oxford Dictionary of National Biography*, OUP, Oxford <http://www.oxforddnb.com/view/article/28766?docPos=2>, accessed 11 April 2012.

Higgins, D. A. (2007) 'A pipeclay figurine', in C. M. Gerrard with M. A. Aston, *The Shapwick Project, Somerset: A Rural Landscape Explored*, SMA monograph 25, Leeds, 684–5.

Higham, N. ed. (2007) *Britons in Anglo-Saxon England*, Boydell Press, Woodbridge.

Hill, J. D. (1995) *Ritual and Rubbish in the Iron Age of Wessex: A Study in the Formation of a Specific Archaeological Record*, BAR British Series 242, Tempus Reparatum, Oxford.

Hillam, J., Groves, C. M., Brown, D. M., Baillie, M. G. L., Coles, J. M. and Coles, B. J. (1990) 'Dendrochronology of the English Neolithic', *Antiquity* 64, 210–20.

Hill-Cottingham, D. (2007) 'The inhabitants of Shapwick

and their occupations in the 19th century', in C. M. Gerrard with M. A. Aston, *The Shapwick Project, Somerset: A Rural Landscape Explored*, SMA monograph 25, Leeds, 1086–9.

Hills, C. (1999) 'Early historic Britain', in J. Hunter and I. Ralston (eds), *The Archaeology of Britain*, Routledge, London, 176–93.

Hinchliffe, J. (1986) 'An early medieval settlement at Cowage Farm, Foxley, near Malmesbury', *Archaeol. J.* 143, 240–59.

Hindle, B. (1988) *Maps and Local History*, Batsford, London.

Hinton, D. A. (1992) 'Revised dating of the Worgret Structure', *Dorset Natur. Hist. Archaeol. Soc. Proc.* 114, 258–9.

Hinton, D. A. (1999) '"Closing" and the later Middle Ages', *Medieval Archaeol.* XLIII, 172–82.

Hinton, D. A. (2005) *Gold, Gilt, Pots and Pins: Possessions and People in Medieval Britain*, OUP, Oxford.

Hobbs, R. (2006) *Late Roman Precious Metal Deposits c.AD 200–700: Changes over Time and Space*, BAR International Series 1504, Archaeopress, Oxford.

Hodges, R. (1982) *Dark Age Economics*, Duckworth, London.

Hodges, R. (1991) *Wall-to-wall History: The Story of Royston Grange*, Duckworth, London.

Hodgkin, R. H. (1935) *History of the Anglo-Saxons*, Clarendon Press, Oxford.

Hoggard, B. (2004) 'The archaeology of counter-witchcraft and popular culture', in O. Davies and W. de Blécourt (eds), *Beyond the Witch Trials: Witchcraft and Magic in the Enlightenment*, MUP, Manchester, 167–86.

Hollinrake, C. and Hollinrake, N. (1992) 'The Abbey enclosure ditch and a late-Saxon canal: rescue excavations at Glastonbury, 1984–1988', *SANH* 136, 73–94.

Hollinrake, C. and Hollinrake, N. (1994) 'Archaeological excavations in Shapwick Park 1994. PVSP94. Wessex Water pipeline', unpublished report 94/57.

Hollinrake, C. and Hollinrake, N. (1996) 'An archaeological evaluation on the site of Lawn Farm, Lawn Lane, Shapwick. SLF96E', unpublished report no. 90.

Hollinrake, C. and Hollinrake, N. (1997) 'Archaeological recording of a ditch section at Pylle Manor House, Somerset', unpublished report.

Hollinrake, C. and Hollinrake, N. (1998) 'An archaeological excavation at Sunnyside Cottage, Edington', unpublished report 126.

Holloway, S. (1996) *The Historical Atlas of Breeding Birds in Britain and Ireland: 1875–1900*, Poyser, London.

Holt, R. (1988) *The Mills of Medieval England*, Blackwell, Oxford.

Homans, G. C. (1941) *English Villagers of the Thirteenth Century*, WW Norton, New York and London.

Hooke, D. ed. (1985) *Medieval Villages*, Oxford University Committee for Archaeology monograph 5, Oxford.

Hooper, M. D. (1970) 'Dating hedges', *Area* 4, 63–5.

Hooper, M. D. (1971) 'Hedges and local history', in *Hedges and Local History*, National Council of Social Service for the Standing Conference for Local History, London, 6–13.

Hooper, St J. (1997) 'Withy Manor: an investigation', unpublished dissertation for a Certificate in Archaeology, University of Bristol.

Hope Taylor, B. K. (1977) *Yeavering: An Anglo-British Centre of Early Northumbria*, HMSO, London.

Hopkinson-Ball, T. (2007) *The Rediscovery of Glastonbury: Frederick Bligh Bond Architect of the New Age*, Sutton, Stroud.

Horne, E. (1940) 'The dovecotes of Somerset', Downside Abbey, unpublished manuscript in Somerset Archaeological and Natural History Society Library, Taunton.

Horner, B. (n.d.) 'Skinner's Wood 1990: Bronze Age trackways on Shapwick Heath', undated typescript.

Horton, M. (1998) 'Vicarage Lane, Shapwick: archaeological evaluation', in M. Aston, T. Hall and C. Gerrard (eds), *The Shapwick Project: An Archaeological, Historical and Topographical Study. The Eighth Report*, University of Bristol, Bristol, 77–83.

Hoskins, W. G. (1955) *The Making of the English Landscape*, Hodder and Stoughton, London (1988 edn with introduction and commentary by C. Taylor).

Hoskins, W. G. (1959) *Local History in England*, Longman, London.

Hoskins, W. G. (1960) *The Western Expansion of Wessex*, Department of English Local History Occasional Paper 13, Leicester University Press, Leicester.

Hoskins, W. G. (1972) *A New Survey of England: Devon*, David and Charles, Newton Abbot.

Housley, R. A., Straker, V., Chambers, F. M. and Lageard, J. G. A. (2007) 'An ecological context for the post-Roman archaeology of the Somerset Moors (South West England, UK)', *J. Wetland Archaeol.* 7, 1–22.

Howard, M. (2003) 'Recycling the monastic fabric: beyond the Act of Dissolution', in D. Gaimster and R. Gilchrist (eds), *The Archaeology of the Reformation 1480–1580*, SMA and SPMA monograph, Maney, Leeds, 221–34.

Howard, P. H. (2007) *Archaeological Surveying and Mapping: Recording and Depicting the Landscape*, Routledge, London.

Howard-Davis, C. (2001) 'Artefacts', in R. Newman, *The Historical Archaeology of Britain, c1540–1900*, Sutton, Stroud, 211–24.

Howell, C. (1983) *Land, Family and Inheritance in*

Transition: Kibworth Harcourt 1280–1700, CUP, Cambridge.

Hunt, T. J. (1960) 'A thirteenth century garden at Rimpton', *PSANHS* 104, 91–5.

Hurst, D. G. and Hurst, J. G. (1969) 'Excavations at the medieval village of Whythmail, Northants', *Medieval Archaeol.* 13, 167–203.

IFA (2001) *Standard and Guidance: For Archaeological Field Evaluation*, Institute of Field Archaeologists <http://www.archaeologists.net/sites/default/files/node-files/ifa_standards_field_eval.pdf>, accessed 21 March 2012.

Ingold, T. (1996) 'Hunting and gathering as ways of perceiving the environment', in R. Ellen and K. Fukui (eds), *Redefining Nature*, Berg, Oxford, 117–55.

Innes, M. (2007) *Introduction to Early Medieval Western Europe 300–900: The Sword, the Plough and the Book*, Routledge, London.

Isaac, P. (1976) 'Coin hoards and history in the west', in K. Branigan and P. J. Fowler (eds), *The Roman West Country: Classical Culture and Celtic Society*, David and Charles, Newton Abbot, 52–62.

Jackson, A. W. (2001) 'Heavy metals in archaeology: an evaluation of chemical residues in the soil associated with past human activity', unpublished PhD dissertation, University of Bristol.

Jacques, D. (1983) *Georgian Gardens: The Reign of Nature*, Batsford, London.

James, S., Marshall, A. and Millett, M. (1984) 'An early medieval building tradition', *Archaeol. J.* 141, 182–215.

Jameson, M. H., Runnels, C. and van Andel, T. H. (1994) *A Greek Countryside: The Southern Argolid from Prehistory to the Present Day*, Stanford University Press, Stanford.

Janes, D. (2002) *Romans and Christians*, Tempus, Stroud.

Jaques, D. (2007) 'Fish remains', in C. Gerrard with M. Aston, *The Shapwick Project, Somerset: A Rural Landscape Explored*, SMA Monograph 25, Leeds, 922–7.

Jenner, L. (2007) *The Monmouth Rebellion and the Battle of Sedgemoor, 1685*, Somerset County Council Heritage Service, Taunton.

John, E. (1982) 'The return of the Vikings', in J. Graham Campbell (ed.), *The Anglo-Saxons*, Penguin, London, 192–213.

Johnson, M. (1993) *Housing Culture: Traditional Architecture in an English Landscape*, UCL Press, London.

Johnson, M. (1996) *An Archaeology of Capitalism*, Blackwell, Oxford.

Johnson, S. (1976) *The Roman Forts of the Saxon Shore*, Elek, London.

Jones, G. R. J. (1979) 'Multiple estates and early settlements', in P. H. Sawyer (ed.), *English Medieval Settlement*, Edward Arnold, London, 9–34.

Jones, J. (1999) 'An overview of the palaeoenvironmental assessment carried out on samples from Trench 1 Wells Road, Glastonbury', report prepared for Avon Archaeological Unit (HER 90128).

Jones, M. (1986) *England before Domesday*, Batsford, London.

Jones, R. and Page, M. (2006) *Medieval Villages in an English Landscape: Beginnings and Ends*, Windgather Press, Macclesfield.

Jope, E. M. (1959) 'Note on the pottery found in the primary material of the rampart in 1940 and 1947', *Medieval Archaeol.* 3, 138.

Jordan, W. E. (1996) *The Great Famine*, Princeton University Press, Princeton.

Kain, R. J. P. and Oliver, R. R. (1995) *The Tithe Maps of England and Wales: A Cartographic Analysis and County-by-county Catalogue*, CUP, Cambridge.

Kapelle, W. E. (1979) *The Norman Conquest of the North: The Region and its Transformation, 1000–1135*, Croom Helm, London.

Keay, J. (1991) *The Honourable Company. A History of the English East India Company*, Harper Collins, London.

Keen, L. and Carreck, A. eds (1987) *Historic Landscape of Weld*, Lulworth Heritage, East Lulworth.

Keil, I. J. E. (1960) 'The garden at Glastonbury Abbey: 1333–4', *PSANHS* 104, 96–101.

Keil, I. J. E. (1964) 'Mills on the estates of Glastonbury Abbey in the later Middle Ages', *Somerset and Dorset Notes and Queries* 28, 181–4.

Kemble, J. M. (1849) *The Saxons in England*, Longman, Brown, Green and Longmans, London.

Kent, O. (1997) 'Ceramic finds from archaeological excavations at Glastonbury Abbey, 1901–1979', *SANH* 140, 73–104.

Keynes, S. and Lapidge, M. (1983) *Alfred the Great, Asser's Life of King Alfred and Other Contemporary Sources*, Penguin, Harmondsworth.

Kitch, M. (1992) 'Population movement and migration in pre-industrial rural England', in B. Short (ed.), *The English Rural Community: Image and analysis*, CUP, Cambridge, 62–84.

Knight, D. (2007) 'Loxley Wood', in C. M. Gerrard with M. A. Aston, *The Shapwick Project, Somerset: A Rural Landscape Explored*, SMA monograph 25, Leeds, 341–6.

Knight, J. (1998) 'The landscape archaeology of Loxley Wood, Shapwick, Somerset', unpublished MA dissertation, University of Bristol.

Knowles, D. (1963) *The Monastic Order in England: A History of its Development from the Times of Dunstan to the Fourth Lateran Council 940–1216*, CUP, Cambridge.

Knowles, D. and Hadcock, R. N. (1971) *Medieval Religious Houses England and Wales*, Longman, London.

Lamb, H. H. (1982) *Climate, History and the Modern World*, Methuen, London.

Langdon, J. and Masschaele, J. (2006) 'Commercial activity and population growth in medieval England', *Past & Present* 190, 35–82.

Langdon, J. and Watts, M. (2005) 'Tower windmills in medieval England: a case of arrested development?' *Technology and Culture* 46(4), 697–718.

Langdon, M. and Fowler, P. J. (1971) 'Excavations near Crandon Bridge, Puriton, 1971', *SANH* 115, 53–4.

Lapidge, M. (1993) 'The cult of St Indracht of Glastonbury', in M. Lapidge, *Anglo-Latin Literature 900–1066*, Hambledon Press, London, 419–52.

Lapidge, M. (2001) 'Dunstan', in M. Lapidge, J. Blair, S. Keynes and D. Scragg (eds), *The Blackwell Encyclopaedia of Anglo-Saxon England*, Blackwell, Oxford, 145–7.

Lapidge, M., Blair, J., Keynes, S. and Scragg, D. eds (2001) *The Blackwell Encyclopaedia of Anglo-Saxon England*, Blackwell, Oxford.

Lawrence, B. (1973) *Somerset Legends*, David and Charles, Newton Abbot.

Lawson, P. (1993) *The East India Company: A History*, Longman, London.

Laycock, S. (2008) *Britannia: The Failed State. Tribal Conflicts and the End of Roman Britain*, Tempus, Stroud.

Le Patourel, H. E. (1969) 'Documentary evidence and the medieval pottery industry', *Medieval Archaeol.* 12, 101–26.

Le Patourel, H. E. (1978a) 'Documentary evidence', in F. A. Aberg (ed.), *Medieval Moated Sites*, CBA Research Report 17, London, 21–8.

Le Patourel, H. E. (1978b) 'The excavation of moated sites', in F. A. Aberg (ed.), *Medieval Moated Sites*, CBA Research Report 17, London, 36–45.

Le Roy Ladurie, E. (1978) *Montaillou: Cathars and Catholics in a French Village 1294–1314*, Scolar Press, London.

Leach, P. J. (1982) *Ilchester Volume 1: Excavations 1974–75*, Western Archaeological Trust monograph 3, Bristol.

Leach, P. J. (2001) *Roman Somerset*, Dovecote Press, Wimborne.

Leech, R. H. (1976) 'Larger agricultural settlements in the West Country', in K. Branigan and P. J. Fowler (eds), *The Roman West Country: Classical Culture and Celtic Society*, David and Charles, Newton Abbot, 142–61.

Leech, R. H. (1980) 'Religion and burials in south Somerset and north Dorset', in W. Rodwell (ed.),

Temples, Churches and Religion: Recent Research in Roman Britain, with a Gazetteer of Romano-Celtic Temples in Continental Europe. Part 1, BAR British Series 77 (i), Oxford, 329–52.

Leech, R. H. (1981) 'The excavation of a Romano-British farmstead and cemetery on Bradley Hill, Somerton, Somerset', *Britannia* 12, 177–252.

Leech, R. H. (1982) *Excavations at Catsgore 1970–73: A Romano-British Village*, Western Archaeological Trust monograph 2, Bristol.

Leech, R. H. and Pearson, T. (1986) 'Excavations at Lower Court Farm, Long Ashton', *Bristol Avon Archaeol.* 5, 12–35.

Leeds, E. T. (1913) *The Archaeology of the Anglo-Saxon Settlements*, Clarendon Press, Oxford.

Leeds, E. T. (1947) 'A Saxon village at Sutton Courtenay, Berkshire: A third report', *Archaeologia* 112, 73–94.

Legg, R. (1997) *A Pioneer in Xanadu. Denys Rolle: 1725–97*, Furrow Press, Whitchurch.

Lethbridge, T. C. and Tebbutt, C. F. (1933–4) 'Ancient limekiln at Great Paxton, Hunts, their relation to the Anglo-Saxon church at Great Paxton, and a tentative scheme for dating pottery of the Late Saxon period', *Proc. Cambridge Antiq. Soc.* 35, 97–106.

Letts, J. (1999) *Smoke-blackened Thatch: A Unique Source of Late Medieval Plant Remains from Southern England*, AML report.

Lewcun, M. (2007) 'The clay tobacco pipes', in C. M. Gerrard with M. A. Aston, *The Shapwick Project, Somerset: A Rural Landscape Explored*, SMA monograph 25, Leeds, 673–84.

Lewis, C. (2003) 'Test pitting medieval settlements – Big Dig 2003', *Medieval Set. Res. Group Annu. Rep.* 18, 46.

Lewis, C. (2005) 'Test pit excavation within occupied settlements in East Anglia in 2005', *Medieval Set. Res. Group Annu. Rep.* 20, 9–16.

Lewis, C. (2007a) 'Test pit excavation within currently occupied rural settlement in East Anglia: results of the HEFACORS project in 2007', *Medieval Set. Res. Group Annu. Rep.* 22, 48–56.

Lewis, C. (2007b) 'New avenues for the investigation of currently occupied medieval rural settlement: preliminary observations from the Higher Education Field Academy', *Medieval Archaeol.* 51, 133–63.

Lewis, C., Mitchell-Fox, P. and Dyer, C. (1997) *Village, Hamlet and Field: Changing Medieval Settlements in Central England*, MUP, Manchester.

Lewis, M., Caffell, A., Jaques, D. and King, A. (2007) 'Human skeletal remains', in C. Gerrard with M. Aston, *The Shapwick Project, Somerset: A Rural Landscape Explored*, SMA Monograph 25, Leeds, 931–3.

Lewis, S. (1848) 'Shabbington – Shapwick', *A Topographical*

Dictionary of England, Volume 2, S. Lewis, London, n.p.

Light, J. M. (2007) 'Marine molluscs', in C. M. Gerrard with M. A. Aston, *The Shapwick Project, Somerset: A Rural Landscape Explored*, SMA monograph 25, Leeds, 927–30.

Lightbown, R. W. (1992) *Medieval European Jewellery: With a Catalogue of the Collection in the Victoria and Albert Museum*, Victoria and Albert Museum, London.

Lilley, K. (2005) 'Urban landscapes and their design: creating town from country in the Middle Ages', in K. Giles and C. C. Dyer (eds), *Town and Country in the Middle Ages: Contrasts, Contacts and Interconnections, 1100–1500*, SMA monograph 22, Maney, Leeds, 223–43.

Lilley, K. D. (1998) 'Taking measures across the medieval landscape: aspects of urban design before the Renaissance', *Urban Morphology* 2, 82–92.

Lilley, K. D. (2004) 'Cities of God? Medieval urban forms and their Christian symbolism', *Trans. Inst. Brit. Geogr.* 29, 296–313.

Linford, P. and Martin, L. (2000) *Archaeomagnetic Dating Report: Beerway Farm, Shapwick, Somerset*, AML report 50/2000.

Lishman, R., Markham, A. and Watkins, D. (1982) 'Shapwick farm buildings survey', unpublished typescript, the Shapwick branch of the Women's Institute.

Locock, M. (1997) 'Rockingham Farm, Avonmouth, 1993–1997: moated enclosures on the North Avon Level', *Archaeology in the Severn Estuary* 8, 83–8.

Losco-Bradley, S. and Kinsley, G. (2002) *Catholme: An Anglo-Saxon Settlement on the Trent Gravels in Staffordshire*, University of Nottingham, Nottingham.

Loveluck, C. (2007) *Rural Settlement, Lifestyles and Social Change in the Later First Millennium AD: Anglo-Saxon Flixborough in its Wider Context*, Excavations at Flixborough Volume 4, Oxbow Books, Oxford.

Loveluck, C. and Atkinson D. (2007) *The Early Medieval Settlement Remains from Flixborough, Lincolnshire: The Occupation Sequence, c. AD600–1000*, Excavations at Flixborough Volume 1, Oxbow Books, Oxford.

Lovis, W. (1976) 'Quarter sections and forests: an example of probability sampling in the northeastern woodlands', *American Antiquity* 41, 364–72.

Lowenthal, D. (1985) *The Past is a Foreign Country*, CUP, Cambridge.

Loyn, H. R. (1970) *Anglo-Saxon England and the Norman Conquest*, Longman, London.

Lucas, A. (2006) 'The role of the monasteries in the development of medieval milling', in S. A. Walton (ed.), *Wind and Water in the Middle Ages: Fluid Technologies from Antiquity to the Renaissance*, Arizona Center for Medieval and Renaissance Studies, Tempe, AZ, 89–128.

Lucy, S. (2000) *The Anglo-Saxon Way of Death: Burial Rites in Early England*, Sutton, Stroud.

McCann, J. and McCann, P. (2003) *The Dovecotes of Historical Somerset*, Somerset Vernacular Building Research Group, Somerset.

McCarthy, M. R. and Brooks, C. M. (1988) *Medieval Pottery in Britain AD 900–1600*, Leicester University Press, Leicester.

McDermott, M. (2006) 'The Somerset dendrochronology project phases 5 and 6', *SANH* 149, 89–96.

McDonnell, R. (1979) 'The Upper Axe Valley, an interim statement', *PSANHS* 123, 75–82.

McDonnell, R. (1984) 'Duck decoys in Somerset, a gazetteer', *PSANHS* 128, 25–30.

McErlean, T. and Crothers, N. (2007) *Harnessing the Tides: The Early Medieval Tide Mills at Nendrum Monastery, Strangford Lough*, Northern Ireland Environment and Heritage Service, The Stationery Office, Belfast.

McFarlane, A. (1977) *Reconstructing Historical Communities*, CUP, Cambridge.

McFarlane, A. (1994) *The British in the Americas 1480–1815*, Longman, London.

MacGregor, A. (1985) *Bone, Antler, Ivory and Horn*, Barnes and Noble, Totowa, NJ.

McOmish, D., Field, D. and Brown, G. (2002) *The Field Archaeology of the Salisbury Plain Training Area*, English Heritage, Swindon.

Macready, S. and Thompson, F. H. eds (1985) *Archaeological Field Survey in Britain and Abroad*, Society of Antiquaries, London.

Maltby, M. (1981) 'Iron Age Romano-British and Anglo-Saxon animal husbandry: a review of the faunal evidence', in M. Jones and G. Dimbleby (eds), *The Environment of Man: The Iron Age to the Anglo-Saxon Period*, BAR British Series 87, Oxford, 155–203.

Mann, J. De Lacy (1971) *The Cloth Industry in the West of England from 1640 to 1880*, Clarendon Press, Oxford.

Manning, W. H. (1976) 'The conquest of the West Country', in K. Branigan and P. J. Fowler (eds), *The Roman West Country: Classical Culture and Celtic Society*, David and Charles, Newton Abbot, 15–41.

Markham, G. (1615; repub. 1986) *The English Housewife*, McGill-Queen's University Press, Kingston.

Marshall, P., Bronk Ramsey, C. and Cook, G. (2007) 'Radiocarbon determinations', in C. M. Gerrard with M. A. Aston, *The Shapwick Project, Somerset: A Rural Landscape Explored*, SMA monograph 25, Leeds, 1185–91.

Marshall, W. (1796; repr. 1970) *Rural economy of the West of*

England, 2 vols, David and Charles, Newton Abbot.

Martins, C. B. (2005) *Becoming Consumers. Looking Beyond Wealth as an Explanation of Villa Variability: Perspectives from the East of England*, BAR British Series 403, Archaeopress, Oxford.

Masters, P. (1975) 'Dating hedgerows in the Vale of Wrington', *Bristol Archaeological Research Group Bulletin* 5, 147–52.

Mattingly, D. (2006) *An Imperial Possession: Britain in the Roman Empire, 54 BC–AD 409*, Allen Lane, London.

Maynard, D. (1988) 'Excavations on a pipeline near the River Frome, Worgret, Dorset', *Proc. Dorset Natural Hist. Archaeol. Soc.* 110, 77–98.

Mays, S., Harding, C. and Heighway, C. (2007) *The Churchyard: Wharram. A Study of Settlement on the Yorkshire Wolds XI*, York University Archaeological Publications 13, Wharram Research Project and Department of Archaeology, University of York.

Meaney, A. (1964) *A Gazetteer of Early Anglo-Saxon Burial Sites*, Allen and Unwin, London.

Members of the Council (1894) *Two Cartularies of the Augustinian Priory of Bruton and the Cluniac Priory of Montacute in the County of Somerset*, Somerset Record Society 8, Wells.

Mercer, E. (1975) *English Vernacular Houses: A Study of Traditional Farmhouses and Cottages*, HMSO, London.

Merrifield, R. (1987) *The Archaeology of Ritual and Magic*, Batsford, London.

Miles, D. (1984) *Archaeology at Barton Court Farm, Abingdon, Oxon*, CBA Research Report 30, London.

Miles, D. (2007) 'The tree ring dating of Shapwick House', in C. M. Gerrard with M. A. Aston, *The Shapwick Project, Somerset: A Rural Landscape Explored*, SMA monograph 25, Leeds, 1135–7.

Miller, E. and Hatcher, J. (1978) *Medieval England: Rural Society and Economic Change 1086–1348*, Longman, London.

Millett, M. (1987) 'The question of continuity: Rivenhall reviewed', *Archaeol. J.* 144, 434–44.

Millett, M. (1990) *The Romanization of Britain: An Essay in Archaeological Interpretation*, CUP, Cambridge.

Millett, M. and James, S. (1983) 'Excavations at Cowdery's Down, Basingstoke, Hampshire', *Archaeol. J.* 140, 151–279.

Minnitt, S. (2001) *The Shapwick Treasure*, Somerset County Museums Service, Taunton.

Minnitt, S. (2007a) 'Coins', in C. M. Gerrard with M. A. Aston, *The Shapwick Project, Somerset: A Rural Landscape Explored*, SMA monograph 25, Leeds, 729–34.

Minnitt, S. (2007b) 'Coins recovered from fieldwork by the Shapwick Project', in C. M. Gerrard with M. A. Aston, *The Shapwick Project, Somerset: A Rural Landscape*

Explored, SMA monograph 25, Leeds, 1158–60.

Minnitt, S. and Coles, J. (1996) *The Lake Villages of Somerset*, Somerset Levels Project and Somerset County Council Museums Service, Glastonbury.

Mithen, S. ed. (2000) *Hunter-gatherer Landscape Archaeology: The Southern Hebrides Mesolithic Project 1988–98. Vol 1: Project Development, Palaeoenvironmental Studies and Archaeological Fieldwork on Islay*, McDonald Institute monographs, Cambridge.

Moore, D. T. (1978) 'The petrography and archaeology of English honestones', *J. Archaeol. Sci.* 5, 61–73.

Moreland, J. (1992) 'Restoring the dialectic: settlement patterns and documents in medieval central Italy', in A. B. Knapp (ed.), *Archaeology, Annales and Ethnohistory*, CUP, Cambridge, 112–29.

Morgan, R. A. (1978) 'Tree ring studies in the Somerset Levels: the Meare Heath Track', *SLP* 4, 40–41.

Morgan, R. A. (1982) 'Tree ring studies in the Somerset Levels: Meare Heath Track 1974–1980', *SLP* 8, 39–45.

Morgan, R. A. (1988) *Tree-ring Studies of Wood Used in Neolithic and Bronze Age Trackways from the Somerset Levels*, BAR British Series 184, Oxford.

Morland, S. C. (1978) *The Somersetshire Quarterly Meeting of the Society of Friends 1668–1699*, Somerset Record Society 75, Yeovil.

Morland, S. C. (1984) 'Glaston twelve hides', *SANH* 128, 35–54.

Morris, C. ed. (1949) *The Journeys of Celia Fiennes*, Cresset Press, London.

Morris, J. (1973) *The Age of Arthur: A History of the British Isles from 350 to 650*, Weidenfeld and Nicolson, London.

Morris, R. (1989) *Churches in the Landscape*, Dent, London.

Morris, R. and Roxan, J. (1980) 'Churches on Roman buildings', in W. Rodwell (ed.), *Temples, Churches and Religion: Recent Research in Roman Britain*, BAR British Series 77, Oxford, 175–209.

Mowat, C. L. (1943) *East Florida as a British Province 1763–1784*, University of California Press, Berkeley.

Mukerji, C. (1983) *From Graven Images: Patterns of Modern Materialism*, Columbia University Press, New York.

Müldner, G. and Richards, M. P. (2005) 'Fast or feast: reconstructing diet in later medieval England by stable isotope analysis', *J. Arch. Sci.* 32(1), 39–48.

Munckton, T. (1994) *Somerset paupers: Unremembered Lives*, Wincanton Press, Wincanton.

Murless, B. J. (2007) 'Post-medieval brick and tile', in C. M. Gerrard with M. A. Aston, *The Shapwick Project, Somerset: A Rural Landscape Explored*, SMA monograph 25, Leeds, 812–19.

Nance, J. and Ball, J. (1986) 'No surprises? The reliability and validity of test pit sampling', *American Antiquity* 51, 457–83.

Neale, F. (1970) 'Early history', in P. J. Fowler (ed.), 'Fieldwork and excavation in the Butcombe area, North Somerset', *Proc. Univ. Bristol Spelaeol. Soc.* 12, 171–5.

Newman, R. (1999) 'Current trends in the archaeological study of post-medieval landscapes in England: context, character and chaos', in G. Egan and R. Michael (eds), *Old and New Worlds*, Oxbow Books, Oxford, 390–96.

Noddle, B. (1992) 'Animal bone', in P. Rahtz *et al.*, *Cadbury Congresbury 1968–73: A Late/Post-Roman Hilltop Settlement in Somerset*, BAR British Series 223, Tempus Reparatum, Oxford.

Ogilby, J. (1675) *Britannia, Volume the First, or, An Illustration of the Kingdom of England and Dominion of Wales*, printed by the author, London.

Oliver, R. (1993) *Ordnance Survey Maps: A Concise Guide for Historians*, Charles Close Society, London.

Oosthuizen, S. (2006) *Landscapes Decoded: The Origins and Development of Cambridgeshire's Medieval Fields*, University of Hertfordshire Press, Hatfield.

Oppenheimer, S. (2006) *The Origins of the British*, Robinson, London.

Orme, B. (1982) 'The use of radiocarbon dates from the Somerset Levels', *SLP* 8, 9–25.

Orton, C. (2000) *Sampling in Archaeology*, CUP, Cambridge.

Orwin, C. S. and Orwin, C. S. (1938) *The Open Fields*, Clarendon Press, Oxford.

Oschinsky, D. (1971) *Walter of Henley and Other Treatises on Estate Management and Accounting*, Clarendon Press, Oxford.

Overton, M., Whittle, J., Dean, D. and Hann, A. (2004) *Production and Consumption in English Households, 1600–1750*, Routledge, London.

Oxley, J. (1986) *Excavations at Southampton Castle, Southampton*, Southampton City Museums, Southampton.

Padel, O. J. (1985) *Cornish Place-Name Elements*, English Place-Name Society, Nottingham.

Page, P., Atherton, K. and Hardy, A. (2005) *Barentin's Manor: Excavations of the Moated Manor House at Harding's Field, Chalgrove, Oxfordshire 1976–79*, Thames Valley Landscapes Monograph 24, Oxford University School of Archaeology, Oxford.

Palmer, M. and Neaverson, P. (2005) *The Textile Industry of South-West England: A Social Archaeology*, History Press, Stroud.

Parker Pearson, M. and Field, N. (2002) *Fiskerton: An Iron Age Timber Causeway with Iron Age and Roman Votive Offerings*, Oxbow Books, Oxford.

Parry, S. (2006) *Raunds Area Survey: An Archaeological Study of the Landscape of Raunds, Northamptonshire, 1985–1994*, Oxbow Books, Oxford.

Payne, N. (2003) 'A resistivity survey on the site of the residence of the medieval bishops of Bath and Wells at Blackford', *SANH* 146, 113–18.

Payne-Gallwey, R. W. F. (1886) *The Book of Duck Decoys, their Construction, Management and History*, J. Van Voorst, London.

Penoyre, J. (2005) *Traditional Houses of Somerset*, Somerset Books, Somerset County Council.

Penoyre, J. and Penoyre, J. (1994) *Decorative Plasterwork in the Houses of Somerset 1500–1700*, Somerset County Council, Taunton.

Penoyre, J., Penoyre, J. and Dallimore, J. (2007a) 'Architectural survey', in C. M. Gerrard with M. A. Aston, *The Shapwick Project, Somerset: A Rural Landscape Explored*, SMA monograph 25, Leeds, 279–322.

Penoyre, J., Penoyre, J. and Dallimore, J. (2007b) 'Shapwick tenants and where they lived in the 17th and 18th century, derived from 18th century documents', in C. M. Gerrard with M. A. Aston, *The Shapwick Project, Somerset: A Rural Landscape Explored*, SMA monograph 25, Leeds, 1131–3.

Penoyre, J., Penoyre, J. and Dallimore, J. (2007c) 'Architectural stonework', in C. M. Gerrard with M. A. Aston, *The Shapwick Project, Somerset: A Rural Landscape Explored*, SMA monograph 25, Leeds, 821.

Percival, J. (1976) *The Roman Villa: An Historical Introduction*, Batsford, London.

Perring, D. (2002) *The Roman House in Britain*, Routledge, London.

Pevsner, N. (1958) *The Buildings of England: North Somerset and Bristol*, Penguin, Harmondsworth.

Pevsner, N. and Cherry, B. (1975) *Buildings of England: Wiltshire*, Penguin, Harmondsworth.

Phelps, W. (1836) *The History and Antiquities of Somersetshire*, volume 1, printed for the author by J. B. Nichols and Son, London.

Philpott, R. (1991) *Burial Practices in Roman Britain: A Survey of Grave Treatment and Furnishing AD43–410*, BAR British Series 219, Tempus Reparatum, Oxford.

Platt, C. and Coleman-Smith, R. (1975) *Excavations in Medieval Southampton 1953–1969*, 2 vols, Leicester University Press, Leicester.

Pollard, J. (2001) 'The aesthetics of depositional practice', *World Archaeol.* 33(2), 315–22.

Polwhele, R. (1793–1806) *The History of Devonshire*, Trewman and Son, Exeter.

Ponsford, M. (1980) 'Bristol Castle: archaeology and the history of a royal fortress', unpublished MLitt thesis, University of Bristol.

Ponsford, M. (2003) 'Excavations at a Saxon-Norman

settlement, Bickley, Cleeve, 1982–89', *SANH* 146, 47–112.

Poole, A. L. (1954) *From Domesday Book to Magna Carta 1087–1216: The Oxford History of England*, Clarendon Press, Oxford.

Postan, M. M. (1952) 'Glastonbury estates in the twelfth century', *Econ. Hist. Rev.* 2nd series V, 358–67.

Postan, M. M. (1956) 'Glastonbury estates in the twelfth century: a reply', *Econ. Hist. Rev.* 2nd series IX, 106–18.

Postan, M. M. (1973) *Essays on Medieval Agriculture and General Problems of the Medieval Economy*, CUP, Cambridge.

Poulsen, J. (1985) 'The pottery', in A. Graham, 'Wimborne Minster, Dorset, Excavations in the Town Centre 1983', *Proc. Dorset Natur. Hist. Archaeol. Soc.* 106, 81–5.

Powlesland, D. (1997) 'Early Anglo-Saxon settlements, structures, form and layout', in J. Hines (ed.), *The Anglo-Saxons from the Migration Period to the Eighth Century: An Ethnographic Perspective*, Boydell Press, Woodbridge, 101–24.

Price, E. (2000) *Frocester, a Romano-British Settlement, its Antecedents and Successors*, Gloucester and District Archaeological Research Group, Stonehouse.

Pryor, F. M. M. (1992) 'Discussion: the Fengate/Northey landscape', *Antiquity* 66, 518–31.

Rackham, J. ed. (1994) *Environment and Economy in Anglo-Saxon England*, CBA Research Report 89, York.

Rackham, O. (1976) *Trees and Woodland in the British Landscape*, Dent, London.

Rackham, O. (1987) *A History of the Countryside*, Dent, London.

Rackham, O. (1988) 'The forest of Neroche and the fuel supply of the Donyatt kilns', in R. Coleman-Smith and T. Pearson, *Excavations in the Donyatt Potteries*, Phillimore, Chichester.

Rackham, O. (1994) 'Trees and woodland in Anglo-Saxon England: the documentary evidence', in J. Rackham (ed.), *Environment and Economy in Anglo-Saxon England*, CBA Research Report 89, York, 7–11.

Radford, C. A. R. (1928) 'The Roman site at Westland, Yeovil', *PSANHS* 74, 122–43.

Radford, C. A. R. (1981) 'Glastonbury Abbey before 1184: interim report on the excavations, 1908–64', in N. Coldstream and P. Draper (eds), *Medieval Art and Architecture at Wells and Glastonbury*, British Archaeological Association Conference Transactions 4, Maney, Leeds, 110–34.

Rahtz, P. A. (1971) 'Excavations on Glastonbury Tor, Somerset 1964–6', *Archaeol. J.* 127, 1–81.

Rahtz, P. A. (1976) 'Buildings and rural settlement', in D. M. Wilson (ed.), *The Archaeology of Anglo-Saxon England*, Methuen, London, 49–98.

Rahtz, P. A. (1979) *The Saxon and Medieval Palaces at Cheddar*, BAR British Series 65, Oxford.

Rahtz, P. A. (1985) *Invitation to Archaeology*, Blackwell, Oxford.

Rahtz, P. (1991) 'Pagan and Christian by the Severn Sea', in L. Abrams and J. P. Carley (eds), *The Archaeology and History of Glastonbury Abbey*, Boydell Press, Woodbridge, 3–37.

Rahtz, P. A. (1993) *Glastonbury*, Batsford, London.

Rahtz, P. A. and Fowler, P. (1972) 'Somerset AD 400–700', in P. J. Fowler (ed.), *Archaeology and the Landscape*, Baker, London, 187–221.

Rahtz, P. A. and Meeson, R. (1992) *An Anglo-Saxon Watermill at Tamworth*, CBA Research Report 83, London.

Rahtz, P. A. and Watts, L. (2003) *Glastonbury Myth and Archaeology*, Tempus, Stroud.

Rahtz, P., Woodward, A., Burrow, I., Everton, A., Watts, L., Leach, P., Hirst, S., Fowler, P. and Gardiner, K. (1992) *Cadbury Congresbury 1968–73: A Late/Post-Roman Hilltop Settlement in Somerset*, BAR British Series 223, Tempus Reparatum, Oxford.

Rahtz, P. A., Hirst, S. and Wright, S. M. (2000) *Cannington Cemetery: Excavations 1962–3 of Prehistoric, Roman, Post-Roman, and Later Features at Cannington Park Quarry, near Bridgwater, Somerset, Britannia* Monograph Series 17, Society for the Promotion of Roman Studies, London.

RCHM (1959) 'Wareham West Walls', *Medieval Archaeol.* 3, 120–38.

RCHME (1970) *An Inventory of Historical Monuments in the County of Dorset – Volume 3: Central Dorset Part 2*, HMSO, London.

Reece, R. (2002) 'Roman coins and pots in fifth-century Britain', *Archaeol. J.* 159, 72–5.

Rendell, I. M. (1963) 'Blackford (Wedmore), the bishop's palace', *PSANHS* 107, 72–8.

Renfrew, C. and Wagstaff, M. eds (1982) *An Island Polity: The Archaeology of Exploitation in Melos*, CUP, Cambridge.

Reynolds, A. (2005) 'From pagus to parish: territory and settlement in the Avebury region from the late Roman period to the Domesday Survey', in G. Brown, D. Field and D. McOmish (eds), *The Avebury Landscape: Aspects of the Field Archaeology of the Marlborough Downs*, Oxbow Books, Oxford, 164–80.

Richards, C. (1992) 'Barnhouse and Maes Howe', *Current Archaeol.* 131, 444–8.

Rippon, S. (1997) *The Severn Estuary: Landscape Evolution and Wetland Reclamation*, Leicester University Press, London.

Rippon, S. (2000) *The Transformation of Coastal Wetlands*, British Academy, OUP, Oxford.

Rippon, S. (2004) 'Making the most of a bad situation? Glastonbury Abbey and the medieval exploitation of wetland resources in the Somerset Levels', *Medieval Archaeol.* 48, 91–130.

Rippon, S. (2006) *Landscape, Community and Colonisation: The North Somerset Levels during the 1st to 2nd millennia AD*, CBA Research Report 152, York.

Rippon, S. (2007) 'Emerging regional variation in historic landscape character: the possible significance of the "Long Eighth Century"', in M. Gardiner and S. Rippon (eds), *Medieval Landscapes*, Windgather, Macclesfield, 105–21.

Rippon, S. (2008a) *Beyond the Medieval Village: The Diversification of Landscape Character in Southern Britain*, OUP, Oxford.

Rippon, S. (2008b) 'Coastal trade in Roman Britain: the investigation of Crandon Bridge, Somerset, a Romano-British transhipment port beside the Severn Estuary', *Britannia* 39, 85–144.

Rippon, S. and Croft, B. (2008) 'Post-conquest medieval', in C. Webster (ed.), *The Archaeology of South-West England, South West Archaeological Research Framework, Resource Assessment and Research Agenda*, Somerset Heritage Service, Taunton, 195–207.

Rippon, S., Jackson, A. and Martin, M. (2001) 'The use of soil analysis in the interpretation of an early historic landscape at Puxton in Somerset', *Landscape Hist.* 23, 27–38.

Rippon, S., Fife, R. M. and Brown, A. G. (2006) 'Beyond villages and open fields: the origins and development of a historic landscape characterized by dispersed settlement in south-west England', *Medieval Archaeol.* 50, 31–70.

Roberts, B. K. (1977) *Rural Settlement in Britain*, Archon, Folkestone.

Roberts, B. K. (1987) *The Making of the English Village*, Longman, Harlow.

Roberts, B. K. (1990) *The Field Study of Village Plans*, Occasional Publication 24, Dept of Geography, University of Durham.

Roberts, B. K. (2008) *Landscapes, Documents and Maps: Villages in Northern England and Beyond AD 900–1250*, Oxbow Books, Oxford.

Roberts, B. K. and Wrathmell, S. (2000) *An Atlas of Rural Settlement in England*, English Heritage, London.

Roberts, C. A. and Cox, M. (2003) *Health and Disease in Britain: From Prehistory to the Present Day*, Sutton, Stroud.

Roberts, C. A. and Manchester, K. (1995) *The Archaeology of Disease*, Alan Sutton, Gloucester.

Robinson, M. (2007) 'Insect remains', in C. M. Gerrard with M. A. Aston, *The Shapwick Project, Somerset: A Rural Landscape Explored*, SMA monograph 25, Leeds, 864–5.

Rodwell, K. and Bell, R. (2004) *Acton Court: The Evolution of an Early Tudor Courtier's House*, English Heritage, London.

Rodwell, W. J. (2001) *The Archaeology of Wells Cathedral: Excavations and Structural Studies, 1978–93*, English Heritage, London.

Rodwell W. J. and Rodwell, K. (1985) *Rivenhall: Investigations of a Villa, Church and Village, 1950–1977, Volume 1*, Chelmsford Archaeological Trust and CBA Research Report 4, Chelmsford.

Roe, F. (2007) 'The stone objects', in C. M. Gerrard with M. A. Aston, *The Shapwick Project, Somerset: A Rural Landscape Explored*, SMA monograph 25, Leeds, 779–90.

Rogers, A. (2007) 'Beyond the economic in the Roman Fenland: reconsidering land, water, hoards and religion', in A. Fleming and R. Hingley (eds), *Prehistoric and Roman Landscapes*, Windgather Press, Macclesfield, 113–30.

Rolle, D. (1766) *To the Right Honourable the Lords of his Majesty's Most Honourable Privy Council. The Humble Petition of Denys Rolls, Esq*, London.

Rolle, H. (1668) *Un abridgment des plusieurs cases et resolutions del common ley: alphabeticalment digest desouth severall titles*, Crooke, Leake, Roper, Tyton, Sawbridge and others, London.

Rolle, H. (1675–6) *Les reports de Henry Rolle serjeant del' ley, de divers cases en le court del' Banke le roy. En le temps del' reign de roy Jacques*, Roper, Tilton, Starkey, Basset, and others, London.

Roud, S. (2006) *The English Year*, Penguin, London.

Rowley, T. ed. (1981) *The Origins of Open-field Agriculture*, Croom Helm, London.

Rynne, C. (1989) 'The introduction of the vertical watermill into Ireland: some recent archaeological evidence', *Medieval Archaeol.* 33, 20–31.

Rynne, C. (2000) 'The early medieval monastic watermill', in J. White Marshall and G. D. Rourke, *High Island: An Irish Monastery in the Atlantic*, Town House and Country House, Dublin, 185–213.

St George Gray, H. (1939) 'Metal vessels found on Shapwick Heath, Somerset', *PSANHS* 85, 191–202.

Salway, P. (1981) *Roman Britain*, Clarendon, Oxford.

Sawyer, P. ed. (1979) *English Medieval Settlement*, Edward Arnold, London.

Sawyer, P. H. (1968) *Anglo-Saxon Charters: An Annotated List and Bibliography*, Royal Historical Society, London.

Scarre, G. (1987) *Witchcraft and Magic in Sixteenth and Seventeenth Century Europe*, Macmillan Education, Basingstoke.

Schrijver, P. (2007) 'What Britons spoke around 400 AD', in N. Higham (ed.), *Britons in Anglo-Saxon England*, Boydell, Woodbridge, 165–71.

Scott, C. E. (1990) *The Time of Memory*, State University of New York Press, Albany.

Scott, E. (1991) 'Animal and infant burials in Roman – British villas: a revitalization movement', in P. Garwood, D. Jennings, R. Skeates and J. Toms (eds), *Sacred and Profane: Proceedings of a Conference in Archaeology Ritual and Religion Oxford 1989*, Oxford University Committee for Archaeology monograph 32, Oxford, 115–21.

Scott, E. (1993) *A Gazetteer of Roman Villas in Britain*, Leicester archaeology monographs 1, Leicester.

Seebohm, F. (1890) *The English Village Community Examined in its Relations to the Manorial and Tribal Systems and to the Common or Open Field System of Husbandry: An Essay in Economic History*, Longmans, Green and Co, London.

Selkirk, A. (1997) 'Shapwick', *Current Archaeology* 151, 244–54.

Serjeantson, D. (2006) 'Birds: food and a mark of status', in C. M. Woolgar, D. Serjeantson and T. Waldron (eds), *Food in Medieval England*, OUP, Oxford, 131–47.

Serjeantson, D. and Woolgar, C. M. (2006) 'Fish consumption in medieval England', in C. M. Woolgar, D. Serjeantson and T. Waldron (eds), *Food in Medieval England*, OUP, Oxford, 102–30.

Shackley, M. (1981) *Environmental Archaeology*, Allen and Unwin, London.

Shammas, C. (1990) *The Pre-Industrial Consumer in England and America*, Clarendon Press, Oxford.

Shennan, S. (1985) *Experiments in the Collection and Analysis of Archaeological Survey Data: The East Hampshire Survey*, Department of Prehistory and Archaeology, University of Sheffield, Sheffield.

Sheppard, J. A. (1974) 'Metrological analysis of regular village plans in Yorkshire', *Agricultural History Review* 22, 118–35.

Sheppard, J. A. (1976) 'Medieval village planning in Northern England: some evidence form Yorkshire', *Journal of Historical Geography* 2(1), 3–20.

Sheppard, J. (1979) *The Origins and Evolution of Field and Settlement Patterns in the Herefordshire Manor of Marden*, Occasional Paper 15, Department of Geography, Queen Mary College, London.

Shoesmith, R. (1980) *Hereford City Excavations*, CBA Research Report 36, London.

Shoesmith, R. (1982) *Hereford City Excavations: Excavations on and close to the Defences, Vol. 2*, CBA Research Report 46, London.

Shorrocks, D. ed. (1998) *Bishop Still's Visitation 1594 and the 'Smale Booke' of the Clerk of the Peace for Somerset 1593–5*, Somerset Record Society 84, Taunton.

Slater, T. R. (1998) 'The Benedictine order and medieval town planning: the case of St Albans', in T. R. Slater and G. Rosser (eds), *The Church in the Medieval Town*, Ashgate, Aldershot, 155–76.

Smith, A. H. (1956) *English Place-name Elements, parts 1 and 2*, English Place-Name Society XXV–XXVI, CUP, Cambridge.

Smith, C. (1977) 'The valleys of the Thame and Middle Trent – their population and ecology during the late first millennium BC', in J. Collis (ed.), *The Iron Age in Britain: A Review*, Sheffield University Press, Sheffield, 51–61.

Smith, C. (1992) *Late Stone Age Hunters of the British Isles*, Routledge, London.

Smith, K. and Petley, D. N. (2009) *Environmental Hazards: Assessing Risk and Reducing Disaster*, Routledge, London.

Smith, R. C. (1996) 'Treasure ships of the Spanish Main: the Iberian–American maritime empires', in J. F. Bass (ed.), *Ships and Shipwrecks in the Americas*, Thames and Hudson, London, 91.

Snape, M. E. (2003) 'A horizontal-wheeled watermill of the Anglo-Saxon period at Corbridge, Northumberland, and its river environment', *Archaeol. Aeliana* 32, 37–72.

Soil Survey of England and Wales (1983) *Soils of south west England*, 1:250,000 map and legend.

Spencer, B. (1990) *Pilgrim Souvenirs and Secular Badges*, Salisbury Museum Medieval Catalogue, Part 2, Salisbury.

Stacy, N. E. ed. (2001) *Surveys of the Estates of Glastonbury Abbey c1135–1201*, OUP, Oxford.

Stamper, P. and Croft, R. A. (2000) *The South Manor area. Wharram: A Study of Settlement on the Yorkshire Wolds VIII*, York University Archaeology Publications 10, York.

Standley, E. (2008) 'Ladies hunting: a late medieval decorated mirror case', *Antiq. J.* 88, 198–206.

Steane, J. (1977) 'The development of Tudor and Stuart garden design in Northamptonshire', *Northamptonshire Past and Present* V, 383–406.

Steane, J. (1993) *The Archaeology of the Medieval English Monarchy*, Batsford, London.

Stell, C. (1991) *An Inventory of Nonconformist Chapels and Meeting Houses in South-West England*, RCHM, HMSO, London.

Stephenson, J. (1989) *William of Malmesbury: A History of*

the Norman Kings (1066–1125), Llanerch Enterprises, Lampeter (facsimile reprint).

Stocker, D. and Everson, P. (2003) 'The straight and narrow way: Fenland causeways and the conversion of the landscape in the Witham valley, Lincolnshire', in M. Carver (ed.), *The Cross goes North: Processes of Conversion in Northern Europe AD 300–1300*, Boydell & Brewer, Woodbridge, 271–88.

Stone, D. J. (2006) 'The consumption and supply of birds', in C. M. Woolgar, D. Serjeantson and T. Waldron (eds), *Food in Medieval England*, OUP, Oxford, 148–61.

Stork, W. (1766) *An Extract from the Account of East Florida, Published by Dr Stork, … with Observations of Denys Rolle, who Formed a Settlement on St John's River, in the Same Province …*, London.

Straker, V., Brunning, R. and Jones, J. (2002) 'The Brue valley, Somerset: Holocene stratigraphy and palaeoecology and the possible influences of sea level change', *Bath Spa University College Occasional Papers in Geography* 2, 31–6.

Straker, V., Campbell, G. and Smith, W. (2007) 'The charred plant macrofossils', in C. M. Gerrard with M. A. Aston, *The Shapwick Project, Somerset: A Rural Landscape Explored*, SMA monograph 25, Leeds, 869–89.

Strong, R. (1979) *The Renaissance Garden in England*, Thames and Hudson, London.

Stroud, G. and Kemp, R. L. (1993) *Cemeteries of the Church and Priory of St Andrew, Fishergate*, The Archaeology of York, The Medieval Cemeteries 12, CBA, York.

Stubbs, W. (1874) *The Constitutional History of England in its Origin and Development*, Clarendon Press, Oxford.

SVBRG (1996) *Somerset Villages – The Vernacular Buildings of Shapwick*, Somerset Vernacular Building Research Group, Crewkerne.

Swanton, M. trans. and ed. (1996) *The Anglo-Saxon Chronicle*, Dent, London.

Sykes, N. J. (2006) 'From *Cu* and *Sceap* to *Beffe* and *Motton*', in C. M. Woolgar, D. Serjeantson and T. Waldron (eds), *Food in Medieval England*, OUP, Oxford, 162–75.

Tabor, R. ed. (2002) 'South Cadbury Environs Project: interim fieldwork report 1998–2001', Centre for the Historic Environment, typescript report, University of Bristol.

Tabor, R. (2004) *Regional Perspectives in Archaeology: From Strategy to Narrative*, BAR International Series 1203, Oxford.

Tabor, R. (2008) *Cadbury Castle: The Hillfort and Landscapes*, History Press, Stroud.

Tabor, R. and Johnson, P. (2000) 'Sigwells, Somerset, England: regional application and interpretation of geophysical survey', *Antiquity* 74, 319–25.

Taigel, A. and Williamson, T. (1993) *Know the Landscape: Parks and Gardens*, Batsford, London.

Tate, W. E. (1951) *The Parish Chest: A Study of the Records of Parochial Administration in England*, CUP, Cambridge.

Taylor, C. (1970) *The Making of the English Landscape: Dorset*, Hodder and Stoughton, London.

Taylor, C. C. (1977) 'Polyfocal settlement and the English village', *Medieval Archaeol.* 21, 189–93.

Taylor, C. C. (1983) *Village and Farmstead: A History of Rural Settlement in England*, George Philip, London.

Taylor, C. C. (1998) *Parks and Gardens of Britain: A Landscape History from the Air*, Edinburgh University Press, Edinburgh.

Taylor, H. M. (1975) 'Tenth century church building in England and on the Continent', in D. Parsons (ed.), *Tenth Century Studies*, Phillimore, London, 141–68.

Taylor, J. (2007) *An Atlas of Roman Rural Settlement in England*, CBA Research Report 151, York.

Templer, A. (n.d.) *The Templer Family from Somerset, Devon & Dorset* <www.templerfamily.co.uk/index.htm>, accessed 22 March 2012.

Thirsk, J. (1964) 'The common fields', *Past and Present* 29, 3–29.

Thirsk, J. (1997) *Alternative Agriculture: A History*, OUP, Oxford.

Thomas, R. M. (2007) 'Food and social boundaries in medieval England', in K. C. Twiss (ed.), *The Archaeology of Food and Identity*, Southern Illinois University Carbondale Occasional Paper 34, Carbondale, IL, 130–51.

Thompson, M. G. (1997) 'The Polden Hill manors of Glastonbury Abbey: land and people circa 1260 to 1351', unpublished PhD thesis, University of Leicester.

Thompson, M. G. (1998) 'Demographic aspects of thirteenth- and fourteenth-century Shapwick with Moorlinch', in M. A. Aston, T. A. Hall and C. M. Gerrard (eds), *The Shapwick Project: An Archaeological, Historical and Topographical Study. The Eighth Report*, University of Bristol, Bristol, 171–80.

Thorn, C. and Thorn, F. eds (1980) *Domesday Book. 8: Somerset*, Phillimore, Chichester.

Thorn, F. R. (1987) *Domesday Book Studies Somerset*, Alecto Historical Edition, London.

Thorn, F. R. (2008) 'Shapwick, Domesday Book and the "Polden Estate"', *SANH* 151, 1–30.

Thorpe, B. (1845) *History of England under the Anglo-Saxon Kings tr. from the German of Dr J. M. Lappenberg*, J. Murray, London.

Thorpe, H. (1975) 'Air, ground, document', in D. R. Wilson (ed.), *Aerial Reconnaissance for Archaeology*, CBA Research Report 12, London, 141–53.

Thorpe, I. J. N. (2000) 'Bare but bountiful: the Later

Neolithic social and physical landscape of Thy, Jutland', in A. Ritchie (ed.), *Neolithic Orkney in its European Context*, McDonald Institute, Cambridge, 71–8.

Thorpe, N. and Gerrard, C. M. (2007) 'Shovel-pits', in C. M. Gerrard with M. A. Aston, *The Shapwick Project, Somerset: A Rural Landscape Explored*, SMA monograph 25, Leeds, 266–78.

Tiller, K. (1992) *English Local History: An Introduction*, Alan Sutton, Stroud.

Tilley, C. (1994) *A Phenomenology of Landscape: Places, Paths and Monuments*, Routledge, London.

Timby, J. R. (1998) *Excavations at Kingscote and Wycomb, Gloucestershire: A Roman Estate Centre and Small Town in the Cotswolds with Notes on Related Settlements*, Costwold Archaeological Trust, Cirencester.

Timby, J. R. (2007) 'Later pre-Roman Iron Age and Roman pottery', in C. M. Gerrard with M. A. Aston, *The Shapwick Project, Somerset: A Rural Landscape Explored*, SMA monograph 25, Leeds, 571–601.

Tingle, M. (1991) *The Vale of the White Horse Survey: The Study of a Changing Landscape in the Clay Lowlands of Southern England from Prehistory to the Present*, BAR British Series 218, Oxford.

Tinsley, H. (2007) 'Pollen analysis of peat samples from borehole A, Shapwick Heath', in C. M. Gerrard with M. A. Aston, *The Shapwick Project, Somerset: A Rural Landscape Explored*, SMA monograph 25, Leeds, 842–52.

Tipper, J. (2004) *The Grubenhaus in Anglo-Saxon England*, Landscape Research Centre, Yedingham.

Todd, M. (2007) *Roman Mining in Somerset: Charterhouse on Mendip: Excavations 1993–5*, Mint Press, Exeter.

Toubert, P. (1973) *Les structures du Latium médiéval*, Ecole Française de Rome, Rome.

Turner, J. (1981) 'The vegetation', in M. Jones and G. Dimbleby (eds), *The Environment of Man: The Iron Age to the Anglo-Saxon Period*, BAR British Series 87, Oxford, 67–73.

Ucko, P. (1969) 'Ethnography and the archaeological interpretation of funerary remains', *World Archaeol.* 1, 262–80.

Van de Noort, R. and O'Sullivan, A. (2007) 'Places, perceptions, boundaries and tasks: rethinking landscapes in wetland archaeology', in J. Barber, M. Cressey, A. Crone, A. Hale, J. Henderson, R. Housley, R. Sands and A. Sheridan (eds), *Archaeology from the Wetlands: Recent Perspectives*, Society of Antiquaries of Scotland, Edinburgh, 79–89.

VCH (1985) *A History of the County of Somerset, Volume 5*, Institute of Historical Research, Oxford University Press, Oxford.

VCH (1992) *A History of the County of Somerset ,Volume 6, Andersfield, Cannington and North Petherton Hundreds (Bridgwater and neighbouring parishes)*, Oxford University Press, Oxford.

VCH (2004) *A History of the County of Somerset, Volume 8, The Poldens and the Levels*, Institute of Historical Research, Boydell and Brewer, Woodbridge.

VCH (2006) *A History of the County of Somerset. Volume 9. Glastonbury and Street*, Institute of Historical Research, Boydell and Brewer, Woodbridge.

Verhaeghe, F. (1991) 'An aquamanile and some thoughts about ceramic competition with quality metal goods in the Middle Ages', in E. Lewis (ed.), *Custom and Ceramics: Essays Presented to Kenneth Barton*, APE, Wickham, 25–61.

Viner, L. (2007) 'Metalwork', in C. M. Gerrard with M. A. Aston, *The Shapwick Project, Somerset: A Rural Landscape Explored*, SMA monograph 25, Leeds, 734–61.

Wade-Martins, P. (1980) *Excavations in North Elmham Park, 1967–1972*, East Anglian Archaeology 9, Norfolk Museums Service, Gressenhall.

Wade Martins, S. (1991) *Historic Farm Buildings: Including a Norfolk Survey*, Batsford, London.

Wainwright, G. J. (1960) 'Three microlithic industries from South-West England and their affinities', *Proc. Prehist. Soc.* 26, 193–201.

Walters, B. (1996) 'Exotic structures in 4th-century Britain', in P. Johnson and I. Haynes (eds), *Architecture in Roman Britain*, CBA Research Report 94, 152–62.

Warren, W. L. (1973) *Henry II*, Eyre Methuen, London.

Warren, W. L. (1987) *The Governance of Norman and Angevin England 1086–1272*, Edward Arnold, London.

Watkin, A. ed. (1947) *The Great Chartulary of Glastonbury, vol. 1*, Somerset Record Society 59, Taunton.

Watkin, A. ed. (1952) *The Great Chartulary of Glastonbury, vol. 2*, Somerset Record Society 63, Taunton.

Watkin, A. ed. (1956) *The Great Chartulary of Glastonbury, vol. 3*, Somerset Record Society 64, Taunton.

Watts, L. and Leach, P. (1996) *Henley Wood, Temples and Cemetery Excavations 1962–69 by the Late Ernest Greenfield and Others*, CBA Research Report 99, York.

Watts, L. and Rahtz, P. (1985) *Mary-le-Port, Bristol: Excavations 1962–3*, City of Bristol Museum and Art Gallery monograph 7, Bristol.

Watts, M. (2002) *The Archaeology of Mills and Milling*, Tempus, Stroud.

Webster, C. J. (1992) 'Excavations within the village of Shapwick', *SANH* 136, 117–26.

Webster, C. J. (2000) 'The Dark Ages', in C. J. Webster (ed.), *Somerset Archaeology*, Somerset County Council, Taunton, 79–83.

Webster, C. J. (2008) 'Early medieval', in C. J. Webster

(ed.), *The Archaeology of South West England: South West Archaeological Framework, Resource Assessment and Research Agenda*, Somerset Heritage Service, Taunton, 169–88.

Webster, G. (1967) 'Excavations at the Romano-British villa in Barnsley Park, Cirencester, 1961–1966', *Trans. Bristol Gloucestershire Archaeol. Soc.* 86, 74–83.

Webster, L. and Brown, M. eds (1997) *The Transformation of the Roman World 400–900*, CUP, Cambridge.

Wedlake, W. J. (1958) *Excavations at Camerton, Somerset*, Camerton Excavation Club, Camerton.

Welch, M. (2007) 'Anglo-Saxon Kent to AD 800', in J. H. Williams (ed.), *The Archaeology of Kent to AD 800*, Kent County Council and Boydell Press, Woodbridge, 187–248.

Wessex Archaeology (2010) 'Sutton Courtenay, Oxfordshire', report 71505.01.

West, J. (1962) *Village Records*, Macmillan, London.

West, S. E. (1985) *West Stow: The Anglo-Saxon Village*, East Anglian Archaeology 24, Suffolk County Planning Department, Ipswich.

White, R. (1990) *Memoirs of a Victorian Farmer: Richard White of Mells, Norridge and Zeals*, edited with an introduction by Michael McGarvie, Frome Society for Local Study, Frome.

White, R. (2007) *Britannia Prima: Britain's Last Roman Province*, Stroud, Tempus.

Whitelock, D. with Douglas, D. C. and Tucker, S. I. eds (1961) *The Anglo-Saxon Chronicle: A Revised Translation*, London.

Whiteman, A. ed. (1986) *The Compton Census of 1676: A Critical Edition*, Clarendon Press, Oxford.

Whittle, A. W. R. (1995) *Europe in the Neolithic: The Creation of New Worlds*, CUP, Cambridge.

Whittle, A. W. R. (1997) 'Moving on and moving around: Neolithic settlement mobility', in P. Topping (ed.), *Neolithic Landscapes*, Neolithic Studies Group Seminar Papers 2, Oxbow Monograph 86, Oxford, 15–22.

Wickham, C. (2009) *The Inheritance of Rome: A History of Europe from 400 to 1000*, Allen Lane, London.

Wilkie, L. A. (2009) 'Interpretive historical archaeologies', in T. Majewski and D. Gaimster (eds), *International Handbook of Historical Archaeology*, Springer, New York, 333–46.

Wilkinson, K. N. (1998) 'An investigation of Holocene peat and intertidal stratigraphy on Shapwick Heath, Somerset: preliminary results', in M. Bell (ed.), *Archaeology in the Severn Estuary 1998*, Annual Report of the Severn Estuary Levels Research Committee 9, Lampeter, 85–90.

Wilkinson, K. N. and Bond, C. (2001) 'Interpreting archaeological site distribution in dynamic sedimentary environments', in T. Darvill and M. Gojda (eds), *One Land, Many Landscapes: Papers from a Session held at the European Association of Archaeologists Fifth Annual Meeting in Bournemouth 1999*, BAR International Series 987, Oxford, 55–66.

Wilkinson, K. N. and Stevens, C. (2003) *Environmental Archaeology: Approaches, Techniques and Applications*, Tempus, Stroud.

Wilkinson, T. J. (2001) 'Surface collection techniques in field archaeology: theory and practice', in D. R. Brothwell and A. M. Pollard (eds), *Handbook of Archaeological Sciences*, John Wiley, Chichester, 529–41.

Williams, A. (1999) *Kingship and Government in Pre-Conquest England c500–1066*, Macmillan Press, Basingstoke.

Williams, H. (1997) 'Ancient landscapes and the dead: the reuse of prehistoric and Roman monuments as early Anglo-Saxon burial sites', *Medieval Archaeol.* 41, 1–32.

Williams, M. (1970) *The Draining of the Somerset Levels*, CUP, Cambridge.

Williams, R. (1989) *Limekilns and Limeburning*, Shire, Aylesbury.

Williamson, T. (1995) *Polite Landscapes: Gardens and Society in Eighteenth-century England*, Alan Sutton/John Hopkins University Press, Baltimore.

Williamson, T. (2003) *Shaping Medieval Landscapes: Settlement, Society, Environment*, Windgather Press, Macclesfield.

Williamson, T. (2007) 'Archaeological perspectives on landed estates: research agendas', in J. Finch and K. Giles (eds), *Estate Landscapes: Design, Improvement and Power in the Post-medieval Landscape*, Society for Post-Medieval Archaeology monograph 4, Boydell and Brewer, Woodbridge, 1–16.

Willmott, H. (2007) 'Glass vessels', in C. M. Gerrard with M. A. Aston, *The Shapwick Project, Somerset: A Rural Landscape Explored*, SMA monograph 25, Leeds, 765–78.

Wilson, D. R. (2000) *Air Photo Interpretation for Archaeologists*, Tempus, Stroud.

Wilson, S. (2000) *The Magical Universe: Everyday Ritual and Magic in Pre-modern Europe*, Hambledon, London.

Windell, D., Chapman, A. and Woodiwiss, J. (1990) *From Barrows to Bypass: Excavations at West Cotton Raunds, Northamptonshire 1985–1989*, Northamptonshire County Council, Northampton.

Winstone, J. H. (1998) 'The bishop's palace at Wookey', *SANH* 141, 91–101.

Winterbottom, M. (1978) *Gildas: The Ruin of Britain and Other Works*, Phillimore, Chichester.

Winterbottom, M. and Thomson, R. M. eds (2002)

William of Malmesbury: Saints' Lives. Lives of SS. Wulfstan, Dunstan, Patrick, Benignus and Indract, Clarendon Press, Oxford.

Woodman, P. C. (1985) *Excavations at Mount Sandel, 1973–77: County Londonderry*, HMSO, Belfast.

Woodward, A. and Leach, P. (1993) *The Uley Shrines: Excavation of a Ritual Complex on West Hill, Uley, Gloucestershire 1977–9*, English Heritage Archaeological Report 17, London.

Wormald, P. (1995) '"Inter cetera bona ... genti suae": law-making and peace-keeping in the earliest English kingdoms', *Settimane do studio del centro italiano di studi sull'alto medioevo* 42, 963–93.

Wrathmell, S. (1996) *Wharram Percy, Yorkshire*, English Heritage, London.

Wrightson, K. (2000) *Earthly Necessities: Economic Lives in Early Modern Britain*, Yale University Press, New Haven.

Wrightson, K. and Levine, D. (1995) *Poverty and Piety in an English Village: Terling 1525–1700*, Clarendon Press, Oxford.

Yates, D. (2007) 'Bronze Age field systems and the English Channel–North Sea cultural region', in A. Fleming and R. Hingley (eds), *Prehistoric and Roman Landscapes*, Windgather Press, Macclesfield, 57–69.

Yates, D. and Bradley, R. (2010) 'Still water, hidden depths: the deposition of Bronze Age metalwork in the English Fenland', *Antiquity* 84, 405–15.

Yentsch, A. E. (1994) *A Chesapeake Family and their Slaves: A Study in Historical Archaeology*, CUP, Cambridge.

Yorke, B. (1995) *Wessex in the Early Middle Ages*, Leicester University Press, London.

Young, D. (2009) 'Excavation of an Early Medieval Site at Brent Knoll, Somerset', *SANH* 152, 105–37.

Zupko, R. E. (1985) *A Dictionary of Weights and Measures for the British Isles: The Middle Ages to the Twentieth Century*, The American Philosophical Society, Philadelphia.

Index

Places without a county indicated are in Somerset – the others are pre-1974 counties
Figures in italic denote illustrations.